A MANUAL OF

UGC NET/JRF Exam

TEACHING AND RESEARCH APTITUDE

Compulsory Paper - I

A MANUAL OF

UGC NET/JRF Exam

TEACHING AND RESEARCH APTITUDE

Compulsory Paper - I

By

Dr. K. Sivarajan
M.A., M.Ed., Ph.D.
Dean
Faculty of Education
University of Calicut

Dr. C. N. Balakrishnan Nambiar
M.A., M.Ed., M.Phil., Ph.D.
Principal
Devaki Amma Memorial College of Teacher Education
Chelembra

UNIVERSITY SCIENCE PRESS
(An Imprint of Laxmi Publications Pvt.Ltd.)

BANGALORE • CHENNAI • COCHIN • GUWAHATI • HYDERABAD
JALANDHAR • KOLKATA • LUCKNOW • MUMBAI • RANCHI • NEW DELHI
INDIA • USA • GHANA • KENYA

A MANUAL OF UGC NET/JRF EXAM—TEACHING AND RESEARCH APTITUDE

Printed and bound in India
New Edition
ISBN 978-93-83828-56-2

Published in India by

UNIVERSITY SCIENCE PRESS
(An Imprint of Laxmi Publications Pvt.Ltd.)
113, GOLDEN HOUSE, DARYAGANJ,
NEW DELHI - 110002, INDIA
Telephone : 91-11-4353 2500, 4353 2501
Fax : 91-11-2325 2572, 4353 2528
www.laxmipublications.com info@laxmipublications.com

Branches

©	Bangalore	080-26 75 69 30	
©	Chennai	044-24 34 47 26,	24 35 95 07
©	Cochin	0484-237 70 04,	405 13 03
©	Guwahati	0361-254 36 69,	251 38 81
©	Hyderabad	040-27 55 53 83,	27 55 53 93
©	Jalandhar	0181-222 12 72	
©	Kolkata	033-22 27 43 84	
©	Lucknow	0522-220 99 16	
©	Mumbai	022-24 91 54 15,	24 92 78 69
©	Ranchi	0651-220 44 64	

C—
Printed at : Repro Knowledgecast Limited, Thane

CONTENTS

Part – II. Previous Years Solved Question Papers

Part – III. Model Question Papers for Practice Test

Appendix

UNIVERSITY OF CALICUT

CALICUT UNIVERSITY P.O., MALAPPURAM (DIST.), 673 635, KERALA, INDIA
Phone: (Off) 0494 - 2400241, 2407102, 2407150, (Resi) 0494 - 2402000, 2400272, 2407600, 2407556, Fax : 0494 - 2400361
E-mail : cashewsalamvc@gmail.com, cashewsalam@yahoo.co.in

Dr. M. ABDUL SALAM
Vice-Chancellor

Foreword

The number of applicants for the UGC NET/JRF examination is increasing every year. Though there were only about six thousand applications in June 2011, the number of applications for UGC test in June 2012 is more than sixteen thousand in the Calicut University Centre. We can imagine the shoot up at the National Level from this data. The more the number of persons appearing for the test the more formidable will be the challenges they have to face. This indicates the need for an authentic and dependable reference material for the aspirants of the test to prepare for it intensively.

I am extremely happy to note that 'A Manual of UGC-NET/JRF Exam' has been written by Dr. K. Sivarajan and Dr. C.N. Balakrishnan Nambiar. I understand that both the authors of this manual are associated with UGC Test Coaching Programmes organized by the Colleges and University departments, including the Minority Coaching Centre of the University of Calicut for the last two decades.

Having gone through this book it is understood that this book consists of three major parts. Part I - The Study Material, Part II - The Solved Question Papers, and Part III - The Model Question Papers.

Part I based on the study material, discusses the theoretical bases of each of the ten components of paper 1 of the UGC test. They are:

1. Teaching Aptitude
2. Research Aptitude
3. Reading Comprehension
4. Communication
5. Reasoning (Including Mathematical)
6. Logical Reasoning
7. Data Interpretation
8. Information and Communication Technology (ICT)
9. People and Environment, and
10. Higher Education System, Governance, Polity, and Administration

Though there are several books for NET Examination already available in book shops an attempt to discuss the theoretical Foundations of each of these components, so comprehensively like this manual, is not available so far. The authors of this book have very seriously and intensively discussed each of these components in separate sections and sufficient number of practice questions are given at the end of each unit. Having scanned these pages, I am convinced that this will broaden the horizons of knowledge of all its readers, there by making them confident in taking the test with better insights and confidence.

Part II of this UGC manual consists of 12 Solved Question Papers of the previous UGC tests. This section will definitely enrich its readers to examine meticulously, all the different approaches adopted for setting of questions for the UGC tests.

Part III is a set of 12 Model Question Papers with their answer keys for the learners to practise further and ensure a cake walk of the UGC test.

We know that the UGC has very carefully selected 10 most important subjects to be included in the test. It is evident that an in depth understanding of each of these subjects is essential for teachers in higher education sector. Each subject is directly related either to teaching or to research. Therefore this book will help, not only the aspirants of the UGC test, but also all teachers in higher education to enhance their professional competence. This can be considered as a bible for teachers and teacher educators for frequent references. Research Scholars and students of courses in education can use this book as a text book for their papers on research and for developing teaching skills.

I am pleased to note that the Calicut University Central Co-operative Stores is publishing this book and congratulate them for bringing out this valuable piece of work for the benefit of the students, teachers and teacher educators.

15/8/12

Dr. M. Abdul Salam
Vice Chancellor
University of Calicut

CU Campus
15th August 2012.

From the authors' desk

We are aware that a good number of publications are available in book shops meant for helping the new generation scholars who intend to take the UGC Test. One would wonder why we have come out with a new book when many others are available in the market. On our acquaintance with the books available for the purpose, we feel that most of them are not comprehensive enough to cater to tune all the competencies expected of a student who takes these tests. One needs a detailed theoretical orientation in some of the new areas. A sound initiation into the basic assumptions and practices relating to educational research, for example, is not in evidence in most of these publications. Understanding the theoretical assumptions and bases of a subject with its various ramifications in the broad perspective, is a basic precondition for developing proper insights about the areas to be included in the test.

The authors have been closely associated with the UGC Test coaching programmes organized by different Universities, Colleges, and other agencies ever since 1993. The authors have contributed articles and columns relating to training programmes in the leading periodicals. Their interaction with the post graduate students preparing for these tests and the confidence they have achieved in this area of work have all contributed to the content of this publication. The authors hope that the candidates will find this publication useful in preparing for the UGC Test. The student friendly approach adopted will help all its users to master the content with greater ease and confidence.

Following are the special features of this book

- It strictly follows the new format adopted by the UGC as on December 2009. The scheme of examination and syllabus are given in the content.
- The book has been divided into three parts, as follows: (1) study material on all the ten units of the syllabus, (2) previous years' solved question papers, and (3) model question papers with answer keys for further practice.
- Since the major objectives of this test are to identify candidates with the right aptitude for teaching and research, these two components are given in an in-depth and comprehensive manner, highlighting the characteristic features of both progressive professional practices in education and covering the major dimensions of educational research.
- Adequate number of practice questions with answer keys are provided at the end of each section so as to enable the learner to practise further.

The authors have made adequate use of all the available materials for preparing UGC Tests and relevant publications by various authors. The authors have consolidated all the available information in a single volume. They would like to express their deep sense of gratitude to all those who have contributed to the present publication.

We are deeply indebted to our most beloved and venerable Guru, Prof. (Dr) A. Sukumaran Nair, former Vice Chancellor of Mahatma Gandhi University for his timely suggestions and expert help and unstinted support which made possible the publication of the present volume. Dr. Nair has been associated with many of the apex bodies, connected with teacher education and higher education like the UGC, NAAC, ICSSR, NCERT, NCTE to name a few. Both the authors of this book were fortunate to be his students and were inspired by his dynamism, expertise and innovative approach to modern education. We have no words to place on record our immense gratitude to our Professor for sparing his valuable time for scrutinizing and correcting the manuscript of this book.

We fail to find out an appropriate word in the dictionary that would convey our deep gratitude to our Hon. Vice Chancellor, Dr. M. Abdul Salam. He has so generously accepted our request to go through this big volume. Though we were hesistant to ask such a busy person to write a forwarding note to this book, the way he accepted our request and the encouragement rendered to us make us bow our heads before his graciousness. Despite his hectic official responsibilities Dr. M. Abdul Salam, who is a scientist by profession, spared his precious time to examine these 850 pages and prepared a foreword to his book. We are deeply indebted to him.

The authors intend to make periodical revisions of this book every year so as to update the content of the book. We will be greatly obliged to those who point out the mistakes or ambiguities, in this edition, or suggestions if any. We assure them that this will be used for improving the future editions.

Wish you all success in the examinations.

–Authors

Part–I

Study Material

Unit - I

TEACHING APTITUDE

1. TEACHING: NATURE, OBJECTIVES, CHARACTERISTICS AND BASIC REQUIREMENTS
2. LEARNER'S CHARACTERISTICS
3. FACTORS AFFECTING TEACHING
4. METHODS OF TEACHING
5. TEACHING AIDS
6. EVALUATION SYSTEMS

Unit - I

TEACHING APTITUDE

One of the prime objectives of the UGC test is to identify candidates with the aptitude to become teachers in the Higher Education Sector. An aptitude does not mean the present ability. It is defined as "present characteristics, indicative of future performance under proper training". For instance, an aptitude to become a pilot does not mean that the person is at present having the abilities to fly a plane. When compared to another person, if the said person at present possesses certain characteristics like depth perception, intelligence, memory, and lack of problems like acrophobia (fear of heights), he can become a good pilot under proper training and future exposures. Similarly an aptitude for teaching means the present characteristics of a person that indicate future performance as a good teacher.

The term given in this test is better described as 'teacher aptitude' than as 'teaching aptitude'. Teaching functions should not be interpreted as standing for classroom interaction alone. Coming to the class to deliver a lecture punctually and giving the lecture systematically and impressively, is certainly, a major function of the teacher. But UGC envisages that a teacher in the higher education sector should also perform additional professional functions like the following:

- ✓ a social engineer
- ✓ a research guide
- ✓ a friend and philosopher
- ✓ a motivator
- ✓ a facilitator
- ✓ an organizer of co-curricular activities
- ✓ an evaluator
- ✓ a guidance and counselling personnel
- ✓ a cognitive tuner
- ✓ a system engineer
- ✓ a role model and so forth.

All these functions are equally important in the professional performance of a teacher. We have to use the term teaching aptitude to stand for teacher aptitude. The items included in this component of the UGC test cover all the above varied functions.

The students in higher education institutions represent an important cross section of the country's population. They are the most vibrant, energetic and responsive group within the population. Guiding them and leading them is a formidable challenge.

Unless those who are entrusted the responsibility of inspiring these potential young adults possess a real aptitude for teaching and in all the other allied activities, it may affect the quality of higher education. The most important objective of education is that of turning out human resources required for meeting the developmental needs of the nation. Superior facilities like air-conditioned class rooms, sophisticated technological facilities, digitalized and updated libraries, superior laboratories are less important than the role played by the classroom teacher. The dedication and enthusiasm of the teacher, the in-depth knowledge of the teacher in his subject, his skill in communicating and involving the students in the process of learning – all play a major role in deciding student learning. The personality qualities of a teacher as a role model are equally important. The teachers' professional skills in group management or his insights into the psychological and emotional problems of his students and his professional skills in the use of various strategies for curriculum transaction and other related qualities are far more important than the physical infrastructure and the mechanical contrivances made available to him.

"Teaching is not everybody's cup of ice" is a popular statement in educational circles. The aptitude to become a teacher is to some extent inborn; but it has to be nurtured properly under expert guidance. A person, who is very intelligent and knowledgeable, need not always be successful as a teacher. If he is an introvert, then he cannot perform his function successfully. An introvert is a reserved person who does not want to mingle with others and share his ideas with others. He often tries to withdraw from interaction with others and prefers to work in isolation. He is likely to be more idealistic than pragmatic. If such a person is assigned the task of teaching in higher education, a profession which demands cordial and congenial interaction and thought – sharing with others, the impact of such interactions are likely to be peripheral. He will not be able to develop a feeling of oneness with his students. A non-accepting relationship with students within itself acts as a detriment to effective learning. Accepting the individuality of the student is a primary requirement for good teaching.

Experts in teaching like Ryans, Good & Brophy and Gage have underlined the fact that the personality of the teacher contributes significantly to teacher effectiveness. Researchers like the above have tried to compare the qualities of best and worst teachers. They have listed and ranked the attributes of the personality traits of effective teacher, collecting responses from students, parents, co-workers and educational supervisors and prepared an elaborate list of characteristics of successful and non-successful teachers and using the technique of factor analysis, reduced such traits to certain essential factors associated with effective teaching. It is significant that the percentage of passes produced by teachers and their instructional efficiency is ranked only thirteenth in the list whereas their dispositions to students (eg. warmth, flexibility, etc.) are ranked much higher on the list of successful characteristics. This indicates further that an effective teacher is not the one who produces high percentage of first classes or distinction, but one who accepts his learners. A good teacher continues to influence the student even after he moves out of the school or even after his death. The everlasting influence of the teacher in the student's personality acts as a motivation for his future life goals. The teacher is one who is a guide, one who motivates and one who understands the learner. He diagnoses learning difficulties and remedies his learning gaps and reciprocates, consoles, supports and facilitates his learners. A teacher has to recognize that "effective teaching means affective teaching". This refers to the emotional aspects of teaching which the teacher has to bear in mind. Learning is not simply an intellectual exercise and information mongering. A teacher who thinks this alone can help his learners to attain the goals of education fails to understand that when a student is in an emotional frenzy, he cannot perform the activity of learning adequately, even when he has the intellectual equipment for learning. "Intellect is a mere speck afloat upon a sea of emotion" is a useful principle which every teacher has to bear in mind. A student's attitude towards the teacher will eventually be transferred to the learning of the subject he is teaching. The teacher's interest in the subject, his motivation, the magnitude of his anxiety (medium level of anxiety is desirable for academic achievement) to perform the role assigned to him are all important. Other things remaining the same, higher the anxiety levels of the teacher, the lower his efficiency as a teacher and vice versa. Absolute absence of anxiety also reduces teaching efficiency. Self confidence and many other emotional factors related to the teacher are also decisive factors which affect instructional efficiency.

The opening statement of the Indian Education Commission (Kothari Commission) report states that "the destiny of the Nation is being shaped in her classrooms" is to be borne in mind by every teacher. This is a very memorable statement to be used by all practising teachers in their professional practice. The new education policy also emphasizes the importance of teachers in the process of student learning. The statement that "the status of the teacher reflects the socio-cultural ethos of the society and it is said that no people can raise above the level of its teachers" is another important reminder of the importance of the teacher in learning.

When India became independent, our political leaders and educational decision makers had lofty ideas to develop our country through proper education of our youth. With a view to fulfilling this goal, the then Prime Minister of India, Jawaharlal Nehru and the then Minister for Education Maulana Abul Kalam Azad, appointed a high power commission with Dr. S. Radhakrishnan as chairman to study the problems of higher education and improve its status and quality. The commission took the bold stand that only if the quality of higher education in the country is assured then the products of the education system will help in the economic and social development of the nation. The commission hoped that those with university education will strive for the upliftment of the citizens at the grass root level. Our experience has shown that these expectations did not materialize. Those who utilize the advantages of higher education often sought employment in foreign countries and were alienated from the common man. The goal of higher education according to the experts who prepared the reports addressed the reframe of education. This commission envisaged 'excellence in personal and national life'. In fact this assumption was a new version of Macaulay's 'downward filtration theory', that if the beneficiaries of higher education dedicate their services and resources to the country and the common mass, the nation's development is sure to be accelerated.

The second education commission in independent India (Secondary Education Commission) with Dr. A. Lakshmana Swami Mudaliar, an eminent educationist, as chairman suggested many new reforms for reforming the secondary education sector in India. Diversification of school education for various occupational and vocational streams during and after secondary education was suggested.

It was only in 1964-66, that we, in India, had a commission which dealt with entire spectrum of education. This commission, the "Indian Education Commission", chaired by Dr. D. S. Kothari, (popularly known as the Kothari commission) recommended to redefine education as 'human resource development' and change the system to include higher levels of economic development and to achieve the development of human resources which will help to modernize the traditional society to become a modern society through proper use of science and technology. Despite earnest attempts, the goal is yet to be achieved. However the various education committees / commissions underlined the need to give a more important role to the teacher. The reports suggested the quality upgradation of the teachers using professional development of the teacher.

In the following unit we deal with the various aspects of teaching like nature and characteristics of teaching, general objectives of teaching, basic requirements for good teaching, characteristics of learners, factors affecting the quality of teaching, ideal methods of teaching, teaching aids, and evaluation procedure in use.

1. TEACHING: NATURE, OBJECTIVES, CHARACTERISTICS, AND BASIC REQUIREMENTS

a. Teaching: Nature

Teaching is both an art and science. It calls for the use of professionalism and the exercise of talent and creativity. It is a professional activity involving teacher and student with a view to achieving changes on the part of the learner. Teaching is a system of professional actions performed by the teacher. This varies content and the initial learning behaviour of pupil. The process of teaching can be analysed into components and assessed separately. The analysis and assessment of this kind provides a feedback to the teacher which he uses for the improvement of students learning. The present practice in teaching is to present the content using words. Present day teaching is dominated by word-based communication by the teacher. Ideal teaching is an interactive process carried out with specific purposes and objectives.

Teaching is a broader term. Terms like conditioning, training, instruction, and indoctrination denote different kinds of teaching. They are part of teaching, but not a synonym for real teaching.

Teachers are among the most influential agents of social change. A teacher does far more than impart factual information. A good teacher guides students through the process of learning: how to acquire information, how to interpret it and how to apply it to their daily lives. But the most vital aspect of teaching is the capacity to instill enthusiasm for a given field of knowledge. Every successful person will be able to identify a small number of teachers who significantly influenced their lives. It is their personal enthusiasm for the subject and the instructional strategies which influenced their students. This quality is the essence of teaching. This cannot be learned or imitated.

Teaching is one of the most important of all professions. But it cannot be said that the special role expected of teachers is not properly fullfilled by most. With a large percentage of the population of the country still illiterate, the higher education sector requires major rejuvenating structural changes. The commitment of teachers to their profession is often in doubt. It is indeed a career for those who are convinced about the importance of education and are willing to commit themselves to the cause of education.

Teachers in higher education often spend several hours researching and preparing for their lectures. Much of the teaching is in the form of lectures on assigned topics. Lecturers aim to develop students' powers of interpretation, analysis and original thought. They are also involved in setting and marking assignments and examinations, carrying out continuous assessment, evaluating research, and monitoring projects. Some of the teachers are engaged in student placement. Lectures last for an hour or more and are attended by a large number of students. Less formal teaching takes place in seminars or tutorials organized for small groups of students. During seminars and tutorials, lecturers may give prepared material, lead discussions and give comments on students' essays or assignments.

Lecturers have to be exposed to the latest developments in their disciplines. They should also be familiar with new practices in higher education. They should be conversant with social development in different forms. Those engaged in research should publish their work in reputed journals owned by reputed professional organizations. The proportion of time devoted to teaching and research varies between persons and institutions. They also carry out administrative tasks such as helping in student admissions, attending workshop, preparing curriculum designs, attend departmental committees, or acting as external examiners for other colleges. Some lecturers render guidance or tutorial help to individual students for helping them in their study, career choice and for solving their personal problems. They may also render their service as wardens of hostels. Lecturers are also assigned the duty of supervising practical work or engage in research on institutional problems

College teachers spend considerable time in making preparations for their lectures. They often spend considerable time in libraries for conferencing and possibly for research.

The teaching profession requires dedication, perseverance and patience. Every teacher has to play decisive role in moulding society. It is the teacher who can influence the thoughts and personality of students. However, the repetitive nature of work makes the task uninteresting unless the teacher is innovative enough to devise new techniques and take interest in giving new shape to student activities, outside his subjects. This entails generally, knowledge of subject as well as a rich experience in different social and co-curricular activities. Every teacher should have the ability to innovate, and be prepared to take many new responsibilities. Tact, patience and the ability to get on with all kinds of people are other essential qualities expected of a teacher.

Lecturers/teachers need an extensive knowledge of their subject. They should update their knowledge about their discipline. They should be able to develop a well-balanced instructional programme using the curricular inputs and course requirements. They should be able to explain facts, concepts and theories in a manner appropriate for proper internalization of knowledge by the learners who have to develop the ability. This requires an analytical mind, self-confidence and good communication skill.

The new generation teachers are expected to go well beyond verbal communication and develop learning situations which would help students to achieve higher – level outcomes like analysis, synthesis, problem solving, critical thinking, creative thinking, etc. What is most important is motivating students to achieve all course objectives and complete the learning requirements as per deadlines. The teacher has to be flexible and to be able to work with large numbers of students and in fostering one-to-one interactions with students. All teachers in higher education should also be able to manage and apply the new knowledge and build their work schedules with maximum efficiency.

b. Teaching: Objectives

Teaching is not to be treated as a profession for all kinds of people. It has to be practised using well-defined psychological and philosophical principles. The guiding principles for action are what we define as instructional / teaching objectives. The important objectives of teaching are:

Learner's all-round development (achieving all socially-desired behaviour changes expected of a human being); this refers to learner's change of behaviour consistent with the instructional outcomes specific to each learning situation. The following are the important behaviour changes:

- Development appropriate forms of cognitive abilities, skills and attitudes
- Improved social adjustment
- Assimilation of broad social values conveyed through the lessons

A pre-condition for this is developing a conducive student friendly environment for learning

Teaching is a bi-polar process where the teacher makes a conscious and planned effort to change each of the students in socially desired direction. This implies the imparting or transmission of knowledge and developing expected skills, and values by the teacher. The direction for such changes is contained in the listing of the objectives of teaching. The objectives are intended to develop an integrated person capable of taking a responsible, active role as a citizen and as a member of the society. We develop an instructional strategy with all these in mind. This is done using a psychological analysis of the objectives of instruction. An accepted model for this is available in the analysis made by Benjamin Bloom and his group – the Taxonomy Group – which made an exhaustive analysis of the expected outcomes of education. The group come out with a first-level clarification of out comes of instruction. The taxonomy of educational objectives postulates that expected out comes of instruction will belong to one of the three following domains of behaviour:

(a) Cognitive outcomes(intellectual abilities / outcomes)

(b) Affective outcomes(emotional outcomes)

(c) Psycho-motor outcomes(practical abilities / skills)

Ideal teaching aims at developing a complete human being with knowledge, skills, values and practice skills. This is to be interpreted as bringing about desirable changes in all the three domains of behaviour. An ideal teacher will conceive teaching as a process of behavioural changes in all the three domains.

i. The cognitive domain

Changes in the cognitive domain stand for intellectual functions like:

- gaining knowledge(recalling and remembering)
- understanding(assuming meaning to knowledge)
- interpreting
- conceptualizing
- defining
- differentiating
- inferring
- analyzing
- synthesizing
- evaluating (criticizing) etc.

ii. The affective domain

Affective domain is related to the emotional changes expected to be created in an individual as a result of teaching. This domain includes behaviour changes like the following:

- attitudes
- appreciations

- interests
- values
- dedication to ideals/social movements, etc
- commitment to work
- optimism

iii. The psychomotor domain

Psychomotor domain refers to the kinesthetic aspect of learning involving the control and use of muscles for achieving certain practical and social ends. All skills are acquired through neuromuscular and skeletal co-ordination. The efficiency achieved in practices of this kind are called psychomotor learning. Examples of psycho-motor skills are abilities like the following:

- writing
- reading
- calculating
- singing
- dancing
- driving
- swimming
- playing a musical instrument
- operating instruments/equipments, etc.

Educational objectives have been given differing but mutually supporting interpretations by educational thinkers. A prominent educational philosopher, Brubacher, has broadly classified the educational objectives in to two:

(1). Proximate aims

(2). Ultimate aims

The first stands for the immediate instructional objectives. For instance, if we teach a lesson about the National Flag, the facts provided to the students in terms of the proportion of the length and breadth of the flag, the symbolism in the use of the three colours and the chakra, etc. indicates the proximate aims. The ultimate aims of instruction in this case are the patriotic values like national pride and respect for the flag. In higher education, particularly, the ultimate aims are also to be borne in mind while teaching.

We teach not just to provide parcels of knowledge which the students have to stack in their minds, but provide experiences which would stimulate the student's passion for learning. If a teacher succeeds in creating in the learner a yearning for knowledge, he has probably done his task satisfactorily.

c. Teaching: Characteristics

Teaching is a very complex process of interaction of personalities. It is presumed that the teacher who is a mature personality well informed, skilled, and has developed a broad vision about the future development of his students, motivates them to achieve higher levels of learning, has probably performed his task in a satisfactory manner. We have to bear in mind the fact that a large number of variables - personality variables of both the teacher and the students, the socio-cultural values imposed by society, the social climate of the classroom and the educational system all influence the process of teaching and learning. The following are some of the characteristics of good teaching:

- Desire of the teacher to share his love of the subject with his students.
- Ability of the teacher to create interest in learning the subject area he has selected for teaching.
- Ability of the teacher to adjust his teaching to the level of understanding of his students.
- Teachers ability to give meaning to his explanations with appropriate practical illustrations.
- Teacher's ability to assess the amount of information to be passed on the students at a particular level with a rationale for its inclusion in the lesson.
- Teacher's concern and acceptance of his students.
- Developing of greater independence in students learning.
- Teachers ability to be creative, ability to adapt to new demands.
- Use of teaching methods and classroom experiences which stimulate self–learning and group work
- Use of valid assessment methods.
- Organizing teaching with focus on key concepts, and student understanding.
- Ability to use feedback on student learning for further learning.
- Ability to use body language for augmenting student learning.
- Ability to relate learning experiences to current events and world developments.
- Competence in using ICT for class teaching.
- Ability to integrate class teaching with guidance and counselling.
- Developing closer student–teacher interaction.
- Expertise in using teaching as an art.
- Expertise in practising education as a science using accepted professional practices.
- Ability to perceive or consider teaching and learning as a continuing process.
- Ability to stimulate students interest for further learning.

- Ability to communicate with maximum efficiency.
- Develop student's disposition to understand his social environment better and make adjustment to conform to the different social perceptions.

(The list is not exhaustive)

The characteristics of effective teaching can be defined as factors which help students achieve greater efficiency in learning. Effective teaching would mean different things in different contests. However, there are certain important factors which are common to all ideal teaching situations. These factors can be roughly divided into three areas: (1) things that foster a proper atmosphere for learning (2) use of proper techniques or teaching approaches and (3) personal qualities essential for effective teaching.

d. Teaching: Basic requirements

Many philosophers of education have termed teaching as a triangular process where teacher, learner and subject matter are treated as the three corners of the triangle. A fourth factor, which needs to be added is the environment where all the other three meet and where teaching-learning process takes place. All these four elements have their own importance. Differing educational levels and differing learning contexts call for different teaching requirements. Obviously the requirements to teach kindergarten level will differ significantly from that of university – level teaching. Consider the practices used in a country like U.S. If you want to teach in a public school in America, you must have a license to teach. Different states do have different requirements but a teaching license is the general rule in most states. One of the basic requirements is a bachelor's degree. A teacher with a master's degree would be eligible for a higher salary. Differing specializations are required to teach different subjects. A teacher has to undergo practical training of an accepted level to be considered for a teaching license.

2. LEARNER'S CHARACTERISTICS

A teacher in a modern classroom is expected to deal with students who differ considerably from each other. A major problem faced by the teacher is that of adjusting his teaching learning strategies to the demands of individuals who differ significantly from each other in their entering behaviour, intellectual ability, aptitudinal dispositions, motivation for learning, social backgrounds and personality, etc. The physical differences are most obvious; psychological differences (differences in intelligence, personality, motivation, etc.) are less obvious. Along with instructional objectives, teaching methods, and evaluation strategies, an understanding of the characteristics of learners is one of the most important factors to be taken in to account by a teacher.

No instructional approach can succeed unless the learner's needs are taken into full account by the teacher. The teacher should address all these needs appropriately, whether he is planning for group learning or for individualized learning.

In any instructional situations the focus is learner, the teacher plays the role of a facilitator and a resource provider. The teacher points to the use of additional learning resources and probes into deeper learning thought - probing questions. His role is to develop a proper setting for learning and to develop the tools for learning, but leaving it to the learner to construct his own knowledge.

While planning for teaching a teacher should have a correct understanding of the ways learners differ from each other. The following are some of the major characteristics of the learners.

- Learners differ in their levels of growth and development
- Learners differ in their interests and aptitudes
- Learners differ in their adjustment to the environment
- Learners are usually nervous in nature
- Learners differ in their level of motivation for learning
- Learners belong to different cultures and family backgrounds
- Learners differ in their receptive power
- Learners differ in their mental abilities
- Learners differ in their creativity.

A common trait of all learners is that they want to learn. Distaste for learning is often the reseult of the wrong approaches of the teachers.

3. FACTORS AFFECTING TEACHING

Teaching is nothing but facilitation of learning. Effective teaching occurs when the learning experiences are properly structured by the teacher to suit to the needs and abilities of the learners. The tasks performed by the learners should be appropriate to achieve the goals envisaged by the teacher. The teacher controls, without his direct entry into the learner's exercise. The organized experiences should result in the development of the learner's knowledge, skills, attitude and values in expected directions. The pupil is made to apply past knowledge as appropriate foundations for next stage of learning. Effective teaching involves complex inter-relationship of a wide range of factors. A major factor which decides the level of student learning is the teacher's understanding of the different ways in which pupils learn. The more the instructional methods match closely with the preferred learning style of the learners, the more effective will be the learning. Subject knowledge, professional skills and professional judgement are all important for effective teaching.

There are many factors that are likely to affect the performance of a teacher. These include certain personal factors, intellectual factors, psychological factors, and most importantly the way he deals with his students. Teacher's knowledge in the subject, his communication skills, level of mental health, facility in dealing with the learners, etc. are also factors which affect the quality of teaching.

4. METHODS OF TEACHING

a. Meaning of the term 'teaching method'

A teaching method in general is used to stand for the strategy or process adopted by the teacher for realising a preconceived educational goal through a sequenced series of teacher - pupil activities. A method of teaching refers to a set of orderly procedures employed by the teacher for achieving his goals of instruction. As applied to class-room teaching, a method is a series of related and progressive acts performed by the teacher designed or devised using his professional knowledge of instruction. It involves regular steps to guide the mental processes of the learner in mastering the subject-matter being presented to him for the realisation of the anticipated goal.

There are a number of methods available for classroom instruction. Each method suits to fulfil a slightly different purpose. Change in the content and structure of the curriculum will demand a different method. A good teacher is the one who knows how to select a method for a specific instructional context. It is often necessary to combine the strong points in different methods for teaching a single lesson. Combining the strong points of a number of approaches (eclectic approach) is often preferred to single-track approaches to teaching.

b. Characteristics of a good teaching method

Following are the major characteristics of a good teaching method: It should:

1. provide a variety of related experiences and activities useful for individual learners as well as for groups; multi sensory experiences.
2. provide scope for the creative expression of the students.
3. help to promote interest and ensure greater student involvement.
4. be useful to develop self-learning practices, including the methods for information processing.
5. stimulate the desire for further study and exploration.

c. Factors which determine the selection of a teaching method

The major aspects to be considered for selecting a teaching method for a learning situation are:

1. The objectives of instruction: The objectives of instruction envisaged for a particular learning context should be the basis for selecting the teaching method.
2. The nature of the student: A method should be selected taking into account the needs of the student. The student should be the centre of all educational programmes and activities. The method of teaching adopted must provide experiences appropriate to the ability level, interest, and learning needs of pupils, as well as with an understanding of their developmental level.
3. The nature of the subject matter: The nature of the subject-matter being presented in the lesson should be taken into account in selecting the method of teaching.

The term subject matter refers to the learning material around which the curricular experiences are to be provided.

4. Classroom environment: The environment of the class-room should also be taken into consideration while selecting a method of teaching.
5. Expertise of the teacher: Mastery of the professional principles of teaching (methods and techniques of teaching) is fundamental to effective teaching. The method selected should be one in which the teacher has sufficient expertise.

d. Major methods of teaching/instructional approaches

Different methods of teaching have been proposed by different educational thinkers. The teacher should have the knowhow of all important methods from which he can make a rational choice for himself. Some of the important methods in use are presented below.

I. Lecture method

Lecture method can be considered as the oldest teaching method. Lecture method is a teacher- centered teaching method involving one way communication by the teacher mostly by way of verbal exposition. Well planned lectures help in communication. But when they are given without planning would result in ineffective transfer of information. Many drawbacks in this method have been pointed out by specialists. But lecture continues to be one of the common methods of teaching as it has certain advantages with the other methods. It can cater to the learning needs of a large number of students at a time. It is a flexible method as teachers can use it for diverse purpose and student groups. The method can be used for different subject contents, student ability levels, time limits, etc. A competent teacher can make the lecture meaningful and interesting by posing problematic situations and by using interesting and illustrative mediators. The vast resources of a teacher's lifelong reading and experience can be communicated most economically to the learners. An important educational expert, Ausubel, has proposed a new model, 'Advance Organiser Model' for meaningful verbal learning through lecture presentations.

II. Descriptive method

In this method, the teacher explains the details of an object or specimen, which he exhibits before the students. There is active participation of the students by way of perception which in turn helps to meaningful learning. This method helps to develop the powers of observation and reasoning of the students. But ambiguous description will have an adverse effect on learning.

III. Project method

This method is the direct outcome of the principles of learning by doing advocated by pragmatic educators. This method is operated by converting the curriculum into activities to be performed by the learners in a natural setting by converting a learning situation into a problem for solution. This method is based on the principle that, true knowledge is acquired not merely by reading books nor by attending lectures, but by solving a real problem using purposive planning and action by the learners themselves. The solution leads to deep and meaningful learning of all concepts connected with the problem. 'Learning by doing', 'learning by living', 'problem orientation' and 'working in natural settings' are the four cardinal principles applied while this method is practised.

IV. Problem solving method

This method is based on the use of the scientific process and the scientific method of solving problems. It pre-supposes the existence of a problem in any learning situation. A problem in this context is designed as challenging situation that warrants additional effort on the part of the learner to arrive at feasible solutions. Problem solving demands the ability to analyse a problem, examine alternatives and finally select a satisfactory course of action which will help to solve the problem. This method encourages a learner to adopt rational set of thought and action processes which will lead to the desired solution.

V. The Dalton Plan

This method was developed around 1920 by Helen Parkhurst of the Dalton High School, Massachusetts in U.S.A. Learning activities in this method of teaching are organised in the form of monthly assignments to pupils to be completed within the course period. There is no rigidity as to the time for submitting an assignment except that the assignments are to be completed before the end of the school session. The student is free to develop the schedule for completing the assignments and to adopt his own learning strategy. The results of the working have to be properly recorded. Along with individual work, group activities and conferences are also organized by teachers. The needed academic help is also being given. The progress of each student is recorded in a separate card meant for him or her. This card is called 'Job Card'. The spirit of the Dalton Plan is even now acceptable and is practised with suitable modifications. The major advantage of this method is that it helps a student to learn at his own pace adopting his own strategies. The method helps to a great extent in meeting individual needs and interests.

VI. The Inductive - Deductive method

Induction and deduction are two processes of reasoning for drawing conclusions and for reaching generalisations. These strategies could be adopted for developing effective methods in teaching different subjects, especially in areas like mathematics and science.

1. Inductive method: In the inductive method, thinking moves from particular to general. From a number of specific examples, the student extracts a commonality which is expressed as a principle. This approach is used to develop the bases of modern science. It gives opportunities for active participation by the student in the process of discovery. This reduces their dependence on memorization and verbal teaching.

2. Deductive method: In this procedure, thinking moves from the general to particular. In this method the learner starts by assuming the validity of a principle and deduces the validity of the sub principle from this general principle. Deductive method has been used by mathematician like Euclid for developing geometry.

Induction and deduction are widely used for teaching.

VII. Analytical and synthetic methods

Analytical and synthetic methods are popularly used for teaching.

1. Analytical Method: The word analytic is derived from the term analysis, which means to break up a thing into its constituent elements. This method generally proceeds from conclusions to the data given for establishing it. Under this method, we are going deep into a problem, phenomena, etc., and trying to find out its hidden aspects and implications by deconstructing the statement/event/conclusions in to its component/contributing statements, which leads to a better understanding of the original conclusion/statement. Here we are starting with known facts, logically analyse this in to its components to identify the unknown facts or components. This method will improve the thinking skills of the learners.

2. Synthetic Method: This is the approach of analysis when components pertaining to a situation are brought together to yield a composite agreement. The word synthetic is derived from the term synthesis, which means "to combine together" various implied aspects of a situation to arrive at a conclusion or solution. It is a process of putting together the bits of information and producing a new knowledge in its totality. In sharp contrast with analysis, it uses a process which proceeds from data to conclusion.

Analytical and synthetic methods are interrelated and complement each other. While applying these strategies in an instructional situation, both the methods are applied together. By the combined use of these procedures, the classroom teaching can be made more effective and logical.

VIII. Demonstration method

Demonstration is another useful instructional method. Demonstration method stands for the use of an appropriate demonstration to give meaning to the task to be presented. It also implies the need to show how something is to be done or how something should not be done. Through demonstration a teacher presents a process skill before the students. The student's role is that of the observer and recorder of information and skills. Demonstration helps to assign meaning to a complex activity which cannot be fully explained using words.

IX. Lecture-cum-demonstration method

Demonstrations serve useful in teaching. The students observe an actual demonstration of what is presented in a lecture. Keen observation during demonstration enables them to comprehend ideas meaningfully through the related 'enaction'. A demonstration is not limited to material objects. It involves observation of a skill in action, a process, functioning of a system or a working model. The observation is enhanced by the explanation provided. A lecturer can combine demonstration with his lectures, so that the students observe and reinforce what is explained. This strategy of using both demonstration and lecture at the same time is known as lecture- cum - demonstration method. This is an improved version of the lecture method.

X. Source method

Source method implies the use of original sources and materials while teaching. A source provides first hand experiences which will lead to a better understanding of the subject. There are primary as well as secondary sources which can be used for the purpose. The advancement in information technology has made the sources easily accessible to the learning community.

XI. Heuristic method

This method is based on the assumption that students can be helped to discover knowledge through use of proper strategies. Prof. Armstrong advocated this method by which pupils were made to find the answer to his problem by unaided efforts with the help of experiments, apparatus or books or logical analysis. Naturally, the procedure adopted will be that of activity method and the reasoning employed will be inductive. The learner invents or discovers knowledge through his efforts. The learners mentally go through the entire process used by a researcher.

5. TEACHING AIDS

a. Approaches in educational technology

Modern education uses the support of technology for augmenting the quality of student learning. There are three approaches in educational technology. They are (1) hardware approach; (2) software approach; and (3) systems approach.

1. Hardware approach: This involves the application of physical science or engineering to education and training system. Using hardware like Radio, Television, Tape Recorder, etc, the teaching-learning process is fast getting mechanised. This approach enables us to deal with an increased number of students at the same time making educational experiences more meaningful. Educational technology can provide the nearest equivalent of real experiences to a large number of learners.

2. Software approach: Software approach is also called instructional technology. It refers to the systematic application of teaching-learning principles for behaviour modification through learning. The basis of instructional technology is the acceptance of the use of the principles of behavioural science for augmenting the quality of learning. Instructional technology involves a scientific sequence of procedures – analysis of an instructional problem, instructional situation, the formulation and use of support materials and instructional strategies for dealing with the instructional situation and for achieving the expected outcomes and the use of appropriate instruments for evaluation.

3. Systems approach: It is a new management approach used for decision making. This technology has influenced educational administration and organisation to a very large extent. It refers to the analysis, designing and evaluation of systems. A system, as used here, refers to a unit of operation capable of certain forms of performance. The whole education machinery is a system. Its sub-components like schools are also systems as per this definition. The term systems approach envisages utilization of scientific procedures and techniques in organisational operations and problems of management as a part of decision making. A classroom in its operational setting is also to be treated as a system and as such systems approach is applicable to classroom instruction as well.

b. Audio visual aids

Audio-visual aids are devices used for helping the learner to gain a wide variety of learning experiences than the usual auditory experiences like verbal teaching. Educational theories/theories of knowledge are based on the assumption that a human being acquires knowledge through the five senses. Classrooms usually depend upon the spoken word of the teacher – auditory experiences. When this is supported by pictures, moving pictures, etc. we refer to this as audio-visual experiences. Whatever be the level of learning or type of learning, the basic learning experiences have to enter the pupil through his five senses; they are treated as the gateways to knowledge. Most of such experiences are visual and auditory. Specially developed materials that help to provide such experiences using more than one sense is what we refer to as audio visual aids. A better term which is used is multi-sensory aids. Radio, Tape Recorder, Film Projector, LCD Projector, etc. are examples of such aids which help to improve the quality of learning.

c. Importance of audio visual aids

Psychological experiments have shown that generally we learn about 1% through taste, 1.5% through touch, 3.5% through smell, 11% through hearing and 83% through sight. We remember 20% of what we hear, 30% of what we see, 50% of what we see and hear, 80% of what we say and 90% of what we say and do. All these highlight the importance of audio visual aids in the teaching-learning process. It is important that we use different media to support our verbal instruction.

d. Classification of teaching aids

Audio-visual aids are classified into three: Projected Aids, Non-Projected Aids and Activity Aids.

Projected aid is found to be more effective than a non-projected aid. Since the darkened room reduces distraction, the bright image on the screen secures the attention of the audience easily. The colour will make the aid more attractive. Motion will make the experience even more realistic. Motion combined with sound will be more effective than the non-projected aids. Films, film strips, slides, film projector, slide projector, episcope, epidiascope and overhead projector are the most important projected aids in teaching. LCD Projectors are most widely used in present-day classroom to achieve higher outcomes of learning.

Non-projected aids can be classified into i. Graphic Aids; ii. Display Boards; iii. Three-Dimensional Aids; and iv. Audio-Aids.

Activity aids are more powerful aids used for instruction than non projected aids. They provide social and educational development of pupils. They create greater involvement of pupils learning and motivate them for learning more. These include Field Trips and Excursions, Exhibitions, Demonstrations, Dramatisation, Museum visits, visits to Planetariums, Aquariums, Terrariums, and Vivariums, Teaching Machine for programmed learning and Computer Assisted Instruction, etc, are also in wide use in advanced educational systems.

e. Abusing the audio visual aids

There is a common complaint that teachers give undue importance to teaching aids and neglect regular instructional activities. Many teachers hold the view that teaching aids can bring about miracles. It should be always borne in mind that audio-visual aids should be used not as a substitute for the teacher but as an additional input for teaching. Teachers have to use their discretion in the use of aids. Use of appropriate aids at the appropriate points of time is helpful for teaching.

6. EVALUATION SYSTEMS

a. The concept of measurement and evaluation

The logical culmination of an instructional process is student evaluation. Teachers look back at the quality and appropriateness of what they have done in the name of teaching by examining the performance of their students by scientifically designed ways of evaluation. This process involves the measurement of the outcomes of instruction (using proper measuring instruments/tools for assessing their level of educational achievement) to be followed by a process of judgement of the adequacy of learning decided based on scientific criteria.

Measurement is the process by which we ascertain the quantity of something. It is merely the assignment of a numerical index to the thing or phenomenon we measure. The aspect measured in educational assessment is the degree of student learning.

Evaluation is the process which follows measurement – the process by which we judge the quality of what we have measured. It represents the process of determining the extent to which the expected objectives have been achieved satisfactorily.

When we evaluate the learning of the student, we test him to find out whether the outcomes of learning have been achieved.

b. Objective based evaluation and the triangle of evaluation

Objective based evaluation: Evaluation in education begins with the determination of specific educational goals expected to be reached by the student. From the point of view of the classroom teacher, instructional objectives are used as the basis for evaluation. This means that educational evaluation is possible only if the instructional objectives are identified even while we design the instructional strategy. Evaluation based on pre-determined objectives is called objective-based evaluation.

The triangle of evaluation: Formulation of objectives, provision of learning experiences and evaluation are three interdependent and inseparable components of evaluation. This inter-relationship of the three processes is illustrated using a diagram called the triangle of evaluation.

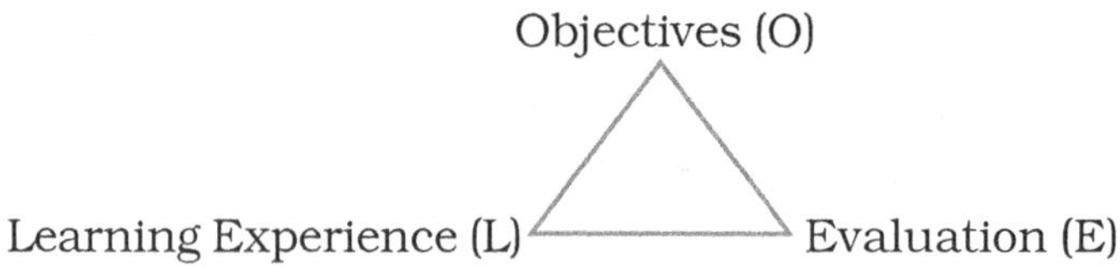

c. Types of evaluation—Formative and Summative

1. Formative Evaluation: This stands for a specialized procedure of evaluation combined with information useful for identifying learning gaps and the reasons which cause such gaps. The content is presented in the form of small teaching points with a view to facilitating easy assimilation followed by sharper methods of evaluation at the end of each of the smaller units to identify the reason for gaps in learning. Students are evaluated with respect to the smaller units and objectives. Thus, weaknesses in learning, if any, are diagnosed at the root and corrected. This procedure will ensure greater mastery of the subject and acquiring all the educational objectives set for the lesson. As this function of evaluation is developmental in nature, it is described as formative evaluation. Formative evaluation provides immediate feedback leading to knowledge of results, diagnosis and remediation. Timely corrections lead to better reinforcement and greater confidence in learning. Use of formative evaluation makes the instructional process more realistic and effective.

2. Summative Evaluation: As the term indicates, summative evaluation is done at the end of a broader learning unit. It is conducted at the end of a term or a course, more as an administrative requirement. It may be at the end of a term covering a number of learning units. Annual examinations, common public examination, etc. are all summative in nature. The result of summative evaluation will give a general picture of the level of attainment of students, again in terms of broader instructional objectives anticipated. But this is used more as a strategy for assessing group performance, institutional performance and for performing administrative functions like promotions, certification, placement, etc.

Though formative and summative evaluation differ in their nature and function, both the forms have certain common functions which vary in their functioning efficiency.

d. Evaluation tools

The word tool literally means implement for mechanical operations. But in educational evaluation, a tool may be defined as an instrument (usually written or oral) used to collect evidences of the student's achievement in a selected area of instructional performance or some of the supporting abilities like intelligence / affective traits like personality, etc. Achievement Tests, Intelligence Tests, Anecdotal Records, Cumulative Records, Check-lists, Rating Scales, Questionnaires, etc. are the main tools used for educational evaluation.

e. Evaluation techniques

A wide range of techniques are used for evaluation. Testing, Observation, Interviews, Case studies, Sociometric Techniques, Projective Techniques, etc. are the major techniques used in educational evaluation. Of these, testing (paper-pencil testing) is the most common technique.

f. Qualities of a good test

The following are the qualities of a good evaluation tool

1. Objectivity
2. Validity
3. Reliability
4. Practicability (administrability & scorability)

Other characteristics covered by the above characteristics are:

(a) Comprehensiveness which is achieved using conditions (2), (3) and (4)

(b) Comparability which is ensured using conditions (2) and (3)

(c) Utility which is covered by condition (4)

Many of the above are overlapping conceptions, though not exactly the same. For example a valid test has to be reliable. But the opposite need not be true. Validity implies comprehensiveness.

g. Achievement test and Diagnostic test

Achievement test: Every teacher wants to measure sharply the progress made by his pupils in the subject he teaches. The measures obtained are interpreted against scientific criteria for judging the appropriateness of learning. It is a complex task to be performed by the teacher on the basis of his interpretation of the measured scores. Achievement in a subject indicates the extent to which the learner has internalized the related learning material. This is decided by student's achievement in all the objectives he has set for his test. Any test designed to assess the achievement in any subject with regard to a set of predetermined objectives is called an achievement test.

Diagnostic test: A test designed to identify and investigate the difficulties, disabilities, inadequacies and gaps of pupils' learning in a specified area of curriculum with a view to helping them overcome those difficulties through remedial instruction is called a diagnostic test. Diagnostic test will also help the teacher to identify his/her own pit falls and inadequacies in transactional strategies. In a broad sense, an achievement test can also be used as a diagnostic test and vice versa. But the two types of tests are developed to satisfy different purposes.

h. Types of test items

A written test is composed of a number of test items. Items differ on the basis of the type of responses they use for measurement. There are items in which responses are free. They are called free response type test items. Here each respondent has freedom to respond in his own way. In fixed response type test items, he does not have this freedom. There are different types of test items coming under these two categories. Generally three types of test items are used. They are objective type, short answer type and essay type (long-answer-type) questions.

i. Norm-referenced and Criterion-referenced tests

A criterion referenced test evaluates an individual's performance in a given situation with respect to specific characteristic expected in the performance. It describes how well the individual does a task expected of him in relation to an envisaged goal. The performance of other individuals is not compared with his performance. For example, when you go to obtain a driving license the authority who gives you the driving test rates your driving skill against set patterns of behaviour expected of a competent driver, irrespective of how others who have taken the test have performed. So if you meet the fixed criteria required for efficient driving you are issued a license. An outcome like speed of writing is measured using the number of letters which we can write per minute. This is not expected in selection to what another does.

The norm referenced test, on the other hand, compares the individual's performance with those of other persons taking the same test. It compares differences in performance among individuals with reference to group norms. The items which are chosen for criterion referenced system, depends on the level of mastery of the key concepts and skills expected of the students.

j. Teacher-made tests and standardized tests

The teachers use two kinds of tests for student evaluation-tests constructed by themselves and standardized tests (tests developed professionally by experts). Standardized tests are preferred because of their technical excellence when compared to teacher made tests. But there are situations where teacher made tests are more appropriate.

A teacher made test is intended to measure the outcomes of learning which a teacher has in mind after completing a lesson unit. A standardized test may not be available for the purpose. The standardized test intends to measure the educational outcomes for a general purpose, prepared for use by different category of consumers, prepared for use of a number of schools and differing measurement purposes. A standardized test is one prepared by an expert in educational evaluation and psychometrics. Experts use higher psychological / educational principles and statistical procedures for test development. Often field testing is used for item validities using item analysis. Item selection is done using scientific indices like discriminating indices, difficulty indices, etc. Scoring procedures are decided using accepted scientific procedures. All the selections are done suing representative sample. Score interpretation is done using norms calculated based on the scores of a number of representative samples.

k. The modern trends in evaluation

The new trends that emerged from attempts to modernise evaluation in order to make it an integral part of the teaching - learning process can be summarised as follows.

1. Evaluation should be continuous. This means that limiting evaluation to the results of the final / terminal examinations only should be discontinued. Internal examinations, are to be conducted frequently.
2. Evaluation should be comprehensive. This means all the objectives (eg. Bloom's Taxonomy or other taxonomies) are to be measured in appropriate forms for deciding the adequacy of learning.
3. Evaluation should be conducted mostly as formative evaluation, namely, immediate feedback leading to knowledge of result, diagnosis and remediation, all aiming at realisation of the anticipated developments, rather than as a final judgement of achievement.
4. The summative function of evaluation should be considered for purposes like certification, promotion, institutional comparison, placement, etc.
5. In order to achieve all the above results, we have to discontinue system of memory-oriented written tests and replace them by a variety of techniques and tools which will help to convert self-fulfilling series of activities which lead to further learning.
6. The system of evaluating various aspects of development in terms of scores/marks suffers from many limitations. These limitations have to be reduced so that the judgements reached by teachers become more valid, reliable and acceptable.
7. Proper forms of grading should be introduced with proper training given to teachers.

8. The practice of giving undue importance to the results of the final examination in determining the future of the learners should be discontinued. The examination system should attempt to reduce the examination anxiety haunting the parents and the pupils alike; use of new alternatives adopted in progressive educational systems will help.

l. Marking system and Grading system in evaluation

1. Marking System: A test is administered to students in order to assess the level of their educational performance. Usually the level of pupil performance is given in terms of numerical scores/marks. The system of assessing student performance on a test by assigning numerical values is called the marking system.

2. Grading System: In the marking system, it is difficult to classify students in terms of their level of performance in tests due to the extremely large number of classificatory units. Small differences in scores do not represent real differences and as much cut offs like 35% (pass-failure classification) or 60% (for deciding a first class) etc. are not scientifically acceptable. In order to overcome this problem, less number of classificatory units has to be opted for while classifying students' level of performance. It will be more reliable if this classification is made on a 5-point, 7-point or 9-point scale. This method grasps a number of students of near-equal performance into a single group and assign them a common label using letters – A, B, C, D, E, etc. If it is done on a 5-point scale the categories may be interpreted as indicating 'excellent', 'good', 'average', 'below average' and 'poor'. This method is in vogue in almost all important educational systems of the world.

m. Internal assessment

The new concept of educational evaluation includes not only quantitative assessment done externally, but also qualitative appraisal done by the teachers concerned. Assessment of learner's behavioural changes qualitatively by way of internal judgment is known as internal assessment. This is done by teachers with specific reference to the qualities which they themselves want to assess, but not expected by the general system. All progressive systems of education use internal evaluation for student certification.

Teaching Aptitude - PRACTICE EXERCISE

1. **In spite of repeatedly trying various strategies, a considerable number of students in your class are highly irregular in completing their assignments. Of the following measures which one do you consider to be most effective?**

   A. Give prizes for regularity

   B. Inform the parents and seek their co-operation

   C. Design an action research for arriving at workable solutions

   D. Discuss the assignments in the class in advance

2. **A student who is normally energetic and attentive in the classroom changes into an inactive and inattentive student; all efforts to change him have failed. Which one of the following steps will you take to change the student back into his original self?**
   A. Ask the parents to consult a psychologist and get him treated
   B. Frequently ask questions to the student during class teaching to get him interested in the lesson
   C. Spend additional time for teaching the subject to the whole class
   D. Render counselling and identify the reasons for the change, before taking a decision

3. **A student continuously creates disturbance in the class in spite of strict warnings of the teacher. Which one of the four actions given below will you adopt?**
   A. Keep him out of the class till he apologises
   B. Inform the parents and ask them to advise him
   C. Make a study of his social and familial background and diagnose the reasons for his behaviour
   D. Provide interesting learning experiences in the classroom to make him more attentive

4. **You come to know that an adolescent in your class is getting attracted to an undesirable peer group. What advice would you give to his parents to put him in the right track?**
   A. Convince the student that the whole family is very worried about his connection with this group
   B. Deny him permission to move out when he has free time
   C. Change the home environment where he is made to feel that the family is a better place for him to move around and he is expected to take more responsibilities in running the family
   D. Advice him to avoid bad company and to see that the advice is accepted by him

5. **While working as a teacher, you get an offer from a business firm for an appointment to an administrative post with better financial prospects and status. How will you react to this?**
   A. Accept the offer provided the salary is considerably higher
   B. Inform the firm that you prefer to continue as a teacher
   C. Accept the offer if attractive service benefits like vehicle, quarters, etc. are provided
   D. Seek the advice of friends and parents before taking a decision

6. **You very much like to select teaching as your future profession. Which one of the following methods will you use to procure the job?**
   A. By giving bribes to the appointing authority to get you selected
   B. By demonstrating your eligibility in the selection interview
   C. By adopting any means that would ensure your selection
   D. By ensuring political support for selection

7. **Following a student agitation two opposing sections of students are about to clash. What step would you adopt as a teacher present in the location?**
   A. Meet the Principal and request to get the help of the police
   B. Ignore the incident since the teachers are expected to teach and not to deal with disciplinary problems
   C. Ask the principal to close the college and send the children home
   D. Intervene and argue with the two groups and disband the two groups

8. **While evaluating the answer books of a class one of your colleagues requests you to give higher marks to one of his pet students. What would you do in this situation?**
   A. Oblige but advise him not to repeat it
   B. Deny the request and find fault with his judgement
   C. Agree to oblige but will not oblige
   D. Evaluate the answer book objectively

9. **Which of the following do you consider is the most important function of a good teacher?**
   A. Prepare the pupils for the examination and enable them to score high marks
   B. Make the teaching interesting to all the pupils
   C. Help the pupils to understand the content of the curriculum
   D. Develop motivation and ability to learn by themselves

10. **Your country is facing a war with another country. Which of the following would you consider as your foremost duty as a responsible citizen?**
    A. Extend your moral support to the soldiers
    B. Give all possible help to the Government to defend the country
    C. Start a strong propaganda against the enemy country
    D. Contribute to the national war fund to defend the country

11. **You are asked to attend, without allowance, a refresher course meant for teachers of your specialization. You have some domestic inconveniences to attend the course. Which one of the following steps would you adopt?**

A. Make arrangements for alternate charge and attend the course

B. Accept the offer only if it is a pre-condition for promotion

C. Agree to attend if you are eligible to receive a substantial amount as TA and DA

D. Persuade the authorities for a postponement of the course till your problems are over

12. All arrangements have been made for taking your students for a study tour. On the previous day the escorting teacher falls ill. You are likely the next choice. Which one of the following courses would you adopt when you are asked to take this responsibility?

A. Will take up the responsibility voluntarily

B. Ask the Principal to postpone the trip

C. Exert pressure on another colleague to take up the responsibility

D. Will not interfere in the issue, but leave the decision to the Principal

13. You are attending a PTA meeting where there is lot of criticism by parents about the way the school functions. How would you behave to the parents?

A. Adopt neutral attitude towards the proceedings

B. Justify the lapses in one or two words in answer to the criticism

C. Be a silent spectator

D. Give adequate importance to criticism and give an assurance that the issues/ points, raised will be corrected

14. A student in your class is ridiculed by his class mates because he gives foolish answers to all questions by the teacher. Which one of the following steps do you consider most appropriate for dealing with this situation?

A. Avoid asking questions to him and ignore him

B. Ask very simple questions to the student so that he can easily find out correct answer

C. Advise the other students privately to stop ridiculing him and give him special consideration

D. Inform his parents and advise the parents to arrange for special tuition so that he can figure out the correct answers

15. While going through a notebook of one of your students, you noticed that he has used one of the pages for drawing which show that the student has unusual artistic abilities. Which of the following will be your reaction?

A. Ignore the drawing and return the note book to the student without any comment

B. Bring this to the notice of his parents and ask them to correct this wrong habit

C. Encourage the student to prepare drawings on the lessons to be taught and display them in the class

D. Tell the student not to disfigure the note books with drawings not connected with the school subject

16. When your Principal uses his official authority and orders the teachers to adopt a wrong step, how will you react?

A. Express your views so that he will not insist his order

B. Make the staff agitate against the Principal's orders

C. Seek the co-operation of the students to resist the move

D. Obey orders, as a subordinate

17. You ask your students to buy a bound note book for writing assignments. One of the students who generally accepts your directions disobeys you. What step will you take?

A. Send him out till he writes the assignments in a bound note book

B. Scold him in the open class

C. Find out the reason for his behaviour and help him if he has genuine reasons for ignoring your directions

D. Ignore his noncompliance

18. A student points out a genuine mistake you committed while explaining a topic in the class. What will be your reaction?

A. Scold him for interrupting the lesson

B. Try to defend your stand

C. Tell the students that it was a slip of the tongue

D. Thank the student and give a correction to the whole class

19. You note that a student in your class is often not following the lecture and dozes quite often. What action would you take?

A. Report the matter to his parents

B. Collect details about his family and domestic background and identify the real reasons for his behaviour and suggest remedies

C. Ask him to go out wash his face and then come back to the class

D. Scold him in public

20. You find it difficult to continue teaching because of loud noise in the neighbouring class. What step would you take?

A. Have a friendly talk with the teacher after the class and find out a solution in consultation with the other teacher

B. Enter their classroom and order the students to be quiet

C. Go to that class and tell the teacher that it is not proper for him to let the students make noise

D. Complain to the Principal and request him to take action

21. A vast majority of the teachers of your school want you to be the secretary of the Staff Association. You are not very confident. How will you react to the proposal?

A. Tell them curtly that you don't like to take up this responsibility

B. Suggest the name of another teacher who you feel is more competent for this position

C. Tell the other teachers that you have no confidence to take up this responsibility

D. Accept the challenge, seeking their co-operation for performing the task

22. In a teachers' meeting, a majority decision is taken on an important issue. You strongly feel that the decision to be taken is not in the interest of the school. What will you do in this situation?

A. Walk out of the meeting, in protest

B. Pressurise your close friends to vote against the decision and defeat the move

C. Present your arguments against the decision and request the members to reconsider

D. Yield to the view-point of the majority

23. Some students of your class approach you with the request to be the editor of a class magazine they would like to bring out. Which one of the following actions would you adopt?

A. Accept the invitation and edit the magazine for them

B. Ask them not to divert their attention from their studies and waste time by taking up activities not connected with learning

C. Encourage them, make one of them the editor of the magazine and help them to bring out a good magazine

D. Tell them that they can do this work by themselves and refuse to respond

24. You strongly feel that an important order sent by your Educational Officer is not just and not acceptable to the teachers. How will you respond?

A. Organise an agitation of the teachers against the order

B. Present your arguments in the teachers meeting and request them to take appropriate steps to get the injustice corrected

C. Give a written complaint to the Principal signed by teachers, against the implementation of the order

D. Send a petition signed by other teachers to the Deputy Director of Education requesting him to quash the order

25. You give a severe punishment to a student of your class. Later you feel that you have overreacted and would like to correct your wrong decision. Following this the students start an agitation against your hasty action. Which one of the following steps would you adopt?

A. Stick to your original stand and get the help of your colleagues to face the agitation

B. Seek the help of the student leaders to withdraw the agitation

C. Tell your students that you are sorry for what happened and request them to withdraw the agitation

D. Request the parents of the student leaders to persuade their wards to withdraw the agitation

26. A group project is expected to be completed by the whole class in about three months. What role would you take in its completion?

A. Give clear instructions to the students from time to time about each step to be taken till the project is completed

B. Form small groups to take up joint responsibilities in its planning and execution and constantly monitor their progress

C. Give them an action plan in the beginning and evaluate the progress when the project is completed

D. Instruct the students do every thing themselves, but ensure that the output is satisfactory

27. In order to teach a topic effectively you require a costly instrument which is not available in your institution. What would you do?

A. Ask the Principal to purchase the aid immediately for the school

B. Try to borrow it from another institution where it is available

C. Tell the students about the advantages of using the instrument and express your inability to procuring it

D. Satisfy with carefully planned verbal explanations

28. You are convinced that a particular instructional strategy will be most effective for teaching a topic in your subject. But most of your colleagues disagree with you. What step will you take to resolve the issue?

A. Look for a theoretical justification from standard books on instructional strategies

B. Adopt the alternative suggested by other teachers

C. Stop with verbal explanations

D. Design an action research to test the validity of the strategy you prefer

29. The curriculum in your subject is revised and you find that there are a number of new topics which are not familiar to you. What will be your reaction?

A. Tell your Principal that you cannot handle the subject effectively and to assign the class to some one else

B. Tell your pupils to learn these topics on their own

C. Read out the textual material in the class and explain

D. Master the topics through self study and discussion with other teachers before teaching the topic

30. You strongly feel that certain decisions taken by your Principal are not good for the interest of the institution. What step will you take to deal with this issue?

A. Ignore the directives and adopt the steps which you feel are appropriate

B. Create a general public opinion against the decisions

C. Present your arguments to the Principal in a strategic manner and convince him

D. Use the pupils to oppose the decisions

31. The Education Department invites projects for action research on instructional problems related to your subject of specialisation. Which one of the following steps would be most appropriate to deal with the situation?

A. Prepare a project on a problem which you have felt

B. Prepare a project for dealing with any problem that is faced by other teachers

C. Refuse to react

D. Prepare a project only if there is an award for the project

32. You come to know that a female student in your class is being teased by a boy in the class. Which among the following is the most appropriate step to deal with this problem?

A. Inform the parents of the boy and ask them to deal with the situation

B. Ask the class leader to deal with the situation

C. Ask the girl to give a written complaint to the Principal

D. Talk to the boy and convince him that his behaviour needs to be corrected and persuade him to apologise to the girl

33. Your students come to you for help in organizing a project not directly connected with your teaching work. How would you respond?

A. Deny help and tell them that it is not your area of specialisation

B. Enquire about the details and help them in case you really appreciate the venture

C. Promise all help without going into the details of the project

D. Ask them to meet another teacher who specializes in this work

34. While in invigilation duty of a public examination, you notice one of your students is trying to copy from a manuscript. How will you react to this situation?

A. Pretend that you have not seen this

B. By gestures make him understand that you don't approve the action

C. Report the incident to the Chief and ask him to take action

D. Tell the student that you will report to the head of the institution and initiate action

35. You follow a particular instructional strategy that you have found to be very effective. Meanwhile another strategy is being popularised by the education department as more effective. How will you react to this situation?

A. Continue your original strategy

B. Try to critically examine your strategy on the basis of established pedagogic theories

C. Analyse the new strategy in the light of the existing pedagogic theories

D. Try-out the new strategy to examine whether it is really superior to your preferred strategy

36. There is a brief news item in news papers regarding a novel educational programme which has successfully been adopted in an advanced country. What step will you take before adopting it?

A. Wait till all the details about the use of the method are published

B. Try to contact the reporter and gather additional details of the programme

C. Ignore the programme because a foreign programme need not work in our country

D. Bring the news to the attention of the colleagues and let them decide on its utility

37. Students of your class tell you that one of your colleagues is not engaging his classes regularly and request your help to complete the lessons. As the class teacher, what step will you take on this issue?

A. Scold the students for complaining about another teacher

B. Tactfully persuade your colleague to complete the lessons

C. Ask the students to complain to the Principal

D. Bring the issue before the Teachers' Association for action

38. You find that many of your students have difficulties in certain topics you have taught. What will you do to correct the situation?

A. Re-teach the whole topic again

B. Ask the students to read the text books several times till they understand the topic

C. Diagnose the learning difficulties and provide remedial steps

D. Dictate questions and their answers to be learnt by heart

39. Your decision on an issue has been criticised by a large number of your colleagues. Which one of the following steps would you adopt for dealing with the issue?

A. Accept the majority suggestions and change your stand

B. Stick on to your original stand point

C. Gather support for your stand from your colleagues

D. Examine the criticisms in an unbiased manner and accept them if you are convinced

40. Your students have to be given a functional knowledge of the working of the Indian Parliament. Which one of the following activities would you organize for the purpose?

A. Present an attractive diagrammatic representation of the structure of the Indian Parliament followed by a verbal explanation

B. Arrange for a show a of video tape of a Parliament session

C. Make pupils organise and enact a mock Parliament session

D. Organise a discussion on the topic with the participation of experts

41. On the basis of a request from students, your principal asks you to be the leader of the school youth festival team and attend the festival. You have certain domestic inconveniences to be away from home. Which one of the following steps would you adopt to deal with this situation?

A. Convince the principal that it is inconvenient to you

B. Persuade a friend of yours to go in your place

C. Accept the responsibility and lead the students

D. Apply for leave for the period and avoid the responsibility

42. You would like to conduct a special class for developing a negative attitude towards war in the minds of the pupils. Which one of the following learning experiences would you organise?

A. Presenting a film which depicts the horrors of war

B. Musical recitation of a poem which describes the horrors of war

C. Organizing a discussion on the effects of war on human communities

D. Conducting an exhibition of the photographs portraying the horrific scenes of a war

43. After attending an in-service course in educational methodologies, you are given the option to select one book from among the four listed below. Which one will be your first preference?

A. A novel written by a famous Indian literary figure

B. A book on innovative instructional strategies

C. The autobiography of your favourite political leader

D. A book on educational philosophy of Mahathma Gandhi

44. While reading a book on educational methodologies, you get interested in a new instructional strategy. Which one of the following steps would you adopt to a follow up your reading?

A. Write an article on the method and publish it

B. Organise a discussion on the method in the teacher's meeting

C. Give a talk on the topic in a teacher's conference

D. Try out the strategy and verify its effectiveness

45. A boy is in the habit of talking to other students while class is going on, even after being warned. Which one of the following actions would you take?

A. Send him out of the class

B. Talk more loudly to attract his attention

C. Make the whole class sit quiet for five minutes, with folded hands

D. Arrange a counselling session for the boy after the class

46. While showing an experiment in Chemistry in the laboratory, a poisonous gas leaks from the equipment. Which step among the following would you adopt to deal with the situation?

A. Explain what has happened and ask the students to go out

B. Get out of the lab and ask the pupils to follow

C. Make all the students go out of the lab within a few seconds and follow them

D. Call for help of other teachers to deal with the situation

47. If you have to choose one of the four following programmes, which will be your first choice?

A. Visiting a film theatre where a famous movie is on the run

B. Five well known poets reciting their poems in the town hall

C. A seminar where some reputed specialists are presenting their views for improving practices in education

D. An exhibition of agricultural products

48. Which one of the following measures would you adopt for ensuring the presence of parents in meetings of the Parent Teacher Association?

A. Make a presentation highlighting the inadequacies in school infrastructure and how this affects the general health of students

B. Make a speech on the need for parental co-operation in education

C. Make the students responsible for bringing their parents for school meetings

D. Prepare an action plan for co-operative effort by parents and teachers for improving school facilities

49. You note that a student from a very poor family is often absent. Which one of the following steps would you adopt for correcting him?

A. Scold him in the class so that others will not adopt this behaviour

B. Report the matter to his parents and ask them to correct him if he is not to be dismissed from the college

C. Report the matter to the Principal and request him to take disciplinary measures

D. Have a friendly talk with the student, and try to help him in his difficulty

50. A student is found to hesitate when asked to take part in class projects. Which one of the following steps would you prefer to correct him?

A. Advise him to be bolder as he has no big challenge

B. Discontinue assigning responsibilities to him in group work

C. Assign lighter responsibilities to him and help him to develop self confidence

D. Ask his class mates not to pass any negative comment about his behaviour

51. Two female students in your class are exceptionally good in music. You know that they have started hating each other and want to excel than

the other in music. Which of the following steps do you think will be the best to create mutual acceptance and appreciation?

A. Call them together, tell them they are equally good and ask them to be friends

B. Develop a music group where the two can work together

C. Bring the fact to the notice of their parents and ask him to advice

D. Have a free talk to each separately and persuade them to be friends

52. You want to motivate the backward learners in the class to work harder. Which of the following steps do you think will be the most appropriate?

A. Exhibit graphs of the results of continuous evaluation of all students and appreciate even the little progress made by the few backward learners and tell them that they can certainly do better in the next test

B. Exhibit graphs of the results of continuous evaluation and make special mention of those who do not show any progress

C. Highlight the failure of low achievers by contrasting it with the success of high achievers

D. Report cases of low achievement to the parents concerned

53. A student is found to perform poorly in your subject, but has won a medal in inter school sports. How will you help him to become a good achiever?

A. Openly tell him that his medal will not help him unless he scores high marks in the school subjects

B. Congratulate him in the open class for his sports performance and tell him that this success will be appreciated much more if he scores high marks as well

C. Tell him not waste any more time for sports till he improves his examination performance

D. Ask him to spend more time for sports even at the risk of neglecting his school work

54. In one of the Parent Teacher Association meetings some parents complain that your pupils are not happy with your teaching. How would you react to this?

A. Identify the pupils who have complained and scold them in the class for complaining

B. Diagnose the real difficulties expressed and organise remedial classes for correcting these difficulties

C. Convince the parents that entertaining such complaints will stand in the way of their learning

D. Persuade the Teachers' Association to protest against such complaints

55. You decide to take action against a student who misbehaved in your class. A considerable number of your colleagues are against this decision. Which step would you adopt to deal with the situation?

A. Stick on to your original decision

B. Gather the support of other teachers and use them to correct the teachers who oppose your decision

C. Withdraw your action and avoid their criticism

D. Analyse the reasons for their opposition and take a final decision, based on your reasoning

56. You and a fellow teacher in your school enter into an educational competition. Your friend wins the prize, while you are defeated. Other colleagues make fun of you. How would you react to this situation?

A. Congratulate the winner and wait for the next chance

B. Tell your colleagues that your colleague won because he influenced the judging committee

C. Ask your colleagues to compare the two entries and make a judgement

D. Write to the organizers stating that there was favouritism in the assessment

57. There is a proposal by the Directorate of Education to organise a compensatory programme for improving the class performance of culturally disadvantaged pupils. This demands considerable extra hard work on the part of teachers. No extra remuneration is provided for the teachers in this project. How will you react to this?

A. Accept the responsibility and do the extra hard work for improving the lot of students' performance

B. Persuade the Teachers Association to complain against this extra work

C. Take up the responsibilities, but demand remuneration for the work

D. Accept the responsibility, but spend only a short time for the work

58. An important student project which will benefit a large number of poor students has been taken up by your college. You are the staff adviser for the project. What particular stand would you adopt for the working of the project?

A. Leave it to the whole group of teachers, giving a few suggestions now and then

B. Prepare a feasible action plan yourself and help the pupils complete the project in time

C. Visit the venue occasionally to ensure that every student participates in the project

D. Make pupils actively participate in the work using a continuous feedback

59. A low achiever in your class is normally withdrawn and is alienated by most of his class mates. You accidently come to know that the boy excels in singing. Which of the following steps would you adopt for dealing with the student?

A. Take him to the teacher's room, make him sing and appreciate him for his talent in the presence of other teachers

B. Inform the parents about their ward's special talents and ask them to encourage him

C. Encourage him to sing in the class and openly appreciate his talent with his classmates and make arrangements with the best students in the class to help him to improve his class performance

D. Tell the class mates that he is a good singer but has to improve his learning methods,

60. Your class, consisting of almost an equal number of boys and girls, is planning to go on a study tour. Which role among the following would you play in the planning of the programme?

A. You will draw up a plan and give it to the students for adoption

B. Will conduct a thorough discussion with your students under your guidance and finalise the plan

C. You will accept the plan prepared by the pupils

D. You give the student leaders the full responsibility to organize and conduct the tour

61. You have noticed that there are students in your class who are good in creative writing and drawing pictures well. Which one of the following steps would you adopt to encourage such students?

A. Mention about the special talents of these students in the open class

B. Bring the fact to the notice of the Principal and other teachers

C. Inform the parents of these students about the special talents of their wards and ask them to encourage them in all possible ways

D. Encourage these students to start a class magazine which can be produced by the talented students

62. A student is found to frequently ask questions to clear his doubts about the area which you teach. Which one of the following steps will you adopt for dealing with the situation?

A. Tell him not to disturb the class asking foolish questions

B. Snub him using sarcastic comments

C. Use the service of the better students in the class to clarify his doubts

D. Teach the whole topic again

63. A meeting of Teachers Association is held to decide the steps to be taken to deal with a controversial issue to develop an action plan for dealing with the issue. What role will you play in the session?

A. Present your views strongly and withdraw

B. Carefully listen to the views of others

C. Declare that you will co-operate with others in implementing the action plan when it is finally accepted

D. Actively participate in the discussion and help the group to arrive at a consensus, and give shape to the action plan

64. As part of your teaching work, you are required to enter into the ideologies and working styles of important political parties of your state. Which one of the following actions would you adopt?

A. Make use of the opportunity to highlight the merits of your preferred political party

B. Highlight the drawback and limitations of the political party you dislike

C. Develop learning situations which will help the students to get an insight into the characteristics of different political parties

D. Just present the facts included in the class text book on the subject

65. There is a suggestion from the Directorate to group students according to their ability and to assign them to different teachers. In that case which one of the following groups would you prefer to teach?

A. The top group

B. The average group

C. The backward group

D. No special preference

66. A student visits your home to share his personal problems with you. Your response will be:

A. Understand his problems and extend reasonable help to him and boost his morale

B. Tell him not to intrude into your private life

C. Talk to the student's parents about his problems and ask them to help him

D. Tell him not to repeat such visits

67. Some people criticise teachers for taking private tuition and receiving remuneration for their extra work. What is your view about this practice?

A. There is nothing wrong in their practice

B. It is desirable as it is an additional service rendered to learners who need extra help

C. It is a controversial issue and hence has no specific preferences

D. Teachers should consider providing free private education as part of his professional duty

68. Suppose an intelligent boy of your class requests you to lend a particular book which you own. What action will you take in this case?

A. Tell him that he will not give any special consideration for a student and that he has taken a wrong decision when he asked for this favour

B. Lend the book for a fixed period

C. Suggest that he should purchase the book for himself

D. Pretend that the book in your possession belongs to another person and hence cannot be lent

69. Suppose an intelligent student is showing probable symptoms of maladjustment, due to some family problems. The student has great faith in your judgement and he comes to you seeking a solution. What action would you take?

A. You contact the student's parents and inform them about what has happened and ask them to help

B. You tell him that you are not competent to give him guidance and so he has to seek help elsewhere

C. You send back the student without any comments

D. You give him a patient hearing and would suggest a few steps to solve his problems

70. You read a touching report about a natural calamity and that the local authorities are seeking the help of service-minded people to raise funds for helping the affected people. As a teacher what step will you take?

A. Read the report about the calamity in the class and request students to sympathise with the sufferers

B. Give leadership to pupils to participate in a programme for mobilizing funds for helping the victims

C. Make pupils write poems, short stories, etc. on the theme as part of your teaching

D. Organise a discussion on the ways and means of dealing with such situation

71. You come to know that the students in your class have represented to the Principal that another teacher be allotted in your place. What will be your reaction?

A. Scold the students in the open class for their action and tell the Principal that you treat this as a personal insult

B. Plead with the students and make them withdraw their representation

C. Ignore the development and continue with your routine work

D. Find out the fact of the complaint and try hard to improve the quality of your teaching

72. In the Parent Teacher Association of your school, some parents complain about the performance of some of the teachers of the school. How would you react to this?

A. Tell curtly that it is none of their business to criticise teachers and that the Department has its own methods of assessing the work of teachers

B. Accept valid criticisms and encourage a detailed discussion to identify specific cases of inefficiency

C. Withdraw from the meeting protesting against such accusations.

D. Request the teachers' union to agitate against such unjust comments

73. While organising a study tour to an exhibition which will help the students to understand history easily, the parent of one of the students refuses permission for his ward to participate in the study tour. In this situation you would:

A. Complain to the Principal about the non co-operation of the parent

B. Ignore the student and go ahead with the tour with the other students

C. Tell the parent that his son will be missing an excellent opportunity to understanding history

D. Convince the father about the importance of the tour and get his permission to include his ward in the tour

74. A few students in your class complain that they have not understood a topic which you taught. Given below are four activities that you would like to correct this shortcoming. Which one among these is most appropriate to deal with the situation?

A. Tell the students that you will be more careful in future

B. Organize peer learning in the evenings with the help of the high achievers in the class

C. Ask the parents to arrange for private tuition to their wards

D. Administer a pre-diagnostic test to identify gaps that exist in their previous learning and arrange remedial teaching

75. A girl student is in the habit of withdrawing herself from the company of other girls. Four steps are suggested below. Of these which one you consider most desirable?

i. Design small group projects and give her specific share in completing one of these projects

ii. Ask her to interact with others since this will make learning easier for her

iii. Profusely appreciate whenever she successfully completes an assigned task on her own

iv. Encourage her to give suggestions for improving the success of a group in learning

A. (i), (iii) and (iv)
B. All the four
C. (i) and (iii)
D. (iii) only

76. You find that you can't make your students learn a topic the way you want because of wide gaps in their pre-requisite learning. What would you do?

A. Give up the effort as the gaps are too wide to be filled within the short time available
B. Ask the parents to arrange for extra tuition in the pre-requisite areas
C. Identify the gaps and arrange for providing compensatory education programmes
D. Use the teaching time more profitably for teaching other new topics

77. The most important task to be accomplished by a teacher in the present scenario of education is:

A. Maintain discipline in the class
B. Prepare students for the final common examination
C. Conduct examinations and give feed back
D. Develop the skill of learning how to learn

78. You note that a vast portion of the time allocated for the PTA meetings used for petty discussions and for discussing non-educational issue. What step would you take to correct this trend?

A. Discuss the matter privately with the Principal and request him to control the proceedings
B. Complain to the authorities of the department

C. Refrain from attending such meetings

D. Present your views that PTA meetings are meant to discuss serious issues and the members have to adopt a different stand

79. Some of your students do not approve your harsh attitude towards them. What would you do to deal with the situation?

A. Summon them to the teachers' room and listen to them patiently to understand the reason for their opposition

B. Take disciplinary action against them

C. Inform the Principal about the situation and get his advice

D. Neglect them and continue your present style of performance

80. You notice some students fighting in the class room when you enter. Which one of the following steps would you take?

A. Suspend all those involved in the clash

B. Report this to the Principal and leave the decision to him

C. Try to understand the root causes of the problem and work out a solution, and give them a warning that fighting in the class room will not be tolerated in future

D. Warn the students sternly against repeating such misconduct

81. Some of the parents complain that their children are found to sit very late to watch night films on the TV in spite of all the measures they take to discourage such behaviour. What step would you take as a teacher to discourage such undesirable practices?

A. Give special advice to such children in the presence of their parents as it will adversely affect their entire life

B. Convince such children that watching late night films will deny them sufficient sleep

C. Scold such children and prevent them from sitting late by giving some homework

D. Ask them to take lessons from the other seniors who do not sit up late to watch films

82. A pupil facing a serious problem asks the teacher: 'What shall I do?' The teacher should:

A. Suggest a course of action after considering the nature of his problems and his special disposition

B. Suggest to the pupil a solution he would adopt if he were a pupil

C. Ask the pupil to take advice from his parents

D. Have an in-depth discussion of the issue with the pupil and provide him an insight which will help him to take a decision himself

83. **Suppose you are travelling in a train and you come across an old student of yours passing by without greeting you, even though he has seen you. What will be your reaction?**

A. Feel insulted as your student who knows you well has ignored your presence
B. Feel disgusted about the degeneration of values among modern youth
C. Assume that he has not seen you properly to recognize you
D. Call him back and introduce yourself and see whether he will respond

84. **When you are busy with an urgent work in the college a senior retired person visits you and starts a long conversation. How will you react to this situation?**

A. Ask him politely to leave as you have some important work to be completed in an hour
B. Receive him and listen to the conversation
C. Greet him warmly, but tell him politely about the urgency of the work you are doing and that you will meet him in his residence in the evening
D. Remain indifferent to his talk and make him leave on his own

85. **Following a serious clash among students, your principal asks you to find out an amicable solution to prevent such occurrences. Which course of action would you adopt for the purpose?**

A. Listen to both the sides and convince the groups that both sides should agree to a compromise
B. Tell the two groups that severe action will be taken if there are new attempts of physical violence
C. Counsel the leaders individually, find out a mid-way and then arrange for a friendly discussion for compromise
D. Arrange for a joint meeting of the groups to sort out the issue

86. **A teacher makes a mistake in spelling a word and a student comes out with the correction. Which one of the following courses should be adopted by the teacher?**

A. Ask him to get the dictionary from the library, find out the correct spelling and ask him write it on the blackboard, and admit that the spelling was wrong
B. Ignore this and proceed with your teaching
C. Tell the class that you will refer to a dictionary, check the spelling and give an answer in the next class
D. Rationalise it by saying he has confused the word with another word

87. You report the behaviour of one of the troublesome students in your class to the Principal and the Principal expels him from the school. Following this, a few friends of the expelled student enters your private room and starts abusing you. How would you deal with this situation?

A. Report the misbehaviour to the Principal for stern action

B. Raise your voice and give an impression that you are prepared to resist them physically.

C. Face them boldly but patiently and tell them that they were given a just punishment by the Principal who has taken his decision in a fair manner after listening to your arguments and that of the expelled students

D. Seek the help of your colleagues to deal with them

88. Suppose you are urged by some of your colleagues to take up membership of a teacher's union. Which of the following decisions do you consider is the most appropriate?

A. Try to avoid an immediate decision and postpone action

B. Take up membership and solve the issue

C. Avoid taking membership in a union as it will offend the school management

D. Tell the group that you will take a decision after a few days

89. You notice that five students out of the 50 in your class have not come anywhere near your expectations. What steps will you take to help them perform better?

A. Inform the parents and get their help in improving their learning styles

B. Advise the students and their parents to take special tuition

C. Arrange for peer teaching with the help of bright students of the class, under your supervision

D. Neglect them, and concentrate your attention on the majority who are doing well

90. A colleague who over hears you making a wrong statement in your class and reports this to you. How will you react to this?

A. Tell him that you never commit any mistakes

B. Discuss with your colleague about your statement if convinced, thank him for correcting you and see that the correction is given in the next class

C. Talk to your colleague that it is not good to criticize other teachers

D. Request your colleague not to report this to other teachers

91. While preparing for a class, you are unable to understand a point in the text book. Repeated reading and reference to other books did not help. What will you do?

A. Avoid presenting the point in the class
B. Present the point as stated in the book
C. Tell the pupils that you have not properly understood the point and need more time comprehend
D. Discuss with senior members of the faculty and clarify your doubts

92. Which of the following instructional strategies would you prefer in your teaching?

A. Enrich the textual material by gathering additional information from other books and by consulting with subject experts
B. Limit learning experiences to what is specifically required for teaching the textual material
C. Discuss probable questions so that the students can do/perform well in the common examination
D. Ask pupils to read the text book in advance and organize class discussions on what is presented there

93. Which of the following, in your opinion, is the most important competence expected of an effective teacher?

A. Competence to plan and provide goal-oriented learning experiences
B. Ability to interpret the content of learning in clear and simple language
C. Skill to dramatise learning situations
D. Ability to generate in the pupils a feeling of confidences

94. As a teacher, what is the ideal role that you have to play while participating in a Parent Teacher Association meeting?

A. Listen patiently to what the parents have to say about the school
B. Give an undertaking that you will implement the suggestions made by the parents and expert teachers in your school
C. Objectively present relevant issues faced by your institution and try to procure the co-operation of the parents for their solution
D. Keep a diary about the general performance of pupils in your class and present relevant points before the parents and make them adopt remedial measures to improve their performance

95. The Principal circulates a code of behaviour to be followed by all teachers of the school. How will you react to this?

A. Accept all the suggestions and act accordingly
B. Organize a thorough discussion on this with other teachers before finalizing these and then practise the general consensus

C. Ignore the behaviour code and continue your normal style of functioning

D. Protest against the act of the Principal by taking the stand that his circulars amounts to interference in one's professional performance

96. Students in your class engage in a demonstration against some disciplinary action taken by the Principal. What role will you play in dealing with the situation?

A. Not to interfere as you are not concerned with the issue

B. Stand firmly with the students and request the Principal to withdraw his decision

C. Support the Principal to help him in maintaining discipline

D. Try to mediate by keeping equal distance from two parties, analyze the situation objectively and make the parties agree for a negotiated settlement

97. A new village road is being constructed as part of a community activity. One of the landowners who oppose the project refuses to give one cent of land free for the project. The volunteers seek your advice and help as you are a popular teacher of the area. Which one of the following courses would you adopt?

A. Advice the group to construct the road ignoring the opposition of the owner

B. Use your influence as a teacher to convince him the need to take a non partial approach and to persuade him to give permission for the construction

C. Co-operate with the committee in filing a suit

D. Use your influence with the local police Inspector and force the owner to give permission

98. You are aware of the fact that your Principal is planning to move against you even when you attend your work properly, but has not been submissive. Your principal is penalizing you. What would you do to deal with this situation?

A. Retort strongly whenever he tries to penalize you

B. Continue to work sincerely, but develop an impression that you will not yield

C. Avoid facing the Principal as far as possible

D. Seek the help of your colleagues to fight against the Principal

99. A colleague tries to create a hostile attitude to you in the mind of the Principal. How will you react?

A. Openly scold him for his indecent behaviour in the presence of other colleagues

B. Ignore the move and allow him to act the way he wants

C. Develop a climate of acceptance through sincere work and proper behaviour

D. Play the same trick against him

100. To what extent should the behaviour of a teacher to his students can be compared with his behaviour towards his own children?

A. The two behaviours should almost be same

B. There is little meaning in comparing the two

C. A teacher has to be more strict in dealing with his pupils than in dealing with his won children

D. Take less interest in students

101. You can convince your students your impartiality by:

A. Speaking eloquently about the need to be impartial

B. Using your teaching talking about how you believe in impartial behaviour

C. Demonstrating your impartiality through fair decisions in your dealing with students

D. Discussing with your students that most teachers are partial in their dealing with students

102. Some parents who want to project another teacher in your college raise some baseless accusations against you in the PTA meeting. What will be your reaction?

A. Explain the real situation to the PTA members

B. Defend yourself using strong language

C. Refuse to react and continue with your work

D. Seek the support of your teachers organisation for defending your innocence

103. You intend to invite your colleagues for your marriage which is to take place shortly. Which among the following methods would you adopt for the purpose?

A. Ask the school peon to distribute your invitation letters to all the colleagues

B. Invite only teachers belonging to your union

C. Seek the help of your close friend and act as per his advice

D. Personally invite every teacher in your school, ignoring other considerations.

104. Which of the following should be your priority in selecting an appropriate goal for the functioning of your college, considering the fact that education should correct the errors of society?

A. The college should help learners to get a reasonable job
B. The college should help to strengthen the political views you hold
C. The college should help students to understand the human beings
D. The college be help students improve their productive efficiency

105. A student is showing signs of withdrawal tendency. What step, do you think, will be most appropriate to deal with this boy?

A. Give the student special help in completing his class assignments
B. Contact his parents and persuade them to give greater attention to his behaviour
C. Ask his classmates to talk to him whenever possible and be friendly to him
D. Give him simple responsibilities in small group projects and persuade other students in his group to accept him as one among them and give him full acceptance

106. A student is in the habit of making comments in the class with the aim of belittling your authority and making fun of you. Which among the following steps would you take to deal with the student?

A. Provide the student opportunities to take up important responsibilities in the running of the class
B. Report the matter to his parents and seek their help to correct him
C. Retaliate by making fun of him every time he makes wrong comments
D. Talk to him personally and tell him that you will take strong action unless he behaves himself

107. You notice certain deficiencies in learning of a few students in your class belonging to socially deprived groups. What step would you suggest to help these students to perform in an equal level with others?

A. Make a scientific analysis of the deficiencies created by social deprivation and organize special compensatory programmes for correcting such deficiencies
B. Provide learning experiences that would suit their impoverished backgrounds
C. Lighten their curricular load and lower the expectation to suit their performance level
D. Empathise with their difficulty and encourage them

108. The father of a student in your class complains that in spite of his stern warning, his son avoids attending classes and spends his time in the company of a few loafers. What will be the initial step you would take to deal with the student?

A. Locate the student along with his friends during a working day and find out they are using their time
B. Trace the student during the working time and take him to the Principal for action
C. Call the student to the teachers' room and warn him in the presence of other teachers
D. Have a personal talk with the student and identify the reason for his truancy

109. A student is found to copy the home assignments of another student and present them as his own. What will you do to correct the boy?

A. Ask the other students not to help this student in preparing assignments
B. Give the student some additional assignment and help to complete them with the help of peers, with instruction that the work is done by the student himself
C. Ignore the student and allow him to do what he wants
D. Meet the boy's father and ask him to arrange for some private tuition

110. In spite of adopting different methods for correction you are not able to ensure that your students are regular and up-to-date in their learning. What would you do?

A. Seek suggestions from other teachers and use what appears to be good
B. Give up your efforts and forget about it
C. Look for new strategies from books on educational psychology
D. Conduct an action research to arrive at a dependable method of solution

111. A very poor boy in your class shows exceptional ability in music. Which one of the following steps would you adopt to deal with the student?

A. Encourage his parents to give him special training
B. Provide his parents with some financial help to give him training in music and prepare him for contests
C. Bring the matter to the notice of the Principal and arrange a school function where the student is given an opportunity to exhibit his talent
D. Give wide publicity to his ability and procure for him maximum opportunities to get better training and exhibit his talent

112. Which of the following, in your opinion, is the best strategy to create and sustain a student's motivation to learn?

A. Ensure that at each stage in the development of a lesson, every student is given an opportunity to play a significant role in the development of the lesson
B. Asking a number of thought-provoking questions based on the material taught

C. Use humorous anecdotes and interesting jokes to make the learning interesting

D. Encourage these students who answer the questions correctly

113. There is a difficult topic in the syllabus, which needs higher technical knowledge which you do not possess. What step would you adopt to tackle this situation?

A. Tell the pupils that as it is a difficult technical area which needs the help of subject experts to teach, and hence it is best that they learn the facts presented in the text book by heart

B. Advice the pupils to ask their parents to seek special help from some outside expert

C. Ask the Principal to procure some additional learning material that would help to understand the topic

D. Identify an expert in the field from the nearby locality invite him to the school and make use of his expertise for dealing with the area

114. One of your senior colleagues is in the habit of influencing the junior members of the teaching staff just to assert his superiority ignoring the ethics of the teaching profession. How would you react to this situation?

A. Form another teacher group to oppose him

B. Try to avoid dealing with him and ignore him

C. Try to develop a counter group to propagate your views strongly among the staff

D. With the co-operation of your colleagues convince him that his 'tactics' will not be accepted

115. You want to instil in your pupils the spirit of democracy. Which of the following strategies do you think, is the most effective for the purpose?

A. Organize a school discussion on the advantages of democracy over other systems and follow this up by circulating a notice to all students about the advantages of a democratic political system

B. Conduct an election for a class assembly and give the representatives certain responsibilities and prove that the democratic style of functioning is superior

C. Maintain a democratic atmosphere in your dealings and make the pupils responsible for class management, assigning duties to the students

D. Invite important local leaders and arrange for their speeches about the worth of democracy

116. Which of the following modalities would you prefer while transacting the curriculum in your class?

A. Present the learning materials in the question-answer form and thus ensure good performance in the examination

B. Conduct frequent test papers where the question papers follow the model used by the common public examinations

C. Explain the concepts and principles clearly and ensure understanding by all the students so that students can perform well in examination irrespective of the question model used

D. Present the learning activities appropriate for the development of the students

117. What, do you think, is the most appropriate role to be played by a teacher in conducting co-curricular programmes?

A. Sincerely discharge duties relating to the conduct of co-curricular programmes if assigned by the Principal

B. Leave all responsibility for conducting co-curricular programmes to the students

C. Critically watch what is happening and report this to other teachers

D. Actively participate and monitor every aspects of the co-curricular activities to give maximum benefit to most students

118. Which one of the following strategies would you adopt to get the appreciation and respect from your pupils?

A. Freely interact with students and act like a friend

B. Champion the needs and demands of students before the authorities

C. Develop an intimacy with the Principal

D. Ensure high-level performance in all the curricular and co-curricular programmes of your school

119. In your opinion, what should be the preferred goal of teaching the topic 'The Second World War' in the history classes for students belonging to the late adolescent stage.

A. To provide learners with a historical perspective of the Second World War

B. Developing in the learner a positive attitude towards world peace

C. To enable students to learn history systematically as a social science

D. To enable students to establish cause effect relation between historical incidents

120. A few students in your class need help in overcoming difficulties in learning your subject. You do not have sufficient time to spare for them. What step will you take to deal with the situation?

A. Arrange for them to have extended study in peer groups involving superior students in the class

B. Send a message to the parents regarding the need to give them additional help in the different areas of your subject

C. Request a friend who takes private tuition to help these students

D. Provide assignments for your students to review the portions taught

121. What step will you suggest to create interest in social activities among your pupils?

A. Organise some programmes each academic year to bring the students into close contact with their locality

B. Organise discussions highlighting the need for engaging in social work

C. Teach life histories of people who brought about revolutionary changes through social work

D. Frequently organize small projects in which the students come into close contact with the local community

122. Which among the following are the most important attribute or attributes of a school teacher? (i) Commitment to social issues (ii) empathy with problems faced by society (iii) gaining mastery of the subject to be taught and (iv) gaining insight into psychological needs of pupils are four attributes.

A. (iii) and (iv)

B. (i), (iii) and (iv)

C. (i), (ii) and (iii)

D. All the four

123. In your view, which of the following is a clear evidence of professionalism of a teacher?

A. Maintaining membership in a teacher organisation

B. Intrinsic motivation to attend in-service courses

C. Engaging the classes assigned to him/her using validated scientific principles and practices

D. Standing in the forefront in the agitations for demanding the rights of teachers

124. You are not sure of certain areas which you are expected to teach. You have four choices suggested below:

(i) Read books other than the text book which deal with the matter

(ii) Seek help from experts in the subject

(iii) Seek help from your colleagues

(iv) Ask students to get help from some other sources.

Which of these is/are most appropriate for dealing with the situation?

A. (i) only B. (i) and (ii) C. (i), (ii) and (iii) D. All the four

125. What strategy would you advocate for ensuring proper classroom discipline?

A. Give appropriate punishment to every student for every mistake

B. Make your classes more effective and interesting

C. Make all students play active roles in class functioning

D. Maintain close contact with the parents and the public

126. Four problem class situations are given below:

(i) One student is unusually withdrawing in his behaviour

(ii) A considerable number of students always score low in your subject

(iii) Some students in your class are in the habit of disturbing the class of a new teacher

(iv) In spite of warning, most of the students of the class are irregular in submitting class assignments.

Which of these solutions (separately or in combination) demand the conduct of action research?

A. (i) All the four B. (i), (ii) and (iv)

C. (ii) and (iii) D. (ii) and (iv)

127. A student in your class approaches you for help in selecting an appropriate optional subject. Which one of the following steps would you adopt to deal with the situation?

A. Avoid answering him since you are likely to be blamed if he makes a wrong choice

B. Try to understand the student and suggest alternatives from which he could make a choice

C. Consider the demand for the subject and recommend one which is in maximum demand

D. Convince him that he should make the selection for himself after consulting with his parents

128. You find that one of the students in your class is absent - minded and inattentive most of the time. What would you do to this behaviour?

A. Report the case to the principal for action

B. Establish close rapport with the student, find out the reason for his behaviour and create in him an interest in learning

C. Punish the student for his negligence

D. Bring the matter to the notice of his parents and make him correct his behaviour

129. You notice that a majority of your students do not follow your teaching. Which step would you adopt?

A. Ensure greater involvement of students in the activities of the class

B. Advise the students to be more attentive

C. Suspend the classes till the students are ready to learn

D. Conduct an action research programme and identify the reason for their lack of interest

130. A student falls down unconscious when your class is in session. Which step would you adopt to deal with the issue?

A. Contact his parents and make them deal with the situation

B. Go to the Principal's office and ask for help

C. Give first aid and take the student to the nearby hospital

D. Contact the doctor in the nearby hospital and seek his help

131. You are taking an examination where you find that the question paper is extremely difficult for you. What will you do?

A. Answer the questions with the needed presence of mind

B. Walk-out from the examination hall

C. Sit through the examination to give the impression that you are performing well

D. Complain loudly about the need to include simple questions

132. Some of your students often imitate the way you treat them. How will you deal with this class?

A. Call the student leaders to the teacher's room for a private discussion and hear them patiently

B. Take disciplinary action against the leaders

C. Inform the principal about the situation and seek his advice

D. Neglect the trouble - makers and continue your style of teaching

133. While dealing with a handicapped student in the class, the best course you would adopt is:

A. feel sorry for him

B. offer him financial help when needed

C. help him to become self - reliant

D. help him to get admitted to an institution for the handicapped

134. A student is found to be in the habit of reading comics when the class is in session. What course of action would you adopt to deal with the student?

A. Ask questions more frequently to make him alert

B. Inform the parents and ask them not to buy comics for him

C. Have free talks with him and identify the reason for his behaviour

D. Adopt teaching methodologies where every student is kept alert

135. Your principal often criticises you in the presence of your students. This affects your self esteem. How will you deal with the situation?

A. Protest in the presence of the students when this happens

B. Make this an issue in the next teachers' meeting

C. Go to the Principal's office after the class and make a strong protest

D. Politely explain your case in private and convince him that what he has done was wrong

136. A colleague of yours is on long leave. The Principal distributes her work among the other members of your faculty. What will be your reaction?

A. Convince the Principal that you can't take it up as you are already over burdened

B. Willingly accept it with a request to get a substitute as early as possible

C. Seek the advice of the teachers in the next teachers meeting

D. Do what the other members of the faculty do

137. The leaders of your teacher organisation in your school plan an agitation. You feel that it is untimely. What will be your course of action?

A. Tell the teachers that you disagree with the move, but will abide by their decision

B. Apply for leave on the day and avoid participating in the protest

C. Present your views to the leader and convince him about the need to change the decision

D. Form a group who agree with your views and agitate against the proposal

138. Some of your fellow teachers are in the habit of cracking filthy jokes in the teacher's room during leisure time which is often overheard by students. What would be your reaction?

A. Convince such teachers that their behaviour is inappropriate for their profession

B. Reprimand them and remind them that they are members of a profession which is expected to teach proper behaviour to the young students
C. Tell them to mind their language while cracking jokes within the college premises
D. Leave the place at once

139. One of your friends is in the habit of opening the letters addressed to you without your permission. How would you deal with him?

A. Give a written complaint to the police
B. Encourage your students to ridicule him for his action
C. Make sure that the post man hands over your letters to you in person
D. Take your vengeance by opening letters addressed to him

140. A girl student was absent for a few days due to illness and she has difficulty in following the classes. How would you deal with this case?

A. Take initiative in inducting some compensatory programme for her with the help of her peers
B. Ask her parents to arrange for special tuition to help her to make up her deficiency
C. Volunteer to give her private tuition for a few months
D. Contact the girl's parents and ask them to take appropriate steps to correct her deficiency

141. You find a cartoon sketch in a student's notebook which is of a good quality. The student has portrayed you as one of the characters in his cartoon. How would you use this information?

A. Give the student a stern warning in the open class and ask him not to waste the pages for trivial purposes
B. Report the matter to the Principal with a request to take urgent action
C. Suspend the student from the class and ask him to meet the Principal
D. Show the cartoon to the whole class and congratulate him for his unusual talent but advise him not to draw cartoons during class hours

142. A villager known to you complains to you about a student in your class making indecent comments every time he sees him on the road. What would you do to correct this behaviour?

A. Advise the villager to attend the PTA meeting and make the complaint to the members
B. Arrange for a meeting of the villager and the student and sort out the problem in the presence of the Principal

C. Tell the villager that you cannot do anything for correcting the behaviour of students outside the school

D. Ask the villager to give a written complaint to the Principal asking for immediate action

143. Suppose a student gives wrong answers deliberately to any question that you put to him. What would you do to correct the student?

A. Punish him by sending him out of the class

B. Report to the Principal and ask him to take disciplinary measures against the student

C. Refuse to ask any question to the student

D. Try to understand the reason for his unusual behaviour and correct it

144. The most important aspect to be considered by a teacher while accepting teaching as his profession is:

A. Salary commemorate with one's qualifications and experience

B. Social status assigned to the profession

C. Freedom and ideal working conditions as a teacher

D. Psychological satisfaction derived from teaching

145. Quite often a student in your class disturbs your teaching by demanding clarifications in what you have said. You know that they are useful questions and the answers will benefit most of the students. How would you react to the situation?

A. Discourage him by making fun of him

B. Ask him not to disturb the class while teaching

C. Make use of his question to clarify the points you have overlooked

D. Ask him to meet you in private and get the doubts cleared

146. Which of the following do you consider is the most important responsibility of a teacher?

A. Ensure the best student performance in the public examination

B. Encourage maximum participants of students in co-curricular activities

C. Establish a strong link between the college and the community

D. Develop an atmosphere in the college for self learning for knowledge construction

147. There is a proposal to start a guidance centre in your college. How would you react to this proposal?

A. Will not play any active role since this is a technical question to be answered by specialists

B. Take up any responsibility prescribed by the Principal and make a specialized study of the issues

C. Take up the responsibility to pool all inputs required

D. Watch the progress of the work and then decide how to react

148. An adolescent in your class is in the habit of engaging himself in destroying school furniture in spite of warnings. What step would you take to deal with the student?

A. Try to convince him that others in the class hate him for creating inconvenience to them

B. Seek the help of his family members to persuade him to stop the habit

C. Make him the leader of class project for improving classroom facilities through community participation

D. Make his class mates to spend more time in his company

149. You are appointed as a teacher in a remote village with a small population and where most of the parents are poor and uneducated. You want to help the community. What would you do to an as initial measure?

A. Teach only the simple topics in the syllabus and make the class examination very simple

B. Orgnise compensatory programmes to give the students additional help they need

C. Contact the authorities to procure extra school facilities to enrich the learning atmosphere

D. Establish close rapport with the parents and get their co-operation in improving standards

150. Your staff council calls for a strike on a non-educational issue in which the union leaders are interested. You strongly feel that the cause is not genuine. How would you react to the demand?

A. Co-operate with the group and participate in the strike

B. Argue against the strike call and try to convince he teachers that the strike will reduce the credibility of teaching community

C. Inform your colleagues that you don't agree to the need for a strike but you are joing the strike to satisfy the others

D. Go on casual leave for a few days and escape from committing a mistake

151. While valuing answer scripts of students of another school public examination, you note that a few candidates have received illegal help from somebody in answering the questions. What action would you take?

A. Ignore what you have noted and give full credit to correct answers to all the correct answers
B. Not to assign marks for items which you feel have been answered with help from others
C. Report to the authorities what you have noticed totake for appropriate action
D. Request the authorities to take action against the invigilator

152. You note that a small group of students are in the habit of disturbing the class through noisy discussions, whistling, use of indecent language, etc. what would you do to discourage such wrong practices?

A. Assert your authority as a teacher and force them to behave properly
B. Expel some students from the class
C. Tackle the rowdy elements with the help of the well behaved students in the class
D. Change your teaching strategy to win over the trouble – making students to your side

153. You note that a student in the last row is disturbing his peers, when you are writing on the blackboard. What do you think is the reason for his misbehaviour?

A. The student has poor eye-sight and hence he is seeking the help of others to read what you have written on the blackboard
B. The student is not interested in noting down what you are writing
C. The student wants to create problems for you
D. All of these

154. You found that an adolescent in your class suffers from anxiety and tension when you are explaining a difficult concept in the class. How would you help him?

A. By trying to understand the student and develop an intimacy with him so that he will share his problems with you
B. By telling him that becoming tense will make learning more difficult
C. By neglecting him totally
D. By making fun of his behaviour in the open class

155. You have to teach a blind student along with normal students in a common class. What special considerations would you give to deal with the blind student?

A. It is not practicable to give extra attention to the students and so I will ignore the student

B. Recommend to the Principal to send him to a special school instead of dealing with him along with regular students

C. Treat him sympathetically and encourage other students to be sympathetic to him

D. Give a seat in the first row and adjust and provide him extra learning experiences wherever needed both during and after the class

156. Your principal is a corrupt person and he urges you to co-operate with him in dealing with college funds. How would you react to his demand?

A. Will not agree to his demand but oppose him openly

B. Remain silent without helping him in any way

C. Persuade him not to adopt steps which would spoil his reputation and that of the school

D. Co-operate with him and ensure that he does not work against you

157. You notice that a large number of students in your class execute their project work with the help of parents or experts from out side the school. Which one of the following steps would you to take to correct the situation?

A. Warn such students that their projects will not be assessed

B. Identify such students and warn them not to adopt this method

C. Will not interfere with the methods adopted by students for completing a project

D. Tell the student that grading will be done purely on the basis of what the student has done.

158. A student belonging to a poor family comes to the school in torn cloth. Other students are in the habit of teasing him for inadequate dressing. How would you deal with the situation?

A. Send the student out of the class and ask him to come back properly dressed

B. Punish the students who tease him

C. Organise a student committee to help the student to purchase his uniform

D. Ignore this situation and continue the usual class teaching

159. The teacher's union declares an indefinite strike one month before the terminal school examination. How will react to this situation?

A. Will not join the strike and help the schools to make arrangements to conduct classes

B. Join the strike

C. Create a teacher group to oppose the move and issue a statement to that effect

D. Persuade the teachers to select a better occasion for striking work

160. A particular parent fails to attend the class PTA meeting repeatedly. What will you do as the class teacher?

A. Will send a note to the parent through the student that he should try to attend every PTA meeting

B. Pay a visit to the family and have a friendly discussion to motivate the parent

C. Try to understand his difficulties and fix the timing to suit the convenience of the parents

D. Complain to the head of institution about the laxity of the parent

161. A student is accused of malpractice in the examination. As a teacher how will you deal with the charge?

A. Give a stern warning to the student and tell him that he will be expelled from school if he is caught again

B. Debar him from taking the examination

C. Inform his parents and tell them that he is likely to be expelled from the school

D. Make him a member of the class committee for conduct of examinations.

162. A biology teacher who intends to teach skeletal system finds that the students are engaged in a discussion about the previous day's cricket match. If you are the teacher how would you deal with the situation?

A. Allow time for the class to finish their discussion

B. Take them to the biology lab and introduce them to the skeletal system

C. Participate in the discussion for a time and lead them to a discussion of the dislocation of bones of sport stars and use this for introducing the skeletal system

D. Curtly tell them that classrooms are meant for teaching and begin the lesson

163. Your colleague does not have the competence to use multimedia for classroom instruction. How will you help her to overcome her difficulty?

A. Encourage her to study the techniques herself before using the multimedia

B. Advise her to continue the traditional modes of instruction till she acquires the needed competencies

C. Give her a standard book which will help her in handling multimedia equipments

D. Operate the multimedia equipments in her class when she is teaching.

164. You find that a student is very weak in your subject. What will you do to help him to overcome his weakness?

A. Give the student more assignments to improve his class performance

B. Direct the student to study the subject with help of peers

C. Provide opportunities to the student to discuss the difficulties with you

D. Identify his learning difficulties and develop strategies for correcting them and integrate this with your regular teaching.

165. Proper evidence of the professional competency of a teacher is:

A. His ability to maintain strict discipline in the class

B. His ability to develop in his students the ability to learn

C. The interest he takes in the welfare of the students

D. Adopting learning strategies which will help him to maintain an ideal learning culture in the classroom

166. As a teacher of biology you have to display a picture of the circulatory system in the class. Which is the ideal way of doing it?

A. Ask the students to refer to the diagram in the text book while explaining

B. Ask a group of students with artistic aptitude to prepare a chart for display

C. Buy a prepared chart and use it

D. Direct the students to copy the picture from the text book before you start your teaching

167. Which one of the following procedures would you consider is the most effective for developing values?

A. Including values as a topic in the curriculum and allot time for teaching this topic like other topics in the curriculum

B. Practising some of the important values in your dealing with students

C. Creating learning situations where the pupils get opportunities to adopt these values

D. Teaching the life history of great personalities with emphasis on the values they practised

168. Which of the following will you accept as a sure evidence for high creativity of a student?

A. Identifying a variety of analogies from life to illustrate a principle learnt

B. Finding out a correct solution for a problematic situation within a short time

C. Working out unusual solutions to a problem

D. Reading books without compulsion for getting new ideas

169. For the proper rehabilitation of a retarded child in a self-help programme, the essential help must come from:

A. teacher's action plan

B. follow up programmes designed by the parents

C. parental participation in the self-help programme

D. combination of all of these

170. Some students have difficulty in understanding a scientific principle taught in the class. Which of the following steps do you consider as most appropriate for dealing with the situation?

A. Explaination of the principle in simple language

B. Instruct the students to discuss the topic among themselves and draw a conclusion

C. Tell the students that when it is difficult to understand a principle it is best that they learn it by heart

D. Analyse the concepts involved in the principle in a sequence and present the principle using this foundation

171. The implications of a scientific phenomenon are not clear to most students. What measures would you suggest to make the meaning of the phenomenon clear?

A. Ask the students to give their own explanations

B. Use some concrete mediators that would help in presenting a visual representation of the phenomenon

C. Explain the phenomenon a number of times again and again until every student understands it

D. Advise the students to seek the help of an outside expert

172. Which of the following learning experiences do you think is the most appropriate to the developmental stage of a sixteen year old learner, while learning a scientific principle?

A. Presenting activities which illustrate the principle

B. Explain the principle with the help of a diagram which illustrates the application of the principle

C. Arrive at the principle inductively by presenting many particular cases and induce the commonality and express it in a principle

D. Memorising the principle for use on future occasions.

173. Which of the following strategies is the most appropriate for enhancing the level of mastery in learning?

A. Providing attractive incentives to high achievers

B. Providing continuous in-service training to teachers
C. Adopting the diagnostic testing and remediation while imparting instruction
D. Use of technological gadgets to make instruction more realistic

174. Which of the following do you think is an essential first step for teaching a topic using mastery learning?

A. Present some interesting anecdotes to prepare learners for the presentation to follow
B. Take steps to identify gaps in pre-requisite learning of the topic, and give remediation wherever needed
C. Ask the students to prepare for the class by learning the topic in advance
D. Make a thorough content analysis of the topic

175. While walking along a village path, a student is in the habit of destroying wild plants on both sides. What is your explanation for the strange behavoiur of the student?

A. He is doing this for fun
B. He wants to show other students that he can be aggressive
C. He wants to release his pent up energy
D. He is not being loved by others and punished by his parents for trivial reasons

176. Which one of the following explanations is most suited to define the teaching profession?

A. A noble profession
B. A man making exercise meant to achieve over all development of the youth
C. A social institution for developing character
D. A system for mastering new ideas for social change

177. Why do you prefer teaching to other professions?

A. It helps to create a new generation who have imbibed many desirable characteristics
B. The memory of some of the best teachers who taught me in school and the respect they received from others motivate me
C. I like young children and would like to help them to become better citizens
D. I can share the knowledge acquired by me with the new generation of students

178. Good teaching is the result of:

A. devotion of the teacher to the profession
B. qualifications acquired by the teacher

C. leadership given by the head of the institution
D. professionalism of the teacher

179. A reputed senior teacher in a discipline has a responsibility to:
A. clarify the doubts of junior teachers who are not familiar with the advanced development
B. explain difficult areas only to those who can pay him for his help
C. use his knowledge only for his own teaching
D. confine his help to a selected few in the teaching community who can understand and use the knowledge

180. A teacher should consider himself as:
A. the final authority on any topic he is expected to teach
B. one with radical ideas relating to his subject
C. one who is able to maintain his status-quo among his colleagues
D. a fairly knowledgeable person

181. If a teacher finds that most of his students are not able to understand what he taught he should:
A. give up teaching
B. start teaching using other methods
C. go to reputed experts and get their help to change his teaching methods
D. make fun of the students and create an impression that the fault lies with the students

182. Which category of teachers will be most successful in the profession?
A. One who teaches in such a way as to develop in the students a real liking for the subject
B. One who comes punctually to the class and prepares students for the examination
C. One who tries to develop a proper value system among his students
D. One who knows his subject well and motivates his students to learn

183. Which among the following categories is least suited to take up teaching as a profession?
A. One who cannot ensure discipline in the class
B. One whose knowledge of the subject is not deep
C. One who has no interest in teaching
D. One who accepts values which are not conducive to the welfare of the society

184. Which of the following qualities of a teacher contributes most to better student discipline in the classroom?

A. Attractive appearance

B. Accepting behaviour and pleasant manners

C. Effective teaching

D. Simple life style

185. A teacher can succeed in his profession if he:

A. has acquired high academic qualifications

B. has a genuine interest in teaching

C. knows his subject thoroughly

D. knows how to enforce classroom discipline

186. The most important reason why we need a total restructuring of educational system is:

A. It does not cater to the harmonious development of students

B. The system caters to the need of the rich people in the community

C. It works using theoretical principles ignoring its impact on the learners

D. It does not practice what is treated as ideal in modern educational practice

187. The prime responsibility of a teacher is:

A. getting the help of parents to improve school facilities

B. imparting instruction using scientific principles

C. creating a healthy classroom climate for teaching

D. establishing close contact with the parents

188. The most important role expected of a teacher in higher classes is to:

A. prepare for his lectures to cover all the details

B. suggest important references and make the students to use them in learning

C. prepare the students for the final examination

D. teach the students to learn on their own

189. 'Peer teaching' means:

A. acquiring the study habits of the members of a peer group

B. helping students to understand the characteristics of their peers

C. two groups of students in a class teaching each another

D. selected student in a class teaching the weaker students

190. Which of the following instructional strategies will be most effective for developing a democratic outlook on social issues by your students?

A. The teacher likes leadership in analysing select social issues and suggesting solutions
B. Arranging seminars on select social issues in which the participation of experts in the field and arrive at solutions
C. Inviting local people and making them present their issues and help them to come out with ways of dealing with such issues
D. Encouraging to present their own views on social issues and present conflicting views

191. Which one of the following strategies would you adopt to ensure students social commitment as a social value?

A. Set apart special time for teaching values
B. Make the students read biographies of famous social workers
C. Give leadership to students to work as volunteers in environmental cleaning of the village close to the school
D. Organize co-curricular programmes to highlight the importance of social commitment

192. Which one of the following characteristics of school principal you consider most appropriate for his job?

A. Plans carefully to cover all the activities of the institution in advance and encourage teachers to implement them
B. Gives complete freedom to teachers to plan and implement various activities
C. Involves the community leaders of the locality in all the activities of the college
D. Develops action plans in staff meetings and continuously monitor their implementation

193. Which of the following is the most appropriate strategy to correct undesirable behaviours of students?

A. Punish students for every undesirable behaviour then and there
B. Never provide opportunities to students to misbehave
C. Tolerate accidental mistakes, but promptly take corrective measures
D. Identify the misbehaving students and give them proper psychological treatment, after identifying the causes for their behaviour

194. Which one of the following measures would you adopt for preventing absenteeism in your class?

A. Punish severely the absentees and use this as a deterrent
B. Give full freedom to students to decide whether they are to attend the classes or not

C. Increase the attractiveness of class teaching with greater student participation in learning

D. Impress on the students the need for attending classes regularly

195. The teachers in modern classrooms are expected to play diverse roles mainly because:

A. they have to deal with a vast expansion of knowledge

B. they have to deal with the complex nature of society

C. they have to fulfil the complex social expectations

D. they have to deal with a large number of students

196. Which of the following qualities is most important for success in the teaching profession?

A. Ability to deal with pupils

B. Systematic planning for instruction

C. Punctuality in attending the college

D. Cordial relationship with pupils

197. You are appointed as a class teacher. The first thing that you will attend to is:

A. identify the problem students in the class

B. establish rapport with the students

C. convince the students that you are a competent teacher

D. enforce discipline in the class

198. The reason why you would like to take up teaching as a profession is:

A. it is most lucrative

B. it provides enough leisure time

C. it is a respectable profession

D. it is a profession in which you can shine

199. The primary duty of the teacher is to:

A. help students to learn

B. enforce classroom discipline

C. provide the latest development in your subject to the students

D. prepare students for the state-level examination

200. Which among the following qualities you consider is the most important requirement a for teacher?

A. Genuine interest in teaching
B. Mastery over the subject you have to teach
C. Ability to express ideas with clarity
D. General communication skill

201. If a majority of students in your class show signs of restlessness and inattention, it could be due to:
A. the inferior intellectual ability of the students
B. the ineffective instructional style adopted by you
C. the inferior infrastructural facilities
D. all the above

202. The duty of a teacher is that of a:
A. philosopher who preaches the need for values
B. guide who helps students in achieving optimal development
C. guardian who protects the interests of the students
D. co-ordinator who organises creative activities

203. The competency of a teacher can be judged on the basis of his:
A. record of work in the profession
B. published works on the subject
C. personality
D. ability to meet the learning needs of pupils

204. The effectiveness of a class is determined by:
A. the proficiency of the teacher in the subject handled by him
B. the ability of the teacher to communicate with his students
C. the ability to ensure the involvement of his students in the teaching-learning process
D. all the above

205. A teacher can promote ideal learning by:
A. covering the syllabus in time
B. teaching students to answer items in question banks
C. encouraging students to ask probing questions
D. evaluating student learning at appropriate points

206. Accountability of a teacher means:
A. accuracy in maintaining accounts of money spent by him

B. maintaining accounts as per the rules prescribed by the school
C. responsibility to perform the educational functions expected of him
D. teaching to satisfy the school inspecting officers

207. In order to help pupils acquire a skill, the first step to be taken is:
A. providing an ideal model to observe and imitate
B. developing knowledge about the principles involved in good teaching
C. let the student learn using the principle of trial and error
D. announce rewards for those who show satisfactory progress

208. A teacher can be considered a successful professional if he:
A. knows his subject thoroughly
B. is able to produce cent percent result in common examinations
C. effectively meets the need of all the learners
D. publishes research papers in reputed research journals

209. The most important challenge for the teacher is to:
A. deal with problems of indiscipline
B. make his evaluation procedures scientific
C. make students understand what he speaks
D. make the teaching process enjoyable and meaningful

210. Students will get interested in a lesson if:
A. the teacher is friendly with them
B. they are able to assimilate the content properly
C. the teacher uses audio-visual aids to supplement his teaching
D. they are told that what is taught is important for further learning

211. A teacher will get maximum appreciation if he:
A. has exceptional good looks
B. empathises with the problems of his students and helps them
C. is friendly with all the students
D. has an attractive voice

212. Which one of the following characteristics reflects the professional commitment of a teacher?
A. Covers all the portions assigned to him much before the examination
B. Attends to the personal problems of the student
C. Ensures active participation of students in the instructional process
D. Maintains proper contact with parents

213. The teacher's philosophy of life influences the pupil because:
A. the student understands the philosophy when taught by a good teacher
B. teacher's philosophy is accepted by the student
C. the teacher's way of living is unconsciously imitated by the student
D. it reflects the philosophy of the society

214. Which among the following is to be avoided in classroom teaching?
A. Ensuring the attention of all students in the class
B. Teasing the students
C. Lecturing using illustrative examples
D. Teaching with the help of appropriate teaching aids

215. The most dependable evidence of good teaching is:
A. high percentage of pass in the common examination
B. developing the ability of students to solve their problems
C. the quantum of information provided through teaching
D. the number of students who opt for the subject as their optional

216. The most crucial teaching skill is:
A. perfect control over the students
B. covering the syllabus within the stipulated time
C. helping students to internalise the matter presented
D. conducting classes regularly

217. While planning a lesson which of the following steps would you consider first?
A. Set the instructional objectives to be attained
B. Identify the various media to be used for improving communication
C. Design learning experiences for curriculum transaction
D. Formulate procedures for effective evaluation

218. Which one of the following would you consider is the most important duty of a teacher?
A. Prepare the pupils for the final examination
B. Conduct the classes punctually and finish the topics
C. Transact the curriculum in conformity with the objectives
D. Enforce proper discipline in the classroom

219. When you have doubts about a specific content to be taught, which one of the following steps would you take?

A. Study the textual matter thoroughly and clear the doubt
B. Refer to other standard books and discuss the area with senior teachers
C. Omit the topic and teach the remaining areas
D. Ask the pupils to get the clarification from experts

220. Which one of the following competencies adds most to the effectiveness of teaching?

A. Subject knowledge of the teacher
B. Ability for class management
C. Construction of proper tools for evaluation
D. Selection of appropriate of learning experiences for conducting the class

221. Which one of the following would you consider as the most important reason for people to select teaching as a profession?

A. It commands considerable respects from others in society
B. It provides ample leisure time
C. It provides opportunities for interaction with the youth and help them in their development
D. It provides a decent salary

222. When a majority of your students do not show any signs of understanding what you teach, the ideal steps to be taken is:

A. Ignore their behaviour and continue your teaching
B. Repeat your explanation using a different strategy
C. Use simple language in your explanation
D. Arrange another class with the help of a senior teacher

223. Which one of the following qualities is most desirable for a dynamic teacher?

A. Plan the classes strictly adhering to the text book
B. Prepare the pupils to perform well in the examination
C. Seek the co-operation of the students by stressing the importance of the topic
D. Developing the ability for self-learning

224. Which of the following methods would you prefer when you want to augment the quality of student learning?

A. Making the learning experiences learner-centered
B. Keeping the students relaxed while teaching
C. Explaining the subject matter clearly and loudly
D. Dictating notes

225. If you are allocating fixed seats for students in your class, which one of the following action would you adopt for the purpose?

A. The heights of students

B. The age of students

C. The academic performance of students

D. The social status of students

226. The ideal method to be adopted by a teacher for introducing a new topic of study is:

A. focussing their attention on the problem using interesting anecdotes

B. use of group discussions on related topics

C. converting the topic into a significant problem to be solved / a worthwhile area to be learnt

D. use of audio-visual presentations

227. A teacher's failure in maintaining discipline is most often due to:

A. inadequate knowledge of his subject

B. inadequate preparation for teaching

C. inadequate knowledge of the psychology of children

D. his displeasing appearance

228. Professional recognitions like teacher awards should be given to teachers who demonstrate:

A. a consistent record of top teaching performance continued with social service

B. purely on the basis of efficiency in teaching

C. on the basis of teaching performance and academic qualifications of the teacher

D. purely on the basis of their service to society

229. Most of the in-service programmes for teachers are not useful for improving the quality of teachers. The most important reason for this is that:

A. the courses are not conducted by experts in the field

B. the courses are not conceived to meet the real needs of the teachers

C. the courses do not cover all the modern developments in the field

D. there is no provision for feed back

230. A teacher with proper psychological insight can be identified using one of the following characteristics:

A. tolerates mistakes committed by students and is willing to explain to the students how to prevent such mistakes in future

B. never tolerates any mistake on the part of his students
C. takes all precautions so that students never commit mistakes
D. gives mild punishment to students every time they commit a mistake

231. The supervising personnel in education should give more stress on:
A. solving disciplinary problems
B. controlling the school activities
C. clarification of rules and regulations
D. monitoring the activities of teachers

232. Unemployment among trained teachers is mainly due to:
A. lack of funds for giving salary to teachers
B. inadequate institutional planning
C. lack of manpower planning
D. teacher's preference to certain places of posting

233. In order to ensure thorough mastery of a skill, the instructor has to:
A. provide for reinforced repetition of the correct model
B. demonstrate the skill with a high degree of perfection
C. take care to avoid undesirable motor actions
D. explain the significance of each step involved

234. What strategy would you adopt in a remotely situated educational institution where facilities and learning materials are very meagre?
A. Resort mostly to lecture method and make the students memorise
B. Gather or improvise locally available inputs and use them to provide meaningful experiences
C. Inform the authorities that classes cannot be handled effectively if the required facilities are not provided
D. Read the text books and explain the content as clearly as possible

235. Based on your assessment of Gandhiyan philosophy of education, which one of the following responses would Gandhiji expect from students when they notice a wrong action from the teacher?
A. Unquestioned obedience to every thing demanded by the teacher
B. To exercise non-violent resistance against implementing the wrong action
C. Do not openly react but try to evade participating in it
D. Organise a strong protest and fight for its cancellation

236. Which one of the following is generally a sound principle of asking questions?

A. Encourage chorus responses and identify mistakes

B. Point out a student and ask him the question

C. Put the question to the whole class gives some time for the students to find out the answer, and ask one student to answer

D. Repeat the correct answers given by student

237. While introducing a new topic of study, which one of the following approaches, will be an appropriate beginning?

A. Directly start with the lesson and proceed

B. Start by asking a few questions on related matters

C. Give the class a broad overview of the topic to be learnt connecting it with familiar knowledge

D. Read some relevant portion from some book

238. The primary function of a teacher is that of a:

A. director who organises and plans learning activities

B. guide, helping the learner progress towards desired development

C. scholar who can provide students maximum knowledge

D. social leader devoted to the preservation and transmission of our cultural heritage

239. Some experts on education consider that a teacher should be a student throughout his carrier. What is your reaction to this?

A. True, but only when he feels necessary to acquire new knowledge

B. This is rather an impracticable suggestion

C. It is enough if the teacher is well versed with the curricular requirements

D. In the light of fast changes in the field of knowledge, this is quite necessary

240. As a teacher, you are expected to read books because:

A. every educated man is expected to read

B. it will help you to become a scholar

C. it updates the knowledge required for a teacher

D. reading books is a joyful experience

241. What is your view regarding the planning to be done by a teacher and prepare for every class he has to teach?

A. It is meaningless to plan afresh if the class has been handled earlier

B. A teacher having enough experience need not have any preparation and planning
C. Classes will be more dynamic if the teacher adjusts to the classroom situation without planning in advance
D. To ensure realisation of goals, teacher has to plan and prepare before handling any lesson

242. Of these, which one is the most important function of a modern classroom teacher?

A. Providing maximum information to pupils
B. Developing problem solving abilities of students
C. Imparting in depth subject matter knowledge
D. Fostering development in all domains of human behaviour

243. The first and foremost duty of a teacher is:

A. implementing the policies prescribed by the institution
B. planning learning experiences for the development of the pupils
C. experimenting new teaching techniques
D. creating a cordial atmosphere in the class

244. The most effective way to foster a positive attitudes of students is:

A. rewarding the students who display a positive attitude
B. leaving children to interact and develop a positive attitude to school all by themselves
C. constantly remind the pupils of the need to develop a positive attitude to school
D. punishing those who show a negative attitude to school

245. The teacher is given the role of leading the students in his class. This is due to the fact that:

A. he can influence his students positively
B. he has authority to control the students
C. he is an elderly as well as a scholarly person who can guide his students
D. he can be a role model for his students

246. The working rules for the conduct of a classroom should be prepared by:

A. school authorities
B. teacher in consultation with his pupils
C. pupils in consultation with their parents
D. teacher who conducts the class in consultation with the authorities

247. Which of the following statements about teachers is the most rational?

A. The teacher should confine to teaching only

B. The teacher should give equal importance to teaching and organizing co-curricular activities

C. The teacher should concentrate more on teaching but should also help in organizing co-curricular activities

D. The teacher should give greater importance to co-curricular activities

248. The most valuable reward for teaching is:

A. the high salary

B. a high and secure job

C. the self-satisfaction of the teacher

D. love and respect of his students

249. What is the most important function of questions asked by the teacher?

A. To stimulate thinking by pupils

B. To add variety to instructional activities

C. To test whether the pupils are attending to what is being taught

D. To identify the bright students in the class

250. It is not a good practice for a teacher to punish his students by inflicting pain. Which one of the following is a justification for this assumption?

A. The student is likely to develop hostile attitude towards the school, the teacher and learning

B. The student is likely to develop negative attitude towards punishment

C. The parents are likely to develop a hostile attitude to the teacher

D. The school will get a bad name

251. The problem faced by a beginning teacher is:

A. fear that the college will not employ him permanently

B. lack of insight about the way college functions

C. controlling the misbehavior of students

D. lack of confidence to face children

252. One will have more chances of becoming a successful teacher if he:

A. is able to understand his students and their learning needs

B. lives close to the college

C. he has higher qualifications

D. has a pleasing appearance

253. Which of the following learning experiences would you provide for developing hatred towards war?

A. Arranging a question answer session about the atrocities committed in wars

B. Conducting essay competitions on the atrocities committed in the world

C. Teaching which will help pupils to empathize with the sufferers in different parts of the world

D. Organizing a few speeches by local politicians

254. A student who is poor in academic performance is often ridiculed by his classmates. How will this influence the student who is ridiculed?

A. Frustration and dislike for schooling

B. Student discontinues his studies

C. Teacher gives more attention to the student

D. The student reports this to his parent and the parent gives a complaint to school authorities

255. The present-day students are often discourteous to teachers. This is because:

A. the type of education provided is not proper

B. the quality of the teachers is substandard

C. students are influenced by cheap literature and movies

D. they develop wrong values at home

256. The impact of the hidden curriculum will be obvious from certain behaviours. Which one of the following behaviours would you attribute to hidden curriculum?

A. Development of the ability for information processing

B. Ability to speak with fluency and speed

C. Acquisition of the habit of critical thinking

D. Internalisation of a positive attitude towards society

257. In the present scenario of higher education in our state, which one of the following statements about student behaviour is most valid?

A. All students can learn well and so all learn

B. All students cannot learn well and no one learns

C. All students can learn well but are not motivated to learn

D. Some students do not have the ability to learn and do not want others to learn

258. Four teacher characteristics are given below:

1. Empathy with problems of children

2. Desire to update knowledge

3. Commitment to the needs of the society

4. Ability to communicate in lucid language

Which of these is most important for a successful teacher?

A. 1 and 2 only

B. 1,2 and 3 only

C. 1,2 and 4 only

D. All the four

259. Given below are some basic teaching competencies

i. Assisting the conduct of co-curricular activities

ii. Motivating students for learning

iii. Adopting proper classroom management styles

iv. Mastery over the subject-matter to be taught

v. Taking interest in the running of the institution

Which one of the following combinations is most appropriate for classroom teaching?

A. (i), (ii), (iii) and (iv)

B. (i), (ii), (iii) and (v)

C. (i), (iii), (iv) and (v)

D. (ii), (iii), (iv) and (v)

260. The major role of a teacher is to:

i. provide information about the subject he teaches

ii. motivate the students to learn

iii. develop learning competencies on the part of his students

iv. prepare students for the final examination

The two characteristics most important among these are:

A. (i) and (ii)

B. (i) and (iii)

C. (ii) and (iii)

D. (iii) and (iv)

261. When the teacher is required to deal with a heterogeneous group of students consisting of slow learners and bright students, it is better for the teacher to:

i. Keep the teaching level high so that the slow learner will eventually catch up

ii. Keep the teaching level low so that every student is benefited

iii. Keep the teaching level moderate and provide enrichment programme for the bright children

iv. Arrange remedial teaching for the slow learners

Which of these are appropriate for the heterogeneous group in the classroom?

A. (i) and (iv)

B. (ii) and (iv)

C. (iii) and (iv)

D. None of the above

262. You note that there is an adolescent student in your class who exhibits symptoms of emotional tension. Which step would you select to help to release his tension?

A. Give him counselling whenever needed

B. Keep him engaged by giving him additional assignments so that he forgets his tension

C. Direct him to the playground and help him to release his pent up energy

D. Develop in him an interest in social work and keep him busy

263. Which of the following teaching strategies will help students most in remembering permanently the new areas taught?

A. Maintain gradation in the learning material presented in the class

B. Make the learning process interesting and meaningful

C. Establish meaningful linkages between the existing and new schemas

D. Repeat the teaching of the area a number of times

264. Which of the following activities would you prefer for spending your leisure time?

A. Participating in social service activities

B. Involving in the activities of the Teacher Association

C. Reading periodicals in the local library

D. Participating in seminars and discussions on educational issues

265. A teacher should read educational journals because it will help him to:

A. acquaint with the new journals in the filed of education

B. understand the reasons for the poor performance of students

C. keep abreast of new developments in the field
D. gather information about the performance of other institutions

266. While organizing a group project in your class, which one of the following steps do you consider is most important?

A. Plan the project systematically and make the students to implement the project following the steps you have prescribed
B. Train a group leader and encourage other students to work as per his direction
C. Monitor the work of the group while they plan and help them to execute the project, leaving the minor details to the group
D. Place the whole responsibility in the pupils and evaluate the work when it is completed

267. Among the four category of teachers presented, which one is most desirable from the point of view of student learning?

A. One who is regular in attending to his work, but does not interact with the students
B. One who is good in teaching, but does not mind students coming late to the class
C. One who gives greater importance for teaching morals than for his subject
D. One who is average in his teaching ability, but is able to motivate his students to do further learning

268. A teacher should attend refresher courses conducted in the Academic Staff Colleges because it helps the teacher to:

A. make better use of his leisure time
B. enhance his professional knowledge
C. develop acquaintance with other teachers and understand them
D. enhance quality for promotion to higher cadres

269. Below are given a few important functions a teacher is expected to perform in the classroom:

(i) promoting group learning and student interaction
(ii) promoting opportunities for knowledge construction by students
(iii) developing a student-friendly environment
(iv) following the directions of the school authorities
(v) following the directions given by the social leaders

Which of the following combinations is most appropriate?

A. (i), (ii) and (iii) B. (i), (ii) and (iv)
C. (i), (ii) and (v) D. (iii), (iv) and (v)

270. Which one of the following approaches in teaching would you adopt as ideal?

A. Enrich the textual material by gathering additional information from other books and experts

B. Limit learning experiences to what is required by the textual material

C. Limiting class teaching to discussion of probable questions

D. Ask pupils in the classroom to read aloud the textbook for the benefit of other students

271. Which of the following steps do you consider most important while transacting the curriculum?

A. Present the learning materials in the question answer form and thus ensure good performance in the examination

B. Conduct test papers frequently using the format used in the public examination

C. Explain the concepts and principles clearly to help all students to understand them

D. Present learning activities using wide range of methods with learner participation for achieving all the instructional objectives

272. To teach effectively at the understanding level, a teacher must:

A. always keep the instructional objectives in mind

B. plan experiences relevant to the objective

C. ensure active participation of all the pupils

D. all the above

273. A university teacher should normally be involved in:

A. doing research in crucial problems in his discipline

B. striking a meaningful balance between teaching, research and extension work

C. helping students to take up political leadership

D. concentrating on his teaching using lecture method

274. Below are given some teaching skills associated with the delivery of a lecture:

i) Using communication boosters.

ii) Varying the stimulus.

iii) Motivating the students.

iv) Connecting with the previous knowledge.

v) Questioning skills.

Which of the following combinations is most appropriate?

A. i, ii and iii
B. i, iii and iv
C. ii, iii and v
D. All the five

275. The most effective strategy for teaching in higher education is:

A. providing the relevant information to students
B. preparing students for the national level competitive examinations
C. leading students to the sources of information and helping them to evolve strategies for processing them to develop new knowledge
D. development of a spirit of competition among for students excellence

276. In higher education, students can become better motivated if a teacher uses:

A. competition among students
B. set up opportunities for personal achievement
C. develop co-operation among students
D. provide individual attention to students

277. Which among the following is the most desirable outcome of teaching a subject to students of higher education?

A. Improving the store of knowledge of students
B. Developing the students' ability to independent thinking
C. Improving the percentage of pass in the final examination
D. Attract more number of students to the subject

278. The most desirable role expected of a new generation teacher in the classroom is:

A. delivering lectures based on the text and doing his own research in his discipline
B. delivering lectures based on the learning demands of the students in relation to the scope of the prescribed course
C. answering questions raised by students and clearing their doubts
D. maintaining disciplinary control where students will have to learn the areas taught

279. Absenteeism in the class can be minimised by:

A. teacher emphasising the need for regularity
B. teacher adopting disciplinary measures to deal with absentees
C. teacher making the classes more effective where the students become aware of the loss of previous learning sessions
D. teacher seeking the help of their administrator

280. Helping students to gain new knowledge should be based on the principle:

A. admitting only the best students to a class

B. from known to unknown

C. avoiding the teaching of trivial areas

D. concentrating on teaching the better students

281. A curriculum may be best conceived as:

A. a means for preparing the students' for an examination

B. the contents of a subject to be taught to students

C. as a framework for achieving all expected behaviour changes

D. as the totality of experiences to be provided to learners under the control of the educational system

282. Meaningful learning takes place when:

A. students accept learning as a joyful experience

B. teaching gives proper explanations to each of the content

C. the new learning content is presented in simple language

D. students get more opportunities to raise questions and get them cleared

283. Which of the following instructional strategies helps to develop a better learning climate in the classroom?

A. teacher-centred teaching

B. subject-centred teaching

C. peer teaching

D. learner-centred teaching

284. Occasional use of peer-teaching would help in developing:

A. better learning among backward learners

B. Developing a superiority among those who are entrusted with peer teaching

C. Developing an inferiority feeling among those who are taught

D. Developing a new classroom climate where teachers are not respected

285. Which among the following should influence most the educational policy of a nation?

A. Man-power planning

B. The demands of the political parties

C. General social and economic objectives of the country

D. The working styles of the government officer of the country

286. In a democratic set up, education is conceived more as:

A. a means for enlightening the citizens

B. an investment in human resource development

C. a tool for changing society

D. a method of training for employment

287. For raising the educational standards of a university we should depend upon:

A. courses designed to meet the demands of the new society

B. courses which cater to the needs of all occupation groups

C. courses over which the government has full control

D. the strategies used in higher education by educationally advanced countries

288. The present educational system in India is criticized for:

A. its inability to reach to the lower strata of society

B. impart common education to all who desire for education

C. over dependence on verbal teaching

D. all the above three

289. For reducing state expenditure on professional education, the best strategy is:

A. promote private institutions to enter the area, collecting higher fee

B. permitting foreign universities to start colleges in the country

C. developing a new cadre of professionals through apprenticeship training and permit them to move to higher positions

D. controlling the functioning of private institutions in the area and make them admit more students based on merit

290. The basic difference in human learning and animal learning is:

A. human learning is based on a well-developed language and other means of communication

B. human being has the capacity for reflective thinking and self-correction

C. the human being is more intelligent and hence can use his brain for assessing the consequences of an action

D. all the above

291. The most serious problem which the country faces is brain drain and wastage of expertise in the country. This is to be attributed to the fact that:

A. people having higher technical qualifications do not have enough employment opportunities in the country
B. people getting higher technical education are not of proper quality
C. people with higher technical education are attracted to the more lucrative posts offered by other countries
D. we have too many technical education institutions in the country

292. The teacher should provide an opportunity for co-operative learning since it:

A. encourages self-study habits among the students
B. prepares the students to learn by sharing experiences and expertise
C. helps students to learn on their own
D. all the above

293. Which of the following strategies is to be preferred in developing better parental attitude towards teachers and school?

A. Teachers to have occasional discussions with parents about the progress of their wards and the problems they face
B. Parents given opportunities to complain about their wards to teachers for corrective measures
C. Parents given opportunities to complain to the teachers about student misbehavior at home
D. All the above

294. In India we are facing the problem of catering to the large number who seek higher education in certain areas. The best solution to the problem is:

A. use satellite facilities to teach all the courses to all who desire for such courses
B. start new institutions in the traditional pattern to meet the demand
C. make higher education costlier so that the demand can be decreased
D. provide alternate educational opportunities for life long learning through distance education

295. The teacher can make classroom communication more meaningful by:

A. organizing supplementary regular classes with the help of experts
B. enhancing the use of mass media in the classroom
C. relating the learning material to the life of the learners
D. asking questions to test whether the learners are following the presentations

296. The teaching profession is respected in our society for the following reasons.

A. Teaching profession gives considerable security to all those who join the profession

B. It is a reasonably well paid profession with minimum working time

C. Education is considered as an investment for national development

D. Teachers play a major role in achieving the national goals of development

297. A teacher should design her/his instructional plan:

A. always by herself/himself

B. in consultation with her/his senior colleagues

C. taking into consideration the available resources

D. in tune with the pattern of the final examination

298. The most critical factor that makes teaching a true profession is:

A. the period prescribed for teacher training

B. active participation of teachers in professional organisations

C. maintenance of a proper work culture

D. adoption of knowledge relating to the profession for practising the profession

299. When you are asking a question to the class, and you do not receive a proper answer from your student, how do you explain this?

A. The question might not be clear to students

B. The students may not be familiar with the content area from which the question has been developed

C. The students did not listen to your question

D. A and B above

300. A class monitor is expected to perform certain important duties. Which in your opinion is the most important among the following?

A. Carrying out the teacher's instructions sincerely

B. Controlling class discipline in the absence of the teacher

C. Checking the homework of the students on behalf of the teacher

D. Attending to the personal needs of teachers who teach the different subjects

301. Which principle would you adopt for assigning seats to students in your class?

A. Bright students be given front seats

B. Seats are to assigned to suit the age and height of children

C. Seats are to be assigned according to mental level of children
D. Mischief-makers are to be given seats in the front row

302. A teacher can plan his/her classroom teaching session in a satisfactory manner:

A. by collecting information from the latest books in class management
B. by discussing with colleagues and using the methods adopted by them
C. by working out a plan which is logically satisfying
D. by getting feedback from students

303. Self-study by students should be encouraged by teachers because:

A. it will help the teacher to confine his teaching to some of the select areas which need the teachers' intervention
B. the habit of self-learning will be promoted
C. it helps to save considerable teaching time
D. this method would help students to learn how to learn

304. Which one of the following characteristics is most appropriate for a successful teacher?

A. Keeping aloof from students
B. Adopting pleasing manner in dealing with children
C. Creating a mild fear in the minds of students through appropriate expressions
D. Cutting jokes and mingling freely with the students

305. The best way to establish rapport with your students is:

A. impress them with knowledge of subject and teaching skill
B. create a feeling that you are willing to help them
C. demand the respect due to you by age and status
D. by mingling with them and acting as if you are one among them

306. Who among the following has the least possibility for becoming an effective teacher?

A. One who knows just enough of his subject, but communicates effectively
B. One who is a strict disciplinarian
C. One who assumes the role of a moralist
D. One who lacks interest and aptitude for teaching, but can create a different impression

307. On the first day of starting a new session a teacher asks his students to introduce themselves. What do you think is the intention in doing this?

A. To know the students better so that he can adjust his teaching to suit their abilities and needs
B. To identify the students who can share different activities relating to instruction
C. Identify students who are good in studies
D. None of the above

308. Which of the following instructional arrangements give greater freedom for the learners to interact among themselves?
A. Small group discussion
B. Classes conducted using audio-video supports
C. Learning using TV lessons
D. Attending class lectures by experts

309. Which is the most desirable outcome of teaching in higher education?
A. Increase the student's store of knowledge
B. Increase their ability to independent thinking and generate new knowledge on their own
C. Enhance the number of first classes in university examination
D. Increase the number of students who opt for your subject of specialisation

310. The following are some of the essential roles of a teacher in higher education institutions:
(i) managing information
(ii) facilitating the development of learning competencies
(iii) motivating students to learn effectively
(iv) helping students to perform well in examination
(v) counselling pupils who are facing problems
Which of the following combinations of roles do you consider the most significant?
A. (i), (ii) and (iii)
B. (ii), (iii) and (iv)
C. (ii), (iii) and (v)
D. (iii), (iv) and (v)

311. Which one of the following statements describes a trait not suitable for a new generation teacher?
A. A teacher should keep pace with the up-to-date developments in his subjects
B. A teacher should be a strict disciplinarian and in order to impose his decisions on students
C. A teacher should encourage students to make independent judgements
D. A teacher should try to understand the personal problems faced by his students

312. Who among the following has the least chance of getting acceptance as an effective teacher?

A. One who knows just enough of his subject, but can communicate effectively and mix with his students

B. One who treats his students as his enemies

C. One who assumes the role of a moralist and tries to find fault with what is done by students

D. One who has no interest or aptitude for teaching, but pretends that he can be a good teacher

313. Which is the most dependable feed back for a teacher?

A. Comments made by the students in the class

B. Remarks of colleagues

C. Remarks made by the Principal

D. Memories of old students

314. Below are given some activities used for introducing a topic in the class:

(i) Relating the topic to what is to be taught

(ii) Relating the topic to the topics already taught

(iii) Testing the students' previous knowledge

(iv) Presenting an overview of the major points to be introduced

(v) Motivating the students for learning the topic

Which of the following combinations is most appropriate?

A. (i), (ii), (iii) and (iv)

B. (ii). (iii), (iv) and (v)

C. (i), (iii) and (iv)

D. (ii), (iii) and (v)

315. Given below are some of the instructional activities used by a teacher during the delivery phase of a lecture:

(i) Checking the previous knowledge

(ii) Using communication boosters

(iii) Reinforcing the content with illustrative examples

(iv) Asking probing questions

(v) Suggesting additional reading material

Which combination is the most appropriate?

A. (i), (ii) and (v)

B. (ii), (iii) and (iv)

C. (iii), (iv) and (v)

D. (ii), (iii) and (v)

316. From the instructional activities listed below select the one which does not relate to the consolidation phase of a lecture.

A. Reviewing and summarizing

B. Motivating the students

C. Giving assignments for additional practice

D. Suggesting additional reading materials

317. You have been included as a member of a selection committee for teacher recruitment. Which one of the following characteristics would you prefer in teacher selection?

A. A candidate with very high academic records, disregarding his ability to communicate

B. A person who has published a large number of research papers in journals, devoid of aptitude for the profession

C. A person with proper aptitude for teaching even though he has only average qualifications

D. A candidate who does not have enough knowledge of his subject, but is willing to accept the post with a lower salary

318. Students learn more from a teacher who:

A. accepts his students

B. can communicate precisely and clearly, but is impersonal in his dealing with students

C. is a thorough gentleman

D. has a pleasing personality

319. Effective teaching is the result of:

A. teachers' scholarship

B. sincerity to the profession

C. liking for the job of teaching

D. ability to use professional principles for teaching

320. Which of the following will make classroom teaching more effective?

A. Cutting jokes in between

B. Using multisensory aids

C. Speaking with authority

D. Use of scientific principles for presenting the content

321. The best way to solve a student's problem is:

A. to help the student to understand the implications and solve the problem himself

B. by developing in the student the ability to solve problem

C. the teacher solves the problem and the student adopts the solution

D. giving proper directions to the parents and make them solve the problem

322. Which among the following is the most effective way for attaining discipline in a classroom?

A. Developing self-discipline among students

B. Enforcing discipline by teachers

C. Leaving the students to decide what is best

D. Forcing students to obey classroom rules strictly

323. Students learn better when:

A. taught in a group

B. individual attention is given

C. students are given supplementary materials

D. forced to memorize the content

324. You want to make a student interested in his work. An effective strategy you would adopt is:

A. praise him in open class when he performs well

B. give him more work practice

C. praise him when he comes to your room

D. pretend that you have not noticed his good qualities

325. Which one among the following statements is not true?

A. What we learn with pleasure, we never forget

B. Repeated reading of a topic is necessary for recall

C. What we learn under compulsion will last longer

D. What we have learnt recently will be remembered more than what we learnt long back

326. A student finds it very difficult to comprehend a topic you have just taught. What will you do to help him?

A. Simplify the presentation and re-teach for the benefit of the student

B. Ask the student to read the topic repeatedly

C. Rearrange the theme and present the area more meaningfully

D. Ask another student who has understood the topic tohelp him

327. Which among the following is an ideal method for developing better self-concept among students?

A. Comparing the class performance of a student with that of a better student

B. Comparing a student's achievement with his own previous achievement

C. Comparing a student's achievement with that of a poor student

D. Avoid comparisons in any form

328. Insulting a student in front of others will:

A. make him realise his mistake

B. develop a feeling of hostility in his mind

C. develop an inferiority feelings in him

D. all the above

329. In order to develop rapport with your pupils you should:

A. develop in the pupils a feeling that they are accepted

B. guide them in the learning process using scientific approaches

C. use your communication ability for the best results

D. all the above

330. Which of the following could be regarded as a principle of good discipline in educational institutions?

A. Framing a code of behaviour through joint discussion of parents and principal

B. Formulating rules and regulations in the beginning of the year by the principal

C. Developing rules and policies in consultation with the students

D. Laying clear rules and principles by authorities and enforcing them

331. To develop proper teaching skills, what is most needed is:

A. work experience under proper supervision

B. training in the professional principles of teaching

C. long teaching experience with out supervision

D. observing video presentation of teaching by senior teachers

332. The best evidence of the professional competency of a teacher lies in his ability for:

A. maintaining proper discipline in the class

B. providing professional leadership to student learning

C. organising co-curricular activities which attract most of the students

D. presenting subject content using technical language

333. Why do you prefer teaching to other professions?

A. It helps me to interact with a large number of human beings

B. Some of my best teachers are my role models

C. I like to interact with the young people

D. I can apply the knowledge I have acquired

334. Which one of the following qualities do you expect from your student?

A. Efficiency in different areas of work

B. Leadership quality and commitment to learning

C. Popularity among his fellow students

D. Smart appearance

335. A teacher feels irritated when he enters a particular class. This is to be attributed to:

A. his dissatisfaction with the behaviour of the students in the class

B. dissatisfaction with their commitment to learning

C. his inability to maintain discipline in the class

D. all the above

336. What do you mean by the statement, "experiments are actions to be performed by students and not as a theme for teacher demonstration"

A. teacher's demonstration of an experiment will not have the impact of an experiment conducted by each student

B. experimentation is a boring work for students and hence the teacher should demonstrate the experiment

C. teacher's experimentation will be more accurate and hence is to be preferred

D. students are to be left to themselves

337. If I get an opportunity to repeat a lesson:

A. I will try to repeat the same lesson with minor changes

B. I will try to improve on my earlier lesson

C. I will start the new lesson with greater confidence

D. I will begin teaching without preparation

338. A teacher becomes successful in his profession because of his:

A. commitment to work

B. qualifications

C. family background

D. financial status of his family

339. Continuing to work in one's school after the working time reflects a teacher's:

A. enthusiasm for work

B. commitment to work

C. motivation for teaching

D. all the above

340. I spend my leisure time after my teaching duties for internet searching to obtain:

A. details of international political developments

B. details about new scientific development

C. details of new developments in instructional methods

D. viewing TV music programmes

341. If you are required to suggest changes in the teaching methods, which one of the following will be your choice?

A. Stick on to conventional methods, but adopt them with all sincerity

B. Tell the authorities that you are not interested in changing the existing teaching methods

C. Search the internet for the innovative teaching methods used by progressive educational systems and recommend them for adoption

D. suggest methods which are recommended by colleagues

342. If you get a chance to help your colleagues in the use of new methods for improving the quality of teaching, which one of the following would you treat as least important for adoption?

A. Enthusiastically use this opportunity and search for new methods in the net

B. Convene a teachers meeting and discuss new methods

C. Get the permission of higher authorities for effecting the changes in the teaching methods

D. Seek the help of the parents for identifying new methods

343. Applying psychological principles for classroom practice is:

A. not practicable and hence can be ignored

B. practicable, but should be adopted carefully

C. not practicable even for the experienced teacher and hence be ignored

D. practicable and hence should be fully used to suit the context

344. In the development of a lesson, a good teacher will always rely on:

A. commonsense and give shape to his teaching strategies

B. professional principles and give shape to his teaching strategies

C. prescribed textbooks for deciding his instructional strategies

D. prepared notes for explaining the course content

345. When you are explaining a difficult topic, a few students ask silly questions to distract you, then you will:

A. shout at them and silence them

B. tell them to meet you after the class for explanations

C. tell them that their questions are no relevant for the topic under discussion

D. develop a new classroom culture where students will not ask questions

346. The moment you start lecturing you develop a feeling that you will not be able to complete the class successfully. This is mainly due to:

A. lack of preparation

B. low teaching ability

C. complexity of the content

D. all the above

347. When you enter the class, you notice that most of the students start making comments in subdued tones. How will you deal with such a situation?

A. Walk out of the class in protest

B. Complain to the Principal

C. Try to find out the reason for this behaviour and then deal with it

D. Ignore this and start teaching

348. You know that you are not good in class management. Which one of the following steps would you take to correct this inadequacy?

A. Undergo an advanced course in education

B. Try to acquire the skills of class management referring to authentic books and adopt the principles given there

C. Get the views of senior expert teachers in the college and use the techniques suggested by them

D. All the above

349. When your class is facing a complex problem, how you would try to deal with the problem?

A. Take a quick decision and implement it

B. Get the help of other experienced teachers

C. Discuss with the Principal and the school managing board and adopt their suggestions

D. Ignore the problem and go ahead with your regular class work

350. As a teacher you have a strong wish that you should be respected and loved by your students. But this is not realized in many situations. This is because:

A. it is based on the principle "you get back what you give"

B. students are not interested in accepting others

C. students are interested only in getting the best from others

D. teacher makes undue demands on students

351. For effective classroom communication, a teacher must:

A. use simple language and systematic communication

B. make students mentally inducted into the learning process

C. provide opportunities to students to use a wide range of learning strategies

D. all the above

352. The ideal learning situation is one where the teacher using the strategy of:

A. teaching one student at a time

B. teaching a small group of students at a time

C. teaching a large number of students using scientific methodologies

D. none of the above

353. The best teacher is said to be one who doesn't teach. This means:

A. a teacher is not expected to teach in the classroom

B. the teacher creates a situation in the classroom for the students where they can learn for themselves

C. The teacher gives the freedom to the students to ask questions to which answers are to be found out by the students themselves under the guidance of the teacher

D. Teaching is not to be equated with verbal explanations

354. The ultimate aim of education is to help the student to:

A. earn an income

B. gain mastery over the content to be taught

C. procure a prestigious job

D. achieve all-around development of personality

355. The best judge of teacher effectiveness is:

A. the principal of the college

B. the coworkers of a teacher

C. the students of the class

D. parents of students in the class

356. You find that all the children in your class fail in a class test given by you. How would you react to this situation?

A. Ask the children to study the same topic and to take a second test

B. Give the same test paper again after giving time for preparation

C. Adopt a new group of strategies to teach the same topic and then give an equivalent test

D. Contact the parents and get their help to step up the quality of learning of their children

357. Continuous absence of the teacher adversely affects the:

A. school routine and student learning

B. learning culture of the class

C. completion of the topics prescribed for the class

D. all the above

358. Some of your colleagues are in the habit of creating problems for you by influencing your students. How will you handle the situation?

A. Tell such teachers that you know how to deal with cowards

B. Ignore the issue and act as if nothing has happened

C. deal with the situation patiently, first by interacting with each of the students individually and converting them to your side

D. Report this to the Principal and leave it to him to handle the issue

359. Teachers are expected to have a good understanding of:

A. the other teachers in the school

B. the superiors and the school decision-makers

C. all students and their strong and weak points

D. all the above

360. There is a common complaint that the quality of education is deteriorating day by day. Which of the following is not a reason for this?

A. Poor management of the system

B. Poor knowledge transaction strategies used by teachers

C. Low intelligence of students

D. Negative attitude of teachers towards teaching

361. How do you justify the use of different teaching aids in your class?

A. To provide multi-sensory learning experiences to students

B. To make teaching interesting

C. To create greater interest for students' learning

D. All the above

362. Who among the following would you prefer to be your child's teacher? A teacher:

A. who has sound knowledge of different subjects

B. who has a pleasing behaviour which will attract children

C. who makes the child do a large number of exercises and heavy homework

D. who can communicate in an interesting manner and understands the limitations of the student

363. Taking into account the popular practices used in present day education, which one of the following statements about grading is true?

A. It is a mechanical process which decreases the accuracy of student assessment

B. It's justification has not been properly understood by teachers

C. It helps to decrease examination tensions among students

D. It has minimized the importance of real learning

364. As a teacher who would you rate as a good student?

A. A student who obeys you with out questioning

B. A student who works very hard but is not a high achiever

C. A student who raises questions and seeks additional explanation

D. A student who does his homework promptly

365. As a teacher what will be your reaction if you find that you are unable to perform an experiment successfully in the classroom:

A. will repeat the experiment after one more study and complete the experiment successfully

B. will identify the reasons for the failure of the experiment, and discuss this before repeating the experiment

C. direct the students to do the experiment at home and report the result in the next class

D. teach the topic avoiding the demonstration of the experiment

Answers keys

1.C	2.D	3.C	4.C	5.B	6.B	7.D	8.D	9.D	10.B
11.A	12.A	13.D	14.B	15.C	16.A	17.C	18.D	19.B	20.A
21.D	22.C	23.C	24.B	25.C	26.B	27.B	28.D	29.D	30.C
31.A	32.D	33.B	34.C	35.D	36.B	37.B	38.C	39.D	40.C
41.C	42.A	43.B	44.D	45.D	46.C	47.C	48.C	49.D	50.C
51.B	52.A	53.B	54.B	55.D	56.A	57.A	58.D	59.C	60.B
61.D	62.C	63.D	64.C	65.D	66.A	67.D	68.B	69.D	70.B
71.D	72.B	73.D	74.B	75.A	76.C	77.D	78.D	79.A	80.C
81.B	82.D	83.D	84.C	85.C	86.A	87.C	88.B	89.C	90.B
91.D	92.A	93.A	94.C	95.B	96.D	97.B	98.B	99.C	100.A
101.C	102.A	103.D	104.C	105.D	106.A	107.A	108.D	109.B	110.D
111.D	112.A	113.D	114.D	115.C	116.D	117.D	118.D	119.B	120.A
121.D	122.D	123.B	124.C	125.C	126.D	127.B	128.B	129.D	130.C
131.A	132.A	133.C	134.C	135.D	136.B	137.C	138.A	139.C	140.A
141.D	142.B	143.D	144.D	145.C	146.D	147.C	148.C	149.D	150.B
151.C	152.D	153.A	154.A	155.D	156.A	157.D	158.C	159.A	160.C
161.D	162.C	163.D	164.C	165.D	166.C	167.C	168.A	169.D	170.D
171.B	172.C	173.C	174.B	175.D	176.C	177.A	178.A	179.A	180.B
181.B	182.D	183.C	184.C	185.B	186.D	187.B	188.D	189.D	190.D
191.C	192.D	193.C	194.C	195.B	196.B	197.B	198.D	199.A	200.A
201.B	202.B	203.D	204.C	205.C	206.C	207.A	208.C	209.D	210.B
211.B	212.C	213.C	214.B	215.B	216.C	217.A	218.C	219.B	220.D
221.C	222.C	223.C	224.A	225.A	226.C	227.B	228.B	229.B	230.A
231.D	232.C	233.A	234.B	235.B	236.C	237.C	238.B	239.D	240.C
241.D	242.D	243.B	244.A	245.D	246.B	247.C	248.D	249.A	250.B
251.D	252.D	253.C	254.C	255.C	256.D	257.C	258.D	259.A	260.C
261.C	262.C	263.C	264.D	265.A	266.A	267.D	268.B	269.A	270.A
271.D	272.D	273.B	274.D	275.C	276.B	277.B	278.B	279.C	280.B
281.D	282.C	283.C	284.A	285.A	286.B	287.D	288.A	289.C	290.D
291.C	292.B	293.A	294.D	295.C	296.D	297.B	298.C	299.B	300.B
301.B	302.A	303.D	304.B	305.B	306.D	307.A	308.A	309.B	310.C
311.B	312.D	313.D	314.B	315.B	316.B	317.D	318.B	319.D	320.B
321.A	322.A	323.B	324.A	325.A	326.C	327.B	328.D	329.D	330.C
331.B	332.D	333.A	334.B	335.D	336.C	337.B	338.A	339.D	340.B
341.C	342.B	343.B	344.B	345.B	346.D	347.C	348.B	349.C	350.A
351.D	352.A	353.C	354.D	355.C	356.C	357.D	358.C	359.D	360.C
361.A	362.D	363.C	364.C	365.B					

EDUCATIONAL PHILOSOPHY

1. **Teachers need to study educational philosophy mainly because:**
   A. most teachers follow undesirable philosophy of life
   B. teachers are incapable of formulating their own philosophy
   C. teachers generally do not have a philosophy of their own and this affects the quality of teaching
   D. it provides answers to basic questions relating to education and gives meaningful direction to instruction

2. **Non-formal education is mainly meant for:**
   A. non-entrants in schools
   B. disadvantaged groups of society
   C. illiterate adults in a society
   D. scheduled castes and scheduled tribes

3. **Open Universities have been created because of:**
   A. economic stringency
   B increased demand for higher education
   C. pressure for compulsory education
   D. educational competition among countries

4. **The expanded form of ECCE is:**
   A. Extension Centre for Child Education
   B. Effective Child Care and Education
   C. Education and Care for Children Everywhere
   D. Early Childhood Care and Education

5. **Which of the following caused a heavy blow to the indigenous schools in India?**
   A. Charter Act of 1813
   B. Macaulay's Minutes of 1835
   C. Woods Despatch of 1854
   D. The Indian Education Commission 1964

6. **Higher education institutions should aim at:**
   A. teaching B. research
   C. extension D. all of the above

7. The most important difference between informal education and non-formal education is that:

A. the former is organised, the latter is not organised

B. the former is not organised, the latter is organised

C. the former occurs within the institution, the latter occurs outside the institution

D. the former is controlled by non-governmental agencies and the latter is controlled by governmental agencies

8. The phrase 'equality of educational opportunity' means:

A. providing equal opportunity to have the type of education for which one is suited

B. provision of the same type of education for all

C. providing opportunity for all to get education at any level

D. ensuring admission to all for the desired stream of education

9. Universalisation of elementary education means:

A. promotion of adult education for the drop outs

B. enhancement of enrolment and prevention of wastage

C. compulsory enrolment of children between 6-14 in schools

D. making provision for elementary education in all parts of the country

10. The primary social function of education is:

A. to foster the skills for practising interpersonal relationships

B. to help students understand the society in which they live

C. to prepare students for social living

D. to develop self-reliant future citizens

11. In which year and where was 'The World Declaration of Education for All' released?

A. 1990, Thailand

B. 1990, Geneva

C. 1993, Newyork

D. 1993, Thailand

12. "A lamp can never light another lamp unless it continues to burn on its own." This statement implies that:

A. the teacher preparation programme should be of high quality

B. the teacher should continuously attend in-service education programmes

C. the teacher should be a learner throughout his life

D. the teacher should have the scholarship and ability to inspire his students

13. The importance of teacher education as a pre-requisite for an efficient educational system in India was first emphasised by:

A. The Woods Despatch

B. The Hunter Commission

C. The Calcutta University Commission

D. The White Paper

14. For Plato, the main role of education is to:

A. cultivate the personality of each individual

B. strengthen the power of perception

C. train each person for a vocation

D. develop the power of contemplation

15. What is the major contribution of Rousseau to modern education?

A. Activity-centred education

B. Education provided by ideal teachers

C. Life-centred education

D. Education based on exposure to social problems

16. Which one of the following recommendations was responsible for instituting the first three universities in India?

A. The Woods Despatch

B. The Charter Act

C. The Macaulay's Minutes

D. The Sargent Report

17. Extension education is to be interpreted as:

A. extending higher knowledge to the door steps of those who need it

B. extending educational opportunities to the deprived

C. a programme for educating the farmers

D. education meant to spread knowledge among villagers.

18. What is the cultural function of education?

A. Preservation and transmission of one's cultural heritage

B. Socialisation of the child

C. Development of scientific attitude
D. Inculcation of democratic values

19. Unemployment among trained teachers is mainly due to:
A. lack of funds
B. inadequate institutional planning
C. lack of man power planning
D. teacher's preference to get posting in schools of their choice

20. To which category of educational agency does the 'home' belong?
A. Formal
B. Non-formal
C. Informal
D. Formal as well as non-formal

21. Name the Chairman of an Indian Education Commission which is described as the "magna carta" of teachers:
A. Dr. S. Radhakrishnan
B. Dr. Malcolm Adiseshiah
C. D.S. Kothari
D. Acharya Rama Murthy

22. Practising democracy in the classroom means:
A. Providing equality of opportunity to all children
B. Giving freedom to pupils in their educational choices
C. Providing learner-centered education in the class room
D. All of the above

23. To provide community experience to students, a teacher should:
A. provide opportunities for working with the community
B. give lectures on community life
C. arrange lectures by eminent members of the community
D. arrange film shows showing details of community life

24. For inculcating national values, which one of the following programmes is not relevant?
A. National song
B. Morning prayer

C. Celebration of the Republic Day

D. Celebration of the Independence Day

25. Which one of the following is the most important instrument of social change?

A. Language B. Religion

C. Science D. Education

26. Which one of the following traits reflects most, the spirit of the Buddhist Philosophy?

A. Service to humanity B. Simplicity

C. Ahimsa D. Truth

27. Modernization of a society is achieved most by:

A. increased use of modern technological contrivances

B. adoption of the life style of a modern society

C. developing a scientific outlook in thinking and working

D. consumption of rich food items and costly life styles

28. The major factor which caused radical social changes in the latter half of the 20th century in India is:

A. political changes

B. technological advancements

C. spread of education

D. all the above

29. The most effective step that would help in the educational upliftment of socially and culturally deprived sections of our society is:

A. compensatory educational programmes

B. financial help for parents of low income families

C. creation of enjoyable atmosphere in schools

D. formation of special teaching groups for dealing with culturally deprived children

30. A broader interpretation of education is:

A. a process which helps one to acquire new knowledge

B. a process used for training of individuals for life

C. a process used for developing vocational skills

D. a process used for aching all-round development of individuals

31. Axiology is the study of the:

A. nature of the universe

B. laws governing reasoning

C. nature of values

D. nature of reality

32. Education and socio economic development of a society are:

A. related in direct proportion

B. related in an indirect proportion

C. related in a few situations and often not related

D. not at all related

33. Social reforms generally aim at changing the:

A. existing values of society

B. existing norms of the group

C. accepted religious practices

D. social and life styles of individuals

34. Which one of the following factors works against giving higher education to girls?

A. Parents do not desire to send their girls to co-education institutions

B. Poverty of parents

C. Using the services of girls for household work

D. All the above

35. The study of educational philosophy is necessary for teachers because:

A. it provides proper sense of direction to the work of a teacher by answering certain fundamental questions relating to teaching

B. teaching without an understanding of philosophy is likely to decrease the effectiveness of teaching

C. teachers ignorant of educational philosophy are likely to adopt unscientific methods for teaching

D. most teachers do not have the ability to formulate their philosophy of education

36. The teacher is a "Friend, Philosopher and Guide" of the students because:

A. he plays a vital role in transforming the society as a whole

B. he helps pupils to inculcate noble human values and styles of living

C. he acts as a major catalyst in student learning

D. all the above

37. Philosophy and education are two sides of the same coin in the sense that:

A. Philosophy helps to give proper meaning to education

B. Effective teaching is not possible without a sound philosophy of life

C. The discipline of education was developed by philosophers

D. Philosophy makes the teacher a better teacher

38. Harmonious development of the child as an aim of education means:

A. development of all the desirable qualities of the mind to the maximum possible extent

B. development of a sound mind in a sound body

C. development of physical, mental, moral and spiritual potentialities of the child in a balanced manner

D. development of the capacity of the child to harmoniously adjust with society

39. 'Equality' as India's constitutional provision in relation to education does not imply:

A. providing identical education for all

B. providing equal opportunity to all according to their endowments

C. providing equal facilities for education to all sections of the society in a judicious manner

D. removing regional imbalances in educational provision

40. If education has to contribute to India's national integration it has to:

A. make children familiar with the concept of 'unity in diversity' in all aspects of our national life

B. reach every child in the country

C. provide free and compulsory education for all sections of our society

D. be free from all religious teachings

41. The family imparts education to every child in the family:

A. formally

B. informally

C. deliberately

D. in all the above ways

42. The most important function to be performed by education in a developing country like ours is:

A. Economic development

B. Human resource development

C. Industrial development

D. social development

43. The most powerful tool in the process of modernisation of a society is:

A. a progressive system of education

B. democratic citizenship

C. adoption of new ways of living by the people

D. science and technology based education

44. As per the Right to Education Act (2009) which among the following is the suggestion on the medium of instruction in elementary classes:

A. English

B. Hindi

C. Mother tongue

D. Any language

Answer keys

1.D	2.B	3.B	4.D	5.B	6.D	7.B	8.A	9.C	10.C
11.A	12.C	13.A	14.D	15.D	16.A	17.A	18.A	19.C	20.C
21.C	22.D	23.A	24.B	25.D	26.B	27.C	28.D	29.A	30.D
31.C	32.A	33.A	34.D	35.A	36.B	37.C	38.C	39.A	40.A
41.B	42.B	43.D	44.C						

EDUCATIONAL PSYCHOLOGY

1. **Piaget's most important contribution to educational psychology is his identification of:**

   A. different rates of growth of children

   B. the cognitive developmental stages in the humans

   C. psycho-social descriptions of human development

   D. stages of social development of children

2. **Learning is best defined as:**

   A. any change in the behaviour of an organism

   B. a relatively permanent change in behaviour due to experience

   C. a change in behaviour due to education or schooling

   D. a relatively permanent change in behaviour due to maturation

3. **One conclusion that can be drawn from Ebbinghaus' work on forgetting is that:**

   A. we can remember only about seven nonsense syllables at a time

   B. most of the forgetting of new materials memorised happens soon after one learns it

   C. the duration of visual-sensory memory is less than half a second

   D. rate of forgetting increases with lapse of time

4. **Which one of the following is an important aim of educational guidance?**

   A. To help students to identify their physical, mental and educational handicaps

   B. To help the students to know more about the avenues for their further education and the requirements expected for getting admission to these courses

   C. To give effective coaching to students on subjects which they have to learn in their higher course

   D. To help the students to adjust themselves to the challenging educational requirements

5. **The main function of the study of educational psychology in teacher education courses is to provide prospective teachers with:**

   A. rules of thumb procedures to deal with every-day class room situations

   B. insight into various aspects of modern educational practice

C. insight into the needs, problems and styles of behaviour of differing learner groups

D. research procedures used for evaluating current teaching practices

6. **Educational psychology should provide prospective teachers with:**

A. validated procedures to be adopted for classroom teaching and screening the system

B. understand the research procedures used for evaluating current instructional strategies

C. obtain insights into various practices used in modern education

D. identify the principles, insights and attitudes which would contribute in effective teaching

7. **An under-achiever is one who:**

A. achieves less than the average of the group

B. achieves below ones mental potential

C. does not show proper progress in the class

D. who has not achieved the minimum essentials of learning

8. **Transfer of learning means:**

A. the process by which the skill learnt in one situation is transformed to a totally different learning situation

B. transfer of an important skill from the teacher to the pupil

C. transfer a skill from one student in the class to another student

D. shifting of learning in one subject to learning of another subject

9. **One should select a career in terms of:**

A. values which he considers important

B. the income associated with the career

C. ones academic qualifications

D. the aptitude he has for the job

10. **According to Piaget, which of the following is the first step the teacher has to take while presenting new knowledge?**

A. Link the new knowledge with the already familiar knowledge relating to the area

B. Create new schemas by presenting concrete examples

C. Introduce the new knowledge using an interesting new situation

D. Create intellectual disequilibrium by creating a related problematic situation

11. In order to ensure that a new topic will be learnt effectively without any difficulty which one of the following steps will be most essential?

A. Ensure that all the pre requisites for learning the new material are mastered in advance

B. Introduce the learning material using a number of interesting situations

C. Analysing the new material into its components and presenting each one after the other

D. Provide enactive experiences to be followed by ikonic and symbolic experiences

12. The modern definition of psychology is:

A. The science of human behaviour

B. The scientific study of human behaviour and mental processes

C. The science of the mind

D. The scientific study of how human beings think and act

13. In psychological discussions, the term 'nurture' refers to:

A. life's experiences B. heredity

C. personality D. the environment

14. The study of how people grow and develop over a period of time is referred to as:

A. social psychology B. humanistic psychology

C. developmental psychology D. differential psychology

15. The process by which a child adjusts to the rules, standards and values of his or her family and culture is termed:

A. bonding B. induction

C. orientation D. socialization

16. Which among the body cells contain just 23 chromosomes?

A. Brain cells B. Bone cells

C. Sperm and egg cells D. Nerve and gland cells

17. The period of development between puberty and adulthood is called:

A. post childhood

B. adolescence

C. early adulthood

D. youth

18. Self-actualization is a process of:

A. separating your real needs from your learned needs

B. learning how to motivate yourself

C. expecting yourself to perform well when your arousal is low

D. achieving everything you aspire to achieve

19. A student is called a problem student when:

A. he suggests wrong solutions to problems discussed in the class

B. he suggests unusual problems for which the teacher has no solutions

C. he is able to solve the problems of other students

D. he exhibits behaviour problems which deviate significantly from normal behaviour

20. Which one of the following is the most effective way to promote student motivation for learning?

A. Give students more freedom to explore what interests them

B. To expose the students to the expectations of the community of which they are members

C. Provide a wide range of curricular and co-curricular learning activities

D. To provide them more opportunities for satisfying their innate desires

21. Child's heredity is determined at the time of:

A. Birth

B. Conception

C. Infancy

D. Early childhood

22. Learning will be most efficient if:

A. the teacher develops a lesson unit using accepted educational practices

B. the teacher fixes a high target for his teaching

C. pupils are given enough curricular activities to practice the content

D. pupils are taught using interesting activities

23. Meaningful learning takes place when:

A. students are really interested in the topics taught

B. cxplanations given are within the reach of students

C. the new content taught is related to the previous knowledge of the student

D. students are given carefully prepared notes for memorizing the content

24. Which of the following factors essentially contributes to effective learning?

i) Learner's motivation

ii) Learning facilities made available to the student by the institution

iii) Adequacy of the curriculum prescribed for study

iv) Learner's active participation in the process of learning ensured through proper teaching

A. (i) and (iv)

B. (i), (iii) and (iv)

C. Only (iv)

D. All the four

25. The aim of a career counselling should be to:

A. help students to collect details relating to different jobs

B. develop the students ability for understanding the nature of jobs and making a meaningful choice of job for himself

C. help every student to make a realistic self-appraisal

D. help the students to obtain vocational placement

26. The most important factor that would help a person to succeed in a job is:

A. Intelligence B. Interest

C. Aptitude D. Attitude

27. Knowledge of group dynamics is essential for the teacher as:

A. it is part of his professional requirement

B. it will help to adopt a dynamic approach to teaching

C. it helps him in improving the socio-emotional climate of the class

D. it helps him to deal with large student groups

28. For dealing with the gifted student, the professional approach used by the educational systems is called:

A. Enrichment B. Acceleration

C. Segregation D. A combination of all these

29. Delinquent persons are those who are deviant:

A. Physically B. Emotionally

C. Intellectually D. Socially

30. Isolates in a classroom are composed of students:

A. who do not attend the class regularly

B. who do not like to mix with other students and keep the member aloof

C. with whom other students in the class do not like to associate

D. who are self-centered introverts disliked by teachers

31. Gifted children are those children who show signs of:

A. originality in their thinking

B. have the ability to contradict popular view

C. have the ability to create new ideas

D. intellectual superiority far more than what is possessed by others

32. Creative people are those who show evidence of:

A. sociability

B. ability to think along new and very unusual ways

C. innovative ideas

D. independent thinking

33. The best agent for managing the psychological climate of a classroom is:

A. the class teacher

B. the subject teacher

C. the school principal

D. the student leader

34. Some children have difficulty in using their reading skill. This is due to:

A. hypertension B. hyper activity

C. dyslexia D. low intelligence

35. "The same fire which melts butter hardens the egg". This statement implies:

A. all individuals react in the same way to the same environment

B. the same environment affects different individuals differently

C. all individuals react in the same way to different environment

D. individual behaviour has nothing to do with his environment

36. Which of the following word is closely related to ZPD?

A. Scaffolding B. Multiple Intelligence

C. Universal Grammar D. Learning Disability

37. The major contribution of Alfred Binet to the study of intelligence.

A. Single factor theory B. Multi factor theory

C. IQ Test D. Theory of Multiple Intelligence

38. In this stage of development, human beings have their own imaginations, role models, etc. Which one of the following stages this is related?

A. Childhood B. Adolescence

C. Infancy D. Adulthood

Answer keys

1.B	2.B	3.B	4.B	5.C	6.D	7.B	8.A	9.D	10.D
11.A	12.A	13.D	14.C	15.D	16.C	17.B	18.D	19.D	20.D
21.B	22.D	23.C	24.B	25.B	26.C	27.C	28.D	29.D	30.C
31.D	32.C	33.A	34.C	35.B	36.A	37.C	38.B		

EDUCATIONAL TECHNOLOGY

1. **Educational evaluation should be:**
   A. a continuous process
   B. a continuous and comprehensive process
   C. a comprehensive process
   D. a process to be attempted at the end of a school term

2. **Education should give stress on desirable changes in the behaviour of learners in the:**
   A. the cognitive domain
   B. the affective domain
   C. the psychomotor domain
   D. all the above domains

3. **A school complex is meant to:**
   A. help schools to solve the complex problem they face
   B. provide expert assistance in identifying the difficult problems faced by schools in general
   C. develop a joint forum for different schools to identify and solve their common problems
   D. create a single organisation of teachers of a few schools in a neighbourhood

4. **The major function of a 'Question Bank' is:**
   A. to reduce the examination phobia of students
   B. developing a large group of questions by teachers using scientific methods
   C. providing scientific guidelines for pupils to learn and teachers to teach
   D. developing test items with the help of students

5. **Objectives selected for teaching a particular topic are called:**
   A. educational objectives B. general objectives
   C. instructional objectives D. subject-specific objectives

6. **For effective teaching a classroom should be:**
   A. limited in size B. well furnished
   C. scientifically planned D. properly ventilated

7. **A system of education meant for national development should adopt:**
   A. annual planning for its working
   B. short-term planning
   C. five year planning
   D. short-term and long-term planning

8. **Education as an investment aims at:**
   A. enhancing productivity
   B. accelerating the cultural development
   C. development of democratic outlook
   D. need satisfaction of learners

9. **Which one of the following instructional strategies would help students learn better?**
   A. Charts and maps
   B. Blackboard presentations
   C. film projection
   D. meaningful verbal explanation

10. **If a teacher has to establish her credibility in evaluating answer scripts she must be:**
    A. strict B. lenient
    C. objective D. prompt

11. **If instruction is treated as a technological endeavour, which items among the following would be considered as inputs?**
    i. The learner
    ii. Instructional objectives
    iii. Evaluational proceedures
    iv. Teacher's expertise
    v. The learning environment
    A. All the five B. (i), (ii), (iii) and (iv)
    C. (ii), (iii) and (v) D. (i), (iv) and (v)

12. **Five major functions of student evaluation are given below:**
    i. Diagnosis
    ii. Placement

iii. Prediction
iv. Certification
v. Ensuring mastery learning

Which of these functions are met by formative evaluation?

A. (i), (ii) and (v) B. (i) and (v)
C. (ii) and (iii) D. (ii) and (v)

13. Five qualities of a good test are listed below

i. Use of a fairly large representative sample
ii. Proof of high reliability
iii. Clear directions for scoring
iv. Provision of different types of norms
v. Evidence of different forms of validity of the test

Which of these are essentially required for a standardised test?

A. (i), (ii) and (v) B. (ii), (iv) and (v)
C. (i), (ii), (iv) and (v) D. all the above

14. Five functions of student evaluation are listed below:

i. Placement
ii. Selection
iii. Gradation
iv. Remediation
v. Prediction

Of these which functions are most important for norm-referenced evaluation?

A. (i), (ii), (iii) and (v) B. (i), (ii), (iii) and (v)
C. (ii), (iii), (iv) and (v) D. (i), (ii) and (iii)

15. Five types of validity are given below:

i. External validity
ii. Empirical validity
iii. Face validity
iv. Curricular validity
v. Construct validity

Which of these are assessed using field testing?

A. (iii) and (iv) B. (i) and (ii)

C. (i), (iii) and (iv) D. (ii), (iv) and (v)

16. **Which of the following is not the characteristic of a good test?**

A. Objectivity B. Subjectivity

C. Validity D. Reliability

17. **The expansion of the abbreviation CAI in Educational Technology is:**

A. Computer Associated Instruction

B. Computer Applied Instruction

C. Computer Assisted Instruction

D. Computer Activated Instruction

18. **The most essential condition for ensuring 'mastery learning' is:**

A. teacher-centred teaching

B. using diagnosis and remediation during every stage of teaching

C. organizing activity-oriented teaching

D. arousing intrinsic motivation to help students to master the content

19. **Which one of the following strategies do you consider the most effective for developing the value 'social commitment'?**

A. Conducting a symposium on the subject

B. Screening a film depicting this theme

C. Narrating stories that illustrate the idea

D. Working with pupils to solve a felt social issue

20. **Which of the following is not to be treated as a sure evidence of teacher's value orientation?**

A. Integrity in dealings with students

B. Commitment to the goals of teaching

C. Visiting temples frequently

D. Empathizing with students facing financial difficulties

21. **The grading system is preferred to the marking system in educational evaluation because:**

A. Marking system demands more work from the teacher

B. Grading is preferred by students

C. Malpractices are more in marking

D. Grading system is a rational method of student assessment

22. (i) Institutional evaluation, (ii) Personal evaluation, (iii) Programme evaluation, and (iv) Systems evaluation, are four processes used in educational evaluation. Of these, which one/which combination of procedures is most useful in educational management?

A. (i) only B. (i) and (ii) only

C. (i), (ii) and (iii) only D. All the four

23. Which of the following statements does not reflect the difference between measurement and evaluation in education?

A. Measurement is quantitative while evaluation is qualitative

B. Measurement is a pre-condition for evaluation

C. Evaluation and measurement are both subjective

D. Evaluation is a continuous process

24. The difficulties of particular learners in mastering a subject content is best identified with the help of:

A. an achievement test

B. a diagnostic test

C. a remedial test

D. a prognostic test

25. Which among the following is not a feature of a standardized test?

A. It is developed using the expertise of the test constructor and not as the basis of empirical testing

B. It is developed using a large and representative population of students

C. Items are selected using statistical techniques like item analysis

D. Validity and reliability are empirically established

26. Which of the following steps would you consider first as an effective communicator?

A. Select the channels of communication

B. Plan the evaluation procedure

C. Specify the objectives of communication

D. Identify the various media for communication

27. A small group of subjects selected from a population for study in order to estimate characteristics of the population is described as a:

A. small group study
B. parameter
C. case study sample
D. representative sample

28. A test designed to measure one's ability to learn effectively in a specified area is called:

A. an achievement test
B. an ability test
C. an intelligence test
D. an aptitude test

29. The major function that Radio and T.V. perform in education is that they are:

A. effective substitutes to teachers
B. useful for information - processing
C. helpful in providing education to several thousand students at a time
D. more convenient for system running

30. Which of the following statements is true about the process of summative evaluation?

A. It aims at providing a feedback to the teacher
B. It aims at reinforcing the student's learning
C. It aims at providing a feedback to both the teacher and the students
D. It aims at providing data useful for taking administrative decisions

31. Observing the behaviours, customs and ways of acting of a group by becoming an active member of the group is known as:

A. direct observation
B. participant observation
C. focussed observation
D. natural observation

32. Diagnostic tests help teachers to:

A. identify individual learning problems
B. identify students with low I Q
C. identify students with dyslexia
D. compare student's achievement

33. The primary function expected of a teacher is:

A. accelerate learning readiness
B. lesson planning
C. maintain student activity
D. curriculum transaction

34. Parent Teacher Associations should be considered as a means for:

A. securing funds for the school

B. ensuring over all development of the school and the students

C. getting the help of parents in controlling students

D. connecting teachers with the local people

35. The relation between anxiety and class achievement of students will be indicated in the form of a:

A. high positive correlation between the variables

B. high negative correlation between the variables

C. low negative correlation between the variables

D. increase of anxiety when the achievement is low

36. What is the full form of NAAC?

A. National Academic Assessment Council

B. National Association of Accredited Colleges

C. National Accreditation and Assessment Council

D. National Assessment and Accreditation Council

37. Education and socio-economic development are:

A. related in direct proportion

B. related in an indirect proportion

C. related in many cases but unrelated in a few cases

D. related but not in a predictable way

38. ICT is the abbreviation for:

A. Information communication technology

B. Information and communication technology

C. Information and computer technology

D. Inter connected technology

39. The most important function served by educational technology is:

A. use of technological aids for augmenting the quality of instruction

B. use of systems approach for designing instruction

C. use of computer assisted instruction in teaching

D. redefining instructional objectives as outputs of instruction

Answer keys

1.B	2.D	3.C	4.C	5.C	6.C	7.D	8.A	9.C	10.C
11.D	12.B	13.B	14.A	15.A	16.B	17.C	18.B	19.D	20.C
21.D	22.D	23.C	24.B	25.A	26.C	27.A	28.A	29.C	30.D
31.B	32.A	33.D	34.B	35.B	36.D	37.A	38.B	39.B	

Unit - II

RESEARCH APTITUDE

1. RESEARCH: MEANING, CHARACTERISTICS AND TYPES
2. STEPS OF RESEARCH
3. METHODS OF RESEARCH
4. RESEARCH ETHICS
5. PAPER, ARTICLE, WORKSHOP, SEMINAR, CONFERENCE AND SYMPOSIUM
6. THESIS WRITING: ITS CHARACTERISTICS AND FORMAT

Unit - II

RESEARCH APTITUDE

One of the objectives of this test is to identify candidates for the award of Junior Research Fellowship (J.R.F). The importance of research for generating new knowledge in any discipline is to be well accepted. The economic development of any country depends essentially on the quality of research in critical areas like agriculture, industry, education, basic science, engineering and technology, health sciences, sociology and behavioural sciences, mathematical and statistical sciences etc. All important wings of administration and important organizations have a Research and Analysis Wing (RAW) which turns out advanced research. We have a number of National Laboratories in our country which do specialized research in areas like Physics, Chemistry, Molecular Biology, etc.

But the vast portion of the research in the country is done by the universities and research institutes located in different parts of the country. They not only train future researchers and confer higher research degrees like M. Phil and Ph. D but conduct research on their own. They also undertake high level research often using funds from external agencies like the DST and bodies like ICSSR etc. One of the most important aims of universities is to promote research endeavours, to provide research guidance, to arrange research facilities, and to publish research journals, abstracts and dissertations. A teacher in a university department can no more confine to classroom teaching only. Rendering research guidance to the research scholars and enhancing one's own fund of knowledge keeping abreast with modern developments in one's own area of specialization and creating new knowledge through one's own research are the most essential functions of a teacher in the universities and colleges. It is disheartening that most of the teachers in higher education institutions are concentrating more on teaching, ignoring the two other major functions expected of higher education viz., research and extension. It is in this context that the UGC has included this component in the UGC test. In the following pages we are going to examine the need, significance, types and characteristics of research, the steps involved in the research process, the methods and tools of research, research ethics etc. We would also examine the difference between research papers, articles and other publications, and also the role played by workshops, seminar, conferences and symposia as methods of disseminating new knowledge. We will also examine the ways in which a research report/dissertation is to be prepared and accepted formats used for writing research reports.

1. MEANING, CHARACTERISTICS AND TYPES OF RESEARCH

Research as the term indicates, is a process of searching for truth especially for interpreting the phenomena we observe in nature and also for solving problems using the scientific method. Problem solving usually is based on identifying the causal factors which lead to problems and predicting the probabilities of occurrence of certain phenomena when certain conditions are satisfied. The findings will directly or indirectly contribute to the growth of existing knowledge and broaden the horizons of knowledge. Research is popularly defined as "a scientific paradigm used for problem solving". We encounter innumerable problems with varied degrees of importance and complexity. The strategies used for solving such problems can be hierarchically represented as shown in the diagram.

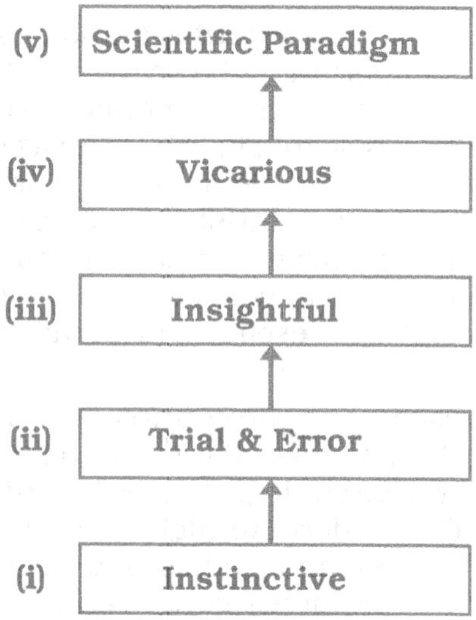

Any living organism, when facing a problematic situation or when anticipating a problem will resort to an instinctive behaviour which is innate, inborn and unlearnt. Ants hoarding food grains in holes before monsoon, the newly hatched baby chicks hiding inside the feathers of the mother hen in response to the alarming sound of the hen, etc. are examples of instinctive learning. We, the homosapiens also behave instinctively when we encounter problems similar to this (e.g. a small child hiding behind its mother when it sees a dog approaching it).

'Trail and Error' is a more complex strategy that sub-humans and human beings adopt under problematic situations. If you are entrusted with a bunch of key and asked to open a lock, or if you have to tune a particular TV station, you adopt trial and error solutions.

'Insightful' problem solving is an 'aha experience' which leads to a sudden flash of the solution of the problem. Experiments have shown that children, animals and birds also can solve problems using insights (The experiments by German psychologists Wertheimer, Kohler and Koffka have shown that children and chimpanzees could gain insights).

The next in the learning hierarchy is 'vicarious problem solving'. This is the process of observation and imitation. Only human beings can imitate others. In the circus tent the training given to one animal will never be imitated by other animals. Each animal requires special individual training for performance expected of it. But human beings have a special talent for imitation. Our style of eating, dressing, and behavioural peculiarities are mostly learnt through imitation. In problem solving also, we often imitate others. The research process is much more complex than all the above four processes.

Research deals essentially with the use of scientific method for problem-solving. The scientific process of problem solving demands a well-defined and logically sequenced series of steps which end up with a dependable solution. Highly systematic, objective and empirical procedures are used for research. Research is described as "a hypothetico-deductive process". A research hypothesis is a tentative solution of a problem. It is also described as "an intelligent guess". The tentative solution is deduced from an established theory, principle or generalization. A hypothesis is verified on the basis of analysis of data and if not validated the hypothesis is rejected. Until and unless it is substantiated by the observed findings, it is not accepted as a worthwhile piece of knowledge. That is why a hypothesis is called a tentative answer to a problem.

Any research endeavour starts with a hypothesis. On the basis of the researcher's own experience, or by reviewing related literature and getting sufficient theoretical bases, the researcher deduces a hypothesis. He sets specific objectives of what he is going to do to test this hypothesis, then develops valid and reliable tools for collecting data relevant to the problem or adopts a valid and reliable tool (tools) already available, and uses the tools for measuring the variables around which the study is conceived. The tools are administered on a representative sample from which data is collected. The data is analysed which helps to draw conclusions as to whether the hypothesis is valid or not. Since research attempts to validate the hypothesis, this method used for research gives meaning to the term 'hypothetico-deductive' process of problem solving.

The purpose of research

We know that the majority of our scholars do research with the intention to acquire higher research degrees. The importance of this objective is not under estimated. But research is a dependable method of adding to existing scientific knowledge in a discipline. The UGC and other such bodies (NCERT, ICSSR, etc) encourage teachers to undertake research projects to help them to contribute to existing knowledge in their disciplines. The Faculty Improvement Programme (FIP) of the UGC has also more important aims in encouraging research. Research also can help researchers in keeping abreast of modern developments in their subject areas. Obviously this will help teachers to improve their instruction. Researches will also help to familiarize teachers with the innovations taking place in teaching and learning. The most important objectives of research are:

i. Developing new principles relating to theory and practice.
ii. To verify the validity of an already established theory to a different setting.
iii. To develop new concepts, theories and new interpretations of phenomena using the logic of science.
iv. To solve problems using systematic steps and methods.

These objectives can contribute significantly to the progress and development of the nation as a whole.

2. TYPES OF RESEARCH AND METHODS OF RESEARCH

Research is classified depending upon the nature of the problem, the purpose of research and the procedures used for conducting research. The following diagram illustrates the various types of research in education and other related social science areas.

a. Cross-sectional Research

Cross-sectional research is the study based on the cross section of an event, phenomenon or population. In fact this is sample study. A sample is the cross section of the population. The term 'population' in research refers to the entire units on which the study is intended. For instance, if a researcher wants to investigate the problems of adolescent school children in Mumbai province, all the adolescents in the Mumbai province are to be studied. In practice, it is difficult to conduct a study on all the individuals constituting a population. Instead the study has to be focused on a portion of the population - a representative sample - a cross-section of adolescents of the area is drawn from various regions, within the geographic area, by selecting the sample to represent other variables like gender, residence, age, etc will be used for study. The sample will be so selected that the findings are generalizable - are applicable to the total population. There are many techniques for selecting a representative sample.

Cross sectional studies are less time-consuming. Statistical techniques are employed to test the probability of errors in sampling and the degree of generalizability can be estimated.

b. Longitudinal Research

Longitudinal studies are lifelong studies. From the origin of the case/problem, up to the present status of the problem, every aspect is considered for the study. Child study researches and case studies are examples of longitudinal studies. In social sciences, especially in psychology, longitudinal study has special relevance. This approach requires long time for completion. But longitudinal studies assume special significance in different areas like child development.

c. Quantitative Research

Quantitative studies imply the use of quantitative methods of the variables covered by the study. In many studies, the data need not be viable for quantification. In quantitative research, tests, questionnaires, check lists, scales of various types, etc. will be employed for data collection. The assumption behind quantification is contained in the statement: "if anything exists, it exists in some quantity; if it exists in some quantity, it is measurable". The quantified data collected are subjected to statistical analysis; and the findings are stated in terms of statistical indices with definite meanings (like correlations, variance, etc) and also using diagrams, graphs and tables.

d. Qualitative Research

In Qualitative or Descriptive studies, numerical data is much less employed as in history, social trends, etc. In a historical study of dynasties, or in a study of the philosophical perspectives of the novels written by famous writers, there is very little possibility of numerical analysis of data. The researcher will have to describe the sequential courses of events in the former example and the excerpts of philosophically pertinent portions in the latter example. Sociological theories, and psychological theories are examples of research using descriptions.

e. Fundamental Research

'Fundamental Research' (also called 'Basic Research' or 'Pure Research'), is done with the sole intention of developing new knowledge about social/natural phenomena without any intention of their use in practical life. Major objectives of this type of research are to develop theories, to verify the existing theories, search of knowledge and many such broad issues. Newton's law of Motion is an example of pure science. These researchers are not much bothered about the application of their findings; rather they are more concerned with finding the truth or explaining a new phenomenon. These laws were used later in areas like Engineering. But the laws were discussed not for their application at the time of discovery. Only experts in research methodology and theoretical foundations can engage in such researches. We know that so many research projects are undertaken in university departments of the country leading to doctoral degrees. Many of these remain as research and are not used for improving practice in relevant areas. This does not mean that such researches have no relevance. Knowledge expands and develops only through research. The progress in various walks of life is determined by the research findings and their applications. Agricultural, medical, pharmaceutical and technological advancements are a few examples of pure research converted into applied research.

f. Action Research

'Action Research' is also known as 'on the spot research' and 'the research of here and now'. This indicates that its goals are proximate and not remote. Whenever a problem is encountered, systematic and scientific approaches of research are adopted for solving the problem then and there in a local setting. Artificial laboratory settings or formal arrangements are not required. The routine functions of the institution or organization, where the study is conducted, need not be disturbed. Research is combined with routine professional practice. Stephen M. Corey who developed this method of research has commented that action research is "like repairing a car while it is running". The objective of this research is not in theory building, nor finding out the ultimate truth; but solving a felt problem which hampers smooth practice. The application of the findings is local and immediate. It can be conducted by any professional who confronts the problem and wants to find out an immediate solution. A research guide's rigid stipulations need not be adopted. But even then, the basic requirements of the scientific methods are met. Hence if a person is using the systematic steps of research in solving his problem, it is action research. The action programme that follows, ie, the use of the results for remedial purposes (action for improvement), is the soul of action research.

g. Experimental Research

Experimental Research is the most systematic approach to research. An experiment is 'an attempt to establish cause-effect relationship scientifically and objectively'. The approach shows that the observed effect is the result of the specific factors, and is not caused by any other factors. Another definition of experimental approach is that "experiment is observation under controlled conditions". What do we observe and what do we control? The answer to these questions is possible only if we are familiar with the variables of an experimental setting. The following diagram shows the various types of variables used in experiments.

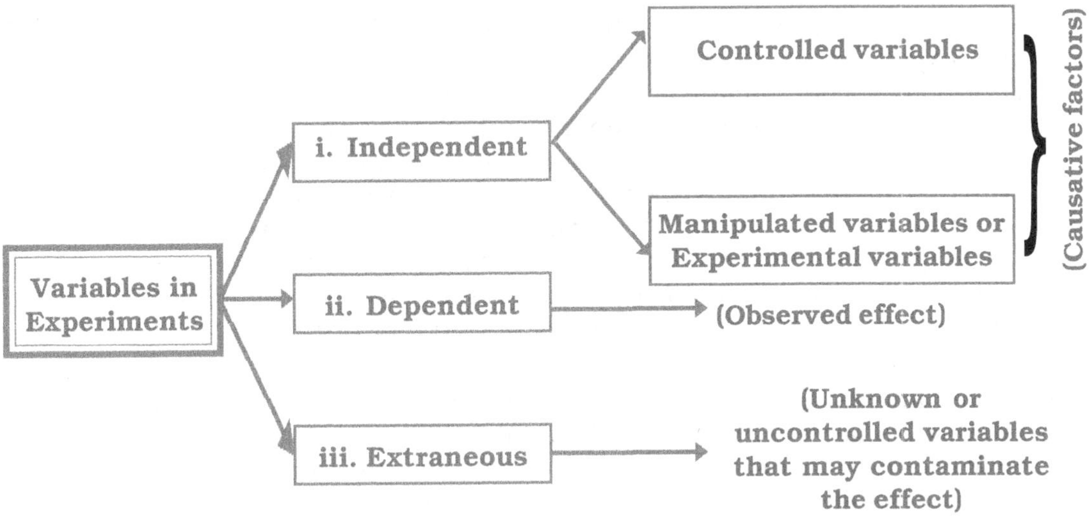

The diagram indicates that we can broadly classify the variables into three, viz, independent variables or causative factors, dependent variables or the observed effects and extraneous variables which enter into the experiment 'uninvited' and are likely to affect the observed effect, which could not be controlled by the experimenter. If a researcher wants to test the effectiveness of a new teaching method he can adopt experimental design for conducting research. This example will help to illustrate the concepts like'experimental control', 'manipulation of variables' 'experimental group, 'control group design', 'pretest – post test design', etc.

In the example cited (testing the effectiveness of a new teaching method), academic achievement of students is the dependent variable. It is called dependent variable because academic achievement is depended upon innumerable factors. The learners' intellectual capacities, anxiety level, interest,aptitude, attitude towards learning particular subjects, teacher effectiveness, learning styles, home environment, facilities, teacher's personality, communication, teaching aids, teaching methods, difficulty level and complexity of task to be learnt etc. are examples of independent variables which describe the level of the dependant variable viz academic achievement. No experimenter can manipulate all these variables at a time, in an experiment. The experimenter selects a few of these most important variables for treatment. These variables are described as the independent variables of a study.

In an experiment, the investigator manipulates anyone of these variables and attempts to test the effectiveness of that variable upon the dependent variable. The independent variable thus manipulated is also called the experimental variable. In the example cited above, the new teaching method is the experimental variable. The investigator is interested in the effectiveness of that teaching method on 'academic achievement'. Therefore he has to ascertain that the other variables do not affect or contaminate the observed effect. The techniques an experimenter uses to ensure that other variables (called extraneous variables) do not influence the result of the study is termed 'experimental control'. The experimenter can control the major variables which are likely to contaminate or vitiate the findings. For example he can select his experimental group (sample) in such a way that they are all of the same level of ability, belong to the same socio-economic status, belong to a common culture, etc and claim that these variables are controlled. Again, the same teacher teaching the same topic, in the same way for the two groups used in the experimental setting (control group and experiment group), will guarantee that the teacher variables are controlled. If he controls all the major extraneous variables, he can ascertain that the observed effect on academic achievement is the result of the new teaching method and not because of the action of any other factors.

The 'experimental group - control group design' is a popular experimental design used in educational research. Students are randomly assigned to two groups - one taught by the new teaching method (called the experimental group) and the other taught using traditional methods (called the control group). After a certain period of teaching, the same test for evaluation is administered on both the groups to find out which group shows better performance. If the experimental group scores more than the control group, it is interpreted as the result of the higher effectiveness of the new method used in the experiment. To make the experiment more precise, experimenters use the 'pretest-post test design'. The 'experimental group' and the 'control group' are created in such a manner that the groups are almost identical or equal. They can be equated with respect to their scores in this pretest. A student getting score 'x' in the pretest in the control group will have a student getting score 'x' (or a score close to x) in the experimental group. There are other methods for equating groups - like equity group on the basis of their mean and standard deviation in the pre-test. When the experimental treatment (teaching the experimental group using the new method and the control group using the conventional method) for a particular period is over, both these groups are again tested using the same test of academic achievement. This is called post test. If the scores in post test of the two groups are significantly different (experiment group showing higher performance) it can be concluded that the difference is the result of the new teaching method employed for teaching the experimental group.

Many improved designs are available for employing experimental and control groups like multi-group designs, where several groups can be compared together. The application of the experimental variable of different magnitudes can be compared using multivariate designs like of variance and co-variance. Experiments can be developed to study the differential effects of an independent variable on the dependable variable.

Though experimental control cannot be accurately and precisely done on human beings and in social sciences, as in the case of the exact science like physics, chemistry and mathematics, the spirit of experimentation can be used for improving the discussions in social sciences. Measuring body temperature is more accurate than measuring intelligence or personality. But social scientists have derived techniques for improving the accuracy of measurement of human behaviour and human learning.

h. Quasi-experimental Research

When an experimental design is planned any technique for controlling variables and measuring variables, it will not be practicable to make random assignment of subjects to experimental and control groups. In such cases we resort to the use of quasi-experimental designs. In these studies the perfect equivalence of the compared groups is not ensured. All other procedures of experimental research are observed in the process.

i. Survey Research and Historical Research

Survey research is essentially cross-sectional in nature. This method is used for analyzing, political, social, economic and educational conditions that prevail in the given area or in a given population. Opinion surveys, trend studies, activity analysis, programme evaluation, etc. are some of the areas where survey research is used.

Surveys can be (i) exploratory, (ii) descriptive and (iii) co-relational. In exploratory research, the investigators are interested in understanding the details of an existing phenomenon. For instance, if a social science researcher is interested in studying the extramarital sex relationship of educated persons, he collects data for analyzing this phenomenon in greater detail and explores the problem adopting accepted procedures.

Descriptive surveys are characterized by:

i. hypothesis formulation and testing
ii. inductive and deductive reasoning for arriving at generalizations
iii. randomization techniques for collecting data from samples
iv. reporting the study in a manner which makes it replicate by other researchers.

In co-relational research, the investigator attempts to find the relationship between two or more variables. Examples are the reaction between alcohol consumption of drivers and automobile accidents. Another is criminality of any member of broken home environment.

The relationship between these variables is estimated using statistical procedures.

When an investigator is interested in the development of a past phenomenon or episode in a specific earlier period, the study is called historical research. For instance, researcher conducting a study of the system of education or an educational practice (promotion practices, teacher promotion practices, etc) in the pre-independence period of India, or about the types of institution for providing Islamic education in India, these can be regarded as examples of historical research. Such researches can be either qualitative or quantitative or a combination of both, depending upon the issues identified for the research. Such studies enable us to understand the 'how' and 'why' of the phenomena being studied. The data are collected from existing books, monographs, periodicals, and monuments, old document, historical relies, etc.

j. Case Study

Case study is a longitudinal study. A 'case' in a case study stands for any social unit that demands an in-depth study. Though the term is derived from clinical practices, a case need not be an individual with a problem. If an investigator attempts to study about an organization, system or institution or a person, for detailed study, in all its various aspects, it can be called a case study. Case study is also called "a social microscope" because it magnifies various aspects of the case and enables the investigator to study meticulously. Data are collected from all available sources and analyzed systematically. The attempt is not to identify the unique characteristics of the case, but to study the typicality of the case. Observation, interviews, questionnaires and inventories, recorded data like letters, reports, biographies, diaries, etc. are all valid sources of data, for conducting case studies.

k. Ex-post facto Research

The 'ex-post facto approach' attempts to investigate about past events or post developments relating to a situation. The recent example is the studies related to the recent Tsunami which affected the eastern coast of India. After the occurrence of the phenomenon, its causes, course and its consequences are studied. The major problem in such studies is that the data available to the researcher need not always be, reliable and valid. This problem is called the 'post hoc fallacy'.

The major limitations of ex-post facto studies are:

i. the independent variables cannot be manipulated.
ii. subjects cannot be randomly assigned for treatment
iii. causes are often multiple and complex, and often not fully identified

In spite of these limitations, the relevance of such studies cannot be underestimated.

3. STEPS IN RESEARCH

As indicated in the first part of this section, research is a systematic process of investigation where the steps are dictated by the methods of science. The research process is accepted because of the acceptability of the steps adopted for validation. The following are the steps adopted in research.

i. Identifying a problem
   Selection of a problem for study
   Delimiting the scope for study

Defining the problem and terms using operationally defined scientific terminology

ii. Stating the hypothesis (hypotheses) of the study (defining expected outcomes of the study)

iii. Setting the objectives of the study (stating specifically what the researcher intends to do to test the hypothesis)

iv. Selecting appropriate methods for conducting the study by:
   - defining the variables involved
   - identifying/developing valid tools for data collection
   - defining the sample for the study
   - defining the research design for conducting the study
   - identifying the statistical techniques to be employed for analysis and interpretation of data

v. Collection of data from the selected sample for the study
   - administering questionnaires, inventories, checklists, tests, rating scales, etc. on the sample
   - conducting interviews if needed
   - making systematic observations of the select aspects to be studied
   - analyzing reports, records, letters, etc.

vi. Analysing data using appropriate statistical techniques(if required.)

vii. Drawing conclusions based on the analysis

viii. Verifying the conclusions
   - validating the hypothesis
   - accepting or rejecting hypothesis

ix. Reporting the findings (in the form of research papers, dissertations, articles, etc.)

The steps listed above are the major ones. Many other sub steps are implied in the research procedure, depending upon the nature of the problem and method of study. A review of related literature is often an unavoidable pre-requisite for understanding the problem in all its aspects. The researcher makes a focused survey of what studies have already been conducted in the area by other researchers, and their findings, the methodology they adopted, what more remains to be explored, etc. The answers to all these questions will be available through a thorough review of literature.

A researcher should also realize that attempting to study every aspect of a problem in areas like education will not be feasible. Delimiting the area or pinpointing the area is a crucial step in research. Penetrating deeper and deeper into a specific area rather than concentrating on very many aspects at a time, is the usual approach adopted in educational research. A researcher decides to "do everything about something rather than something about everything".

4. RESEARCH ETHICS

Human beings are generally the subject matter of social sciences. Even the study of social institutions implies the study of the contributions of human being in the functioning of institutions. Certain types of experiments cannot even be imagined to be conducted on human beings. Imagine that an investigator administers some psychotropic drugs on college students to study its impact on behaviour and its susceptibility to addiction! We have to uphold certain values in conducting research on humans or on what has been done by humans. Some of the values one has to keep in the forefront in conducting social science research are:

- People have the right to privacy; our right to enter into the privacy of others is limited
- Every individual has right for self-determination
- One should never do harm to another person intentionally

These values are listed as ethics in research. This refers to the proper moral duty and obligation of a researcher. A researcher can never encroach on the privacy of another person without his consent. It is the moral responsibility of a researcher to ensure confidentiality of the facts disclosed to him by a subject if it has social taboo attached to it. Deception of any sort has to be avoided at all costs.

According to Monette et. al 1986 (Applied Social Research, Tools for the Human Services. Duane R Monette, Thoas J. Sullivan and Cornell R. De Jong. Holt Rinehart and Winston Inc. 1986), there are seven ethical issues in social science research.

1. Informed consent
2. Confidentiality
3. Privacy (anonymity)
4. Physical or mental distress (absence of)
5. Problems in sponsored research (the probability and violation of ethics is more in sponsored research when it is entrusted to agencies)
6. Disclosure of research results (against the assurance given to subjects)
7. Scientific advocacy (argument that science is value free and truth and objectivity are the only concern)

Mistreatment of any section of the society, harm to vulnerable respondents rigid adherence to doctrines, etc. have to be totally banished from the process.

5. PAPER, ARTICLE, WORKSHOPS, SEMINARS, CONFERENCES AND SYMPOSIA

A paper in the context of research is either a read or published work on the basis of an original investigation or study conducted by a person. It is read to an audience or society which consists of a group of learned individuals or scholars or is published in a research journal. A research paper essentially includes the title and definition of the problem, the objectives of the study, the major hypotheses, the methodology, the findings and their interpretation.

An article is any essay based on a specific topic which is published in any periodical or journal. An article may often highlight the special features of a phenomenon or a crucial issue. For instance one can think of an article on the 'Importance of Instructional Understanding' or on 'Global Warming'. Articles are published in a magazine or weekly or even in a journal, but need not fulfil the rigid format of the research paper. It is a non fictional essay which comes out with new arguments, new viewpoints, and new vision about issues.

A workshop, as the name indicates, is aimed at the production of some materials based on the deliberations of its participants. A workshop will have well designed objectives. A curriculum revision workshop, a handbook preparation workshop, an evaluation tool development workshop, etc. are examples. The materials produced in the workshop will be provided to the participants either in the form of printed materials or CD's. The outcome of the workshop is published in magazines or journals.

Seminars are organized when an in-depth study is required by a scholarly group, especially through collecting data using experiments or library work or exploring the findings of research abstracts in journals or other publications. The different dimensions of a topic are assigned to different scholars and they are required to present their views systematically before a motivated and informed audience. A seminar will be moderated by an expert or chairperson who leads the discussions and invites clarifications. The chairperson can contribute his views and enrich the deliberations.

A symposium consists of different teams of presenters. Each team is led by a scholar. It also has the possibility of presenting the various aspects of the problem by various teams. Each team will present their views about the same theme one by one in a preplanned sequence. Then the open forum will deliberate upon the presentations and end up with conclusions. A chairperson initiates and regulates the proceedings.

In a conference, mutual consultation and discussion is the major objective. Conferences are regularly held by some scholarly associations and organizations for evolving various strategies of their modus operandi. In conferences, the proceedings are initiated and regulated by a chairperson and the minutes of the deliberations are recorded and signed by all its participants and countersigned by its chairperson.

6. THESIS WRITING: ITS CHARACTERISTICS AND FORMAT

The Research Report is a highly formalized presentation of a research study conducted by professionals. It is expected to follow a rigid and conventional pattern. The pattern suggested for writing reports are given in 'style manuals' which specify the way in which the title, introduction, method, result, discussion, references and appendices etc. are to be presented in the report. A research report or thesis or dissertation follows these conventions in paraphrasing, numbering and citing references, pagination, presentation of tables, figures, graphs etc. Researchers have to follow the specifications and stipulations given in the prescribed style manuals.

Example: Chicago Manual of Style 14th ed. (1993).

The MLA Handbook for Writers of Research Papers 5th ed. (Gibaldi 1999).

Form and Style: Research Papers, Report, Theses. 11th ed. (Slade 2000).

A Manual for Writers of Term Papers, Theses and Dissertations 6th Ed. (Turabain. 1996) etc. A common pattern is usually prescribed in all these style manuals which are internationally adopted. They all generally require the following:

i. Introduction and the statement of the problem

This section should state the need and relevance of the problem. The scope and objectives of he study, the major hypotheses, the social implications, etc. are to be mentioned in this section. It is also desirable to state how the investigator was motivated to take up the project. This section should define the problem with operational definitions of the key terms. The objectives of the study and the hypotheses should be listed clearly in this section.

ii. Review of related literature/studies

A review of the related literature bringing out the history of the problem and major research endeavours undertaken in the area is an indispensable part of a dissertation. The numerous citations of the work done in each area will provide a broader perspective of the problem. This also will help to avoid unnecessary duplication of the work done by other researchers.

iii. The methods adopted by the study

This section describes the procedures adopted for conducting the study. This includes details like the following: population on which the study is conducted including how the sample was selected to ensure that it is representative of the population to be studied, the strategy used for sampling (random sampling, stratified sampling, snowball sampling, incidental sampling, etc.) the number of cases included in the sample, the sample size, etc. is to be mentioned and to be followed by the variables used in the study (independent variable, dependent variable, intervening variables, etc) and the measures adopted to control the extraneous or confounding variables, etc. It is important to state the validity and reliability of the tools used for collection of data, and details relating to the tools whether tools developed and standardized by the investigator or whether an already standardized tool with established validity and reliability was used, etc. The researcher is expected to spell out the details of the steps adopted for administering the tool, precautions adopted for collecting the data and statistical techniques employed for the analysis of data, etc.

iv. Analysis and interpretation of data

This section is expected to provide details of how the data collected form the representative sample using the prescribed tools, and techniques, was analysed and interpreted objectively. Statistical techniques are often employed in quantitative researches for calculating statistical indices like mean scores, standard deviation of scores, correlations between variables, etc. The techniques of inferential statistics are used for interpreting the data and determining the probability of errors, prediction and reaching generalisable results.

v. The results

This section consists of the straight forward presentation of the findings based on the analysis. The presentation is to be supported by graphs, statistical diagrams like histograms, pi-diagrams and tables for providing an understanding of what is presented. (These types of representations are not always possible in researches based on qualitative data).

vi. Discussion

This section is meant for interpretation of results like validity of the hypotheses. Each hypothesis is to be tested based on the findings and has to be either accepted or rejected. The broader implications of the findings of the study are to be identified. The practical and social relevance of the findings etc. also are to be mentioned in this section. It is also customary to state the limitations of the study and to suggest problems for further study which emerged from the present study.

vii. References

In this section a list of all the works cited in the study are presented using internationally accepted conventions. For doing this 'The Harvard Method' is commonly used by social science researchers. The author's last name and date of publication are placed in parenthesis at the end of the sentence. The references are to be listed in the alphabetical order by the author's last name.

Another popular format is called 'the serial method'. In this the citations are indicated numerically in the body of the text. The references are then given in the section for references, following the same order. Journals, textbooks, abstracts, etc. should be listed separately.

viii. Appendices

The last part of the report should present models of the tools used, the scoring keys adopted and other details of tools, etc. and such other relevant items which will throw adequate light on the procedure adopted.

In writing the thesis, the language should be simple and straight forward. The investigator has to remind himself that writing a dissertation is a process rather than a product. Clarity in communication is far more important than the use of flowery, literary narrations. Rewriting each section is essential for ensuring accuracy in communication and to minimize errors. Paraphrasing and numbering each sub titles, proper use of capital letters in typing, spacing between the lines and every aspect of thesis writing is to be carefully observed under the guidance of an expert.

Research Aptitude – PRACTICE EXERCISE

1. **The selection of variables in a research endeavour is to be presented as part of:**
   A. Data analysis
   B. Statement of hypothesis
   C. Interpretation of data
   D. Definition of the research problem

2. **A questionnaire is to be preferred over an interview when:**
   A. data are collected from a dispersed sample
   B. the information sought is of an impersonal nature
   C. written communication conveys the responsibilities
   D. all the given options are to be met

3. **Selection of a statistical technique for a research problem is reported in the section which presents:**
   A. statement of the hypothesis
   B. analysis of data
   C. data collection procedures
   D. identification and formulation of the problem

4. **Reliability of a research study is concerned with the:**
   A. replicability of findings
   B. generalizability of findings
   C. interpretability of findings
   D. all the above

5. **Validity of a test is based on whether:**
   A. the test measures what it intends to measure
   B. the test yields the same result on repeated administration
   C. the test items are easily understandable
   D. the responses can be converted into scores easily

6. **Which of the following statements is incorrect.**
   A. It is not possible to estimate the validity of a questionnaire using quantitative techniques
   B. Estimating the reliability of a tool with open-ended questions is difficult
   C. In item analysis of an attitude scale, it is not necessary to estimate the difficulty value of each item
   D. All the given options are correct

7. **Which of the following is correct when we want to establish the reliability of a standardized test?**
   A. Parallel form method B. Test-retest method
   C. Odd-even method D. All the above options

8. **Which one of the following statistical tests is described as a non-parametric tests?**
   A. Test of significance for mean differences
   B. Test of significance for difference between correlations
   C. Chi-square test
   D. None of the above

9. **The reason why we estimate or calculate the reliability of a psychological tool by different methods is:**
   A. None of the methods is a complete method in itself
   B. Use of different methods would help to increase the reliability of the tool
   C. Using different methods ensures greater faith in the quality of the tool
   D. None of the given options is correct.

10. **Which one of the following statements is not correct?**
    A. Reliability does not ensure validity
    B. Validity coefficient of a test can be negative
    C. Reliability coefficient of a test can be negative
    D. All valid tests are also reliable

11. **Which one of the following statements about the reliability and validity is not accurate?**
    A. Validity ensures reliability, but the reverse is not true
    B. A standardized test is expected to be both valid and reliable
    C. Reliability of a test can be ensured by making all the test items objective
    D. A larger test will be more reliable than a shorter test

12. **Interest inventories are used mainly for:**
    A. identifying the occupation for which a student is best suited
    B. opening communication with students in career counselling
    C. identifying psychological differences in vocational interests of students
    D. selecting candidates who like an available job in the job market

13. **The validity of a test is determined by correlating the scores obtained:**
    A. using two forms of the same test administered to the same group

B. on a newly-developed test with another test used as an external criterion
C. on the test with each item of a class achievement test
D. by administering the same test twice to the same group

14. The selection of a proper method of research has to be decided as part of:
A. formulation of the problem
B. part of data collection for the study
C consolidating the findings of the study
D. identifying the scope of the study

15. Which of the following technique is most suitable for assessing a student's 'job preference'?
A. Interviews B. Anecdotal records
C. Questionnaire D. Vocational inventory

16. A researcher wants to select the best items from his draft test while developing an attitude scale using item analysis. The researcher should find out:
A. both difficulty value as well as discrimination index of each item
B. the scale value to be assigned to each item
C. difficulty index of each item
D. discrimination index of each item

17. Which one of the following statements is not a justification for the use of the interview technique in research?
A. oral communication is most dependable
B. written communication should not be taken as the last word
C. people prefer to talk rather than write when they express themselves
D. oral communication gives more appropriate to the respondent to code up his views to suit the views of the questioner

18. Which one of the following research tool is different from the others in the group?
A. Rating Scale B. Sociometry
C. Semantic Differential D. Questionnaire

19. Which one of the following tools is not appropriate for studying the use of environmental inputs in the science text books used in primary schools of your state?
A. Rating scale B. Achievement test
C. Questionnaire D. Content analysis

20. **For standardisation of an achievement test in a school subject, item analysis is to be done. Item analysis will be done to assess:**

A. only the discrimination index of each item in the draft test

B. only the difficulty index is to be calculated

C. both difficulty as well as discrimination indices are to be calculated

D. neither difficulty nor discrimination indices will help to select the best items in the draft

21 **The objective of sociometry is to study:**

A. social distance among the members of a group

B. interaction pattern of students within a classroom

C. group cohesiveness within a community

D. all the above

22. **Which one of the following methods is most appropriate for establishing the validity of an achievement test?**

A. Construct validity B. Concurrent validity

C. Predictive validity D. All the above

23. **Which one of the following tools yields data which is most difficult to be interpreted?**

A. Questionnaire B. Observation schedule

C. Unstructured interview D. Structured interview

24. **To study the impact of a development project on a group of stake holders, it is best that the data is to be collected using:**

A. participant observation B. structured interview

C. rating scale D. a psychological test

25. **Which tool among the following uses 'equal-appearing' interval scale?**

A. Test of attitude B. Personality Inventory

C. Checklist D. Aptitude test

26. **The selection of the tools for research will be decided mostly by the:**

A. hypothesis of the study

B. variables used for the study

C. statistical techniques expected to be used

D. methods to be used for data analysis

27. The selection of sample for research will be decided mostly by:

A. the time available for conducting the study
B. professional expertise of the researcher
C. tools to be used for data collection
D. technique expected to be used for hypothesis testing

28. Participant observation is appropriate when the purpose of the research is to collect data in situations where:

A. data relating to a large number of variables are to be collected
B. dependable data will not be available through the usual methods
C. regularities underlying a phenomenon are to be identified
D. all the above

29. To study the effect of new instructional strategies for developing creativity of students, the best method of research is comparison of control and experimental groups using:

A. Survey Method B. Experimental Method
C. Semi-discriptive Method D. Nonparametric Method

30. Findings of a research conducted on sample of tenth grade students do not hold good for college fresher's, it is another way of stating that the new study:

A. lacks internal validity
B. lacks external validity
C. has not used a representative sample
D. uses an experimental design not suitable for college fresher's

31. Which one of the following type of research uses quantification techniques in a big way?

A. Survey Research B. Historical Research
C. Philosophical Research D. Experimental Research

32. Which one of the following statements is not true of a deductive inference?

A. The validity of a deductive inference depends upon the soundness of the deduction
B. The validity of a deductive inference depends upon the soundness of the assumptions used for deduction
C. A deductive inference is always valid
D. A deductive inference is always based on concrete experience

33. To study the status of women's education from 1870 to 1910, the most appropriate methodology to be used is:

A. Analytical method using original data
B. Experimental method using quantified data
C. Survey method using available data
D. Historical method using validated data

34. **In which type of research the manipulation of variables is not necessary?**
A. Experimental research
B. Survey research
C. Historical research
D. Ethnographic research

35. **Internal criticism is used in historical research to:**
A. give meaning to a source material
B. decide the authenticity of a given source
C. give credibility to a source
D. decide the date of occurrence of an event

36. **Scientific method involves inferences which are based on:**
A. inductive reasoning
B. statistical reasoning
C. deductive reasoning
D. inductive and deductive reasoning

37. **Lack of consistency in research findings is described as:**
A. lack of reliability
B. lack of validity
C. lack of both reliability and validity
D None of the given options is correct

38. **In historical research, external criticism refers to the process used by researchers to:**
A. the use of a document relevant for a research problem
B. the acceptability of a historical document for use in a research problem
C. identify the data that is useful for a research problem
D. establish the trustworthiness of a data source

39. **A researcher wants to study the effect of Intelligence and Socio Economic Status on creativity of college entrants. For this the most appropriate method of research is:**
A. Historical Method
B. Descriptive Survey
C. Survey Method
D. Experimental Method

40. A mathematics teacher wants to study the reasons for the poor learning of the concept of rational numbers by her/his students. The type of research most suited for dealing with the problem is:

A. Action research B. Applied research

C. Survey research D. Experimental research

41. Premise(s) in a deductive argument offer:

A. incomplete evidence for the acceptance of the conclusion

B. conclusive evidence for the acceptance of the conclusion

C. partial evidence for the acceptance of the conclusion

D. None of the above options

42. Which of the following research procedure is not essential in historical research?

A. Hypothesis formulation B. Sample selection

C. Internal validities of data D. External validities of data

43. Which one of the following procedures is not relevant for historical research?

A. Collection of source material

B. Criticism of collected data

C. Application of the method of internal and external validation of data

D. Quantification of data

44. Which one of the following definitions describe survey method?

A. A study which determines the relationship among selected sociological or psychological variables

B. A research study which focuses on immediate classroom problems

C. A study conducted using questionnaires

D. A study which does not use an experimental design

45. An interview is to be preferred to a questionnaire when we want to

A. collect information within a short time

B. reduce the time and effort

C. collect valid information about an event

D. get valid information about sensitive issues

46. A researcher wants to select the best method for teaching English from among the available methods. Which one of the following research procedures should be adopt?

A. Comparing the performance of the same class when it is taught using each of the methods

B. Comparing the performance of three identical groups taught using the three methods

C. Collecting the reactions of teachers who have used each of the different methods

D. None of the above

47. A researcher who wants to study gender differences in Mathematics learning assessed the achievement of boys and girls using a standardized achievement test in Mathematics and by comparing the mean scores of the two groups. This type of research is best described as:

A. Philosophical research
B. Quantitative research
C. Experimental research
D. Survey research

48. Reliability of a research study depends upon:

A. replicability of the study
B. usefulness of the findings
C. generalizability of findings
D. all the above options

49. Induction is based on:

A. validity of a conclusion based on a number of particular cases

B. validity of a conclusion based on common observations

C. validity of a conclusion by deciding its agreement with an accepted general principle

D. None of the above options

50. Statistical hypothesis is used:

A. when the nature of the differences is not known

B. to increase the precision in defining differences in statistical properties of compared examples

C. to increase precision by using quantitative methods

D. as a precondition in an experimental setup

51. To study the effectiveness of Computer Aided Instruction on class achievement in science of the Xth standard students, the ideal research procedure to be used is:

A. the experimental method

B. the analytical method

C. the philosophical method

D. the quantitative method

52. When we design a research study to compare the effectiveness of Programmed Learning Material and the Advance Organizer Model for teaching English in 10th standard, the study has:

A. two dependant variables

B. only one independent variable

C. two independent variables

D. none of the given options is correct

53. Which one of the following is an incorrect statement?

A. Induction will not help to establish fully the truth of an inference

B. Inductive inference becomes more probable if the number of observations is increased

C. Deduction refers to the process of inferring a less general truth from a more general truth

D. Induction is always more dependable than deduction

54. Which of the following statements describes a developmental study correctly?

A. It studies the way a sample had made progress during a span of time

B. It studies how a cross section of several samples made progress during a span of time

C. It studies the way a sample should progress during a specified span of time

D. None of the given options is correct

55. Which sampling technique is most appropriate for an experimental study?

A. Purposive sampling technique

B. Stratified sampling technique

C. Random sampling technique

D. None of the given options is correct

56. The most appropriate strategy to be adopted by a teacher for identifying the effectiveness of his teaching strategy is:

A. Action research B. Fundamental research

C. Quantitative research D. Experimental research

57. Which one of the following is not a precaution for improving the reliability of an interview?

A. Use of trained interviewer to conduct the interview

B. Choosing the competency of the interviewer in conducting the interview

C. Interviewer to establish a good rapport with the interviewee

D. Choosing only those who are known to you for the interview

58. Action research is usually conducted

A. as part of his class teaching/professional performance

B. by expert researcher with in the class room

C. using descriptive methods

D. by the class teacher to solve problems common to all teachers

59. Statistical inference is not essential in conducting:

A. Experimental Research
B. Historical Research
C. Ex-Post Facto Research
D. Survey Research

60. For conducting a research for comparing the creativity of males and female students of class IX, a most appropriate method of research is the use of:

A. test of significance for difference between the means of male and female students in their creativity

B. correlating the creativity scores of the group with their class performance

C. studying the creativity of the top boys with that of the top girls in the class

D. use of covariance for comparing the creativity and class achievement of the group of boys and girls

61. In philosophical research, the data will be:

A. descriptive

B. both quantitative and qualitative

C. real and imaginary

D. none of the above

62. "An analytical study of the concept of equality of educational opportunity" it is an example of:

A. Survey Research
B. Philosophical Research
C. Experimental Research
D. Ex-post Facto Research

63. An in-depth and intensive study of an institution is described best as:

A. an institutional assessment study

B. an in-depth sample study

C. a cross sectional study

D. a case study

64. Which one of the following statements about historical research is correct?

A. a primary source is better than a secondary source

B. a secondary source from a reliable individual is more valuable than primary source

C. a secondary source when subjected to historical criticism will make it more valuable than a primary source

D. review of related literature will help to throw full light in a historical problem

65. External criticism in historical research refers to:

A. criticism of a source to find out whether the source is genuine

B. critical assessment of a data to find out its usefulness for a study

C. criticism of a data source for use in research problem

D. none of the above

66. In experimental study, the nature of the data is:

A. descriptive

B. both quantitative and qualitative

C. only quantitative

D. none of the above

67. A researcher studied the status of the education of women in India during the Mughal period. This type of research is best described as:

A. Historical research B. Action research

C. Case study research D. Descriptive research

68. The objective of an experimental design is to:

A. minimise treatment variance only

B. maximize treatment variance but minimise error variance.

C. maximize treatment variance only

D. All the given options are correct

69. Internal validity of an experiment refers to the:

A. replicability of the findings of an experiment

B. applicability of the findings of an experiment

C. procedures which help interpretability of the findings of an experiment

D. generalizability of the findings of an experiment

70. Which one of the following represents a quasi- experimental design?

A. Use of intact groups of subjects in an experiment

B. Use of post-test and pre-test groups in an experiment

C. Design which uses statistical procedures

D. Design using quantification techniques for results

71. If the heterogeneity of the population increases, the sample size should:

A. decrease
B. increase
C. both increase or decrease
D. none of the above

72. Which type of sampling method belongs to the category of probability sampling?

A. Random Sampling
B. Stratified Random sampling
C. Sequential Sampling
D. Multi-stage Sampling

73. Which of the following is the non-probability sampling?

A. Quota Sampling
B. Judgement Sampling
C. Purposive sampling
D. All the above

74. Whenever data are collected from the entire population and mean is computed the mean is called:

A. a sample value
B. a parameter
C. non-parametric value
D. a statistic

75. Which of the following statements is correct?

A. Sample is a representative portion of the population
B. Sample will have all the properties of the population
C. Sample will be smaller than the population
D. All the given options are correct

76. A sample should be representative of a population. The representation should be in terms of:

A. criterion variable
B. independent variable selected for the study
C. intervening variables entering into the study
D. dependent variable selected for the study

77. In case of random sampling method, the probability of the selection of any subject in the population in the sample is:

A. the same
B. different
C. cannot be decided before hand
D. None of the given options is correct

78. Whenever the population is homogenous, the best method of sampling is:

A. stratified
B. random
C. purposive
D. incidental

79. If the population is heterogeneous, then a representative sample may be selected using the:

A. stratified sampling method
B. quota sampling method
C. cluster sampling method
D. random sampling method

80. Sampling refers to the technique of:

A. selecting small portion of a universe
B. selecting a large portion of a universe
C. selecting a representative portion of a population
D. selecting small portion of a population

81. The mean anxiety scores of males and females can be compared best by collecting data from a sample selected using:

A. Cluster sampling method
B. Purposive sampling method
C. Random sampling method
D. Stratified random sampling method

82. If a researcher wants to study the relationship between 'job satisfaction' and 'professional competency of Middle Level Managers of Medium Scale Industries' the most appropriate sampling technique will be:

A. Systematic Sampling
B. Random Sampling
C. Purposive Sampling
D. Multi-stage Sampling

83. Which one of the following is NOT used as the base for forming a research hypothesis?

A. Professional experience reported by professionals about the phenomenon
B. Commonsense views about the phenomenon
C. Discussions by experts in the area
D. Conclusions reached by researchers reported in journals

84. Which of the following statements is correct?

A. A research hypothesis can be tested through a statistical hypothesis

B. A research hypothesis can be tested without reference to a statistical hypothesis

C. A statistical hypothesis precedes a research hypothesis

D. None of the options are correct

85. Which one of the following is the most appropriate wording of a research hypothesis regarding the relationship between intelligence and mathematics achievements of secondary students?

A. There is a significant relationship between intelligence & mathematics achievement of secondary school students

B. There is a high correlation between intelligence & mathematics achievement of secondary school students

C. There is a positive relationship between intelligence & achievement in mathematics of secondary school living students

D. The intelligence scores of secondary school students will correlate positively with their achievement score in mathematics

86. A researcher wants to study the effectiveness of peer teaching on the understanding of science concepts. An appropriate hypothesis for the study is:

A. There will not be any difference in the understanding of science concepts before and after peer teaching

B. The mean scores of two groups – one based on peer teaching and a control group – in understanding science concepts will differ significantly

C. Peer Teaching will not significantly affect understanding of science concepts in schools

D. The science concepts of experimental group taught by peer teaching and control group taught using conventional teaching will differ significantly with the experimental group having an advantage over the control group

87. A hypothesis may not be indispensable for:

A. Experimental Research

B. Quasi-Experimental Research

C. Trend Survey

D. Historical Research

88. Which one of the following statements about a hypothesis is a correct statement?

A. Hypothesis stands for what appears to be true before conducting a study

B. Hypothesis stands for a definition of the end result of study, based on facts available at the commencements of the study.

C. Hypothesis is an unproved assumption about the outcome of a study when part of the study is completed

D. Hypothesis is an intelligent guess based on incomplete data

89. **A researcher wants to know the effectiveness of the translation method of teaching English. Which one of the following is the most appropriate research hypothesis for the study?**

A. The means scores in English language achievement of males and females taught through the translation method do not differ significantly

B. The mean scores in English language achievement of students taught using the translation method differ significantly from that of students taught using conventional procedures

C. The means scores of the experimental group taught using the translation method will be significantly greater than that of control group taught using conventional teaching methods

D. None of the above

90. **The selection of the variables of a study is done during:**

A. the statement of hypothesis of the study

B. data collection

C. sample selection

D. scientific definition of the problem

91. **To establish the superiority of the concept attainment model over the advance organizer model for teaching science concepts the most appropriate research hypothesis will be:**

A. There is no relationship between the understanding of the concepts of science and the models used for teaching science

B. There is significant difference between the understandings of science concepts of school students when taught using the concept attainment model and other models of teaching

C. The means science concept scores of school students taught using the concept attainment model will be significantly higher than that of students taught using the advance organizer model

D. There is no significant relationship between the understanding of science concept of school students and the teaching strategies used in different models of teaching

92. **Which of the following is an ideal definition of Hypothesis?**

A. A hypothesis is the statement of a probable solution of a research problem

B. A hypothesis is an imagined result of a research study with which we begin an experimental study

C. A hypothesis is the expected solution of a research problem formulated at the beginning of a study

D. None of the above options is correct

93. Hypothesis generation for a problem is generally done by a researcher using:

A. personal experience as a professional

B. the results of previous studies

C. consultation with experts

D. all the above

94. An investigator wants to study the relationship between sex of school students and their achievement in science. It can be done by using:

A. Rank difference method of correlation of the science achievement scores for the two sex groups

B. Product-moment correlation of the science achievement scores of the two groups

C. Mean difference of science scores for the two groups

D. None of the above

95. A researcher wants to study the effectiveness of peer teaching on the understanding of science concepts of secondary schools. Which of the following would you treat as intervening variables in this study?

A. Time of teaching

B. Gender of students

C. Teaching effectiveness of the peers

D. All the above

96. If an investigator wants to compare the mean scores of language achievement of students taught through peer teaching modes and concept attainment model, the independent variable(s) of the study is (are):

A. language achievement B. concept attainment

C. models of teaching D. peer teaching and concept attainment model

97. In a study of the effectiveness of process approach in science teaching the concomitant variable(s) are:

A. teacher effectiveness in using process approach for science teaching

B. seating arrangements in the class

C. interpersonal relationship between the teacher and his students

D. appropriateness of the strategies used for developing scientific processes

98. Which of the following is/are the characteristic(s) of good research?

A. It has to confirm to the methods of science

B. It has to be problem-oriented

C. It has to be designed using valid research strategies

D. All the above

99. The review of related literature helps to identify a research problem because:

A. It helps to identify inconsistencies in the findings of different researchers

B. it helps to identify gaps in existing research

C. it helps to asses the quality of the procedures used by different researchers

D. All the above

100. Research is a process wherein the proper sequence of the steps to be adopted are:

A. statement of hypotheses, data analysis, conclusions

B. identification of problem, statement of hypothesis, data collection, data analysis, conclusion

C. data collection, identification of problem, data analysis, conclusion

D. data analysis, data collection, conclusions, verification of hypotheses

101. At which stage of research is the study of related literature least relevant?

A. Statement of the problem

B. Identification of the problem

C. Data analysis

D. Data collection

102. Which of the following statements does NOT represent the criterion for selecting an area of research?

A. Researcher's area of specialization

B. Research facilities available in the institution related to the area of research

C. Researcher's understanding of the area

D. Area of special interest of the institution in concentrating its research projects

103. In a study of the correlation between intelligence and science achievement of higher secondary students, the dependent variable(s) is (are):

A. Achievement in Science

B. Intelligence and Achievement in Science

C. Intelligence

D. None of the above

104. Which of the following objectives' are most appropriately worded?

A. To understand the influence of gender on achievement in English of class VI students

B. To identify the influence of gender on achievement in English of class VI students

C. To asses the influence of gender of class of students on their achievement in English of class VI students

D. Identification of the learning disabilities of boys and girls of class VI in teaching teaching English

105. In the study of the relationship between job - satisfaction and professional competency of middle level managers of medium scale industries, the variables are:

A. job-satisfaction and professional competency of managers

B. job-satisfaction, professional competency and level of management

C. job-satisfaction, professional competency, level management and size of industry

D. job-satisfaction, professional competency and size industry

106. Which of the following are not important in choosing a research problem?

A. Library facilities available for study

B. Specialization of supervising teacher

C. Funds available for conducting the research

D. Cultural context of the locality where the research is to be conducted

107. If a researcher wants to compare the anxiety level of rural students with that of urban students of Class IX in private schools of a locality. Which of the following is to be treated as a research variable for the study?

A. Rural-urban localities of schools

B. Rural-urban localities of Private schools

C. Urban students

D. None of above.

108. Which one of the following titles is most appropriate for a research study on history of Indian education?

A. Contributions of Akbar to the spread of secular education

B. History of Indian education during the reign of Akbar

C. Education system in India during the reign of Akbar

D. The spread of the concept of secular education during the reign of Akbar

109. Which of the following research titles is most appropriate?

A. Comparison of the examination anxiety of students taking state run and centrally run secondary examinations

B. A comparative study of the examination anxiety of students taking the CBSE examinations in India

C. Examination anxiety of secondary school students

D. A survey of examination anxiety of high school students

110. Which of the following statements is NOT correct?

A. Good researchers always begin research with a research hypothesis

B. Some researchers generate a hypothesis after a research study

C. A progressive hypothesis helps to fix the procedure to be adopted for a study

D. The best way to conduct a research study is to analyze the data and evolve a hypothesis

111. Which of the following statements about research is NOT correct?

A. A discrete variable cannot be converted into continuous variable

B. In all researches, we have to deal with both continuous and discontinuous variables

C. In all experimental research situations we are concerned with relationship existing among variables

D. Measuring tools used for research should yield scores which are both valid and reliable

112. Which of the following statements about educational research is not correct?

A. Research refers to the tentative solution of a problem

B. Research solutions in education should always help to solve class room problem

C. Research is intended to provide a solution which is applicable to all educational institutions

D. Research provides dependable new knowledge about education

113. In the identification of a research problem, the researcher should begin with:

A. defining the title

B. deciding the variable(s), title and the objective(s)

C. decide the hypothesis

D. decide the title and the variable(s)

114. After reviewing the related research literature for a study, a researcher becomes familiar with:

A. consistency in findings of different researchers

B. inconsistencies in the findings of different researchers

C. gaps in the area of research

D. general problems faced by the educational system

115. Which of the following statements is correct?

A. The qualitative information always provides discontinuous variables

B. Any continuous variable can be made discontinuous

C. Researchers use different criteria of dichotomizing the variables

D. All the given options are correct

116. Which of the following statements is correct?

A. The objectives can be stated either in the form of a statement or in a question form

B. The objectives should be stated only in statement form

C. The objectives should be stated only in question form

D. None of the given options is correct

117. For every problem in educational research.

A. there may not be any solution

B. there is only one correct solution

C. there may be more than one correct solution

D. there will be one solution which is true only for the sample selected

118. A sample should be representative of a population. The representation has to be in terms of:

A. criterion variable B. intervening variables

C. independent variable D. dependent variable

119. A researcher wants to know the best method of teaching English for developing reading comprehension in high school students. He has an 'experimental group' taught using a method he has developed and a 'control group' taught using conventional teaching strategies. Which of the following can be the most appropriate objective of this research?

A. To compare the means of reading comprehension scores of the experimental groups with that of the control group

B. To compare the means of reading comprehension scores of male and female students in the sample

C. To study the influence of intelligence on the scores of English reading comprehension of all boys and girls in total sample

D. None of the above

120. Which of the following is a continuous variable?

A. Bloodcount

B. Attitude towards academic work

C. Number of words per line

D. Gender of student in a sample

121. Which of the following can be the source of research problem?

A. Talk given by a researcher in a conference

B. Findings of a Ph.D research study

C. Article in a news paper

D. All the above

122. A study is to be conducted on the effectiveness of Programmed Learning Material on achievement in Mathematics of Class VIII students in Government schools. The independent variable of the study is:

A. Programmed Learning Material

B. Mathematics Achievement

C. Mathematics curriculum of standard VIII

D. Instructional Efficiency of Government Schools

123. In the study "the Relationship between Teaching Experience and Effectiveness of Science Teachers in Secondary Schools", the independent variable is:

A. Length of the teaching experience of teachers covered by the study

B. Quality of professional training given to science teachers

C. Quality of science teaching provided to students

D. Quality of science teachers covered by the study

124. Delimitation in research report refers to:

A. defining the research problem using scientific terminology

B. limitations of the researcher in studying the problem

C. setting limits to the problem of research and pin pointing the area

D. all the above

125. Which statement does not describe the continuity of a research variable adequately?

A. The variable can take any value within a given interval

B. It is difficult to assign a single value for a variable

C. There are infinite values between any two values of the variable

D. None of the above

126. A variable measured on Ratio Scale can certainly be measured on:

A. Ordinal Scale
B. Interval Scale
C. Nominal Scale
D. All the above

127. In induction, if the premises are true, the conclusion:

A. may not always be true
B. is never true
C. is always true
D. none of the above

128. A scale of Attitude Towards Teaching is usually measured using :

A. An Interval Scale
B. A Nominal Scale
C. A Ratio Scale
D. An Ordinal Scale

129. Classification of students according to their gender and caste is an example of a (an):

A. Interval Scale
B. Ordinal Scale
C. Nominal Scale
D. Ratio Scale

130. There is a high negative correlation between variables X and Y, while there is a high negative correlation between variables Y and Z. Variables X and Z are likely to be:

A. negatively correlated
B. positively correlated
C. uncorrelated
D. difficult to control

131. Which of the following type of inference is free from empirical observation?

A. Inductive inference
B. Commonsense inference
C. Deductive inference
D. None of the above

132. A researcher measured height of Class X students. The measurement of height is expressed using the:

A. nominal scale
B. ordinal scale
C. interval scale
D. ratio scale

133. The intelligence scores of father, son and grandson are high, average and low respectively. It shows that intelligence is correlated with age:

A. negatively B. positively

C. zero D. intelligence declines from one generation to another

134. Correlation is used in testing to establish the:

A. Validity of a test

B. Predictability of success in a field

C. Reliability of a test

D. All the above

135. In the study of the relationship between the intelligence of students and their achievement in science, the dependent variable is:

A. Intelligence and Achievement in Science

B. Intelligence

C. Achievement in Science

D. None of the above

136. Which of the following is an incorrect statement?

A. Deduction refers to the process of inferring less general conclusions from a more general statement

B. Deduction establishes the truth of particular cases under a general category

C. Induction will help to establish the truth of all possible cases in a category

D. Inductive inference becomes more probable if numbers of observations are increased

137. What happens if the length of the test is increased?

A. Both reliability and validity will decrease

B. Its reliability increases but validity decreases

C. Validity as well as reliability will increase

D. Its validity increases but reliability decreases

138. Statistical inference is not essential in:

A. Historical Research B. Experimental Research

C. Ex-post Facto Research D. Survey Research

139. In philosophical researches, the nature of the data will be:

A. Only qualitative B. Both quantitative and qualitative

C. Only quantitative D. None of the above

140. Scientific method involves inferences which are:

A. Deductive B. Inductive

C. Statistical D. All the above

141. The quality of research is depended upon:

A. The expertise of the research supervisor

B. The availability of advanced research facilities

C. The generalizability of the findings

D. All the above

142. Examine the following statements about research and choose the best combination of statements.

i) Research aims at contributing to the existing fund of knowledge

ii) A researcher should penetrate deeper into some specific aspect of the research area

iii) A researcher should collect as much data as possible

iv) A researcher often develops new theories/improves on existing procedures

v) Quality of research depends upon the culture of the institution where the research is conducted

A. i , ii, and iii B. ii , iii, and iv

C. i , ii, and iv D. iii , iv, and v

143. If a researcher wants to find out the effectiveness of a new teaching method, the most suitable research approach is:

A. experimental comparison of the new method with the existing methods

B. expert consultation

C. review research literature

D. use of advanced statistical techniques

144. Which of the following is not essential in reporting research endeavours.

A. The statement of hypothesis and objectives

B. Use of international conventions for research reporting

C. The use of figurative literary style of language

D. Scientific description of the study to help replication

145. A research hypothesis is one which is:

A. suggested by experts in the area

B. deduced from existing theories or experiences

C. emerges while reviewing related literature

D. one which is not covered by the above illustrations

146. In research, which one of the following is to be avoided by a researcher?

A. Understand everything in the area rather than concentrating on specific areas

B. Collect as much data as possible to make the study comprehensive

C. Concentrate on specific sub-areas and study it meticulously

D. Ignore the confounding variables that may disprove the hypothesis set for the study

147. A research hypothesis is best defined as:

A. an intelligent guess

B. a mere hunch

C. the final solution to the problem under investigation

D. an assumption which gives proper direction to the study

148. The purpose of conducting research is to:

A. procure a higher research degree to be used for placement and promotion

B. to enhance the status and reputation of the researcher

C. to fulfil the requirements of the employer

D. either explain a new phenomenon or to verify the existing theories and expand the fund of existing knowledge

149. A theory is acceptable because:

A. a large number of scholars have supported it

B. it has been stated in ancient literature

C. it is advanced by a reputed person and he has published several books on the subject

D. it has been supported by empirical and objective data

150. Arriving at a generalization based on the analysis of sample data is called:

A. statistical inference

B. statistical analysis

C. prediction of consequences

D. factorial analysis

151. Some major steps in research are listed below. Select the correct sequence of steps from the given alternatives.

i) Setting objectives

ii) Selecting a research design

iii) Collecting proper data

iv) Arriving at conclusions

v) Analyzing the data

vi) Testing the hypothesis

A. (ii), (i), (iii), (v), (vi), (iv)

B. (i), (ii), (iii), (iv), (vi), (v)

C. (i), (ii), (iii), (v), (iv), (vi)

D. (i), (vi), (ii), (iii), (v), (iv)

152. An operational definition of a term used in the title of research means:

A. A most acceptable definition of the term

B. A comprehensive definition of the term

C. A definition quoted in glossaries or dictionaries

D. A definition that gives meaning to the term and helps into quantification

153. Which of the following statements about research will you endorse as the most suitable?

A. A teacher in higher education should concentrate more on research than on teaching

B. A teacher in higher education should concentrate more on teaching than on research

C. A teacher in higher education should maintain a balance between teaching and research and should concentrate on both

D. A teacher in higher education should concentrate only on the subject being taught by him

154. Which of the following is the most acceptable description about educational research?

A. Surveying and compiling all the existing researches in the area

B. Penetrating deeper into the specific area of the subject

C. Solving a problem based on an established theory

D. Scientific paradigm for problem solving using accepted logical procedures assumptions

155. Which one of the following does not describe the qualities of a good researcher?

A. One with a proper understanding of the methods of science

B. One with the ability to understand the deep implication of a problem to be solved

C. All who can transcend above subjective prejudices

D. One who can interpret the data to support his hypothesis

156. Which of the following is not true of research?

A. One research leads to another research

B. A researcher should be scientific in his approach and disposition

C. Research findings should be congruent with social and physical realities.

D. New researches should refute the findings of all existing research findings

157. Random sampling in research means:

A. Using mechanical devices to select the units to be included in the sample.

B. Selecting items giving weightage to all categories to be represented in the sample

C. Ascertaining that each unit in the population has equal chance to be included in the sample

D. Choosing only relevant items to be included in the sample

158. Which of the following combinations of qualities of a research report is most acceptable ?

(i) Comprehensiveness with survey of related literature

(ii) Scholarly language and metaphoric interpretations

(iii) Precision in prescribing and explaining objectives, hypothesis, methodology and findings

(iv) Voluminous report

(v) Validation of hypothesis, suggestion for further studies and a reference to scope and limitations of the study

A. (i), (ii) and (iii) B. (ii), (iii) and (iv)

C. (iii), (iv) and (v) D. ((iii) and (v)

159. To study the relationship of family size and family income an investigator classifies the population into different income slabs and draws samples from each of these slabs. Which sampling technique is being adopted?

A. Random sampling B. Stratified sampling

C. Cluster sampling D. Systematic sampling

160. Which one of the following is correct about experimental research?

A. It is conducted in a laboratory

B. It involves only independent and dependent variables

C. It is an attempt to establish cause-effect relationship under controlled conditions

D. It is suitable only for science subjects

161. One of the given alternatives is not the purpose of research. Identify the alternative:

A. Research often attempts to give new explanations to known theories

B. Research is hypothesis testing adopting scientific procedures

C. Research is always an attempt to disprove existing popular notions in a subject area

D. Research aims at disproving certain established theories and develop more valid new theories

162. If a researcher engaging in studying the course and causes of an event or phenomenon after its occurrence, what is the term we use to describe this research?

A. Experimental research

B. Survey research

C. Ex post facto research

D. Case study research

163. Which one of the following statements about research is not correct?

A. Conduct a pre-analysis of part of the data to frame a hypothesis

B. Collect data that are relevant to the problem

C. Collect data that is sufficient to test the hypothesis

D. Collect data using standardized tests as far as possible

164. What is the possible relationship of the social status of the family on the phenomenon of 'school dropouts'?

A. No significant relationship

B. Can only be ascertained after a study

C. The lower the social status of the family, the higher the drop-out rate

D. Relationship is unpredictable, as research findings vary

165. A good researcher concentrates on:

A. a specific area with a view to understand all minute details connected with the area

B. several areas relating to the problem in order to get a comprehensive coverage of the issues

C. an area which provides manpower and funding for the selected area

D. a problem which can be completed within a short time with least effort

166. A good research always begins with:

A. a felt problem to be thoroughly tackled

B. preparation of the plan and design for study

C. study of different research procedures

D. study of the relevant research by others

167. Generalizability of a new teaching method can be through research across:

A. different cultural contexts
B. different school subjects
C. different educational levels
D. all of the above

168. In research, which of the following sources will be most acceptable for establishing a fact?

A. Opinion of a large number of scholars

B. Practised by educational institutions over a long period of time

C. Availability of empirical data in support of the fact

D. References in past publications

169. Lack of consistency in research findings is described as:

A. lack of reliability B. lack of validity

C. lack of practicability D. lack of objectivity

170. Which one of the following is the accepted sequence of scientific inquiry?

A. Observation - Verification - Hypothesising - Theorising

B. Experimentation - Observation - Verification - Hypothesising

C. Observation - Hypothesising - Experimentation - Theorising

D. Theorising - Observation - Experimentation - Hypothesising

171. In every field, research pursuits promote systematic and gradual advancement of knowledge, but innovative discoveries are rare because:

A. research is often understood using conventional assumption

B. a discovery requires divergent thinking which is not very common

C. most people have not developed the mind-set for making a discovery

D. all the above

172. Which one of the following is not a description of a research hypothesis?

A. A hypothesis should be based on facts

B. A good hypothesis is one which helps to create original knowledge

C. A hypothesis always contradicts existing knowledge

D. A good hypothesis will suggest a suitable design for a study

173. Teaching and research are two different activities in higher education which:

A. cannot go together as these are different

B. should go together

C. should go together and supplement each other

D. none of the above

174. How would you decide whether a theory is correct?

A. When it is advocated by an established scholar in one of his important books

B. When it is supported by a large number of scholars

C. When it has been accepted by a large number of people

D. When the deductions from the theory match with experience

175. Which of the following is not correct?

A belief becomes a scientific truth when it:

A. is accepted by many people

B. is established experimentally and reported properly

C. is accepted by important organizations

D. can be converted into an experimental situation

176. A researcher would like to study the influence of the family environment on the language development of a child. Which one of the terms would describe the variable 'family environment' in this study?

A. Independent variable
B. Dependent variable
C. Intervening variable
D. Control variable

177. In an attempt to predict the winner in the forthcoming general elections, The New Indian Express contacts a representative sample of the voting population and gathers their opinion and uses the data for predicting the election outcomes. How would you name this research?

A. Correlational
B. Survey
C. Case Study
D. Descriptive

178. The research tool generally used in the survey method of research is:

A. Observation
B. Questionnaire
C. Interview
D. All of the above

179. The most appropriate strategy used for scientifically studying the behaviour of abnormal children is:

A. Focused Observation
B. Interview
C. Psychological Testing
D. Study of Family History

180. Which among the following is least important in reporting the research?

A. Use of scholarly language

B. Statement of objectives

C. Description of the methodologies used

D. Explanation of the major findings

181. "A good teacher is essentially a good researcher also." How do you react to this statement?

A. Fully agree with the statement

B. Partially agree with the statement

C. Disagree completely with the statement

D. The statement does not merit consideration by a professional

182. Objectivity in research implies:

A. the use of a set of procedures which will ignore the researcher's preferences

B. search for findings consistent with reality

C. research reporting in a manner which will help to replicate the study

D. all the above

183. What is statistical inference?

A. Inferring the properties of a population using the data relating to a sample

B. Techniques used for analysing statistical data for drawing conclusion

C. Applying statistical methods for data collection

D. Making quantitative study of the properties of a sample

184. For gathering opinion of university students in a specific issue, a researcher sent a questionnaire to every twentieth person on the list of students of the institution. The sample has been selected using the technique of:

A. Quota sampling

B. Stratified sampling

C. Random sampling

D. Purposive sampling

185. The most important question that a researcher interested in the application of statistical techniques in the analysis of research data has to ask is:

A. whether the data could be quantified

B. whether statistical techniques appropriate for the objectives are available

C. whether analysis of data would help to verify the hypothesis

D. whether worthwhile inferences could be drawn form the available data

186. A researcher calculates the correlation between scores obtained on two halves of an abstract reasoning test developed by him. What characteristic of the test is he trying to determine?

A. Reliability of the test

B. Construct validity of the test

C. Difficulty level of the test

D. Discriminating power of the items

187. Judgement sampling can be based in:

A. qualitative research

B. quantitative research

C. qualitative and quantitative research

D. none of the above

188. Raju scores 60% marks in an English language test, the mean score of which is 50 with a standard deviation of 15. Gopi scores 60% in another English language test having a mean score of 50 and a standard deviation of 8. Which of the conclusions is justifiable?

A. Comparison is possible only if the same test is given to both

B. Gopi's performance in his group is better than Raju's in his group

C. Raju's performance in his group is better than Gopi's in his group

D. None of the above

189. Which of the following is a typical example for a hypothesis in an action research programme?

A. The language achievement of a pre-primary child will depend upon the cultural level of his home

B. The quality of handwriting of primary school children in any school can be improved by presenting proper models to children for imitation

C. Vocabulary development is faster in girls than in boys

D. Drill in proper handwriting will help in improving different psychomotor skills

190. Action research means:

A. research related to school activities

B. research related to school improvement

C. research geared towards scientific solution of felt classroom problems integrated with teaching

D. research on classroom activities of pupils

191. The originator of the term 'Action Research' is:

A. Lehmann
B. Travers
C. Corey
D. Dewey

192. One of your high school students has recently developed withdrawing tendencies: the friendly efforts and counsels by you and other teachers do not help to change her irrational behaviour. What type of study would you think is most suitable for dealing with this situation?

A. Survey
B. Observational
C. Case study
D. Experimental

193. A few traits are listed below

i. Keenness of observation

ii. Persistence

iii. Industry

iv. Sociability

v. Logical reasoning

Which of the above qualities do you consider essential for a researcher?

A. (i), (ii), (iii) and (iv) B. (ii), (iii), (iv) and(v)

C. (i), (ii), (iii) and (v) D. (i), (iii), (iv) and (v)

194. Four problematic situations are given below:

i) A student is abnormally withdrawing in nature

ii) A considerable number of students always score low in your subject

iii) A considerable number of students of your class create disturbances in your class

iv) In spite of warning most of the students of your class are irregular with assignments.

Which of these situations suggest the adoption of action research?

A. All the four B. (i), (ii) and (iv)

C. (ii), (iii) and (iv) D. (ii) and (iv)

195. Research reports can be reviewed in the light of:

(i) investigator bias evident in the study

(ii) emphasis given to the cultural context of the study

(iii) appropriateness of the methodologies used in the study

Of these the ones that are relevant is/are

A. (i) and (ii) B. (i) only

C. (iii) Only D. All the three

196. Which is/are quite essential for a good research report?

(i) Clarity in reporting the procedure

(ii) Use of simple and straight forward language

(iii) Adequacy of the objectives to test the hypothesis

A. (i) only B. (ii) and (iii)

C. (i) and (ii) D. All the three

197. When the population is heterogeneous, which of the following sampling methods would yield authentic conclusions?

A. Cluster sampling B. Stratified sampling

C. Random sampling D. Purposive sampling

198. Action research is ordinarily concerned with problems:

A. which are basic to professional education

B. that will help to establish universal truths

C. issues of immediate concern calling for immediate solutions

D. having long-term implications for the discipline

199. On the spot research aimed at the solution of an immediate problem is known as:

A. Survey research
B. Fundamental research
C. Action research
D. Pure research

200. The first question that a researcher should ask is:

A. whether the tools for data collection are available

B. whether the study will make an original contribution to knowledge

C. whether a good research library is available for consultation

D. whether the research endeavor will help him to secure the research degree within a short time

201. Which one of the following functions is not expected of a researcher?

A. study the existing literature in the area selected for the study

B. generate new principles and theories

C. critically evaluate the concepts used by other researchers in the field

D. yield results which will be accepted by higher authorities in the field

202. The method used for official census conducted once in ten years by Government is best described as:

A. the case study method
B. the census method
C. the survey method
D. the descriptive method

203. the hypothesis is most appropriate for:

A. fundamental research
B. participatory research
C. survey research
D. experimental research

204. Which among the following data sources is most suitable for assessing the social adjustability of a student in the classroom?

A. A projective test of personality

B. An in-depth interview with the student

C. A performance test of intelligence

D. A sociogram relating to the members of his peer group

205. Research is best described as:

A. an activity having only theoretical value

B. an interesting activity for the researcher

C. an activity helps a researcher to become popular

D. an activity which contributes positively to the growth and development of the discipline concerned

206. "A good teacher is essentially a good researcher" is a statement:

A. which is not true

B. which is abused since teaching skills are different from research skills

C. which highlights the fact that good teachers will always be looking for better procedures for teaching

D. which is a mere expectation

207. Quality of research always depends upon:

A. use of sophisticated technologies

B. available library facilities and guidance

C. training given to researchers

D. dedication on the part of the researcher

208. Which one of the following will help to give authority for establishing a fact?

A. Opinion of a large number of people

B. A principle accepted true for a long time

C. Observable valid evidences

D. Acceptance of a principle in ancient religious literature

209. A research hypothesis is validated on the basis of:

A. its agreement with established theories

B. accepted beliefs of several scholars

C. empirical findings of expert researchers

D. inter-researcher agreement

210. The quality of a research project is judged by the:

A. the social relevance of the research problem

B. adequacy of the development of the methodology proposed to be used

C. scientific approaches proposed to be used during each stage of the project

D. reputation of the researcher in the area of research

211. Which of the following is not the purpose of conducting research?

A. To discover new truth and expand the vistas of knowledge

B. To identify weaknesses in earlier research

C. To explain a newly confronted phenomenon

D. To verify an existing theory and enhance its authenticity

212. The Following are some of the steps used in scientific research is:

(i) Formulating hypothesis and listing objectives

(ii) Reaching at conclusions

(iii) Analysing the data

(iv) Reviewing related literature

(v) Developing valid and reliable tools for data collection

(vi) Collection of data

Which answer choices indicates the correct sequence in a research study?

A. (iv), (ii), (iii), (i) (v) and (vi)

B. (i), (v), (iv), (vi), (iii) and (ii)

C. (i), (iv), (v), (vi), (iii) and (ii)

D. (vi), (iii), (ii), (v), (i) and (iv)

213. If a researcher/teacher wants to find out the effectiveness of two teaching methods, the best strategy for investigation is:

A. Experimental Research

B. Survey Research

C. Case Study

D. Ethnographic Research

214. The most important quality expected of a good researcher is:

A. an in-depth understanding of the nature of the discipline

B. knowledge of statistical techniques

C. experience in conducting research

D. experience in teaching research methods

215. Our attitude towards knowledge should be:

A. to accept what is scientifically proved with empirical evidences cited in support of the problem

B. to accept what is reported by a researcher

C. not to accept anything until it is personally verified

D. to accept an idea supported by a good number of scholars

216. Which of the following is not the requirement for formulating a research hypothesis? It should:

A. be based on facts

B. be evolved from concrete experience/the results of previous studies

C. not conflict with the views held by earlier researchers

D. when verified, help in extending the horizons of existing knowledge

Answer keys

1.B	2.D	3.B	4.A	5.A	6.D	7.D	8.A	9.A	10.D
11.A	12.B	13.B	14.B	15.A	16.A	17.A	18.D	19.B	20.C
21.D	22.D	23.C	24.A	25.C	26.B	27.C	28.B	29.B	30.B
31.C	32.D	33.D	34.D	35.D	36.D	37.A	38.D	39.C	40.A
41.B	42.D	43.D	44.C	45.C	46.B	47.D	48.A	49.B	50.C
51.D	52.C	53.A	54.C	55.B	56.C	57.D	58.D	59.B	60.B
61.A	62.B	63.D	64.D	65.C	66.B	67.A	68.B	69.C	70.C
71.B	72.C	73.D	74.B	75.D	76.C	77.D	78.B	79.A	80.D
81.D	82.B	83.D	84.A	85.A	86.B	87.C	88.C	89.C	90.D
91.D	92.D	93.D	94.D	95.D	96.A	97.A	98.D	99.D	100.B
101.D	102.D	103.D	104.C	105.A	106.D	107.D	108.B	109.C	110.D
111.B	112.B	113.B	114.D	115.D	116.A	117.C	118.B	119.C	120.B
121.D	122.B	123.C	124.C	125.B	126.D	127.A	128.A	129.C	130.B
131.C	132.D	133.B	134.D	135.D	136.	137.	138.A	139.A	140.D
141.C	142.C	143.A	144.C	145.B	146.C	147.A	148.D	149.D	150.A
151.C	152.D	153.C	154.D	155.B	156.D	157.C	158.D	159.B	160.C
161.D	162.C	163.B	164.C	165.A	166.A	167.D	168.C	169.C	170. C
171.B	172.C	173.C	174.D	175.A	176.A	177.B	178.D	179.B	180.A
181.A	182.B	183.A	184.C	185.B	186.A	187.A	188.B	189.B	190.C
191.C	192.C	193.C	194.D	195.D	196.D	197.B	198.C	199.C	200.B
201.B	202.C	203.D	204.B	205.D	206.A	207.D	208.C	209.C	210.C
211.B	212.C	213.C	214.D	215.A	216.C				

Unit - III

READING COMPREHENSION

READING PASSAGE
WITH
COMPREHENSION QUESTIONS

Unit - III

READING COMPREHENSION

Reading comprehension questions asses your ability to read and understand a unit of communication presented as a passage. This type of question can be used for testing different abilities and competencies. These include your ability to understand the main ideas in the passage, and your ability to recognize both explicitly stated facts in the passage and the implicit assumptions underlying statements or arguments in the passage together with the implications of the statements.

The ability to read and understand the contents of a language communication and understand it is a vital cognitive function. In most of the competitive examinations comprehension questions are included to test this ability. The UGC test gives equal weightage to this component in paper I. Formerly there were two passages in the UGC test, each followed by four questions, thereby making 16 percent weightage (each questions carrying 2 marks – $8 \times 2 = 16$). This indicates the importance given to the ability to read and grasp. In the recent revision equal weightage is given to all the ten components of the test i.e., 10 percent for each, including reading comprehension.

It is unimaginable, how a teacher in the higher education sector can function with out the ability to read and comprehend. He or she has to refer to several books, articles, etc. and has to be a continuous reader throughout his/her career. Only a person who has developed reading ability can succeed as a teacher in higher education classrooms. Reading broadens the horizons of a teacher, provides him insights that leads him to higher levels of understanding and promotes greater confidence and professional satisfaction. Keeping abreast of the modern trends in the subject area of one's specialization is an essential challenge to any teacher of any levels of in higher education.

The ability to read and comprehend is perhaps one of the most important competencies expected of a researcher. Review of related literature is one of the major activities in any new research endeavour. The research scholar will have to explore several authentic written documents – Encyclopedias, Research Abstracts and other scholarly publications along with dissertations, critical reviews of research, etc. The books published in one's area of research will have to be meticulously explored by a researcher. Searching the web-cites warrants almost the same skill. The ability to scan swiftly and grasp the message in the passage is an important performance skill expected of a researcher. Rapid silent reading with full comprehension is regarded as one of the basic objectives of teaching languages even in schools. The more one gets practice in reading and grasping, the better would be his reading comprehension ability. Ability to read and comprehend is included as an important ability in the

UGC tests since it is the most useful cognitive function to be performed by both teachers and researchers.

The most important factor to be noted is we have to acquire the ability to answer many questions within a limited time. Please note that to answer 50 questions, the total time available is just 75 minutes. This includes the time to read the instructions given in general and the time available for answering each question, and the time needed for completing the other test formalities. This means that only less than one minute will be available to answer one question in this section. Reading a passage (passages) spread over one or two pages, then reading the questions to be answered and then to workout the answer to five questions all within a maximum of 7 minutes poses a real challenge to the examinees.

In this section, passages and 5 questions to be answered based on each passage are given. The questions that follow the passage are of varying difficulty and range. The test will assess your ability to read a passage, comprehend its meaning, and make certain critical judgement about what is presented. Normally a step by step method is to be adopted to answer these questions. The following method is advised.

i. Always start by reading the questions and understand what is expected of you. This will give you a better idea about what one has to look for in the passage.
ii. Underline keywords in the question as they will help you to locate what is expected when you read the passage.
iii. Read the passage quickly and try to locate the keywords you have identified.
iv. As a general rule, make it a habit to read the articles in newspapers and magazines critically and use this as a training for taking this particular test. This will eventually pay in the long run.

Normally the questions asked are those which require you to formulate:

i. the title for the passage
ii. what is discussed in the passage
iii. the central idea of the passage
iv. the content presented in the passage, and identify the details
v. make inferences from what is presented in the passage
vi. the author's main trend of thinking about the theme discussed

We have selected a few passages for practice, each passage followed by 5 questions. The candidates are advised to practise this exercise nothing the time taken for answering each. You should verify the answers, after answering all the questions. Self monitoring and self-feed back are always beneficial to check up the accuracy of your answers and boost your confidence.

Examples:

1. Read the following passage carefully and answer questions 1 to 5

I am familiar with the superstition that self-realization is possible only in the fourth stage of life, ie Sannyasa (renunciation). But it is a matter of common knowledge that those who defer preparation for this invaluable experience until the last stage of life attain not self-realization, but old age amounting to a second and pitiable childhood, living as a burden on earth. I have a full recollection that I held these views even whilst I was teaching, though I might not then have expressed them in identical language. How then was this spiritual training to be given? I made the children memorize and recite hymns and read to them from books on moral training. But that was far from satisfying me. As I came into closer contact with them, I saw that it was not through books that one could impart training of the spirit. Just as physical training was to be imparted through physical exercises, and intellectual through intellectual exercises, even so the training of the spirit was possible only through the exercise of the spirits entirely dependent on the life and character of the teacher. The teacher has always to be mindful of his P's and Q's whether he was in the midst of his students or not.

1. **Which among the following is the most suitable title for the passage?**
   A. Intellectual training for all
   B. Importance of the teacher in spiritual training
   C. Importance of memory training
   D. Renunciation as spirit training

2. **The superstition among people about self-realization is that; it is:**
   A. a continuous process
   B. possible only through training
   C. attained through renunciation
   D. a phenomenon which can be easily achieved

3. **Spiritual training of the children according to the author is hinged mainly upon the character of:**
   A. Parents B. Peer group C. Social leaders D. Teachers

4. **The original view held by the author about old age was that, it is:**
   A. an appropriate stage for self-realization
   B. spiritual training can be given by memorizing hymns
   C. defining preparation for self-realization
   D.training of the spirit is best done through experience of the spirits

5. **What does the author indicate through P's and Q's of the teacher, in the context of this passage?**
   A. the spiritual & moral qualities of the teacher
   B. his concern about students
   C. student's commitment to society
   D. the teacher's strength and weakness

Answer keys

1.B 2.C 3.D 4.B 5.A

2. Read the following passage and answer question Nos.1 to 5

The Bible has said that he who lives by the sword shall perish by the sword. It is one of the tragedies of history that the greatest exponents of non-violence, the most powerful opponents of the cult of the sword have died as a result of the sword succeeding over the principle of ahimsa. Christ died on the cross, Gandhiji was assassinated and the latest instance is the death of Dr. Martin Luther King. Is non-violence then an empty dream?; a mere dialectic in philosophy which seeks to conceal the seething passions which sway both the individual and the nation?

That is not true. Caesar dead is more powerful than Caesar alive. The crucification of Christ resulted in a great religion coming to birth which has moulded the thoughts and ideas of millions of people. The death of Gandhiji has brought into existence a philosophy which is not only the basis of statecraft in our own country but has influenced people all over the world and for ought we know the murder of Dr.King may hasten the removal of blot of apartheid from the face of the world.

There is always one great danger every prophet runs – his sayings and his message taking on the fixed mould of immutability. A prophet must be judged in the context of the time he lived and the problems that he had to face. Times change and old problems get solved and new ones present their challenge. But we refuse to give dynamism to the prophet's thoughts. We convert his preaching to empty slogans and refuse to permit any 'deviation' from what he wanted his followers to do however meaningless such an action might have become and however divorced might it be from the true essence of his philosophy.

Gandhiji has suffered the same fate. There is hardly a platform where his name is not uttered and I am afraid, very often in vain. The most dishonest, the most defamed and the most corrupt politicians capitalize on his name and every day he is being assassinated again not in the body but in the spirit.

Undoubtedly, Gandhiji's great contribution to political philosophy is his doctrine of non-violence. But it is a mistake to think that he merely preached physical non-violence. It has become abundantly clear now that unless the minds and spirits of men are cleansed war will not be abolished and the menace of destruction will hang dangerously over the head of mankind. But the threat of physical violence is no less. In South Africa, in Rhodesia, in the USA, racial arrogance and racial divisiveness is getting more and more marked. In our own country, the upsurge of regionalism and communalism emphasizes spiritual intolerance. Even in government there is a marked tendency towards a monolithic society. Independent and autonomous organs are under constant attack and non conformity can only be practised at the risk of political and even social ostracism. The age of old tradition of our society has been tolerance and compassion. The great Buddha preached it and Gandhiji worked on it to make it a world creed and to give it a name and a flag. The second great contribution of Gandhiji was the application of the doctrine of the dignity of man to Indian society. For centuries, we have treated a large section of our fellow citizens as sub-human denying them elementary human rights. No one did more than Gandhiji to wipe out this blot from our society. If our constitution proudly proclaims the abolition of untouchability, it is largely due to the awakening that Gandhiji brought about in the mind of upper caste Hindus. He himself performed all kinds of labour in order to prove that no shame is attached to any kind of work, however menial.

1. **Gandhiji worked to remove untouchabilty because:**
   A. he believed that menial work is no shame
   B. he wanted the Indian constitution to abolish it
   C. he wanted to change the minds of the upper caste Hindus
   D. he wanted the dignity of man to be restored

2. **Preaching of a prophet becomes empty slogans because:**
   A. we take it in its letter, not in spirit
   B. we do not find the principle very relevant to the present way of life
   C. we use it for achieving our selfish motives
   D. we think that the preaching is for others to follow and not for us

3. **Martin Luther King's name is associated with:**
   A. removal of social inequality B. removal of apartheid
   C. removal of poverty D. removal of illiteracy

4. **Non-violence implies:**
   A. merely physical non-violence B. conformity and dependence
   C. tolerance and compassion D. maintaining the dignity of man

5. **The examples of Christ, Gandhiji and Martin Luther King are quoted in this passage to show that:**
   A. non-violence will always subdue violence
   B. violence will ultimately succeed
   C. the cult of the sword will end with the sword
   D. the tragedy of the opponents of violence is that they become victims of violence

Answer keys

1.D 2.A 3.B 4.C 5.D

3. Read the following passage carefully and answer questions 1 to 5

The past decade has upset many preconceptions about development and thus, more than anything else makes it difficult to be overly definite about what the next decade has in store. But there are a few things that one can assert with some confidence.

First, education, health and productive employment are crucial both for growth and for equity we have tended to assume that all of these are the consequences of rapid economic growth and that only growth can generate the resources required for these purposes. But, increasingly it appears that those are better seen as the causes rather than as consequences of development. Virtually every case of successful development involves a prior improvement in literacy, technical skills, health, status and access to productive work.

Second, technological competence is the most important resource endowment and it explains a far larger proportion of growth in output and trade than more conventional factors like natural resources for capital accumulation. The competence required is not just in research. In fact, technological dynamism in the factory and the farm is more important than the presence of a larger research establishment.

Third, the environmental imperative can no longer be ignored. Today as an international issue, it is second only next to disarmament. Naturally, the developmental consequences of environmental neglect are increasingly obvious.

In the Indian context there are at least two further factors which reinforce the above propositions. The first is population growth. Given the pace of expansion of the population and the work force, human resource development acquires an added urgency. Population growth is also one, but not necessarily the most important factor which underlines environmental stress in rural and urban areas. The second factor is that as a large country we cannot carve out an independent position in the global system without building up a substantial capacity for self reliant growth. The acquisition of technical competence is crucial for this purpose.

Until now we have tended to treat human resource development, technology issues and environment as subsidiary to the main task of planning. The thrust has been on: Quantitative expansion of infrastructure and production with a focus on production targets like tones of steel, Kilowalts of electricity etc. capacity targets like number of schools and students, numbers of villages electrified, catching up with known technologies, fuller use of natural resources, maximum mobilization of financial resources, etc.

1. **According to this passage we have so far placed more emphasis on:**

   A. increased number of basic facilities and meeting number targets

   B. optimum use of available natural resources

   C. maximum utilization of available finances

   D. All of the above

2. **With passage of time, the effects of which of the following are being felt at the national level?**

   A. Expansion of work force of high quality

   B. Lack of attention and action for protecting environmental wealth

C. Progressive degradation of technological competence in urban areas

D. Emphasis on slow rate of disarmament as compared to other nations

3. **Which of the following statements is not true in the context of the passage?**

A. We have to emphasize new aspects of human resource development

B. Technological competence has to be given due priority over more conventional factors

C. We will have a bright future by only catching up with known technologies.

D. Optimum self-reliance is the need of the day

4. **What seems to be the purpose of the author in writing this passage?**

A. A review of world affairs with special emphasis on developed countries

B. To prove how his predictions have turned out to be correct

C. To show how the policy makers have failed

D. Review of the past with a view to evolving positive directions for future

5. **What seems to be the approach of the author regarding the present status of research?**

(A) He desires that more research establishments should come up

(B) Application of new technologies in factories and the field is more vital than setting up of research laboratories

A. Neither A nor B   B. Both A and B

C. Only A   D. Only B

Answer keys

1.D   2.B   3.C   4.D   5.C

4. Read the following passage and answer questions 1 to 5

Men and women are the two wheels of the universe; one cannot exist without the other. Though their field of activity differs yet they are inseparable. The present condition of woman in India is bifurcated. A recent report titled 'Women and children in India' and a nearly simultaneous report on 'Indian women – their health and economic productivity' highlight the international importance being given to the problems of the progress of Indian women. Unfortunately both the reports failed to either convey a fresh understanding of the issues or to suggest innovative and workable approaches for women's development. The ratio of the women and men remains below its natural levels and is related to other parameters, such as the level of literacy and the availability of primary health care. A variety of approaches of women's development has been tried out all over the world and in India; the State has made a strong political and economic commitment to the welfare of women. In 1990, the National Commission of

Women was established. The government released two major policy decisions in 1989. Ever since the 8th Five Year Plan, there has been a special section on socio-economic programmes for women. Poverty alleviation programmes have a thirty percent target for women. Special programmes like development of women and children in rural areas have also been started.

SEWA's (Self Employed Women's Association) and WWF's (Working Women's Forum) approach of using bank credits to organize self-employed women has worked well. Women's literacy programme in Kerala is also remarkable.

On the other hand some of the legislated reforms like Dowry Prohibition has not worked well. The issue of whether women should be identified as separate participants in the development process was also controversial. It is disappointing to read in the Government Report and of the government's targets for the nineties ought to aim at fostering 'an ethos of caring in the community - not to let a child go to bed hungry, be subjected to a preventable disease or remain without learning opportunity – this could mark the beginning of a social process towards a more humane order'. Is that report saying then that Indians do not love their children as a matter of cultural practice? Both the reports are likely to be highly influential on opinion leaders and policy makers. It is very unfortunate that these reports have become superficial and do not delve sufficiently deep into the real problems.

For the development of women in India, Prime Minister Atal Bihari Vajpayee launched two new insurance schemes for women and girls in New Delhi in March 1999 as 'Bhagyasree Child Welfare Policy' and 'Rajarajeswari Woman Welfare Policy'. Mahatma Gandhi and Jawaharlal Nehru tried to develop the status of Indian women. Indian men also need an attitudinal change in their oulook toward women so that male chauvinism may come to an end. As, Rabindranath Tagore said "We are waiting for the time when the spirit of the age will be incarnated in a complete human truth and the meeting of men and women will be translated into the unity of men and women".

1. Which of the following is specifically put forward as a major reason for the unequal sex ratio in the population?

A. Natural causes B. Economic development

C. Literacy level D. Socio economic programmes

2. Which of the following is true in the context of the passage?

A. Some developmental programmes have failed in India

B. Women literacy programmes are held all over India

C. Indian women do not manage their finance well

D. Culturally Indians do not love their children

3. Which of the following is correct in the context of the passage in regard to development schemes?

A. All people are of the view that women should not be given special status

B. Some people hold the view that special status given to women will not solve the problems they face

C. No one feels that women should be given special status

D. There is no controversy that women in India be given special status

4. **Which of the following would indicate the same meaning as the phrase 'go to bed hungry' as it has been used in the passage?**

A. without food

B. with out parental attention

C. Given the food they dislike

D. Given food which fails to give proper nourishment

5. **The two reports 'Women and Children in India' and 'Indian Women – Their health and Economic Productivity' according to the author of the passage fail to:**

A. highlight the real plight of women

B. clear misconceptions about the problem faced by women

C. convey the real understanding of the issue

D. give a convincing picture of problems faced by women

Answer keys

1.C 2.A 3.D 4.D 5.C

5. *Read the following passage and answer the questions given below it.*

Two principles are involved in the controversy about the presence of foreign-controlled media in the country: the free flow of ideas and images across the borders, and the need to safeguard the national interest and preserve cultural autonomy. Both are valid, but both are at loggerheads because each has been used to promote less lofty goals. The first principle conforms to a moral imperative: freedom of expression, which cannot rhyme with restrictions imposed by any government. But the free flow rhetoric also clouds the fact that the powerful Western, especially American media can and often do present, subtly or brazenly, news in a manner which promotes Western political, ideological and strategic interests. Besides, Western entertainment programmes with present lifestyles and values cherished by traditional societies. All this explains why so many Indian newspapers, magazines and news agencies have sought protection from the courts to prevent foreign publications and news agencies from operating in the country. Their arguments are weak on two counts. As the bitter debate on a new world information and communication order demonstrated in the late seventies and early eighties, many of those who resent Western 'invasion' of the information and cultural fields are no great friends of democracy. Secondly, the threat of such an 'invasion' has been aired by those media groups in the developing countries who fear that their business interests will be harmed if Western groups, equipped with large financial and technological resources and superior management skills, are allowed to operate in the country without let.

The fear is valid but it goes against the grain of the economic reform programme. The presence of foreign newspapers and television channels will increase competition which, in course of time, can only lead to the upgradation of dynamic Indian newspapers and television channels even while they drive the rest out of the market. One way to strike a balance between the two antagonistic principles would be to allow foreign media entry into the country, provided the Indian state treats them on a par with the domestic media on all fronts. On the import of technology, for instance, foreign media cannot be allowed duty concessions denied to their Indian counterparts. Foreign media will also have to face the legal consequences, should they run foul of Indian laws. Why, for example, should the BBC, or Time Magazine or the The Economist get away with showing the map of Kashmir which is at variance with the official Indian map? Why should they go scot-free when they allow secessionists and terrorists to air their views without giving the government the right to reply? Or when they depict sexually explicit scenes which would otherwise not be cleared by the Censor Board? Since the government can do precious little in the matter, especially about satellite broadcasts, what if it should consider attaching the properties of the offending parties? Demands of this kind are bound to be voiced unless New Delhi makes it clear to the foreign media that they will have to respect Indian sensibilities especially where it concerns the country's integrity and its culture. It may be able to derive some inspiration from France's successful attempts in the GATT to protect its cinematographic industry.

1. **In what way will the presence of foreign-controlled media be most beneficial to the country?**

   A. Their presence will help us promote our cultural autonomy

   B. Their presence will help us know about Western lifestyles

   C. They will project undesirable trends in the West

   D. Their presence will help the free-flow of ideas and from the rest of the world

2. **What does the phrase 'at logger heads' mean in the context of the passage?**

   A. Opposite to each other B. Not fully agreeable

   C. Unusual D. Out of place

3. **In what way will the presence of foreign media be harmful to our country?**

   (1) The foreign media will never present news pertaining to India in an objective manner.

   (2) They will present news in a manner which promotes Western interests.

(3) Their entertainment programmes will present Western lifestyles which are at loggerheads with what we want the country to practice.

(4) They will monopolise the print and visual media in India.

A. Only (1) is correct. B. (2) & (3) are correct

C. (1) & (4) are correct D. (2) & (4) are correct.

4. **What in fact is the reason for the opposition of the media in the developing countries to the presence of foreign-controlled media?**

A. They fear that they will lose their position of importance in society.

B. They fear that their drawbacks and blemishes will be exposed.

C. They fear that their business interests will be affected.

D. They fear that they will be totally at the mercy of the powerful foreign media.

5. **Which of the following means 'without let'?**

A. permission to practice

B. practice without restrictions

C. practice without approval

D. practice without charging for the farmer

Answer keys

1.D 2.A 3.B 4.C 5.B

6. *Read the following passage and answer the questions given below it.*

William Coyne headed research and development at 3M, the company behind Ace Bandages, Post-it-notes, Scotch Tape, and other inventions for over a decade. Shortly after retiring, Coyne spoke to a group of hundreds of executives about innovation at 3M and his own management style. He said he'd started at 3M as a researcher and learned firsthand how well-meaning but nosy executives who proffer too many questions and suggestions which can undermine creative work. So when he became head of R&D, he was determined to allow his teams to work for long stretches, unfettered by intrusions from higher-ups. Coyne understood his colleagues' curiosity; if successful, an R&D project could generate millions in new revenue. But he limited their interference (and his own) because, he said, "After you plant a seed in the ground, you don't dig it up every week to see how it is doing".

Coyne knew that the performance of his employees as well as his career and the company's success depended on shielding them from threats. This notion that management buffers the core work of the company from uncertainty and external perturbations is an old theme in organizational theory, going back at last to James D. Thompson's 1967 classic 'Organizations in Action'. The best bosses are committed to letting their workers work, whether on creative tasks such as inventing new products or on routine things such as assembling computers, making McDonald's burgers, or flying planes. They take pride in being human shields, absorbing or deflecting heat from inside and outside the company, doing all manner of boring and silly tasks, and battling idiots and slights that make life harder than necessary on their people.

The best bosses shield their people from disruption and distress, but they aren't martyrs who always put employee performance and happiness first. Wise leaders balance the need to protect their people against other, sometimes more crucial, considerations.

If your immediate reaction is to fight for your people without considering its effect on your influence and reputation, you're undermining your own power. That, in turn, does you and your team a disservice.

A fact of organizational life for most bosses is that no matter how hard you work to build a great team, you will hire or be assigned some weak and destructive people. Your job is, of course, to help them learn and improve. If they don't change, however, it's best to send them packing.

Research by Will Felps and his colleagues on bad apples, bolsters this point. They identified three kinds of destructive characters, whom I call deadbeats (withholders of effort), downers (who express pessimism, anxiety, insecurity, and irritation), and 'ass...es' (who violate interpersonal norms of respect). Felps estimates that, compared to teams without bad apples, those with just one suffer a performance disadvantage of 30% to 40%. Rotten apples sap time and energy that could be devoted to useful tasks. Their negativity is also contagious – it infects coworkers, turning them into deadbeats, downers, and 'ass..es' just like them.

Good bosses balance their followers' needs for protection with their own needs. They treat the job like a marathon, not a spirit. Bosses who never tend to their own mental and physical health, families' needs, and careers are doomed to failure. If you don't take time away from work to recharge, you will eventually bun out.

My wife, Marina Park, a hardworking boss for decades, first as managing partner of a large law firm and now as CEO of Girl Scouts of Northern California, uses the airplane safety analogy: Secure your own oxygen mask before helping others. After all, if you're choking for air, you can't save someone else. Similarly, if you as a boss are not breathing feely, you can't clear the air for others.

Good bosses shield their employees from distress and distraction in diverse ways, whether behind the scenes or publicly. They work day after day to enhance their self-awareness; stay in tune with followers' worries, hot buttons, and quirks; and foster a climate of comfort and safety. They also learn to identify which battles their people consider crucial to fight, and which they see as unimportant. When bosses can't protect people – for example, from layoffs, pay cuts, or tough assignments – the best ones convey compassion, do small things to allay fears, and find ways to blunt negative consequences. Operating in this way helps bolster your people's performance and well-being. And a nice by-product is that they will have your back, too.

1. **At 3M William headed the company which:**
   A. manufactured ace bandages of a different kind
   B. developed a routine work culture
   C. produce quality scotch tapes
   D. practised a distinctive management style

2. **Coyne allowed his research teams to work:**
   A. with the help of execution who asked too many questions
   B. without intervention from higher ups
   C. for the organization by ignoring trivial questions
   D. without shielding them from threats

3. **Coyne knew that he could best serve his employees by offering them:**
   A. top salaries B. a level playing field
   C. unlimited power to defend themselves D. himself as a shield

4. **The notion that management buffers core work of an organization is:**
   A. an outdated organizational theory
   B.an accepted organizational theory
   C. a theory which is accepted to a certain extent
   D.an inner active practice which has become popular

5. **Effective managers fight for the right of their employees to:**
   A. help their workers work B. help them to get recognition
   C. put their own interests first D. work as human shields

Answer keys

1.D 2.B 3.D 4.A 5. A

7. *Read the following passage and answer the questions given below.*

It is evident that there is a close connection between the capacity to use language and the capacities covered by the verb 'to think'. 'Indeed, some writers have identified thinking with using words – Plato coined the aphorism, in thinking the soul is talking to itself – Many thinking situations are hardly distinguishable from the skillful use of language, although there are some others in which language is not involved. Thought cannot be simply identified with using language. It may be the case of course that the non linguistic skills involved in thought can only be acquired and developed if the learner is able to use and understand language.

At the common sense level it appears that there is often a distinction between thought and the words we employ to communicate with other people. We often have to struggle hard to find words to capture what our thinking has already grasped, and when we find words we sometimes feel that they failed to do their job properly. Again, when we report or describe our thinking to other people we do not merely report unspoken words and sentences. Such sentences do not always occur in thinking, and when they do they are merged with vague imagery and the limit of unconscious of subliminal activities going on just out of range. Thinking as it happens, is more like struggling, striving or searching for something than it is like talking or reading. Words do play their part but they are rarely the only feature of thought.

1. **Thinking and using language according to the author are:**
   A. unrelated B. closely related C. identical D. mutually exclusive

2. **Plato's aphorism quoted in the passage expresses his belief in:**
   A. The soul's capacity to talk to itself
   B. The difference between thinking and use of language
   C. Thinking as unexpressed speech
   D. Complete identity between thinking and speech

3. **To strengthen his point of view the author brings in the authority of:**
   A. a well-known philosopher
   B. a scholar who shares a popular view
   C. empirical evidence
   D. commonsense understanding of human thought

4. **Words fail to express our thought fully because**
   A. our knowledge of any subject is inadequate
   B. words are not the only means of expression
   C. some thoughts are too subtle to be expressed through language
   D. we are often forced to communicate to others what we do not fully understand

5. **The best title for this passage is:**
   A. communicating new ideas
   B. inability of language to express all ideas
   C. how rhetories can mislead
   D. how do we communicate human thought

Answer keys

1.B 2.A 3.D 4.C 5.B

8. Read the following passage carefully and answer the questions:

There is a general, if vague agreement among most people that television is not a good thing. Why it is not is, again fairly well known: every now and then, there is an outcry against it. Its effect on children, its hypnotic, compelling nature, the negative value it projects, its essential superficiality and the intense commercialism that keeps it going: the need to sell, the insistent advertising which leads to mindless consumerism and so on. Yet, television keeps growing at an exponential rate, attracting more and more of the advertising spending countries across the regions, certainly in India. Television advertising has been accused of inducing youngsters to emulate what they see on the screen and die in the process. There is the sad and much talked about care of a child trying to sort of bungee jump without any rope or support in the manner of a character in a soft drink commercial: the character bounces back with the drink for his girl, but the child, lost his life. The premise in Jery Mander's book 'Four Arguments for the Elimination of Television' that television is a dangerous medium with a variety of frightening ill effects is consequently not new. One has to remember, however that his book was first published in the U.S. in 1978, and its Indian reprint has come out. In any event, while the actual arguments may be familiar to many, the reasons leading upto the conclusions Mander presents are carefully researched and written with a clarity and easiness that is admirable.

Mander takes one back from television to the nature of advertising and even further to the quality of life as it is in the U.S. and as it, no doubt will be in other parts of the world sooner or later. He argues most persuasively that man has, over the past sixty or seventy years, been manipulating the manner in which we live and work and indeed, the environment. The evidence he has gathered is formidable, from the effect of artificial light on human body and, worse on the mind, to the manner in which television images become the reality in which children grow up and millions of adults live and how these are manipulated by a handful of people for purely commercial ends.

1. **The most important reason why television as a channel of communication (according to the author) is not to be encouraged because:**

   A. there is an out cry against its use now and then

   B. it has a mesmerizing effect on children

   C. it leads to mindless consumerism

   D. its superficiality

2. **The main theme of the passage is:**

   A. four arguments for rejecting TV

   B. how TV corrupts the new generation

   C. evils of TV

   D. television images is dangerous

3. **Indicate which one of the statements is not true according to the writer:**
   A. the intense commercialization of the process of communication
   B. it has changed the quality of life of the people in an undesirable direction
   C. it is a dangerous medium with frightening its effects
   D. its failure to achieve exponential growth

4. **Which of the following is not correct?**
   Television is considered immoral as it has a wrong effect on:
   A. The living styles of human beings
   B. Physical health of human beings
   C. An individual's social functioning
   D. Nature and content advertising

5. **What is the most hazarduous effect of television according to the author?**
   A. Its hypnotic compelling effect on the viewers
   B. Intense commercialism which often leads to the propagation of wrong ideas
   C. Projecting unreal images as real
   D. Encourages youngsters to emulate what they see on the screen

Answer keys

1.C 2.C 3.D 4.C 5.D

9. Read the following passage and answer the questing based on the passage

It is necessary to be clear about the definition and scope of the word science, as also its distinction from technology. Among the few powerful forces that hold the key to the future of mankind, science is perhaps the only important one that enjoys the unique position of being accepted by all, practically without exception. Even in the case of those rare individuals who seem to entertain an antipathy to science, a casual conversation with them will bring out the fact that they are actually opposed not to science, but to technology which is concerned with the applications of the findings of science to satisfy diverse human needs.

By science we mean today the fundamental knowledge of our world and its environment, the controlled study and pursuit of that knowledge in all its aspects, without necessarily a desire to use it for public ends. And by technology we refer to the numerous ways of pressing science into human service, the concerned study of the ways in which things may be made or changed for human ends. To make a concrete differentiation between the two, one cites examples from the presently highly popular fields of nuclear science and technology. It is science here when measurements are made of the number and nature of the particles emitted in the break up or fission of the nucleus of the heavy metallic element Uranium. It is however, technology when this scientific knowledge is used either to design and make an atomic bomb or to design a nuclear power reactor. As such, it is technology which acquires ethical overtones and can be labeled as moral or immoral. Science is neutral or amoral and can never be opposed to ethics or human welfare, although a scientist as a human being, technologist can be.

1. **The writer of the passage is trying to:**
   A. plead for a better attitude to science
   B. suggest we apply science for public good
   C. study ethical science rather than physical science
   D. distinguish between science and technology

2. **According to the writer, science:**
   A. is the only force which determines the future of mankind
   B. is the one of the few determining forces which shape human destiny
   C. will be the only concern of human beings in the future
   D. is one of the many obstacles which retards the progress of human societies

3. **This passage is best described as a:**
   A. a logical analysis of the relation between science and technology
   B. a descriptive presentation of the nature of science and technology
   C. a narrative of the interplay of science and technology
   D. an expository presentation of the role of technology

4. **The study of fission of the nucleus of Uranium can be thought of as:**
   A. an example of modern technology
   B. application of the principle of electromagnetic induction
   C. a technology which cannot be labeled as amoral
   D. a process which contribute to human welfare

5. **The major difference between science and technology is**
   A. Science is based on measurements while technology is not
   B. Science is more concerned with the theory of something while technology is concerned with its use
   C. Science is fundamental knowledge while technology does not use fundamental knowledge
   D. Science is concerned with controlled observation while technology does not use controlled observation

Answer keys

1.D 2.A 3.B 4.A 5.B

10. *Read the following passage carefully and answer the questions given below it.*

Where does the strength of India lie? Not in numbers, not necessarily in our moral stance on international issues. In modern times, the strength of a nation lies in its achievement in science and technology. This is not to say that other fields do not count.

In the five decades after independence, we have yet to demonstrate our originality in applied science and technology. Though Japan also started like us, by cultivating the technology of the West, the Japanese adapted, improved and displayed originality in several areas of science and technology. The generation which is at the helm of affairs in science and technology in our country after independence, mostly consists of self-seekers. By and large, with a few exceptions, the science and technology managers in India concentrated in gaining power and influence. They loved publicity. Most of them stopped doing science while they managed science. Things would have been better had they been humble enough to acknowledge the difference between doing and managing science. Instead, they claimed they were the foremost in science and technology, simply because they were at the helm of affairs. As a result, they ceased to inspire the younger lot. India continues to be a borrower of science and technology, even though its potential for originality is substantial.

Our achievement in nuclear science and technology may be dazzling to our people. But in worth and originality they are ordinary and routine. While our own people remain ignorant, the people of other countries know all about the pretensions to knowledge of our nuclear science and technology managers. One subtle way of sabotaging our nuclear goals is to help allow persons reach and remain at the helm of affairs. International bodies came in as handy tools in that subtle process. The veil of secrecy effectively protects the mismanagement in our nuclear establishments. The talk of national security comes as an easy weapon to prevent any probe into mismanagement. On nuclear matters, the media in our country, by and large, avoid the investigative approach. As a result, the mismatch between promise and performance in the nuclear field does not get exposed as much as the management in other fields.

1. **What is the yardstick for measuring the achievement of a nation, according to the author?**

   A. Its moral stance on intellectual issues

   B. Its large population

   C. Its achievement in science and technology

   D. Its achievements in fields other than science and technology

2. **What according to the author, should India do to demonstrate originality in applied science and technology?**

   A. India should adapt western technology and improve and display originality in science and technology

B. India should identify the self-seekers among the men of science

C. Science and technology mangers should not waste their time for gaining power and influence

D. India should lay the foundation for developing science and technology without copying western technology

3. **What did the 'self-seekers' in science and technology do or want?**

(i) The self-seekers concentrated in gaining power and influence

(ii) They loved publicity

(iii) They stopped doing science while they managed science

(iv) They did not acknowledge the difference between doing science and managing science

(v) They ceased to inspire the younger lot with their wrong pretensions

Identify the correct answer form the following

A. Only (i) is correct
B. (i) and (ii) are correct
C. (i), (ii) & (iii) are correct
D. All are correct

4. **Which one of the following represents what is common between the Indian and the Japanese scientists?**

A. Both have displayed originality in science

B. Both have cultivated the technology of the West

C. Both have adapted and improved in western technology

D. Both have excelled the scientists of the West

5. **Doing science and managing science as used by the author stand for:**

A. failure to do scientific research of quality by decision-makers and concentrating on administration

B. Doing an activity and watching the activity

C. Originality and adaptability

D. Practice and precept

Answer keys

1.A 2.A 3.D 4.B 5.C

11. *Read the following passage carefully and answer the questions given below it.*

It is not a nation that counts for me, what counts for me is whether a man is good or bad: this is the only criterion which I recognize. I do not think that everyone outside my nationality, whom I regard as alien, is wicked or bad, nor do I think that all men who belong to my nationality are good. I do not adopt such ideas. If you wish to have a symbol of the true universal spirit – the spirit which in the western world has been put forth by Socrates, and which was exemplified by many others in later years. – it can be sought in intellectual sincerity and universal love. Whatever one may say of the great achievements of science and technology, and their possibilities for bringing an end to this world, the one good thing that they have done is to bring the nations, race cultures and civilizations of the world together. They have come together – never again to part. We have to settle down and work together as members of one community. Our true nationality is the human race, the world is our home. It is this kind of society that is emerging today. We will see that the tumult, the agitation, the violence, the anger, which we come across in the world are all the birth-pangs of a new world order.

This world has progressed from a state of molten mass of fire to that of life, first of animals then of human beings. But men have now come to the state where they are divided by doubts and discord. The revolution, however, is not complete; men have to become perfect before they can become citizens of a world community.

We are accustomed today to the nation-state and also to the military method of solving our international disputes. Both have now become out of date. With all its nuclear weapons, the military method is not likely to help in achieving our ends. Secondly conflicts are inevitable in the very concept of the nation-state with our belief that we are the elect of God and designed to be educators of the human race.

We have to settle down to a situation where we think that we are all the children of the Supreme, and that every nation has a particular contribution to make to the richness, variety and the wealth of human society. It is this kind of society that we have to work for.

How can we get it? We know the way in which the nation-state was formed. People then had their private, armies and we come to the conclusion that if all these disputes between groups and tribes were to be over, we must surrender our right to private violence and hand over whatever powers of coercion we had to a central authority called the state.

There will be source of unrest, source of upheavals, dissensions, etc, so long as people are not treated on a fair basis, so long as they do not have opportunities by which they can rise to their full stature, so long as few illustrious men enjoy all the privileges while the large numbers suffer from privation, poverty and unemployment.

So if a nation-state is to be stabilized, all the citizens of that state should have the right to express themselves. Opportunities for self-expression and self-development must be accorded to them.

If we hand over the instruments of coercion to a central authority, and also try to remove all the causes which bring about social unrest, we shall then have a national purpose, some commitment to ideals, some objectives which bind all the citizens together. If we have that, the nations become stable ones. Surrender of national armies, settlement of differences among the people, and the development of common objectives for common purposes. We have to transfer all this to the international scale. Some part of the sovereignty of the nations of the world will have to be given over to a central authority.

1. Which of the following is considered most important by the author?

A. a good nation, whatever it be

B. A good compatriot, whoever he be

C. The intellectual sincerity of man

D. A good man, irrespective of his nationality

2. How does the author view those outside his nationality?

A. The author regards them as wicked

B. To him all those outside his nationality are good

C. He regards them just as he regards his compatriots

D. He regards them as intellectually more sincere than his compatriots

3. Which of the following is/are true in the light of the observations in the passage?

i. Science and technology have shown the dreaded possibility of bringing an end to this world

ii. Science and technology have been working as great unifiers

iii. The whole world is our home

iv. A new world order is emerging fast

A. Only (i) is true B. (ii) and (iv) are true

C. All are true except (iii) D. All are true

4. What, in the opinion of the author, divides human beings?

A. Nation-states B. Doubts and discords

C. Revolutions D. Tumult, agitation, violence, anger, etc.

5. Why does the author regard the concept of 'nation-state' as unacceptable?

i. The concept causes conflict

ii. It paves the way for international disputes

iii. It hinders the birth of a unipolar world

iv. It necessitates the use of military method of solving international disputes.

A. (i) only is true B. (i) and (ii) are true

C. All except (iv) are true D. All are true.

Answer keys

1.D 2.C 3.D 4.B 5.A

12. *Read the following passage carefully and answer the questions given below it.*

The misfortunes of human beings may be divided into two classes: first, those inflicted by the non-human environment, and second, those inflicted by other people. As mankind has progressed in knowledge and technique, the second class has become a continually increasing percentage of the total. In old times, famine for example, was due to natural causes, and although, people did their best to combat it, large numbers of them died of starvation. At the present moment, large parts of the world are faced with threats of famine, but although natural causes have contributed to the situation, the principal causes are human. For six years (1939-1945) the civilized nations of the world devoted all their best energies to killing each other, and they find it difficult suddenly to switch over to keeping each other alive. Having destroyed harvests, dismantled agricultural machinery and disorganized shipping, they find it no easy matter to relieve the shortages of crops in one place by means of superabundance in another, as would easily be done if the economic system were in normal working order. As this illustration shows, it is now man that is man's worst enemy. Nature, it is true, still sees to it that we are mortal, but with the progress in medicine it will become more and more common for people to live until people have had their fill of life. We are supposed to wish to live for ever and to look forward to the unending joys of heaven, of which, by miracle, the monotony will never grow stale. But in fact, if you question any candid person who is no longer young, he is very likely to tell you that, having tasted life in this world, he has no wish to begin again as a 'new boy' in another. For the future, therefore, it may be taken that the most important evil that mankind has to consider are those which they inflict upon each other through stupidity or malevolence or both.

It would be easy to multiply instances in support of the thesis that human beings justify cruelty and cruel impulses within them. When we pass, in review, the opinions of former times which are now recognized as absurd, it will be found that nine out of ten they were such as to justify the infliction of suffering. Take, for instance, medical practice. When anesthetics were invented, they were thought to be wicked as being an attempt to thwart God's will. Insanity was thought to be due to diabolic possession, and it was believed that the demons inhabiting a mad man could be driven out by inflicting pain upon him, and so making them uncomfortable. In pursuit of this opinion, lunatics were treated for year on end with systematic and conscientious brutality.

1. The author cites 'famine' as an instance of the misfortune of human beings inflicted by:

A. the non-human environment

B. Other people

C. both the non-human environment and other people

D. dictators

2. **In what ways the human beings contributed to the threat of famine in the present-day world?**

   i. Destruction of harvest

   ii. Dismantling of agricultural machinery.

   iii. Disorganization of shipping

   iv. Creating shortage of crops

   A. Only (i) is correct B. Only (ii) is correct

   C. (i), (ii) and (iii) are correct D. All are correct

3. **Which of the following does the author indicate as the single-most powerful cause of the misfortune that humankind has brought upon itself?**

   A. War B. Pestilence

   C. Ignorance D. Human actions

4. **Why does the author say that 'man is man's worst enemy'? It is because:**

   i. Man unsuccessfully tries to control the non-human environment

   ii. Man wages wars and kills fellow human beings

   iii. Man upsets or destroys the normal working order of the economic system of other nations

   iv. In times of war, man creates famine and starvation by destroying crops.

   Chose the correct answer:

   A. Only (i) is correct B. (ii), (iii) and (iv) are correct

   C. (i), (ii) and (iii) are correct D. None of them are correct

5. **What evidence does the writer provide from medical science in support of his statement that human beings are cruel towards others?**

   A. The idea that the use of anesthesia is an attempt to thwart God's will

   B. By filling our minds with irrational thoughts

   C. By filling our minds with ideas about heaven

   D. By developing medicines which failed to relieve the pain

Answer keys

1.C 2.D 3.A 4.B 5.A

13. ***Read the following passage carefully and answer the questions given below it.***

"If we stop thinking of the poor as victims or as a burden and start recognizing them as resilient and creative entrepreneurs and value conscious consumers, a whole new world of opportunity will open up." That "simple proposition" begins a controversial new management book that seems destined to be read not just in boardrooms but also in government offices. "The Fortune is at the Bottom of the Pyramid. Eradicating Poverty Through Profits" (Wharton School Publishing), is essentially a rallying cry for big business to put serving the world's 5 billion or so poorest people at the heart of their profit-making strategies. It has already been praised by everyone from Bill Gates ("A Blueprint for Fighting Poverty – to a former American Secretary of State (Madeleine Albright). Who says " if you are looking for fresh thinking about emerging markets, your search is ended".

The management has come out with new ideas about management. After becoming a management professor at the University of Michigan via a job at Union Carbide and study at the Indian Institute of Management and Harvard, he wrote "Competing for the Future" (Harvard Business School Press) with Gary Hamel in 1994. This work was regarded as perhaps the best business book of the 1990s.

As the two gurus searched for their next hit, Mr.Hamel stumbled across Enron, a then-thriving energy conglomerate that he eulogized in "Leading the Revolution" (Harvard Business School Press). Mr. Prahalad, by contrast, "after searching for a couple of years, saw that the big idea was creating wealth at the bottom of the pyramid". He has been evolving his ideas about how firms should focus on the bottom of the pyramid – a phrase he shortens to BOP, to contrast with those wealthy folk at the TOP.

He is a fierce critic of traditional top-down thinking on aid, by governments and non-governmental organizations alike. They tend to see the poor as victims to be helped, he says, not as people who can be part of the solution – and so their help often creates dependence. Nor does he pin much hope on the "corporate social responsibility" (CSR) programmes of many large companies. If you want serious commitment from a firm, he says, its involvement with the poor" can't be based on philanthropy or CSR". The involvement of big business is crucial to eradicating poverty, he believes, but BOP markets must "become integral to the success of the firm in order to command senior management attention and sustained resource allocation."

Mr.Prahalad reckons that there are huge potential profits to be made from serving the 4 billion – 5 billion people on under $2 a day – an economic opportunity he values globally at $ 13 trillion a year. The win for the poor of being served by big business includes, he says, being empowered by choice and being freed from having to pay the currently widespread "poverty penalty". In shanty towns near Mumbai, for example, the poor pay a premium on everything from rice to credit – often five to 25 times what the rich pay for the same services. Driving down these premiums can make serving the top, he argues, and points to a growing number of leading firms – from Unilever in India to Cemex in Mexico and CAsas Bahia in Brazil – that are profiting by doing precisely that.

1. **Prahlad's book suggests that the poor should be thought of as:**
   A. Victims B. A burden on society
   C. Opportunities D. Consumers

2. **Prahlad advocates the economic strategy of eradicating profits through:**
   A. Collaboration with Bill Gates
   B. The construction of model pyramids
   C. The need for fresh thinking about emerging markets
   D. Profit-making ideas aimed at the poorest of the poor

3. **The best business book of the 1990's was:**
   A. The Fortune at the Bottom of the Pyramid
   B. A Blueprint for Fighting Poverty
   C. Competing for the Future
   D. Leading the Revolution

4. **Prahlad worked with Union Carbide:**
   A. Before joining the faculty of the University of Michigan
   B. Before he joined the IIM
   C. Before his study at Harvard
   D. After he left the University of Michigan

5. **Mr. Prahlad is credited for the strong views he expressed about:**
   A. the error in top-down thinking on aid
   B. poor at the bottom to be treated as victims to be helped
   C. co-operate social responsibility
   D. BOP markets can be ignored

Answer keys

1.D 2.D 3.C 4.A 5.A

14. ***Read the following passage carefully and answer the questions given below it.***

In modern times Abraham Lincoln stands as the model of a compassionate statesman. He showed this quality not only in striving for the emancipation of the American Blacks but in the dignity with which he conducted the American Civil War.

Lincoln did not fancy himself as a liberator. He thought it would be better for all if emancipation was a gradual process spread over many years. He proposed compensation for slave-owners in US bonds and grants for the rehabilitation of Blacks. The haste with which the South wanted to break away from the Union with the North, compelled him to move faster than he expected. Perhaps more than most men of his time, he had thought through the issue of slavery. 'We must free the slaves', he said, 'or be ourselves subdued'. Before reading his first draft of the Proclamation of Emancipation, he told his colleagues, 'In giving freedom to the slaves, we assure freedom to the free'.

On September 22, 1862, Lincoln set his hand on the Proclamation of Emancipation declaring that on the first day of January 1863, 'all persons held as slaves within any state shall be then and forever free'.

Lincoln's revulsion for slavery left him without any moral indignation or passion against the slave-owners. The guilt of the slave-owners, he felt, should be shared by the whole country, the North and South, for it seemed to him that everyone in the nation was an accomplice in perpetuating that system. To have whipped up any hatred against slave-owners would, to him, have been an act of malice.

'I shall do nothing in malice', he wrote, 'what I deal with is too vast for malicious dealing'. As the Civil War was coming to a successful conclusion, a Northerner demanded of Lincoln: 'Mr.President, how are you going to treat the Southerners when the war is over?'

Lincoln replied, 'as if they never went to war?'

When the news came of the victory of the Northern against the Confederate forces, some one suggested that the head of the Confederation Administration, Jefferson Davies, really ought to be hanged. 'Judge not, that ye be not judged', Lincoln replied. As to the demand for the prosecution of rebels, Lincoln replied, 'We must extinguish our resentments if we expect harmony and union'. This was his last recoded utterance.

1. Which of the following statements is/are correct?

i. Lincoln strove for the emancipation of the American Blacks as a gradual process.
ii. Lincoln conducted the Civil War with dignity.
iii. He wanted the rehabilitation of the Blacks as part of their emancipation.
iv. He hoped there would be a change of heart in the slave-owners.
v. He was vindictive towards the Confederate leaders.

Choose the correct answer:

A. Only (i) is correct
B. (ii) and (iii) are correct
C. (ii), (iii) and (iv) are correct
D. All except (v) are correct.

2. Which of the following statements about Lincoln could be taken as evidence of his days convictions about the right to freedom for the slaves?

A. Lincoln asked the Northerners to harbour no malice towards the former slave-owners and also to treat the vanquished Southern leaders with compassion
B. He wanted the slave-owners to free the slaves by accepting compensation in US bonds

C. He proposed payment of grants for the rehabilitation of the Blacks

D. It seemed to Lincoln that the American people as a whole were accomplices in perpetuating slavery

3. **What was Lincon's stand in respect of prosecuting the rebels in the civil war?**

A. That they have to be dealt with severely

B. The guilt has to be shared by the whole country

C. The rebels were figuring on a principle which all the people accepted as correct up to the time

D.All work will only breed more ill-will

4. **The sentence "in giving freedom to the slaves, we assure freedom to the free" means,**

A. If we give freedom to the slaves, they will serve us better

B. If we do not grant freedom to the slaves, they will fight for freedom

C. By freeing slaves we will be honouring the concept of freedom

D. By freeing slaves we are safeguarding our own interests

5. **According to Lincoln, the culprits of the system of slavery were**

A. The salve-owners alone

B. The slaves themselves

C. Both the salves and the slave-owners

D. The American people as a whole

Answer keys

1.D 2.D 3.B 4.C 5.D

15. ***Read the following passage carefully and answer the questions given below it.***

Although cynics may like to see the government's policy for women in terms of the party's internal power struggles, it will nevertheless be churlish to deny that it represents a pioneering effort aimed at bringing about sweeping social reforms. In its language, scope and strategies, the policy document displays a degree of understanding of women's needs that is uncommon in government pronouncements. This is due in large part to the participatory process that marked its formulation, seeking the active involvement right from the start of women's groups, academic institutions and non-government organizations with grassroots experience. The result is not just a lofty declaration of principles but blueprint for a practical programme of action. The policy delineates a series of concrete measures to accord women a decision-making role in the political domain and greater control over their economic status. Of especially far reaching impact are the devolution of control of economic infrastructure of women, notably at the gram panchayat level, and the amendments proposed in the Hindu Succession Act of 1956 to give women coparency rights.

An enlightened aspect of the policy is its recognition that actual change in the status of women cannot be brought about by the mere enactment of socially progressive legislations. Accordingly, it focuses on reorienting development programmes and sensitizing administrations to address specific situations, as for instance, the growing number of households headed by women, which is a consequence of rural-urban migration. The proposal to create an equal-opportunity police force and give women greater control of police stations is an acknowledgement of the biases and the callousness displayed by the generally all-male law-enforcement authorities in cases of dowry and domestic violence. While the mere enunciation of such a policy has the salutary effect of sensitizing the administration as a whole, it does not make the task of its implementation any easier. This is because the changes it envisages in the political and economic status of women strike at the root of power structures in society and the basis of man-woman relationships. There is also the danger that reservation of women in public life, while necessary for their greater visibility, could lapse into tokenism or become a tool in the hands of vote seeking politicians. Much will depend on the dissemination of the policy and the ability of elected representatives and government agencies to reorder their priorities.

1. **Which of the following is/are incorrect in the light of the government's policy for women?**

   i. The policy represents a pioneering effort aimed at bringing about sweeping social reforms

   ii. The policy document displays an obvious understanding of women's needs

   iii. It is a blue print for a practical programme of action

   iv. The policy provides women with greater control of economic infrastructure at the gram panchayat level

   A. (i) & (iii) are incorrect
   B. (ii) & (iv) are incorrect
   C. Only (iii) is incorrect
   D. None are incorrect

2. **Which one of the following ideas can be considered to be an enlightened aspect of the new policy for women?**

   A. Recognition that the status of women can change through a proper legislation

   B. Recognition that a change in the status of women cannot be brought by a legislation alone

   C. Taking note of the higher incidence of rural-urban migration

   D. Giving women greater control in the police stations

3. **According to the passage, which of the following is a consequence of the rural-urban migration?**
   A. Many households are headed by women
   B. Women have no time to participate in the developmental activities of their grama panchayats
   C. Unemployment rate has shot up in rural areas
   D. The police force of rural areas consists of women only

4. **Which of the following statements regarding the new policy for women is not true?**
   A. The new policy will go a long way towards empowering women
   B. The policy was formulated without consulting any women's body any or organization
   C. There is a proposal in the policy to create an equal opportunity police force
   D. The gender bias displayed by the generally all-male law-enforcement authorities can be reduced to a considerable extent

5. **Why does the writer say that the task of implementation of the policy is not easy?**
   A. It is because those who formulated the policy have not understood its implications
   B. The policy is likely to be implemented without commitment
   C. The elected representatives are not keen on implementing the policy
   D. It is because the changes it envisages in the status of women strike at the very root of power structures in society

Answer keys

1.D 2.B 3.A 4.B 5.D

16. Read the following passage and answer the questions 1 to 5.

Children are part and parcel of the social and political philosophy of a country. The attitude that are meted out to them, are the important factors determining whether their basic needs will be fulfilled and they get their rights. Every forward looking society will take this matter seriously that children should be given proper care from the early childhood. We deeply regret to say that there is no provision in many parts of the world to bring up children with the feeling of peace and brotherhood. The most dreadful record of war and terrorism that we see in the newspapers depicts the pictures of small children and infants crying near the dead bodies of their families in their devastated houses. Some of these infants are too small to weep. Children either in countries experiencing hostilities or in societies in which such actions are glamourised will reflect the life events and or societal acceptance of such events, causing us all to wonder whether the millions of children affected by such national philosophies have any likely-hood of achieving their rights to grow up in a spirit of peace. And certainly discrimination based on race, colour, sex, religion or national or social origin, either singly or in some combination keeps millions of children from the fulfillment of these rights in spite of the universality of the needs upon which rights are based.

1. **Which one of the following is conducive to the development of a spirit of peace and brotherhood among children?**

   A. When elders expose children to the horrors of war

   B. When adults practise racial discrimination

   C. When the political philosophy of a nation pleads for universal brotherhood

   D. When society glamourizes war activities

2. **Adults have a duty towards children. How well children are looked after in a particular society, can be inferred from:**

   A. What is done for them in disaster

   B. How much they care for the adults

   C. How responsive adults are to their rights

   D. How affluent the society is

3. **The author of the passage holds that:**

   A. Children achieve their rights to live in peace in spite of war situations

   B. Children's rights should be dependent upon the social conditions prevailing in a society

   C. Children have a right to grow in a spirit of peace

   D. National philosophers uphold children's right

4. **War activities in many societies:**

   A. tend to make children ignore cruelty

   B. are unlikely to achieve their rights to grow up in peace

   C. are not given the importance they deserve

   D. are treated as adults

5. **Why does the author comment that he has deep regret about children?**

   A. In many parts of the world there is no provision to rear children in an atmosphere of peace and brotherhood

   B. The media reports depicts the dreadful pictures of children and infants crying near the dead bodies of their relatives

C. Societies are glamorizing war activities

D. Discrimination based on race, sex, colour, religion and nationality is not condemned

Answer keys

1.C 2.C 3.C 4.B 5.A

17. Read the following passage and answer the questions 1 to 5.

It is time we looked at the latent causes. Where does the strength of India lie? Not in numbers, not necessarily in our moral stands on international issues. In modern times the strength of a nation lies on its achievements in science and technology. This is not to say that other fields do not count.

In the five decades after independence, we have yet to demonstrate our originality in applied science and technology. Though Japan also started like us, by cultivating the technology of the West, Japanese adopted, improved and displayed originality in several areas of science and technology. The generation which is at the helm of affairs in science and technology in our country after independence, mostly consisted of self-seekers. By and large, with a few exceptions, the science and technology managers in India concentrated in gaining power and influence. They loved publicity. Most of them stopped doing science while they managed science. Things would have been better had they been humble enough to acknowledge the difference between doing and managing science. Instead, they claimed they were the foremost in science and technology simply because they were at the helm of affairs. As a result they ceased to inspire the younger lot. India continues to be a borrower of science and technology, even though its potential for originality is substantial.

Our achievements in nuclear science and technology may be dazzling to our people, but, in worth and originality they are ordinary and routine. While our own people remain ignorant, the people of other countries know all about the pretension to knowledge of our nuclear science and technology managers. One subtle way of sabotaging our nuclear goals is to help hollow person reach and remain at the helm of affairs. International bodies come in as handy tools in that subtle process. The veil of secrecy effectively protects the mismanagement in our nuclear establishments. The talk of national security comes as an easy weapon to prevent any probe into mismanagement.

On nuclear matters the media in our country, by and large, avoid the investigative approach. As a result, the mismatch between promise and performance in the nuclear field does not get exposed as much as the mismanagement in other fields.

1. What does the author of the passage mean by 'doing science'?

A. Demonstrating exaggerated performance

B. Managing the administrative functions of research

C. Concentrating on innovative researches

D. Displaying genuine performance in pure science

2. **Science and technology managers in India have:**

A. set unrealistic targets and failed to achieve them

B. most practitioners did not believe in science management

C. most practiced science without understanding

D. mostly self-seekers

3. **The author of the passage is not happy with Indian nuclear scientists because:**

A. the power crazy Indian technocrats have received publicity

B. they followed the model of Japanese scientists

C. they have concentrated more on gaining power and influence

D. they have unreasonably criticized the Indian politicians

4. **Which of the following is the correct assessment of Indian's post independence nuclear and scientific advancement?**

A. Originality and adaptability have been displayed

B. Achievement in nuclear science and technology is dazzling

C. Achievement is of low quality and of routine nature

D. Our scientists have done all that needed to cater to the developmental needs of nuclear science in the country

5. **The author is fully convinced that:**

A. most of the managers of science havemoved away from the real issues of research.

B. India's strength lies wholly on its moral stands on international issues

C. India's potential for originality in science and technology

D. our scientists are recognized abroad, though they are criticized in India

Answer keys

1.C 2.D 2.C 3.A 4.C 5.A

Unit - IV

COMMUNICATION

COMMUNICATION: NATURE, CHARACTERISTICS, TYPES, BARRIER AND EFFECTIVE CLASSROOM COMMUNICATION

Unit - IV

COMMUNICATION

The rapid industrialization and advancement of new technology has changed the face of the earth. Modernization and urbanization have already transformed the life style of mankind. It has induced greater mobility from traditional village to modern urban centres. Such vast change has occurred within the last 50 years. The reason for such a change is traceable in the advancement of science and technology. It has reached the people only through the technology of communication. Information explosion is due to the expansion of mass media, which is an essential component of communication.

1. NATURE AND CHARACTERISTICS OF COMMUNICATION

Skill in communication is essential for both teachers and researchers. In fact teaching is basically a process of communication. Effective classroom interaction is possible only if the communication in classroom is interesting, motivating and realistic. It is a two way process involving, so many factors like:

- Communicator's personality, knowledge base, skill in presentation, attitude, organized and life related illustrations, facial expressions, actions, movements, body language, eye contact, interest in the subject, commitment, insights, etc.
- The infrastructural and environmental factors like physical environment, free from noise and other disturbances, technological facilities, appropriate furniture, sound systems, display boards, availability of internet & down loading facilities, etc; and
- The receiver's mental ability, linguistic facility, grasping capacity, past experiences, motivation, interest, attitude, anxiety levels, involvement, etc.

It is evident that the listed attributes in each of these sections are not exhaustive.

All the above factors are operative when it comes to reporting of research by a research scholar. The researcher is often required to present seminar papers, or the articles through which he has to make his listeners comprehend what he actually desires them to grasp. The skill in communication and the know-how of making it effective and interesting is very important. A good teacher is essentially a vibrant communicator. So is a good researcher. The minimum, the distortions in communication and physical distractions, the maximum will be the effectiveness of communication.

Communication is the exchange of ideas, information, opinions, attitudes and emotions between the 'source' and the 'receiver(s)'. The source is the person who wants to share some of his views or the facts at his disposal to the receivers. In the example of classroom communication, the teacher or textual material can be regarded as the source. In radio transmission of a talk, the speaker is the source. In the case of an editorial printed in a periodical, the editor is the source. In the examples cited, the students, the listeners of the radio talk and the readers of the periodical respectively are the receivers. The receivers are the beneficiaries or target groups of the communication process.

There are certain other elements which are important in communication. A 'message' is being delivered from a source. This (viz the source) is most important element of the communication process. If the message does not reach the receiver, or if it reaches the receiver in a distorted or incomplete manner, the purpose of the process will not be achieved.

The message is conveyed to the receiver through different 'channels' or 'media'. In a face to face communication, the message is conveyed orally through auditory symbols, which are supplemented with visual stimuli. In a telephonic conversation, the wire is the medium. The TV channel communication through the invisible electronic medium. Cartoons, posters and prints are often used as effective media for communication. In the public functions held by political parties, public address systems (microphones and loud speaker) are used as medium for communication to a large audience. Radio stations use 'air' as their medium for transmission of messages.

Yet another important element in communication is the 'feedback'. Feedback may occur in various forms. Feedback stands for the reactions of the receivers to the messages they receive sent back to the source in different forms. Take the example of the letters to the editor in a newspaper or weekly or the clarifications sought by a student after listening to a classroom lecture, or the letters of criticism or appreciation sent to Doordarsan by its spectators, about the quality of a programme which they have telecast. These are all examples of feedback. The five most important elements of communication can be diagrammatically represented as shown below.

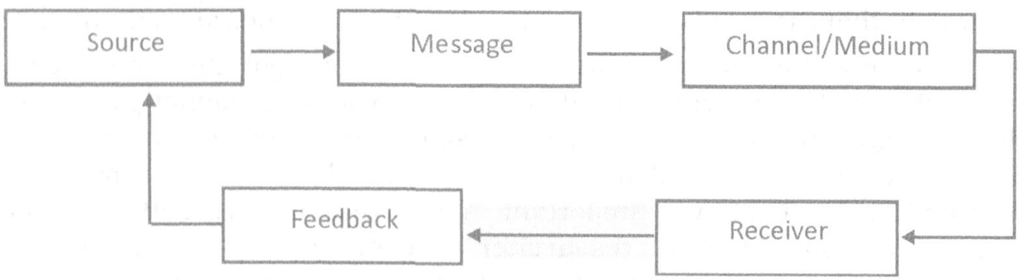

2. TYPES OF COMMUNICATION

Communication can be classified into different ways based on its context, nature, process and media.

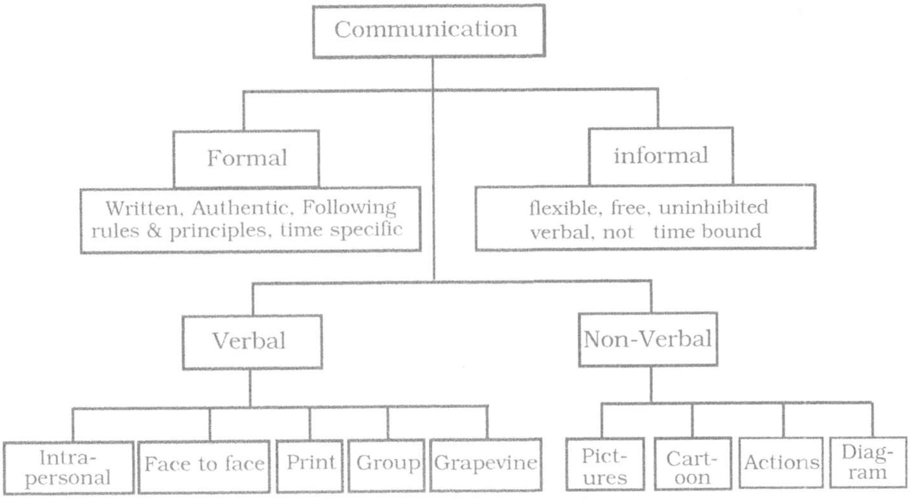

1. Face-to-Face Communication

Face-to-face communication comes in many forms. Some are one-to-one meetings, either scheduled or arranged at the spur of the moment. Others involve small groups of people, gathering spontaneously or in formal meetings. Still other forms of face-to-face communication occur in large groups, where one or more speakers make presentations to an audience. Whatever the setting and number of people, all types of face-to-face communication possess the same qualities.

Advantages:

i. Speed: Once a communicator makes contact with his/her audience, there is no time lag between the transmission of a message and its reception. This is especially important when time is a major consideration: if you need information regarding the price of an article or check the amount in your bank account, putting in a written request or memo won't be of much help in providing the needed information in time.

ii. Control: You may spend hours drafting a memo or a letter and seek information or action only to have the recipient scan it superficially or not read it at all. In a personal contact, however, you have much more command over the receiver's attention. The listener at least has to pretend to pay attention—and if you use the speaking skills described in the following chapters, your messages ought to be clear and interesting enough to capture the attention of your audience.

iii. Instantaneous feedback: When a teacher speaks directly to one or more students at a time, she/he can respond to questions as soon as they arise. You can rephrase or elaborate when your listeners seem confused, and you can speed up if details aren't necessary. You can revise hurriedly if you see you have used the wrong word or has offended or confused your audience.

iv. Personal quality: When a personal meeting goes well, the relationship that communicators develop can help solve problems that might have been more difficult when handled at a distance. Personal meetings are especially important in some cultures, where failure to visit someone in person is treated as an insult. The same principle can occur closer to home. People who don't show up for meetings may (intentionally or unintentionally) suggest to others that they are too important or too busy or too apathetic to be present.

Drawback: Although face to face communication has many advantages, it has its drawbacks as well. The biggest drawback of personal contacts is the difficulty in arranging for the event. Even when communicators are in the same building, scheduling a meeting can be difficult and frustrating. When the people who need to meet are separated by greater distances, personal contact is expensive and time-consuming. Even a cross-town trip for a half-hour meeting can take most of the morning or afternoon, depending on factors like traffic and weather.

A personal encounter might also be unproductive if the contact antagonizes one or more of the participants. If the personalities or the subjects are likely to make someone angry or defensive, then less confrontational forms of communication might be better.

2. Telephone and Voice Mail

A telephone conversation lacks the visual feedback that often reveals how your message is getting across to the interested persons. But the telephone still communicates vocal cues such as tone of voice, pauses, interruptions, pitch and rate. Telephone conversations also make it harder to hold the attention of your listener. Recall, for instance, all the fingernail cleaning and paper clip sculpting you have done while unsuspecting speakers have rattled on. The drawbacks of telephone communication are offset by one tremendous advantage: It lets you contact a receiver at any time and bridges distances. You can talk to someone halfway around the world in a very short time. The telephone can even help you get through to busy people who are nearby.

3. Written Communication

Written messages have a different set of advantages and drawbacks than their spoken counterparts have. Unlike speech, written communication is permanent. Once your words are down on paper, they are saved for future reference. While people may have trouble accurately recalling what you spoke to them a few hours ago, they can refer to your written remarks even years later. Even if the receiver has lost or forgotten your message, you can always supply its copy from your files.

Along with its permanence, written communication can be easier to understand than speech. Readers can study complex passages as many times as necessary something they can't do when the same message is delivered orally. They can take a break if their interest wanes and, after a cup of coffee or a quick stretch, come back to what they were reading in refreshed mood.

Perhaps the greatest advantage of written communication is that you can compose it in advance. You can take as much time as necessary to shape a message just as you want it, pondering on every word if necessary. You can try out several versions on test readers to anticipate the reactions of your real audience, and you can make changes until you get the desired response.

Finally, written messages are less prone to errors. Even the best-rehearsed oral presentations can go awry. You can misplace an important set of papers or forget to mention a key idea. Sometimes attempt to improvise might sound confusing or lame, and the joke you thought would make the perfect icebreaker might fall flat. Every speaker would have wished hours after a conversation, "If only I'd said..." When you communicate in writing, you have time to choose exactly the right words and present right communication.

4. Electronic mail (or e-mail)

E-mail allows communicators to send and respond to one another's written messages via a computer. Like telephone and faxes, e-mail is virtually instantaneous: once you push the "send" key on your computer, the message will be waiting for the addressee, in a matter of minutes. Along with being a tool for external communication, e-mail is used as an alternative to telephones and personal contacts within an office, where it is often labelled as part of an Intranet—an infrastructure that allows people within an organization to exchange information in digital form.

E-mail possesses some characteristics of voice mail. Besides its speed, it allows for leaving messages for others to read at their convenience. However, because the ideas appear in writing, e-mail communication (like letters and faxes) makes it easier to comprehend lengthy, detailed messages. Because it's easy to send a message to several people virtually anywhere in the world simultaneously, e-mail expedites the speed and reach of communication in ways that cannot be achieved through most other forms of communication.

Along with speed, e-mail provides an astonishing degree of access to people you otherwise might not be able to reach through other sources. Once you have located someone's e-mail address the chances for getting your messages delayed, when sent through other sources can be avoided. Your messages get delayed when transmitted through secretaries, gatekeepers and other intermediaries. The electronic source has become a way of providing a more open system of communication in all areas of human interaction, especially in public administration.

E-mail differs from most others forms of written communication in one important respect: its informal, almost spontaneous in nature. Communicators using e-mail have almost no concerns with the kind of formatting that is important in other business correspondence, and the ease of 'logging on', and sending a message which increases the frequency and informality of the contacts. For this reason, some users have termed e-mail a "conveyor belt for ideas". But along with ease of use comes the risk of spontaneous messages that the sender might later regret—especially since they can be stored and printed out, unlike an 'off-the-cuff' spoken remark.

The speed and easy-to-use nature of e-mail also makes it a tool for improving personal relationships on the job. Speeding up routine communication leaves more time for personal contacts, which the medium also makes more possible.

5. Mass Communication

When one needs to communicate with a large number of people at the same time, it is necessary to use the tools of mass communication. These are: newspapers, radio, television, 'webcast' and 'podcast'. Traditionally, the first three have been used to inform a large population about events and places. Advertisers can use these to reach out to a large population in a very short span of time. Mass marketing rests on instruments of mass communication.

With the advent of technology, webcast and podcast have become means of targeting marketing messages to specific audiences. Since devices like the cellphone and iPod have become common, messages to these devices from a central source are called podcast. When messages are sent over the Internet it is called a webcast.

Teachers can use the mass media in two ways. First, it can be used to reach students living in far places. Teaching through television and now through the Internet has picked up over the years. Second, mass media can be used in the classroom to enhance the learning experience. Modern classroom teaching is aided by multimedia techniques. The message to be transmitted more effectively when the verbal communication is supported by diagrams and animation.

Which channel to use?

In general, oral communication is best for messages that require a personal dimension. Oral channels are also best for ideas that have a strong need for visual support— demonstration, photos or slides, and so on. Spoken communication is also especially useful when there is a need for immediate comments, such as question-and-answer sessions.

Written communication (with the exception of the e-mail) works best in formal communication. Writing is often better than speaking when you want to convey complicated ideas that are likely to require closer study and deeper comprehension by the receiver. It is also smart to put your message in writing when you want it to be the final word, with no feedback or discussion. Finally, writing is the best for any message if you want a record to exist. In business and the professions, sending confirmation letters and memoranda is common practice, as is keeping minutes of meetings. These steps guarantee that what is said will be a matter of record, useful in case of later misunderstandings or disputes and in case anyone wants to review the history of an issue.

3. BARRIERS IN COMMUNICATION

Communication often gets distorted by several factors. These factors are called barriers in communication. The following are the usual barriers:

i. The factors associated with the source: The ambiguity and confusion on the part of the communicator is the major problem affecting communication. A good communicator should be one who is thorough with the subject he is communicating, the levels at which the subject is to be delivered (its depth), the objectives of communication, and the needs of the recipients of the message and strategies to deliver it systematically. All these require a lot of home work and expertise. The ability of the communicator - clarity in explanation, the verbal facility and the ability to use simple language, the skill in using communication boosters, the voice modulation, the stress and intonation, the facial expression and gestures, the skill in eliciting and asking probing questions and leading questions, patience to listen to the questions being asked, the histrionic talents, the use of illustrations, etc. are all important in communication. The absence of any one of them would lead to distortion of communication.

ii. The Physical environment: In a noisy environment, what is being communicated will be either partially or inadequately heard; this will result in wrong understanding of what is communicated. Even the time used for communication is a factor. The infrastructural inadequacies will adversely affect the quality and effectiveness of communication. Imagine a large class of more than 150 students, without a public address system! Use of defective technological devices also can act as a barrier in communication.

iii. The Receiver - related factors: Several factors like intellectual, emotional and social incapabilities are also likely to cause barriers in communication. Inability to comprehend the oral or written presentations, inadequate background knowledge to assimilate new information, lack of span of attention, etc. are the intellectual limitations. Negative attitudes, lack of motivation, excessive anxiety, lack of interest, lack of confidence etc. are certain affective factors. Familial, economic and peer-group influences are also likely to create barriers in communication. Even the reputation and status of the speaker (source) becomes an important factor which affect the efficacy of communication.

4. EFFECTIVE CLASSROOM COMMUNICATION

a. Effective communication

What are the basic factors which determine the effectiveness of communication? They are:

1. Knowledge of the audience for communication - demographic and socio-economic characteristics of the audience, their needs, tastes, social traditions, awareness of issues and their levels of comprehension, attitudes, values, motivation etc.

2. Empathy on the part of the communicator: empathy which stands for the psychological sensitivity to perceive the emotional reactions of the target audience. The sender should be in a position to feel imaginatively the recipients state of mind and possible mental reactions.

b. Variables controlling effective communication (7Cs)

How effectively a message is communicated depends on several most important factors. These are often used as a check-list for evaluating the effectiveness of communication.

1. Credibility	2. Capability	3. Context	4. Content
5. Channel	6. Clarity	7. Continuity	

1. Credibility: Credibility refers to the extent of belief a receiver is willing to attribute to the content of communication. The receiver must have confidence in the sender and hence accepts what he conveys through his message.

The confidence in the source is essential to ensure acceptance of the message. It continues as long as the trust is maintained and breaks when faith and confidence are lost. The credibility of the medium and also the credibility of the' communicator (i.e character credibility) are equally important.

2. Capability: An effective communication should be one which is understood by the audience (digested) with minimum effort. The perception of images and their interpretation by the receivers depend largely on their level of education, exposure to other media, cultural background, social background, earlier acquaintance with the area, their values, etc. Communication must, take into account the nature and capability of the audience. As such, in evaluating the effectiveness of the message, we have always to see whether the target audience can comprehend the symbols / messages at the same level as the sender of the message.

3. Context: Communication should take into account the present-social context. This means it has to fit in with local conditions and capability when it is development-oriented. Recent studies in SITE show that the rural audience is often more interested in messages dealing with their specific local needs and issues. The communicator has to ensure that no contradictions creep into the communication. As far as possible what is communicated should be in consonance with what prevails in the target area. The context, as far as possible, should help in greater participation and involvement provided for and play back. It must confirm the message.

4. Content: A programme for communication must have a meaning and a purpose to the audience. For this it must fit in with the social and economic context and the interests of the target group. The message must, to the extent possible, be compatible with the receiver's beliefs and value system. It must also have some relevance for him. Usually, there exists the problem to select a message which promises the audience highest rewards and returns. A need-based content will be better accepted by the audience than one with imaginary advantages.

5. Channel: Before pushing the message it is essential to ascertain whether the channel to be used is within the reach of the audience. Multi-media approach, if it is well coordinated, is very helpful in supplementing one another. Channels have differing levels of reach depending upon their nature. This factor needs to be taken into account in communication.

6. Clarity: The effort should be to deliver the message accurately in clear and unambiguous terms. Any loss of accuracy will have a negative effect in communication. Communication should be simple and straight forward. We should, as far as possible, keep the information load to the minimum. The message must be put in simple terms and reduced to a minimum for best effects.

7. Continuity: The flow of message should be smooth and continuous. Irrelevant sequences should be avoided, if the consistency is disturbed, we have to think of reinforcement to produce better results. Repetition with variation can contribute to better communication.

c. Effective classroom communication

The tremendous and breath-taking expansion and growth of the communication system presents several possibilities for augmenting the quality of communication. Any information available in any part of the world is available to us within seconds at the touch of a button. Classroom communication also has considerably changed because of the speed with which information can be downloaded by users. Direct linking of satellite transmission channels to classrooms helps educational institutions to make better instruction. Open universities like the IGNOU started teleconferencing, debates and discussions decades back. Formerly, Insat IB transponders were hired for telecasting these academic programmes. Now we have the 'edusat' channel which can be used exclusively for telecasting educational programmes. Many UGC programmes are transmitted to the distant learners using these advanced facilities. The use of LCD projectors for presenting the teacher-made power-points and video clippings that would boost communication are becoming popular in the new educational set-up. Print media, visual media, electronic media, voice recorders, video tapes, audio tapes, VCDs, etc. are all utilized in class rooms for making the teacher's communication more effective.

The concept of the conventional classroom has also changed, especially in the context of the new developments. Open University systems, Country Wide Class Rooms (CWCR) are common practices in distance education. The same class being attended by students spread over the entire country and interacting with the resource persons either telephonically or by Yahoo chatting makes the classroom a CWCR. Through such programmes the students can be exposed to very rich direct experiences, by national level expert faculty. Certain learning experiences which cannot be developed in the ordinary classrooms can now be provided to the learners more effectively through the new communication networking systems.

Communication - PRACTICE EXERCISE

1. **Which one of the following steps would you consider important for effective communication?**

   A. Selection of channels of communication
   B. Planning the efficacy of the method of communication
   C. Specifying the objectives of communication
   D. Identifying the various media to be used for communication

2. **The most important barrier affecting communication in a classroom is:**

   A. noise inside the classroom
   B. noise outside the classroom
   C. failure of the teacher to identify the barriers in communication
   D. failure to use teaching aids

3. **Any good communication system employs a feedback system in order to help to:**

   A. make necessary modifications in the content or process to be used for communication
   B. understand more about the content to be communicated
   C. identify the weak points of the communicator
   D. identify the difficulties of the receiver

4. **Effective communication does not require:**

   A. the proper use of language by the communicator
   B. use of appropriate gestures while communicating
   C. mastery of the content to be communicated
   D. pleasing appearance of the communicator

5. **One will be an effective communicator if he:**

   A. is a speaker with a good sense of humour
   B. has histrionic talents needed for effective presentation
   C. has clear ideas about the objectives of communication
   D. has the ability to quote the views of authorities

6. **Effective communication should aim at making the receivers:**

   A. enjoy receiving the communication
   B. accept the content of the communication
   C. remember the communication for future use
   D. reflect upon what has been communicated and build on it

7. **A teacher will be an effective communicator if he:**
   A. uses communication boosters
   B. asks probing questions
   C. illustrates his views with examples
   D. does all the above

8. **Which of the following activities would help a teacher to communicate effectively?**
   A. Use of instructional aids wherever needed
   B. Help students to get new meanings to what is taught and construct new knowledge
   C. Asking questions in between teaching, with a view to evaluate the efficacy of his teaching methods
   D. Helping students to find out the correct answers to questions

9. **Which one of the following instructional aids can be most effectively used in distance education for teaching the working of an electric bell?**
   A. Television B. Overhead Projector
   C. Video D. Computer

10. **A classroom discussion will be more effective if the topic for discussion:**
    A. is introduced for the first time in the class
    B. is stated a few minutes before starting the discussion
    C. written on the black board just before the discussion
    D. is announced to the students a few days earlier

11. **What should be the ideal mode of talking to be adopted by a teacher while giving a classroom lecture?**
    A. Loud enough and high pitched to prevent students from ignoring any single word
    B. Just high enough to be heard by all
    C. Just loud enough and slow enough to be heard and assimilated by all students
    D. Very loud in order to rouse the attention of every student in the class

12. **What do you mean by the term 'feed back' in print media communication?**
    A. Special articles published in newspapers
    B. Views raised in the editorials of newspapers
    C. Editor's comments on the news published in the news paper
    D. Letters to the editor published in the news paper

13. Which of the following is an example of 'verbal communication'?

A. Ravi recites a poem while in the bathroom

B. Arjun describes to his teacher the details of an accident which killed his classmate

C. A small child cries aloud to attract his mothers attention

D. A dumb man gestures to get him water for drinking

14. Teacher uses teaching aids for:

A. making his teaching interesting

B. making his teaching more meaningful

C. attracting the attention of his students

D. to create an impression of good teaching

15. The term used in the communication process to describe the ;facial expression' of a student' in the classroom, relates to:

A. The message B. The receiver

C. The channel D. the sender

16. Which one of the following will facilitate communication most?

A. The teacher who makes good use of the black board

B. The teacher who speaks clearly and loudly

C. The teacher who will not allow his students to stir in the classroom

D. The teacher who explains the difficult aspects of the content in clear terms

17. Books can be powerful source of communication if:

A. the content is precisely presented using words

B. the content is presented with proper illustrations and illuminating examples

C. the content is presented clearly in the mother tongue

D. the matter is presented in bold colour print

18. The major limitation of mass communication is that:

A. it is very costly

B. the feedback system is weak

C. more time is required to produce the message

D. the success largely depends upon the producer

19. Effective teaching depends largely on:

A. teacher's grasp of the subject taught

B. student's level of intelligence

C. teacher's skill in communication
D. the quality of teacher's planning and preparation for teaching

20. **Classroom communication will be more effective if the teacher:**
A. is a master of his subject
B. uses a number of aids for his teaching
C. discusses the question papers of a number of previous examinations
D. starts his teaching from what students already know and builds new knowledge on them

21. **Which of the following provides greater freedom for the learners to interact actively?**
A. Small-group discussions
B. Large-group interactions
C. Viewing connected educational programmes in the TV
D. Listening to lectures by experts

22. **Which is the most valuable feedback for a teacher, about his teaching?**
A. Comments made by students
B. Comments made by parents
C. Comments made by the co-workers
D. Comments made by the senior administrators

23. **1 will appreciate most a teacher:**
A. who has the ability to keep all students in the class under control
B. who is capable of making interesting extempore presentations in the class
C. who establishes good rapport with his students through proper communication
D. who produces 100 percent result in common examinations

24. **Which one of the following statements is not correct?**
A. Histrionic talents will help a teacher to become a better communicator
B. A speaker with a sense of humour will be an effective communicator
C. Lack of interest of students in what is presented decides the quality of a teacher's communication
D. Effectiveness of the method of communication used by a teacher can be boosted using colourful teaching aids

25. **Which process of communication is best for controlling inattention and noise in a class-room?**

A. Repeat saying "don't talk", loudly, to attract student attention
B. Raising one's voice above the noise of the classroom
C. Involve students in your presentations through questions, activities to be performed encouraging good work, small group discussion, etc.
D. Raise your voice and continue teaching ignoring the noise

26. The test of effectiveness of communication is:
A. the pacing and tone of the words used for communication
B. use of appropriate media for communicating
C. testing the quality of the reception assessed in terms of what is expected by the sender
D. the speed of receiving the message of communication

27. Overhead Projector (OHP) is most appropriately used for:
A. displaying transparencies
B. substituting the blackboard
C. presenting sketches difficult to be drawn
D. magnifying the diagrams for better understanding

28. Which of the following will make classroom communication most effective?
A. Cutting commonplace jokes from time to time
B. Teaching using ideal methods of communication with proper student participation
C. Speaking with authority and asserting by the teacher
D. Permitting students to cut jokes about their classmates

29. There will be better communication if the teacher:
A. reads out from notes prepared after referring to authentic sources
B. gives extempore talk without usual preparation
C. prepare the sequence in advance and refer to the points before teaching
D. rearranging the topics in a logical sequence and frequently quotes from various other sources

30. Verbal communication is least effective for the development of:
A. attitudes B. relationships
C. concepts D. skills

31. Failure of the teacher to communicate his ideas properly to the students may result in:
A. classroom indiscipline
B. loss of interest among students

C. increase in the number of drop-outs

D. all the above

32. Of the following mass media, the one most effective for deep level learning is:

A. News paper B. T.V discussions

C. Radio discussions D. Referring periodicals

33. Which of the following is not a teaching aid?

A. Blackboard B. Calculator

C. Television D. Computer

34. Communication in the class room often fails because:

A. students do not follow the presentation

B. teacher is ineffective in delivering the message

C. students are generally not interested in classroom learning

D. there is no proper learning atmosphere in schools

35. The teacher's communication in the class will be more effective if the lecture begins with:

A. questions for testing previous learning on the topic

B. presentation of an overview of what is to be learnt

C. highlighting of the relevance of the topic

D. stressing the importance of the topic for the final examinations

36. In communication, perception, retention and recall are:

A. source variables B. message variables

C. channel variables D. receiver variables

37. Four strategies related to teacher-pupil communication are given below:

1. the teacher comes fully prepared and delivers the lecture

2. the students come fully prepared and engage in active discussion among themselves

3. teacher and students discuss different aspects of the topic and evolve their conclusions

4. teacher explains the sub-topics with the help of multisensory aids

Which combination of the above is the ideal method of communication?

A. (1) only B. (2) and (3)

C. (1) and (2) D. (1), (3) and (4)

38. **The most important hurdle in communication is:**
A. the human factor
B. the language factor
C. the absence of the technology for teaching
D. none of the above

39. **To make one's teaching more effective one should depend most on his:**
A. knowledge of subject-matter
B. feed back from students
C. the efficacy of one's class management
D. careful use of teaching aids

40. **Which one of the following is most important for effective teaching?**
A. Systematic use of black board
B. Ability to speak clearly and loudly
C. maintaining classroom discipline
D. Skill in explaining difficult aspects of content in lucid terms with illustrative example

41. **Which of the following will not hamper effective communication in the class?**
A. Use of lengthy statements
B. Use of ambiguous statements
C. Use of self-explaining statement using simple language
D. Use of statement which help the student to draw his/her own conclusions about what is taught

42. **The most effective teaching of a complex learning unit can be done if the learners are helped to:**
A. make profuse use of charts, maps and diagrams
B. make wide use of black board presentations
C. making lesson presentations with the help of a film projector
D. making the lesson meaningful using proper verbal explanations

43. **Classroom communication will be most effective if:**
A. it is delivered slowly and clearly
B. it is delivered in a peaceful classroom atmosphere
C. it is done in such a way that reaches all the receivers completely
D. it reaches the receiver as intended by the sender

44. **Effective communication takes place in a classroom when:**
    A. the source is attractive and authoritarian
    B. the message is designed with the learners as the focal concept
    C. modern communication technologies are widely used
    D. receivers are treated as passive recipients of knowledge

45. **A teacher delivering a lecture will be able to augment the quality of his communication if he:**
    A. prepares teaching notes in advance and uses it for his teaching
    B. refers to a note he has prepared while lecturing
    C. gives extempore talk interspersed with familiar examples and anecdotes while delivering the lecture
    D. uses eloquent language and humorous episodes

46. **The most important duty of the teacher as a communicator is:**
    A. making the students to reflect on the issue and draw conclusions based on this
    B. imparting knowledge through verbal explanations
    C. discussing the subject collectively in the classroom
    D. using colourful teaching aids for student motivation

47. **T.V. makes stronger impact on students because:**
    A. it is an efficient technological device
    B. it provides visual as well as auditory perceptions which are close to reality
    C. it shows the events of life in a realistic manner
    D. it helps to communicate authentic information in a credible manner

48. **The teacher can make classroom communication more meaningful to the learners by:**
    A. inviting outside experts to deliver lectures
    B. bringing mass media into the classroom
    C. relating the learning material to their life
    D. asking questions to students to test their level of learning

49. **Which of the following can become barriers to the source of communication?**
    (i) Confusion about the message
    (ii) Prejudices of the sender
    (iii) Inability to identify the spirit of the message
    (iv) Disturbed mental state of the sender

A. None of the above B. (i), (ii) and (iv)
C. Only (iii) D. All the four

50. An important limitation of the mass media is that:
A. they are used only by the literate sections of the society
B. the audience is often loosely identified
C. the mass media does not provide any feedback from its users
D. there is no chance for two-way communication

51. The main purpose of a communication process is to:
A. transmit one person's important thoughts to others
B. transmit verbal messages to another person
C. transmit non-verbal messages to another person
D. share thoughts between communicators and receivers

52. The best venue for communication between a teacher and his students is:
A. the class-room
B. a spot visited by people interested in sight seeing
C. the school assembly
D. all the above

53. Communication of teacher's thoughts to students means:
A. imparting knowledge
B. imparting social skills
C. transmission of human thought
D. training in the use of knowledge

54. Below are given some of the major components of teacher's communication in the class room. Which of the following combinations of these components is most appropriate?
Components (i) audible (ii) effective (iii) pictorial (iv) continuous (v) interesting
A. (i), (ii) and (iii) B. (i), (ii) and (iv)
C. (i), (iii) and (Iv) D. (i), (ii) and (v)

55. Informal communication network within the organization is known as:
A. Interpersonal Communication
B. Intrapersonal Communication
C. Mass Communication
D. Grapevine Communication

56. Which state brings out the maximum number of periodicals for public information?

A. Uttar Pradesh B. Tamil Nadu
C. Kerala D. Punjab

57. The main objective of a public broadcasting system is:

A. Information, Entertainment and Education
B. Entertainment, Information and Interaction
C. Education, Interaction and Entertainment
D. Entertainment only

58. The competency of an effective communicator can be judged on the basis of:

A. the personality of the communicator
B. experience of the communicator in the field
C. effectiveness of the interaction of the communicator with his target audience
D. ability of the communicator to meet the needs of his target audience

59. An effective communication does not require:

A. changes in the speech pattern used by the communicator
B. appropriate changes in the gestures used by the communicator
C. mastery of content by the communicator
D. the communicator to have a pleasing personality

60. The instrument used to project opaque and transparent objects.

A. Overhead Projector B. Episcope
C. Slide Projector D. Epidiascope

61. Which of the following provides the most valuable feed back for a teacher?

A. Comments by his present-day students
B. Analysis of student responses in their answer sheets
C. Comments by his colleagues
D. Comments of his former students

62. One major difference between the class room teacher and the country wide classroom teacher is that:

A. The country-wide class room teacher has different media at his disposal
B. The country-wide class room caters to the needs of a large audience
C. The country-wide class room teacher takes the learners outside the class room
D. All the above

63. **In what way does communication in small group differ from that of large group?**
   A. Small group provides more interaction among the participants
   B. Interaction in a small group will be more restrictive
   C. Small group requires less time to communicate a message
   D. Large-group communication provides for larger feedback facilities

64. **Effective communication requires all the following except:**
   A. voice modulation
   B. use of illustration
   C. an impressing appearance
   D. student motivation

65. **The teacher's communication will be more effective:**
   A. if the teacher is a master in the subject
   B. if he is an authority in communication
   C. if he relates the message to the already known aspects of the subject
   D. if he is very enthusiastic in communicating ideas

66. **I will appreciate most, a teacher:**
   A. who has a strict disciplinary control over his students
   B. who is capable of making attractive extempore presentations
   C. who establishes rapport with his students through the magic of his communication
   D. who produces 100% result in the examinations

67. **The teacher's communication in the class will be more effective if the lecture is begun with:**
   A. questions leading to the topic presented
   B. the presentation of a global concept of which the new topic will be a sub-topic
   C. a verbal introduction of the relevance of the topic
   D. an explanation of how learning of the topic will be useful for the common examination to follow

68. **Effective communication takes place when:**
   A. the source of communication is credible
   B. message delivering strategy has been designed keeping in view the characteristics of the receivers
   C. modern communication technology is used for communication
   D. message is communicated through the medium of mother tongue

69. We can observe a person's internal feelings through:

A. the way he walks B. his facial expression

C. his mode of dressing D. the language he uses for communication

70. A good listener is one who:

A. listens to everything the other person wants to tell you

B. gives his ear only to listen to important matters

C. listens with appreciation whatever the other person has to say

D. notes down everything the other person wants to tell you

71. A good speaker is one who:

A. speaks fluently

B. conveys matters speedily

C. takes into account the need and nature of his audience

D. reads out the matter from a prepared note

72. Failure of the teacher to communicate his ideas well to the students may result in:

A. classroom indiscipline

B. loss of students' interest in the topic

C. increased number of absentees in the class

D. all of the above

73. Communication in the classroom often fails because:

A. the students have no interest in the topic being taught

B. there is lot of noise around the classroom

C. the students dislike learning

D. the method used by the teacher is ineffective

74. Which one of the following statement most appropriately describes an effective teacher?

A. All good communicators are teachers

B. All teachers are good communicators

C. Effective communicators alone can become effective teachers

D. All effective teachers are effective communicators

75. Which one of the following statements describes best the term 'classroom communication'?

A. Formal B. Informal

C. Nonformal D. None of the above

76. Communication inside the classroom and communication outside the classroom are:

A. different

B. not different

C. have few things in common

D. are never meant to be the same

77. Four elements of communication are give below. Arrange the elements in the order of decreasing importance.

1. Context 2. Message 3. Receiver 4. Source

A. 1, 4, 3 and 2 B. 4, 1, 3 and 2

C. 3, 1, 2 and 4 D. 2, 3, 1 and 4

78. In classroom communication, select the source from the following

A. Teacher only B. Students only

C. Teacher and students D. None of the above

79. Classroom communication (teaching) is not effective when:

A. channel used for communication is inappropriate

B. appropriate feedback is not practised

C. message is not received properly

D. the messages are not sent properly

80. Encoding is to source (sender) as decoding is to:

A. message B. receiver

C. channel D. feedback

81. In classroom communication, which one of the following types of communication is predominant?

A. Verbal B. Nonverbal

C. Intra-personal D. All of the above

82. Effective classroom communication includes:

A. verbal communication

B. Nonverbal communication

C. Verbal and nonverbal communication

D. None of the above

83. There will be better communication in the class if the teacher:

A. prepares a proper teaching design

B. sends the message using appropriate strategies

C. uses the verbal channel exclusively

D. uses verbal and nonverbal channels inter-changeably

84. **A lecture-demonstration is effective than lecture method in the sense that the former provides:**

A. multi sensory channels for students

B. single channel for communication

C. varying stimuli for students/teacher

D. uses feedback in the communication

85. **Which one among the following is not a barrier in classroom communication?**

A. Feedback from communication

B. Ineffective language used for communication

C. Emotional problems of the communication

D. Lack of previous knowledge of the receiver

86. **A teacher will be an effective communicator if she/he:**

A. is clear about 'why and what' of his communication

B. makes extended use of ICT in the classroom

C. uses humorous episodes

D. has lots os histrionic talents

87. **Which among the following will be a better strategy of communication?**

A. Speaking loudly than anyone in the group

B. Demanding the attention of the group and speak when the group is calm

C. Forcing the members of the group to listen to the communication

D. Sharing the ideas with others, by waiting for ones turn

88. **Which of the following provides for a better feedback analysis?**

A. Presentation using LCD projector

B. Use of small group discussion

C. Viewing country wide classroom programmes

D. Lecture presentation by experts

89. **The major purpose of feedback analysis is:**

A. to modify the content presented

B. to find fault with what is received

C. to find fault with the source of the communication

D. to modify the process of communication

90. **Communication will be effective if:**

A. the source is authoritative

B. the content is need-based

C. the content is presented using power point

D. more opportunities are provided to the receiver to ask questions

91. **What is the major demerit of communication in the country-wide classroom (CWCR) system?**

A. Inadequate feed back

B. Insufficient time

C. Transmission distractions

D. Inaccessible lessons (materials)

92. **Which of the following is an example of a verbal communication?**

A. Seta reads her lessons loudly

B. Ravi uses sign language because he is deaf.

C. The postman reads out a letter to the blind lady

D. The baby cries to attract its mother's attention.

93. **Which is the most valuable feedback for a teacher in higher education?**

A. More students get distinction in his subject

B. More students opt his subject for study

C. The appreciation of the head of the institution

D. The appreciation of the co-workers

94. **Communication can be more effective if:**

A. the source uses a lot of teaching aids

B. the receivers are highly motivated

C. the message is illustrative

D. the electronic media are used

95. **Retention and recall are:**

A. message variables

B. receiver variables

C. feedback variables

D. source variables

96. Which of the following will provide better interpersonal interaction?

A. Small group discussion

B. Lecture presentation

C. Viewing films followed by discussion

D. Seminar presentation by experts

97. Which of the following diagrams represents communication process best?

A 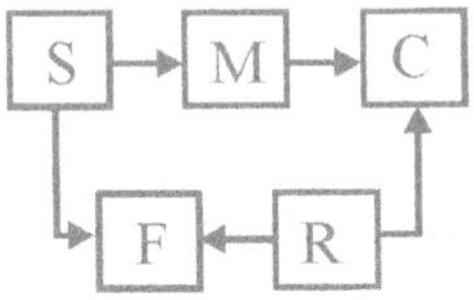

B 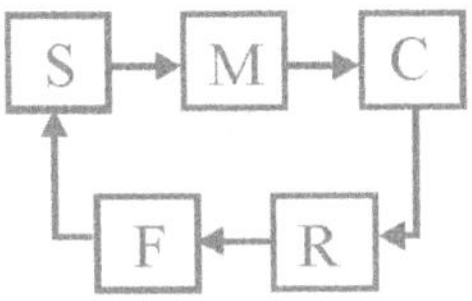

C 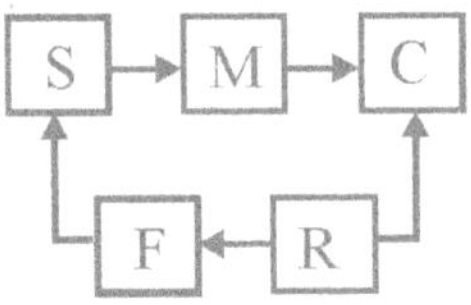

D 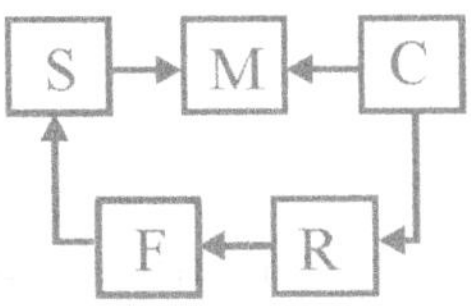

98. Which one of the following situation will not distort classroom communication?

A. Reversing, evaluating, focussing

B. Evaluating, focussing, illustrating

C. Evaluating, focussing, exaggerating

D. Focussing, reversing, illustrating

99. In distance education, multimedia approach is adopted because:

A. it enables self learning

B. it helps the learner to get acquainted with realities of the world outside

C. the quality of education improves with the use of modern technology

D. multimedia compensates for the limited interpersonal interaction between peers and teachers

100. The teacher's communication in the classroom will be more effective only if she/he:

A. uses multi sensory instructional aids

B. supplements the textual materials with life's experiences

C. motivates the students and understands their learning needs

D. can use language effectively

101. Which is the best feedback for a university teacher?

A. Evaluation of answer sheets and marks scored by students

B. Praise and comments made by students to others about the teacher

C. Appreciation from co-workers and authorities

D. The level of student's involvement and enthusiasm in attending her class

102. Which one of the following provides the maximum interpersonal communication?

A. Lecture presentation

B. Group discussion

C. Seminars

D. Brainstorming sessions

103. Feedback in the communication system helps to:

A. make the communication exact and precise

B. understand more about the content

C. helps to identify the defects in the methods used for communication

D. helps to identify the drawbacks of the receiver of the communication

104. Which one of the following will present the distortion of effective communication in the classroom?

A. Explanations by the teacher in a form which enables the students to draw their own conclusions

B. Extempore lectures by the teacher

C. Objective-based precise deliberations

D. Teacher quoting from different authors different sources to create interest

105. Classroom interaction based on the topic will be more effective if the topic of discussion is:

A. made known to students earlier to prepare the background for learning
B. written on the blackboard just before the commencement of the class
C. stated before the beginning of the class
D. only implicitly stated and students encouraged to discover it

106. Which of the following is associated with the element 'feedback' in the classroom communication?
A. Regular attendance of students
B. Questions raised by students
C. Illustrations used by the teacher
D. Respect and adoration for the teacher

107. While presenting your ideas in a classroom it is better to:
(i) recognise that there can be other views
(ii) recognise that students are not a homogenous group
(iii) take dissenting views also into consideration
A. (i) and (iii) B. (iii)
C. (ii) and (iii) D. (i), (ii) and (iii)

108. Perception, retention and recall are:
A. source variables B. message variables
C. receiver variables D. channel variables

109. What is more desirable in a classroom?
A. A teacher delivering a lecture on the basis of the text and his own research
B. A teacher delivering a lecture on the basis of course content and standard books
C. A teacher developing his teaching by helping the students to answer their questions
D. A teacher maintaining strict discipline and paying least attention to student needs

110. Modern communication technology is used in distance education to ensure:
A. their students get a wider and effective understanding of the instructional material
B. their students understand the use of modern technology in education
C. that higher standards are achieved by all students
D. that teaching efficacy can be enhanced and better interpersonal links are established

111. The efficacy of classroom communication often goes down because:

A. the students are mostly inattentive

B. the teacher adopts wrong methods for delivering the message

C. the students have very little interest in the lesson being taught

D. there is lot of disturbance and noise in and around the classroom

112. Which of the following will make communication more effective?

A. Cutting jokes in between

B. Using multi-sensory teaching

C. Speaking with authority

D. Pointing out to the listeners that what is taught is useful

113. Three of the following four terms are alike in a certain way and so they form a group. Which is the one that does not belong to the common group?

A. Interpersonal communication

B. Intrapersonal communication

C. Group communication

D. Grapevine communication

114. Students learn more from a teacher who:

A. in friendly and affectionate to his students

B. has the ability to communicate his ideas precisely and clearly

C. is gentle and soft to the students

D. is hard-working and expects his students to do hard work

115. Which one of the following statements is not correct?

A. A good communicator is one who can teach complex subjects in schools

B. A good communicator is one who has a good sense of humour

C. A good communicator is one who is widely read

D. A good communicator is one who has a good command over language

116. The most powerful barrier to communication in the classroom is:

A. noise in the classroom

B. confusion about how to present a topic on the part of the teacher

C. outside disturbance while teaching

D. non-availability of proper teaching aids

117. There will be better communication in a lecture if a teacher:

A. reads from prepared notes

B. prepares the notes well in advance and uses them as a guide

C. gives an extempore talk

D. talks extempore, but supplementing them with diagrams and illustrations

118. Which is the most desirable procedure to be adopted by a teacher to make teaching effective?

A. Should make good use of the blackboard

B. Should speak clearly and loudly

C. Should not allow students to make noise in the class

D. Should explain difficult topics using simple language

119. When a teacher cannot find a good answer to a question asked by a student he should:

A. not hesitate to give a wrong answer to save his face

B. say that he would answer the question the next day after consulting the concerned books

C. ask the student to meet him after the class for further discussion

D. discourage the student to ask questions in the class

120. T.V channel launched for covering only engineering subjects is known as:

A. Gyan Darshan

B. Vyas

C. Eklavya

D. Kisan

121. The service launched by India to combat Radio Cylone is called:

A. Gyan Vani B. Yuva Vani

C. Vividh Bharati D. Ekalavya

122. The competency of an effective communicator can be judged by:

A. the personality of communicator

B. the experience of the communicator in the field

C. the efficacy with which the communicator interacts with the target audience

D. ability of the communicator to meet the needs of his target audience

123. A group discussion is a form of:

A. Dyadic communication B. Multiadic communication

C. Mass communication D. None of these

124. Dyadic communication means the transfer of a message from one person:

A. to another person B. to a group of persons

C. to a mass audience D. none of these

125. Which one of the following is true for informal communication?

A. It has a high speed

B. It helps to increase high speed

C. It enhances performance of people through grapevine

D. It promotes harmony and helps to solve problem

126. National Press Day is celebrated on:

A. December 14 B. March 15

C. November 16 D. July 30

127. Effective communication produces:

A. happiness on the part of the receiver

B. acceptance on the part of the receiver

C. access to other people

D. deeper thinking about the theme communicated

128. Orkut is a part of:

A. Intrapersonal communication

B. Mass communication

C. Interpersonal communication

D. Group communication

129. What is paid news syndrome?

A. Paying politicians for news

B. Taking money for publishing views as news

C. Paying agents for news

D. Offering money to news sources

130. In downward communication, messages:

A. flow from bottom to the top of an organization

B. flow from the top to the bottom of organization

C. get exchanged between the members of the top brass

D. none of the above

131. Closed circuit television is useful:

A. only for a restricted audience at a place

B. for large group communication

C. only for the poor students of a classroom

D. none of the above

132. Television education programme is useful because:

A. it can present the natural phenomenon of the world in natural setting

B. it can magnify microscopic forms of life which can be presented through the TV

C. it allows large audience to view it clearly

D. all these

133. Teaching on T.V is superior to classroom instruction because:

A. very large class size is possible when TV is used

B. experts can be used more economically for teaching difficult topics

C. teaching matters can be recorded for reuse

D. all of these

134. Which one of the following skills has the largest share in communication in schools and colleges?

A. Listening B. Reading

C. Writing D. Speaking

135. All the following are components of listening except:

A. hearing B. attending

C. answering D. remembering

136. Effective teaching is by and large a function of the teacher's:

A. scholarship

B. professional efficiency

C. ability for verbal expression

D. aptitude for the profession

137. The messages are changed into symbols through the process of:

A. encoding B. decoding

C. sign language D. none of the above

138. Communication basically is a ....process.

A. one way B. two way

C. multiway D. complex

139. What are the three types of communication?

A. Written, Oral, Verbal

B. Oral, Verbal, Nonverbal

C. Verbal, Nonverbal, Gestural

D. Written, Oral, Gestural

Answer keys

1.C	2.C	3.A	4.D	5.C	6.D	7.D	8.B	9.A	10.D
11.C	12.D	13.B	14.B	15.B	16.D	17.B	18.B	19.C	20.D
21.A	22.A	23.C	24.C	25.C	26.C	27.A	28.B	29.D	30.D
31.D	32.B	33.B	34.B	35.B	36.D	37.C	38.A	39.B	40.D
41.C	42.C	43.D	44.B	45.C	46.A	47.B	48.C	49.B	50.C
51.D	52.A	53.C	54.D	55.D	56.C	57.A	58.D	59.D	60.D
61.A	62.D	63.A	64.C	65.C	66.C	67.B	68.B	69.B	70.C
71.C	72.D	73.D	74.D	75.A	76.A	77.A	78.C	79.A	80.B
81.A	82.C	83.D	84.A	85.A	86.A	87.D	88.B	89.D	90.B
91.A	92.C	93.A	94.B	95.B	96.A	97.B	98.B	99.D	100.A
101.D	102.B	103.A	104.A	105.A	106.B	107.A	108.C	109.C	110.D
111.B	112.B	113.D	114.B	115.A	116.B	117.B	118.D	119.B	120.C
121.C	122.D	123.B	124.A	125.C	126.C	127.D	128.D	129.B	130.B
131.A	132.D	133.D	134.D	135.C	136.C	137.A	138.B	139.D	

Unit - V

REASONING (INCLUDING MATHEMATICAL)

1. MATHEMATICAL REASONING TEST
2. INSERT THE MISSING TEST
3. NUMBER SERIES TEST
4. LETTER SERIES TEST
5. CODING – DECODING TEST
6. BLOOD RELATIONSHIPS TEST
7. CLASSIFICATION TEST

Unit - V

REASONING (INCLUDING MATHEMATICAL)

The basic idea behind all sorts of reasoning tests is to assess an individual's intelligence which in popular language means an individual's ability to reason using abstractions - abstract concepts and processes involving abstractions. This is a test to see how well you can solve problems involving deep analysis and unusual/original thought processes. The questions are designed to assess your ability to deal with different abstract ideas and symbols and deduce their interrelationships and use them for problem solving. A careful study and practice of these questions would familiarize you with the techniques employed for setting the questions so that you can take the examination with greater confidence.

If we examine the syllabus of the UGC test and analyze the question papers of the previous NET/JRF examinations, we can see that the items given below are typical of the items included in the test.

1. MATHEMATICAL REASONING TEST

This section deals with questions on simple mathematical operations, which measure one's ability in numerical reasoning. The four fundamental items are based on the arithmetical operations – addition, subtraction, multiplication and division. The questions involving these operations have been prepared using incorrect symbols. The candidate has to substitute the real symbols and solve the problems.

Example

If $19+1 = 18$

$33+3 = 30$

$14+2 = ?$

A. 12 B. 16 C. 28 D. 7

Correct answer is 12. The plus sign is used in the place of the minus sign. Hence 14+2 is really $14 - 2 = 12$.

Another example

$3 \times 4 = 28$

$4 \times 5 = 45$

$5 \times 6 = 66$

$6 \times 7 = ?$

The answer is 91. $3 \times 4 = 28$ stands for $(3 + 4) \times 4 = 7 \times 4 = 28$

$4 \times 5 = 45$ stands for $(4 + 5) \times 5 = 9 \times 5 = 45$

$5 \times 6 = 66$ stands for $(5 + 6) \times 6 = 11 \times 6 = 66$

Hence 6×7 is $(6 + 7) \times 7 = 13 \times 7 = 91$

Similarly you can work out the problems below:

1. If $4 + 5 = 20$
   $6 + 6 = 36$
   $6 + 7 = ?$

   A.36 B.42 C.54 D.49

2. If $8 \times 3 = 26$
   $16 \times 5 = 82$
   $32 \times 2 = ?$

   A.99 B.64 C.66 D.18

3. If $2 \times 2 = 8$
   $3 \times 3 = 18$
   $4 \times 4 = ?$

   A.16 B.64 C.32 D.18

4. If $5 \times 4 = 45$
   $6 \times 3 = 54$
   $7 \times 2 = 63$
   $8 \times 4 = ?$

   A.48 B.96 C.72 D.36

5. If $8 \times 7 = 65$
   $9 \times 2 = 81$
   $5 \times 7 = 53$
   $6 \times 4 = ?$

   A.24 B.42 C.34 D.46

6. Supply the missing number
   $45 - 24 = 4524$
   $92 - 81 = 9281$
   $13 - 11 = ?$

   A.1113 B.1310 C.1311 D.1111

7. Supply the missing number.

5	8	3
3	7	4
4	?	5

A.15 B.6 C.3 D.9

8. Supply the missing number.

3	6	4
12	18	?
4	3	7

A.27 B.21 C.28 D.18

9. Supply the missing number.

8	6	10
1	2	?
7	4	7

A.2 B. 5 C. 3 D. 1

10. If we assume $64 \times 52 = 17$
$48 \times 56 = 23$
$74 \times 35 = 19$
What can 84×37 be?
A.22 B.20 C.21 D.18

11. If $65 - 54 = 2$
$86 - 40 = 10$
$324 - 312 = 3$
$94 - 82 = ?$
A.3 B.12 C.20 D.10

12. Supply the missing number
$56 - 72 = 99$
$62 - 34 = 56$
$23 - 16 = 35$
$42 - 51 = ?$
A.66 B. 74 C.20 D.36

13. If $52 \times 45 = 30$
$73 \times 21 = 23$
$84 \times 52 = 42$
$62 \times 43 = ?$
A. 20 B. 30 C. 24 D. 32

14. If 53 ÷ 31 = 2
    45 ÷ 45 = 1
    69 ÷ 32 = 3
    97 ÷ 26 = ?

    A. 1 B. 2 C. 3 D. 4

15. If 4 2 5 = 2 2
    6 4 8 = 5 2
    7 4 1 = 1 1
    5 3 8 = ?

    A. 33 B. 42 C. 43 D. 15

16. If 8 7 9 = 8
    6 2 5 = 1
    5 8 6 = 9
    7 8 5 = ?

    A. 7 B. 0 C. 9 D. 6

17. Find out the missing number in the fourth column. You may assume that the numbers in each column follow the same rule.

6	5	8	9
7	3	3	2
1	2	3	2
42	30	72	?

    A. 60 B. 36 C. 102 D. 112

18. Fill in the missing number in the arrangement.
    They are arranged on the basis of a common principle.

5	7	9
9	6	4
36	36	?

    A. 40 B. 32 C. 36 D. 42

19. The following arrangement is based on certain principle.
    Keeping this in mind, fill in the vacant space.

8	6	4
3	?	7
14	16	18

    A. 4 B. 5 C. 6 D. 8

20. Supply the missing number in the matrix assuming that the numbers have been arranged following a common principle.

4	3	5	7
7	6	8	9
8	2	12	?
20	16	28	50

A. 13 B. 14 C. 16 D. 18

21. If $58 \times 12 = 4$

$37 \times 96 = 5$

$11 \times 20 = 2$

$42 \times 12 = ?$

A. 2 B. 3 C. 4 D. 5

22. If $5 + 3 = 16$

$7 + 3 = 40$

$9 + 3 = ?$

A. 70 B. 71 C. 72 D. 73

23. If 5+3+2 = 151022

9+2+4 = 183652

8+6+3 = 482466

5+4+5 = 202541

7+2+5 = ?

A. 143547 B. 351447 C. 471435 D. 144735

Answers with explanation

1.B. The symbol + denotes ×. So, $6 \times 7 = 42$

2.C. It is $(32 \times 2) + 2 = 66$

3.C. It is $(4 \times 4) \times 2 = 32$ or sum of the squares

4.B. $8 \times (8 + 4) = 96$

5.B. Invert the product

6.C. Delete the – to get the answer

7.D. It is $4 + 5 = 9$

8.C. It is $4 \times 7 = 28$

9.C. It is $10 - 7 = 3$

10.A. It is $8 + 4 + 3 + 7 = 22$

11.A. (1) 94 − 82 = 12, 1 + 2 = 3
(2) 9 − 8 = 1, 4 − 2 = 2, 1 + 2 = 3
(3) 9 + 4 = 13, 8 + 2 = 10, 13 − 10 = 3

12.D. It is sum of 1st × sum of 2nd ie. (4 + 2) × (5 + 1) = 36

13.C. It is 6 × 2 = 12, 4 × 3 = 12, 12 + 12 = 24

14.B. It is 9 + 7 = 16, 2 + 6 = 8, 16 ÷ 8 = 2

15.C. (5 × 8) + 3 = 43

16.D. It is (5 + 8) − 7 = 6

17.B. It is 9 × 2 × 2 = 36

18.B. It is (9 − 1) × 4 = 32

19.B. It is (16 − 6) ÷ 2 = 5 or (3 + 7) ÷ 2 = 5

20.A. It is 7 × 9 − X = 50
X = 63 − 50
= 13

21.B. It is 4 + 2 + 1 + 2 = 9, Square root of 9 is 3

22.C. Square of 9 = 81 and square of 3 = 9.
It is 81 − 9 = 72

23.A. It is 7 × 2 = 14, 7× 5 = 35
14+35− 2 = 47.
Therefore, the answer is 143547

2. INSERT THE MISSING TEST

This test is presented using a diagram. Certain numbers are given in the diagram. The numbers follow a pattern which you have to identify. Use this pattern to identify the missing number in the diagram.

1. Which number will replace the question mark in the diagram given below?

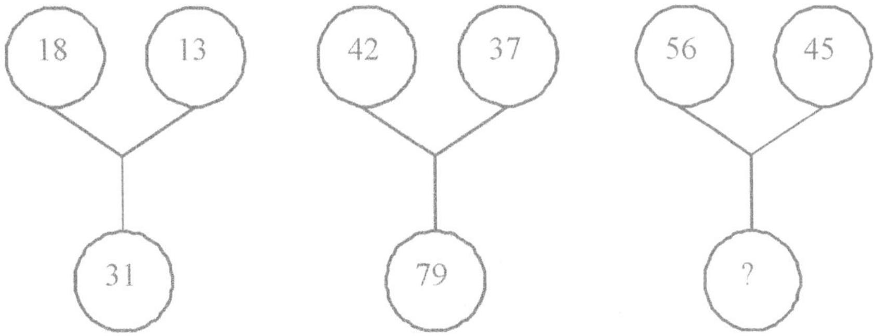

A. 20 B.99 C. 101 D. 110

Note: Pattern. By adding the numbers in the top two circles, we can get the number in the bottom circle. The missing number = 56+45 = 101.

2. Find the missing number

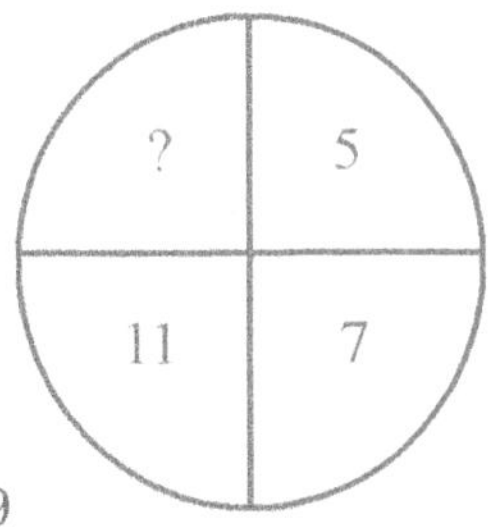

A. 16 B.14 C. 13 D. 9

Hint: By adding 2 with the number in the upper section will give you the number in the lower section. The missing number = 9. Since 9+2 = 11.

3. Find the missing number in the following figure

3	8	19
11	9	10
16	13	?

A.7 B.6 C.1 D.14

Hint: Add columns/rows you have to get 30. Thus we can find the missing number in the third column/third row is 1.

4. Which number is required to replace the question mark?

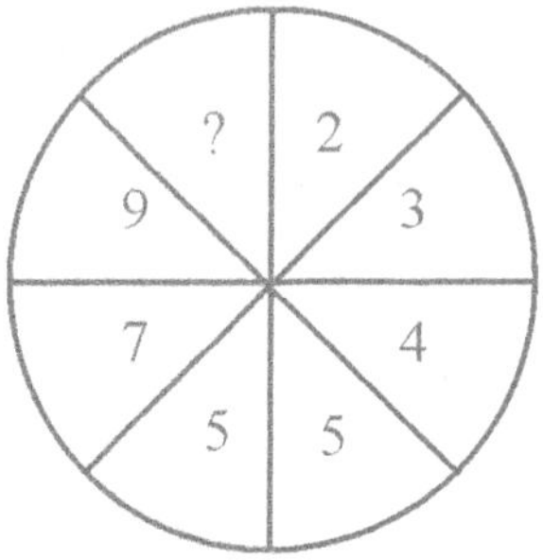

A.10 B.11 C.12 D.13

Hint: On the right continuous numbers and on the left alternative numbers are given in the clockwise direction. Hence the missing number = 11.

5. Find the missing number

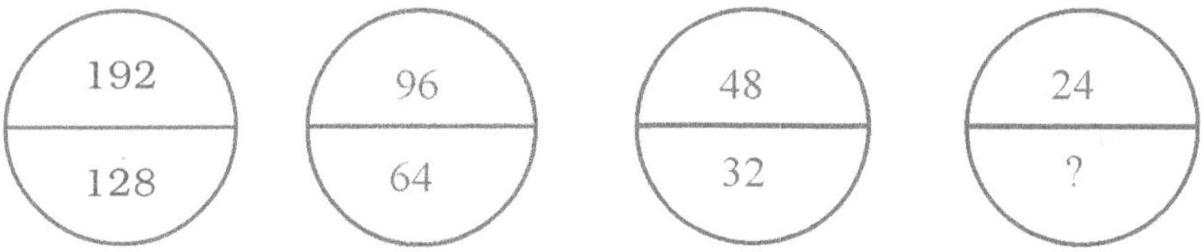

A. 8 B.10 C. 16 D. 21

Hint: Number in the upper half of the circle are formed as follows:

8×24, 8×12, 8×6 and 8×3

The number in the lower half of the circle are found as follows:

8×16, 8×8, 8×4 and 8×2

The missing number = $8 \times 2 = 16$

6. Find the missing number in the space indicated by the question mark.

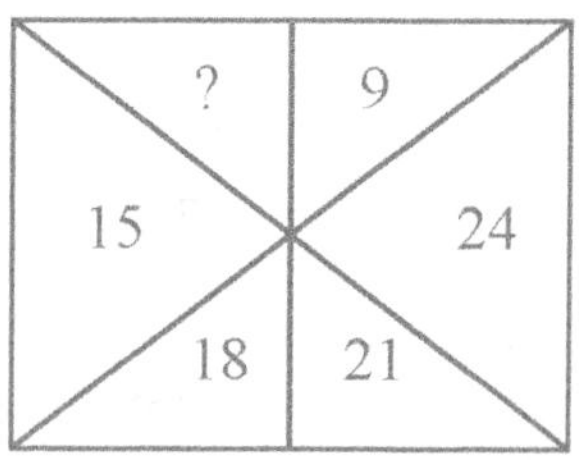

A.27 B.12 C.30 D. 42

Hint: The pattern followed is: 3 is added in the anti clockwise direction. Hence 9 + 3 = 12.

7. Insert the missing number in this series of circles given below:

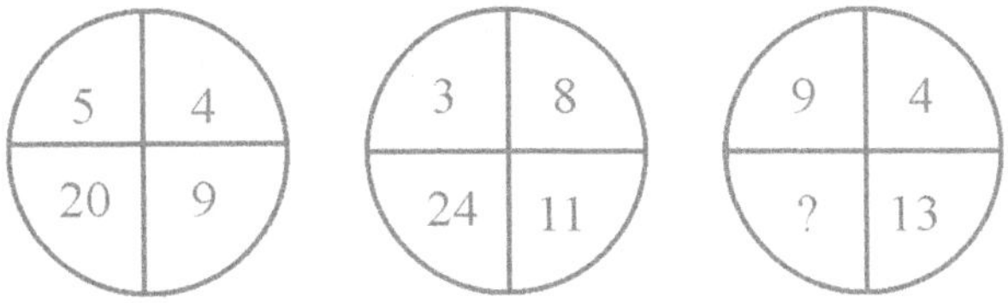

A.117 B.36 C.32 D.26

Hint: On the right hand bottom the sum of the two numbers in the upper section and the left bottom the product of the numbers at the top are given. Hence the answer is $9 \times 4 = 36$

8. Find the missing number in the figure below:

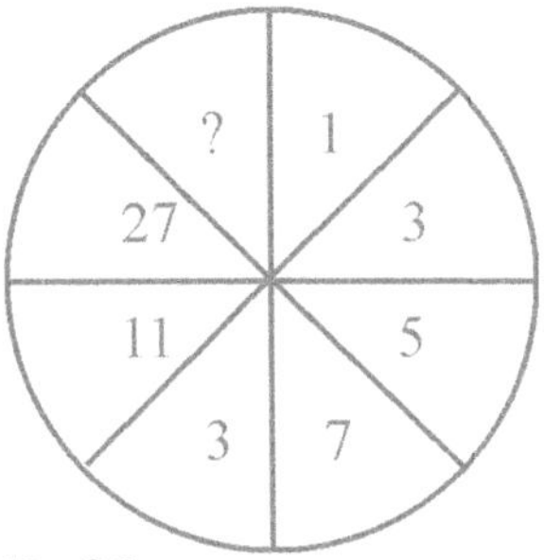

A. 51 B.59 C. 43 D. 36

Hint: The numbers on the right hand side of the sections of the circles are 1, 3, 5, 7. The numbers opposite each number are:

$1 \rightarrow 1^2 + 2 = 3$

$3 \rightarrow 3^2 + 2 = 11$

$5 \rightarrow 5^2 + 2 = 27$

$7 \rightarrow 7^2 + 2 = 49 + 2 = 51$

9. Insert the appropriate numbers in the place of the 2 question marks in the series formed by the four sequences given below:

256	225	?	169
246	205	?	129

A. $\frac{225}{205}$ B. $\frac{196}{166}$ C. $\frac{169}{225}$ D. $\frac{196}{129}$

Hint: The numbers in the upper portion: $16^2, 15^2, 14^2$ *and* 13^2

ie., 256, 225, 196 and 169

Number in the lower portion = $16^2 - 10, 15^2 - 20, 14^2 - 30, 13^2 - 40$

ie., 246, 205, 166 and 129. Hence the missing number is $\frac{196}{166}$

10. Insert the missing number in the small triangle:

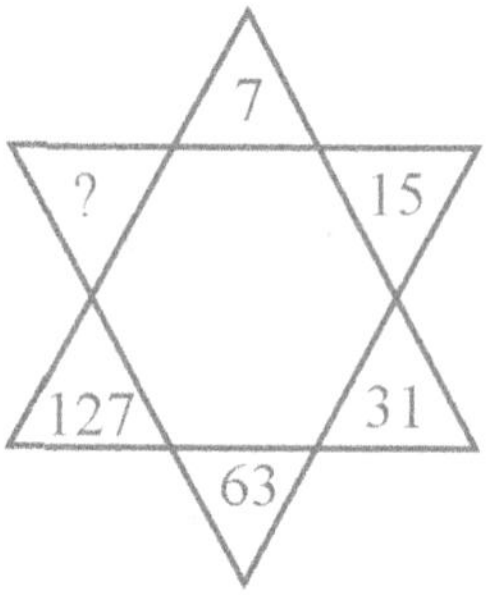

A. 190 B.221 C. 236 D. 255

Hint: The numbers in the small triangles at the end of the whole figure starting from 7 are: 7, 15, 31, 63, 127, ?

This follows the law 7, $(7 \times 2)+1$, $(15 \times 2)+1$, $(31 \times 2)+1$, $(63 \times 2)+1$ and $(127 \times 2)+1$

ie., 7, 15, 31, 63, 127, 255

Hence missing number = 255

11. Insert the missing number

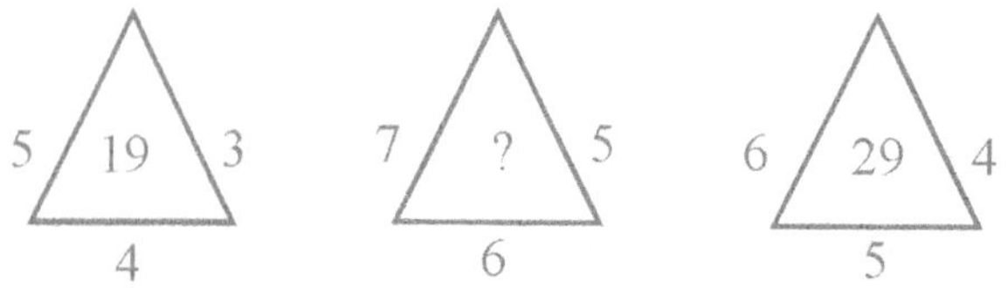

A. 25 B.37 C. 41 D. 45

Hint: The law which governs the numbers within the triangles: Multiply the two figures on the right and left of each triangle and add the figure at the bottom will give the figure within the triangles. Therefore the Ist triangle, the numbers within = 19 = $5 \times 3 + 4$. For third triangle the number within = $6 \times 4 + 5$. For this second triangle the number within = $7 \times 5 + 6 = 41$

12. Which is the correct number to replace the question mark in the figure?

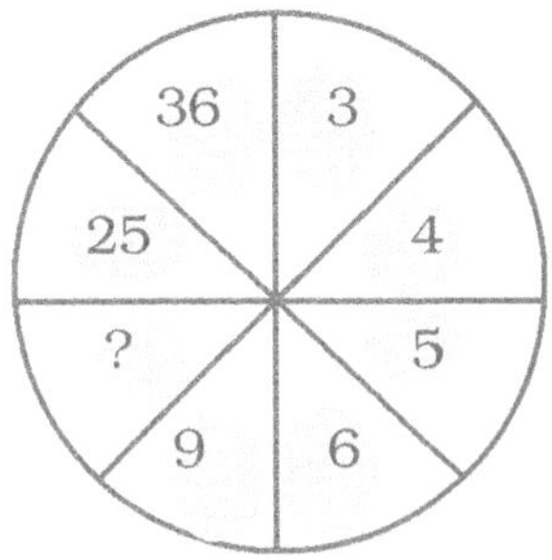

A. 10 B.12 C. 24 D. 16

Hint: Squares are given at the opposite sides. Hence the answer is D.

13. The numbers in each of the three columns and four rows are formed as per certain rules. Using these, identify the missing number in the place of the question mark.

14	9	4
12	7	2
10	5	0
16	11	?

A. 9 B.7 C. 3 D. 6

Hint: The relation existing among the columns. ie., a + b – c = d

14 + 12 – 10 = 16

9 + 7 – 5 = 11

4 + 2 – 0 = 6

Hence the answer is 6.

14. Which number will replace question mark in the fourth circle of the series below?

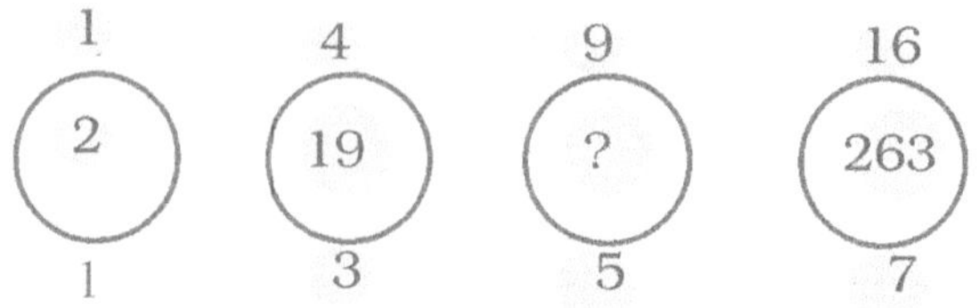

A. 38 B.86 C. 36 D. 258

Hint: The numbers above each circle are 1, 4, 9, 16 viz 1^2, 2^2, 3^2 *and* 4^2.

The number below the circle are 1,3, 5,7 (Ist four odd numbers)

Th number within each circle are $1^2 + 1$, $4^2 + 3$, $9^2 + 5$, *and* $16^2 + 7$ viz 2, 19, 86, 263

The missing number is 86

15. Write the appropriate number in the place of the question mark

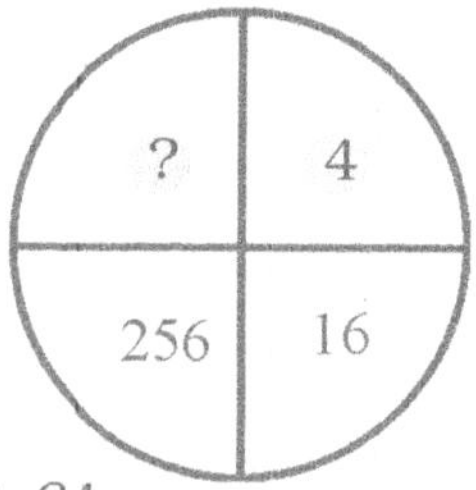

A. 8 B.16 C. 32 D. 64

Hint: Squares are given on left hand side. Hence the missing number is 16

16. Find the missing number

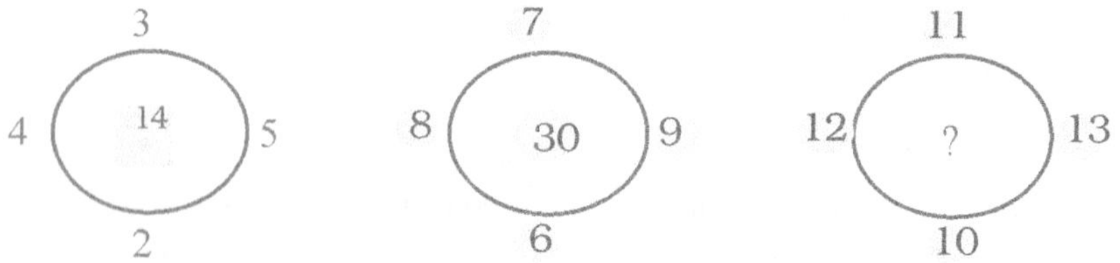

A. 12 B.25 C. 46 D. 48

Hint: The sum of the numbers arround the circle equals the number in the centre of the circkle. The answer is C = 12 + 11+ 13 + 10 = 46

17. Find the missing number

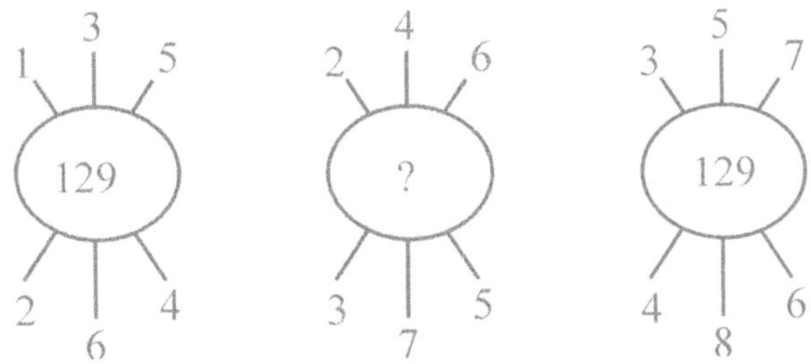

A. 486 B. 129 C. 258 D. 135

Hint: Top number is deducted from the bottom number to get the centre number.

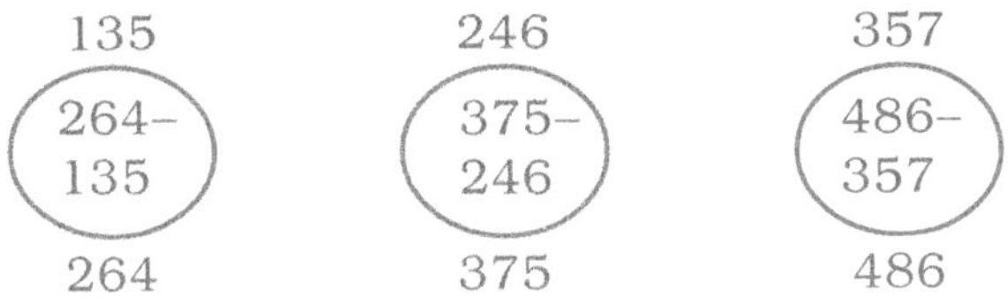

Missing number = 375 – 246 = 129

18. Find the missing number in the following figure

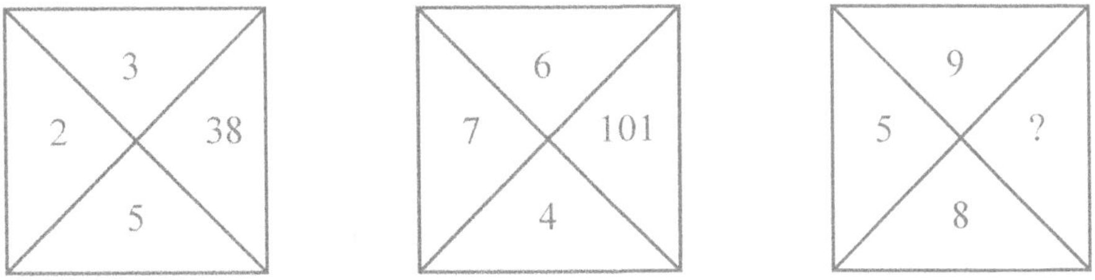

A. 120 B. 141 C. 170 D. 156

Hint: The sum of the squares of the three numbers in the top, left and bottom triangle = number in the right side of the triangle as shown below:

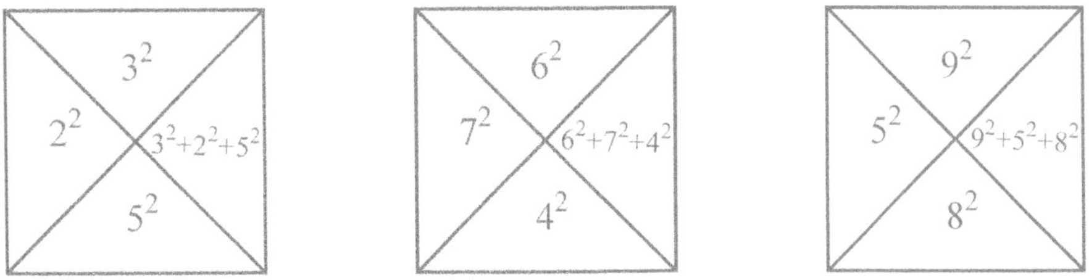

Missing number = $9^2 + 5^2 + 8^2 = 170$

19. Insert the missing number

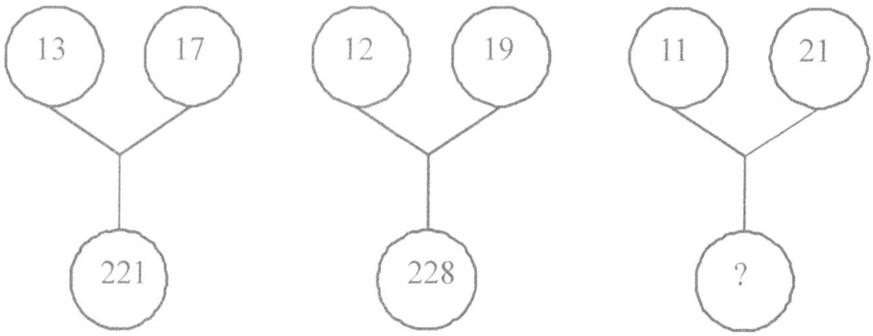

A.229 B.222 C.231 D.331

Hint: Product of numbers in the two upper circles = numbers in the lower circle. Hence 11 × 21 = 231

20. Find the missing number

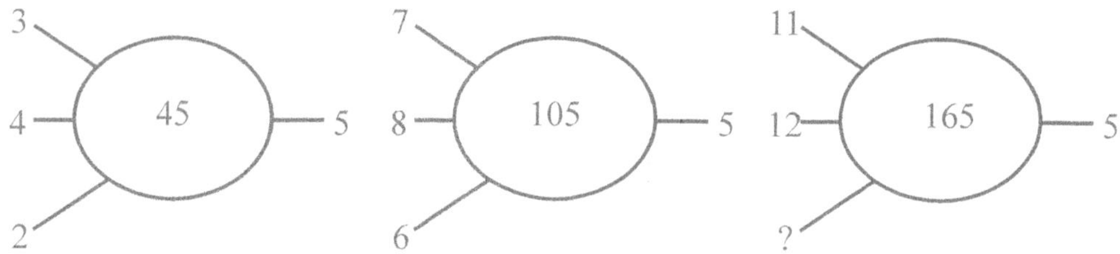

A. 5 B.11 C. 25 D. 10

Hint: The sum of numbers in the left of the circle multiplied by the number on the right of the circle will give the number within the circle. Hence the answer is 10.

21. Fill in the column in the figure given below

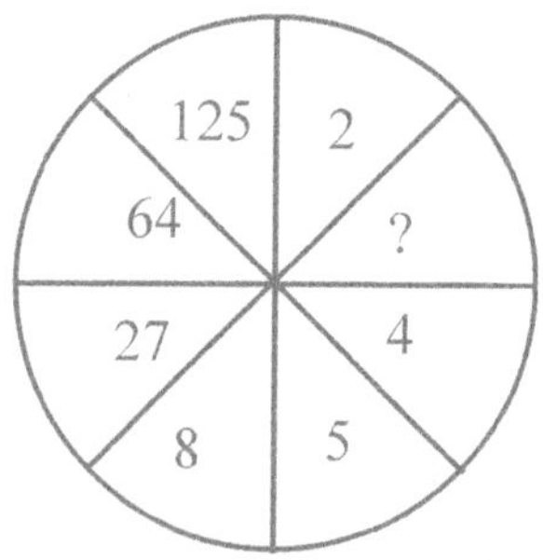

A. 1 B.3 C. 6 D. 64

Hint: Cube of every number on the right side of the circle appears opposite to it as the left side sector of the circle. The missing number is the number whose cube is 27. Hence this number is 3.

22. Select the missing number from the given responses

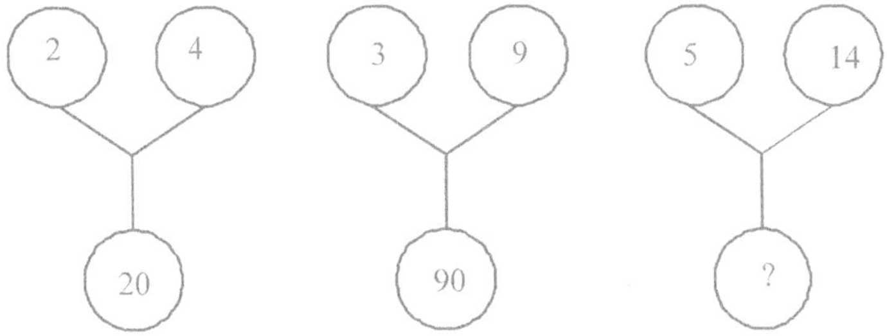

A. 20 B.19 C. 221 D. 110

Hint: The number in the lower circle = sum of the squares of the two numbers in the upper two circles.

Missing number = $5^2 + 14^2 = 221$

23. Find the missing number

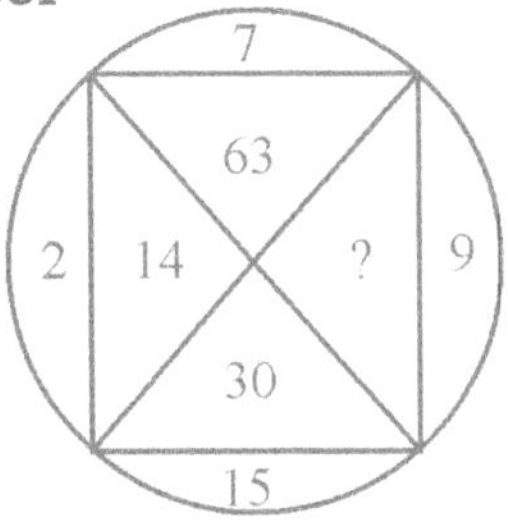

A. 18 B.33 C. 135 D. 145

Hint: Rule - $I \times II = VI$

$II \times III = VII$

$III \times IV = VIII$

$IV \times I = V$

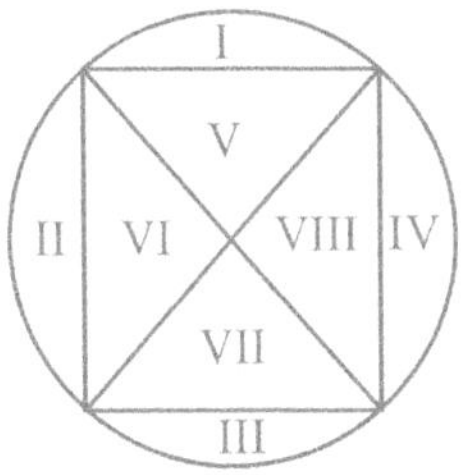

Missing number = $III \times IV = 15 \times 9 = 135$

24. Select the missing number from the given responses

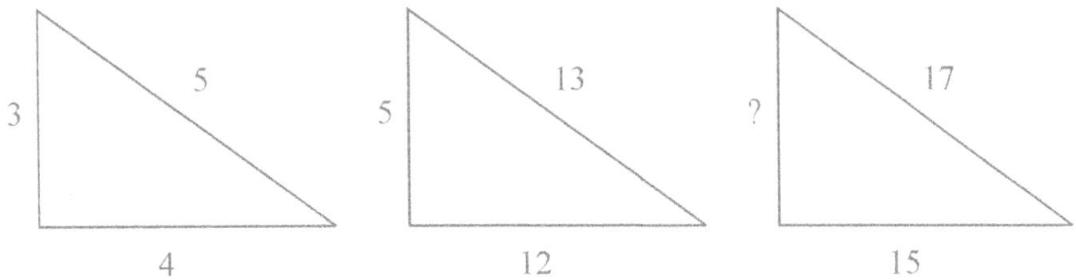

A. 8 B.9 C. 5 D. 6

Hint: The longest side = sum of the squares of two smaller sides.

Thus $3^2 + 4^2 = 5^2$

$$5^2 + 12^2 = 13^2$$

$$x^2 + 15^2 = 17^2$$

Using the last equation $x^2 = 17^2 - 15^2$

$$= 289–225$$

$$= 64$$

$$\therefore x = \sqrt{64}$$

$$= 8$$

25. What is the appropriate number which will replace the question mark at the centre of the third circle?

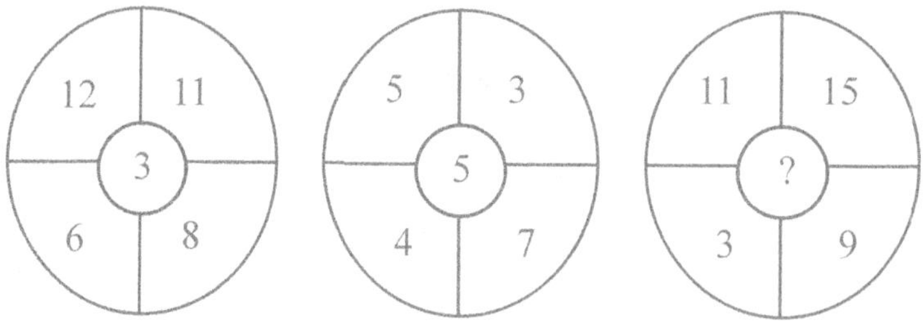

A. 30 B.2 C. 6 D. 38

Hint: Number at the centre of each circle can be found out by summing opposite numbers and finding out the difference between the two sums.

For circle 1 the number at the centre = (12 + 8) – (11 + 6) = 20 – 17 = 3

For circle 2 the number at the centre = (5 + 7) – (3 + 4) = 12 – 7 = 5

For circle 3 the number at the centre (missing number) = (11 + 9) – (15 + 3) = 20 – 18 = 2. Hence the answer (missing figure) = 2.

26. Find the missing number in the series (third figure)

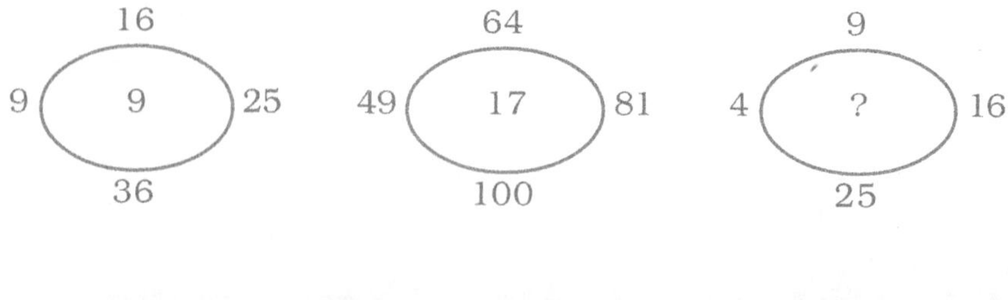

A. 6 B.7 C. 8 D. 9

Hint: For every circle, the following rule is valid

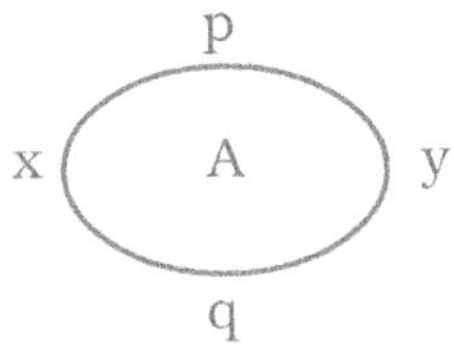

$$A = \frac{1}{2}\left(\sqrt{x} + \sqrt{y} + \sqrt{p} + \sqrt{q}\right)$$

For the last circle answer $A = \frac{1}{2}\left(\sqrt{4} + \sqrt{9} + \sqrt{16} + \sqrt{25}\right)$

$$= \frac{1}{2}(2 + 3 + 4 + 5)$$

$$= \frac{1}{2}(14) = 7$$

27. Which number would meaningfully replace the question mark in the figure below?

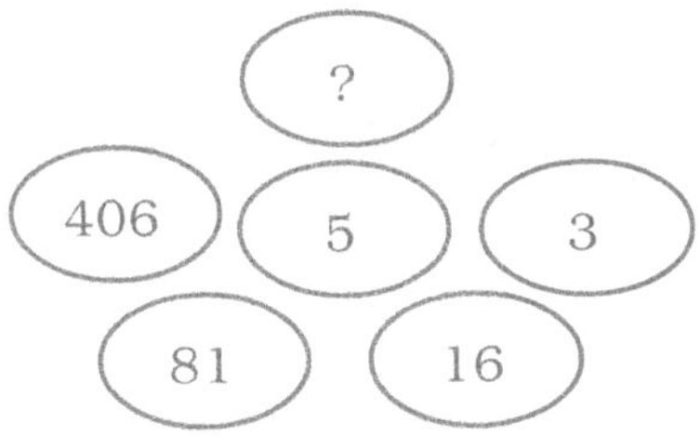

A. 2031 B.731 C. 1625 D. 1

Hint: The numbers in the outer circles starting from 3 can be used to work out the next number as follows:

$(3) \times 5 + 1 = 16$

16 can be used to find out the number in the outer circle next to 3, viz 16 as follows:

$(16) \times 5 + 1 = 81$

81 can be used to find out the number in the outer circle next to 81, viz 406 as follows:

$(81) \times 5 + 1 = 406$

406 can be used to find out the missing number next to 406 in the outer circles, as follows: $(406) \times 5 + 1 = 2031$

Correct answer is 2031

28. Find the missing number

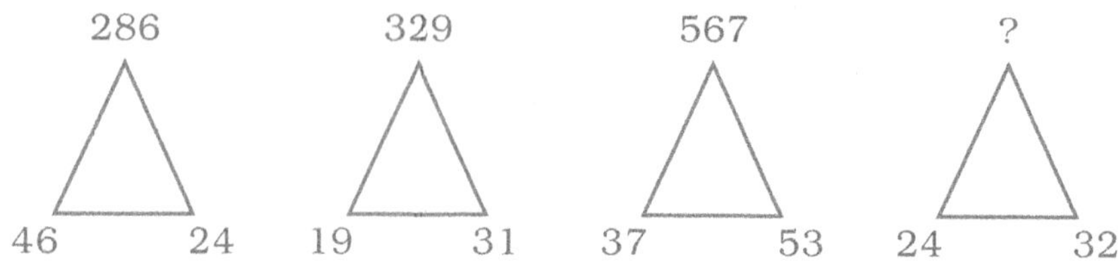

A. 343 B.334 C. 344 D. 442

Hint: For every triangle the rule connecting the three numbers at the three vertices are:

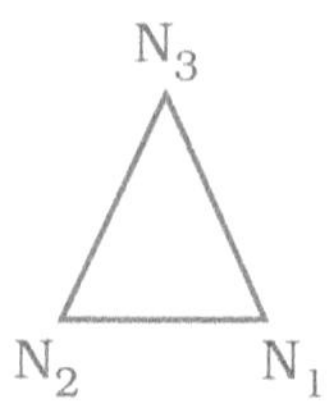

$N_3 = 10\, N_1 + N_2$

For the last triangle $N_1 = 32,\ N_2 = 24$.

Hence the missing number $N_3 = 10N_1 + N_2 = 10 \times 32 + 24 = 344$

29. Which number will replace the question mark in the following figure?

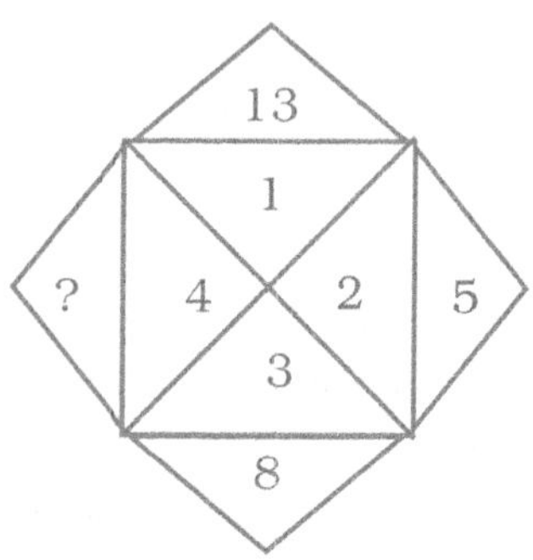

A. 10 B.12 C. 13 D. 14

Hint: The numbers inside the inner square are numbered N_1, N_2, N_3, N_4. The numbers outside the inner square are numbered M_1, M_2, M_3, M_4.

The following figure will help:

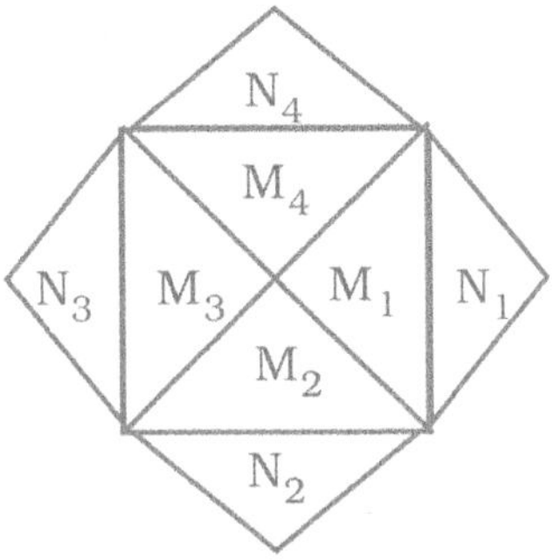

We can see that $N_1 + M_2 = N_2$

$$N_2 + M_3 = N_3$$

$$N_3 + M_4 = N_4$$

The second equation can be used for calculating N_3.

The missing number $N_3 = N_2 + M_3$

$$= 8 + 4 = 12$$

The missing number = 12.

30. Which number would replace the question mark in the figure?

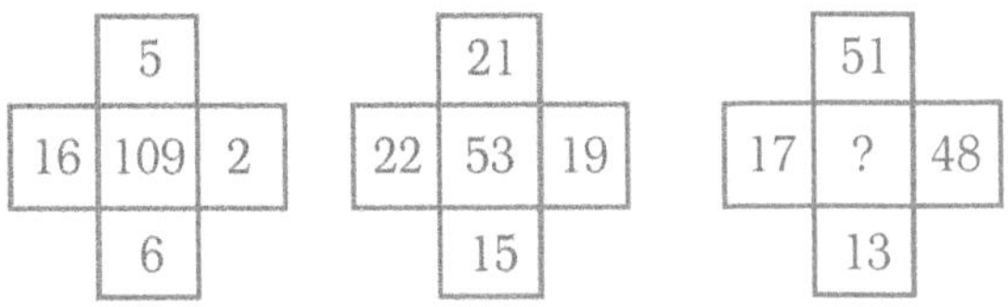

A. 7 B.25 C. 49 D. 129

Hint: We have to find out the law connecting the figures in the four outer squares with the figure in the central square.

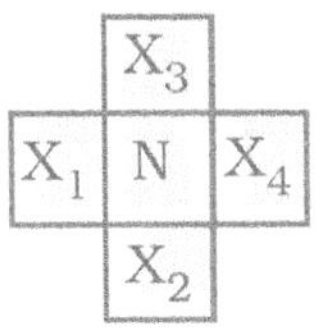

$$N = (X_1 - X_2)^2 + (X_3 - X_4)^2 = (17 - 13)^2 + (51 - 48)^2 = 4^2 + 3^2 = 16 + 9 = 25$$

31. Which number is appropriate to replace the question mark in the figure?

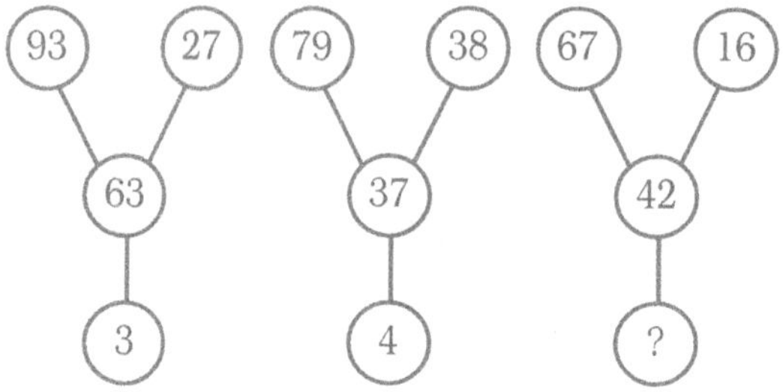

A. 5 B.6 C. 8 D. 9

Hint: The following rule can be found:

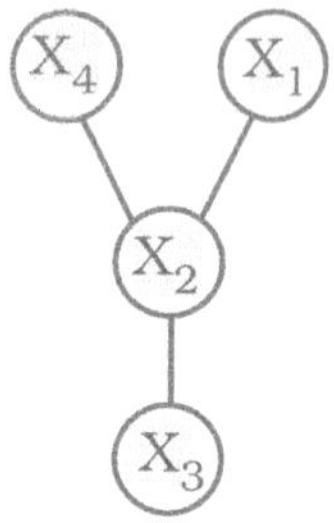

$X_1 + X_2 + X_3 = X_4$

ie., $16 + 42 + X_3 = 67$

$\therefore 58 + X_3 = 67$

$\therefore X_3 = 67 - 58 = 9$

Missing number = 9.

32. What should replace the question mark?

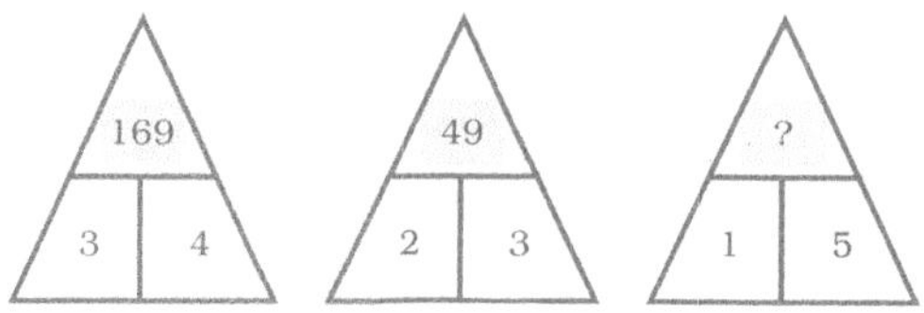

A. 36 B.156 C. 64 D. 92

Hint:

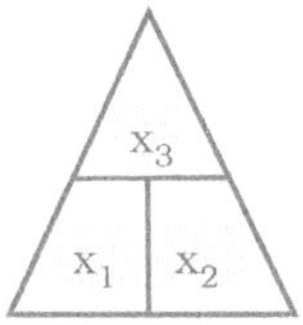

The numbers x_1, x_2, x_3 in all the triangles are found according to the rule:

$$[(x_1)\times(x_2)+1]^2 = x_3$$

For the first triangle the top number is $[(4\times3)+1]^2 = (12+1)^2 = 13^2 = 169$

For the second triangle the top number $= [(2\times3)+1]^2 = (6+1)^2 = 7^2 = 49$

For the third triangle the top number is $[(1\times5)+1]^2 = (5+1)^2 = 6^2 = 36$

Hence the answer = 36

33. What should replace the question mark?

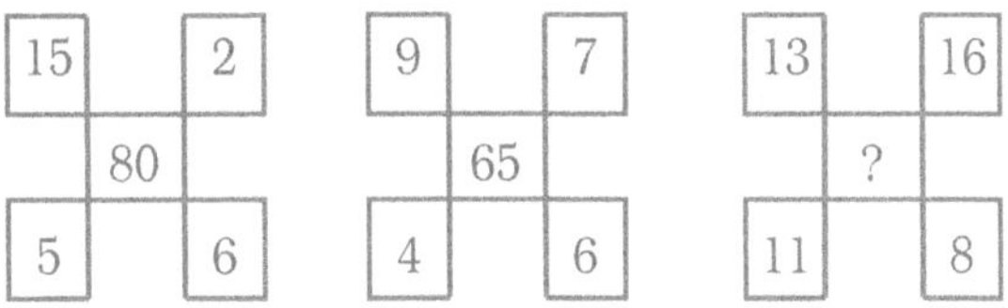

A. 35 B.48 C. 72 D. 120

Hint:

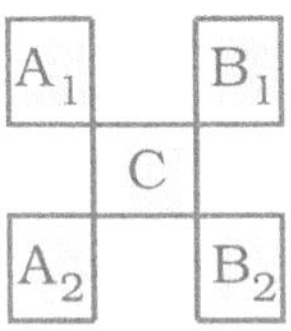

The rule connecting the five numbers (in all the three figures) follows the law given below:

$$C = (A_1 - A_2)\times(B_1 + B_2)$$

For the last figure, the missing figure C is given by $(13-11)\times(16+8) = 2\times24 = 48$

Hence the missing number is 48.

34. Which number should replace the question mark in the following diagram?

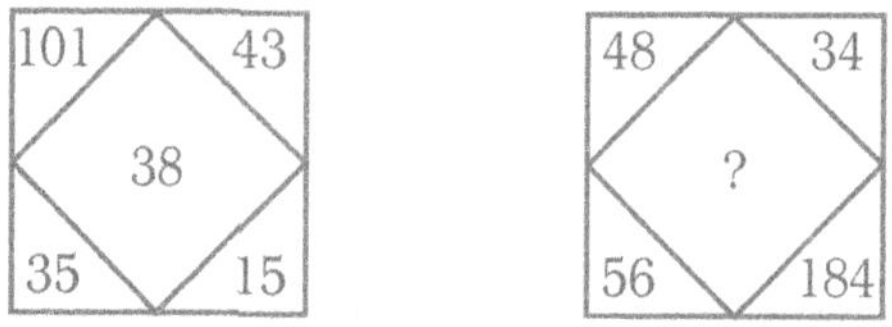

A. 127 B. 142 C. 158 D. 198

Hint: Both the squares follow a common rule given below:

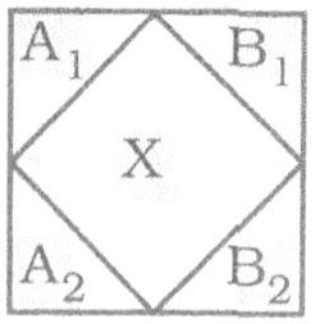

$$X = (A_1 + B_2) - (A_2 + B_1)$$

Hence for the second square the missing number

$$X = (48 + 184) - (56 + 34) = 232 - 90 = 142$$

35. Numbers in the figures given below are arranged in a particular order. Find out the missing number?

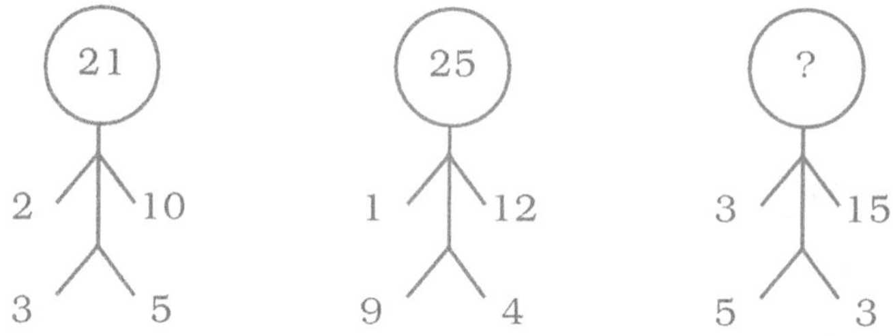

A. 29 B. 32 C. 10 D. 33

Hint: The numbers in each of the figures is related as follows:

$$X = (A \times B) + (C + D)$$

Missing number $X = (3 \times 5) + (15 + 3)$

$= 15+18$

$= 33$

36. Find the missing number indicated by a question mark?

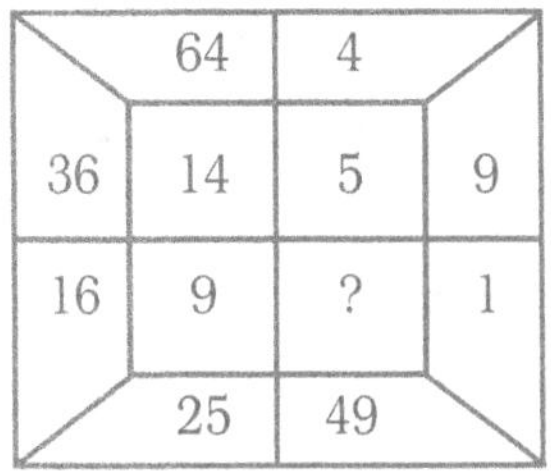

A. 11 B.7 C. 8 D. 9

Hint: The equivalent figure with symbols X_1, X_2, X_3, X_4 and Y_1, Y_2, Y_3, Y_4 and then the relationship with the 4 number in the central square are given to facilitate calculations.

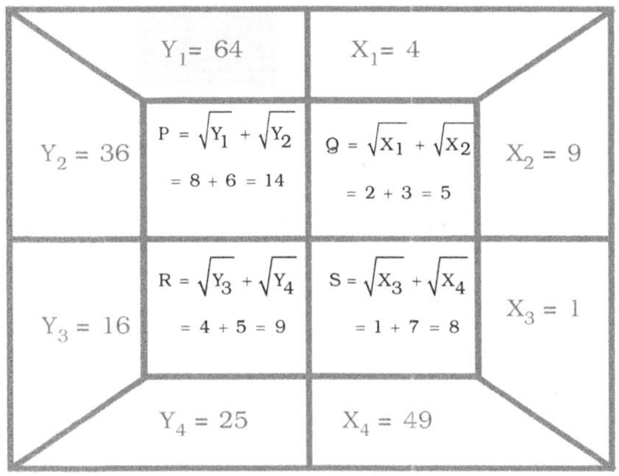

Missing number = S

$= \sqrt{X_3} + \sqrt{X_4}$

$= \sqrt{1} + \sqrt{49}$

$= 1 + 7 = 8$

Answer = 8.

37. Replace the question mark with a number.

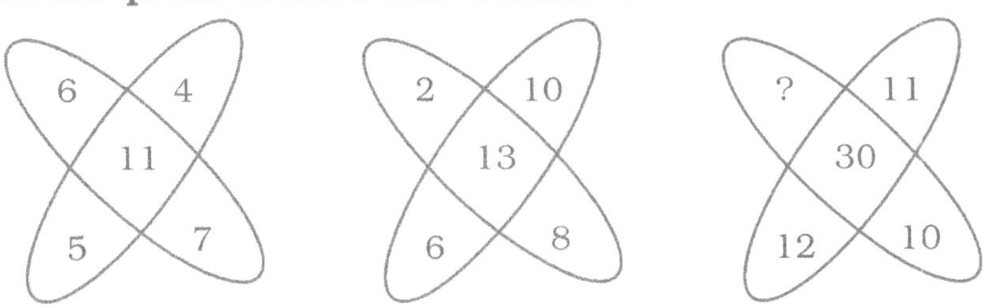

A. 8 B.15 C. 4 D. 27

Hint: Each of the three figures satisfies the following rule:

Half sum of the 4 outer numbers = central number

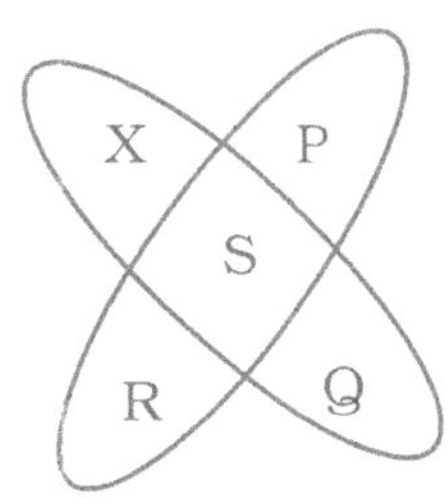

For the last figur $\dfrac{X+P+Q+R}{2}$ ie., $\dfrac{X+11+10+12}{2} = 30$

ie., $\dfrac{X+33}{2} = 30$ ie., $X + 33 = 2 \times 30$ ie. $X+33 = 60$.

$\therefore$ $X = 60 - 33 = 27$

38. Which number will appropriately substitute the question mark in the following figural arrangement?

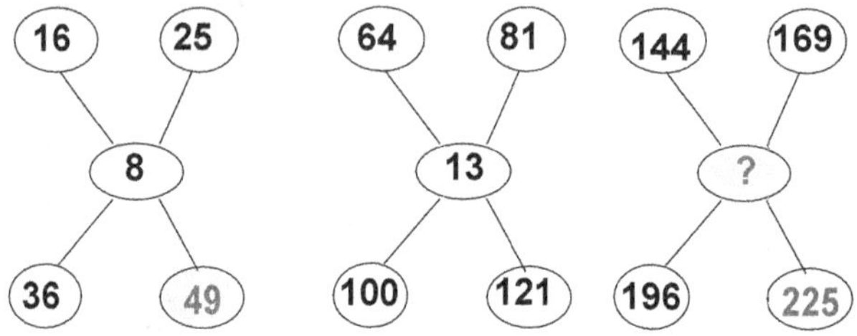

A. 7 B.6 C. 10 D. 9

Hint: Using symbols find out Q = difference of the numbers $(X_1 + Y_1)$ and $(X_2 + Y_2)$ Find out sum of the digit of the number Q. This will give P.

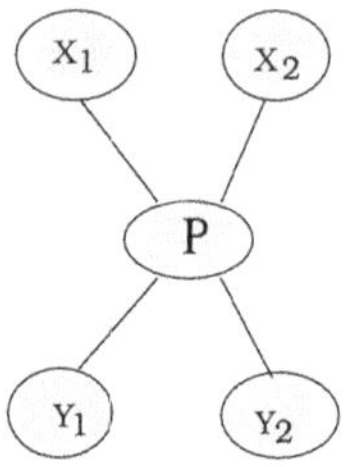

$(X_1 + Y_1) = 144 + 196 = 340$

$(X_2 + Y_2) = 169 + 225 = 394$

Difference = $394 - 340 = 54$

Sum of the digits of 54 = 5 + 4 = 9

$\therefore$ P = 9

Missing number = 9.

39. Which number will replace the question mark in the fourth square?

Square 1		Square 2		Square 3		Square 4	
5	6	4	7	8	3	7	9
3	0	2	8	2	4	?	3

A. 4 B.5 C. 6 D. 7

Hint: The product of the number in the top row in each square when splitting into its 2 digits will give the 2 digits in the lower row.

Ist square = $5 \times 6 = 30$

3 and 0 are the numbers at the bottom corners.

This is true for all the other three squares. For the last square product of the numbers in the top row = $7 \times 9 = 63$. These are the two digits of the 2 lower corners. These are 6 and 3. Answer = 6.

40. Replace the question mark with a suitable number.

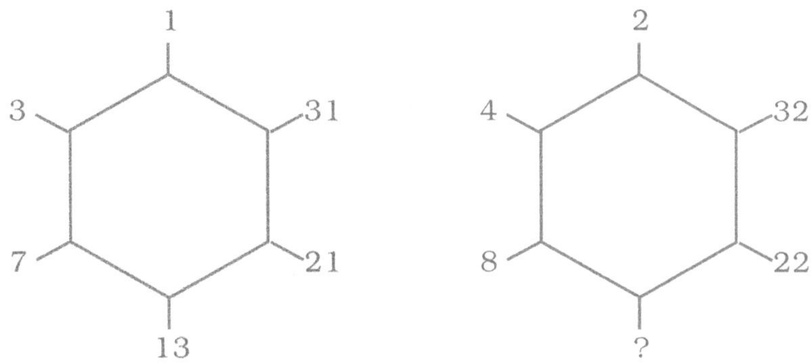

A. 16 B.17 C. 18 D. 14

Hint:

Figure 1 Figure 2

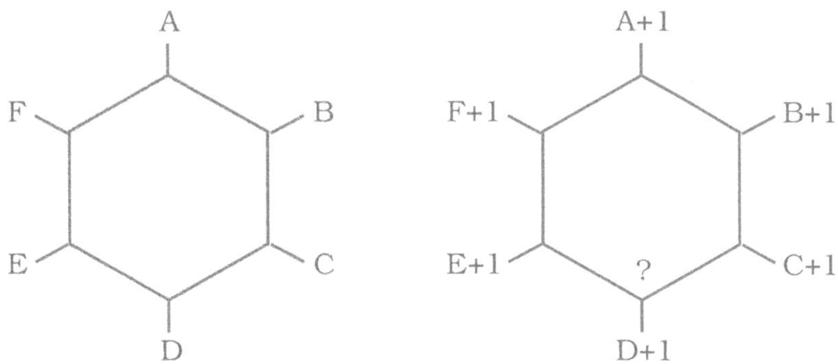

The numbers at the vertices of the second figure are one more than the figure in the corresponding portion of the first figure.

A = 1, B = 31, C = 21, D = 13, E = 7 and F = 3

∴ The corresponding numbers in the second figure is 1+1, 31+1, 21+1, 13+1, 7+1, and 3+1.

Missing number = 13+1 = 14.

41. Replace the question mark

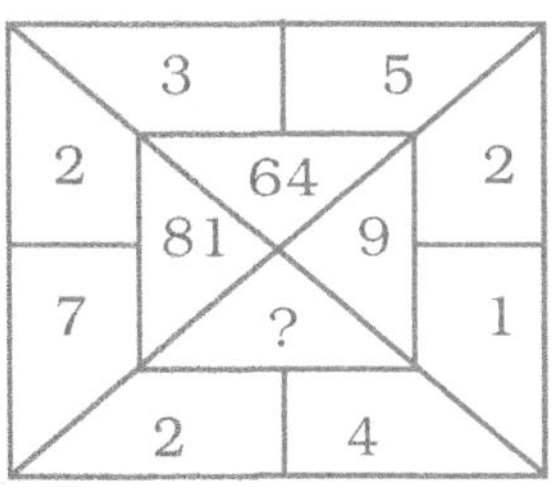

A. 22 B.26 C. 36 D. 14

Hint:

Missing number = $(4+2)^2$

= 36

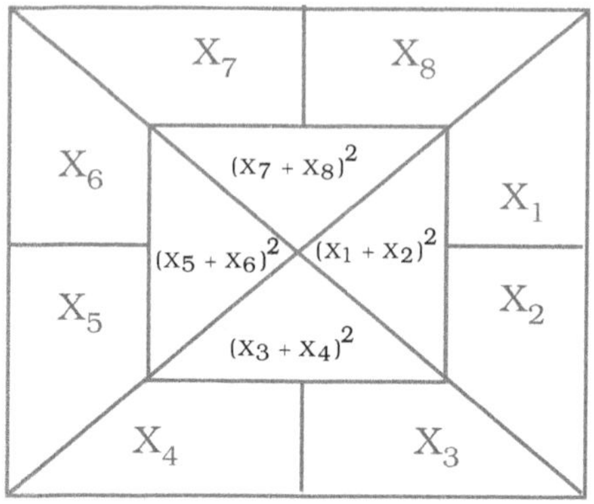

42. Find the missing number in the following.

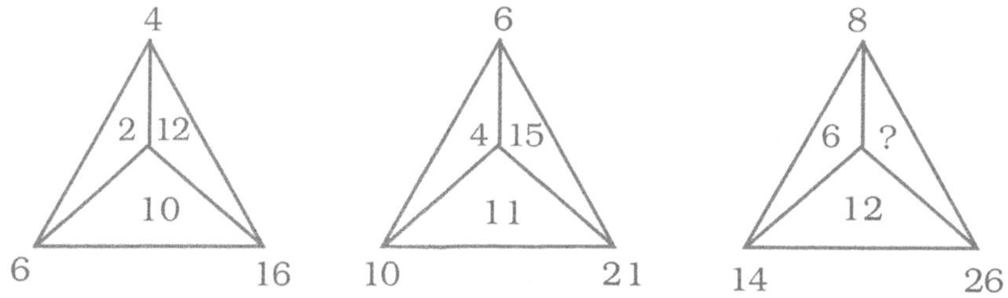

A. 18 B. 15 C. 34 D. 14

Hint: Answer =18

Since Z = 26

X = 8

and hence Z–X = 18

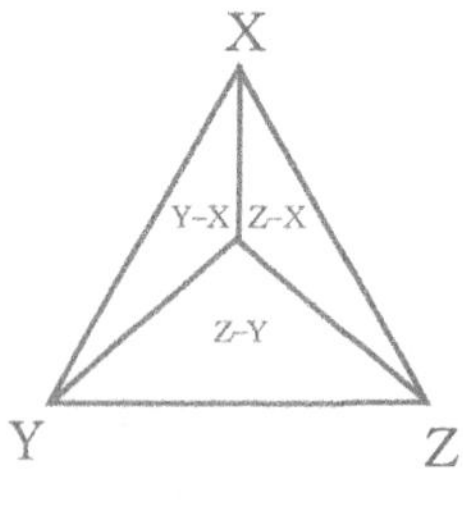

43. Replace the question mark

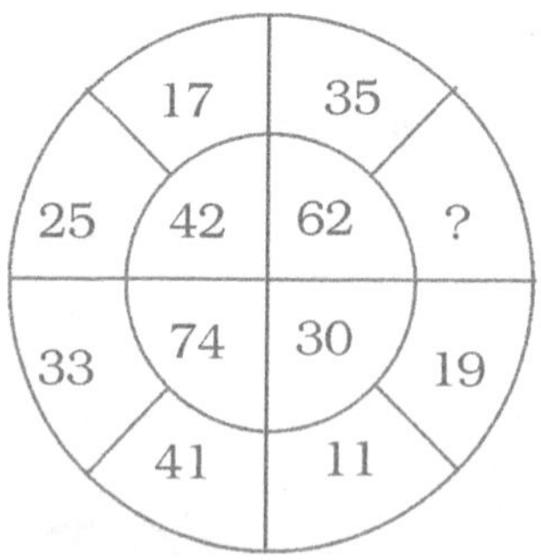

A. 27 B. 32 C. 33 D. 8

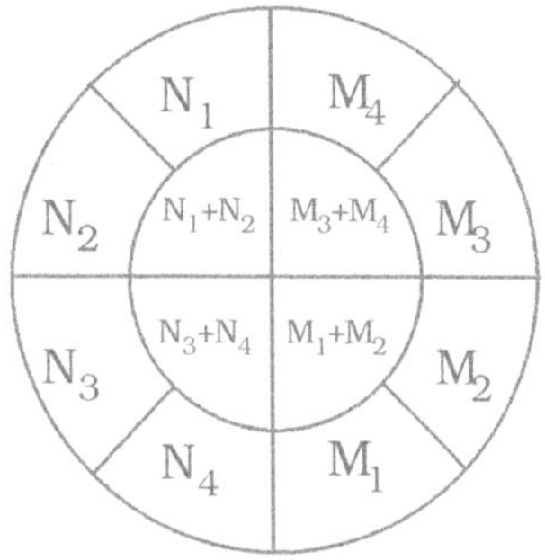

Hint: X = 17 Y = 11

$N_1 = X$ $M_1 = Y$

$N_2 = X+8$ $M_2 = Y+8$

$N_3 = X+16$ $M_3 = Y+16$

$N_4 = X+24$ $M_4 = Y+24$

Missing number = $M_3 = Y+16 = 11+16 = 27$

44. Insert the missing number

963	2	844
464	?	903

A. 1 B.2 C. 3 D. 4

Hint: This rule is valid for the 2 rows.

First row the difference = 2

For the second row the missing number = (4+6+4)–(9+0+3)

= 14 – 12 = 2

X_1, X_2, X_3	$(X_1 + X_2 + X_3) - (Y_1 + Y_2 + Y_3)$	Y_1, Y_2, Y_3
X_1, X_2, X_3	$(X_1 + X_2 + X_3) - (Y_1 + Y_2 + Y_3)$	Y_1, Y_2, Y_3

45. Numbers in the figures given below are arranged in some order. Find out the missing number in the figure.

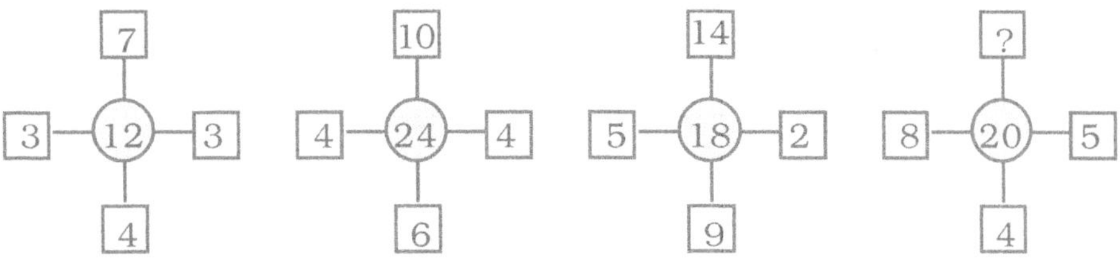

A. 16 B.20 C. 12 D. 18

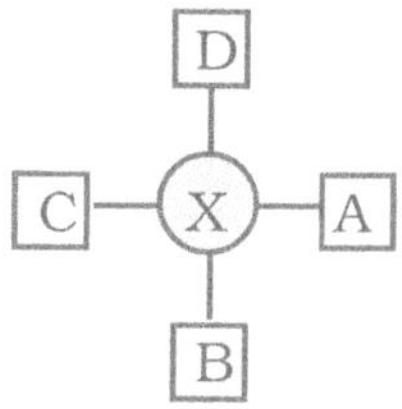

Hint: The law connecting the numbers in the four squares and the number at the centre within the circle is as follows:

For each figure, product of the right hand figure and the bottom figure = figure at the centre. ie. $A \times B = X$

Also For each figure, the sum of the bottom figure and the figure on the left = the figure at the top. ie., $B+C = D$

We have to find out D for the last figure = sum of the figures at the bottom and at the left, using the result $B+C = D$, we get D as $4+8 = 12$.

46. Which number is appropriate to replace the question mark?

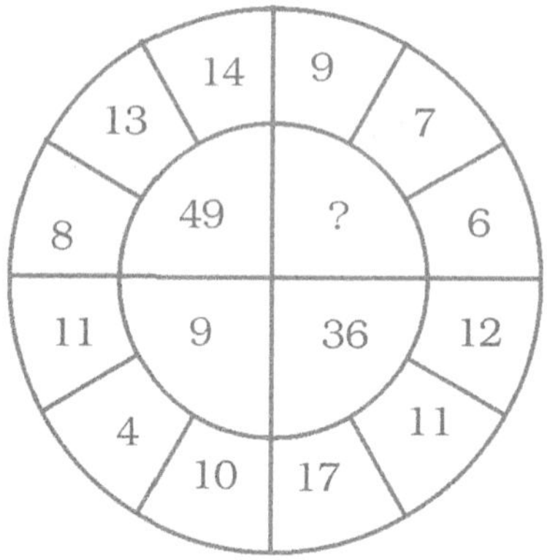

A. 4 B. 25 C. 64 D. 100

Hint: The numbers within each quarter of the circle that represent I, II, III, IV are formed as following:

Number in Region I = $(A + B - C)^2$

Number in Region II = $(P + Q - R)^2$

Number in Region III = $(L + M - N)^2$

Number in Region IV = $(X + Y - Z)^2$

The missing number in Region I = $(9 + 7 - 6)^2$

$= (16 - 6)^2 = 10^2 = 100$

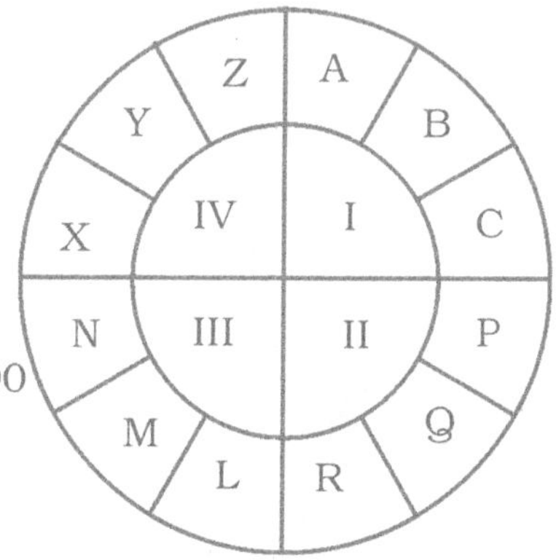

47. Find out the missing number in the following diagram.

5	20	25
7	42	49
9	72	?

A. 57 B. 63 C. 81 D. 54

Hint:

The pattern is given below:

A	$A^2 - A$	A^2
B	$B^2 - B$	B^2
C	$C^2 - C$	C^2

Missing number = C^2, viz

48. Replace the question mark with a suitable alternative.

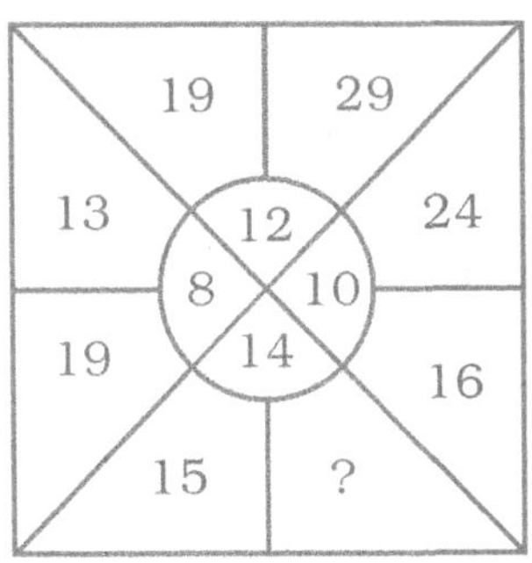

A. 35 B. 29 C. 41 D. 27

Hint: For every triangle, the sum of the end figures are divided by 4 to get the number in the corresponding portion of the circle as below:

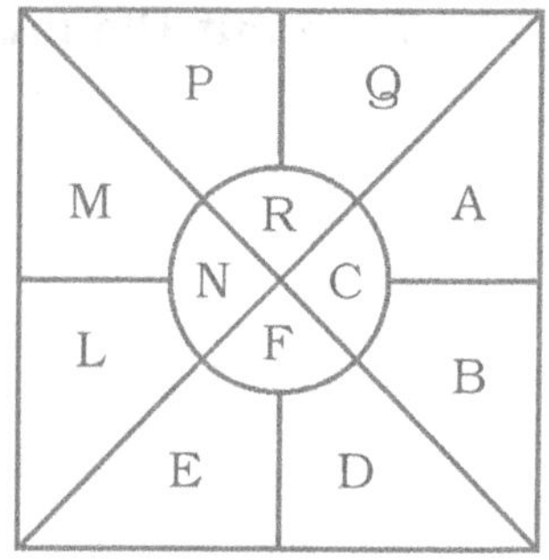

We know that $\frac{A+B}{4}=C$

$\frac{D+E}{4}=F$

$\frac{L+M}{4}=N$ and

$\frac{P+Q}{4}=R$

From the second equation $\frac{D+E}{4}=F$, $\frac{D+15}{4}=14$

$\therefore D=41$

49. Replace the question mark in the following arrangement with the appropriate number

4	5	3	2	0
7	3	4	4	21
6	4	4	5	22
9	6	5	5	?

A. 34 B. 42 C. 44 D. 45

Hint: Assume that the numbers in every row are represented by letters A, B, C, D, and E, they follow a common rule: $E=(A\times D)-(B+C)$

A	B	C	D	E

For the last row missing number

$E=(9\times 5)-(6+5)$

$=45-11=34$

50. Which number is to be substituted in the place of the question mark?

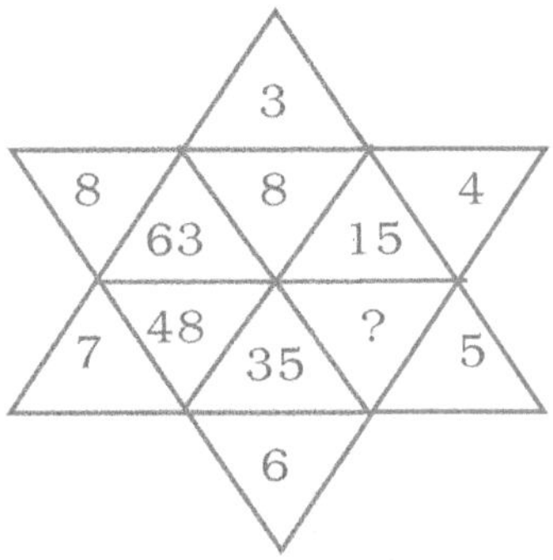

A. 25 B. 24 C. 64 D. 36

Hint: The number in the six projecting triangles of the star shaped are A, B, C, D, E, F. The numbers in the inner six triangles are P, Q, R, S, T, U. We can see that the numbers in the inner triangles are formed from the numbers in the outer triangles as follows.

$P = A^2 - 1$

$Q = B^2 - 1$

$R = C^2 - 1$

$S = D^2 - 1$

$T = E^2 - 1$

$U = F^2 - 1$

The question mark in the place of $Q = B^2 - 1 = 5^2 - 1 = 24$

Answer = 24.

51. Insert the missing number from the centre of the fourth triangle.

A. 29 B. 18 C. 41 D. 11

Hint: Inorder to get the number at the centre, the square root of the small number in the periferel is to be subtracted from the product of the big numbers in the periferel. In the fourth triangle square root of 4 = 16. Product of 9 and 5 = 45. Therefore 45 − 16 = 29. Answer 29.

3. NUMBER SERIES TEST

This deals with questions in which a series of numbers formed in a particular order are given. Each number in the series is generally called a term of the series. The terms in the series follow certain pattern **throughout.** The candidate is required to recognize this pattern and identify one number which is missing. In some cases two numbers will be missing. The questions can be of four types. You will be required either to fill up the blank space in the series or to complete the given series with the most suitable alternative or to find out the wrong term in the series or required to replace the question mark in the series by the appropriate number.

Knowledge of addition, subtraction, multiplication, division, squaring and finding square root, etc. are the pre-requisite skills for answering questions in the series test. Most of the questions under the series test are application of these operations. The most basic requirements will be to identify the principle used for generating one term from the preceeding term. The hint for solving the practice problems are given at the end of the question. On the basis of the rule, you have to decide as to what would be the missing number/numbers.

It will be useful if you are able to identify whether the terms in the series are arranged in the ascending order or descending order. If the preceeding terms are in the ascending order, you must understand that the missing can be obtained from addition or multiplication, squaring, etc. which is implied. If the terms are in the descending order, you must conclude that it is either subtraction or division, finding square root, etc.

1. Which number would replace question mark in the series?

2, 7, 14, 23, ?, 47

A. 28 B. 34 C. 31 D. 38

Hint: The given series is formed starting with two and the remaining terms formed by adding odd numbers 5, 7, 9, 11, etc. to the previous number. Hence, the missing number is 23+11 = 34.

2. Fill up the blank in the series

47, 32, ——, 11, 5, 2

A. 27 B. 20 C. 15 D. 12

Hint: The first term is 47. From this we have to subtract multiples of three starting with 15 (which is 5×3) to get the next number, then by subtracting 12 (which is 4×3) 9 (which is 3×3), 6 (which is 2×3), ... etc. the missing number is the third term which is $32 - 12 = 20$.

3. Complete the series

10, 5, 9, 5, 8, 5, ———, ———

A. 7, 5 B. 8, 5 C. 9, 5 D. 10, 5

Hint: The odd number of terms follow the pattern 10, 9, 8, 7, 6,........ The even number of terms follow the pattern 5, 5, 5, 5, 5. The combined series will be 10, 5 9, 5 8, 5 7,5 6,5 5, 5. The missing two terms are 7, 5.

4. Find out the missing term in the following series

31, 40, 48, 55, ——, 66, 70

A. 60 B. 61 C. 62 D. 53

Hint: The given series is formed by adding 9,8,7,6,5 and 4 to the first, second third, ——, —— terms. Hence the answer is 61.

5. Identify the missing number in the series

1, 4, 9, 16, 25, 36, 49, ———

A. 54 B. 56 C. 64 D. 81

Hint: The given series is formed by squairing numbers 1,2,3,4,5,6,7,8. The next number in the series will be square of 8 = 64.

6. Fill up the next term in the series

1, 2, 5, 16, 65, ———-

A. 326 B. 271 C. 196 D. 131

Hint: The rule is starting with the first term multiply by one and add one to get the second number; multiplied the previous number by two and add one to get the third number; multiplied the third number by three and add one to get the fourth number; multiplied the fourth number by 4 and add 1 to get the fifth number; multiplied the fifth number by 5 and add one to get the sixth number; multiplied the sixth number by 6 and add one to get the seventh number, multiplied the seventh number by seven and add one to obtain the eighth number etc. What we have to find out is the sixth term = $(5^{th}$ term $\times$ 5) + 1 = (65 $\times$ 5) + 1 = 325+1=326.

7. Find the next term in the series

120, 80, 60, 40, 30, 20, ———, 10

A. 25 B. 30 C. 18 D. 15

Hint: Two series of alternative terms 120, 60, 30, 15 (odd terms) and 80, 40, 20, 10 (even terms). The terms are divided by 2. Missing term = 15.

8. Complete the series

5, 6, 8, 9, 11, 12, 14, ———-

A. 16 B. 15 C. 17 D. 13

Hint: Combination of two series; odd terms: 5, 8, 11, 14; even term: 6, 9, 12, 15; Missing term is 15.

9. Fill up the blank in the series

5, 9, 17, 33, ——, 129

A. 66 B. 78 C. 65 D. 128

Hint: Given one term, the next term can be found by doubling the term and subtracting one from it.

Answer: double 33 and subtract one which is 65.

10. Find the next term in the series

1, 5, 14, 30, 55, ———

A. 104 B. 98 C. 121 D. 91

Hint: Add 2^2 to the first term to get the second term; add 3^2 to the second term to obtain the third term; add 4^2 to the third term to obtain the fourth term; add 5^2 to the fourth term to obtain the fifth term; add 6^2 to the fifth term to obtain the sixth term, etc.

Missing term = 6th term = 5th term + $6^2 = 55 + 36 = 91$

11. Fill up the blank in the series with a suitable alternative

6, 12, 60, 120, ——, 1200

A. 240 B. 600 C. 780 D. 740

Hint: Multiply every preceeding term by 2 and 5 alternatively to get the next term

ie., $6 \times 2 = 12$	$12 \times 5 = 60$	$60 \times 2 = 120$	$120 \times 5 = 600$	$600 \times 2 = 1200$
↓	↓	↓	↓	↓
IInd term	IIIrd term	IVth term	V^{th} term	VIth term

Missing term = V^{th} term = 600 OR

Combination of two series. The terms are multiplied by ten.

12. Supply the next term of the series

3, 14, 33, 60, ———

A. 95 B. 100 C. 105 D. 110

Hint: The terms are $2^2 - 1$, $4^2 - 2$, $6^2 - 3$, $8^2 - 4$ and $10^2 - 5$

Missing term is $10^2 - 5 = 95$

13. Find out the correct alternative to fill up the blank

260, 600, 128, 400, 62, 200, ———

A. 39 B. 29 C. 32 D. 34

Hint: The odd term follow one rule, while the even term follow another rule.

The series formed by the odd term are 260, 128, 62, ? We have to find out the fourth term of the series. The rule is half of the first term – 2 = IInd term, half of the second term – 2 = IIIrd term, half of the third term – 2 = IVth term.

The fourth term = half of the third term – 2 = 31 – 2 = 29

14. Complete the series

4, –8, 16, –32, 64, ———

A. 128 B. –128 C. 192 D. –192

Hint: Each number in the series is the preceding number multiplied by –2

Therefore, the missing number will be $64 \times (-2) = -128$

15. Which one of the following alternatives will complete the series?

4, 3, 6, 5, 8, 7, 10, 9, 12, ——, ———

A. 11, 14 B. 12, 13 C. 13, 12 D. 14, 11

Hint: The odd terms form one series following one rule while the even terms follow another rule. The two series are going. The first series is 4, 6, 8, 10, 12. The next term of the first series = 14. The second series is 3, 5, 7, 9. The next term in the second series = 11. The next two series of the combined rule is 11, 14.

16. Which number would replace the question mark in the series?

3, 7, 15, ? , 63, 127, 255

A. 33 B. 39 C. 30 D. 31

Hint: Any succeeding term can be found out from the preceeding term by doubling this term and adding one to it.

Thus
$7 = (2 \times 3) + 1 = 7$
$15 = (2 \times 7) + 1 = 15$
$? = (2 \times 15) + 1 = 31$
$63 = (2 \times 31) + 1 = 63$
$127 = (2 \times 63) + 1 = 127$
$255 = (2 \times 127) + 1 = 255$ OR

The terms are addition of the multiples of 4.

17. Choose the correct alternative that will fill in the blank space in the series

2, 5, 10, 50, 500, ——

A. 5000 B. 25000 C. 10000 D. 1000

Hint: Product of first & second term = third term.
Product of second & third term = fourth term.
Product of third & fourth = fifth term.
Produt of fourth & fifth term = sixth term
The missing term = sixth term = fourth term × fifth term = $50 \times 500 = 25000$.

18. Find out the term to fill in the blank space

5, 10, 13, 26, 29, 58, 61, ——

A. 122 B. 125 C. 128 D. 64

Hint: Any succeeding term can be found from the preceeding by alternate use of (a) multiplication by 2 or (b) addition of 3. Next term to 61 is by multiplication by 2 of the last term viz 61. The terms are alternatively multiplied by 2 and added by 3.

Answer $61 \times 2 = 122$.

19. Find out the next term in the series

240, 120, 40, 10, ——

A. 5 B. 20 C. 4 D. 2

Hint: Rule: succeeding term by multiplication successively by $\frac{1}{2}, \frac{1}{3}, \frac{1}{4}, \frac{1}{5}$, etc.

The missing term = $\frac{1}{5} \times 10 = 2$

20. What will be the next number in this series ?

2, 5, 9, 19, 37, ——

A. 74 B. 75 C. 76 D. None of these

Hint: The alternative terms follow different rule. First to second (Previous term $\times$ 2) + 1. second to third (Previous term $\times$ 2) – 1. This will repeat.

Missing term = $(37 \times 2)+1 = 74+1 = 75$

21. Fill up blank in the following series

4, 4, 9, 3, 16, 2, ——, 1, 36

A. 25 B. 32 C. 12 D. 18

Hint: This is combination of two series.

Odd term series: 4, 9, 16, ——, 36. Which is $2^2, 3^2, 4^2$, ——, 6^2

Even term series 4, 3, 2, 1, 0

Missing term (fourth in the first series) is $5^2 = 25$

Answer = 25.

22. Which is the next term of the series?

3, 14, 27, 44, ——

A. 63 B. 64 C. 47 D. 85

Hint: Difference between second term and first term = $14 - 3 = 11$

Difference between third term and second term = $27 - 14 = 13$

Difference between fourth term and third term = $44 - 27 = 17$

All are prime numbers in a sequence.
Difference between fifth term and fourth term = the next prime number = 19
If the missing number is X then
Difference between fifth term and fourth term = X – 44.
We know that X – 44 = 19 (the next prime number)
$\therefore X = 19 + 44 = 63$. The missing term = 63.

23. Complete the series

6482, 7582, 5739, ——, 9784

A. 9348 B. 6759 C. 3684 D. 6857

Hint: The sum of the digits follow the pattern 20, 22, 24, ——, 28.
Missing number is one were digits add up to 26. This number is 6857.

24. Which is the number that has to come next in the sequence?

9, 8, 8, 8, 7, 8, 6, ——

A. 5 B. 6 C. 8 D. 4

Hint: This is a combination of two series.
Odd term series: 9, 8, 7, 6, ...
Even term series: 8, 8, 8, 8, ...
The missing term is the fourth term of the second series which is 8.
Answer = 8.

25. Complete the series

462, 420, 380, ——

A. 342 B. 330 C. 370 D. 335

Hint: The series 462, 420, 380, ——, etc. follow a pattern.
Difference between a number and its preceeding number follow the pattern 42, 40, 38, ——. If the missing term is X, then $380 - X = 38$
$\therefore X = 380 - 38 = 342$. Hence the missing term = 342.

26. Identify the next number in the series

4, 9, 20, 43, ——

A. 90 B. 84 C. 96 D. 95

Hint: (First term $\times$ 2) + 1 = (4 $\times$ 2) + 1 = 9 = second term
(Second term $\times$ 2) + 2 = (9 $\times$ 2) + 2 = 20 = third term
(Third term $\times$ 2) + 3 = (20 $\times$ 2) + 3 = 43 = fourth term
(Fourth term $\times$ 2) + 4 = (43 $\times$ 2) + 4 = 86 + 4 = 90 = fifth term

27. Complete the series

3, 6, 12, 15, 30 ——

A. 33 B. 35 C. 45 D. 60

Hint: First term = 3

Second term = 3 + 3 = 6

Third term = 6 × 2 = 12

Fourth term = 12 + 3 = 15

Fifth term = 15 × 2 = 30

Sixth term = 30 + 3 = 33

28. Complete the next term of the given series

4, 9, 19, 39, 79, ——

A. 169 B. 159 C. 119 D. 139

Hint: The series 4, 9, 19, 39, 79, follows this rule:

2 times first term + 1 = second term

2 times second term + 1 = third term

2 times third term + 1 = fourth term

2 times fourth term + 1 = fifth term

2 times fifth term + 1 = sixth term

Missing term = sixth term = 2 × fifth term + 1

= (2 × 79) + 1 = 158 + 1 = 159

Answer = 159.

29. Identify the next number in the series

5, 15, 35, 65, 105, ——

A. 175 B. 75 C. 170 D. 155

Hint: The series is generated as follows:

First term = 5

Second term = first term + 10 = 15

Third term = second term + 20 = 35

Fourth term = third term + 30 = 65

Fifth term = fourth term + 40 = 105

Sixth term = fifth term + 50 = 155

The term to be identified = sixth term = 155.

30. Complete the following series

3, 2, 7, 6, 11, ——

A. 13 B. 8 C. 4 D. 10

Hint: The series 3, 2, 7, 6, 11, —— is composed of two series:

Odd term series: 3, 7, 11, ——

Even term series: 2, 6, 10, ——

For both series, the difference is 4. The missing term is 10.

31. What is the next term?

7, 13, 25, 49, ?

A. 99 B. 97 C. 89 D. 87

Hint: The series is formed as follows

First term = 7

Second term = 7 + 6 = 13 (First term + 6)

Third term = 13 + 12 = 25 (second term + 12)

Fourth term = 25 + 24 = 49 (third term + 24)

Fifth term = 49 + 48 = 97 (fourth term + 48)

Missing number = 97

32. Complete the following series

5, 6, 10, 19, ——

A. 28 B. 37 C. 36 D. 35

Hint: Series is 5, 6, 10, 19, ——

The series is formed as follows:

First term = 5

Second term = $5 + 1^2 = 6$ (first term + 1^2)

Third term = $6 + 2^2 = 6 + 4 = 10$ (second term + 2^2)

Fourth term = $10 + 3^2 = 10 + 9 = 19$ (third term + 3^2)

Fifth term = $19 + 4^2 = 19 + 16 = 35$ (fourth term + 4^2)

Missing term = Fifth term = 35

33. Find the next term in the series

8, 9, 20, 63, ——

A. 256 B. 252 C. 246 D. 242

Hint: Series is 8, 9, 20, 63, ——

The series is formed using the following rule:

First term = 8

Second term = (first term × 1) + 1 = (8 × 1) + 1 = 9

Third term = (second term × 2) + 2 = (9 × 2) + 2 = 20

Fourth term = (third term × 3) + 3 = (20 × 3) + 3 = 63

Fifth term = (fourth term × 4) + 4 = (63 × 4) + 4 = 256

Missing term = Fifth term = 256.

34. Substitute the missing number in the following series

8, 12, 24, ——, 180, 630

A. 48 B. 60 C. 36 D. 64

Hint: The series is 8, 12, 24, ——, 180, 630

The rule for finding the succeeding terms beginning with the first term is: (Multiply successively by 1.5, 2, 2.5, 3, 3.5, etc.)

First term = 8

Second term = 8 × 1.5 = 12

Third term = 12 × 2 = 24

Fourth term = 24 × 2.5 = 60

Fifth term = 60 × 3 = 180

Sixth term = 180 × 3.5 = 630

The missing term = fourth term = 60.

35. Fill up the blank in the series

10, 18, 34, ———, 130, 258

A. 32 B. 60 C. 68 D. 66

Hint: The series is 10, 18, 34, ——, 130, 258

From any term, we can get the next term by doubling the previous term and subtracting 2 from it.

First term = 10

Second term = (10 × 2) – 2 = 18

Third term = (18 × 2) – 2 = 34

Fourth term = (34 × 2) – 2 = 66

Fifth term = (66 × 2) – 2 = 130

Sixth term = (130 × 2) – 2 = 258

The missing term = fourth term = 66.

36. Fill up the blank in the following series

3, 128, 6, 64, 9, ———, 12, 16, 15, 8

A. 32 B. 12 C. 108 D. 72

Hint: The series is 3, 128, 6, 64, 9, ——, 12, 16, 15, 8

The series have been combined, each following a different rule

Odd series: 3, 6, 9, 12, 15 (Rule: Add 3 to the previous term to get the next term)

Even series: 128, 64, ——, 16, 8 (Rule: Every succeeding term is half of the previous term)

The missing term in the second series = $\frac{1}{2} \times 64 = 32$

37. Fill up the missing term in the series

9, 11, 20, 31, ———, 82

A. 41 B. 51 C. 60 D. 71

Hint: The series is 9, 11, 20, 31, ———, 82

The term follow the common rule: The sum of any two succeeding terms will be the value of the third term. If X is the missing term.

Third term = 20 = sum of First Term and Second Term = 9 + 11

Fourth term = 31 = sum of Second Term and Third Term = 11 + 20

Fifth term = X = sum of Third Term and Fourth term = 20 + 31 = 51

Sixth term = 82 = sum of Fourth Term and Fifth Term = 31 + 51 = 82

The missing term = Fifth term = 51.

38. Complete the series by supplying the next term

1, 3, 4, 8, 15, 27, ———

A. 37 B. 44 C. 50 D. 55

Hint: Rule used for generating the terms: The sum of any three consecutive terms = the next terms. Thus:

Fourth term = 1 + 3 + 4 = 8

Fifth term = 3 + 4 + 8 = 15

Sixth term = 4 + 8 + 15 = 27

Seventh term = 8 + 15 + 27 = 50

Missing seventh term = 50

39. Complete the following series

4, 9, 20, 43, 90, ———

A. 180 B. 182 C. 179 D. 185

Hint: The terms follow the rule : Double the previous term and add 1, 2, 3, 4.... to get the succeeding term

First term = 4

Second term = (4 × 2) + 1 = 9

Third term = (9 × 2) + 1 = 20

Fourth term = (20 × 2) + 3 = 43

Fifth term = (43 × 2) + 4 = 90

Sixth term = (90 × 2) + 5 = 185

Missing term = sixth term = 185

40. Fill up blank in the series

1, 4, 10, ———, 46

A. 20 B. 22 C. 24 D. 19

Hint: The series is 1, 4, 10, ———, 46

The rule for generating the term is as given below:

First term = 1

Second term = First term + 3 = 1 + 3 = 4

Third term = Second term + 6 = 4 + 6 = 10

Fourth term = Third term + 12 = 10 + 12 = 22

Fifth term = Fourth term + 24 = 22 + 24 = 46

Missing term = Fourth term = 22

Answer = 22.

41. Fill up blank space in the series

5, 17, 37, 65, ———, 145

A. 95 B. 97 C. 99 D. 101

Hint: The series is 5, 17, 37, 65, ———, 145

The terms satisfy a common rule given below:

First term = 5 = $2^2 + 1$

Second term = 17 = $4^2 + 1$

Third term = 37 = $6^2 + 1$

Fourth term = 65 = $8^2 + 1$

Fifth term = X = $10^2 + 1$

Sixth term = 145 = $12^2 + 1$

Missing term = X = $10^2 + 1$ = 101.

42. Which of the alternative figures would correctly fill in the blank space in the following series of numbers?

6, 5, 24, 25, ———

A. 175 B. 210 C. 164 D. 144

Hint: The series is 6, 5, 24, 25, ——

We have to identify the 5th term

The pattern need for generating the series is:

Third term = 4 times the first term = $4 \times 6 = 24$

Fourth term = 5 times the second term = $5 \times 5 = 256$

Fifth term = 6 times the third term = $6 \times 24 = 144$

The missing number = 144.

43. Which one of the number given below would come next in the series of numbers?

7, 13, 21, 31, ———

A. 41 B. 43 C. 37 D. 39

Hint: The series is 7, 13, 21, 31, ———

We have to identify the fifth term

The series is generated by adding numbers 6, 8, 10, 12, etc. to the first, second, third term, as shows below:

First term = 7

Second term = 7 + 6 = 13

Third term = 13 + 8 = 21

Fourth term = 21 + 10 = 31

Fifth term = 31 + 12 = 43

The missing number = Fifth term = 43.

44. Which one of the four numbers shall come next in the series?

6, 3, 12, 6, 24, ———

A. 12 B. 18 C. 30 D. 48

Hint: The series is 6, 3, 12, 6, 24, ———, 48

This is a combination of two series.

Odd items series : 6, 12, 24, 48

Even item series : 3, 6, ———, 24

Both the series follow the some rule : any term will be twice the previous term. Hence the missing term (in the even series) is 12.

The Answer = 12.

45. Which number will come next in the given series?

1, 1, 6, 6, 11, 11, ?

A. 11 B. 13 C. 16 D. 17

Hint: The series is 1, 1, 6, 6, 11, 11, ?

The term first, second two, third two two proximate numbers are repeated; the difference between the first two and the next two is 5, which is repeated.

Hence the next two times are to be 16, 16.

The next missing term is 16.

46. Fill up the blank in the series below

0, 1, 8, 27, 64, ?

A. 122 B. 125 C. 128 D. 256

Hint: The series is 0, 1, 8, 27, 64, ——

This is really $0^3, 1^3, 2^3, 3^3, 4^3,$ ——

The next missing term = $5^3 = 125$

47. Complete the following series by filling the blank:

5, 14, 27, 44, 65, ?

A. 150 B. 90 C. 88 D. 180

Hint: The difference between 2nd and Ist terms, 3rd and 2nd term, 4th and 3rd terms, etc. are given below:

Second – Ist term = 14 – 5 = 9

Third term – Second term = 27 – 14 = 13

Fourth term – Third term = 44 – 27 = 17

Fifth term – Fourth term = 65 – 44 = 21

Sixth term – Fifth term should be 25

Sixth term – Fifth term + 25 = 65 + 25 = 90

Hence missing term = 90.

48. Which is the number that has to come next in the series ?

30, 24, 19, 15, 12, ?

A. 6 B. 8 C. 10 D. 11

Hint: The series is 30, 24, 19, 15, 12, ——

Let the missing term be X.

We can see that

Ist term – Second = 30 – 24 = 6

Second term – Third term = 24 – 19 = 5

Third term – Fourth term = 19 – 15 = 4

Fourh term – Fifth term = 15 – 12 = 3

Hence, Fifth term – Sixth = 12 – X = 2

Solving the equation

$12 - X = 2$

$-X = 2 - 12$

$-X = -10$

$\therefore X = 10$

$\therefore$ Missing term = 10.

49. Find missing term in the following series

4, 6, 12, 14, 28, 30, ——

A. 32 B. 64 C. 62 D. 60

Hint: The series is 4, 6, 12, 14, 28, 30, ——

This can be looked upon as a combination of two series:

Odd term series : 4, 12, 28, ——

Even term series : 6, 14, 30, ——

We have to find out the missing term (fourth term) is the odd term series above.

The terms in the odd series follow the rule shown below:

Ist term = 4

Second term = First term + 8 = 4 + 8 = 12

Third term = Second term + 16 = 12 + 16 = 28

Fourh term = Third term + 32 = 28 + 32 = 60

Hence the missing term in the original series = Fourth term of the odd term series = 60.

50. Which is the number that comes next in the series?

5, 16, 51, 158, ——

A. 1452 B. 483 C. 481 D. 1454

Hint: The series is 5, 16, 51, 158, ——

The rule connecting we have to identify the Fifth term two successive term is as follows:

First term = 5

Seond term = (First term $\times$ 3) + 1 = (5 $\times$ 3) + 1 = 16

Third term = (Second term $\times$ 3) + 3 = (16 $\times$ 3) + 3 = 51

Fourth term = (Third term $\times$ 3) + 5 = (51 $\times$ 3) + 5 = 158

Fifth term = (Fourth term $\times$ 3) + 7 = (158 $\times$ 3) + 7 = 481

Hence the missing term in the series = 481.

4. LETTER SERIES TEST

In order to find answers to this type of questions candidates have to maintain a chart assigning place value to the English alphabets like A-1, B-2, C-3, etc. to X-24, Y-25, Z-26. We can also assign numbers in the reverse order also like Z-26, Y-25, X-24 to C-3, B-2, A-1. and with the solving problem in this section.

A useful arrangement is given below:

1	2	3	4	5	6	7	8	9	10	11	12	13	14	15	16	17	18	19	20	21	22	23	24	25	26
A	B	C	D	E	F	G	H	I	J	K	L	M	N	O	P	Q	R	S	T	U	V	W	X	Y	Z
26	25	24	23	22	21	20	19	18	17	16	15	14	13	12	11	10	9	8	7	6	5	4	3	2	1

1. Complete the following series

BHL, DJN, FLP, ———

A. HNR B. HOS C. IOS D. INR

Hint: Replace the ulters by equivelent numbers the series becomes

(2, 8, 12); (4, 10, 14); (6, 12, 16)

The next term here to be (8, 14, 18) converted into letters, it is HNR

2. Fill up the blank in the series

ACE, GIK, ———, SUW, YAC

A. MNP B. MOP C. MOQ D. MPQ

Hint: The equivelent series in numbers is:

(1, 3, 5), (7, 9, 11), ———, (19, 21, 23), (25, 1, 3)

Missing term is (13, 15, 17). In letters, (MOQ)

3. Fill in the blank

AZBY, ———, EVFU, GTHS

A. BYCZ B . CYDR C. EXDZ D. CXDW

Hint: The remaining problem in this section:

Replace letters by their equivalent numbers and convert them into a number series and find the solution in numbers convert the solution is in numbers into equivalent letters to find the answers.

(1, 26, 2, 25), ———, (5, 22, 6, 21), (7, 20, 8, 19)

Missing term is (3, 24, 4, 23). In letters, CXDW

4. Complete the following series

AHQ, DJR, GLS, JNT, ———

A. LPU B. MPU C. MQU D. MPV

Hint: The equivelent number series is (1, 8, 17), (4, 10, 18), (7, 12, 19), (10, 14, 20), ———

The missing term (Fifth term) = (13, 16, 21) = MPU

5. **Complete the series**

nsi, org, pqe, qpc, ———

A. rod B. pqa C. aor D. roa

Hint: The equivalent number series is:

(14, 19, 9), (15, 18, 7), (16, 17, 5), (17, 16, 3)

The next term (Fifth term which is missing) is (18, 15, 1) which is 'roa'.

6. **Complete the following series**

ANBO, CPDQ, ERFS, GTHU, ———

A. IVJW B. JWKX C. KXZB D. HSIT

Hint: The equivalent number series (1, 14, 2, 15), (3, 16, 4, 17), (5, 18, 6, 19), (7, 20, 8, 21), ———

Missing term (Fifth term) = (9, 22, 10, 23) = IVJW

7. **Fill up the blank space in the series**

BU, ET, ———, KR, NQ, QP

A. BS B. HS C. PS D. SH

Hint: The equivalent number series (2, 21), (5,20), ———, (11, 18), (14, 17),

Missing term (Third term) = (8, 19) = HS

8. **Complete the series**

BY, EV, HS, KP, ———

A. YB B. VE C. NM D. MN

Hint: The equivalent number series (2, 25), (5, 22), (8, 19), (11, 16), ———

The first number in each pair increases by 3 (2, 5, 8, 11, etc.) while the second number in each pair decreases by 3 (25, 22, 19, 16, etc.)

The missing number (Fifth term) = (14, 13) = NM

Answer = MN.

9. **Complete the series**

ABC, BCD, CDE, DEF, ———

A. DFE B. EFG C. GHI D. GIH

Hint: The equivalent number series (1, 2, 3), (2, 3, 4), (3, 4, 5), (4, 5, 6), ———

Th next term (missing term) is (5, 6, 7)

Expressed in letters, this becomes EFG.

Answer = EFG.

10. **Complete the series with a suitable alternative**

LONM, NQPO, PSRQ, RUTS, ———

A. TWVU B. VZYX C. ZCBA D. TWVX

Hint: The equivalent number series (12, 15, 14, 13), (14, 17, 16, 15), (16, 19, 18, 17), (18, 21, 20, 19), ———
The next missing term is (20, 23, 22, 21)
Expressed in letters, this becomes TWVU
Answer = TWVU

11. Complete the following series

AC, EG, ______, MO, QS

A. IC B. GH C. IK D. LN

Hint: The equivalent number series (1, 3), (5, 7), ______ (13, 15), (17, 19).
Missing term (9, 11) = IK

12. Complete the following series

E, J, 0, ______, Y

A. P B. X C. T D. Z.

Hint: The equivalent number series 5, 10, 15, 20, 25
Missing term = 20
Equivalent letter = T
Missing term = T

13. Complete the following series

AG, CI, EK, ______

A. FG B. GM C. FL D. ZH

Hint: The equivalent number series is (1, 7), (3, 9), (5, 11), (7, 13)
Missing term = Fourth term = (7, 13) = GM

14. Complete the following series

ACE, FHJ, KMO, PRT, ______

A. TVX B. RTU C. UWY D. ZBG

Hint: The equivalent number series is (1, 3, 5), (6, 8, 10), (11, 13, 15), (16, 18, 20), (21, 23, 25)
Missing term = Fifth term = (21, 23, 25) = (UWY)

15. Complete the following series

AG, BH, CI, ______

A. DJ B. DI C. EL D. HM

Hint: The equivalent number series is: (1, 7), (2, 8), (3, 9), (4, 10)
Missing term = (4, 10) = DJ

16. Fill up the blank in the series

AFK, BGL, ______, DIN, EJO

A. CIN B. CHM C. CGL D. CIM.

Hint: Equivalent number series (1, 6, 11), (2, 7, 12), ______, (4, 9, 14), (5, 10, 15)

Missing third term = (3, 8, 13) = CHM.

17. Fill up the blank in the series

ADG, GJM, MPS, ______

A. SVX B. SUX C. SWZ D. SVY.

Hint: Equivalent number series is: (1, 4, 7), (7, 10, 13), (13, 16, 19), ______

Missing fourth term = (19, 22, 25) = (SVY)

Missing term = SVY.

18. Fill up the blank in the series

KU, LV, ______, NX, OY

A. MY B. HM C. MW D. MU

Hint: Equivalent number series is: (11, 21), (12, 22), ______, (14, 24), (15, 25)

Missing third term = (13, 23) = MW.

19. Complete the following series

AK, CM, EO, GQ, ______

A. JT B. IS C. JP D. HR

Hint: Equivalent number series is: (1, 11), (3, 13), (5, 15), (7, 17), ______

Missing fifth term = (9, 19) = IS.

20. Complete the following series

AGM, BHN, CIO, DJP, ______

A. EPR B. EKP C. EMS D. EKQ

Hint: The equivalent number series is: (1, 7, 13), (2, 8, 14), (3, 9, 15), (4, 10, 16), ______

The fifth term to be identified. This is (5, 11, 17) which in letters is EKQ.

21. Complete the following series

SJA, TKB, ULC, VMD, WNE, ______

A. XPF B. XNF C. XOG D. XOF

Hint: The equivalent number series is: (19, 10, 1), (20, 11, 2), (21, 12, 3), (22, 13, 4), (23, 14, 5). The three numbers in every term increases by 1 to get the three numbers in the next term.

The missing term is obviously (24, 15, 6) which in letters is XOF.

Missing term = XOF

22. Complete the following series

QIA, SKC, UME, ______

A. XOH B. WOG C. TLD D. VPG

Hint: The equivalent number series is: (17, 9, 1), (19, 11, 3), (21, 13, 5) ______

The term are generated using the principle: Every numbers in every term increased by 2 to get the next three numbers.

Hence the next (fourth term) term is (23, 15, 7) = WOG.

23. Complete the following series

CJQ, DKR, ELS, FMT, ______

A. GNU B. GOV C. GNW D. NOV

Hint: The equivalent number series is: (3, 10, 17), (4, 11, 18), (5, 12, 19), (6, 13, 20), ______

Every higher term can be found by adding are to each, the three numbers in the preceeding term.

Hence the missing term is (7, 14, 21) = GNU

24. Complete the following series

AJQ, BKR, CLS, DMT, ______

A. BJQ B. IOT C. ENU D. FNV

Hint: The equivalent number series is: (1, 10, 17), (2, 11, 18), (3, 12, 19), (4, 13, 20), ______

Add one to each if the three numbers in a preceeding term will give the next higher number

The missing term = (5, 14, 21) = ENU

25. Fill up the blank in the series

GPW, FOV, ENU, ______, CLS

A. DMT B. DKR C. DMR D. DLT

Hint: Equivalent number series is: (7, 16, 23), (6, 15, 22), (5, 14, 21), ______, (3, 12, 19)

The three numbers in each term to be decreased by 1 to get the three numbers in the next higher term.

Hence the missing term is (4, 13, 20) = DMT

26. Complete the following series

EIMQ, FJNR, GKOS, ______

A. IMQU B. KOSW C. HLPT D. HLPU

Hint: Equivalent number series is: (5, 9, 13, 17), (6, 10, 14, 18), (7, 11, 15, 19), ______
The next term is: (8, 12, 16, 20) which is HLPT. Answer: HLPT.

27. Complete the following series

NIFA, OJGB, PKHC, ______

A. QRHD B. QRID C. QLID D. QLDI

Hint: Equivalent number series is: (14, 9, 6, 1), (15, 10, 7, 2), (16, 11, 8, 3), ______
The next term is (17, 12, 9, 4) which is QLID.

28. Complete the following series

UME, VNF, WOG, ______

A. QIA B. XPH C. XTL D. XPD

Hint: Equivalent number series is: (21, 13, 5), (22, 14, 6), (23, 15, 7) ______
Missing term = (24, 16, 8) = XPH

29. Complete the following series:

ABCDE, FGHIJ, KLMNO, ______, UVWXY

A. ZABCD B. PQRST C. PQSRT D. XYZAB

Hint: The equivalent number series is (1, 2, 3, 4, 5), (6, 7, 8, 9, 10), (11, 12, 13, 14, 15), ______, (21, 22, 23, 4, 25)
Missing term: (16, 17, 18, 19, 20) = PQRST.

30. Fill up the blank in the series

YWVU, TRQP, OMLK, ______, ECBA.

A. JHGF B. JIHF C. JHFG D. FGHJ

Hint: The equivalent number series is:
(25, 23, 22, 21), (20, 18, 17, 16), (15, 13, 12, 11), ______, (5, 3, 2, 1)
Rule: Subtract 5 from each of the four numbers to get this next term.
The missing term = (10, 8, 7, 6) = JHGF.

31. Complete the following series

YMA, ZNB, AOC, ______

A. BND B. CPC C. BPQ D. BPD

Hint: The equivalent number series is:

(25, 13, 1), (26, 14, 2), (1, 15, 3), ______

Rule: Add 1 to all the three numbers of the previous term to get the next.

The missing term = (2, 16, 4) = BPD.

Additional note: The first number in the series increases by 1. We get 25, 26, 27and 28. When the number is more than 26, subtract 26 and write the remaining number. Then 27 becomes 1, 28 becomes 2, 29 becomes 3 etc.

32. Complete the following series

YVSP, UROL, QNKH, ______

A. MIGD B. MJFC C. MJGD D. MKHE

Hint: The equivalent number series in the disorder form is (2, 5, 8, 11), (6, 9, 12, 15), (10, 13, 16, 19), ______

Rule: Add four to each of the four numbers of every term to get the next

The missing term = 14, 17, 20, 23 = MJGD.

33. Complete the following series

AGPU, BHQV, CIRW, ______

A. DOSX B. DJSY C. DJSX D. DISX

Hint: The equivalent number series is:

(1, 7, 16, 21), (2, 8, 17, 22), (3, 9, 18, 23), ______

Rule: Add one to each of the four numbers of every term to get the next

The missing term = (4, 10, 19, 24) = DJSX.

34. Complete the series

ZXV, TRP, ______, HFD

A. MLJ B. GLJ C. NLJ D. SXV

Hint: The equivalent number series is:

(26, 24, 22), (20, 18, 16), ______, (8, 6, 4)

Rule: Subtract 6 from each of the three numbers in a term to obtain the next term in the series. The missing term is (14, 12, 10) = NLJ.

35. Which group of letters will replace the question mark (?) in the following series?

ADH, DHM, ?, MSZ

A. HPZ B. HMR C. HMS D. HMT

Hint: The series in formed in the following pattern

$$A \xrightarrow{+3} D \xrightarrow{+4} H \xrightarrow{+5} M$$
$$D \xrightarrow{+4} H \xrightarrow{+5} M \xrightarrow{+6} S$$
$$H \xrightarrow{+5} M \xrightarrow{+6} S \xrightarrow{+7} Z$$

So 'HMS' is the missing group.

Answers with explanation

1.A. In the given series B-2, H-8, L-12 next 4, 10, 14 next 6, 12, 16. Hence next will be 8, 14, 18 ie. HNR

2.C. Assign place value to the concepts. This is alphabets representing odd numbers like 1,3,5,7,9, 11. Hence next is 13, 15,17 ie.MOQ

3.D. The sequence of the letters is as follows. First group 1, 26, 2, 25. Third group 5, 22, 6, 21. Fourth group 7, 20, 8, 19. Hence second group will be 3, 24, 4, 23 ie. CXDW

4.B. In each group first one is the third letter, second letter is second letter and the third letter is the next letter. Hence MPU

5.D. While assigning place value in every group first letter is jumbled in the forward direction by one step, second letter is jumbled in the backward direction by one step and third letter is jumbled in the backward direction by two steps. Hence answer is roa.

6.A. Split the English alphabets into two half; from A to M and N to Z. First letter of the first half and first letter of the second half and second letter of the first half and second letter of the second half. Continue this pattern. Hence the answer is IVJW.

7.B. While assigning place value, each group will get 2-21, 5-20, —, 11-18, 14-17, 17-16.

This shows that first number is added by 3 while the second number is subtracted by 1. Hence the next number will be 8-19. ie. HS

8.C. The group consists of letters of both sides of the vowels. Hence the next group will be letters of both sides of U. is TV

9.B. Last two letters of each group are combined with the next letter to form the next group. Hence EF should be combined with G to get the next group.

10.A. Assign place value to the letters and find the order. This is 12 15 14 13, 14 17 16 15, 16 19 18 17, 18 21 20 19. Hence next will be 20 23 22 21. Ie TWVU.

11.C. The series includes the alternate letters.

12.B. The series includes 5th, 10th, 15th, 20th, and 25th letters.

13.C. Group of 1st and 6th letters.

14.C. Group of 1st, 3rd and 6th letters.

15.A. Group of 1st and 6th letters, 2nd and 7th, similarly 3rd and 8th letters.

16.B. Group of 1st, 6th & 11th alphabets.

17.D. Group of 1st, 3rd and 6th alphabets.

18.C. Group of 1st and 10th alphabets starting from K.

19.B. Group of 1st and 11th alphabets starting from A, skipping an alphabet in between.

20.D. Group of every 7th letter starting from A.

21.D. Group of every 9th letter in reverse order of Z to A.

22.B. Group of every 9th letter in reverse order of Z to A starting from Q to W skipping an alphabet in between.

23.A. Group of every 8th letter starting from C.

24.C. Group of 1st, 10th and 18 alphabets in series starting from A to E.

25. A. Group of 1st, 10th and 17th letter in series, starting from G and going in reverse, G-A.

26.C. Group of 1st , 5th, 9th and 13th alphabets starting from E to H.

27.C. Alphabets arranged in order of 1st, 6th, 9th and 14th alphabets arranged in reverse order.

28.B. The series includes 1st, 9th and 18th alphabets in reverse order from U to X.

29.B. The set of five consecutive alphabets starting from A.

30.A. Group of four alphabets starting from Y in reverse order, skipping one alphabet in 1st and 2nd.

31.D. Group of 1st, 10th and 25th alphabets in reverse order starting from Y to B(Y, Z, A, B)

32.C. Group of four alphabets, the alphabets are taken in reverse order, skipping two alphabets in between the consecutive alphabets in the group.

33.C. Group of four alphabets, the alphabets are 1st, 6th, 16th and 21st starting from A to D.

34.B. Group of 26th, 24th and 22nd alphabets.

35.C. HMS. The series is formed as $H \xrightarrow{+5} M \xrightarrow{+6} S$

5. CODING - DECODING TEST

Use of coding (converting a message using an unfamiliar language to achieve secrecy) is a popular strategy used in modern societies. We know that coding and decoding secret messages have become an integral part of communication particularly in areas like military intelligence or diplomatic communications. The codes are always based on a system of symbols into which regular communication gets converted. The new symbols are based on a pattern which follows a certain set of assumptions known to both the sender and the receiver, but not to others. The coding-decoding test is used to judge a candidates' ability to decipher the law used for developing the code used a particular message and break the code to reveal the content of the message. In this type of tests, you will be given a word with its coded form. You have to find out the principle used for coding the word. Then you are required either to use this information to develope a code for conveying a word, or to decode the coded form of a communication, applying the known principle.

The following are the principles commonly used for coding.

I. Jumbling

1. Forward Jumbling
   eg. GHIJKL – HIJKLM
   (G replaced by H, H by I, etc.)

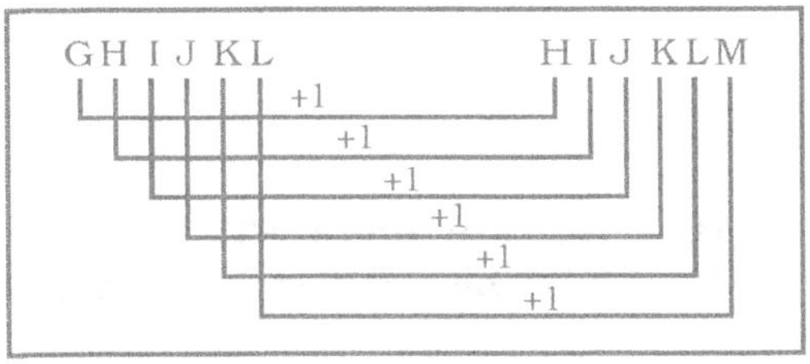

2. Backward Jumbling
   eg. GHIJKL – FGHIJK
   (G replaced by previous letter F, etc.)

II. Reversing

1. Reversing as it is
   (the spelling of the entire word reversed (first as last, last as first, etc.)
   eg. GHIJKL – LKJIHG
2. Split into half and reversing
   (word split into two halves and each reversed; GHI into IHG etc.)
   eg. GHIJKL – IHGLKJ

III. Interchanging

1. Pairing and interchanging
   eg. GHIJKL – HGJILK
   (two adjacent letters reversed, GH into HG, IJ into JI, etc.)
2. Order and disorder
   eg. GHIJKL – TSRQPO

GHIJKL are $7^{th,}$ $8^{th,}$ $9^{th,}$ $10^{th,}$ 11th and 12th letters when we write the English alphabets in the proper order. TSRQPO are $7^{th,}$ $8^{th,}$ $9^{th,}$ $10^{th,}$ 11th and 12th letters when we write the English alphabets in the reverse order. It is advisable that you prepare a chart with letters of the alphebet and their series number as follows:

1	2	3		24	25	26
A	B	C	....	X	Y	Z
26	25	24		3	2	1

This can be used for coding and decoding.

It should also be remembered that a combination of two or more techniques mentioned above is also used for coding. The solution of problems in this section depends upon one's ability to identify the principle used for converting the original message into code language.

QUESTIONS

1. If in a certain language, FIELD is coded as GJFME, how is SICKLE coded in that code?

A. RHBJKD B. RHJBKD

C. TJDLMF D. TJDMLF

Hint: The code uses the principle: replace every letter by its next letter in the alphabet.

Thus	S	I	C	K	L	E
becomes	T	J	D	L	M	F

2. In a certain code STABILISE is written as UVCDKNKUG. How would CRICKET be written in that code?

A. ETKFMVG B. ESLEMGV

C. ETKATCR D. ETKEMGV

Hint: Code: Replace every letter by its second letter to obtain the code.

S	T	A	B	I	L	I	S	E
U	V	C	D	K	N	K	U	G
Hence		C	R	I	C	K	E	T
becomes		E	T	K	E	M	G	V

3. If ROAD is coded in a certain language as URDG, how SWAN will be coded?

A. VXDQ B. VZDQ

C. UXDQ D. VZCQ

Hint: Replace every letter by its third letter as below:

R	O	A	D
U	R	D	G
S	W	A	N
V	Z	D	Q

Answer = VZDQ

4. If MPOEPO means LONDON, what does NPTDPX mean?

A. MOSCOW B. MSOCOW C. MSOCWO D. MOSWCO

Hint: M P O E P O

L O N D O N

Rule: Replace every letter by its previous letter

Hence N P T D P X becomes

M O S C O W

Answer = MOSCOW

5. If the word LPPHGLDWH is coded as IMMEDIATE, how is WRSVHFUHW coded in that code?

A. YUVKIXKYL B. DECITEFUL

C. TOPSBRASS D. TOPSECRET

Hint: L P P H G L D W H

I M M E D I A T E

Principle: Replace every letter by a letetr which is 3 letters behind this letter.

Hence W R S V H F U H W

becomes T O P S E C R E T

6. In a certain code, CLOCK is written as F O R F N.
How is ATTEND written in that code?

A. BDDWGQ B. DOOWQG C. DHHWQG D. DWWHQG

Hint: The rule can be found from the following:

C	L	O	C	K
(3)	(12)	(15)	(3)	(11)
↓	↓	↓	↓	↓
F	O	R	F	N
(6)	(15)	(18)	(6)	(14)

Rule: Three added to the serial order of the letter in the original will give the letter in the second word C is 3rd; this becomes F which is sixth letter, etc.

Use the rule to code the word A T T E N D as follows:

A	T	T	E	N	D
(1)	(20)	(20)	(5)	(14)	(4)
↓	↓	↓	↓	↓	↓
D	W	W	H	Q	G
(4)	(23)	(23)	(8)	(17)	(7)

Answer: D W W H Q G

7. If in a certain language METAPHER is coded as RJYFUMJW, how is NORMAL coded in that code?

A. SWTRFQ B. TSWRFQ

C. ONMRAL D. STWRFQ

Hint: The rule can be found from the following:

M	E	T	A	P	H	E	R
(13)	(5)	(20)	(1)	(16)	(8)	(5)	(18)
↓	↓	↓	↓	↓	↓	↓	↓
R	J	Y	F	U	M	J	W
(18)	(10)	(25)	(6)	(21)	(13)	(10)	(23)

Add 5 to serial number of every letter in the original word to get the letters in the coded language. Use this principle to represent the word NORMAL

N	O	R	M	A	L
(14)	(15)	(18)	(13)	(1)	(12)
↓	↓	↓	↓	↓	↓
(19)	(20)	(23)	(18)	(6)	(17)
S	T	W	R	F	Q

Answer: S T W R F Q.

8. In a code, PEN is written RGP.

How would INK be written in that code?

A. KPM B. KMP C. LRT D. JOL

Hint: Rule: Add 2 to get the new letter.

P	E	N	I	N	K
(16)	(5)	(14)	(9)	(14)	(11)
↓	↓	↓	↓	↓	↓
R	G	P	(11)	(16)	(13)
(18)	(7)	(16)	K	P	M

Answer: K P M.

9. A military code writes TARGET as RATTEG. Using the same code, how would you write BRIDGE?

A. DGEBRI B. IRBDGE C. BRIEGD D. IRBEGD

Hint: The principles used: Word split into two parts:

'T A R' replaced by 'R A T' and

'G E T' replaced by 'T E G'

Using the same principle,

'B R I D G E' has to be split 'B R I' and 'D G E' and each reversed to yield 'I R B' and 'E G D' and combining them, we get his word 'I R B E G D' as answer.

10. If BOARD is written as ERDUG, how will you write DREAM?

A. FUDEO B. GUHDP C. GUHEP D. ESEBN

Hint: Principle used

B	O	A	R	D
(2)	(15)	(1)	(18)	(4)
↓	↓	↓	↓	↓
E	R	D	U	G
(5)	(18)	(4)	(21)	(7)

Rule: Add 3 to each number corresponding to each letter to obtaon the corresponding number in the coded word.

Using this principle, the word DREAM will change as follows:

D	R	E	A	M
(4)	(18)	(5)	(1)	(13)
↓	↓	↓	↓	↓
(7)	(21)	(8)	(4)	(16)
G	U	H	D	P

Answer: G U H D P.

11. In a certain code MISFIT is written as SIMTIF.
How will you write GROCER in that code?

A. OCRLER B. ORERCE C. ORGREC D. ORCRCE

Hint: The modification of 'MISFIT' into 'SIMTIF' uses the principle of splitting the original word into two - as 'MIS' and 'FIT' and reversing the end letters of the two parts to obtain 'SIM' and 'TIF', which are to be combined into one word SIMTIF.

Using this principle, GROCER will split into 'GRO' and 'CER', each of which should reverse their first and last letters to obtain 'ORG' and 'REC'. When these are combined, we get the word 'ORGREC' as our answer.

12. In a certain code COURSE is written as FRXUVH.
Then how would RACE be written in that code?

A. HFDU B. UCFH C. UDFH D. UDHF

Hint: Principle used

	3	15	21	18	19	5
Original word:	C	O	U	R	S	E
Coded word :	F	R	X	U	V	H
	6	18	24	21	22	8

Principle: The letters in the new word can be obtained by adding 3 to each of the numbers in the original word.

The change in the word R A C E will be as shown:

	(18)	(1)	(3)	(5)
Original word:	R	A	C	E
Coded word :	(21)	(4)	(6)	(8)
	U	D	F	H

Answer: UDFH.

13. If in a certain language, HOUSE is coded as INVRF, how is CROWD coded in that code?

A. BGNVC B. DQPVK

C. DQPVE D. DSPXE

Hint:

Original word:	H	O	U	S	E
	(8)	(15)	(21)	(19)	(5)
Coded word :	I	N	V	R	F
	(9)	(14)	(22)	(18)	(6)

Rule: The number in word I and word II are formed as per to a rule: adding and subtracting alternatively one from the numbers in the first word. Use this to find the transformed word for CROWD.

This can be done as follows:

Original word:	C	R	O	W	D
	(3)	(18)	(15)	(23)	(4)
Coded word :	(4)	(17)	(16)	(22)	(5)
	D	Q	P	V	E

Answer: DQPVE.

14. If in a certain language PROSE is coded as PPOQE, how is LIGHT coded in that language?

A. LIGFT B. LLGFE

C. LGGFT D. LGGHT

Hint:

Original word:	P	R	O	S	E
		(18)		(19)	

Coded word :	P	P	O	Q	E
		(16)		(17)	

Principle used for changing: end letters and middle letter do not change. The other two changes (R to P and S to Q) are effected by reducing the original numbers by 2 to obtain the corresponding number in the second word.

Using this we can find out hero LIGT gets coded

Original word:	L	I	G	H	T
		(9)		(8)	
Coded word :	L	(7)	G	(6)	T
	L	G	G	F	T

15. If in a certain language PRACTICE is coded as PUDCTLFE, how will GUARDIAN be coded using the same principle?

A. GDXRDLDN B. XGDRDLDN

C. GXDRDLDN D. GXDRLDDN

Hint: Original word:		(18)	(1)			(9)	(3)	
	P	R	A	C	T	I	C	E
Coded word :	P	U	D	C	T	L	F	E
		(21)	(4)			(12)	(6)	

Rule: Letters at either end, and the middle two letters remain without change. For the remaining letters, add 3 to the original number to obtain the corresponding number in the coded number.

(eg. $R \to U,\ 18 \to 21;\ A \to D,\ 1 \to 4;$

$I \to L,\ 9 \to 12;\ C \to F,\ 3 \to 6;$

Using then, we can find the code for GUARDIAN.

Code for GUARDIAN can be found as follows.

G	U	A	R	D	I	A	N
same	(21)	(1)	same		(9)	(1)	same
↓	↓	↓	↓	↓	↓	↓	↓
↓	↓	↓	↓	↓	↓	↓	↓
	(24)	(4)			(12)	(4)	
G	X	D	R	D	L	D	N

Answer: GXDRDLDN.

16. If in a certain language, HAPPY is coded as GBOQX, how will CROSS be coded in the same language?

A. BSPTR B. BSNRT

C. BSNTR D. BNSTR

Hint: Original word: (8) (1) (16) (16) (25)

	H	A	P	P	Y
	(8)	(1)	(16)	(16)	(25)
	↓	↓	↓	↓	↓
Coded word :	G	B	O	Q	X
	(7)	(2)	(15)	(17)	(24)

Rule: Alternatively decrease by 1 and inrease by 1

as shown: $8 \rightarrow 7$, $1 \rightarrow 2$; $16 \rightarrow 15$, $16 \rightarrow 17$, $25 \rightarrow 24$;

Use the same rule for coding CROSS

(3)	(18)	(15)	(19)	(19)
C	R	O	S	S
↓	↓	↓	↓	↓
(2)	(19)	(14)	(20)	(18)
B	S	N	T	R

Answer: B S N T R.

17. If in a certain language, TIGER is coded as RIGET, how will CROWN be coded in the same language?

A. NROWC B. NOWRC C. RRWCO D. NOWCR

Hint: Rule: Interchange the first letter with the last letter.

Then CROWN becomes NROWC

18. In a certain code, JUDICIAL is written as ICLAUJID. How will you write GLORIOUS in the same code?

A. OISULGRO B. IOSULGRO C. OIUSLGRO D. OSIULGRO

Hint: Split the word JUDICIAL into four groups as below:

$$\frac{JU}{I}\ \frac{DI}{II}\ \frac{CI}{III}\ \frac{AL}{IV}$$

We get the coded word for JUDICIAL as follows:

(a) Interchange groups I and III after reversing the letetrs in each group (I and III)

(b) Interchange groups II and IV after reversing if the letters in each group (II and IV)

We get the coded word ICLAJUID. Use this rule to obtain the coded word for 'GLORIOUS'

GL	OR	IO	US
I	II	III	IV

Interchange I with III after reversing the letter in each group (OI, LG) group. Also interchange II and IV after reversing the letters (SU, RO) we get the coded word.

Number with reversed letters

LG	RO	OI	SU
(i)	(ii)	(iii)	(iv)

Number with interchange (i) with (iii) and (ii) with iv):

OI SU LG RO

Answer: OISULGRO.

19. In a certain language, WOMEN is written as OWMNE, what is the equivalent of NOTES in the same code?

A. OTNES B. NOETS C. SETON D. ONTSE

Hint:

Original:	W	O	M	E	N
Coded:	O	W	M	N	E

The second word is formed from the first word as follows:

(a) Middle letetr (M) remain the same in both

(b) The first two letters in the original word are reversed to obtain the first two letters in the second word.

(c) The last two letters in the original word an reversed to obtain the last two letters in the second word.

Using these rules, the word NOTES will transform as follows:

Original:	N	O	T	E	S
Coded:	O	N	T	S	E

Answer: ONTSE.

20. If PRAMOD be coded as SODJRA in a certain language, how will KESHAV be coded?

A. NBUEDS B. NBVECS C. NBVFDS D. NBVEDS

Hint:

	16	18	1	13	15	4
Original:	P	R	A	M	O	D
Coded word:	S	O	D	J	R	A
	19	15	4	10	18	1

Rule: Add 3 to the odd letters and subtract 3 from even letters of the original word to obtain the coded word as shown above.

(16 → 19; 1 → 4; 15 → 18); (18 → 15; 13 → 10; 4 → 1)

Apply the same principle for coding KESHAV as shown below:

11	5	19	8	1	22
K	E	S	H	A	V
14	2	22	5	4	19
N	B	V	E	D	S

Answer: NBVEDS.

21. In a certain code MONKEY is written as XDJMNL. How is TIGER written in that code?

A. SHFDQ B. QDFHS C. SDFHS D. QDHJS

Hint:

Original:	M	O	N	K	E	Y
	(13)	(15)	(14)	(11)	(5)	(25)
Decrease by 1:	12	14	13	10	4	24
Reverse:	24	4	10	13	14	12
In letters:	X	D	J	M	N	L

The above rule can be used to code the word TIGER as follows:

Original:	T	I	G	E	R
	(20)	(9)	(7)	(5)	(18)
Decrease by 1:	19	8	6	4	17
Reversed:	17	4	6	8	19
In letters:	Q	D	F	H	S

Answer: QDFHS

22. In a certain code SEQUENCE is coded as HVJFVMXV. How is CHILDREN coded in that code?

A. XSRMWIVM B. XSROWIVM

C. DSROWIUN D. MVIWORSX

Hint:

Original Word:	S	E	Q	U	E	N	C	E
	(19)	(5)	(17)	(21)	(5)	(14)	(3)	(5)
Coded:	H	V	J	F	V	M	X	V
	(8)	(22)	(10)	(6)	(22)	(13)	(24)	(22)

The rule: Numbers corresponding to the origial + number corresponding to its coded equivalent = 27

Then, H + S = 27, E + V = 27, ...

Using this we can find the coded equivalent of CHILDREN.

Original:	C	H	I	L	D	R	E	N
	(3)	(8)	(9)	(12)	(4)	(18)	(5)	(14)
Coded Number Equivalent:	24	19	18	15	23	9	22	13

Letter Equivalent:	X	S	R	O	W	I	V	M

Answer: XSROWIVM

23. In a certain code QUESTION is written as NXBVQLLQ. How is REPLY written in that code?

A. OBMIV B. UHSOB C. OHMOV D. OFMMV

Hint:

Original Word:	Q	U	E	S	T	I	O	N
	17	21	5	19	20	9	15	14
Coded Word:	N	X	B	V	Q	L	L	Q
	14	24	2	22	17	12	12	17

Rule for coding:(a) Odd letters: Subtract 3 from the top letter to get its equivalent letter at the bottom

(b) Even letters:Add 3 to the top letter to get its equivalent letter at the bottom.

Example of odd letters:Q – N = 17 – 4 = 3, E – B = 5 – 2 = 3, T – Q = 20 – 17 = 3, O – L = 15 – 12 = 3

Example of even letters:U + 3 = 21 + 3 = 24 = X; S + 3 = 19 + 3 = 22 = V; I + 3 = 9 + 3 = 12 = L ; N + 3 = 14 + 3 = 17 = Q etc.

Use this for encoding the word REPLY

Original:	R	E	P	L	Y
	18	5	16	12	25
Coded Numbers:	18 – 3, = 15	5 + 3, = 8	16 – 3, = 13	12 + 3, = 15	25 – 3 = 22

Letters corresponding to this above is:

15	8	13	15	22
O	H	M	O	V

Answer: OHMOV

24. In a certain code DIVISION is written as DVISIOIN. How is STATES written in that code?

A. SATETS B. STAETS C. SATTES D. SAETTS

Hint: The transformation is an below

Original:	D	IV	IS	IO	N
	↓	↓	↓	↓	↓
Coded:	D	VI	SI	OI	N

Rule:(a) End letters in changed. Mid letters, two close numbers taken two at a time in this original will be reversed in the coded form.

Then IV → VI, IS → SI and IO → OI.

Applying the same rule,

Original:	S	T	A	T	E	S
	↓	↓		↓		↓
Coded:	S	A	T	E	T	S

Answer: SATETS.

25. In a certain code SCRIPT is written as TCQIQT. How is DIGEST written in that code?

A. TIHETT B. EIFETT C. TIFETT D. EIFERT

Hint:

Original:	S	C	R	I	P	T
	(19)	(3)	(18)	(9)	(16)	(20)
Coded word:	T	C	Q	I	Q	T
	(20)	(3)	(17)	(9)	(17)	(20)

Difference between odd numbered letters above and below = 1

Difference between even numbered letters above and below = 0

Difference between S and T, R and Q, P and Q are all = 1

Difference between C and C, I and I, and T and T, are all = 0

This rule can be used to find the code for 'DIGEST'

Original:	D	I	G	E	S	T
	(4)	(9)	(7)	(5)	(19)	(20)
Coded word:	(5)	(9)	(6)	(5)	(20)	(20)
	E	I	F	E	T	T

The numbers were so obtained to follow the rule above and converted into equivalent letters. Diffences between corresponding odd terms = 1, odd difference between corresponding even terms = 0.

Hence the new word is: EIFETT.

26. The word TENDER has been coded in four different ways. Find out which pattern/rule is used for coding it, if MELLOW is coded as TLSSVD.

A. UFOEFS B. SDMCDQ

C. REDNET D. ALUKLY

Hint:

Original:	M	E	L	L	O	W
	13	5	12	12	15	23
Coded word:	T	L	S	S	V	D
	20	12	19	19	22	4

Rule: Difference between the numbers representing equivalent term = 7 ie. 13 and 20, 5 and 12, 12 and 19, 12 and 19, 15 and 22, and the difference between 23 and 4 is not to be treated as 19; it can be treated as the number of letters to be counted for moving forward from W to D, ie. letters X, Y, Z, A, B, C, D = 7. Hence all the six letters obey the same law.

Answer: ALUKLY.

27. In a code, INSTITUTION is written as NOITUTITSNI. How is PERFECTION written in that code?

A. NOITCEFREP B. NOITCRERPF

C. NOITCEFRPE D. NOITCFERPE

Hint:

Original:	I	N	S	T	I	T	U	T	I	O	N
Coded:	N	O	I	T	U	T	I	T	S	N	I

Method of changing → reversing the spelling of the original word by letter interchanging the last letter with the first letter last but one with the second letter, ... the second letter with the last but one letter, and the first letter with the last letter etc.

The same principle can be applied for coding the word 'PERFECTION'

Reversing the spelling of original, we get the answer.

Original:	P	E	R	F	E	C	T	I	O	N
Coded:	N	O	I	T	C	E	F	R	E	P

Answer: NOITCEFREP.

28. In certain code, BOXER is written as AQWGQ. How is VISIT written in that code?

A. UKRKP B. UKRKS C. WKRKU D. WKRKS

Hint:

	(2)	(15)	(24)	(5)	(18)
Original:	B	O	X	E	R
Coded:	A	Q	W	G	Q
	(1)	(17)	23	(7)	(17)

Rule for coding:

Odd letters: replace with a letter one step behind

Even letters: replace with a letter two steps ahead

Odd letters : B → A; X → W; R → Q

Even letters : O → Q; E → G

Use this for encoding the word VISIT

V	I	S	I	T
(22)	(9)	(19)	(9)	(20)
↓	↓	↓	↓	↓
(21)	(11)	(18)	(11)	(19)
U	K	R	K	S

Answer: UKRKS.

29. In a certain code, MOUSE is written as PRUQC. How is SHIFT written in that code?

A. VKIRD B. VKIDR C. VJIDR D. VIKRD

Hint:

Original:	13	15	21	19	5
	M	O	U	S	E
Coded:	P	R	U	Q	C
	(16)	(18)	(21)	(17)	(3)

Method of change (a) Letter at the centre → no change (U → U)

(b) Two letters before the letter at the centre → Add 3 to the original letter to get the coded letters (M → P; O → R; 13 → 16; 15 → 18)

(c) Two letters following the letter at the centre → subtract 2 to the original to get the coded letters.

(S → Q; E → C)

(19 → 17; 5 → 3)

Use this to code the word SHIFT

	19	8	9	6	20
Original:	S	H	I	F	T
Coded:	(22)	(11)	(9)	(4)	(18)
	V	K	I	D	R

Answer: VKIDR

30. If POND is coded as RSTL, how is HEAR written in that code?

A. GHIJ B. GHIZ C. JIGZ D. JCIZ

Hint:	(16)	(15)	(14)	(4)
Original:	P	O	N	D
Coded:	(R	S	T	L
	(18)	(19)	(20)	(12)

Rule for coding: Add 2, 4, 6, 8 respectively to the numbers corresponding to the four letetrs of the original word to obtain the numbers corresponding to the coded word. Coded word numbers are for and as follows:

	16+2	15+4	14+6	4+8
ie,	18	19	20	12

In letters, this is RSTL

Use the same rule to obtain the coded word for 'HEAR'.

	(8)	(5)	(1)	(18)
Original:	H	E	A	R
Coded:	(8+2)	(5+4)	(1+6)	(18+8)
	10	9	7	26
Letters:	J	I	G	Z

Answer: JIGZ

31. In a code language if POSE is coded as OQNPRTDF, then TYPE will be coded as:

A. SUXZOQFD B. SUXZQOFD C. SUXZOQDF D. SUXZQODE

Hint:

Original:	P	O	S	E
Coded:	OQ	NP	RT	DF
	(18)	(19)	(20)	(12)

Method of coding: Two letters on either side of P are used to replace P; From OPQ, omit P, we get OQ as the replacement of P.

Replacement of O is obtained from NOP omiting O; we get NP as replacement of O

Replacement of S is to be obtained from RST, omiting E, we get DF.

The word TYPE can be coded as below from STU, XYZ, OPQ and DEF omit the middle letters to obtain the replace

viz, SU, XZ, OQ, DF

The coded word on SUXZOQDF

32. In a certain code, BACK is coded as GFHP. How MIST would be written in this code?

A. YZON B. QMVW

C. PSKX D. RNXY

Hint:

	(2)	(1)	(3)	(11)
Original:	B	A	C	K
Coded:	G	F	H	P
	(7)	(6)	(8)	(16)

Rule: Add 5 to the number representing each letter to get the equivalent letter in the coded language. Use this we find the code for M I S T

	(13)	(9)	(19)	(20)
Original:	M	I	S	T

Coded:	(18)	(14)	(24)	(25)
	R	N	X	Y

Answer: RNXY

33. In a certain code, METAL is coded as LNDFSUZBKM. How would BODY be written in this code?

A. CAPNECZX B. ACNPECZX

C. ACNPCEXZ D. ZCMOEFUY

Hint:

Original:	M	E	T	A	L
Coded:	LN	DF	SU	ZB	KM
	(7)	(6)	(8)	(16)	

The code is generated as follows:

LMN:	mid letter (M) original; side letters LN are the coded equivalents.						
DEF:	,,	E	,,	;	,,	DF	,,
STU:	,,	T	,,	;	,,	SU	,,
ZAB:	,,	A	,,	;	,,	ZB	,,
KLM:	,,	L	,,	;	,,	KM	,,

Note: letters are not supposed to end with z; A and B are the next two letter.

The code word for BODY can be found as follows

Original:	B	O	D	Y
	ABC	NOP	CDE	XYZ
Coded:	AC	NP	CE	XZ

BODY is to be replaced by ACNPCEXZ.

34. In a certain code, MASTER is coded as NOBCTUUVFGST. How would SCHOOL be written in this code?

A. TUDIJPSPMN B. TUDEIJPQPQMN

C. UVDEIKPQPQNO D. KPEDIJQSQSMN

Hint:

Original:	M	A	S	T	E	R
	↓	↓	↓	↓	↓	↓
	MNO	ABC	STU	TUV	EFG	RST
	↓	↓	↓	↓	↓	↓
Coded:	NO	BC	TU	UV	FG	ST

Use this principle for coding SCHOOL

Original:	S	C	H	O	O	L
	↓	↓	↓	↓	↓	↓
	STU	CDE	HIJ	OPQ	OPQ	LMN
	↓	↓	↓	↓	↓	↓
	TU	DE	IJ	PQ	PQ	MN

The code word for SCHOOL is TUDEIJPQPQMN

Answer: TUDEIJPQPQMN.

35. In a certain code, POND is coded as QRSPQROPQEFG. How would the word HEAR be coded?

A. IJKGHIBCDSTU B. EFGCDEXYZOPA

C. IJKFGHBCDSTU D. GHDEZAQR

Hint:

Original:	P	O	N	D
	↓	↓	↓	↓
	PQRS	OPQR	NOPQ	DEFG
	↓	↓	↓	↓
Coded:	QRS	PQR	OPQ	EFG

Use this principle to code the word HEAR

Original:	H	E	A	R
	↓	↓	↓	↓
	HIJK	EFGH	ABCD	RSTU
	↓	↓	↓	↓
	IJK	FGH	BCD	STU

The code word is IJKFGHBCDSTU.

Answer: IJKFGHBCDSTU.

36. In a certain code, PRIVATIZE is coded as EZZITAAVIRRP. How will the word EDUCATION be coded in the same language?

A. OOINTAACUDDE B. NOIJTAACUDDE

C. NOOITAACUDDE D. NOOITCAAUDEE

Hint:

	I	II	III
Original:	'PRI'	'VAT'	'IZE'
Coded:	'EZZI'	'TAAV'	'IRRP'
	(i)	(ii)	(iii)

The rule: reversed of each group I, II, III with the change: the second letter is repeated as below:

PRI → IRRP, VAT → TAAV, IZE → EZZI

Using this rule we can transform the word EDUCATION by dividing it into 'EDU' 'CAT' 'ION'

EDU → UDDE, CAT → TAAC, ION → NOOI

Combine the three transformed terms in the reverse order, we get the answer as: NOOI, TAAC, UDDE.

37. In a certain code, DISTRIBUTION is coded as SIDIRTTUB. How will the word DIFFICULT be coded?

A. FIDCIFTLU B. FIDICFTLU C. IFDCIFTLU D. FDTICFTLU

Hint:

Original:	'DIS'	'TRI'	'BUT'	'ION'
Coded:	'SID'	'IRT'	'TUB'	'NOI'

Each group in the 'original' is converted into a new group by reversing the letter group; example: DIS → SID, TRI → IRT, etc.

Using this principle we can code the word DIFFICULT.

Original:	'DIF'	'FIC'	'ULT'
	'FID'	'CIF'	'TLU'

Method: DFF → FID, FIC → CIF, ULT → TLU

Answer: FIDCIFTLU.

38. In a certain code, DISTRESS is coded as IDSTERSS. How will the word FICTITIOUS be coded?

A. ICFTTIIOSU B. OFCTTIIOSU C. IFCTIOUSTU D. IFCTITIOSU

Hint:

Original:	DI	ST	RE	SS
	↓	↓	↓	↓
Coded:	ID	ST	ER	SS

Rule: odd numbered with groups are reversed even numbered letter groups are retained.

Using this

Original:	FI	CT	IT	IO	US	becomes;
	↓	↓	↓	↓	↓	
	IF	CT	TI	IO	SU	

Answer: IFCTTIIOSU.

39. In a certain code, the word REPATRIATE is coded as RFQBUSTBUE. How will the word REPERTOIRE be coded?

A. PFQFOUSISE B. RFFQSUPISE

C. RFQFSPUSJE D. FRFQFSUPJSE

Hint:

Original:	R	E	P	A	T	R	I	A	T	E
	↓	↓	↓	↓	↓	↓	↓	↓	↓	↓
Coded:	R	F	Q	B	U	S	J	B	U	E

Rule: (a) First and Last letters - no change.

(b) For other letters, replace each letter by its next letter.

Use this to code the word: R E P E R T O I R E

Using the rules (a) and (b), the word above changes as follows:

R	E	P	E	R	T	O	I	R	E
↓	↓	↓	↓	↓	↓	↓	↓	↓	↓
R	F	Q	F	S	U	P	J	S	E

Answer: RFQFSUPJSE.

40. In a certain code language MASTER is coded as AMTSRE. How will the word HILTON be coded in the same language?

A. IHTLNO B. HITLNO

C. IHLTON D. INHOTL

Hint:

Original: M A S T E R

Split the word into three groups (as shown), each containing two letetrs MA, ST, and ER. Reverse each letter group, to get the coded equivalent. Thus:

MA	ST	ER
↓	↓	↓
AM	TS	RE

Using this principle

HI	LT	ON
↓	↓	↓
IH	TL	NO

The coded word is IHTLNO.

41. In a certain code language, UNITED is coded as QOJUFE. How will the word MOSCOW be coded in the same language?

A. NPTPPX B. IPTDPX

C. WOCMOS D. PXDTIP

Hint:

Original:	U	N	I	T	E	D
	↓	↓	↓	↓	↓	↓
	Q	↓	↓	↓	↓	↓
	↓	↓	↓	↓	↓	↓
	Giving back to the 4th letter back words QRSTU	One letter forwards (0)	One letter forwards (J)	One letter forwards (U)	One letter forwards (F)	One letter forwards (E)

The coded word is QOJUFE

Use the same rule for coding MOSCOW as below:

M	O	S	C	O	W
IJKLM	↓	↓	↓	↓	↓
↓	↓	↓	↓	↓	↓
I	P	T	D	P	X

Coded word is: IPTDPX.

6. BLOOD RELATIONSHIP TEST

This test is based on the relationship of human beings, especially blood relationships. We know that a blood relationship/marriage relationship between A and B will become different when it refers to a relationship of B to A.

The relationships are expressed using standard terms. The important terms used to define relationships are listed below. Those who attempt to take the tests in this section are expected to familiarise themselves with these terms before taking the tests. They are also expected to be familiarise themselves with certain terminologies used for defining the problem. Examples are: "daughter of my fathers wife". 'Father's wife' refers to your mother and hence 'daughter of my father's wife refers to your sister. A large number of equivalent examples are contained in the representative problems given here. Read through the problems and connect them with the solutions to acquaint yourself with similar usages in this group of problems. Try these problems a number of times if you want to familiarise yourself with the solution of question of this type.

We are expected to have a fair knowledge of blood relations. This test is designed to asses the candidates level of knowledge in this subject. Some of the blood relationships are summarized below to help you to understand this group of problems..

1. Mother's or Father's son : Brother
2. Mother's or Father's daughter : Sister
3. Mother's or Father's brother : Uncle
4. Mother's or Father's sister : Aunt
5. Mother's or Father's mother : Grand mother
6. Mother's or Father's father : Grand father
7. Son's son or Daughter's son : Grand son
8. Son's daughter or Daughter's daughter : Grand daughter
9. Father's wife : Mother
10. Mother's husband : Father
11. Daughter's brother : Son
12. Son's sister : Daughter
13. Son's wife : Daughter-in-law
14. Daughter's husband : Son-in-law
15. Husband's mother or wife's mother : Mother-in-law
16. Husband's father or wife's father : Father-in-law
17. Husband's sister or wife's sister : Sister-in-law
18. Husband's brother or wife's brother : Brother-in-law
19. Sister's husband : Brother-in-law

20. Brother's wife : Sister-in-law
21. Brother's son or sister's son : Nephew
22. Brother's daughter or sister's daughter : Niece
23. Uncle's son or daughter or aunt's son or daughter: Cousin

The question paper setters often club three or four relationships together and frame questions.

What we have to do when we want to untie the knots after putting a number of knots? First we have to untie the last knot - the knot at the end. Similarly we have to start over solution of a problem by beginning with the relationship at the end of the chain; not from the beginning. The qustions given below will illustrate the procedure or solution.

QUESTIONS

1. **Anil introduces Rohit as the son of the only brother of his father's wife. How is Rohit related to Anil?**

   A. Cousin B. Son
   C. Uncle D. Son in law

2. **Vinayak is the brother of the son of Sekharan's son. What relation is Vinayak to Sekharan?**

   A. Brother B. Son
   C. Cousin D. Grandson

3. **Pointing to a photograph, a man tells his friend, she is the daughter of the only son of my father's wife. How is the girl related to the man?**

   A. Daughter B. Cousin
   C. Mother D. Sister

4. **X introduces Y saying, "He is the husband of the only grand daughter of the father of my father". How is Y related to X?**

   A. Brother B. Son
   C. Brother-in-law D. Sister-in-law

5. **Showing the man on the stage, Rita said he is the brother of the daughter of the wife of my husband. How is the man on the stage related to Rita?**

   A. Son B. Husband
   C. Nephew D. Cousin

6. **Pointing out to a lady, Ramesh said, "She is the daughter of the women who is the mother of the husband of my mother". How is the lady related to Ramesh?**

A. Aunt B. Grand Daughter
C. Daughter D. Sister

7. **While walking with his friend, Mahesh meets another man whose mother is the wife of Mahesh's father's only son. How is the man related to Mahesh?**
A. Son B. Nephew
C. Cousin D. Uncle

8. **If X is the brother of the son of Y's son, how is X related to Y?**
A. Son B. Brother
C. Cousin D. Grandson

9. **Introducing a man to her husband a woman said, "His brother's father is the only son of my grand father". How is the woman related to this man?**
A. Mother B. Aunt
C. Sister D. Daughter

10. **Rita told Mani, the girl I met yesterday at the beach was the youngest daughter of the brother in law of my friend's mother. How is the girl related to Rita's friend?**
A. Cousin B. Daughter
C. Niece D. Friend

11. **Deepak said to Nitin, "That boy playing with the football is the younger one of the two brothers of the daughter of my father's wife". How is the boy playing football related to Deepak?**
A. Son B. Brother
C. Cousin D. Nephew

12. **Asok said, "This girl is the wife of grandson of my mother". Who is Asok to the girl?**
A. Husband B. Father
C. Grandfather D. Father-in-law

13. **Pointing to a photograph, a woman says, "this man's son's sister ismy mother-in-law". How is the woman's husband related to the man in the photograph?**

A. Grandson B. Son
C. Son-in-law D. Nephew

14. Neelam, who is Rohit's daughter, says to Indu, "Your mother Reeta is the yonger sister of my father, who is the third child of Soman". How is Rohit related to Indu?

A. Maternal-uncle B. Father
C. Grandfather D. Father in law

15. Pointing to a person, Rohit said to Neha, "his mother is the only daughter of your father". How is Neha related to the person?

A. Aunt B. Mother
C. Daughter D. Wife

16. Pointing out to a lady, a girl said, "She is the daughter-in-law of the grandmother of my father's only son". How is the lady related to the girl?

A. Sister-in-law B. Mother
C. Aunt D. Mother-in-law

17. Pointing to a photograph, Vipul said, "She is the daughter of my grandfather's only son". How is Vipul related to the girl in the photograph?

A. Father B. Brother
C. Cousin D. Data inadequate

18. Pointing to a gentleman, Deepak said, "His only brother is the father of my daughter's father". How is the gentleman related to Deepak?

A. Father B. Grandfather
C. Brother-in-law D. Uncle

19. Pointing to a man a woman said, "The daughter of his father is the only daughter of my mother". How is the husband of that woman related to that man?

A. Brother-in-law B. Sister's son
C. Son-in-law D. Son

20. Pointing at a photo, Dinesh said, "His father is the only son of my mother". The photo belongs to:

A. Father and Mother B. Father and daughter
C. Dinesh's father D. Dinesh's son

21. Introducing a lady, a man said, "Her mother is the only daughter of my mother-in-law". What is the man to the lady?

A. Uncle B. Brother

C. Father D. Husband

22. Looking at a portrait of a man, Sanjay said, "His mother is the wife of my father's son. Brothers and sisters I have none". At whose portrait was Sanjay looking?

A. His son B. His Nephew

C. His cousin D. His father

23. Pointing to a boy, Ramesh said, "His only brother's mother is my father's wife". How is Ramesh related to that boy?

A. Uncle B. Father

C. Nephew D. Brother

24. Introducing a woman, a man said, "Her mother's husband's sister is my aunt". How is the man related to the woman?

A. Nephew B. Brother

C. Uncle D. Cousin

25. A and B are brothers. C and D are are sisters. A's son is D's brother. How is B related to C?

A. Father B. Brother

C. Uncle D. Grandfather

26. Old man's son is my son's uncle, then what relation has the old man to me?

A. Brother B. Father

C. Grandfather D. Uncle

27. Leela, who is Sohan's daughter, says to Latika, "Your mother Alka is the younger sister of my father who is the third child of Gajanan". What is the relation of Gajanan to Latika?

A. Father B. Uncle

C. Grandfather D. Father-in-law

Answers with explanation

1.A. Father's wife : Mother
Mother's brother : Uncle
Uncle's son : Cousin

2.D. Son of Sekharan's son : Sekharan's Grandson
Grandson's brother : Grandson

3.A. My father's wife : My mother
My mother's only son : Myself
So the girl is man's daughter

4.C. Father of my father : My grandfather
My grand father's grand daughter : My sister
Sister's husband : Brother in law

5.A. Wife of my husband : Myself
Brother of my daughter is my : Son

6.A. Husband of my mother : My father
Father's mother : Grandmother
Grandmother's daughter : Father's sister/Mother's sister
Father's sister/Mother's sister : Aunt

7.A. Mahesh's father's only son : Mahesh
Mahesh's wife in the mother of the man
So, the man is Mahesh's son

8.D. Son of Y's son : Y's grandson
Brother of Y's grandson : Y's grandson

9.C. Only son of my grandfather : My father
Man's brother's father : Man's father
So, man's father is her father, ie. She is the man's sister

10.A. Daughter of brother in law is niece
Mother's niece : Cousin
So, the girl is the cousin of Rita's friend

11.B. Father's wife : Mother
Mother's daughter : Sister
Sister's brother : My brother

12.D. Grandson of my mother : My son
My son's wife : My daughter-in-law
Hence Asok is her Father-in-law.

13.A. Man's son's sister : Man's daughter

So, the man's daughter is the mother of the woman's husband. Thus, woman's husband is the grandson of the man in the photograph.

14.A. From the information given in the question, it is concluded that Soman is the father of Rohit and Reeta, who is the mother of Indu. Therefore, Rohit is the mothers brother of Indu or maternal-uncle.

15.B. Only daughter of Neha's father : Neha herself

Therefore, statement in other words implies that Neha is mother of the man.

16.B. My father's only son : My brother

Grandmother of my brother : My grandmother

Daughter-in-law of my grandmother : My mother

17.D. My grandfather's only son : My father

So, the girl is the daughter of Vipul's father ie. Vipul is the girl's brother

18.D. Father of Deepak's daughter's is daughter's father is the father of Deepak and brother of father is the uncle. Hence, gentleman is related as brother of Deepak.

19.A. Only daughter of her mother : She herself

So, the man is her brother and her husband is the man's brother-in-law.

20.D. Only son of the mother of Dinesh : Dinesh

Therefore, the photograph belongs to Dinesh's son.

21.A. Since, the mother-in-law of the man is mother of the mother of the lady, therefore the lady is the daughter of the man.

22.A. Since Sanjay has neighbour a sister nor a brother, therefore Sanjay is the only sone of his father. Hence, the mother of the portrait is the wife of Sanjay. Therefore the portrait was of Sanjay's son.

23.D. The mother of the only brother of the boy is the wife of Ramesh's father. Therefore, she is mother of Ramesh. Hence, Ramesh is the brother of the boy.

24.B. He mother's husband means her father and her father's sister is man's aunt. Therefore, the man and woman may be cousin.

25.C. C and D are the daughters of A and B is the uncle of C.

26.B. Since, the old man's son is my son's uncle, therefore, old man's son is my brother. Hence, the old man is my father.

27.C. As Alka is the sister of Sohan and Sohan is the third child of Gajanan, therefore, Alka will be the daughter of Gajanan. But Latika is the daughter of Alka, therefore, Gajanan will be granddaughter of Latika.

7. CLASSIFICATION TEST

Classification means to group the items in a list as belonging to a specific group. In this test, you are given a group of four items. Out of these four three are alike in some manner or the other. One is different and hence does not belong to this group. The candidate is required to choose this item which does not fit in the given group. You have to pick the one that does not belong to the group. This test is also known as **'odd man out'** test.

Find out the common **quality** based on which three words out of the four given words can be grouped. Once the common properly in detected, you will be able to locate the word which does not posses this particular quality.

QUESTIONS

1. Find the odd term in the following:

A. Blade B. Axe

C. Dish D. Scissors

Hint: A, B, D are instruments; C is different.

2. Find the word which does not belong to the group:

A. Walk B. Run

C. Jump D. Think

Hint: D is different; it involves a process different from what is described as A, B and C.

3. Four of the five words given below are alike in a certain way and so form a common group. But one is dissimilar from the rest. Which is the one is dissimilar?

A. Sofa B. Chair

C. Table D. Ashtray

Hint: A, B, C are furniture items, while D is not

4. Which one of the following does not belong to the group to which others belong?

A. Boy B. Girl

C. Man D. Infant

Hint: A, B, C indicates the gender but D does not indicate this.

5. Find the odd group out:

A. 4,8,6,2 B. 10,20,15,5

C. 2,4,3,1 D. 6,12,9,3

Hint: B, C, D Contain numbers which are odd multiples of 2, 4, 3, 1. A is an even multiple of 2, 4, 3, 1.

6. Choose the word which is dissimilar to others in the group:

A. Crab B. Lizard

C. Prawn D. Fish

Hint: A, C, D are creatures which live in water. B does not belong to this group.

7. Which is the one that does not belong to the group?

A. Ring B. Bracelet

C. Skirt D. Bangle

Hint: C is name of a dress item, all others are ornaments.

8. Choose out the odd one:

A. Himachal Pradesh B. Haryana

C. Punjab D. Chandigarh

Hint: D is name of a Union Territory, all others are names of states in India

9. Identify the one which is different:

A. Ear B. Eye

C. Tongue D. Tooth

Hint: Except D, all others are sense organs

10. Spot out the outsider in the following:

A. Diving B. Swimming

C. Jumping D. Bathing

Hint: C not connected with water; other activities are connected with water

11. Select the odd one from the following:

A. Weep B. Love

C. Hate D. Enjoy

Hint: D is not an emotion; others are

12. Choose the odd one from the following:

A. Transport B. Bus

C. Car D. Train

Hint: A not a conveyance others are conveyances.

13. Choose the one that does not belong to the rest:

A. Delhi B. Beiging

C. Rangoon D. Pakistan

Hint: A, B, C are name of cities, D is the name of a state.

14. Which one of the words given below is different from the rest?

A. Mango B. Apple
C. Brinjal D. Grape

Hint: A, B, D are sweet fruits, C is non-sweet vegetable.

15. Find out the pair which is different from the other given pairs:

A. Cow and Buffalo B. Cock and Hen
C. Horse and Mare D. Dog and Bitch

Hint: B, C, D pair words which represent the male and female of a group, but A sands for two different animals.

16. Find the odd one from the following:

A. Carpenter B. Blacksmith
C. Goldsmith D. Sailor

Hint: D names a work category, A, B, C stands for category of standard workers.

17. Find the odd one from the following:

A. Deer B. Zebra
C. Jackal D. Giraffe

Hint: A, B, D represent herbivorous animals, C for a carnivorous animal.

18. Choose the stranger from the following:

A. Physics B. Chemistry
C. Botany D. Economics

Hint: A, B, C are names of science subjects, D is a social science subject.

19. Select the odd one:

A. Ear B. Kidney
C. Eye D. Heart

Hint: A, C, B are human organs which occur in pairs, D occurs singly.

20. Find the odd one from the following:

A. Newton B. Faraday
C. Bethovan D. Rutherford

Hint: A, B, D are names of scientists, C is the name of a musician

21. Select the odd one from the following:

A. Cow B. Deer
C. Donkey D. Goat

Hint: A, B, D are animals with horns, C is an animal without horns.

22. Choose the odd one from the following:

A. Sun B. Moon

C. Star D. Comet

Hint: D seen only on occassions; others are permenently present.

23. Identify the one which is different:

A. Tiger B. Lion

C. Fox D. Cat

Hint: A, B, C are wild animals, D is a domestic animal.

24. Find the odd one:

A. Deer B. Pear

C. Fear D. Near

Hint: A - 'ear' part of the spelling missing, it is present in B, C and D.

25. Choose the number which does not belong to the rest:

A. 1375 B. 5079

C. 5934 D. 1753

Hint: C is the only number which contains an even digit.

26. Choose the odd letter group from the following:

A. EGIK B. MOQS

C. ACEG D. UWYZ

Hint: UWYZ contains an even - numbered letter (viz Z) ; all others are formed using odd numbered letters.

27. Choose the term which does not belong to the rest:

A. GROUSE B. GROVEL

C. GRIEVE D. GROCER

Hint: A, B, D all begin with letters 'GRO' while C begins with 'GRI'.

28. Identify the one which is different:

A. 1 49 B. 9 41

C. 9 42 D. 4 91

Hint: For A, B, D, every digit is the square of numbers 1, 2, 3, where as for C, the last digit does not obey this principle.

29. Find the odd one:

A. Indian
B. British
C. Tropical
D. Canadian

Hint: A, B, D, refer to countries C refer to a region

30. Choose the odd letter group from the following:

A. DFHJ
B. LNPR
C. TVXZ
D. ACEF

Hint: Last group of letters (D) does not follow the pattern found in A, B, C viz. the beginning letter is followed by its 3rd letter, 5th letter and 7th letter. This is not true of D.

31. Which one of the following does not belong to the group of others?

A. Bus
B. Car
C. Bike
D. Lorry

Hint: ABC used to transport people. D used to transport goods.

32. Choose the word which in least like other words in the group:

A. Snake
B. Lizard
C. Turtle
D. Whale

Hint: ABC are reptiles, D is not a reptile.

33. Find the odd one:

A. Blue
B. Orange
C. Rose
D. Red

Hint: C-Rose is a flower and all rests are colours.

34. Choose the month which does not belong to the rest:

A. April
B. July
C. January
D. February

Hint: D-February has two possibilities of 28 and 29 days.

35. Identify the one which is different:

A. Bull
B. Cow
C.Horse
D. Lion

Hint: B - It is the only female animal in the group.

36. Choose the word which is dissimilar to others in the group:

A. Weaver B. Tailor

C. Clerk D. Carpenter

Hint: C - It is the only professional involved in white collar jobs.

37. Spot out the outsider in the following:

A. Circle B. Cone

C. Cylinder D. Area

Hint: Except D all are geometrical figures while area in a measurement.

38. Select the odd one:

A. Rubber B. Gold

C. Salt D. Petrol

Hint: A is the only material that is obtained from trees.

Unit - VI

LOGICAL REASONING

1. STRUCTURE OF ARGUMENTS
2. DEDUCTIVE AND INDUCTIVE REASONING
3. ANALOGY
4. LOGICAL DIAGRAM
5. VENN DIAGRAM
6. ANALYTICAL REASONING

Unit - VI

LOGICAL REASONING

1. STRUCTURE OF ARGUMENTS

Forcefulness of Arguments

The term 'argument' is fairly well-known to need any special discussion. It stands for an accepted mode of arguing for the validity of a stand which one is taking in respect of a problem area about which different opinions are held by different people.

An argument could be effective (carries conviction to most) or ineffective depending upon the force of the logic used in support of the argument and the communication techniques used for the purpose.

We can identify the basic criteria used for judging the appropriateness of an argument. An 'argument' can either be **strong** or **weak.** There is no fixed rule for reaching the solution; what is possible in a situation you can evolve a few dependable guidelines to help you in locating the 'strength of an argument'.

The following guidelines can be used as the basis for taking decisions about the degree of conviction an argument carries (strength):

Guideline I: Before an in depth analysis, test the argument for the following:

i. The argument should not be based on an assumption that in itself appears to be untenable.

ii. The argument should not be based on factually incorrect statements.

iii. The argument should not be ambiguous (uncertain assertions).

iv. The words and phrases used in statements should be used with the same meaning throughout an argument.

v. The arguments that are too simple or too trivial should not be used.

vi. The arguments that contain questions in response to the well-defined statements should be avoided e.g. "Ya, why shouldn't we?"

vii. Arguments with ambivalent implications should be avoided; eg. "both conditions have their pros and cons".

Guideline II: Once your argument satisfies the above test, check further to find out whether:

i. the argument is an established fact – universally accepted or scientifically proved

ii. the argument is in conformity with historically accepted facts

iii. the argument is logically feasible

iv. the argument makes an overuse of previous examples.

Guideline III: Finally, check the following:

i. Whether the argument is factually correct, but not relevant to the stand you take.

ii. Whether the argument takes note of all the above presumptions.

STRENGTHENING AND WEAKENING AN ARGUMENT

1. Strengthening an Argument

Almost every premise has contained hidden assumptions within it and a conclusion follows from these. The set of arguments that would support the conclusion in the given premise can 'strengthen' it. This points to the fact that, amongst the many given arguments (all of which may or may not support the main premise), the one that supports its basic assumption is the strongest argument.

The following points are worth considering in this context:

i. An argument is strong only if it is a fact.

ii. The argument is an extra statement not included in the total communication that supports the conclusion in the relevant communication.

iii. The argument must be related to the conclusion.

2. Weakening an Argument

Argument is weakening if it gives some fact that contradicts the conclusion of a given premise. Such arguments may weaken the conclusion by using some contradictory examples or by contradicting hidden assumptions of the premises. The statement that contradicts the basic assumption of given passage is the most weakening argument. However, as in the case of strengthening arguments, the arguments used for weakening a conclusion should also be (a)factual, (b) extra statements, and (c) relevant to the context.

FALLACIES IN ARGUMENTS

Fallacy literally means misleading arguments. The term 'sophism' is used to describe such statements. It is used in a technical sense in logical reasoning. We know that logic formulates certain rules and regulations for valid thinking. The violation of any of the rules in an argument amounts to committing a fallacy. There are several forms of fallacies. The common fallacies in arguments come under any of these following categories:

1. Deductive fallacies

The deductive fallacies often arise because of the defective formation of arguments, which lead to misleading conclusions. Deductive fallacies are either inferential or non-inferential.

1. Inferential Deductive Fallacies are those which result from the violation of rules or principles formulated for various inferential processes of reasoning. These fallacies are of two types: (i) fallacy of immediate inference which involves the faulty process of conversion, obversion, contraposition and inversion, as used in logical deduction; and (ii) fallacy of mediate inference which involves the faulty process of the syllogistic form of reasoning, viz. violating the rules of categorical, hypothetical-categorical syllogism and dilemma.

2. Non-Inferential Deductive Fallacies are those which arise out of the violation of the rules of logical definition or logical division, such as, redundant definition, accidental definition, too wide or too narrow, incomplete, obscure and figurative definitions, synonymous or negative definitions, cross division, incomplete or too narrow division, overlapping, too wide division, metaphysical partition, etc. These are not inferential because they do not involve reasoning.

2. Semi-logical Fallacies

This fallacy occurs due to the faulty use of language which creates ambiguity. There are eight forms of this fallacy - emphibology, accent, accident, converse accident, composition, division, equivocation, and paronyms. Some of the important forms which have become part and parcel of examinations are the following:

1. Fallacy of Emphibology results when a sentence is wrongly constructed e.g.

Alexander, Darius will conquer.

In this it is not clear who will conquer whom.

2. Fallacy of Accent arises from shifting emphasis from one word to another, and in the process changing the very meaning of the sentence, e.g.

We cannot bear false witness against our neighbour.

If the emphasis is on the word 'neighbour' the very meaning of the sentence will change. It means that we can bear false witness against those who are not our neighbours.

Note: Both the fallacies, of emphibology and of accent, are not inferential fallacies.

3. Fallacy of Accident occurs due to confusion between the essential and accidental properties. What is true of a thing in its peculiar or accidental circumstances may not be true for its real nature. e.g.

Killing of man is a crime.

A murderer is a man.

∴ Killing a murderer is a crime.

Converse of accident also leads to a fallacy where what is true accidentally is taken as true generally e.g.

Killing of a murderer is legally justified.

A murderer is a human being.

∴ Killing of a human being is legally justified.

4. Fallacy of Composition and Division are converse of each other and occur due to use of a term both distributive and collective i.e., shift from using it for each member separately to using it for all the members taken together, or vice-versa.

Example of composition

(a) One can read Othello in a day, Tempest in a day, As You Like It in a day, Merchant of Venice in a day. All these are works of Shakespeare. Therefore one can read the whole of Shakespeare in a day.

(b) Seven and eight are odd and even. Fifteen is eight and seven. Hence fifteen is odd and even.

Both the arguments exhibit a shift of term and its distributive use i.e., for each member separately to its collective use i.e., for all members collectively.

Example of Division

(a) All works of Shakespeare cannot be read in a day.

Othello is a work of Shakespeare.

∴ Othello cannot be read in a day.

(b) Fifteen is an odd number.

Eight and seven are fifteen.

∴ Eight and seven are odd numbers.

Both the above examples exhibit fallacy of division from a collective major to a distributive conclusion through a distributive minor premise.

5. Fallacy of Equivocation occurs when a term is used with more than one meaning in an argument which leads to an ambiguous conclusion. e.g.

The end of life is perfection.

Death is the end of life.

∴ Death is perfection.

Here, the word 'end' is used ambiguously. In the major premise it stands for idealism or 'goal' and in the minor premise it denotes the termination of life. Hence, the argument is faulty.

3. Material Fallacies

Besides these logical and semi-logical fallacies there are some other forms of fallacies known as material fallacy or non-verbal fallacies; its important forms are given below.

1. Irrelevant Conclusion: Popularly known as *egnatio elanchi* in logic occurs when used for an argument which goes outside the issue, what we popularly describe as 'beating around the bush'. See the following examples.

(i) "You cannot accuse me of theft because you were convicted for theft last year." Here an accused tries to defeat his adversary on an irrelevant argument – using the fact that he is not himself an upright person. This form of argument is known as *argumentum ad hominem.*

(ii) How can you do away with the caste system?

Lord Krishna has suggested it in the Bhagavad Geeta.

The above fallacy is based on quoting authorities for purposes other than for the actual issue (caste system). This is known as *argumentum adverecundian.*

(iii) "If people will elect me, I will protect their religious sanctity", another example where instead of straight reasoning, an appeal is made to the sentiments of the people, known as *argumentum ad populam.*

(iv) "This lad has committed a mistake, leave him, he is an orphan."

An appeal for pity is used in the place of reasoning. This is known as *argumentum ad miser ignonatium.*

(v) "His failure to disprove the argument is taken as proof against his case."

Instead of advancing a valid argument, the opponent is using his opponent's other forms of weaknesses. This is known as *argumentum ad ignonatium.*

(vi) "Confess your crime or I will break your head."

Here reasoning fails and attempt is to make a person agree to an untruth at pistol point.

2. Begging the Question *(pettio principii)*: This involves 'argument in a circle' i.e., the very conclusion that is required to be proved or drawn is already assumed as the premise and the remaining arguments are based on this. Example:

"Opium produces sleep because it has a soporific quality."

Here 'opium produces sleep' and 'opium has a soporific quality' (sleep producing effect) mean the same.

3. Fallacy of Complex Questions: Here a complex, tricky question is asked which involves in itself more questions. This fallacy is committed when an 'Yes' or 'No' answer is expected, which itself implies admitting other facts without a knowledge of which he is admitting.

"Have you stopped cheating?"

This question creates a puzzling situation. If one says 'yes' it means that he is cheated in the past, if one says 'no' then it implies that one continuing his cheating even now.

4. Fallacy Due to False Cause or No Cause: Sometimes absurd conclusions follow the argument *(reductio ad absurdum).* e.g.

It is ridiculous to suppose that resources are the source of development of a state. Bihar is a state rich in minerals, but 70% of the state's population live below the poverty line.

The cause which is used to falsify the statement is in itself a false cause.

We will examine a few illustrative examples.

The question below consists of a statement followed by two arguments numbered I & II. Decide which is 'strong' argument and which is 'weak' argument.

Statement:

Should there be a restriction on the migration of people from one state to another in India?

Arguments:

I. Yes, because this is the way to effect an equitable distribution of resources across states in India.

II. No, any Indian citizen has a basic right to stay at any place of their choice in India and hence cannot be prevented from moving to another state.

Solution:

Let us take up Argument. I

Argument I is not assumption. It is a fundamental right supported by law.

It is factually correct.

It is not ambiguous.

It contains no word(s)/phrase(s) that convey a different meaning.

No scope for any superfluous interpretation or further questioning.

Hence Guideline I is satisfied.

The argument is established fact and logical; hence it satisfies Guideline II

It is fully related to the topic of discussion; hence it satisfies Guideline III

Hence Argument I is a **strong argument**.

Argument II satisfies the first guideline that this is not an assumption; but is based on a factually incorrect assumption.

Hence, Argument II is a **weak argument**.

Practice Exercise

In each question given below a statement is followed by two arguments numbered I and II. You have to decide which of the arguments is a 'strong' argument and which is a 'weak' argument.

You have to choose one of the following alternatives as your answer:

A. Only argument I is strong

B. Only argument II is strong

C. Both I and II are strong

D. Neither I nor II is strong

Examples:

1. *Statement:*

Should parliamentary elections in India be held every three years as against five years at present?

Arguments:

I. Yes; this will help the voters to change non-performing representatives from parliament.

II. No; the elected representatives will not have enough time to settle down and concentrate on the country's development.

2. *Statement:*

Should the elections for the Lok Sabha and Rajya Sabha be conducted simultaneously?

Arguments:

I. Yes; it will reduce cost of elections and precious time which could then be used for constructive purposes.

II. No; it is unconstitutional, as mid-term polls would have to be conducted in the same states too, which is in contradiction to the provisions of the constitution.

3. *Statement:*

Should there be a complete ban on import of food grains by India?

Arguments:

I. Yes; India produces enough food grains and does not need to import—which may affect interest of the Indian farmers.

II. No; India should keep the option of imports open to tackle any future abnormal food situation.

4. *Statement:*

Should private parties be allowed to run air services in India?

Arguments:

I. Yes; private parties in India are capable of providing reliable air services.

II. No; we should not follow the practice adopted by foreign countries.

5. *Statement:*

Should junk food be disallowed in schools?

Arguments:

I. Yes; Junk food has no nutritious element and is injurious to human health and well-being.

II. No; Junk food can be prepared easily and in less time while regular food takes time to cook.

6. *Statement:*

Should all farmers in India be provided free electricity for agricultural activities?

Arguments:

I. Yes; many developed countries in Western Europe provide lot of subsidies to the farmers to encourage them to remain engaged in agricultural activities.

II. No; many rich farmers will unduly be benefitted at the cost of exchequer.

7. Statement:

Should the government impose a blanket ban on the use of animals in entertainment industry?

Arguments:

I. No; instead the entertainment industry may be encouraged to use animals with proper care.

II. Yes; animals used in entertainment industry are treated badly and hence should be banned.

8. Statement:

Should the post of Governors be abolished in India?

Arguments:

I. Yes; it puts strains on the federal structure envisioned by the forefathers of the Constitution.

II. No; Governors are agents of Centre in the States; thus they are important for maintaining the unity of the country.

9. Statement:

Should the markets in City 'X' in India be permitted to function till late night?

Arguments:

I. Yes, why not? Other metros like Lahore, London, New York have markets which are open till late in the night.

II. No; it will give encourage consumerism, which is detrimental to family savings.

10. Statement:

Should foreign surgeons be allowed to conduct surgeries in India?

Arguments:

I. No, their bonafides could be false, leading to fatal mishandlings.

II. No, because Indian surgeons are not allowed to perform operations in foreign countries.

11. Statement:

Should power theft be made a cognizable offence?

Arguments:

I. Yes; people employ dishonest tricks to utilize power and cheat the public.

II. Yes; this will reduce anti-social activities in our society.

12. Statement:

Should exit polls be banned in India?

Arguments:

I. Yes; Indian voter is not mature for the task and any such poll at initial phases of the polling will affect and influence uncommitted voters during the subsequent phases of the poll.

II. No; citizens have the right to information, at all times, which will help a voter for adopting the right decision in voting.

13. Statement:

Should we open five new IITs (Indian Institute of Technology) in the country?

Arguments:

I. Yes; India needs more well-qualified technical manpower to meet its diverse technological needs.

II. No; It would be a wastage of national resources as many of the individuals trained in IITs leave the country.

14. Statement:

Should all the political appointees, as heads of different organizations other than administration, resign at the time of change of government?

Arguments:

I. Yes; such a practice is followed up in USA as the system of spoils is more effective.

II. No; such appointments should be kept free from political influences and each of them should be allowed to complete their tenures.

15. Statement:

Should Non-Resident Indians (NRIs) be entitled to dual citizenship?

Arguments:

I. Yes; this will help cultivation of intimacy of NRIs with their place of origin.

II. No; this move will have limited success as many countries in which NRIs may be residing have no provision of dual citizenships.

16. Statement:

Should sale and purchase of human organs be made legal in India?

Arguments:

I. Yes; in many countries it is not considered illegal.

II. No; this may open the floodgates for the sale of human organs.

17. Statement:

Is the pen mightier than the sword?

Arguments:

I. Yes; written words influence the way of thinking of a large number of people.

II. No; one can conquer the world by use of physical force.

18. Statement:

Should the press in India be given the complete freedom?

Arguments:

I. Yes; only then people will get the correct information on which to act.

II. No; absolute freedom to the press in a developing country like India will confuse issues.

Answer keys

1.D. Parliamentary elections require huge sum of resources, so Argument I is not strong. What guarantee is there that the people will choose the right representatives if the elections are held after three years'? Hence Argument II is disputable. If three years are not enough for settling then five years may also be insufficient!

2.A. Only Argument I is strong, as conducting of elections to Lok Sabha and various State Assemblies simultaneously will save time and money. Argument II is not valid as midterm polls could be conducted if necessary. So it is a weak argument.

3.D. Argument I is factually incorrect while Argument II is too simple to be an argument since it is not based on an in-depth analysis of the situation.

4.A. Argument 1 is strong as it is based on fact. Indian private entrepreneurs are capable of operating airlines. Argument II is not strong since it is based on comparisons that make tend to weaken the argument.

5.A. Good health is desirable. Hence Argument I is strong. Argument II raises the issues which are of superfluous importance; so it is not strong.

6.D. If other countries are providing subsidies, it does not mean that India should also provide free electricity. So Argument I is not strong. Argument II is not strong since it proposes not to make electricity free, using wrong arguments.

7.B. This uses the argument for idealistic behaviour. Could it be achieved? It is debatable. So Argument I is weak. Argument II is strong as it is based on experience and observation.

8.B. Argument I is weak as it is false. The governor's office-does not contradict with the federal structure envisioned in India. Argument II is strong.

9.D. Argument I is not strong as it is based on comparisons. Argument II is not strong; it sounds ridiculous. Such ideas are not plausible.

10.D. This is a wrong assumption, and hence is a weak argument. Argument I cannot be the reason to allow or not to allow something, since bonafides could be ascertained.

11.D. Both are not strong.

12.A. Argument I is strong because it is plausible. Argument II is not strong since the results of exit polls may not be factual and the voter is likely to be misguided.

13.A. Argument I is strong as it is based on valid assumptions. Argument II is weak.

14.D. What is followed in USA and is found to be effective there may not be effective in India. So Argument I is weak. Argument II also does not provide an answer to as why the appointees should resign. It is not a valid argument. Hence Argument II is also not strong.

15.A. Argument I is strong as entitlement of NRIs with their place of origin may be beneficial to the Indian Economy. Argument II is not strong as a move cannot be derailed only because it is not availed by all kinds of people.

16.D. Argument I is not strong; in fact that certain act is legal in many countries does not support that stand that it has to be followed in India. Argument II is untrue and lacks substance.

17.A. Argument I is strong because influencing the ways of thinking of different people rationally to bring about radical changes in the world is an acceptable change; but conformity achieved with the help of physical force will cease to exist once the force is taken away. So Argument II is not strong.

18.D. Argument I is not strong; the word 'only' decreases its validity. Argument II is also not strong as it does not specify how the move will confuse issues.

2. DEDUCTIVE AND INDUCTIVE REASONING

The logical reasoning of an individual is his ability to identify the unknown from the presently known facts. The logical inference is a cognitive process (intellectual process) of arriving at a conclusion. The inference can be inductive or deductive. The inference is said to be inductive when one move from several particular cases to one general case, the inference is said to be deductive when one moves from a general principle to a particular principle contained within the general principle.

It is necessary that we define some of the terms used for the present discussions.

A **'Term'** means the *subject* or *predicate* of a logical proposition. A **proposition** is the statement of a certain relation between two terms. The standard form of a proposition is *Quantifier + Subject + Copula + Predicate.*

1. **Quantifier:** The words 'all', 'no' and 'some' are called quantifiers because they help to quantify some term used in the proposition.
2. **Subject:** The subject in a proposition is a term about which something is said.
3. **Predicate:** The predicate is the part of the proposition denoting something about the subject that which is affirmed or denied about the subject.
4. **Copula:** The copula is that part of the proposition which denotes the relation between the subject and the predicate.

e.g.	All	men	are	animals
	Quantifier	Subject	Copula	Predicate

Four-fold classification of proposition:

Based on **quantity** propositions can be classified into universal and particular. A proposition is said to have a **universal** quantity if it begins with universal quantifier, and a **particular** quantity if it begins with a particular quantifier. Propositions can be further classified on the basis of **quality** viz affirmative and negative. Proposition which assent something about the inclusion of the whole or a part of one set in the other are said to have **affirmative** quantity, while those which deny the inclusion of the whole or a part of one set in the other are said to have a **negative** quantity. Also, a term is distributed in a proposition if it refers to all members of the set of objects denoted by the term. Otherwise, it is said to be undistributed. Based on the above facts, propositions can be classified into four types.

1. **Universal Affirmative Proposition**: It distributes only the subject. i.e the predicate is not interchangeable with the subject.

   All snakes are reptiles.

   We cannot conclude that 'All reptiles are snakes'.

2. **Universal Negative Proportion**: It distributes both the subject and the predicate. i.e an entire class of predicate term is denied to the entire class of the subject term.

   No boy is intelligent.

3. **Particular Affirmative Proposition**: It distributes neither the subject nor the predicate.

   e.g. Some men are foolish.

   Here, the subject term 'men' is used not for all but only for some men and similarly the predicate term 'foolish' is affirmed for a part of the subject class. So, both are undistributed.

4. **Particular Negative Proposition**: It distributes only the predicate.

   e.g. Some animals are not wild.

   Here, the subject term 'animals' is used only for a part of its class and hence is undistributed while the predicate term 'wild' is denied entirely to the subject term and hence is distributed.

The four types of propositions are represented using letters for sharpness and brevity. The following letter symbols are used for each:

Universal Affirmative Proposition : A

Universal Negative Propostion : E

Particular Affirmative Proposition : I

Particular Negative Proposition : O

The details of the different classification categories are presented in the following table:

Statement Form	Quantity	Quality	Distribution
A : All S is P	Universal	Affirmative	Within S only
E : No S is P	Universal	Negative	In both S and P
I : Some S is P	Particular	Affirmative	In neither S nor P
O : Some S is not P	Particular	Negative	Within P only

LOGICAL DEDUCTION

The phenomenon of deriving a conclusion from a single proposition or a set of given propositions is known as **logical deduction.** The given propositions are also referred to as the premises for deduction.

Two Inferential Processes of Deduction

Inferences are of two types – *inductive and deductive.* Intelligence testing, mostly tests a person's deductive reasoning ability. Deductive inference may be further classified as **Immediate** inference and **Mediate** inference. These are taken up in the next few sections.

I. Immediate Deductive Inference

In this method of reasoning, the conclusion is derived from a single premise, by any of the three ways – *Conversion, Obversion, and Contraposition.*

1. Conversion: The conversion proceeds with interchanging the subject term and the predicate term i.e. the subject term of the premise becomes the predicate term of the conclusion and the predicate term of the premise becomes the subject of the conclusion. The given proposition is called **convertend,** whereas the conclusion drawn from it is called its **converse.**

Table of Valid Conversions

Convertend	Converse
A: All S is P eg. All students are bright.	**I :** Some P is S Some bright people are students.
E: No S is P eg. No man is virtuous.	**E :** No P is S No virtuous being is a man.
I : Some S is P eg. Some boys are poets.	**I :** Some P is S Some poets are boys.
O: Some S is not P	No valid conversion

Note that in a conversion, the quality remains the same and the quantity may change.

2. Obversion: In obversion, we change the quality of the proposition and replace the predicate term by its complement.

Table of Valid Obversions

Obvertend	Obverse
A : All birds are mammals.	**E :** No birds are non-mammals.
E : No poets are singers.	**A :** All poets are non-singers.
I : Some nurses are doctors.	**O :** Some nurses are not non-doctors.
O : Some politicians are not statesmen	**I :** Some politicians are non-statesmen.

3. Contraposition: To obtain the contrapositive of a statement, we first replace the subject and predicate terms in the proposition and then exchange both these terms with their complements. Here a double change takes place. First the change is to obverse and then to converse.

Table of Valid Contrapositions

Proposition	Contrapositive
A: All birds are mammals	**A:** All non- mammals are non-birds
I : Some birds are mammals.	**I :** Some non-mammals are non-birds

Note that in valid converse, obverse or contrapositive of a given proposition always logically follows from the proposition.

Practice Exercise

Directions: Following questions have a statement followed by a few conclusions. Find out which of these is definitely true.

1. *Statement:*

Some I.A.S officers are corrupt.

Conclusions:

A. Some I.A.S officers are not corrupt.
B. A few I.A.S officers are honest.
C. A few corrupt human beings aren't I.A.S officers.
D. A few corrupt human beings are I.A.S officers.

2. *Statement:*

All I.A.S officers are corrupt.

Conclusions:

A. Some I.A.S officers are not corrupt.
B. All corrupt officers are I.A.S officers.
C. No corrupt officer is an I.A.S officer.
D. Some corrupt officers are I.A.S officers.

3. *Statement:*

Most of the policemen beat suspects to get a confession from them.

Conclusions:

A. Some policemen beat their suspects to make them confess.
B. There are no policemen who don't beat their suspects to get their confession.
C. There are some policemen who don't beat their suspects to get their confession.
D. All policemen beat their suspects.

4. *Statement:*

No beggar is poor.

Conclusions:

A. Some beggars are poor.
B. None of the poor is a beggar.
C. Beggars are rich.
D. Some poor beings are beggars.

5. *Statement:*

All women are beautiful.

Conclusions:

A. Some beautiful human beings are women.

B. Some beautiful human beings are not women.

C. All beautiful human beings are women.

D. None of the above is true.

6. *Statement:*

All lovers are blind.

Conclusions:

A. None of the blind is a lover.

B. Some blind people are lovers.

C. A few lovers may have eyes.

D. None of these.

Answer keys

1.D. 'I' has 'I' type convertend.

2.D. 'A' has 'I' type of conclusion.

3.A. Since conclusion of 'A' type is 'I'.

4.B. 'E' type is converted to 'E' only.

5.A. The statement is 'A' type, hence conclusion would be of 'I' type with subject & predicate interchange.

6.B. It is of 'A' type of statement so has 'I' type conclusion.

II. Mediate Deductive Inference (SYLLOGISM)

First introduced by Aristotle, a syllogism is a deductive argument in which a conclusion has to be drawn from two propositions referred to as the premises.

Example:
1. All lotus are flowers
2. All flowers are beautiful
3. All lotus are beautiful

Clearly, the propositions 1 and 2 are the combined premises for proposition 3. Proposition 3, which follow from the first two propositions, is called the conclusion.

Syllogism is concerned with three terms:

1. Major Term: It is the predicate of the conclusion and is denoted by P (first letter of 'Predicate')

2. Minor Term: It is the subject of the conclusion and is denoted by S (first letter of 'Subject')

3. Middle Term: It is the term common to both the premises and is denoted by M (first letter of 'Middle')

Example: **Premises** : 1. All dogs are animals.
2. All tigers are dogs.

Conclusion : All tigers are animals.

'Animals' is the predicate of the conclusion and so, it is the major term, P.

'Tigers' is the subject of the conclusion and so, it is the minor term, S.

'Dogs' is the term common to both the premises and so, it is the middle term, M.

Premises.

1. **Major premise** is that in which the middle term is the subject.
2. **Minor premise** is that in which the middle term is the predicate.

Rules for deriving the conclusion from two given premises

1. The conclusion does not contain the middle term.

Example. **Statements** : 1. All men are girls.
2. Some girls are students.

Conclusions : 1. All girls are men.
2. Some girls are not students.

Since both the conclusions 1 and 2 contain the middle term 'girls', neither of the two conclusions will follow.

2. No term can be distributed in the conclusion unless it is distributed in the premises.

Example. **Statements** : 1. Some dogs are goats.
2. All goats are cows.

Conclusions : 1. All cows are goats.
2. Some dogs are cows.

Statement 1 is an I – type proposition which distributes neither the subject nor the predicate.

Statement 2 is an A – type proposition which distributes the subject i.e. 'goats' only.

Conclusion 1 is an A – type proposition which distributes the subject 'cows' only.

Since the term 'cows' is distributed in conclusion 1 without being distributed in the premises, conclusion 1 cannot follow.

3. The middle term should be distributed at least once in the premises. Otherwise, the conclusion cannot follow.

For the middle term to be distributed in a premise,

(i) M must be the subject if premise is an A proposition.

(ii) M must be subject or predicate if premise is an E proposition.

(iii) M must be predicate if premise is an O proposition.

Note that in an I proposition, which distributes neither the subject nor the predicate, the middle term cannot be distributed.

Example. **Statements :** 1. All fans are watches.
2. Some watches are black.

Conclusions : 1. All watches are fans.
2. Some fans are black.

In the premises, the middle term is 'watches'. Clearly, it is not distributed in the first premise which is an A proposition as it does not form its subject. Also, it is not distributed in the second premise which is an I proposition. Since, the middle term is not distributed even once in the premises, and hence no conclusion follows.

4. No conclusion follows:

(i) if both the premises are particular.

Example. **Statements :** 1. Some books are pens.
2. Some pens are erasers.

Conclusions : 1. All books are erasers.
2. Some erasers are books.

Since both the premises are particular, no definite conclusion follows.

(ii) if both the premises are negative.

Example. **Statements :** 1. No flower is mango.
2. No mango is cherry.

Conclusions : 1. No flower is cherry.
2. Some cherries are mangoes.

Since both the premises are negative, neither conclusion follows.

(iii) if the major premise is particular and the minor premise is negative.

Example. **Statements :** 1. Some dogs are bulls.
2. No tigers are dogs.

Conclusions : 1. No dogs are tigers.
2. Some bulls are tigers.

Here, the first premise containing the middle term 'dogs' as the subject is the major premise and the second premise containing the middle term 'dogs' as the predicate is the minor premise. Since the major premise is particular and the minor premise is negative, no conclusion follows.

5. If the middle term is distributed twice, the conclusion cannot be universal.

Example. **Statements :** 1. All fans are chairs.
2. No tables are fans.

Conclusions : 1. No tables are chairs.
2. Some tables are chairs.

Here, the first premise is an A proposition and so, the middle term 'fans' forming the subject is distributed. The second premise is an E proposition and so, the middle term 'fans' forming the predicate is distributed. Since the middle term is distributed twice, the conclusion cannot be universal.

6. If one premise is negative, the conclusion must be negative.

Example. **Statements :** 1. All grasses are trees.
2. No tree is a shrub.

Conclusions : 1. No grasses are shrubs.
2. Some shrubs are grasses.

Since one premise is negative, the conclusion must be negative. So, conclusion 2 cannot follow.

7. If one premise is particular, the conclusion must be particular.

Example. **Statements :** 1. Some boys are thieves.
2. All thieves are dacoits.

Conclusions : 1. Some boys are dacoits.
2. All dacoits are boys.

Since one premise is particular, the conclusion must be particular. So, conclusion 2 does not follow.

8. If both premises are affirmative, the conclusion must be affirmative.

Example. **Statements :** 1. All women are mothers.
2. All mothers are sisters.

Conclusions: 1. All women are sisters.
2. Some women are not sisters.

Since both the premises are affirmative, the conclusion must be affirmative. So, conclusion 2 does not follow.

9. If both the premises are universal, the conclusion must be universal.

10. If the major premise is affirmative, the conclusion has to be particular.

Example. **Statements** 1. All plays have a dramatic edge.
2. Some movies have plays.

So, we cannot have a conclusion like "All plays are movies".

Let us study the various possible cases and draw all possible inferences in each case, along with verification through venn diagrams.

Case 1. All men are boys. All boys are students.

Immediate deductive inferences:

The converse of first premise i.e. 'some boys are men' and converse of the second premise i.e. 'some students are boys' both hold.

Venn diagram	**Inferences**
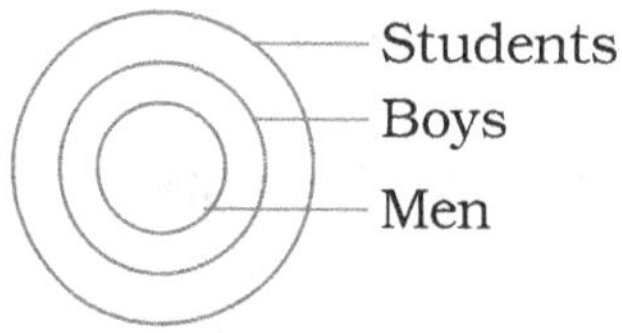	1. Some boys are men. 2. Some students are boys 3. All men are students 4. Some students are men

Mediate deductive inferences:

Since both the premises are universal and affirmative, the conclusion must be universal affirmative. Also, the conclusion should not contain the middle term. So, it follows that 'All men are students'. The converse of this conclusion i.e. 'Some students are men' also holds.

Case 2. All birds are animals. All fishes are animals.

Immediate deductive inferences:

The converse of the first premise i.e. 'Some animals are birds' and converse of the second premise i.e. 'Some animals are fishes' both hold.

Venn diagram	**Inferences**
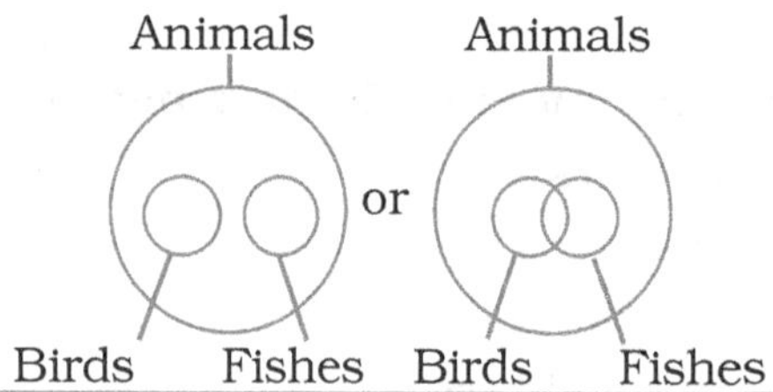	1. Some animals are birds. 2. Some animals are fishes. 3. Either 'No bird is fish' or 'Some birds are fishes' as E and I-type propositions form a complimentary pair.

Mediate deductive inferences:

Both, being A-type propositions, distribute subject only. Thus, the middle term 'animals' is not distributed even once in the premises. So, no definite conclusion follows.

Case 3. All puppets are dolls. Some dolls are rattles.

Immediate deductive inferences:

Venn diagram	**Inferences**
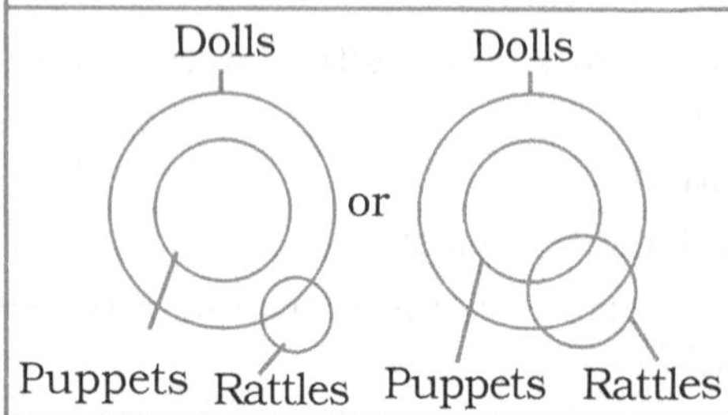	1. Some dolls are puppets 2. Some rattles are dolls 3. Either 'No puppet is rattle' or 'Some puppets are rattles' as E and I-type propositions form a complimentary pair.

The converse of the first premise i.e. 'Some dolls are puppets' and the converse of the second premise i.e. 'Some rattles are dolls', both hold.

Mediate deductive inferences:

First premise, being an A-type proposition, distributes the subject only while the second premise, being an I-type proposition, distributes neither subject nor predicate. Since the middle term 'dolls' is not distributed even once in the premises, so no definite conclusion can be drawn.

Case 4. Some writers are players. All players are musicians.

Immediate deductive inferences:

The converse of the first premise i.e. 'Some players are writers' and the converse of the second premise i.e. 'Some musicians are players', both hold.

<table>
<tr><th>Venn diagram</th><th>Inferences</th></tr>
<tr><td>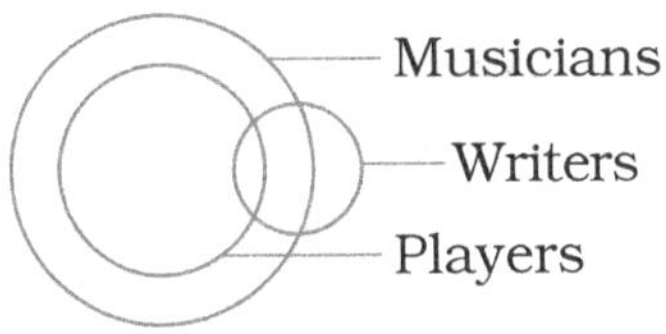
</td><td>1. Some players are writers
2. Some musicians are players
3. Some writers are musicians
4. Some musicians are writers</td></tr>
</table>

Mediate deductive inferences:

Since one premise is particular, the conclusion must be particular and should not contain the middle term. So it follows that 'Some writers are musicians'. The converse of this conclusion i.e. 'Some musicians are writers' also holds.

Case 5. All boxes are toys. Some boxes are clips.

Immediate deductive inferences:

The converse of the first premise i.e. 'Some toys are boxes' and the converse of the second premise i.e. 'Some clips are boxes', both hold.

<table>
<tr><th>Venn diagram</th><th>Inferences</th></tr>
<tr><td>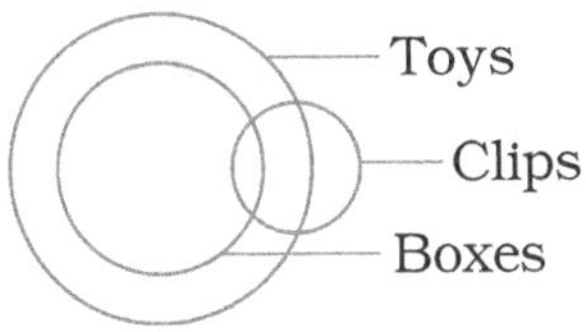
</td><td>1. Some toys are boxes.
2. Some clips are boxes.
3. Some toys are clips.
4. Some clips are toys.</td></tr>
</table>

Mediate deductive inferences:

Since one premise is particular, the conclusion must be particular and should not contain the middle term. So it follows that 'Some toys are clips'. The converse of this conclusion i.e. 'Some clips are toys' also holds.

Case 6. All buses are vans. Some cycles are vans.

Immediate deductive inferences:

The converse of the first premise i.e. 'Some vans are buses' and the converse of the second premise i.e. 'Some vans are cycles', both hold.

Venn diagram	Inferences
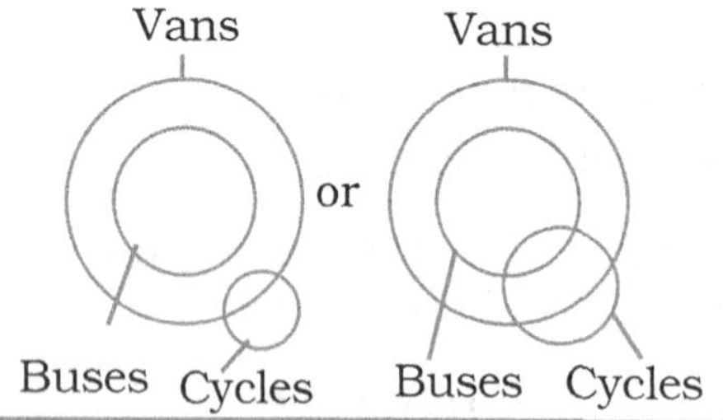	1. Some vans are buses. 2. Some vans are cycles. 3. Either 'No bus is cycle' or 'Some buses are cycles' follows.

Mediate deductive inferences:

First premise, being an A-type proposition, distributes the subject only and the second premise, being an I-type proposition, distributes neither subject nor predicate. So, the middle term 'vans' is not distributed even once in the premises. Hence, no definite conclusion can be drawn.

Case 7. Some radios are cameras. Some cameras are statues.

Immediate deductive inferences:

The converse of the first premise i.e. 'Some cameras are radios' and the converse of the second premise i.e. 'Some statues are cameras', both hold.

Venn diagram	Inferences
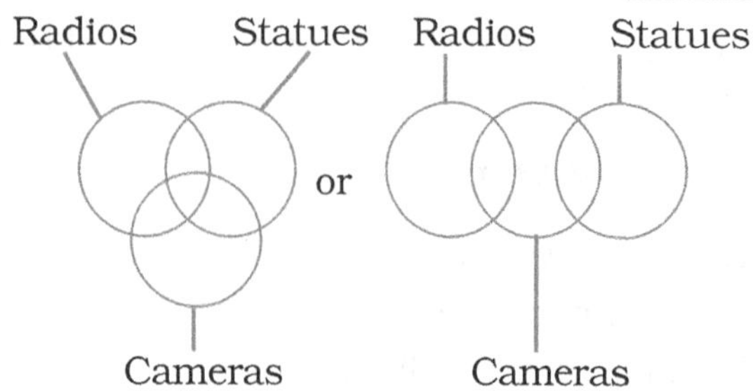	1. Some cameras are radios. 2. Some statues are cameras. 3. Either 'some radios' are statues or 'no radio is statue' follows as I and E-type propositions form a complim-entary pair.

Mediate deductive inferences:

Since both premises are particular, no definite conclusion follows.

Case 8. All cakes are candles. No candle is pastry.

Immediate deductive inferences:

The converse of the first premise i.e. 'Some candles are cakes' and the converse of the second premise 'No pastry is candle' both hold.

Venn diagram	**Inferences**
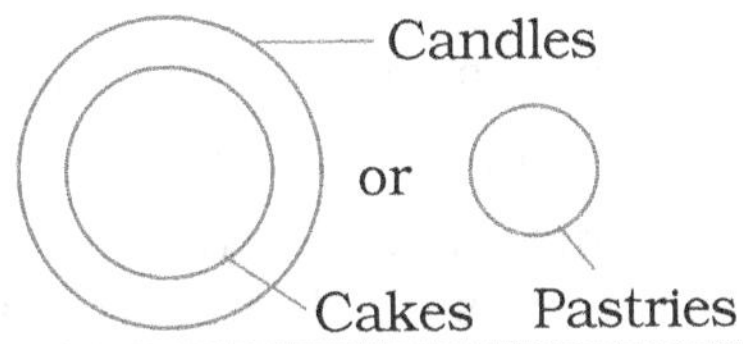	1. Some candles are cakes. 2. No pastry is candle. 3. No cake is pastry. 4. No pastry is cake.

Mediate deductive inferences:

Since both premises are universal, the conclusion must be universal. Since one premise is negative, the conclusion must be negative. So, it follows that 'No cake is pastry'. The converse of this conclusion i.e. 'No pastry is cake' also holds.

Case 9. No coin is ring. All rings are bangles.

Immediate deductive inferences:

The converse of the first premise i.e. 'No ring is coin' and the converse of the second premise i.e. 'Some bangles are rings' both hold.

Venn diagram	**Inferences**
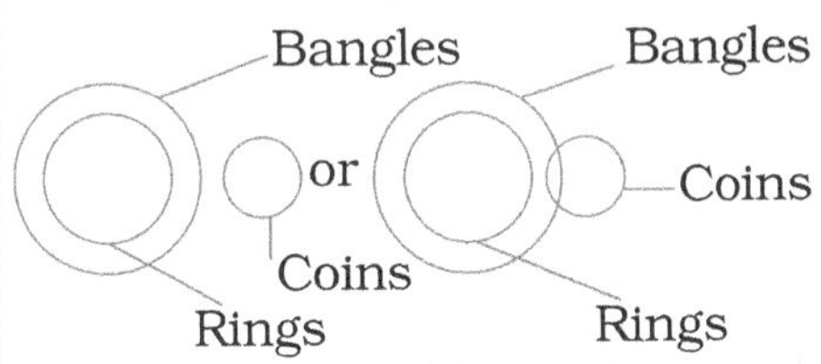	1. No ring is coin. 2. Some bangles are rings. 3. Some bangles are not coins. 4. Either 'Some coins are bangles' or 'No coin is bangle' follows as E and I-type proposition form a complimentary pair.

Mediate deductive inferences:

First premise, being an E-type proposition, distributed both the subject and predicate. Second premise, being an A-type proposition, distributes the subject. Thus, the middle term 'ring' is distributed twice in the premises. So, the conclusion cannot be universal. Also, since one premise is negative, the conclusion must be negative. Thus, the conclusion must be particular negative i.e. O-type. So, it follows that some bangles are not coins.

Case 10. Some lamps are candles. No candle is bulb.

Immediate deductive inferences:

The converse of the first premise i.e. 'Some candles are lamps' and the converse of the second premise i.e. 'No bulb is candle' both hold.

Venn diagram	**Inferences**
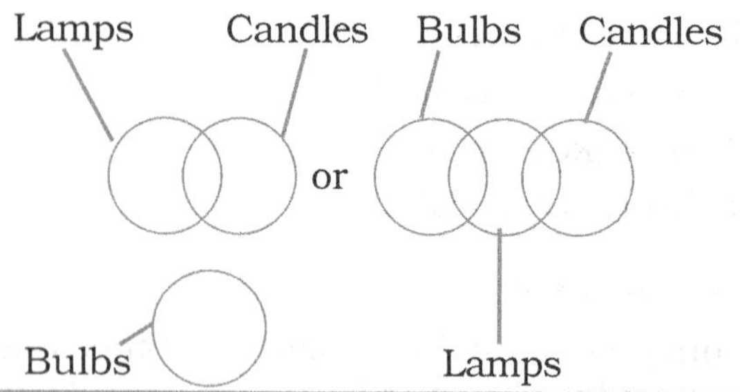	1. Some candles are lamps. 2. No bulb is candle. 3. Some lamps are not bulbs. 4. Either 'some lamps are bulbs' or 'no lamp is bulb' follows as E and I-type propositions form complimentary pair.

Mediate deductive inferences:

Since one premise is particular and the other negative, the conclusion must be particular negative i.e. O-types so, it follows that 'some lamps are not bulbs'.

Some important point to remember:

While deriving logical conclusion, always remember that the following conclusions hold:

1. The converse of each of the given premises.
2. The conclusion that directly follows from the given premises in accordance with the rules of syllogism.
3. The converse of the derived conclusions.

Practice Exercise

Directions: Given below are the two statements followed by two conclusions. Disregarding commonly known facts, taking statements to be thoroughly true, mark your answer as:

A. Only I follows
B. Only II follows
C. Both I and II follow
D. Neither I nor II follows

1. *Statements:*

I. All bats are blind.

II. All snakes are blind.

Conclusions:

I. Some snakes are bats.

II. No snake is a bat.

2. *Statements:*

I. Arunachal Pradesh has the earliest sunrise in India.

II. XYZ is in Arunachal Pradesh.

Conclusions:

I. XYZ has the earliest sunrise in India.

II. Other states don't have the earliest sunrise.

3. *Statements:*

I. Some birds can fly.

II. Flying things should be light-weighted.

Conclusions:

I. All light-weighted things are birds.

II. Some birds are light-weighted.

4. *Statements:*

I. Some housewives are educated.

II. I am educated.

Conclusions:

I. I am a housewife.

II. Some educated people are housewives.

5. *Statements:*

I. Sania Mirsa is a tennis player.

II. Tennis players are all tall.

Conclusions:

I. All tall people are tennis players.

II. Sania Mirsa is tall.

6. Statements:

I. All long boots are made of leather.

II. No leather is wooden.

Conclusions:

I. No long boot is wooden.

II. No wooden thing is long boots.

7. *Statements:*

I. All sheep are mammals.

II. No sheep will lay an egg.

Conclusions:

I. Some sheep lay egg.

II. No sheep will lay an egg.

8. *Statements:*
   I. Some politicians are illiterate.
   II. Men are politicians.

Conclusions:
   I. Some illiterates are politicians.
   II. Some men are illiterate.

9. *Statements:*
   I. All huts are mansions.
   II. All mansions are temples.

Conclusions:
   I. Some temples are huts.
   II. Some temples are mansions.

10. *Statements:*
   I. All water is divine.
   II. All temples are divine.

Conclusions:
   I. All water is temple.
   II. All temples are water.

11. *Statements:*
   I. Some hens are cows.
   II. All cows are horses.

Conclusions:
   I. Some horses are hens.
   II. Some hens are horses.

12. *Statements:*
   I. Some adults are boys.
   II. Some boys are old.

Conclusions:
   I. Some adults are not old.
   II. Some boys are not old.

13. *Statements:*
   I. All fish are tortoise.
   II. No tortoise is a crocodile.

Conclusions:
   I. No crocodile is a fish.
   II. No fish is a crocodile.

14. *Statements:*

I. All road are poles.

II. No pole is a house.

Conclusions:

I. Some roads are houses.

II. Some houses are poles.

15. *Statements:*

I. No gentlemen is poor.

II. All gentleman are rich.

Conclusions:

I. No poor man is rich.

II. No rich man is poor.

16. *Statements:*

I. Some desks are caps.

II. No cap is red.

Conclusions:

I. Some caps are desks.

II. No desk is red.

17. *Statements:*

I. No bat is ball.

II. No ball is wicket.

Conclusions:

I. No bat is wicket.

II. All wickets are bats.

18. *Statements:*

I. Many scooters are trucks.

II. All trucks are trains.

Conclusions:

I. Some scooters are trains.

II. No truck is a scooter.

19. *Statements:*

I. Most teachers are boys.

II. Some boys are students.

Conclusions:

I. Some students are boys

II. Some teachers are students.

Answer keys

1.D. Middle term is not distributed.

2.A. We cannot say anything about other States as premise does not talk of it.

3.B. Again 'A' and'I' type premises have 'I' type Conclusion.

4.D. Middle term "educated" is not distributed even once.

5.B. Since both Statements are 'A' type, conclusion has to be 'A' but "tall" is not distributed in premises. Hence cannot be distributed in Conclusion II.

6.C. 'A' and 'E' type of Statements have 'E' type conclusions.

7.D. Conclusion I is absolutely wrong with respect to Statement II and Conclusion II.

8. A. Conclusion 1 follows directly from Statement I and Conclusion II follows 'A' and 'I' type of premises together give'I' type of Conclusion.

9. C. Since both the premises are universal and affirmative, the conclusion must be universal affirmative. 'All huts are temples'. I is the converse of this conclusion and so it holds, II is the converse of the second premise and so it also holds.

10.D Since the middle term 'divine' is not distributed even once in the premises, no definite conclusion can be drawn.

11.C Since one premise is particular, the conclusion must be particular and should not contain the middle term. So, II follows. I is the converse of II and so it also holds.

12.D. Both the premises are I-type propositions and as such, the middle term 'boys' is not distributed even once in the premises. So, no definite conclusion follows.

13.C. Since both the premises are universal and one premise is negative, the conclusion must be universal negative. Also, the conclusion should not contain the middle term. So, II follows. I is the converse of II and thus it also holds.

14.D. Since both the premises are universal and one premises negative, the conclusion must be universal negative. So, neither I nor II follows.

15.D. The first premise is an E-type proposition. So, the middle term 'gentlemen' forming the subject is distributed. The second premise is an A-type proposition. So, the middle term 'gentlemen' forming the subject is distributed.

16.A. Since one premise is particular and the other premises is negative, the conclusion must be particular negative and should not contain the middle term. So, it follows that 'some desks are not red'. However, I is the converse of the first premise and thus it holds.

17.D. Since both the premises are negative, no definite conclusion follows.

18.A. Since the first premise is particular, the conclusion must be particular and should not contain the middle term. Thus, only I follows.

19.A. Since both the premises are particular, no definite conclusion follows. However, I is the converse of the second premise and thus it holds.

3. ANALOGY TEST

Analogy means correspondence or similarity. Analogy tests are meant to assess candidate's ability for eduction of correlates. The ability to educe the relation is the best indicator of intelligence according to Spearman.

Some basic knowledge about the kinds of relationships is required for these tests. Hence let us look into it first.

1. Study and topic relationship

We know that Botany is the study of plants.

Botany	:	Plants
Zoology	:	Animals
Anthropology	:	Man
Astrology	:	Future
Ornithology	:	Birds
Pathology	:	Diseases
Semantics	:	Language
Nephrology	:	Kidney
Hematology	:	Blood
Entomology	:	Insects
Taxonomy	:	Classification
Cardiology	:	Heart

2. Worker and tool relationship

Axe is the tool used by a Woodcutter.

Woodcutter	:	Axe
Soldier	:	Gun
Doctor	:	Stethoscope
Barber	:	Scissors
Carpenter	:	Hammer
Tailor	:	Needle
Labourer	:	Spade
Sculptor	:	Chisel
Farmer	:	Plough
Author	:	Pen
Warrior	:	Sword
Painter	:	Brush
Butler	:	Chopper
Astronomer	:	Telescope
Mechanic	:	Screwdriver
Chef	:	Knife

3. Tool and action relationship

Knife	:	Cut	Knife is used for cutting.
Gun	:	Shoot	
Spoon	:	Feed	
Needle	:	Sew	
Sword	:	Slaughter/Cut	
Filter	:	Purify	
Steering	:	Drive	
Shovel	:	Scoop	
Chisel	:	Carve	
Spade	:	Dig	
Loud Speaker	:	Amplify	
Pen	:	Write	
Microscope	:	Magnify	
Spanner	:	Grip	

4. Tool and object relationship

Screwdriver	:	Screw	Screwdriver is intended to drive screw.
Pen	:	Paper	

5. Action and object relationship

Drive	:	Car
Hit	:	Ball
Kick	:	Football
Smoking	:	Pipe

6. Worker and working place relationship

Farmer	:	Field	Farmer works in the field.
Pilot	:	Cockpit	
Actor	:	Stage	
Lawyer	:	Court	
Chef	:	Kitchen	
Warrior	:	Battlefield	
Sailor	:	Ship	
Beautician	:	Parlour	
Artist	:	Theatre	
Mechanic	:	Garage	
Scientist	:	Laboratory	
Teacher	:	School	

Doctor	:	Hospital	
Clerk	:	Office	
Servant	:	Home	
Waiter	:	Restaurant	
Worker	:	Factory	
Gambler	:	Casino	
Engineer	:	Site	

7. Worker and product relationship

Author	:	Book	An author writes a book.
Tailor	:	Dress	
Butler	:	Meat	
Cobbler	:	Shoe	
Carpenter	:	Furniture	
Farmer	:	Crop	
Goldsmith	:	Ornament	
Poet	:	Poem	
Editor	:	Newspaper	
Teacher	:	Education	
Chef	:	Food	
Judge	:	Justice	
Producer	:	Film	
Architect	:	Design	
Hunter	:	Prey	
Mason	:	Wall	

8. Product and raw material relationship

Book	:	Paper	Book is made of paper.
Butter	:	Milk	
Shoe	:	Leather	
Wine	:	Grapes	
Prism	:	Glass	
Wall	:	Brick	
Furniture	:	Wood	
Pullover	:	Wool	
Metal	:	Ore	
Jaggery	:	Sugarcane	
Cloth	:	Fiber	

Omelette	:	Egg	
Oil	:	Seed	
Paper	:	Pulp	
Jewellery	:	Gold	

9. Instrument and measurement relationship

Scale	:	Length	Scale is an instrument used to measure the length.
Balance	:	Mass	
Rain Gauge	:	Rain	
Barometer	:	Pressure	
Thermometer	:	Temperature	
Odometer	:	Speed	
Ammeter	:	Current	
Screw Gauge	:	Thickness	
Seismograph	:	Earthquakes	
Hygrometer	:	Humidity	

10. Quantity and Unit relationship

Mass	:	Kilogram	Kilogram is the unit of mass.
Length	:	Meter	
Time	:	Seconds	
Capacity	:	Liter	
Resistance	:	Ohm	
Power	:	Watt	
Potential	:	Volt	
Work	:	Joule	
Current	:	Ampere	
Area	:	Hectare	
Temperature	:	Degree	

11. Animal and Young one relationship

Cow	:	Calf	Calf is the young one of cow.
Cat	:	Kitten	
Sheep	:	Lamb	
Dog	:	Puppy	
Horse	:	Pony	
Butterfly	:	Caterpillar	
Insect	:	Larva	
Hen	:	Chicken	

Lion	:	Cub	
Duck	:	Duckling	
Man	:	Child	
Pig	:	Farrow	
Frog	:	Tadpole	
Tortoise	:	Turtle	

12. Individual and dwelling relationship

Pig	:	Sty	Pig lives in Sty.
Rabbit	:	Burrow	
Cow	:	Shed	
Lion	:	Den	
Snake	:	Hole	
Birds	:	Nest	
Dog	:	Kennel	
Fish	:	Aquarium	
Monk	:	Monastery	
Poultry	:	Farm	
Horse	:	Stable	

13. Male and female relationship

Lion	:	Lioness	Lioness is the female lion.
Son	:	Daughter	
Nephew	:	Niece	
Gentleman	:	Lady	
Horse	:	Mare	
Tiger	:	Tigress	
Boy	:	Girl	
King	:	Queen	
Dog	:	Bitch	

14. Word and intensity relationship

Wish	:	Desire	Desire is of higher intensity than wish.
Quarrel	:	War	
Error	:	Blunder	
Refuse	:	Deny	
Kindle	:	Burn	
Famous	:	Renowned	
Unhappy	:	Sad	

Crime : Sin
Warm : Hot
Frown : Anger
Anger : Rage
Sink : Drown

15. Word and Synonym relationship

Vacant : Empty
Solicit : Request
Dearth : Scarcity
Brim : Edge
Blend : Mix
Ban : Prohibition
Assign : Allot
Abduct : Kidnap
House : Home
Substitute : Replace
Presume : Assume
Enormous : Huge
Muddy : Unclear

Vacant means almost the same as empty. Thus empty is the synonym of vacant.

16. Word and antonym relationship

Attack : Defend
Cruel : Kind
Best : Worst
Initial : Final
Fresh : Stale
Ignore : Notice
Create : Destroy
Sink : Float
Gentle : Harsh
Deep : Shallow
Cordial : Hostile
Lethargy : Alertness
Lend : Borrow
Correct : Wrong
Good : Bad
Purity : Evil

Attack means the opposite of defend. Thus, defend is the antonym of attack.

17. Cause and effect relationship

Work	:	Fatigue	Work causes fatigue.
Germ	:	Disease	
Smoke	:	Pollution	
Fast	:	Hunger	

18. Whole and part relationship

Pen	:	Nib	Nib is part of a pen.
Hand	:	Finger	
Circle	:	Arc	
Aeroplane	:	Cockpit	
Room	:	Window	
Fan	:	Blade	
Home	:	Kitchen	
Book	:	Chapter	

19. Purpose relationship

Net	:	Fish
Air gun	:	Birds

20. Individual and class relationship

Snake	:	Reptile	Snake belongs to the class of reptiles.
Cow	:	Mammal	
Nose	:	Sense organ	
Man	:	Mammal	
Butterfly	:	Insect	

21. Place relationship

India Gate	:	Delhi
Tajmahal	:	Agra
Red Square	:	Moscow
Kutab Minar	:	Delhi
Red Fort	:	Delhi

22. Sequential relationship

November	:	December
Sunday	:	Monday
Spring	:	Summer

23. Symbol relationship

Green light	:	Move
Red light	:	Stop

24. Associated relationship

Students : Teachers
Patients : Doctors

25. Stage relationship

Girl : Woman
Infant : Child

26. Individual and group relationship

Man : Crowd
Singer : Chorus
Sailors : Crew
Cattle : Herd
Soldiers : Army
Sheep : Flock
Flowers : Bouquet
Artist : Troupe

27. Body part and disease relationship

Trachoma : Eye
Pyorrhea : Teeth

Analogy is of 4 types – word analogy, letter analogy, number analogy and figure analogy.

1. Word Analogy

King : Crown :: Policeman : ? Ans. Cap

2. Letter Analogy

ACE : PRT :: MOQ : ? Ans. BDF (Remember that after 'Z' there will come 'A' in the sequence because the counting is circular)

3. Number Analogy

5 : 25 :: 6 : ? Ans. 36

4. Figure Analogy

△ : □ :: □ : ? Ans. ⬠

Word analogy is a common question in NET examination. In this type of question, a particular relationship is implied in the first part of the question and the same relationship has to be identified from the alternatives provided. The selection and placement should depend upon the 'eduction of relationships' (deducing implied relationships) between the two words given on other side.

In word analogy tests one pair of related words are given on one side of the sign '::' and one word from a second pair with a question mark on the other side. The relationship which obtains between the words on the left side of the sign :: is to be found out and used for finding out the missing word on the right, indicated by question mark. The missing word is included as one of the alternatives given as answers. Select the correct alternative from this list.

This is just like balancing. If we want to maintain a proper balance between two sides we have to recognize the relationship between the two words given on one side of the symbol '::' and use the **same** relationship on the other side to fill in the blank, by select a suitable word from among the alternatives.

Practice Exercise

1. **Book : Paper :: Table : ?**
   A. Forest B. Wood C. Carpenter D. Wood Cutter
2. **Ocean : Ship :: Desert : ?**
   A. Horse B. Elephant C. Sledge D. Camel
3. **Diving : Water :: Skating : ?**
   A. Ice B. Sky C. Mountain D. Space
4. **Brave : Coward :: Praise : ?**
   A. Applaud B. Scold C. Comment D. Appreciate
5. **Smoke : Pollution :: War : ?**
   A. Victory B. Death C. Enemy D. Army
6. **News paper : Editor :: Film : ?**
   A. Actor B. Director C. Audience D. Producer
7. **Cobbler : Shoe :: Carpenter : ?**
   A. Furnitue B. Gold C. Wood D. Iron
8. **Grapes : Wine :: Wheat : ?**
   A. Grain B. Maize C. Bread D. Field
9. **Child : Father :: Book : ?**
   A. Author B. Publisher C. Editor D. Library
10. **Pyorrhea : Teeth :: Trachoma : ?**
    A. Eye B. Skin C. Lungs D. Ear
11. **Gun : Bullet :: Chimney : ?**
    A. House B. Ground C. Roof D. Smoke
12. **Ancient : Modern :: Often : ?**
    A. Commonly B. Repeatedly C. New D. Seldom

13. Mother : Daughter :: Aunt : ?

A. Cousin B. Brother C. Sister D. Niece

14. Cow : Calf :: Lioness : ?

A. Lion B. Cub C. Pub D. Chick

15. Feather : Soft :: Diamond : ?

A. Light B. Hard C. Sharp D. Costly

16. Cloth : Metre :: Gold : ?

A. Gram B. Litter C. Ton D. Sovereign

17. Doctor : Medicine :: Teacher : ?

A. Students B. Class C. Principal D. Knowledge

18. Monday : April :: Friday : ?

A. August B. Tuesday C. July D. Saturday

19. House : Wall :: Wall : ?

A. Brick B. Roof C. Paint D. Sand

20. Ankle : Knee :: Wrist : ?

A. Hand B. Foot C. Elbow D. Finger

21. Kangaroo : Australia :: Giraffe : ?

A. Africa B. India C. France D. Japan

22. House : Windows :: Man : ?

A. Eyes B. Brain C. Speech D. Emotion

23. Crocodile : Crawl :: Frog : ?

A. Walk B. Hop C. Jump D. Creep

24. Fire : Ashes :: Explosion : ?

A. Flame B. Death C. Sound D. Debris

25. Professor : Lecture :: Doctor : ?

A. Hospital B. Disease C. Treatment D. Patient

26. King : Throne :: Rider : ?

A. Seat B. Horse C. Saddle D. Chair

27. Car : Garage :: Aeroplane : ?

A. Port B. Waiting Shed C. Airport D. Landing Ground

Answer keys

1.B. Book is made of paper and table is made of wood. 'Product' 'raw-material' relationship is to be used

2.D. Ship is the vessel to travel in ocean while the camel is the animal used for travel in a desert

3.A. Diving is doing in water while skating is done on ice

4.B. Coward is the antonym of brave and scold is the antonym of praise, ie. word - antonym relationship

5.B. Smoke causes pollution and war causes death. Cause - effect relationship

6.B. Editor is responsible for the subject matter published in the newspaper, while the Director of a film is responsible for the content of the film

7.A. Shoe is made by the cobbler while furniture is made by the carpenter. Worker - produce product relationship is implied

8.C. Wine is prepared from grapes while bread is prepared from wheat; raw material and product relationship is implied

9. A. Father-child relationship is the same as author-book relationship

10.A. Pyorrhea is the disease of teeth while trachoma is the disease of eye. What is implied is relation between affected part of the body and the name of the disease

11.D. Bullet is discharged by the gun while smoke is discharged through the chimney

12.D. Ancient is the antonym of modern; seldom is the antonym of often. We use the word - antonym relationship for finding the answer

13.D. Since mother is to daughter, aunt is to niece (similarly in relationship between senior and junior members of the family)

14.B. Cub is the young one of lioness; Animal and its young-one relationship is implied

15.B. Feather is known for its softness;, similarly diamond is known for its hardness. We have to deal with opposites for an answer

16.A. Metre is the measure of cloth; similarly gram is the measure of gold

17.D. As the doctor prescribes medicine for patient, in the same way the teacher imparts knowledge to students.

18.A. Friday comes three days after Monday; likewise August comes three months after April.

19.A. As house is constructed with walls, the wall is constructed with bricks.

20.C. Similarly placed joints (last two joints) of the leg compared to similarly placed joints (last two joints) of the hand; C is the answer. As ankle is the lowest part of the knee, the same way wrist is the lowest part of elbow.

21.A. As natural habitat of the Kangaroo is Australia, similarly the natural habitat of the Giraffe is Africa.

22.A. Windows help us to see the outside of the house, eyes help us to see the surroundings.

23.B. Crocodile crawl from one place to another; frog hop from one place to another.

24.D. Fire followed by ashes; similarly an explosion is followed by its debries.

25.C. Professor gives lectures to students, while the doctor gives treatment to his patients.

26.C. A king sits on a throne while a rider sits on his saddle.

27.C. Car–garage relationship the same as aero plane-airport relationship; C is the answer.

4. LOGICAL DIAGRAMS

This type of questions aims to analyze a candidate's ability to identify and classify a given group of items presented in the form of diagrams. Circles are needed to represent a category of similar objects ie. object belonging to a class. A class is used here to stand for a homogeneous group of items (items which posses a common property). Class of 'human being' is those who are human (irrespective of their sexes), but no other item or object can be included in this class.

On the basis of the notion about class, it has to be decided whether the objects will form a set, a subset (part of a bigger set) or a disjoint set (a set which does not share a common object with another set), etc. Intersection or union of sets (part of a set which shares with another set) can also be diagrammatically represented.

Study the following diagrams

Here are a few different types of venn diagrams with their implications made clear. Suppose you are given a group of three items. Then:

1. If the items evidently belong to three different groups, the venn diagram representing it would be *three independent circles* as shown below.

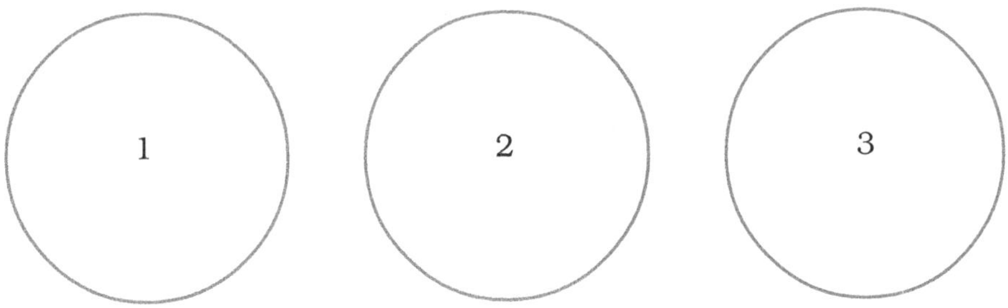

2. If one item belongs to the class of second while third item is entirely different from the two, then they may be representing by *circle one subset the second circle and third is an adjoint circle.*

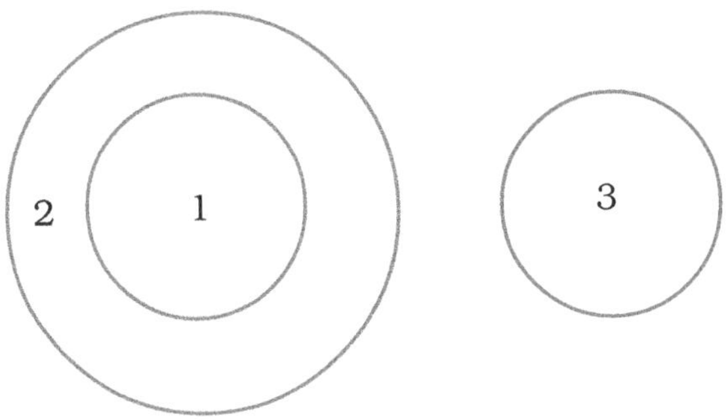

3. If one item belongs to the class of the second and the second belongs to the class of third, then the representation is in the form of *three concentric circles.*

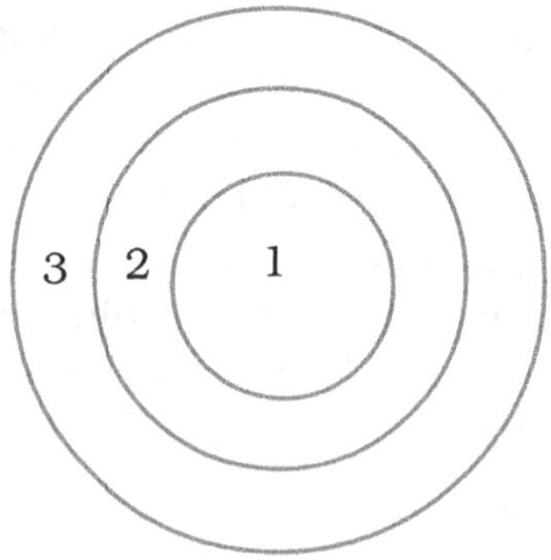

4. If two items are partly related to each other and the third item is entirely different from the two, they are represented by *circle one intersect the second circle and third is an adjoining circle.*

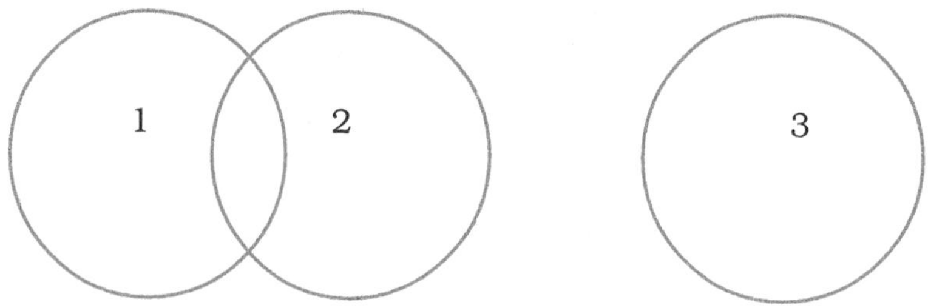

5. If two items are partly related to the third and are themselves independent of each other they are represented by *two circles intersect the third circle.*

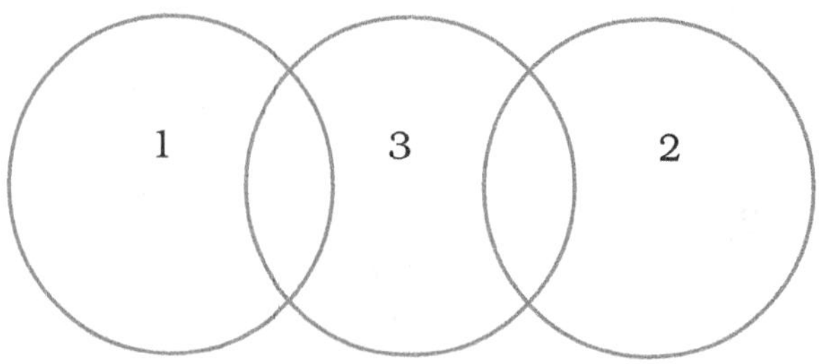

6. If the three items are partly related to each other they are represented as *three intersecting circles.*

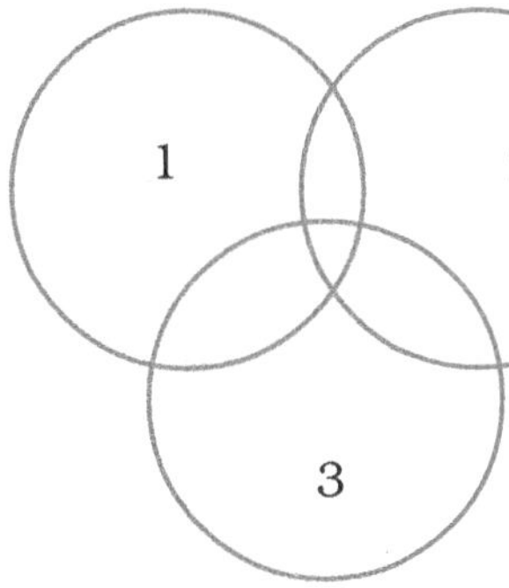

7. If one item belong to the class of second and third item is partly related to the second, they are represented as *circle one subset the second circle and the third circle intersect the second circle.*

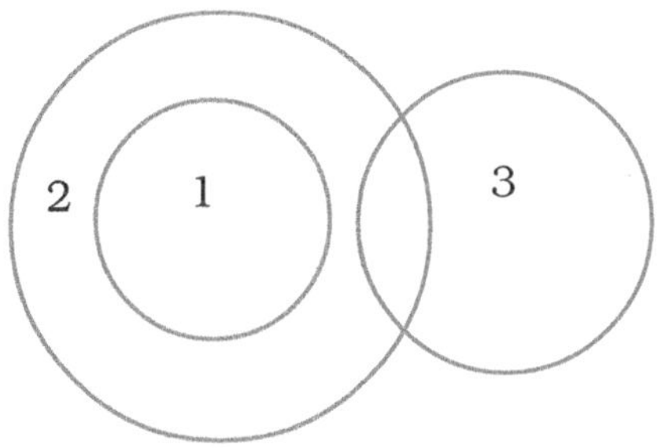

8. If one item belongs to the class of second and the third item is partly related to these two they are represented *circle one subset the second circle and the third circle intersect the two circles.*

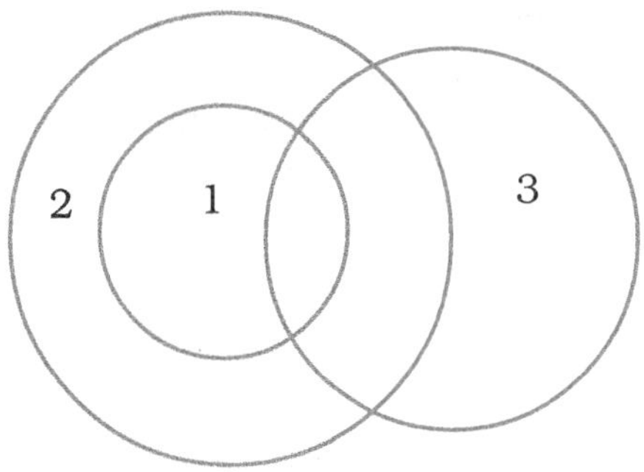

9. If two separate items belong to the class of the third, they are represented by the *two disjoint circles subset the third circle.*

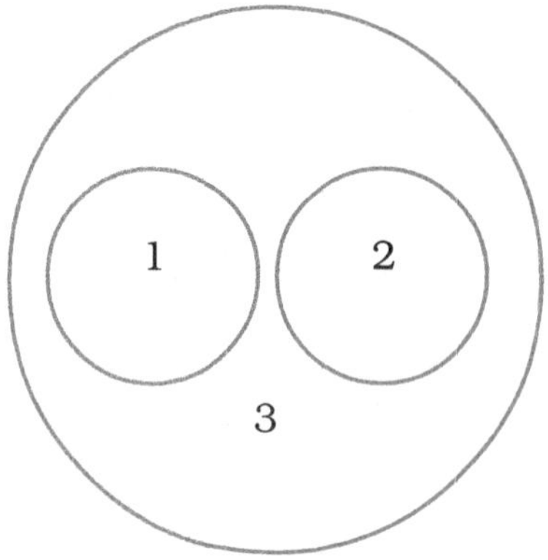

10. If two items belong to the class of the third such that some items of each of these two groups are common in relationship, they are represented by *two intersecting circles subset the third circle.*

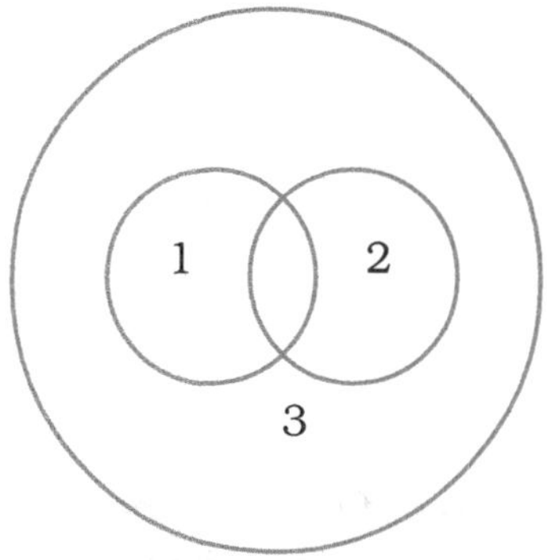

Although the questions are easy and tackled with training, familiarity with their operations will save your precious time, when it is needed for taking competitive tests where power and speed in test-taking becomes important. Some important clues and suggestions for dealing with problems using diagrams of this kind are given below.

Exercises

1. Draw a figure that best illustrates the relationship among Carrot, Food and Vegetables.

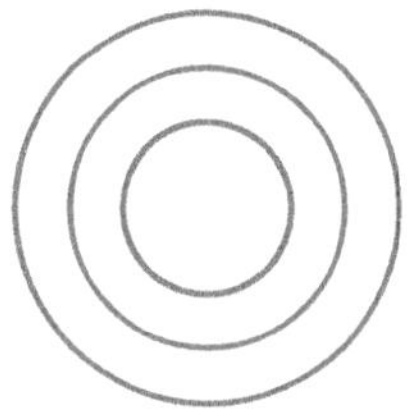

2. Draw a figure that best illustrates the relationship among Mothers, Sisters and Females.

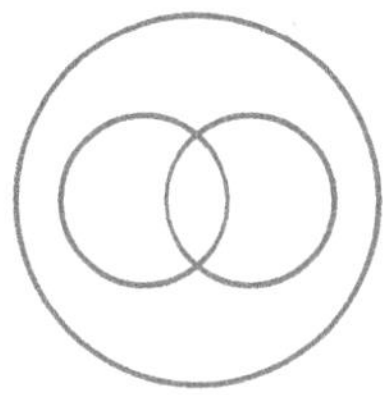

3. Draw a figure that best illustrates the relationship among Pencil, Stationery and Car.

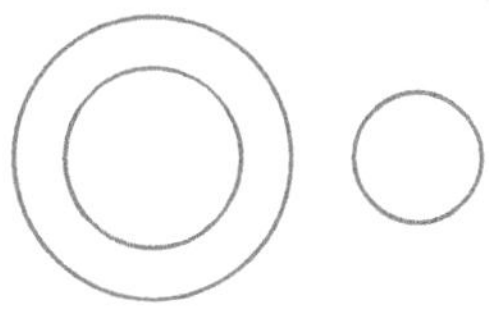

4. Draw a figure that best illustrates the relationship among Vegetable, Brinjal and Cauliflower.

5. Draw a figure that best illustrates the relationship among Dogs, Pets and Cats.

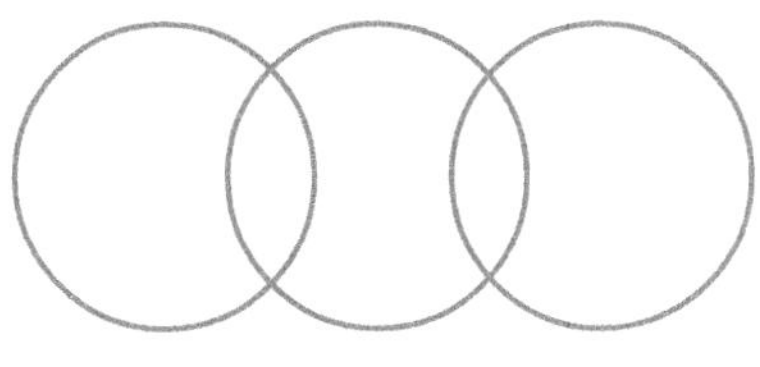

6. Draw a figure that best illustrates the relationship among Yak, Zebra and Bear.

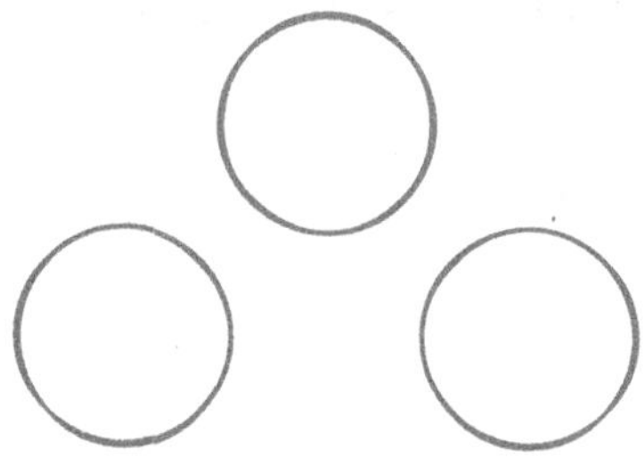

7. Draw a figure that best illustrates the relationship among Blue-eyed, Females and Doctors.

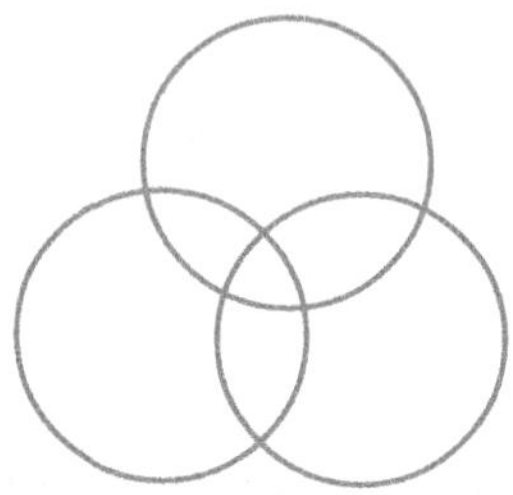

8. Draw a figure that best illustrates the relationship among Women, Mother and Doctor.

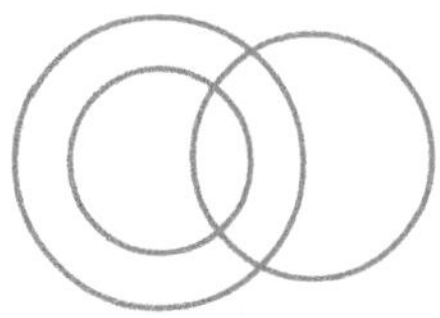

9. Draw a figure that best illustrates the relationship among Male, Doctors and Stethoscope.

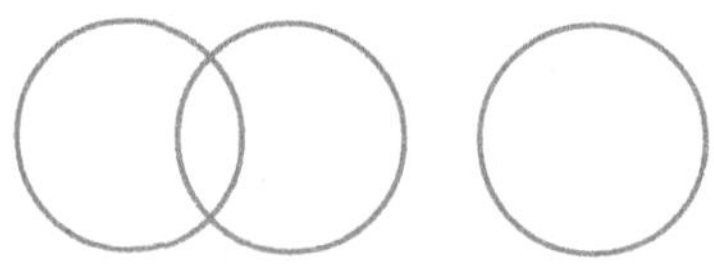

10. Draw a figure that best illustrates the relationship among Wines, Alcoholic liquids and Medicines

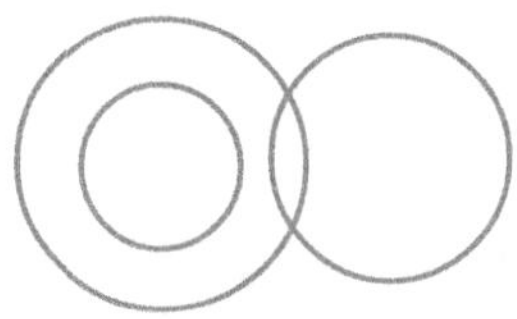

Practice Questions

In this type of questions, a set of four different figures is given in options. Each figure represents a logical pattern of certain groups of related words wherein each word represents a class. Identify the most appropriate logical figure for the set of words given.

1. Which one of the following diagrams represents Qutab Minar, Delhi and Eiffel Tower?

A. 

B. 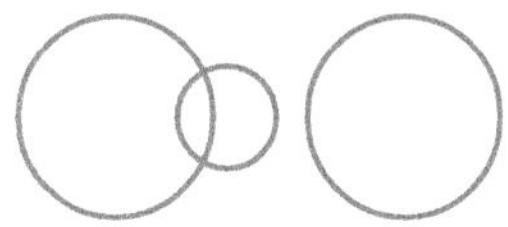

C. 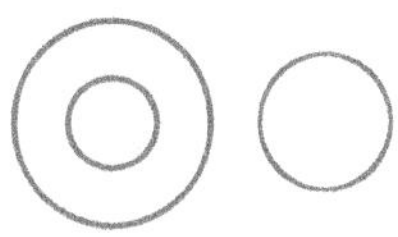

D. 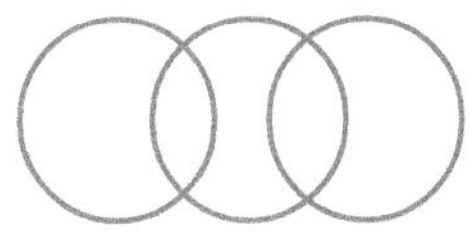

2. The following diagrams represent relationship between members of 3 groups. Select the diagram which best represents the relationship between the members of these groups - Bread, Butter and Food

A. 

B. 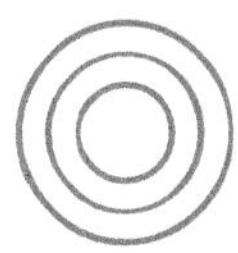

C. 

D. 

3. Which one of the following combination of circles best represents athletes, sprinters and marathon runners?

A. 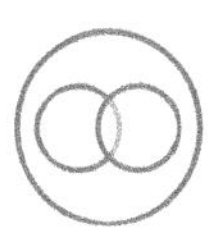

B. 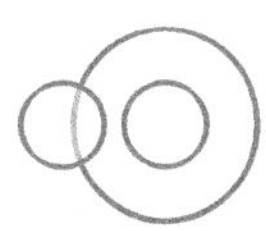

C. 

D. 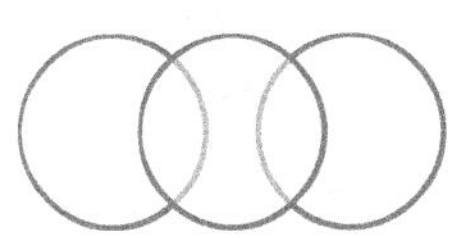

4. If criminals, hard-core criminals and terrorists are represented by diagrams, which one of the following diagrams shows the correct relationship between these three groups?

A. 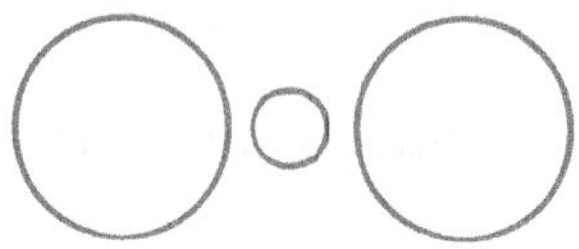

B. 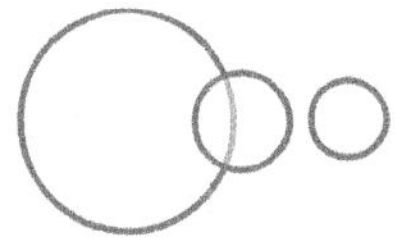

C. 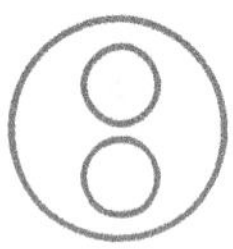

D. 

5. Which one of the following represents cousins, nephews and males?

A. 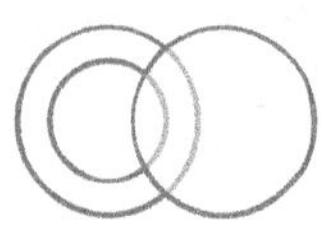

B. 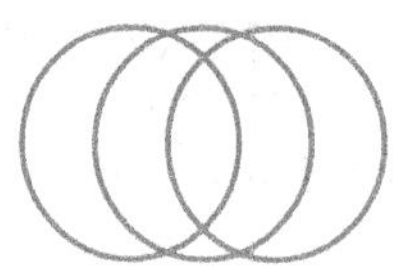

C. 

D. 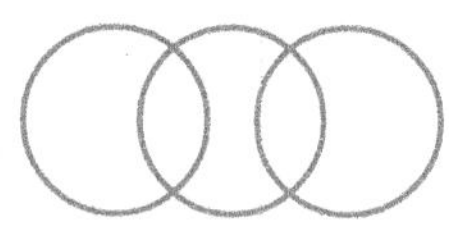

6. The following question is based on the diagram given below. If the two big circles represent animals living on land and those living in water and the small circle stands for the animals that both live on land and in water, which figure represents the relationships among them?

A. 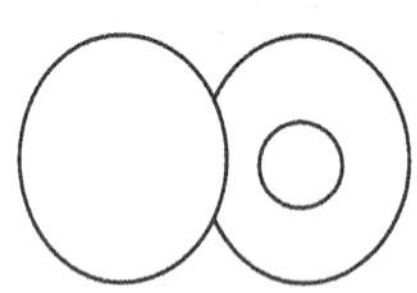

B. 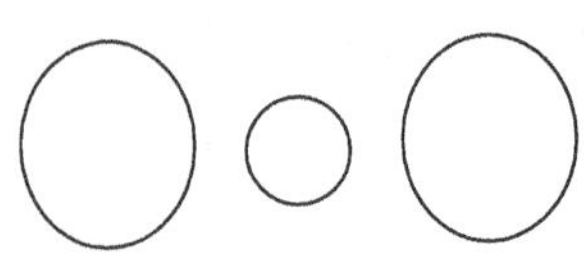

C. 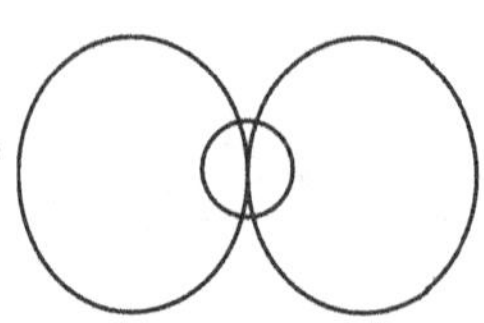

D. 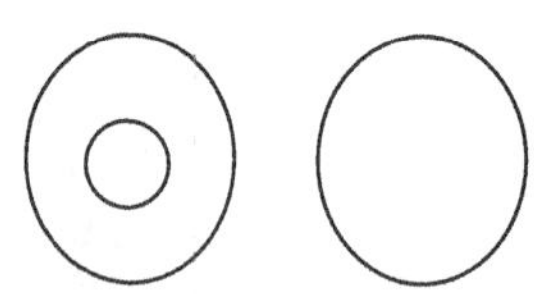

7. The relationship between three professional groups such as Teacher, Doctor and Engineer is indicated by the following diagrams. Which is the most appropriate?

A. 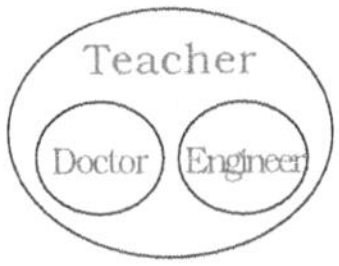

B. 

C. 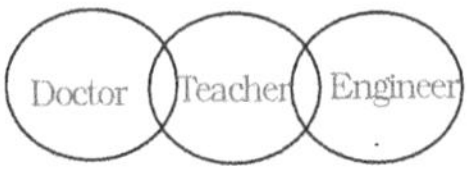

D. 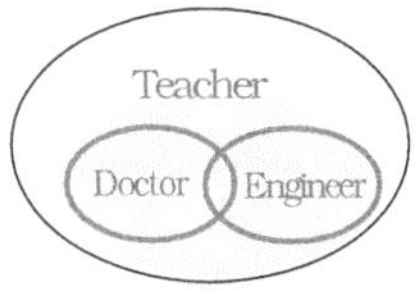

8. Which of the following Venn Diagram best represents relationship among Doctor, Male and Actor ?

A. 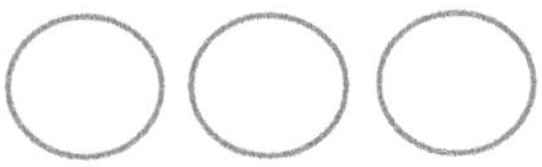

B. 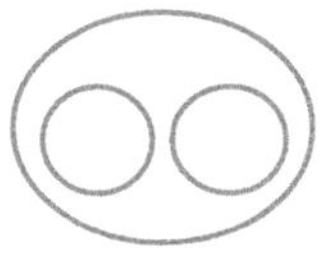

C. 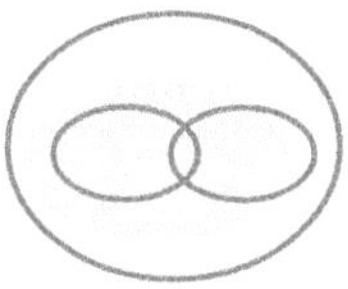

D. 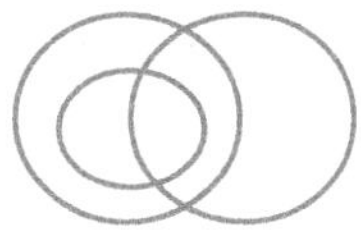

9. Which one of the following diagrams represents Bachelors, Men, and Hockey players?

A. 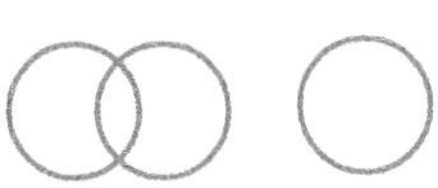

B. 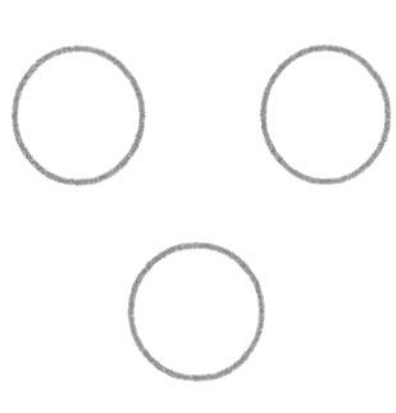

C. 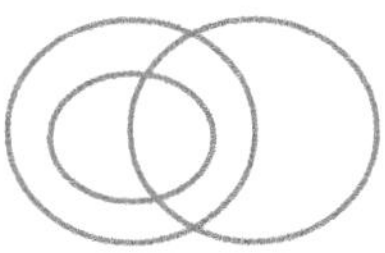

D. 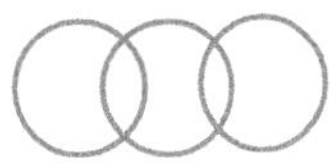

10. Which of the diagrams represents Eagles, Birds, and Dogs?

A. 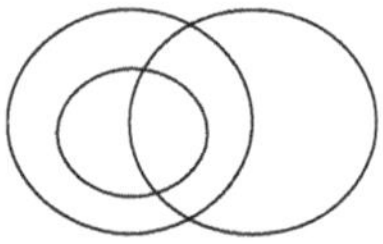

B. 

C. 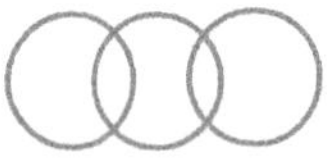

D. 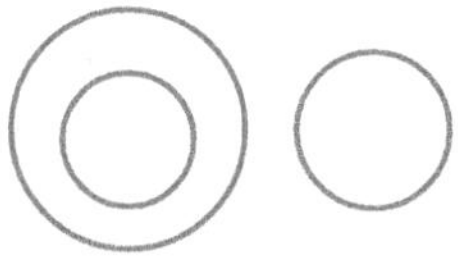

11. Draw a diagram that will represent Americans, Scholars, and people.

A. 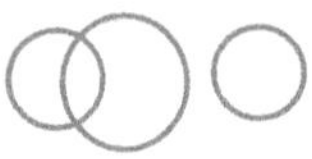

B. 

C. 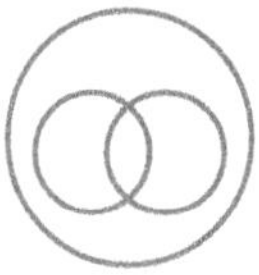

D. 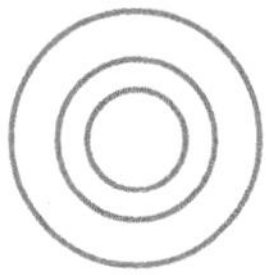

12. Which of the diagrams represents Artists, Painters, and Cricket fans?

A. 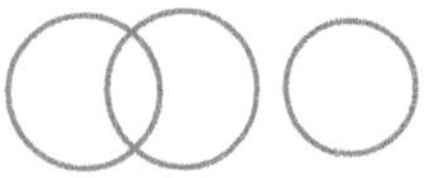

B. 

C. 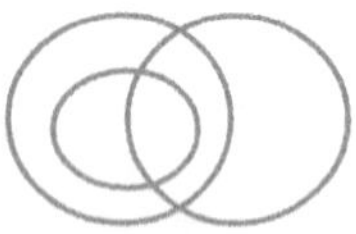

D. 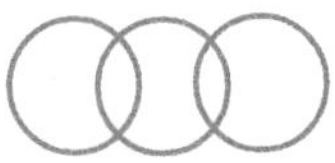

13. Draw a diagram which can represent Bricks, Iron, and Building materials.

A. 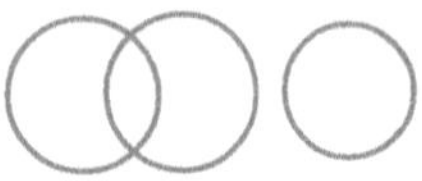

B. 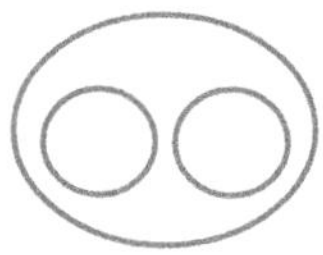

C. 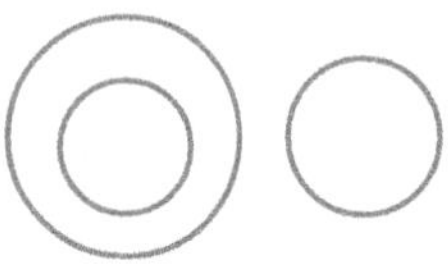

D. 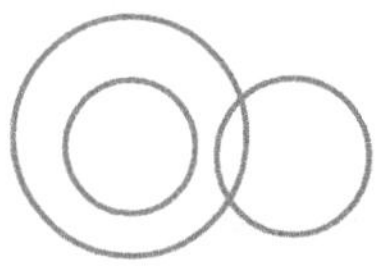

14. Choose the diagram which best illustrates the relationship among Sun, Moon, and Stars.

A. 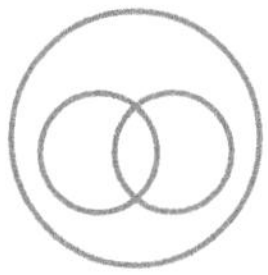

B. 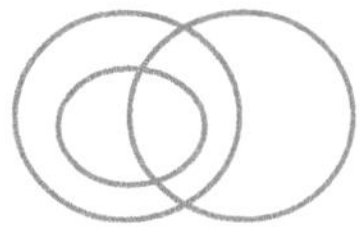

C. 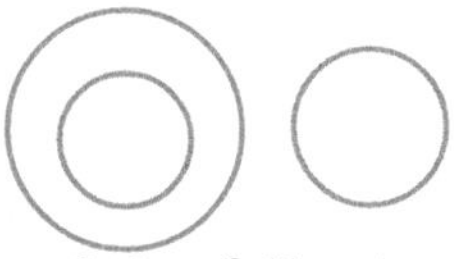

D. 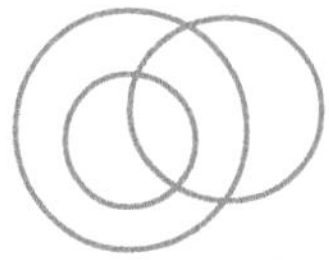

15. Which of the following diagrams correctly represents the relationship among Smokers, Bidi smokers, and Cancer patients?

A. 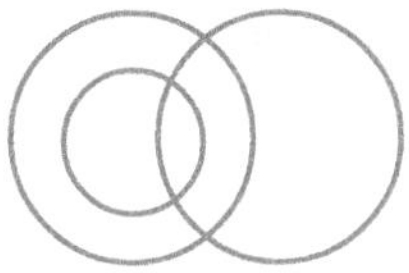

B. 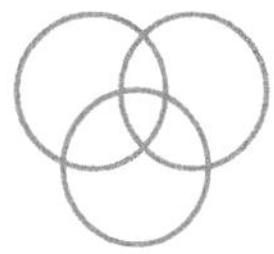

C. 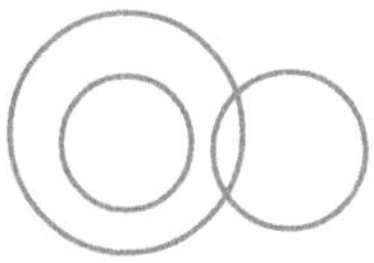

D. 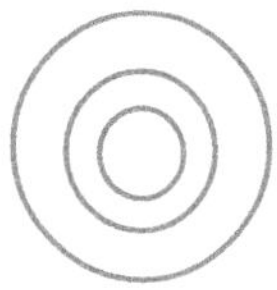

16. Which of the following diagrams correctly represents the relationship among Tennis fans, Cricket players, and Students?

A. 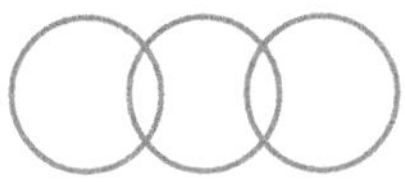

B. 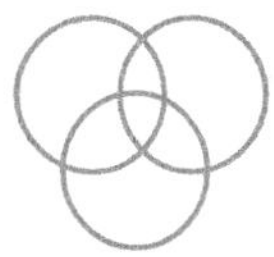

C. 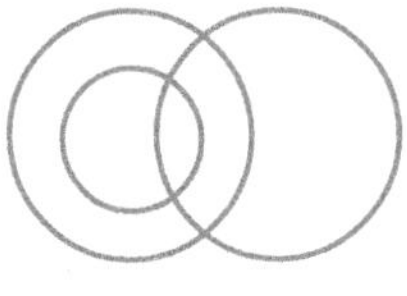

D. 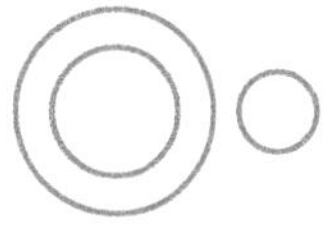

17. Which of the following figures correctly represents the relation between Languages, English, and Hindi?

A. 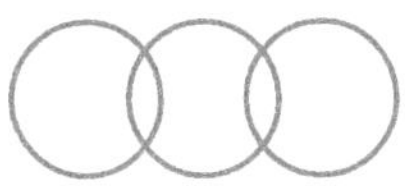

B. 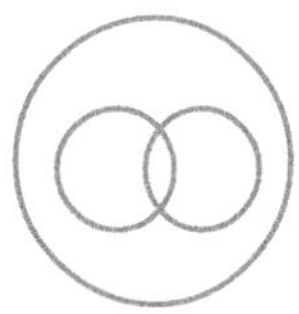

C. 

D. 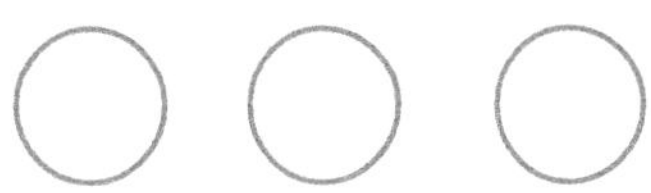

18. Which of the following diagrams indicates the best relation between Judges, Thieves, and Criminals?

A. 

B. 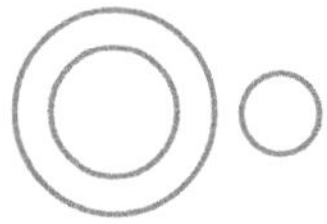

C. 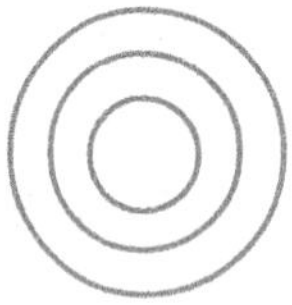

D. 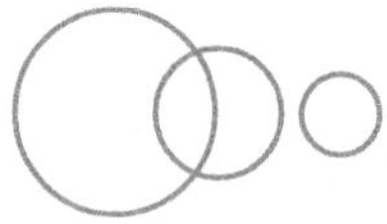

19. Which of the following diagrams represents the relation between Red, Clothes and Roses most appropriately?

A. 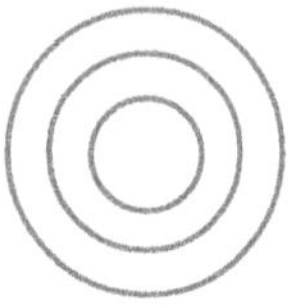

B. 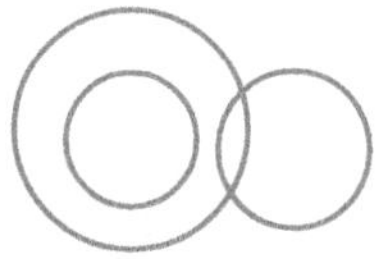

C. 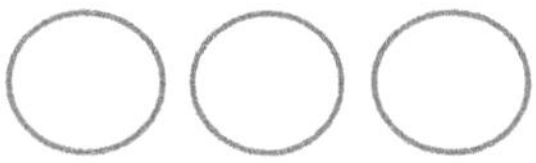

D. 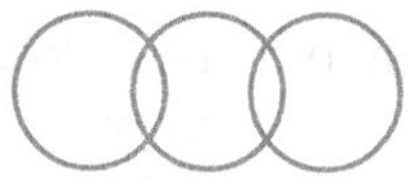

20. Which one of the following four diagrams correctly represents the relationship among the classes: Musicians, Instrumentalists and Violinists?

A. 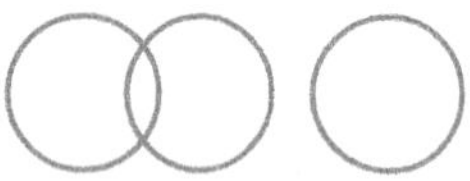

B. 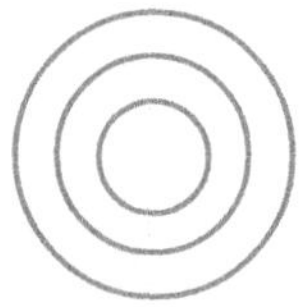

C. 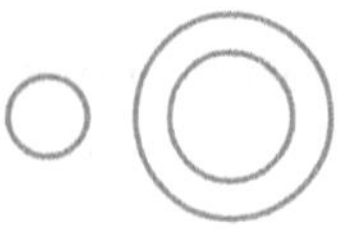

D. 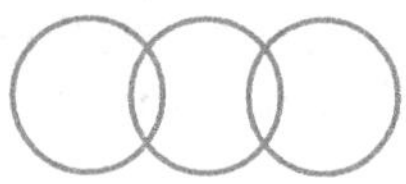

Answer keys

1.C. Qutab Minar is in Delhi. But Eiffel Tower is a separate entity in this figure.

2.D. Since Bread and Butter are food D is correct.

3.A. Sprinters and marathon runners are athletes. So, athletes is a general category, which is represented by the bigger circle. Now, some athletes can be sprinters and marathon runners too. So, they overlap each other.

4.B. Terrorists form a separate group. However, criminals and hard-core criminals have some overlap.

5.A. All males are nephews. Some cousins can be nephews as well as males. But there will be cousins who are females too.

6.D. There are animals living in soil and there are animals living in water.

7.D. Some Doctors are Teachers as well as some Engineers also Teachers.

8.C. All actors are male. Some doctors are males and vice –versa. Some actors are doctors and vice-versa.

9.D. All Bachelors are Men and Hockey players could be both.

10.C. Dogs is an entirely separate set.

11.D. People include both Americans and Scholars.

12.D. Artists and Painters could be Cricket fans.

13.A. Both Bricks and Iron are Building materials.

14.D. Sun is a Star but Moon is entirely different.

15.B. Bidi smokers is a subset of smokers and cancer patient may be a smoker, bidi smoker and non-smoker. Hence third object shares a common relationship with first and second object as well.

16.A. Some Tennis fans may be Cricket players and some not be, some Cricket players may be student and some not be and some student may be Tennis fans and some not be. So, all terms touch to each other partly.

17.D. As English and Hindi both come under language.

18.A. Thieves come under the grouping of criminals, whereas Judges are a separate group.

19.C. Some Clothes are Red as well as some Roses also Red.

20.A. Violinists come under Instrumentalists and Instrumentalists come under Musicians.

5. VENN DIAGRAMS

John Venn was a famous 19th century mathematician developed diagrammatic methods for obtaining the solutions to certain complicated problems. These diagrams are known as 'Venn Diagrams'.

Venn diagram is a figural representation of ideas which help to represent relationships between the members of different sets. This method starts with the representative of one group of objects with a common property by a circle. Two non-overlapping circles are used to stand for two groups of objects which have no common member. Such groups are called disjoint sets. Two or more over lapping circles stand for the fact that the objects have certain common properties which justify the inclusion in two or more circles. The overlapping parts of the circles help us to identify number of members with common properties, and other implied relationships.

Practice Exercise

1. 130 families reside in a housing colony, where 95 families own motorbikes and 80 families own cars. Among them a total of 55 families own both bikes and cars. If so, how many families are there who own neither a car nor a bike?

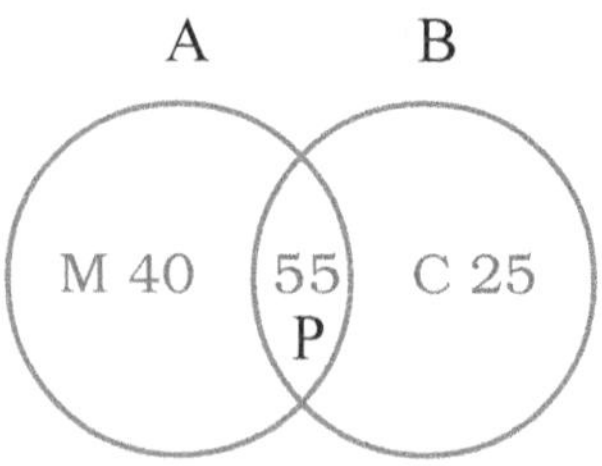

A = Families which own motor bikes
B = Families which own cars
P = Common region for A and B
= Families which own both bikes and cars.

Families owning different vehicles = 40 + 55 + 25 = 120

Families not having either a car or a bike = 130 − 120 = 10

2. 60% students in a dance school learn Bharatha Natyam. 55% students learn Kuchipudi while 35% students learn both Bharatha Natyam and Kuchipudi. Rest of the students in this dance school is students of Kathakali. What is the percentage of students who learn Kathakali?

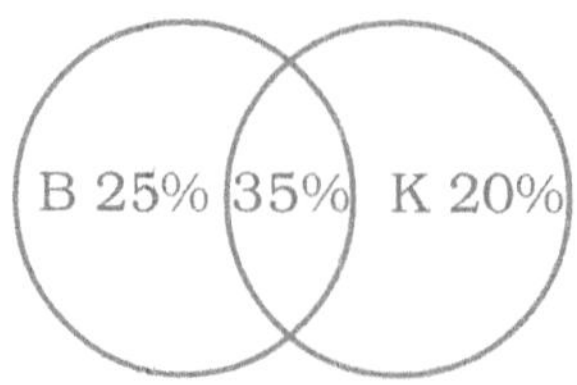

Percentage of students learning Kathakali = 100 - (25 + 35 + 20) = 20%

3. 200 students reside in a hostel block. 85 students know Malayalam. 80 students know Tamil. 90 students know Kannada. Only 10 students know Malayalam, Tamil and Kannada. 15 students know Malayalam and Tamil only. 20 students know Kannada and Malayalam only. 25 students know Tamil and Kannada only. How many students are there in this hostel who does not know any of these three languages?

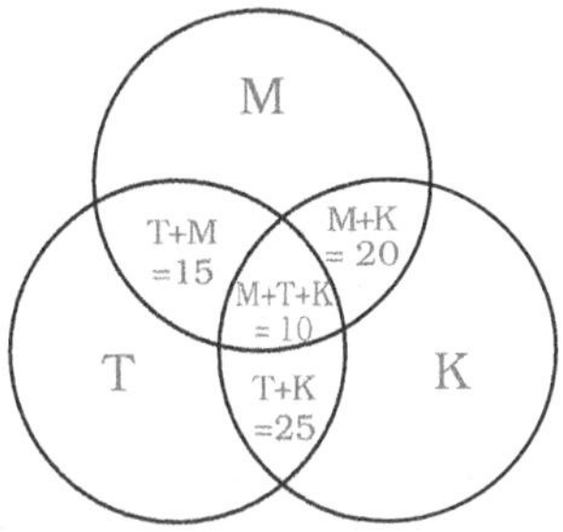

The students who do not know any of the languages = 200 – (40+20+15+10+30+25+35) = 200 – 175 = 25

4. In a survey of 150 students it was found that 50 are studying Physics, 50 Chemistry and 50 Mathematics. 6 students are studying all the three subjects while 10 are studying Physics and Chemistry, 11 Chemistry and Maths and 12 Physics and Maths. Calculate the students studying none of the subjects.

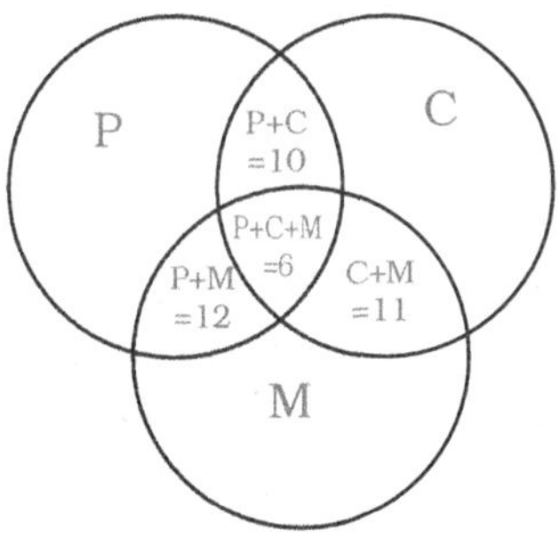

Ans. 45. (50+11+44) = 105   150 – 105 = 45

5. There are 70 players in the college team. 16 of them play all the three games football, hockey and cricket. 8 play hockey and cricket, 6 play football and cricket. 10 play football and hockey. Equal number of students plays only one of these games. How many students play hockey?

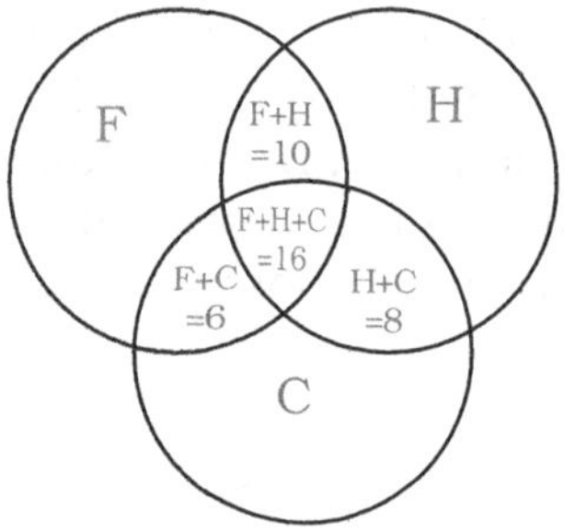

Hockey players = 70 – (16+8+6+10) = 30/3 = 10

16+10+8+10 = 44

6. There are 58 players in a sports college. The college provides coaching in three games. 10 players practice all these three games. 30 players practice only two games. 8 players practice volleyball and cricket only. 10 players practice football and cricket only. The number of players who undergo practice only in a single game is equal. If so, how many players are there who practice the game of football?

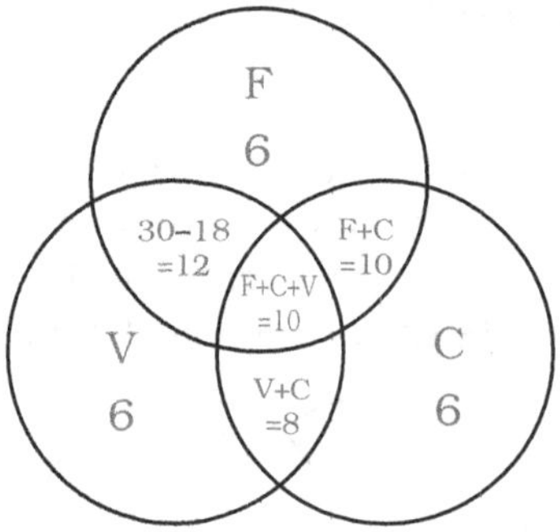

Players practicing football = 10 + 10 + 12 + 6 = 38

7. There are 50 national level players in a college. The college specializes in three games. 9 players play all the tree games. 17 play only two games. 5 play Volleyball and Tennis. 7 play Volleyball and Criket. Equal number of players plays only Criket, Tennis or Volleyball. How many plays Criket?

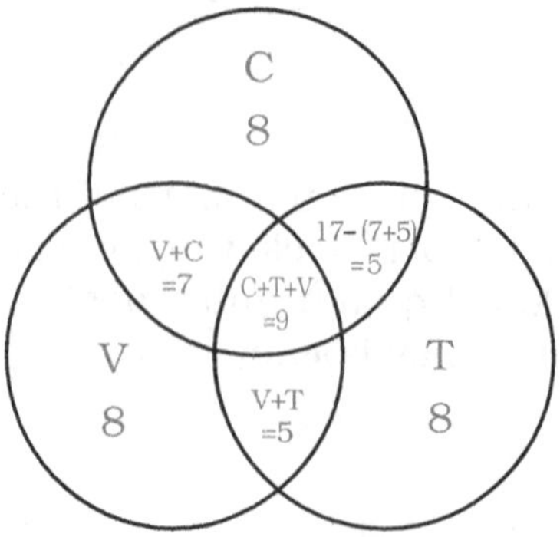

Cricket Players in 3 games players = 9
Cricket Players in 2 games players = 12 (7 + 5)
Cricket Players in 1 game players = 8 (24/3)
Total Cricket Players = 29

8. There are 56 houses in a housing colony. Out of the 56, the number of houses possessing computer, car and bike is 10. 22 houses own any two out of the tree mentioned above. 9 houses have both car and bike. 5 houses own only bike and computer. The number of houses which possess only one each among the three is equal. Then how many computers, cars and bike are there in this housing colony?

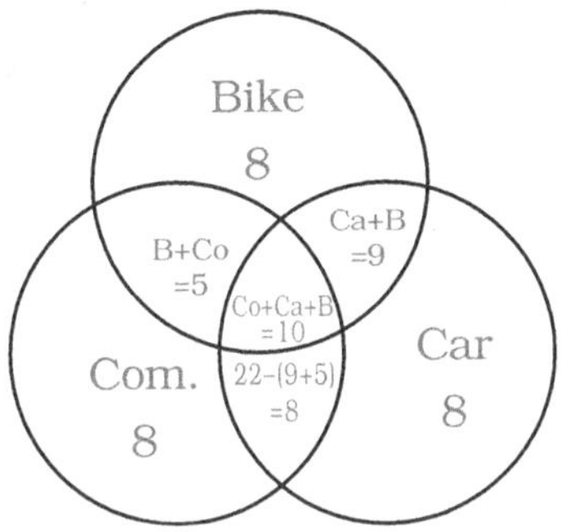

Total Computer = 8 + 8 + 5 + 10 = 31
Total Car = 8 + 8 + 9 + 10 = 35
Total Bike = 8 + 5 + 9 + 10 = 32

9. In a private tuition centre there are 100 students. 22 study all the three subjects, Maths, Physics and Chemistry, 24 study Physics and Chemistry, half of those who study Physics and Chemistry are enrolled in Chemistry and Maths combination. 18 students have registered in Maths and Physics group. Equal number of students studies only one subject. How many students study Maths?

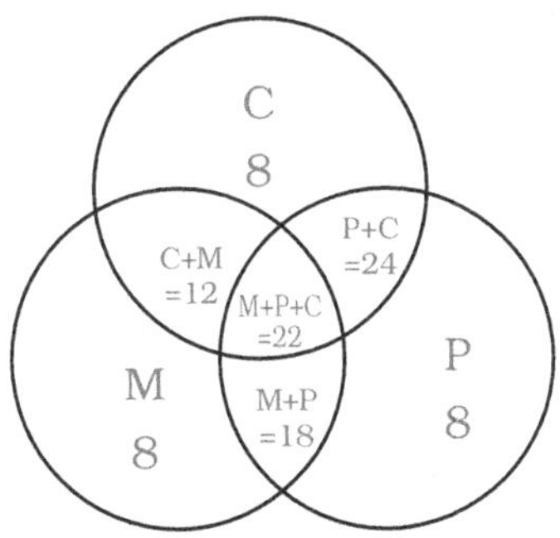

From the given diagram, the enrolment of 76 students (22 + 24 + 12 + 18) is clear
Remaining 24 students are equally divided into 3 ie. 8
Therefore students study Mathematics = 22 + 18 + 12 + 8 = 60

10. In a college there are 40 students in each of Maths, Physics and Chemistry main groups. 8 students from these groups study all the 3 subjects. There are 2 students more in Maths-Physics combination than in Maths-Chemistry combination and 5 students more in Physics-Chemistry combination than in Maths-Chemistry combination. 15 students study only Chemistry. How many students study only Mathematics?

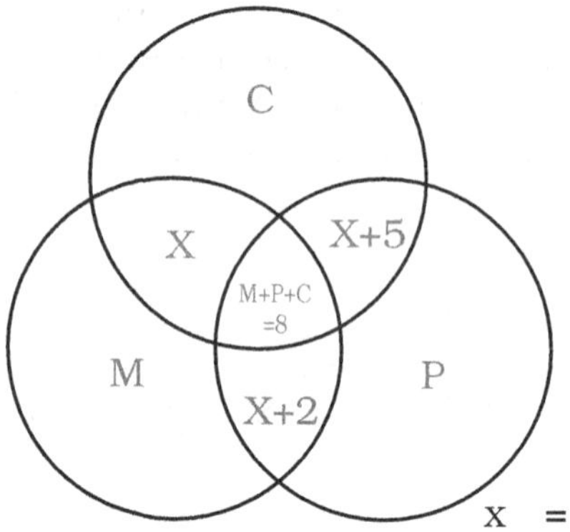

$15 + 8 + x + (x+5) = 40$

$28 + 2x = 40$

$2x = 40 - 28 = 12$

$x = 6$

$x = 40 - (15+8+x+5)$

$= 40-(28+x)=40 - 28-x$

$2x = 40 - 28=12$

$x = 12 \div 2 = 6$

Students studying Mathematics only $= 40 - (8 + 6 + 8)$

$= 40 - 22 = 18$

11. In a college 50 students each study in the main groups of Mathematics, Physics and Chemistry. Out of them10 students study all the three subjects. The number of students who study Mathematics and Physics is 4 more than those studying Mathematics and Chemistry. Similarly the number of students studying Physics and Chemistry is 6 less than those studying Mathematics and Chemistry. There are 22 students who study only Chemistry. If so, how many students study only Mathematics? How many students study only Physics?

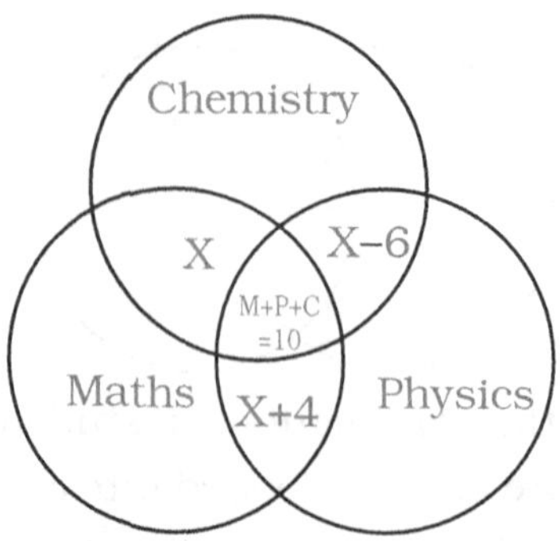

$$\begin{aligned}
\text{Students studying Chemistry only} &= 50 - 22 + 10 + x + (x - 6) \\
&= 50 - 26 + 2x \\
2x &= 50 - 26 = 24 \\
x &= 12 \\
\text{Students studying Mathematics only} &= 50 - 10 + 12 + (x + 4) \\
&= 50 - 22 + 16 \\
&= 50 - 38 = 12 \\
\text{Students studying Physics only} &= 50 - 10 + (x + 4) + (x - 6) \\
&= 50 - 10 + 16 + 6 \\
&= 50 - 32 = 18
\end{aligned}$$

12. A factory works in 8 hour shifts. The total number of workers is 210. The minimum number of workers required per shift is 80. No worker can work for more than 16 hours in a day. What is the minimum of workers who work 16 hours a day?

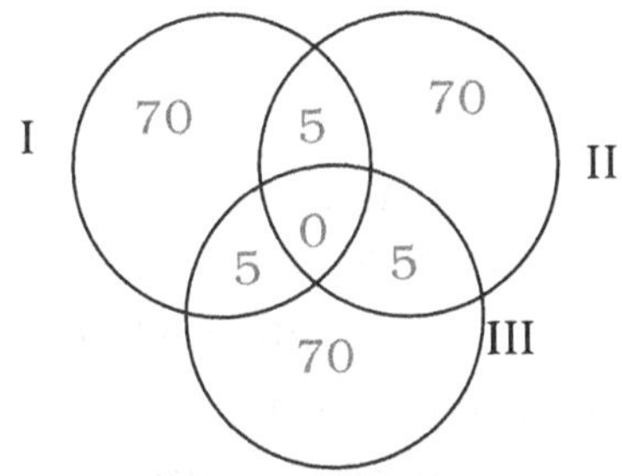

Make a Venn diagram of shift I, II and III. Intersection of 3 shifts is 0. Each shift = 80 and total = 210. So intersections of two shifts = 30, which mean ten each circle leaving 70 outside. As there are 10 in 2 intersections, there must be 5 workers in both. So the workers who work 16 hours are 5+5+5= 15

13. In a group, 18 boys play Badminton, 19 plays Cricket and 16 plays Football. 6 play Badminton only, 9 play cricket only, 5 play Badminton and Cricket, 2 play cricket and Football. How many play all 3 games?

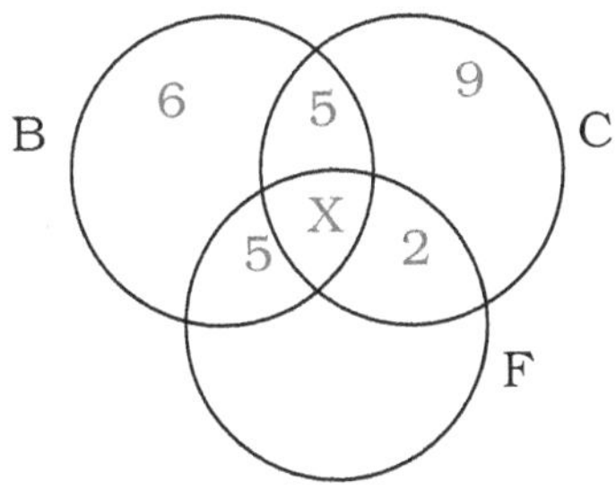

Draw a Venn diagram. The circle representing Cricket with some other game is 19 – 9 = 10. This consists of both games (5+2) and 3 games (X). Therefore x = 10 – 7 = 3

14. Five hundred candidates appeared in an examination comprising tests in English, Hindi and Mathematics. The diagram gives the number of candidates who failed in different tests. What is the percentage of candidates who failed in at least two subjects?

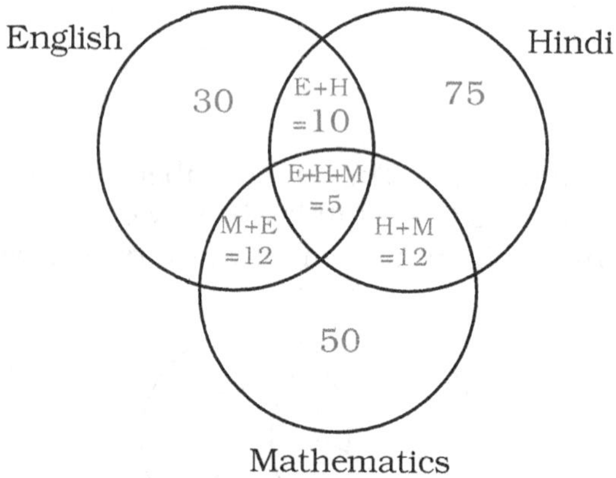

Number of candidates who failed in English and Hindi = 10

Number of candidates who failed in Hindi and Mathematics = 12

Number of candidates who failed in Mathematics and English = 12

Number of candidates who failed in all the three subjects = 5

Therefore the number of candidates who failed in at least two subjects = 10+12+12+5 = 39

Total number of candidates = 500

Hence, required percentage = $\frac{39}{500} \times 100 = 7.8$

6. ANALYTICAL REASONING

The test of Analytical Reasoning given here involves problems dealing with the counting of geometrical figures in a given complex figure. The method of solving the problem would be clear from the following examples.

1. One figure is missing. Can you say which is missing?

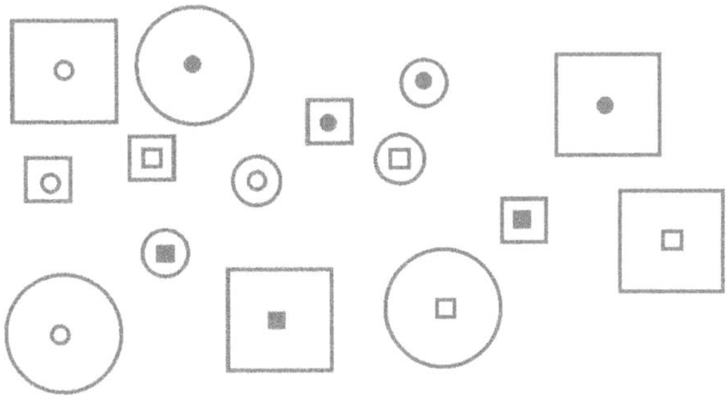

There are 15 figures in all. By symmetry we expect one more to complete the sequence below. The figures can be re-classified as follows:

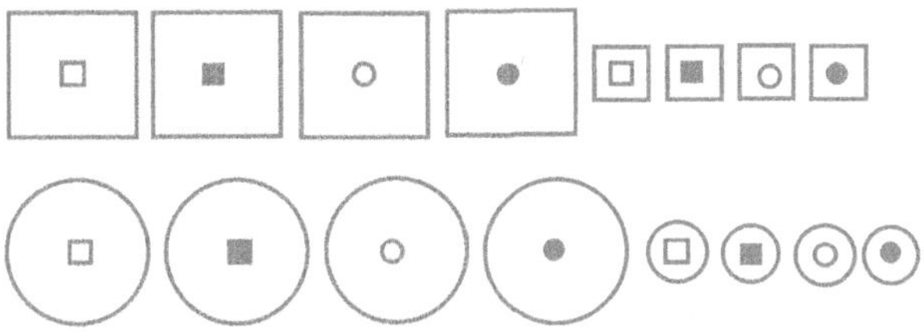

What we would expect is one more figure to complete the 16 figures.

There are 4 big squares, 4 small squares, 4 big circles and 4 small circles as shown above. The missing figure to complete the sequency is a 'big cicrle' with a black square inside.

Ans: Big circle with black square inside

2. How many circles are there in the figure given below?

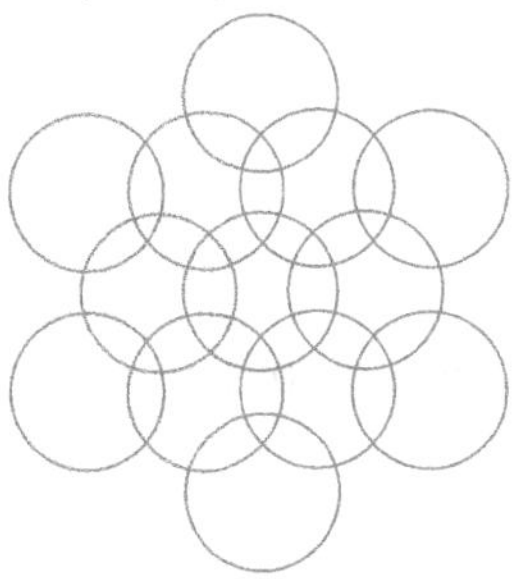

Ans: 13 Circles can be classified into three groups:

(a) one at the centre

(b) 6 surrounding the centre circle

(c) 6 forming the outer circle.

3. What is the number of straight lines in the following figure?

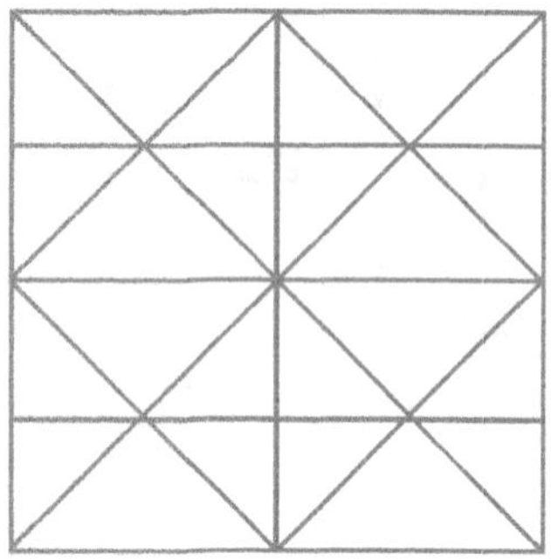

Ans: 14 Horizontal lines = 5, Vertical lines = 3, Slanting lines = 3+3 = 6

4. State the minimum number of straight lines required to make the figure given below

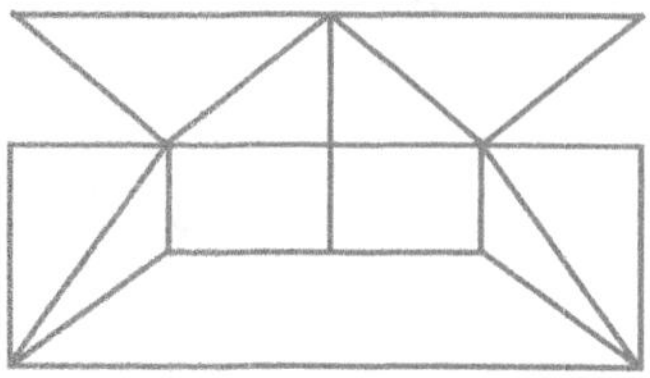

Ans: 17 Horizontal lines = 4, Vertical lines = 5, Slanting lines = 8

5. How many line segments are there in the following figure?

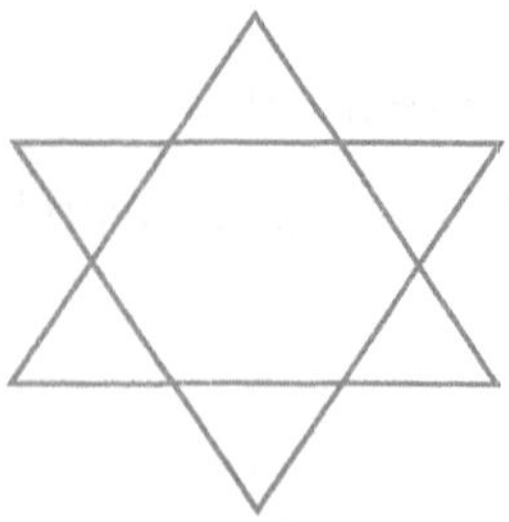

Ans: 18 There are 3 line segments in one line. There are 6 such lines.

6. Find the number of triangles in the following figure.

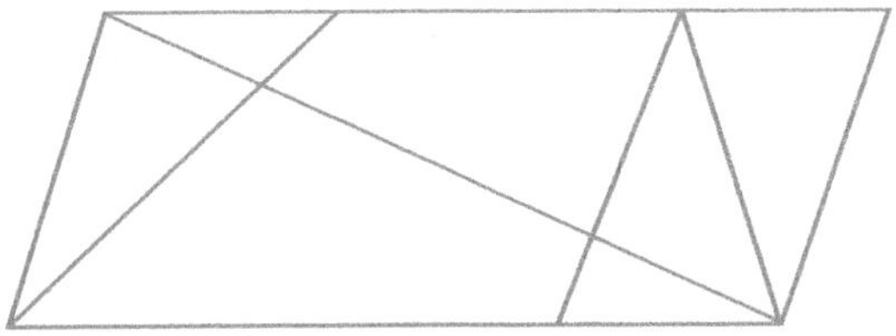

Ans: 12

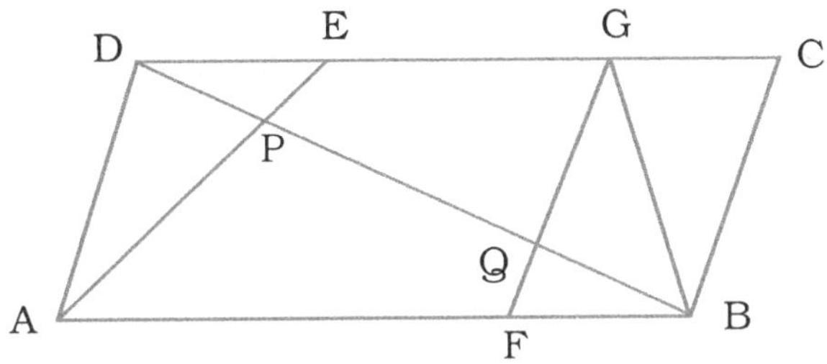

Identify the possible triangles by locating a line segment which becomes the base of a triangle, with a third point viz its vertex. Note down all such triangles. There are 12 triangles in all viz., ADP, ADE, ADB, DGB, DCB, GCB, FBG, FQB, QGB, GFB, APB and DEP. Avoid repetitions of the same triangle - eg: ABD, ADB, etc.,

7. How many triangles are there in the figure given below?

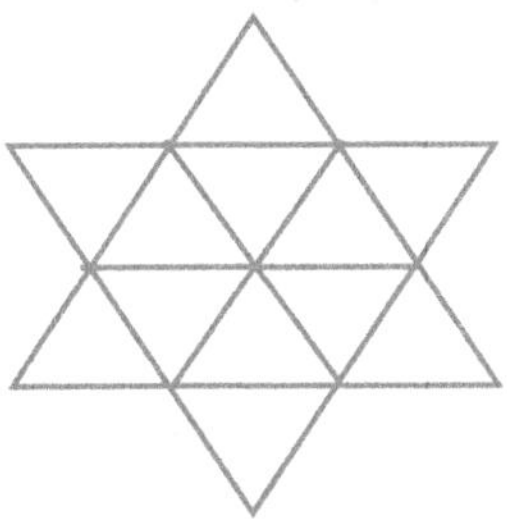

Ans: 20. The figure consists of (a) 12 small triangles (b) 6 bigger triangles (each composed of 4 small triangles.) (c) 2 very big triangles (each composed of 9 small traingles).

Note down the number of large and small triangles. 2 very large triangles, 1 facing upwards and another facing downwards.

(a) 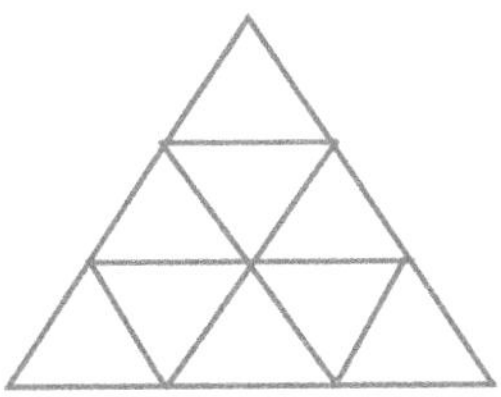 Very big triangle (of 9 small triangles)

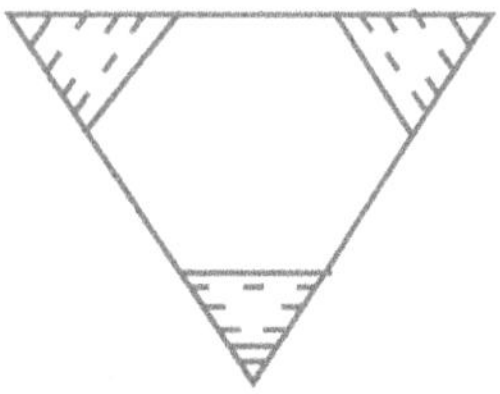

3 Small triangles not in the top triangle

(b)

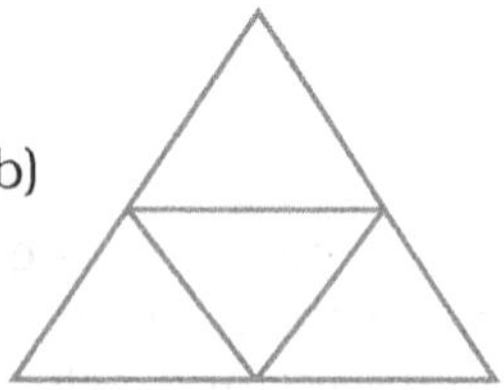

Big triangles consists of 6 this type of triangles

(c) The figure consists of 2 very big triangles.
The total number of triangles = a+b+c = 12+6+2 = 20

8. How many cubes are there in this figure?

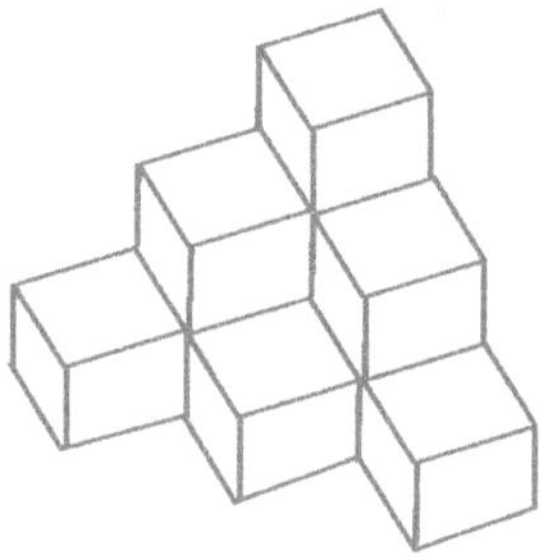

Ans: 10 Ground layer = 6, Second layer = 3, Third layer = 1

Total = 6+3+1 = 10

You are required to identify the number of cubes in this arrangement. You are expected to count what can be seen and what can be guessed as belonging to this arrangement.

9. Find the number of triangles in the following figure

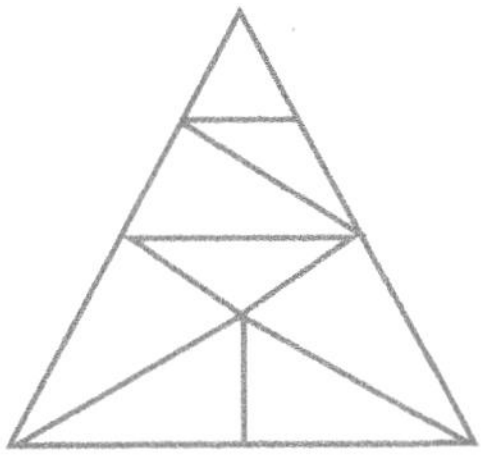

Ans: 19

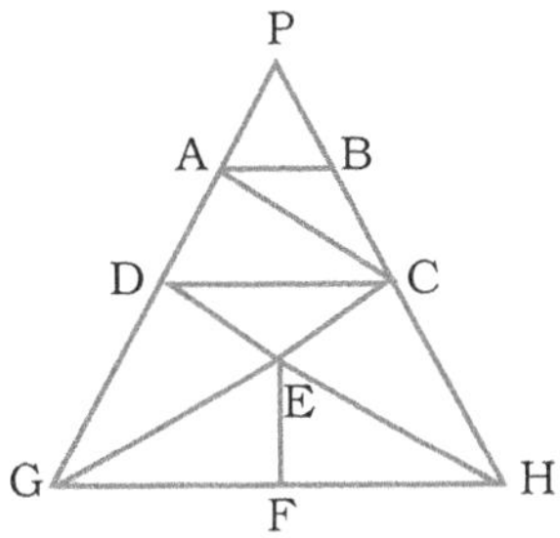

(a) Number of small independent triangles - 8 numbers
GFE, HFE, ECH, DEG, DEC, DCA, CAB, BAP

(b) Number of triangles formed by a combination of 2 triangles - 4 numbers
GFE+HFE, GDE+EDC, HCE+ECD, CAB+BAC

(c) Number of triangles formed by a combination of 3 triangles - 4 numbers
GFE+EFH+HEC
HFE+EFG+GED
DCA+ACB+BAP
GED+DEC+DCA

(d) Number of triangles formed by a combination of 5 triangles - 2 numbers
HEC+CED+CDA+ACB+BPA
GED+DEC+CDA+ACB+BAP

(e) Number of triangles formed by a combination of 8 triangles - 1 number
GEF+EFH+EHC+EGD+ECD+DAC+CBA+APB

10. How many squares are there in the following figure?

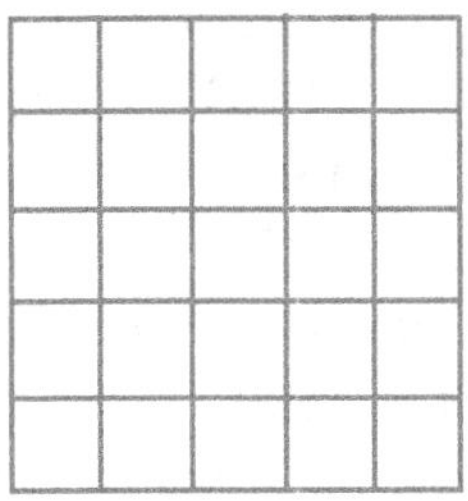

The total number of squares is $5^2 + 4^2 + 3^2 + 2^2 + 1^2 = 55$

Ans: 55

Number of squares with:

No. with side 1 = $1^2 = 1$

No. with side 2 = $2^2 = 4$

No. with side 3 = $3^2 = 9$

No. with side 4 = $4^2 = 16$

No. with side 5 = $5^2 = 25$

Total = 55

11. What is the number of rectangles in the following figure ?

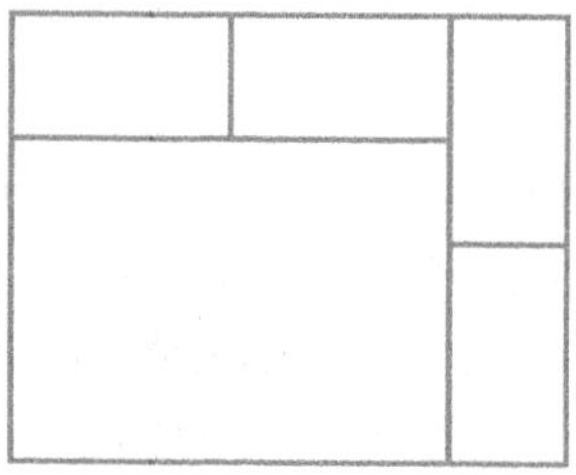

Ans: 9

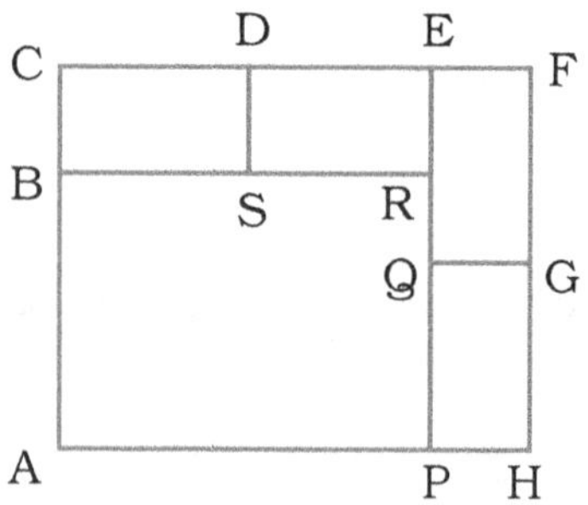

Number of single rectangles = 5
(figures APRB, PHGQ, QGFE, EDSR, DSBC)
combination of 2 rectangles = 2
(figures CBRE, PHEF)
combination of 3 rectangles = 1
(figures APEC)
combination of 5 rectangles = 1
(figures AHFC)
Total number of rectangles = 5+2+1+1 = 9

12. Determine the number of triangles in the following figure

Ans: 36

Type I Triangle

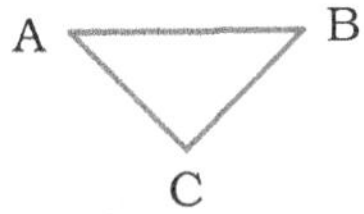

Type II Triangle

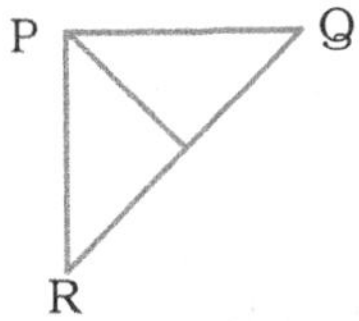

Type III Triangle

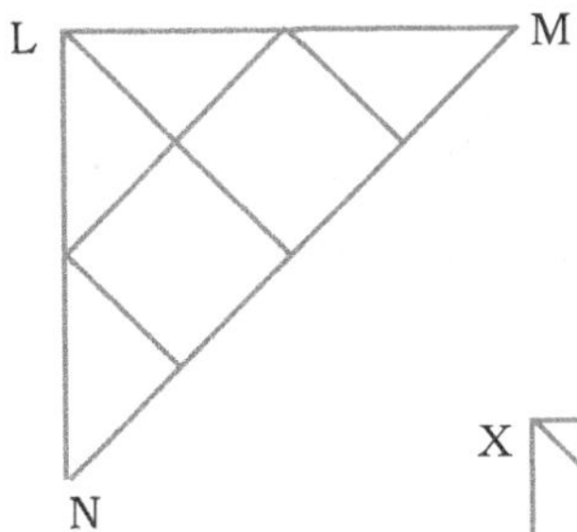

Type IV Triangle

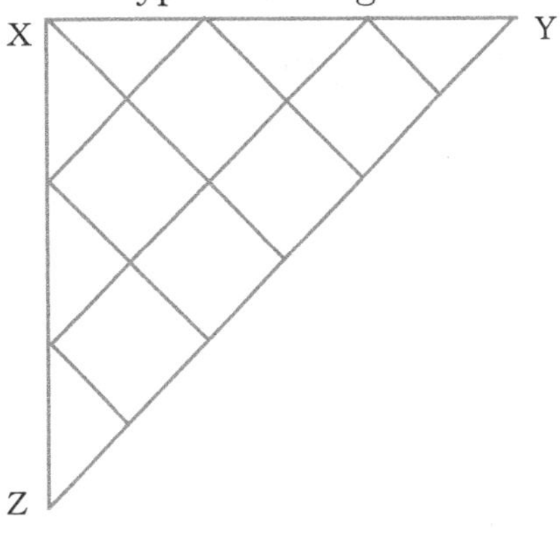

Type V Triangle

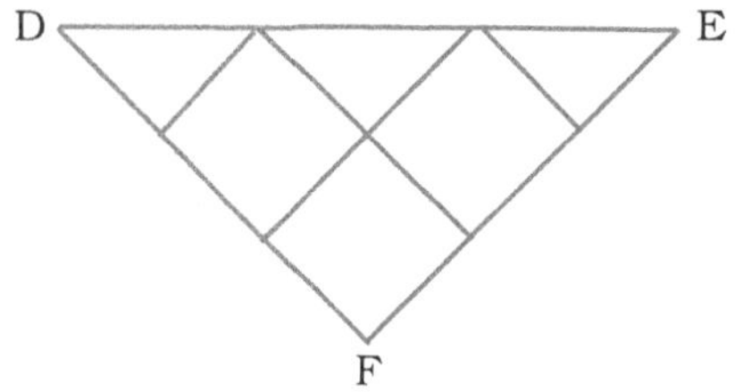

Type VI Triangle

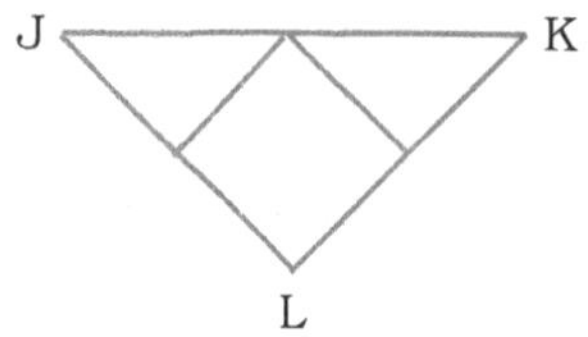

Note: We can locate four kinds of triangles in this figure. These are shown above:

(a) Type I triangles (smallest in the figure) Triangle ABC type. There are 3 for each side. Total for 4 sides = 3 × 4 = **12 triangles.**

(b) Type II triangles (combination of 2 triangles) Triangle PQR type. There will be 4 triangles at each of the 4 corners = **4 triangles.**

(c) Type III triangles (like LMN) With 4 small triangles and two small squares. There will be 4 triangles of this kind in 4 corners = **4 triangles.**

(d) Type IV triangles (like XYZ) There will be 4 such triangles corresponding to each of the 4 corners of the square = **4 triangles.**

(e) Type V triangles (like DEF) There will be 4 such triangles corresponding to each of the 4 corners of the square = **4 triangles.**

(f) Type VI triangles (like JKL) There will be 2 triangles for each corner: Total **8 triangles.**

Total number of triangles = **36**.

13. Count the total number of triangles

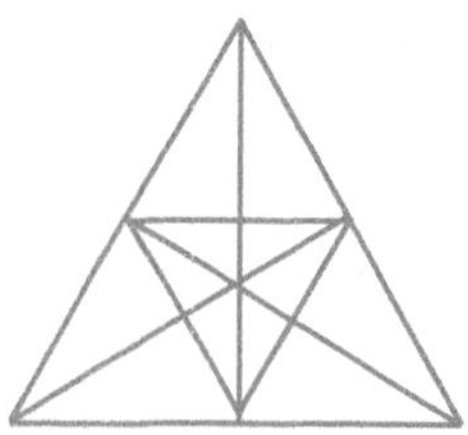

Ans: 47

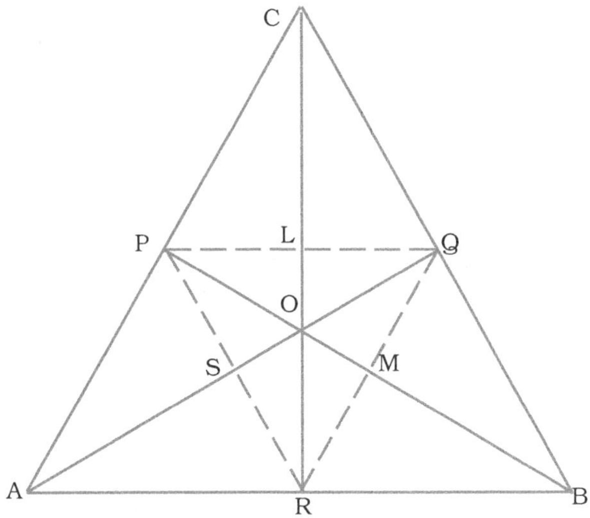

Number of triangles in the figure:

(a) One-triangle figures: (12 numbers)
ASR, ASP; RMB, QMB; QLC, PLC;
SOR, SOP; MOR, MOQ; LOQ, LOP;

(b) Two-triangle figures: (12 numbers)
ROB, ROA; POA, POC; QOB, QOC;
RBQ, RAP; PCQ, POR; ROQ, QOP;

(c) Three-triangle figures: (6 numbers)
SRQ, SPQ, RMP, QMP, LQR, LPR

(d) Four-triangle figures: (9 numbers)
ARQ, BRP, BQP, APQ, CQR, PCR, AOC, BOC, ABO

(e) Six-triangle figures: (7 numbers)
BRC, ARC, BQA, APB, CQA, CPB, PQR

(f) Twelve-triangle figures: (1 number)
ABC

Total 47 triangles.

14. Count the number of squares in the figure given below

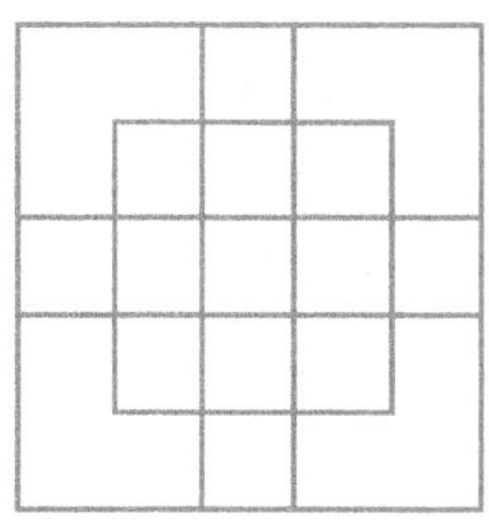

Ans: 27 1 = 13, 2 = 4, 4 = 4, 7 = 4, 9 = 1, 17 = 1

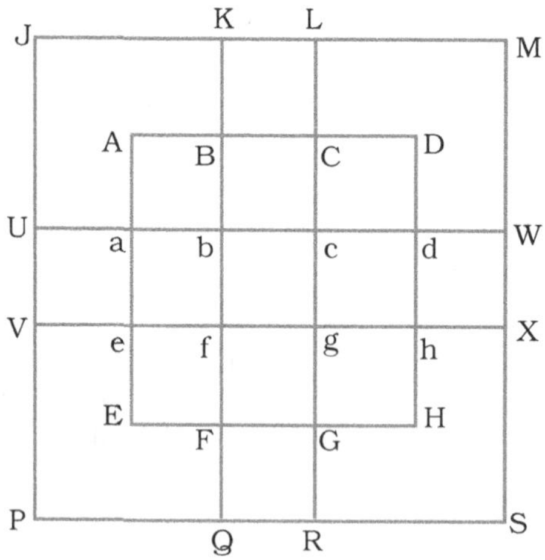

Single squares (13 numbers)

ABba, BCcb, CDdc

abfe, bcgf, cdhg

efFE, fgGF, ghHG

UaeV, dWXh

KLCB, FGRQ

Two square (small square with in a large square) **Pattern** (4 numbers)

JKbU, LMWc

VfQP, bdHF

Four square Pattern (4 numbers)

ACge, BDhf

acGE, bdHF

Seven figure pattern (6 squares, and L shaped area) (4 numbers)

UcRP, bWSQ

VgLJ, fXMK

Nine figure pattern (3×3 squares) (1 number)

ADHE

Seventeen figure pattern (1 number)

PSMJ

Total squares 13+4+4+4+1+1 = 27

15. How many rectangles does the following figure have?

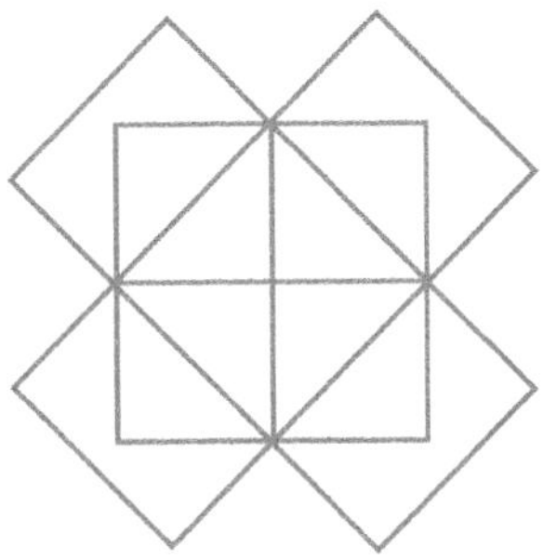

Ans: 14

Note: Square not treated as a rectangle

We can split the figure in to 2 separate sheets (since this can be done without affecting any rectangular shapes in the combination) and discussed seprately.

Fig. I

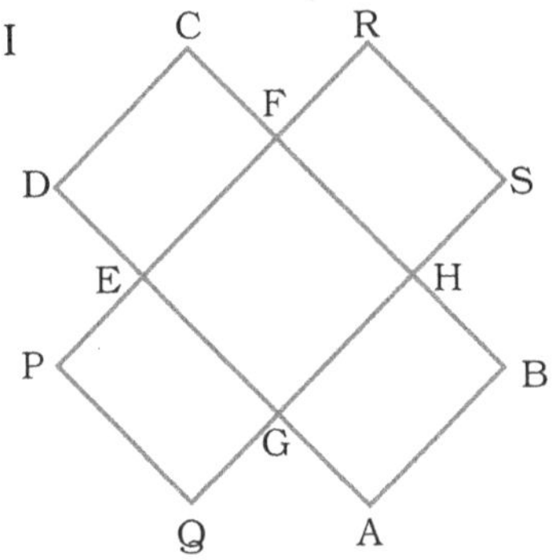

The following are the rectangles in figure 1

(a) without combination (4 numbers)

EDCF, AGHB

FRSH, PEGQ,

(b) with combination of one rectangle with the square (4 numbers)

GHCD, ABFE

GERS, FHQP

(c) Combining the square with two rectangles on either side (4 numbers)

ABCD, PQSR (2 numbers)

Fig. II

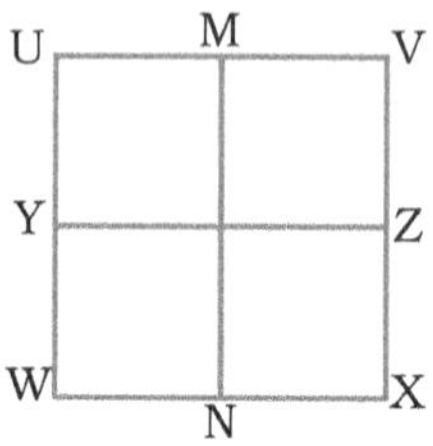

The following are the rectangles in figure II.

Combining two squares (4 numbers)

UVZY, YZXW

UMNW, MVXN

Total number of rectangles = 4+4+2+4 = 14

16. How many parallelograms are there in the figure below?

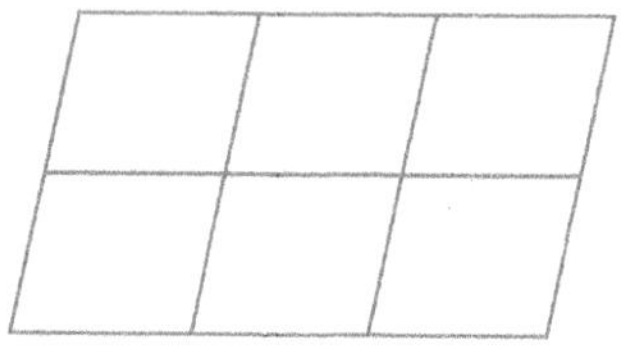

Ans: 18

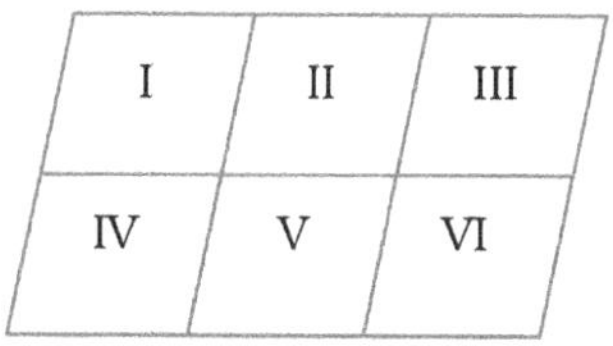

(a) Counting one small parallalogram at a time

I, II, III, IV, V, VI (6 numbers)

(b) Adding 2 small parallalograms at a time

I+II, II+III, IV+V, V+VI

I+IV, II+V, III+VI (7 numbers)

(c) Adding 3 small parallalograms at a time

I+II+III, IV+V+VI (2 numbers)

(d) Adding 4 parallalograms at a time

I+II+IV+V, II+III+V+VI (2 numbers)

(e) Adding 6 parallalograms at a time

I+II+III+IV+V+VI (1 number)

Total = 6+7+2+2+1 = 18

17. Count the number of pentagons in the following figure

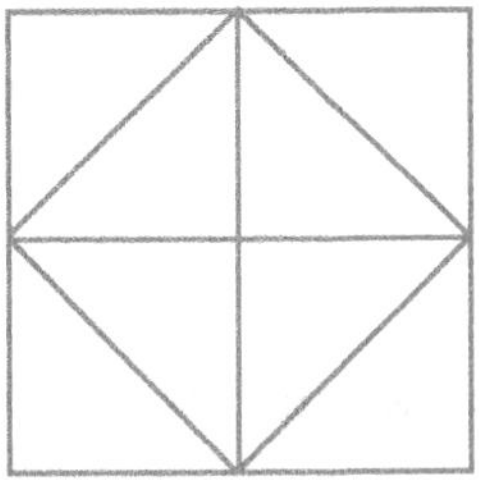

Ans: 12

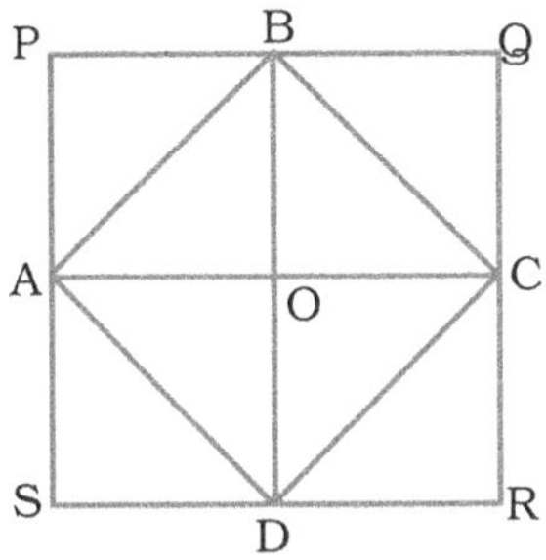

3 groups of pentagons (4 each) are possible. They are:

(a) ASRCB, DRQBA, CQPAD, BPSDC

(b) ADCBP, DCBAS, CBADR, BADCQ

(c) ADCBO, DCBAO, CBADO, BADCO

Ans: 12 pentagons.

18. Determine the number of hexagons in the following figure

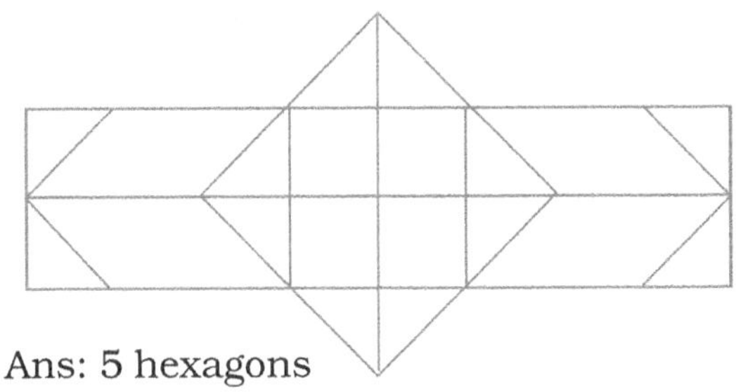

Ans: 5 hexagons

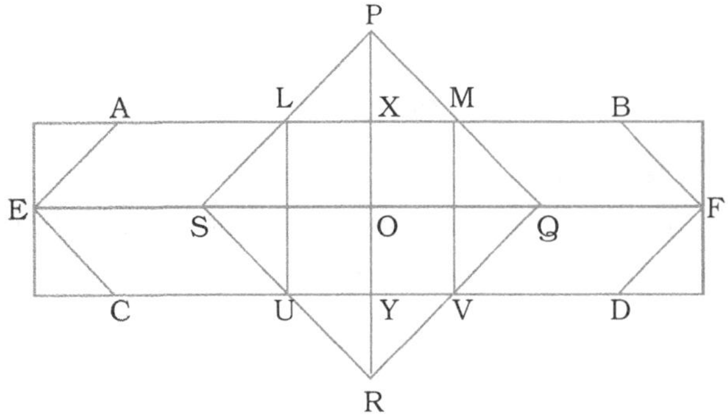

The following hexagons are possible:

ALSUCE, BMQVDF

AMQVCE, BLSUDF

ABFDCE

Ans: 5 hexagons

19. How many triangles and squares are there in this figure?

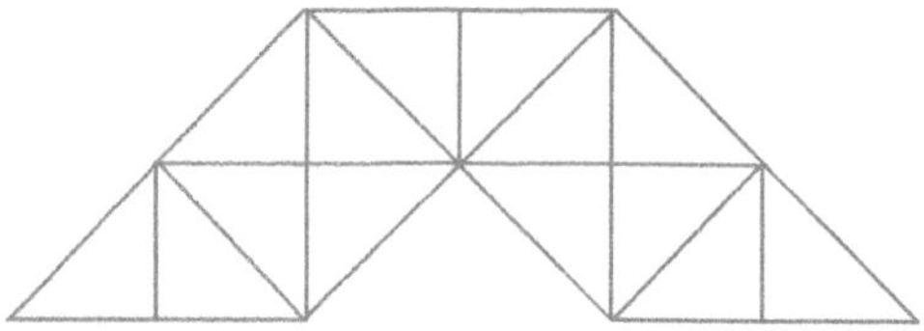

Ans: Triangles = 29
Squares = 6

Squares

(a) small squares formed by the combination of 2 small triangles = 4

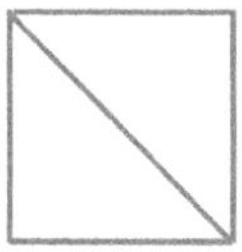

(b) bigger squares formed by the combination of 4 small triangles = 2

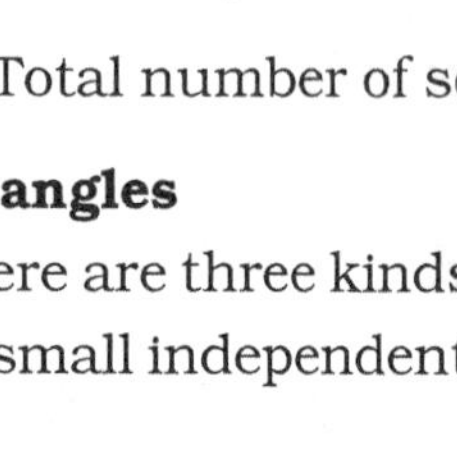

Total number of squares = 4=2 = 6

Triangles

There are three kinds of triangles in this figure

(a) small independent triangles

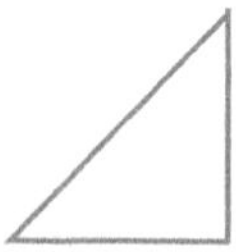

(b) medium size triangles formed by combining 2 triangles of the type in (a)

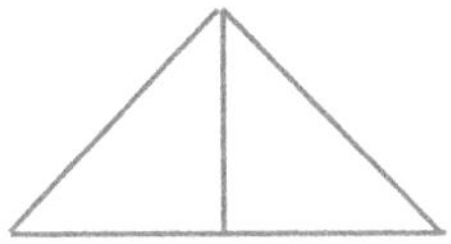

(c) bigger triangles formed by doubling medium sized triangles in (b) with four small triangles.

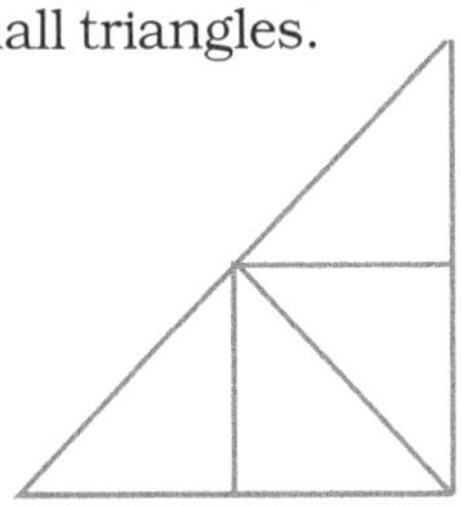

Number in category (a) = 14

Number in category (b) = 11

Number in category (c) = 4

Total = 14+11+4 = 29

20. How many squares and triangles are there?

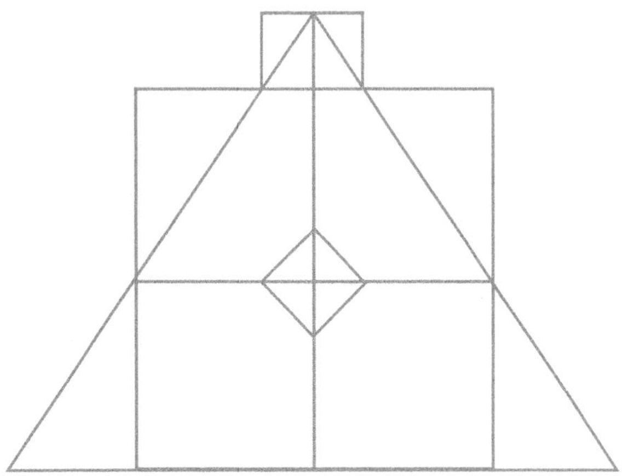

Ans: Square = 7

Triangles = 22

Number of Squares:

2 very small squares (centre and edge)

4 medium size squares, and

1 large square formed by the 4 medium sized squares.

In all there are 2+4+1 = 7 squares

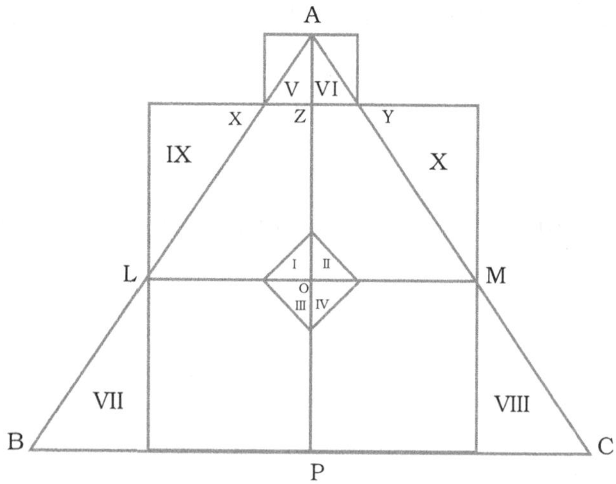

Besides the 10 smaller triangles indicated by Roman letters, there are bigger triangles BPA, CPA, LOA, MOA, XYA, LMA, ABC.

There are combination triangles formed as follows: V+VI, I+II, III+IV, I+III, II+IV.

There are 22 triangles in all

21. How many triangles and squares are there?

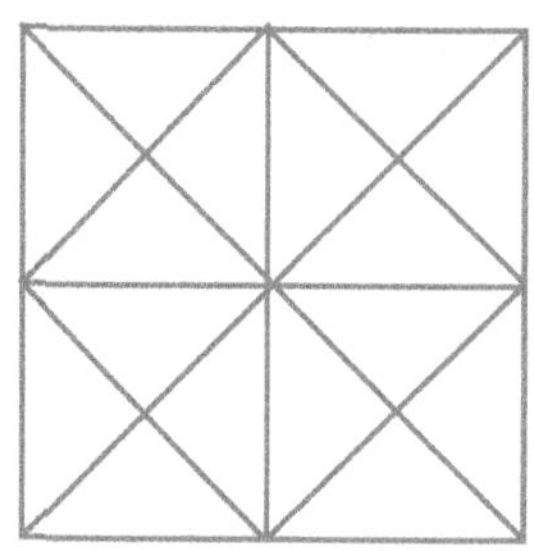

Ans:	Triangles = 44	(1 = 16, 2 = 16, 4 = 8, 8 = 4)
	Square = 10	(2 = 4, 4 = 4, 8 = 1, 16 = 1)

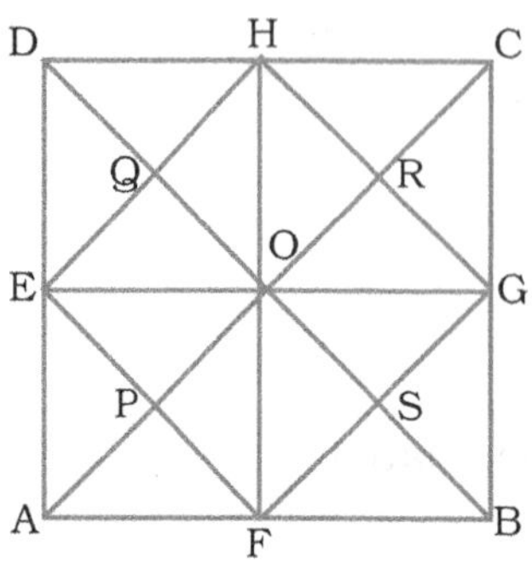

(a) Number of **independent triangles** (smallest possible) in the figure = 16

(b) Number of bigger triangles, each composed of **2 small triangles** are the following:

EOF, FOG, GOH, HOE

AFO, BFO, BGO, CGO, CHO, DHO, DEO, AEO

EAF, FBG, GCH, HDE

The number of triangles in this case = 16

(c) Number of bigger triangles, composed of **4 small triangles** are the following:

AOB, BOC, COD, DOA

EFG, FGH, GHE, HEF

Total number of triangles in this case = 8

(d) Number of bigger triangles, each composed of **8 small triangles** are the following:

ABC, BCD, CDA, DAB

Total number of triangles in this case = 4

Total number of triangles in the figure = 16+16+8+4 = 44

Number of squares

Whole figure → ABCD

Inner square of ABCD → EFGH

Four corner squares → EOFA, GOFB, GOHC, EOHD

Inner squares of EFGH → PFSO, RGSO, QHRO, QEPO

Total number of squares in the figure = 1+1+4+4 = 10

22. How many triangles and squares are there?

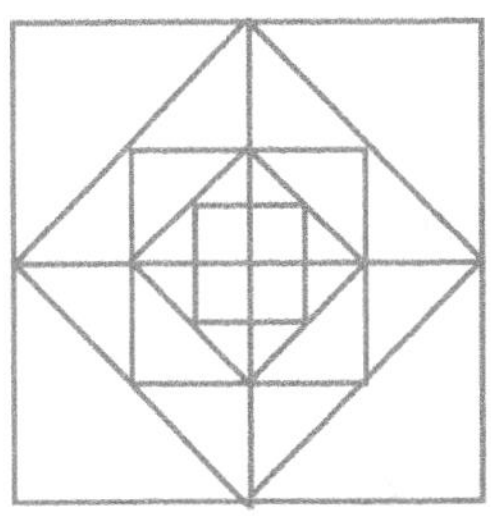

Ans: Triangles = 48 (1 = 24, 2 = 8, 3 = 4, 6 = 8, 12 = 4)

Square = 17 (1 = 4, 4 = 5, 7 = 4, 12 = 1, 16 = 1, 24 = 1, 28 = 1)

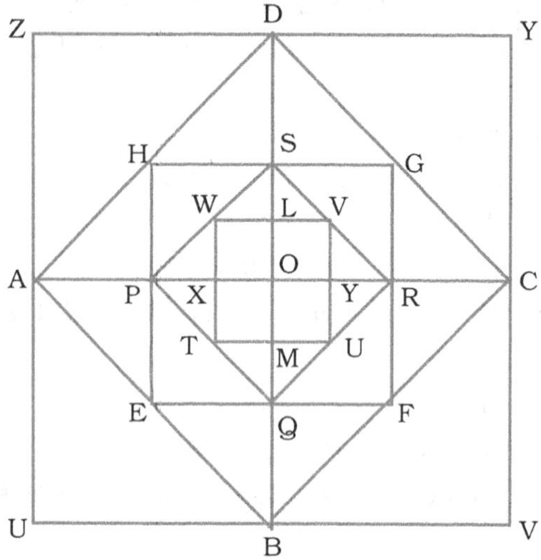

(a) One independent triangle as unit

AUB, BVC, CYD, DZA

(EBQ, FBQ), (FCR, GCR), (GDS, HDS), (HAP, EAP)

PEQ, QFR, RGS, SHP

(TQM, UQM), (URY, VRY), (VSL, WSL), (WPX, TPX)

24 triangles.

(b) 2 triangle combination of bigger triangles

(EBF, FCG, GDH, HAE)

(TQU, URV, VSW, WPT)

8 triangles

(c) 3 figure combination (2 triangles and 1 square)

QOR, ROS, SOP, POQ

4 triangles

(d) 6 figure combinations (4 triangles and 2 squares).

(RSP, PQR), (QRS, SPQ)

4 triangles

(e) 6 figure combinations (5 triangles and 1 square)

BOC, COD, DOA, AOB (4 triangles)

(f) 12 figure combinations (10 triangles)

BCD, CDA, DAB, ABC (4 triangles)

Total number of triangles = 24+8+4+4+4+4 = 48

23. Count the number of straight lines, triangles and squares

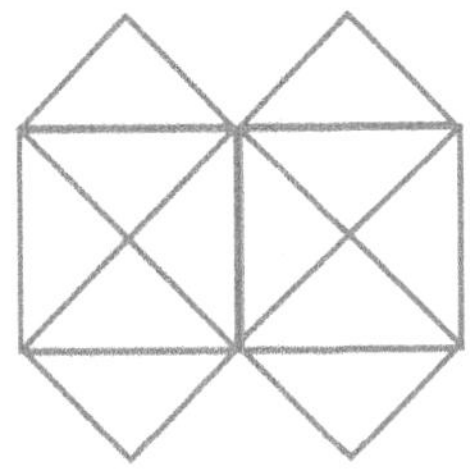

Ans: Lines = 17
Triangles = 22
Square = 7

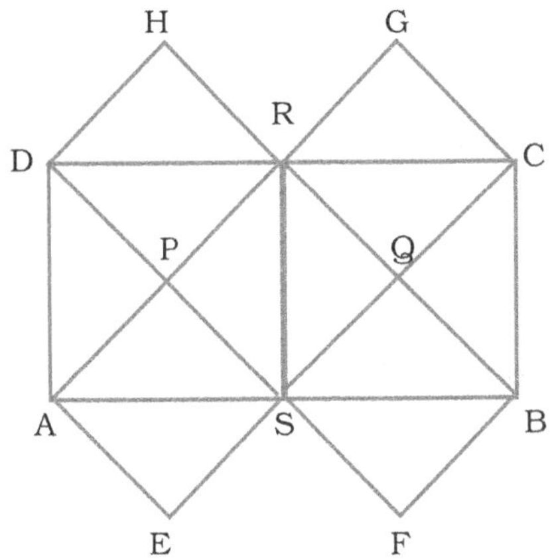

Number of complete line segments

(a) Horizontal line segments
AB, CD

(b) Vertical lines segments
AD, SR,BC

(c) Slanting line segments
DH, HR, RG, GC, AE, ES, SF, FB, DF, HB, GA, CE
Total number of line segments = 2+3+12 = 17

Number of triangles

(a) Single triangles:
AES, SFB, RGC, RHD,
APS, PSR, RPD, DPA,
SQB, BQC, CQR, RQS
(12 triangles)

(b) 2 triangle combinations:
ASR, SRD, RDA, DAS,
SBC, BCR, CRS, RSB
(8 triangles)

(c) 4 triangle combinations:
DSC, ARB
(2 triangles)

Total number of triangles in this figure = 12+8+2 = 22.

Number of squares

(a) Squares with slanting sides (2 triangle combinations)
DHRP, APSE, PRQS, RGCQ, SQBF
Total 5 squares

(b) Squares with vertical sides (4 triangle combinations)
ASRD, SBCR
Total 2 aquares.
Grand total 5+2 = 7

24. Count the number of squares, rectangles and triangles

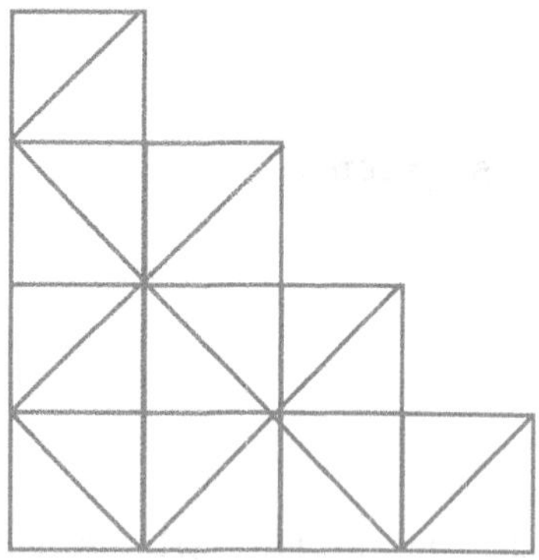

Ans: Squares = 14
Rectangles = 22 (excluding squares)
Triangles = 39

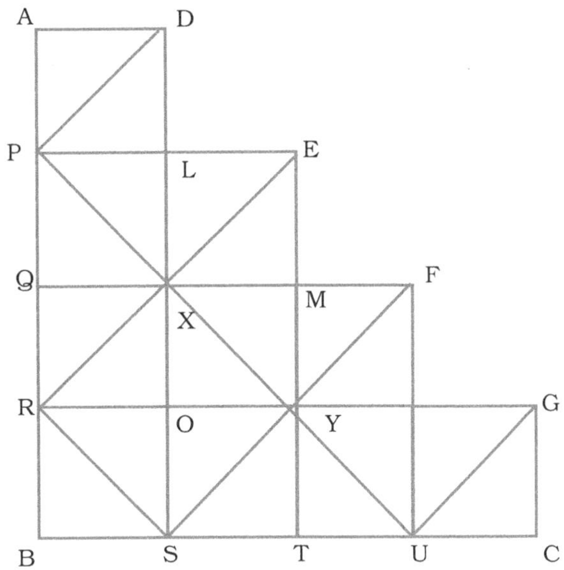

Squares

(a) Single squares (formed by combining two triangles):

RBSO, OSTY, YTUN, NUCG,

QROX, XOYM, MYNF,

PQXL,LXME,

APLD

Total 10 squares

(b) Bigger squares (formed by four square/eight triangle combination):

BTMQ, RYEP, SUFX

Total 3 squares

(c) Slanting square (formed by four triangle combination):

XYSR

Total 1 square

Grand total squares = 10+3+1 = 14

Rectangles (excluding squares)

Two groups of rectangles are persive, viz horinzontal combination squares/vertical combination squares.

(a) Rectangles formed by combinining two squares vertically viz,

ADXQ, PLOR, QXSB,

LEYO, XMTS;

MFUT

Total = 6

(b) 2 squares horizontally vix.,

GCTY, NUSO, YTBR,

FNOX, MYRQ,

EMQP

Total = 6

(c) Rectangles formed by combining three squares vertically viz.,

ADOR, PLSB,

LETS

Total = 3

(d) Rectangles formed by combining three squares horizontally viz.,

GCSO, NUBR,

FNRQ

Total = 3

(e) Rectangles formed by combining four squares vertically

ADSB

Total = 1

(f) Rectangles formed by combining four squares horizontally

GCBR

Total = 1

(g) Rectangles formed by combining six squares vertically

PETB

Total = 1

(h) Rectangles formed by combining six squares horizontally

FUBQ

Total = 1

Grand Total = **22 rectangles.**

Triangles

There are 39 kinds of triangles in this figure. There are the smallest triangles obtained by dividing the smallest squares in the figure, then the bigger triangles formed by combining two triangles, the still bigger triangles formed by combining four triangles, and the biggest triangles formed by combining 9 small triangles. These are:

(a) Small independent triangles (obtained by dividing the smallest square in the figure).

Since there are 10 small squares, there are **20 small triangles** in the figure.

(b) Bigger triangles formed by combining 2 small triangles. These are:
PXE, EYX, XYR, RPX
XFY, XYS, SRX, SYU
FYU, YUG
10 triangles

(c) Still bigger triangles formed by combining 4 small triangles. The triangles of this kind are:
For the square PEYR, the triangles are:
RYE, YRP, YEP, EPR.
For the square XFUS, the triangles are:
SUF, USX, UFX, FXS.
There are **8 triangles**

(d) Biggest possible triangle formed by combining 9 triangles.
Only **1 triangle** of this kind, viz. PBU,
In all there are 39 triangles in the figure.

Unit - VII

DATA INTERPRETATION

1. SOURCES, ACQUISITION, AND INTERPRETATION OF DATA
2. QUANTITATIVE AND QUALITATIVE DATA
3. GRAPHICAL REPRESENTATION AND MAPPING OF DATA

Unit - VII

DATA INTERPRETATION

An important intellectual skill expected of a researcher is the ability to understand, represent and interpret the data collected for research in the forms which are either self – interpreting or can be understood using standard conventions. Data collected can be converted into tables, diagrams, and graphs of different kinds - like histograms, bar diagrams and pie diagrams, etc. Even while planning a research project, the researcher will have to think about the collection of data, tools appropriate for collecting data, and the analysis and interpretation of data using the different methods listed earlier. For a researcher who reads the related studies in journals, dissertations, research abstracts, etc. the ability to interpret the presentations by researchers is very crucial. Most of the researchers use the diagrammatic and graphical techniques to present their findings in a more intelligible form.

These skills have to be developed even at the planning stage of research. Researchers have to develop tools and techniques for quantifying the different variables. We know that certain forms of research require the use of quantitative data, whereas certain other types of research will be based on qualitative data.

The use of statistical techniques for analyzing the data will enable the researcher to arrive at valid conclusions and generalizations. The findings are thereafter represented in the form of tables or different types of graphs. This mode of presentation of data enables the researcher to understand the implications of the result at a glance. Graphical modes enable comparisons between groups and between variables. This is why data interpretation is included as a compulsory component in the test for identifying the research aptitude of applicant for the award of a J.R.F.

Teachers in the higher education institutions are expected to have acquired this ability. The rationale behind this assumption is:

1. A teacher in higher education is essentially a researcher since he/she has to get acquainted with the latest development in one's discipline. The teacher is expected to train and prepare future researchers, besides conducting his/her research. We may recall in this connection the functions of teachers in higher education. A teacher of higher education has to be a continuous researcher for the entire period of his employment and even beyond. A teacher has to be up to date in surveying research literature in his/her area of specialization. All these demand that the teacher should acquire the ability to read and judge the continuous research publications

2. Another reason for assessing the ability of a would-be teacher in data interpretation is that all teachers will have to use different kinds of data and interpret them in their lecture classes. For eg: a teacher of economics presenting his arguments relating to the level of development of a country like India will have to support his arguments with data and interpret them properly. The findings of his own research in publications will have to be presented before academic groups in seminars, conferences, debates etc., where again the interpretation of data becomes important. Visual presentation would make the debates more meaningful and impressive. Data presentation (numerical, diagrammatic, etc) and interpretation are important strategies for effective communication. These skills are widely used in the publication of research papers.

In the following pages, we intent to familiarize our readers the related details:

a. Source of Data

b. Qualitative and Quantitative Data.

c. Primary and Secondary Data.

d. Tabulation, Classification and Interpretation of Data.

e. Diagrammatic Presentation of Data

The representative questions based on the above information are also given as practice exercises.

1. SOURCES OF DATA

It is too well known that any scientific investigation is based on valid data collected for the purpose. "Truth is buried in the data" underline that research conclusions are drawn from the relevant data which contain the conclusions for those who have the ability to see through what is collected as data. Remember that data is a plural word of the Latin term datum. When these bits or pieces of data are processed, we can derive information. Such information has to be processed and presented in a logical and organized form if one has to comprehend and identify often hidden inter-data relationships and enable their comparison. Data for a research problem are collected using several accepted methods using tools like questionnaires, rating scales, check-lists., etc. Data can also be collected from printed materials like books, journals and other data communication strategies like internet browsing. Quantified data is used for experimentation. Data thus collected can be broadly classified into two types; Quantitative Data and Qualitative Data.

2. QUANTITATIVE AND QUALITATIVE DATA

The former is directly measured data, expressed in terms of measured units. Such data are generally expressed using distinct numerical indices. They are mostly in the terms of integers without any fractional parts. If an investigator is interested in estimating the number of employees in an industry who belong to a particular community or gender or if he wants to measure the intelligence level (IQ) of the students in a class, the data can be expressed in the form of numbers. These are examples of quantitative data.

When the data deal with approximations which cannot be reduced to numbers, we have to use qualitative descriptions like 'high', 'excellent', 'low', 'average', etc. There are examples of terms like 'social change', 'social acceptance', etc. are qualitative descriptors.

3. PRIMARY AND SECONDARY DATA

Primary data in research refers to the pieces of information collected directly by the investigator / data are collected from original or first-hand sources. They represent first-hand information. Secondary data, on the other hand are data collected by someone else, probably for some other purposes, but made available to another investigator either directly or from published or other communication sources. The borrower uses such data because he is satisfied that it is valid for the purpose of his study and hence adopts it. Primary data is also known as 'internal data' and secondary data as 'external data'. The information obtained by an investigator form the institution which is responsible for its generation/creation is internal data. The information collected by the researcher about the same institution from publications or interviews about the same institution by an outsider is example of 'external data'.

4. INTERPRETATION OF DATA

The data collected by an investigator are the raw materials for research in its crude form. These raw data need to be analyzed to discover hidden results / implied trends, etc. The statistical treatment of the data is done by editing, classifying, and tabulating the data to make interpretation easy. We often edit data. This refers to the identification and correction of probable mistakes. Classifications of data may be based on the purpose of the study – its objectives, what we want to find out from the data. Editing (reorganizing data) is often required. One example of reorganization is classification of data into tables. Data relating to a large number of observations/people are converted into class intervals. The following is an example of the percentage of marks obtained in Geography in a classroom of 50 students.

Marks: 35, 19, 30, 70, 75, 00, 23, 59, 15, 22, 90, 81, 87, 28, 30, 40, 36, 40, 50, 89, 56, 27, 89, 91, 22, 21, 22, 50, 89, 56, 70, 65, 89, 75, 65, 85, 22, 03, 12, 41, 28, 89, 50, 87, 22, 50, 72, 82, 87, 17.

This is ungrouped data. It is difficult to draw conclusions from 50 such different measures. If we arrange them into class intervals like 0-10, 11-20, etc., and find out the number falling into each interval, (frequency of each interval) we can draw more definite conclusions from the data. The number in each class interval is first entered as tally marks (see the table) and this tally marks are converted into their equivalent numbers. Note that the number in the interval '0-10' is 2. See the underlined two numbers in the original data. This can be repeated for all the 50 marks were we get the table given below. The term 'cumulative frequency' stands for the number of students getting scores below the upper limit of a class interval. The cumulative frequency for the class interval 31-40 is 20 means, 20 people in this group get scores at or below 40.

Class interval	Number of student	Frequency	Cumulative frequency
0-10	II	02	02
11-20	IIII	04	06
21-30	~~IIII~~ ~~IIII~~	10	16
31-40	IIII	04	20
41-50	III	03	23
51-60	III	08	31
61-70	I	01	32
71-80	~~IIII~~	05	37
81-90	I	11	48
91-100	II	02	50
	50	50	50

It is clear that the table presents the original data in a different manner. Data presented in this form help in getting a better understanding of the data. It is easier to interpret the data in a better way than in the original form. Identification of the cumulative frequency is one example. Looking into the frequency distribution one can see for example, that eleven students have scored between 81 and 90 marks, where as only one student has scored between 61 and 70 marks. This table also helps to present the data in the form of graphs / diagrams.

Given below is an example of how the data given earlier can be presented in the form of a graph, called the bar-diagram.

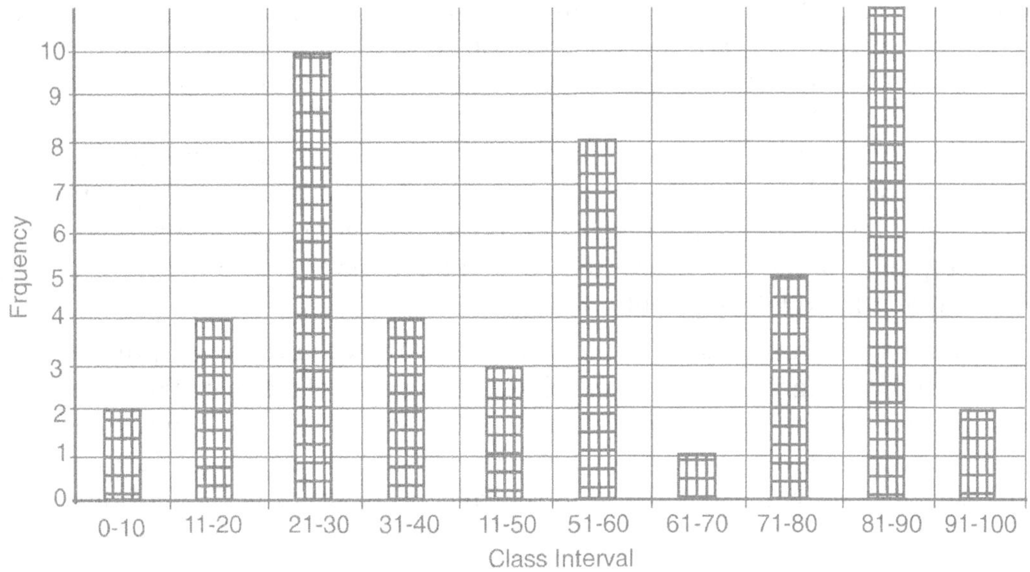

Bar diagrams are used when we have to compare frequencies in different class intervals.

The data above can be presented in the form of another graph called the 'frequency polygon. This is given below.

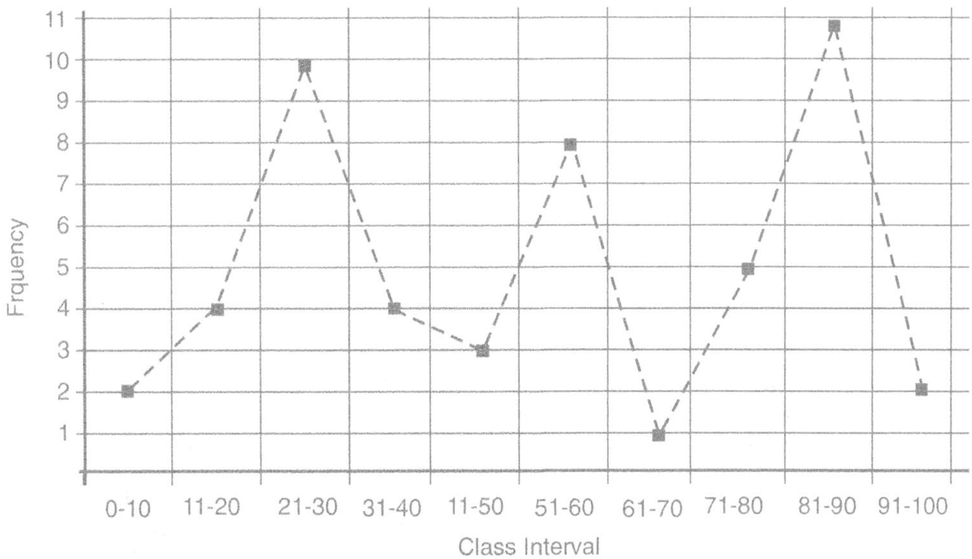

In this form of the graph (frequency polygon), the mid points of the 10 class intervals are connected using dotted lines. If the data are presented in a single line (mostly to represent a single variable), 'it is also called a histogram'. A frequency polygon can be converted into a frequency curve if through the vertices of the polygon is gained by a smooth freehand curve. This is to be encouraged only when the width of the class intervals is small enough.

Numerical data is often converted into a 'cumulative frequency' curve, also called the 'ogive'. This graph also can be smoothed by free hand curve in appropriate cases. The upper limits of the classes are taken as *x* coordinate and the cumulative frequencies up to the top limit of the just preceding class interval as the 'y co-ordinate' and the points are plotted and joined to obtain an ogive.

Another most commonly used way of presenting the data in the graphical form is what is called 'pie diagrams'. Pie (p) is related to the area of a circle. We know that a circle subtends 360° at its centre. Taking this as cent percent of a group, the sub-group can be represented by sectors where the angle subtended by the sub-group is decided as properties of the angle 360. In the following diagram each of the four sections of the circle divided by straight lines represents 25% (90°).

eg: a village where 50% of the people are 'below poverty line', 25% belong to the 'average income group', 20% belong to 'high income', and remaining are nomadic (5%).

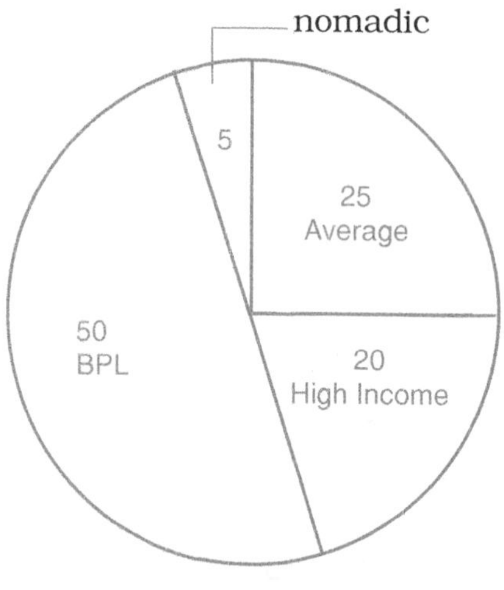

The data can be interpreted using these principles. In the pie diagram, the annual expenditure incurred by a family on various items, or the area of allocation of land by a farmer for cultivating agricultural product, or any such data can be presented.

Data presented using different types of graphs (including pie diagrams and other two dimensional visuals) make the numerical presentation more effective. In dissertations and research abstracts the data presented in these visual forms facilitate the readers to understand, compare, and arrive at sharper judgments about the implications contained in the numerical representations.

QUESTIONS

Note: Proportions are to be decided by the angle mentioned at the centre (measured in degrees) by a category. The allocation of 360^0 to each category is the basis of this division.

I. PIE DIAGRAM

I. Study the pie diagram given below and answer questions 1 to 4. The diagram represents the annual expenditure incurred by a family.

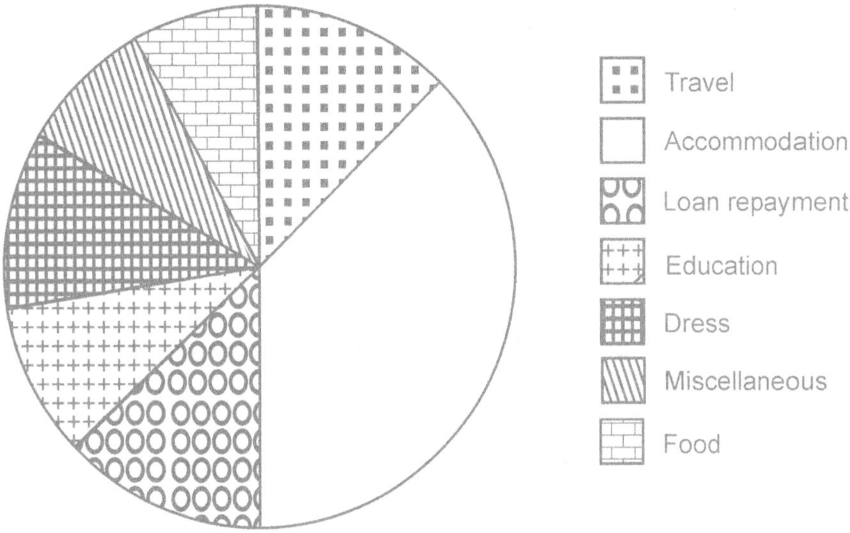

Note: Education + Food = one half of a quadrant + one third of a quadrant = 75^0. Identify the portion which subtends 75^0 at the centre.

Which of the following conclusions would you draw from the graph?

1. The family spends annually as much expenditure on education and food as on:

A. accommodation　　B. loan repayment and miscellaneous
C. travel, dress and loan repayment　　D. miscellaneous, travel and dress

2. What percentage of the total expenditure is spent on food, education and loan repayment?

A. 25%　　B. 37%　　C. 33.33%　　D. 35%

3. What percentage of the total expense is spent on accommodation?

A. 37.5%　　B. 30%　　C. 42%　　D. 45%

4. Expenditure on accommodation is equal to:

A. loan repayment, miscellaneous and food.
B. dress, education and travel.
C. education, loan repayment and dress.
D. education, food, dress and miscellaneous.

II. Study the pie diagram given below and answer questions 5 and 6. The diagram represents the expenses incurred by a family on various items.

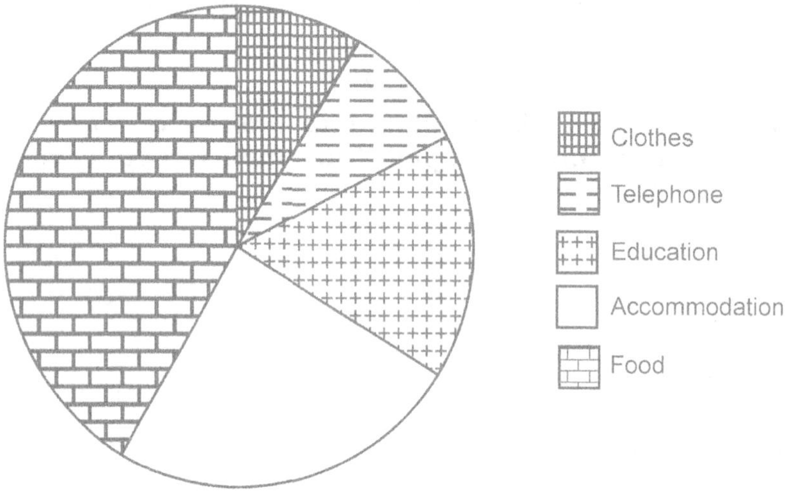

5. What is the percentage of total expenditure incurred on accommodation and clothes together?

A. 37.5 B. 50 C. 33.3 D. 25

6. The expenditure incurred on food is as much as on:

A. Education and Accommodation B. Education and Telephone.

C. Accommodation and Clothes D. Telephone and Clothes

III. Study the following pie diagram and answer the questions 7 and 8. The diagram indicates the area used by a farmer to cultivate various agricultural products.

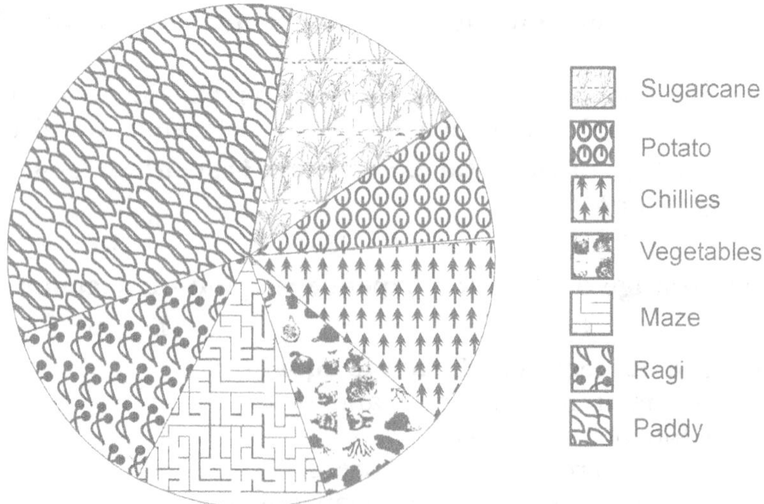

7. **The farmer utilizes land for cultivating paddy as much as on:**
   A. Ragi, Maze and Potato
   B. Maze, Vegetables, Chillies and Potato
   C. Potato, Sugarcane and Vegetables
   D. Ragi, Sugarcane, Chillies and Vegetables
8. **What percentage out of the total area is utilized by him for cultivating sugarcane, potatoes and chillies?**
   A. 25% B. 37.5% C. 33.3% D. 28%

IV. Study the pie diagram given below and answer questions 9 & 10.

PROPORTION OF EXPENSES INCURRED BY A FAMILY

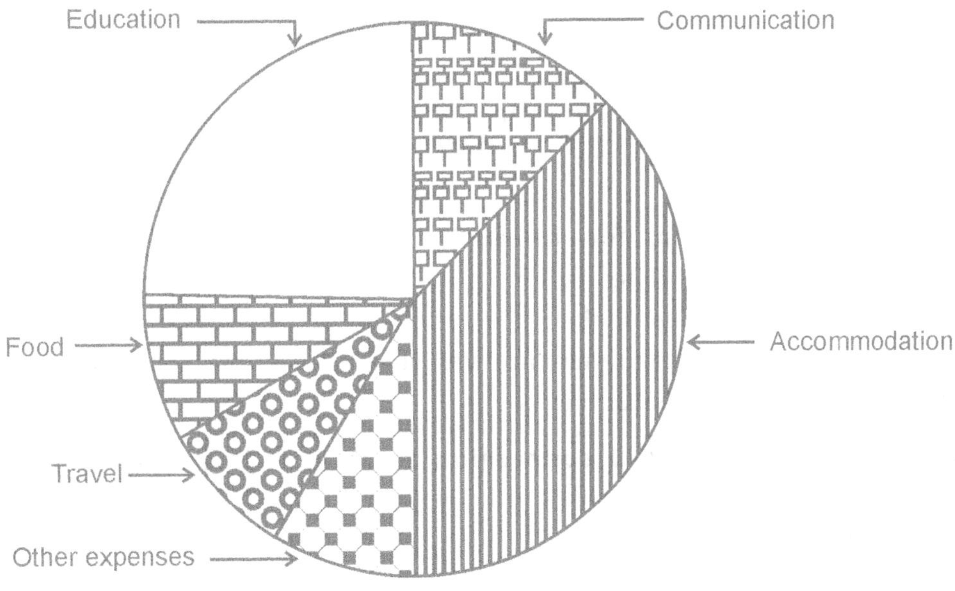

9. **The family spends as much as on accommodation as on:**
   A. Communication, Education and Food
   B. Other expenses, Travel, Food and Communication
   C. Education, Food and Other expenses
   D. Travel, Food and Education
10. **The percentage of expense incurred on Education and Communication is:**
    A. 75 B. 40 C. 37.5 D. 33.5

V. The following diagram indicates the expenditure of a student. Read the diagram and answer questions 11 to 13.

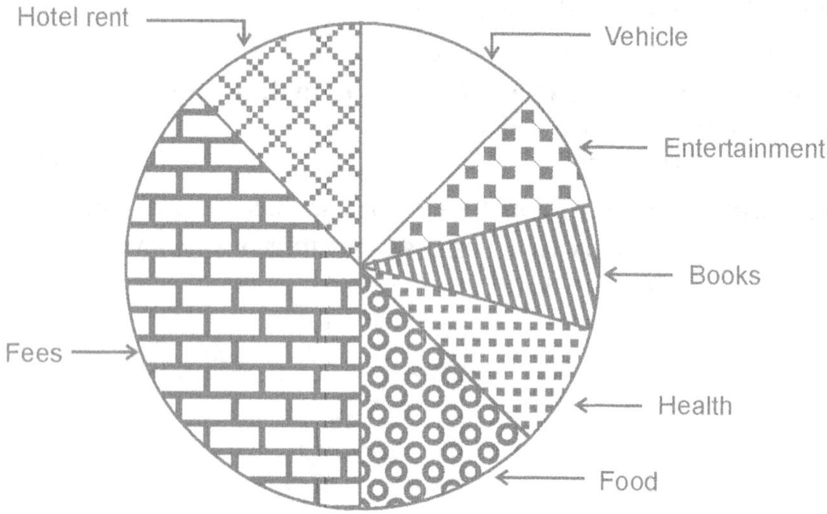

11. The student spends on fees as much as on:

A. hostel rent, food and health

B. hostel rent, food and books

C. health, books, entertainment and vehicle

D. hostel rent, food, health and books

12. If the student gets 1/3 concession in fees, that amount equals the expenditure on:

A. health

B. books

C. entertainment

D. food

13. If the student has to increase expenditure on books, he will most probably save on:

A. fees and food

B. hostel rent and food

C. food and entertainment

D. entertainment and vehicle

VI. Study the pie diagram and choose the correct answer.

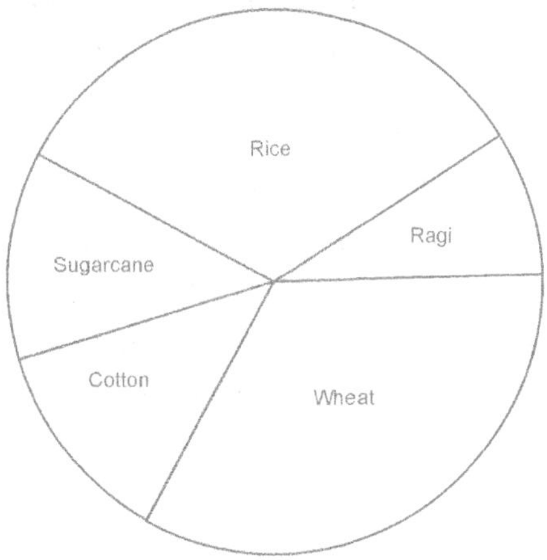

14. Which of the following is true about the areas under cultivation?

A. Rice + Ragi= Wheat

B. Rice = Wheat-Ragi

C. Cotton = Wheat-Rice

D. Cotton + Wheat = Rice + Sugarcane

VII. Study the following pie diagram and answer questions 15 & 16.

Distribution of Students in Graduate Level in 10 Subjects

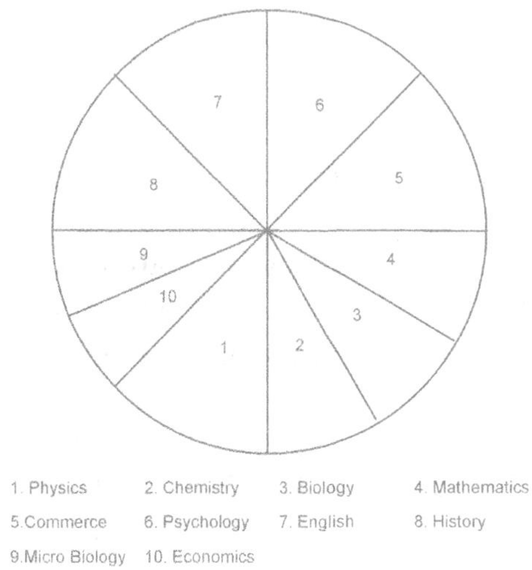

15. If the total number of graduates enrolled in all these subjects is 2500 how many are studying History and English put together?

A. 360 B. 478 C. 625 D. 600

16. Which of the following is the correct statement based on the data given in the pie diagram if the total number of graduates is 1250?

A. Total students enrolled in Physics, History, Commerce and Psychology are 625.

B. In Physics, Chemistry and Biology, there are more students when compared to Maths, Commerce and Psychology.

C. Equal number of students have enrolled in Psychology and Commerce.

D. Total number of students in English, Maths and Microbiology are 400.

VIII. The pie diagram given here shows the spending of a country on various sports during a particular year. Study the diagram carefully and answer the questions given below it.

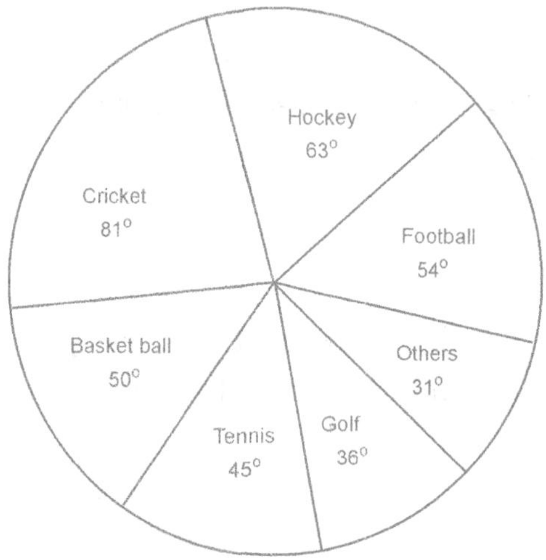

Note: Treat the total as 360°, and work the percentages of each group as a part of 360°. Hockey for example will account for (63/360 × 100) %. Football will account for (54/360 × 100) %. Etc.

17. What percent of the total spending on sports is on Tennis?

A. 12.5 %   B. 22 .5%   C. 25%   D. 45%

18. What is the percentage difference between the expenditure on Hockey and the expenditure on Golf?

A. 27%   B. 35%   C. 37.5%   D. 75%

19. How much percent less is spent on Football than that on Cricket?

A. 22 2/9 %   B. 27%   C. 33 1/3%   D. 37 ½%

20. If the total amount spent on sports during the year was ₹ 2 crores, the amount spent on Cricket and Hockey together was:

A. ₹ 8,00,000   B. ₹ 80,00,000

C. ₹ 1,20,00,000   D. ₹ 1,60,00,000

21. If the total amount spent on sports during the year be ₹ 1,80,00,000, the amount spent on Basketball exceeds that in Tennis by:

A. ₹ 2,50,000 B. ₹ 3,60,000

C. ₹ 3,75,000 D. ₹ 4,10,000

Answer keys

1.B	2.C	3.A	4.D	5.C	6.A	7.A	8.C	9.B	10.C
11.C	12.D	13.C	14.D	15.C	16.A	17.A	18.D	19.C	20.B
21.A									

2. OVERLAPPING DIAGRAMS

I. Study the following figure carefully and answer questions 1 to 4.

Note: We have to identify common areas of overlap to answer the problems below.

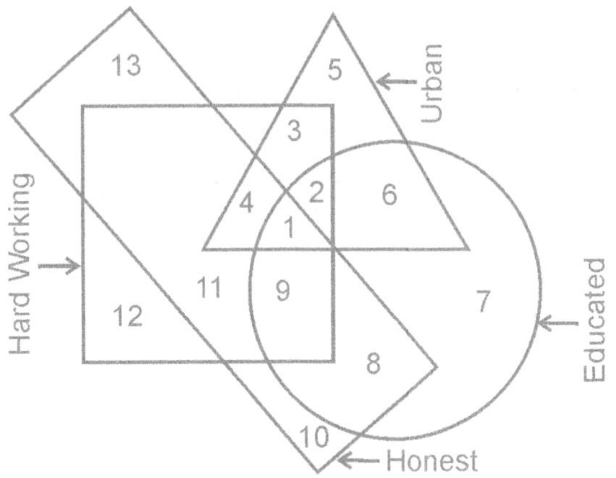

1. **Urban and educated persons are represented by the area numbered 6, 2 & 1 represent urban & educated:**

   A. 1& 2 B. 2 & 6 C. 3 & 6 D. 6, 2 & 1

2. **Honest and educated persons are represented by the area numbered 8, 9 & 1:**

   A. 1 & 9 B. 4 & 8 C. 8, 9 & 1 D. 9

3. **Urban, educated and honest persons are represented in the figure with the numbers:**

   A. 1 B. 2 & 3 C. 2 & 9 D. 1,3 and 4.

4. **Area numbered 4 represents:**

   A. Honest, hard working persons

   B. Honest, hard working, urban persons

C. Urban, educated, honest persons
D. Hardworking, honest, educated persons

II. Study the following figure and answer questions 5 and 6.

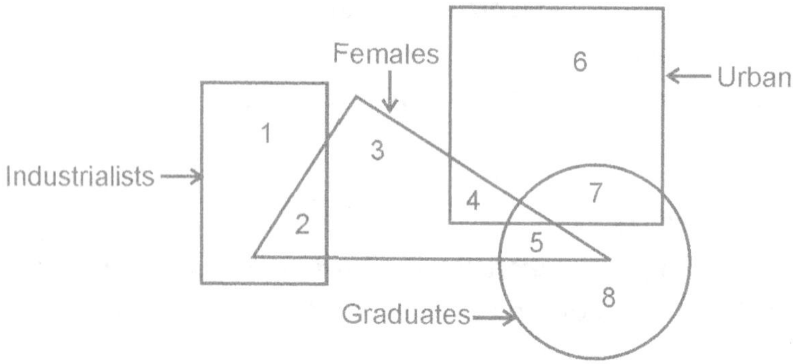

5. Graduate females are represented by the area numbered:

A. 4 B. 5 C. 6 D. 8

6. Graduate industrialist females are not represented by the area numbered:

A. 3 B. 5 C. 6 D. 8

III. Study the diagram and answer the question 7.

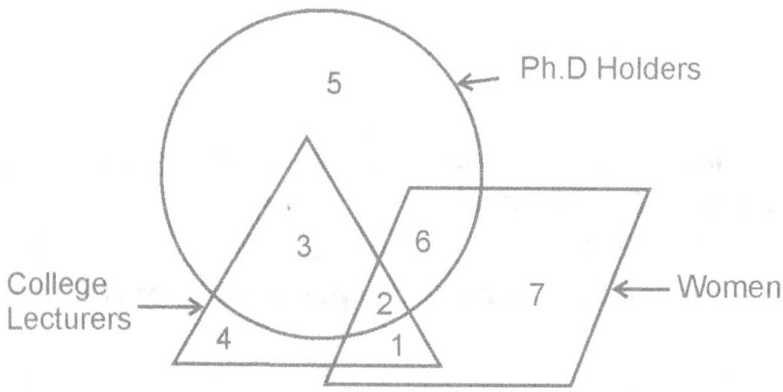

7. Which number indicate (s) women lectures who are Ph.D holders?

A. 2 B. 3 C. 2&6 D. 2&3

IV. Study the diagram and answer the question based on it. The diagram represents the students admitted to a college under different quotas.

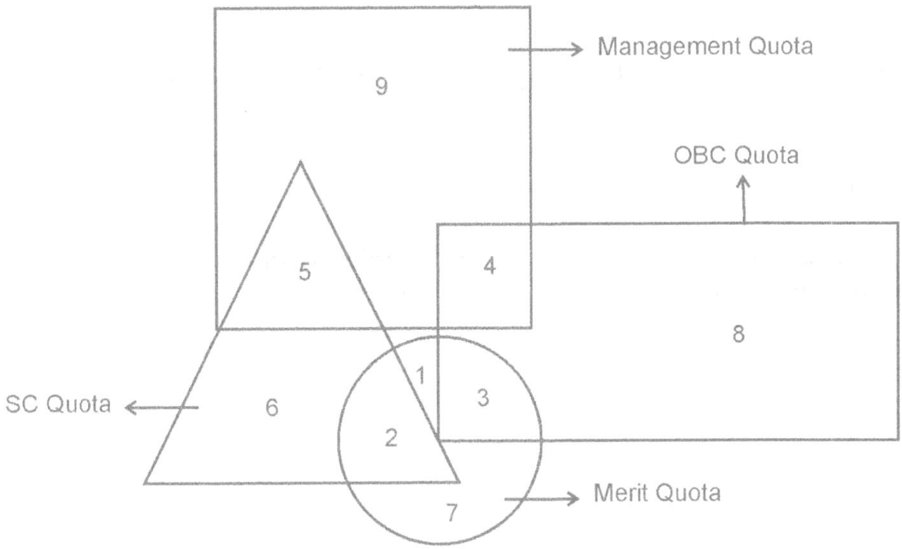

8. **The number of SC students admitted in the merit quota and management quota respectively are represented by columns numbered.**

   A. 5 and 2　　B. 6 and 2

   C. 2,5 and 6　　D. 2 and 5

V. Study the following diagram and answer the questions 9 and 10.

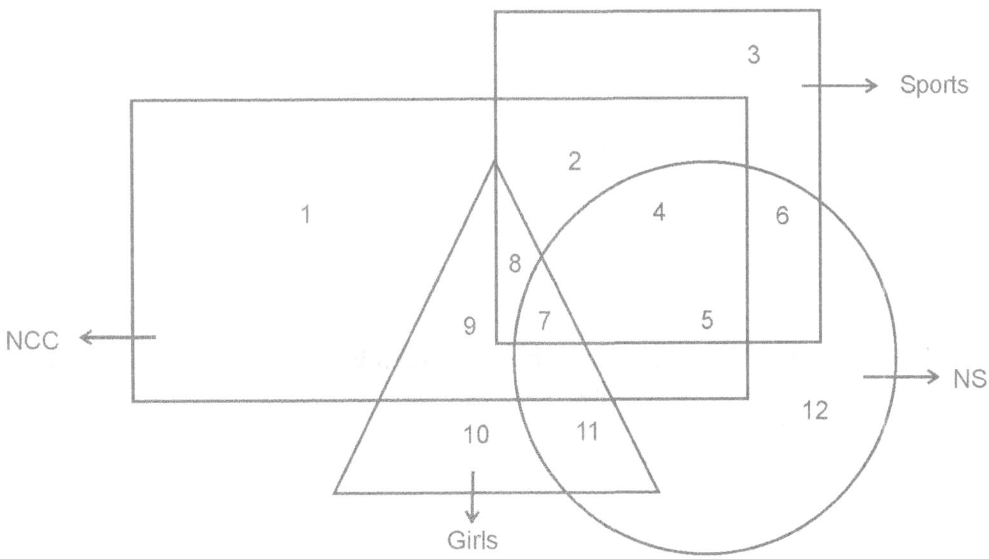

9. **The girls who have joined the NSS are indicated in columns numbered:**

A. 7 and 11 B. 10 and 11

C. 5 and 12 D. 4,5,7 and 11

10. **Students involved in sports, NSS and NCC are indicated in column numbered:**

A. 7 and 8 B. 2, 4 and 8

C. 2,4,5,7 and 8 D. 4,5 and 7

VI. Study the diagram representing the various quota for admission to a college, and answer the question based on it.

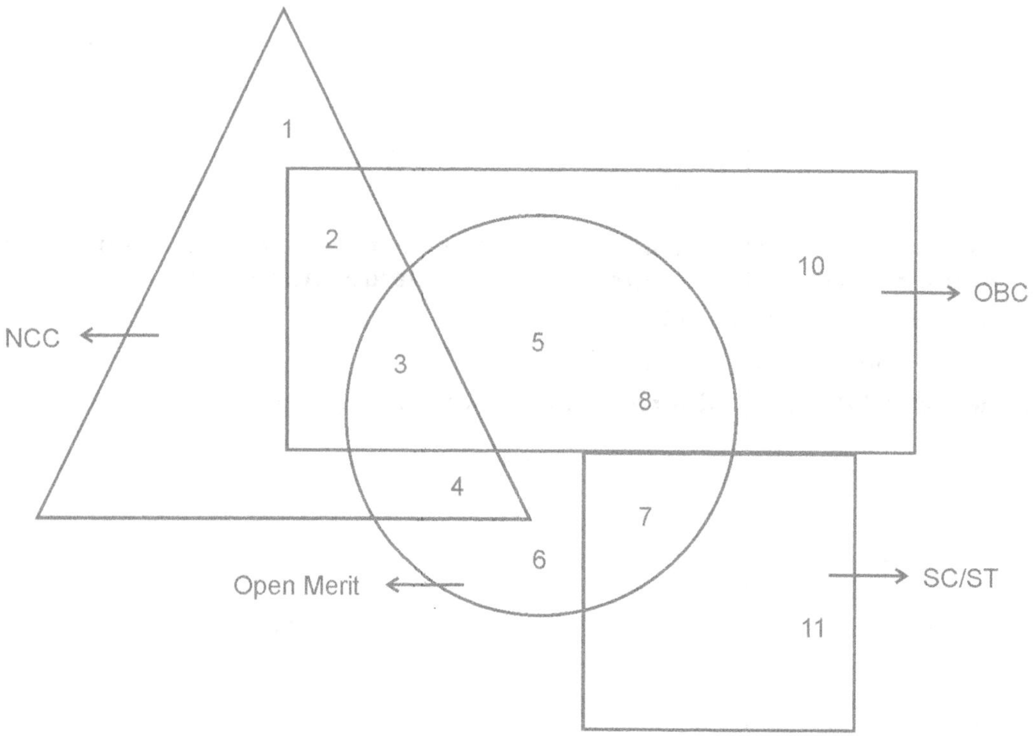

11. **The NCC cadets admitted in the merit quota belonging to OBC group are represented by the area numbered.**

A. 11 B. 7

C. 6 D. 3

VII. Study the following figure carefully and answer question below.

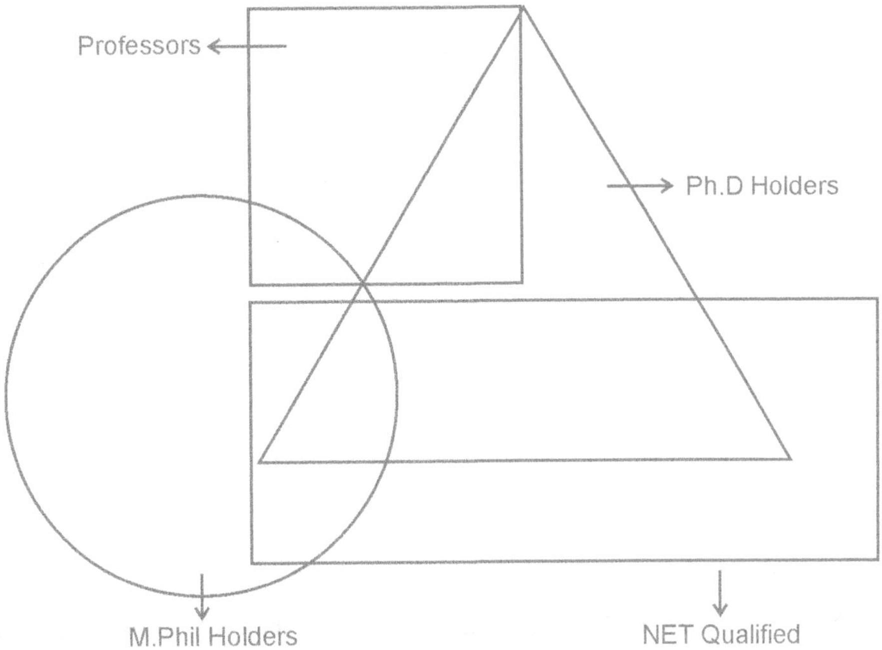

12. Choose the most valid conclusion based on what is represented by the diagram.

A. All the professors are Ph.D or M.Phil holders

B. None of the professors is NET qualified

C. Almost all the teachers have M.Phil, Ph.D and NET

D. None of the teachers in the college is fully qualified

Answer keys

1.D 2.C 3.A 4.B 5.B 6.C 7.A 8.D 9.A 10.D

11.D 12.B

3. LINE GRAPH

I. Study the graph given below and answer questions 1 and 2.

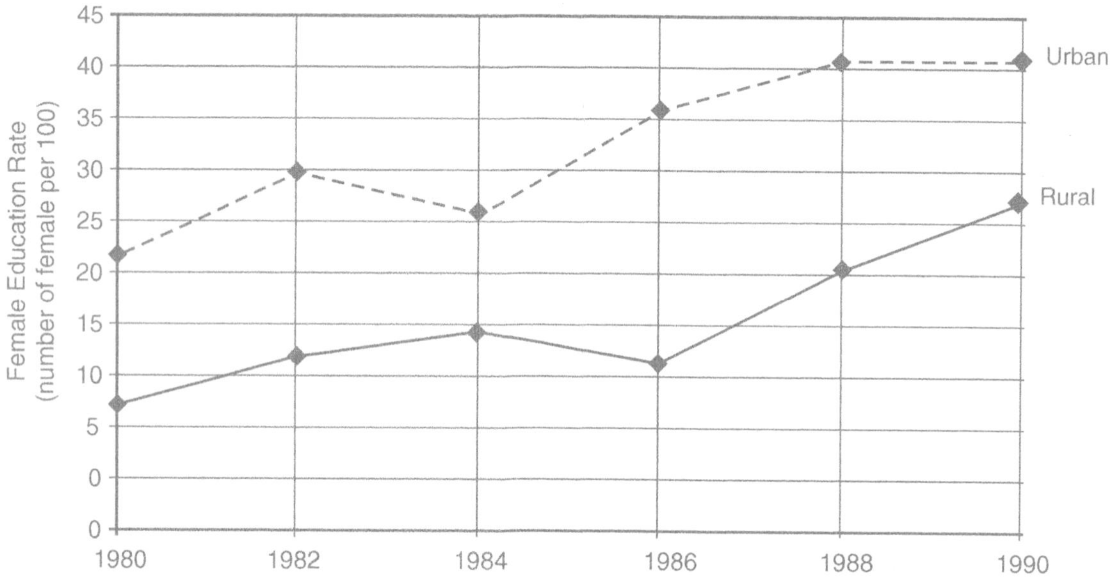

1. Which one of the following statements is true about female education rate in India?

A. Maximum discrepancy in female education between rural and urban population was in the year 1980.

B. Minimum difference between rural and urban females in education was in the year 1984.

C. The lowest overall rate in education of females was in 1984.

D. The highest overall rate in female education was in 1988.

2. Which one of the following statements is definitely wrong?

A. There is an overall increase in female education rate between 1980 to 1990.

B. Rural women show definitely high rate in their education when compared to the urban counterparts.

C. 1986 witnessed a down fall in the educational rate of the rural women.

D. Over these 10 years the rate of female education has shown a considerable increase.

II. The following graph represents the cumulative number of applications for admission to 2 subjects over a week. Study the graph and answer questions 3 & 4.

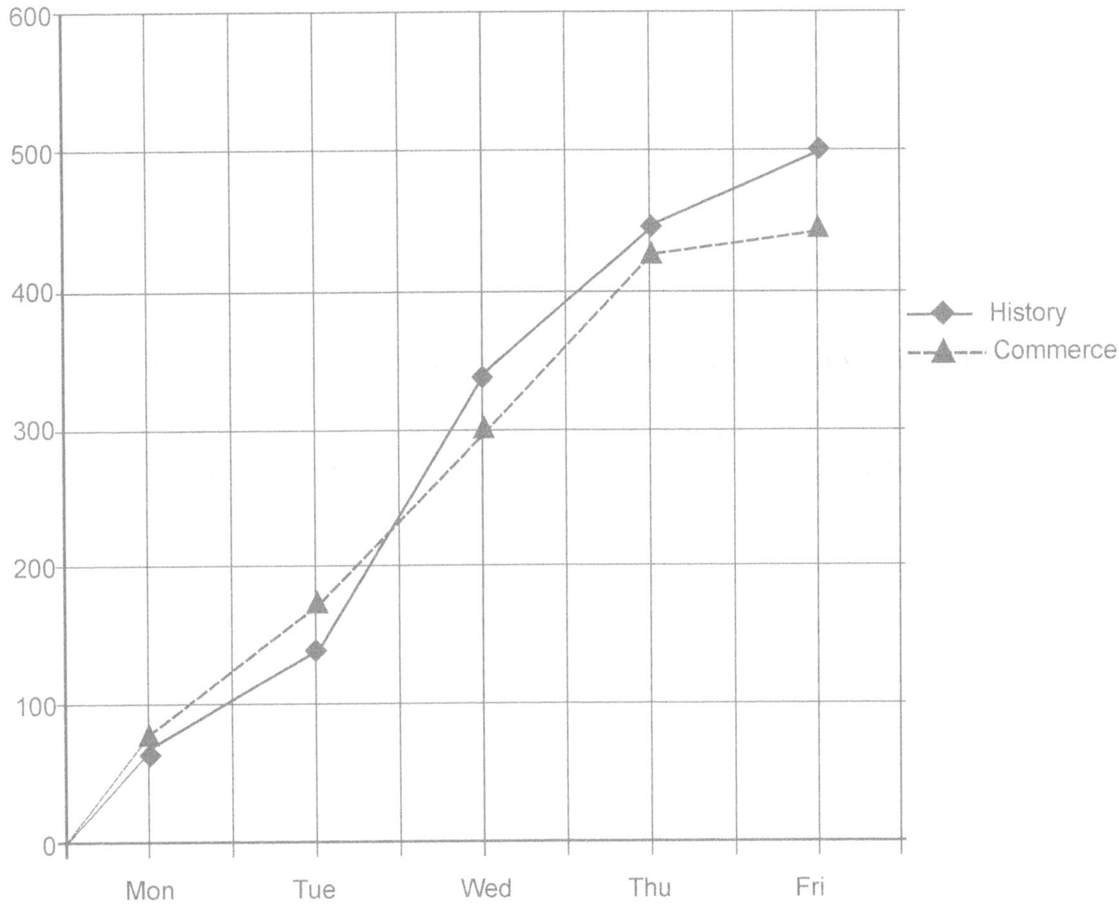

3. **For which subject the largest number of applications were received, and which day?**

A. Tuesday in Commerce

B. Friday in both the subjects

C. Wednesday in History

D. Thursday in both the subjects

4. **How many applications were received for both these subjects on Friday?**

A. 950. B. 500 C. 100 D. 940

III. Study the following diagram indicating rainfalls in various years and answer Question 5.

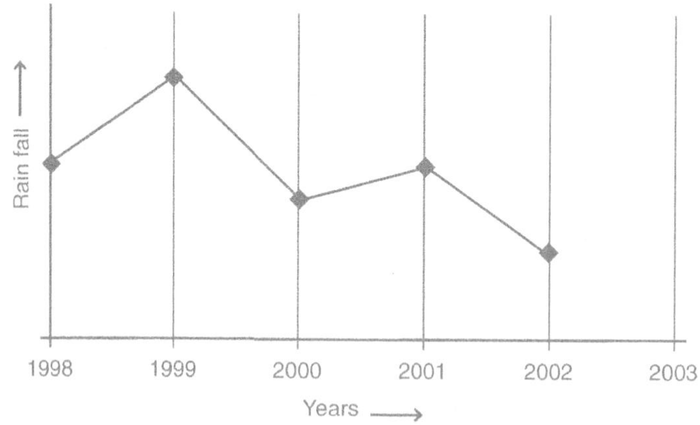

5. Which of the following could be a reasonable forecast of rain for the year 2003?

A. There will be more rain in 2003 than in 2002.

B. There will be slightly more rain in 2003 than in 2002; but it will be much less than the rainfall in 1999.

C. The rain fall will be more or less the same as in 2002.

D. We cannot forecast rain based on the data in the graph.

IV. Study the graph given below and answer question 6.

INSURANCE PREMIUM PAID BY EMPLOYEES

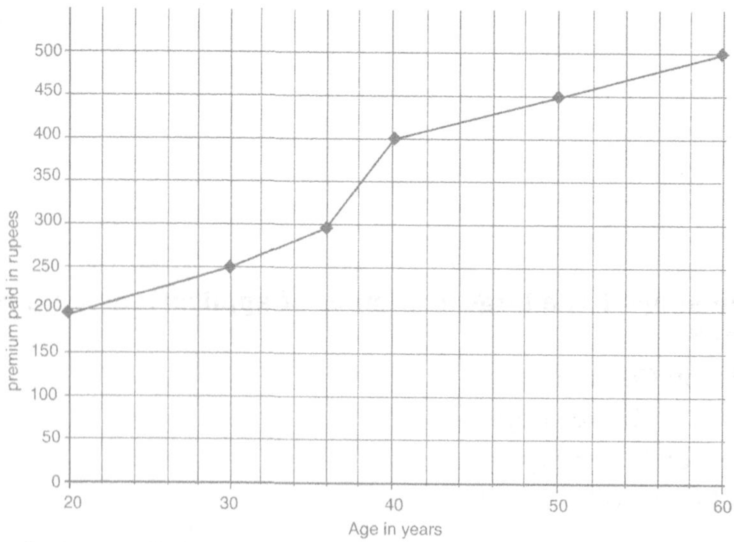

6. How much more of the premium was paid by 50 year old employees than 30 year old employees?

A. 220.50 B. 175.00 C. 400 D. 270.05

V. The graph below shows rainfall in centimeters in the cities E, F, G and H from the year 1991 to 95. Study the graph and answer questions 7 and 8.

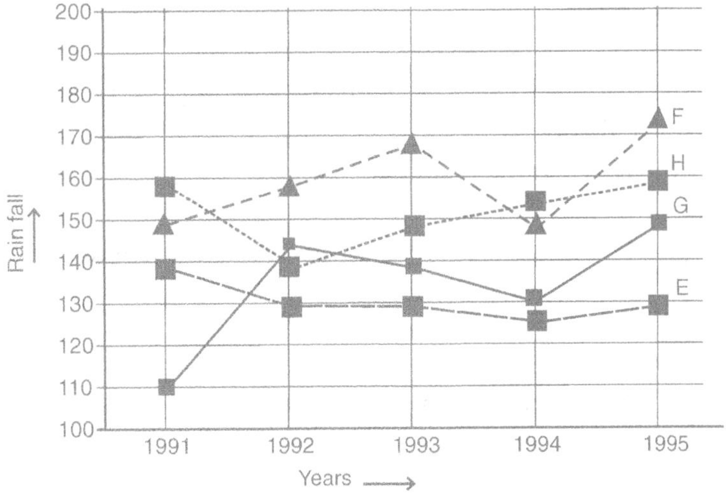

7. Which city has recorded the maximum average rainfall for the period 1991-95?

A. E B. F C. G D. H

8. Which city has the widest range of rain fall over these years(1991-1995)?

A. E B. F C. G D. H

VI. Study the graph showing the variation in temperature in a city over a week and answer the questions 9 to 13.

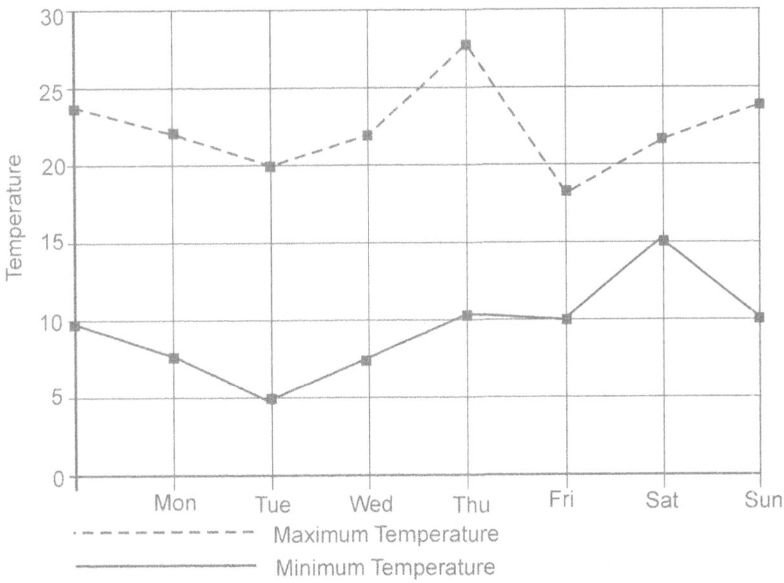

9. On which day of the week did the difference between the maximum and minimum temperature was least?

A. Monday B. Thursday

C. Friday D. Saturday

10. On which day did we record a minimum increase in temperature from minimum to maximum?

A. Wednesday B. Thursday

C. Saturday D. Sunday

11. On which day of the week was the highest temperature recorded for the week?

A. Wednesday B. Thursday

C. Friday D. Saturday

12. On which day of the week was the lowest temperature recorded for the week?

A. Monday B. Wednesday

C. Tuesday D. Friday

13. On which day was the temperature variation (difference between the highest and lowest temperature) the minimum?

A. Tuesday B. Thursday

C. Saturday D. Sunday

VII. Study the graph and answer questions 14 to 17.

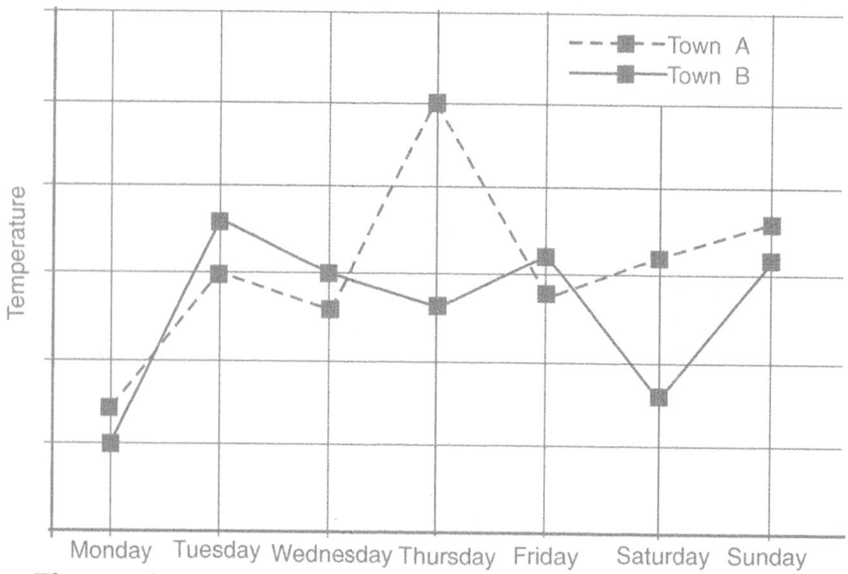

The graph represents temperature of two towns during a week

14. Between which two days was the difference in temperature the highest in town A?

A. Friday and Saturday
B. Saturday and Sunday
C. Wednesday and Thursday
D. Thursday and Friday

15. Between which two days was the difference in temperature the lowest in Town B?

A. Thursday & Friday
B. Monday & Tuesday
C. Friday & Saturday
D. Wednesday & Thursday

16. In which Town the fluctuation in temperature is the highest and between which days?

A. Monday & Tuesday, Town B
B. Wednesday & Thursday, Town A
C. Thursday & Friday, Town B
D. Thursday & Friday, Town A

17. On which day did town B have the same temperature as that of town A on Friday

A. Saturday
B. Friday
C. Wednesday
D. Tuesday

VIII. Study the graph given below, indicating the fluctuations of prices of 3 vegetable items over a period of one week, and answer questions 18 & 19.

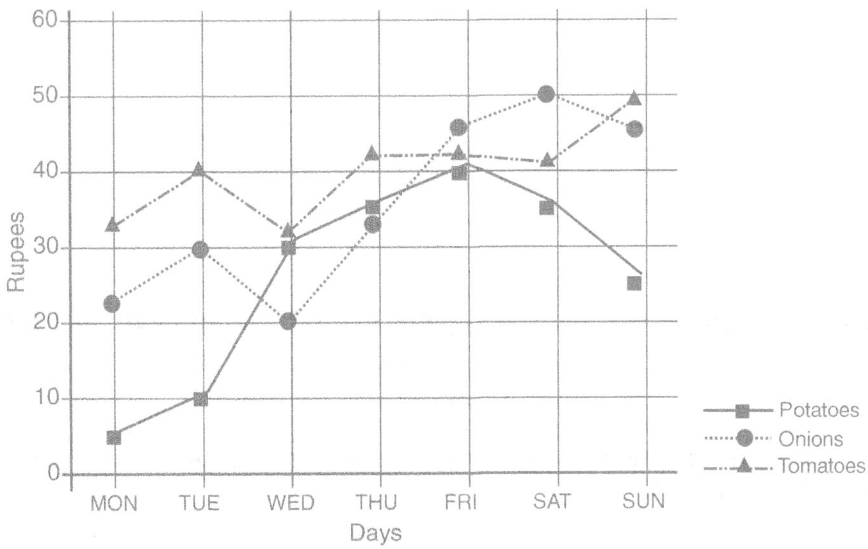

18. On which day the price of onion and tomato showed the same rise?

A. Friday B. Tuesday

C. Thursday D. Saturday

19. On which day did the peak rise in the price of potatoes match with that of tomatoes?

A. Tuesday B. Thursday

C. Friday D. Saturday

IX. Study the following graph and answer questions 20 & 21. The upper two lines in the graph represent per head income and the lower two indicate per head plan assistance.

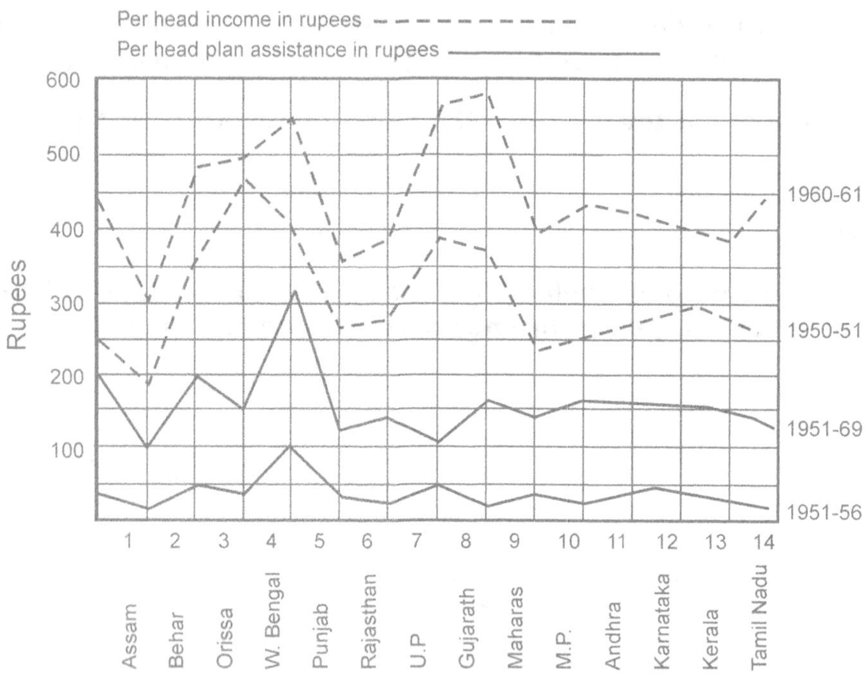

20. As per the graph, which state received the highest per head plan assistance?

A. West Bengal B. Punjab

C. Gujarat D. Kerala

21. For which state there is minimum increase in per head income from 1950-51 to 1960-61?

A. Bihar B. Rajastan

C. Utterpradesh D. West Bengal

X. The following graph gives the variation in the "ratio of the amounts of imports by a company to the amount of exports" by a manufacturing company over the period from 1995 to 2001. Examine the graph and answer the questions 22 and 23

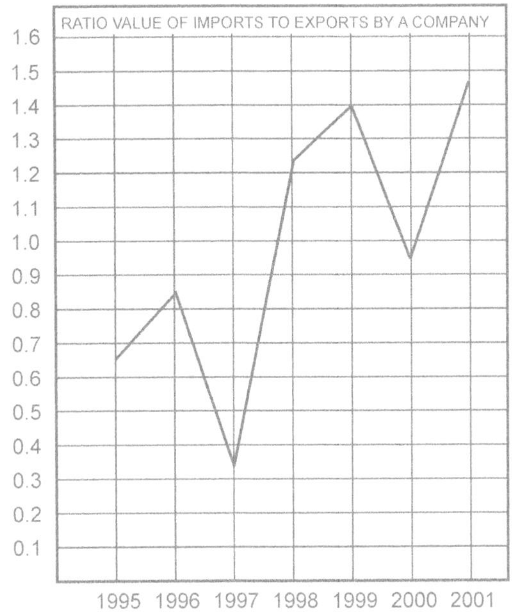

22. In how many of the given years were the exports more than the imports? (Note: Years for which the ratio exceeds are)

A. 1 B. 2

C. 3 D. 4

23. The ratio of the imports to exports is minimum during the year:

A. 1995 B. 1996

C. 1997 D. 2000

XI. Graph showing the Annual Rainfall in Four Cities (E, F, G and H) During 1991-95

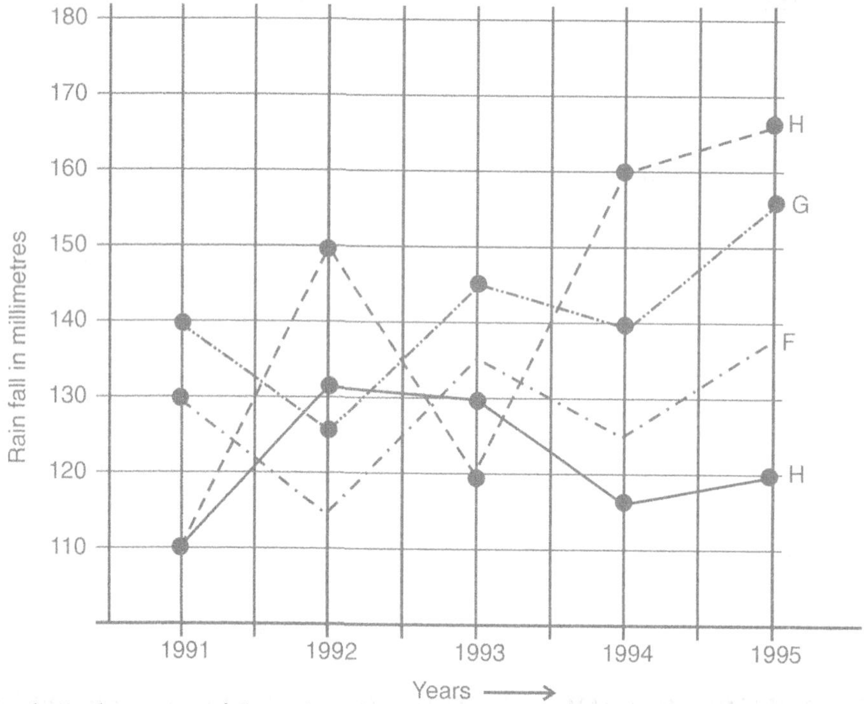

The graph below provides data relating to annual rainfall of four cities (named E, F,G, H) for 19991-1995.

Examine carefully the graphs for this four cities and answer the following questions:

24. The most heavy rainfall among for the four cities was in:

A. City H, Year 1994　　B. City H, Year 1995

C. City G, Year 1994　　D. City F, Year 1992

25. The lowest rainfall for the five years is registered for:

A. City G, City F　　B. City F

C. City E　　D. City E, City F

26. City with rainfall higher than that of cities E and G the year 1993 is:

A. City E　　B. City H

C. City E　　D. None of these

27. The highest recorded rainfall for the period 1991-1993 was in city ______

A. City H　　B. City E

C. City G　　D. City F

28. The recorded rainfall was identical for two cities during the period 1991-1993; there were:

A. City E, City G
B. City E, City H
C. City E, City F
D. City F, City G

29. This cities which registered higher rainfall than city during the period 1991-1993 are:

A. City F, City G
B. City E, City F
C. City E, City G
D. None of above

30. The lowest recorded rainfall for the period 1993-95 among the four cities was for:

A. City F
B. City E, City F
C. City E
D. None of above

31. Which registered a lower rainfall than 1994 are:

A. City E
B. City G
C. City H
D. None of these

32. Among the two cities which registered the two lower levels of rainfall in 1995, the one which registered a just higher level of rainfall than the lowest is:

A. City G
B. City F
C. City H
D. City E

33. The two cities which registered the two lowest levels of rainfall in 1991 are:

A. City E, City G
B. City E, City F
C. City E, City H
D. City F, City H

34. The average annual rainfall of city H in an 1995 is close to:

A. 165mm
B. 155mm
C. 150mm
D. 160mm

35. The difference between the annual rainfall of city F and city H in the year 1994 is:

A. 300mm
B. 350mm
C. 200mm
D. 100mm

Answer keys

1.B	2.B	3.C	4.D	5.B	6.A	7.B	8.C	9.D	10.A
11.B	12.C	13.C	14.C	15.D	16.A	17.C	18.C	19.C	20.A
21.A	22.D	23.C	24.B	25.D	26.B	27.D	28.C	29.B	30.C
31.C	32.A	33.B	34.B	35.C					

4. BAR DIAGRAM

I. Study the following bar diagram of the income and expenditure of an industrial concern from 1995-96 to 1999-2000 and answer questions 1 & 2.

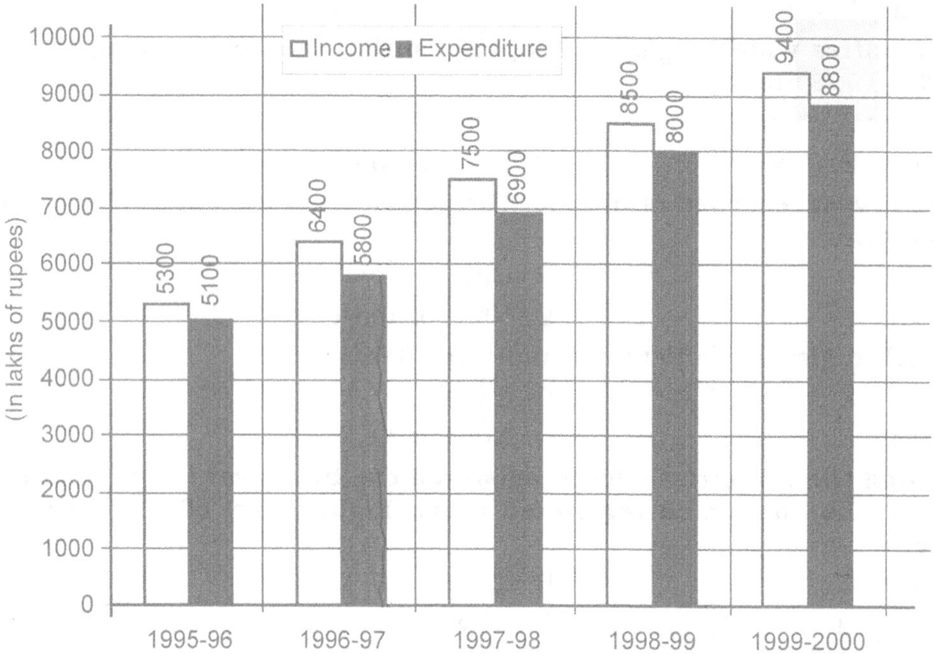

Note:

Income for 1995-96 = ₹ 5300 lakhs

Income for 1997-98 = ₹ 5300 lakhs

Income (Difference) = ₹ 7500-5300 lakhs

= ₹ 5300 lakhs

Income percentage = 2200/5300 X 100 =41.5 approximately

1. **What is the approximate percentage of increase in the income of 1997-1998 over the income of 1995-96?**

   A. 33.9 B. 20.7

   C. 41.5 D. 17.0

2. **Which is the most valid inference based on the data presented in the bar diagram?**

   A. The difference between income and expenditure was the same in 1996 – 77 and 1999-2000.

   B. Expenditure during all the years is more than the income.

   C. Income all these years is less than the expenditure.

   D. The difference between income and expenditure is lowest during the year 1997-98

II. Study the graph of the crude oil import during the year 2000-2006 and answer questions 3 to 6.

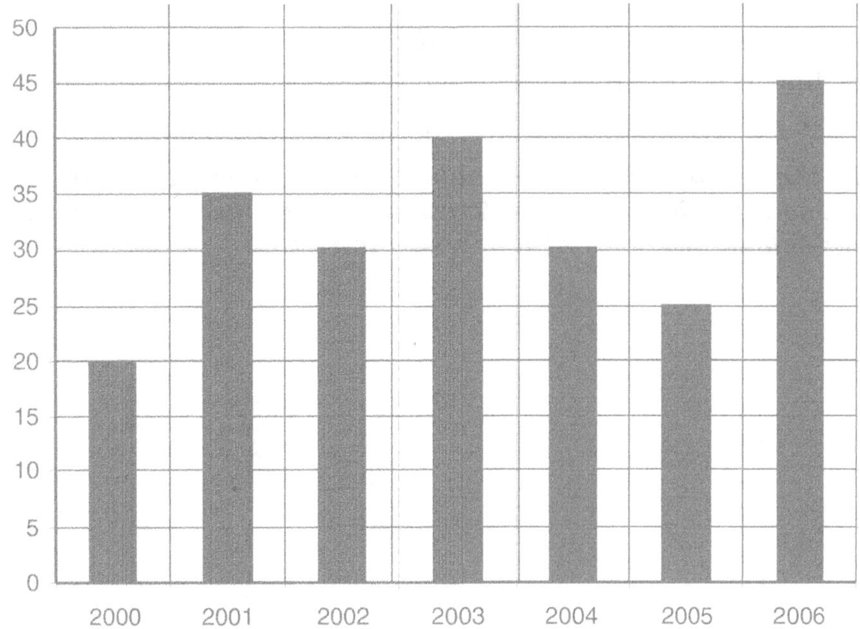

Crude Oil Import in India

3. The percentage reduction in the import of crude oil in India from the year 2001-2002 is:

A. 16.6 B. 18.1 C. 8.3 D. 14.3

[Barrels (Lakhs)

2001 – 35

2002 – 30

Reduction – 5 lakh barrels

Percentage reduction = $\frac{5}{35} \times 100 = \frac{100}{7} = 14.3$ approx

4. What is the percentage increase in the combined imports of 2004 and 2005 over the import of 2003?

A. 14 B. 12 C. 13.5 D. 37.5

combined imports of 2004 and 2005 = 30+25 = 55 lakh of barrels

Import of 2003 = 40 lakh of barrels

Increase in the year 2003 = 55 – 40 = 15 lakh barrel

Percentage increase = 15/40 × 100 = 37.5

5. If the price of one barrel of crude oil was ₹ 256.00 during the year 2005, what was the total value of import during that year?

A. 640 crores B. 640 lakhs

C. 64 crores D. 82 crores

Note. Import during 2005 = 25 lakh barrels

Price at ₹ 256 per barrel = 256 × 25,00,000 = 64 crores

III. Study the bar diagram given below and answer questions 6 and 7. The data is based on the scores in 7 standardized achievement tests of 300 secondary school students of a school district.

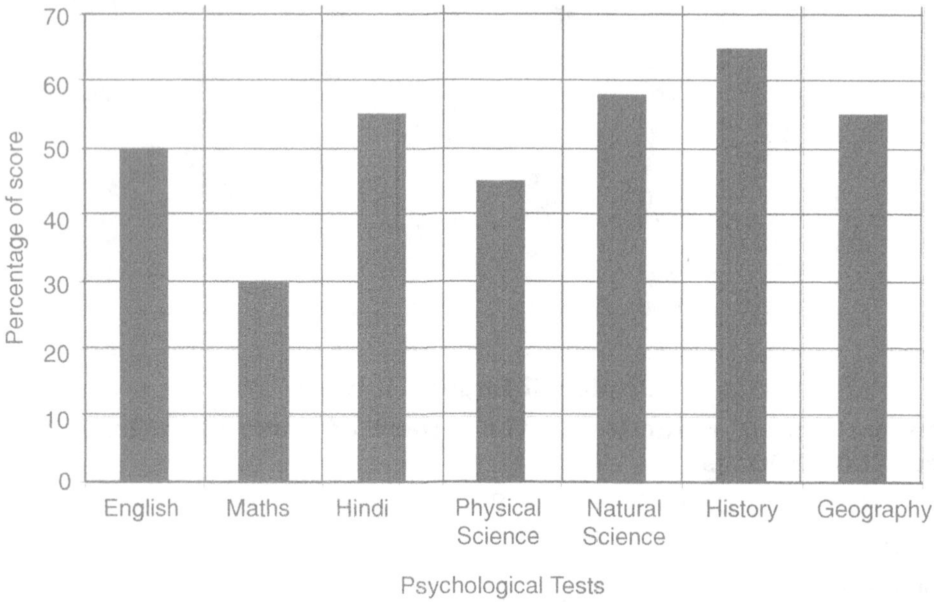

6. Which of the following is the correct inference from the given table?

A. Most of the students show higher performance in Hindi than in English.

B. Most of the students perform badly in Physical Science.

C. On the whole, top performance students in Geography.

D. All the students in the group perform poorly in Mathematics.

7. Which of the following statements is not correct?

A. The average scores in History of the group is more than double that for Mathematics.

B. The average performance of the group in Mathematics is more than average performance of the group in Physical Science.

C. Average performance of the group in Hindi is better than for Natural Science.

D. All the students in the group are poor achievers.

IV. Study the following graph which shows number of road accident deaths during the rainy season in a country; and answer questions 9 to 11.

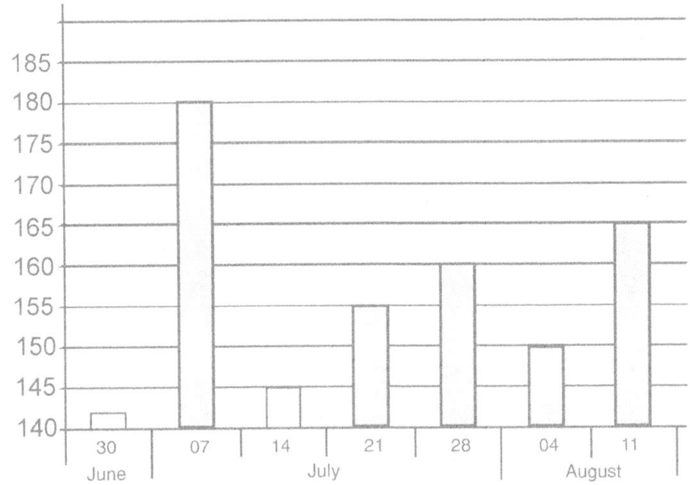

8. Between which two consecutive weekends was the rise in the number of deaths greatest?

A. 14th to 21st July B. 30th June to 7th July

C. 4th August to 11th August D. 21st July to 28th July

9. For many weeks during the entire period were there more than 147 road accident deaths?

A. 1 B. 2 C. 3 D. 4

10. For how many weeks were there less than 150 deaths by road accidents?

A. 0 B. 1 C. 2 D. 3

V. Study the graph given below of the number of barrels of crude oil import to the country (in lakhs) and answer question 12.

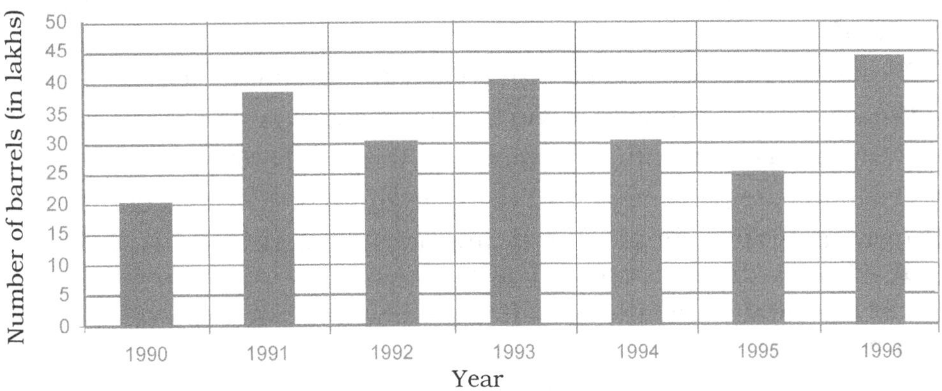

11. What was the total value of import for the year 1995, if one barrel of crude oil cost ₹ 25.60 that year?

A. ₹ 64.00 crores

B. ₹ 64.00 lakhs

C. ₹ 6.4 crores

D. ₹ 8.2 crores

Note:

Number of barrels imported in 1995 = 25 lakhs

Cost per one lakh barrels = 25.6 × 100,000 = ₹ 2560000

Therefore, cost of 25 lakh barrels = 6.4 cores rupees

Answer keys

1.C	2.A	3.D	4.D	5.C	6.A
7.A	8.A	9.D	10.B	11.C	

5. TABULAR CHART

I. Study the following table showing details of candidates who appeared and passed in a test for recruiting lower division clerks, and answer questions 1 and 2.

Category	*Number who appeared for the examination*	*Number who Passed*
General	52000	1300
OBC	22000	600
Scheduled Caste	15000	500

1. Which of the following is the correct inference which can be drawn from the data?

A. The lowest pass percentage within each group is for the OBC.

B. The lowest pass percentage within each group is for the SC.

C. The total pass percentage is more than that for the SC.

D. The total pass percentage for the whole group is twice that of the OBC.

Note: Percentage passes for the three categories. General – 2.5%, OBC – 2.72%, SC – 3.33%, Total group – 2.7%

2. Out of the total number of candidates who attended the test, percentage failure is close to:

A. 11 percent B. 13 percent C. 27 percent D. 33 percent

II. The following table shows the annual income of 3 men and 2 women during 4 years (in rupees). Answer questions 3 to 6, using the figures given in the table.

Year / Name	2005	2006	2007	2008
Arun	12,000	16,000	20,000	24,000
Anand	10,000	14,000	16,000	20,000
Ranjith	9,000	12,000	15,000	20,000
Neethu	12,000	12,000	15,000	17,000
Sitha	20,000	25,000	30,000	37,000

3. **Who is the male member whose average income for the four-year period is ₹ 14,000?**

   A. Arun B. Anand

   C. Ranjith D. Sitha

4. **Who are the two people in the group whose average incomes (for the four-year period) are equal?**

   A. Arun and Neethu B. Anand and Ranjith

   C. Ranjith and Neethu D. Neethu and Sitha

5. **What is the ratio of total income earned by the men to the income earning by women during the four-year period?**

   A. 32:27 B. 15:16 C. 23:21 D. 18:17

   Note:

   Total income for men = ₹ 64,000

   Total income for women = ₹ 54,000

   Ratio of income of men to women = 64:54 = 32:27

6. **Which of the following are the correct conclusions which we can drawn from the data given in the table?**

   A. The total income of Anand during the four year period is just the half of Sitha's income for the period.

   B. The income of each of the 3 male members in 2008 is twice what they earn in 2005.

   C. The total income of Neethu and Ranjith during the 4 year period put together is equal to that of Sitha during the same period.

   D. If the four persons are ranked with respect to their total income for the 4 year period, Sitha comes at the top, while Neethu comes second.

III. Study the following table which provide estimates of 7 parameters (listed below) of the different states in India and the whole of India and answer questions 7 to 9

Values of various parameters

Sl. No	States	1	2	3	4	5	6	7
1	Rajastan	44.00	38.55	16.9	31	49.03	11.83	23.302
2	Madhya Pradesh	66.1	44.20	29.2	45	67.88	22.52	38.261
3	Orissa	31.6	49.09	15.5	30	66.38	12.98	15.694
4	Assam	22.40	52.89	11.8	23	44.15	8.33	11.735
5	West Bengal	68.1	57.70	39.2	17	67.28	18.81	41.603
6	Uttar Pradesh	139.1	41.60	57.8	65	70.03	34.97	69.120
7	Bihar	86.4	38.48	33.2	50	46.86	14.46	29.341
8	Delhi	09.4	75.29	7.0	1	13.18	11.37	11.201
9	Haryana	16.50	55.85	9.1	16	32.33	05.11	18.057
10	Himachal Pradesh	05.2	63.86	3.3	12	12.78	2.72	2.798
11	Punjab	20.3	58.51	11.8	14	32.93	7.51	26.002
12	Andhra Pradesh	66.5	44.09	29.3	23	100.89	17.40	45.187
13	Tamil Nadu	55.8	62.66	45.0	23	63.08	21.53	48.185
14	Karnataka	45.0	56.04	25.2	20	80.04	14.42	42.926
15	Kerala	29.1	89.81	26.1	14	32.94	12.80	19.585
16	Gujarat	41.3	61.29	25.3	19	58.02	13.87	32.240
17	Maharashtra	78.9	64.87	51.2	30	137.85	32.80	91.208
18	Others	20.6	52.21	10.7	69	46.18	6.94	99.404
19	India	846.3	52.21	441.8	502	1021.83	270.37	615.273

Headings of various columns: 1. Population in millions, 2. Literacy Rate, 3. Literate Population in Millions, 4. No. of Districts, 5. No. of High/Higher Secondary Schools in Hundred, 6. Enrolment in High/Higher Secondary Schools in ten thousand, 7. Net Domestic Product in ₹ one thousand crores.

7. **Compared to the total population of India, the population of Uttar Pradesh and Bihar together is:**

   A. less than one-fourth B. equal to one-fourth

   C. more than one-fourth D. above two-third of it.

8. **Regarding literate population, which of the following inferences are correct?**

   (i) Literate population in Bihar is more than the literate population in the most other states.

   (ii) Literacy rate in Bihar is the lowest in India.

   (iii) Uttar Pradesh and Bihar account for about 25% of India's literate population.

   A. (i) and (iii) are true B. (ii) and (iii) are true

   C. (i) and (ii) are true D. (i), (ii) and (iii) are true

9. **Maximum number of High/Higher Secondary Schools per million is in:**

   A. Maharashtra B. Andhra Pradesh

   C. Kerala D. Orissa

IV. Read the following table and answer the questions 10 to 12.

Unemployment Rate

Year	Primary Level	Secondary Level	Higher Education Level
1960	47	20	10
1965	30	15	05
1970	20	10	15
1975	15	12	09
1980	10	15	20
1985	18	16	05
1990	10	12	16

10. **What is the overall trend of unemployment from 1960 to 1990?**

    A. Increasing B. Decreasing

    C. Neither increasing nor decreasing

    D. Sometimes increasing & some times decreasing.

11. **The highest percentage of unemployment from 1960 to 1990 was at the level of:**

    A. Secondary Education B. Higher Education

    C. Primary education D. None of these.

12. The ratio among total unemployment figures from 1960 to 1990 for all the three levels is:

A. 15:10:8 B. 5:3:2 C. 8:10:15 D. 2:3:5

V. Four students P,Q,R, and S appeared for four papers, I,II, III and IV in an examination. Their scores out of 100 in the four subjects are given in the table below.

Students \ Papers	I	II	III	IV
P	60	81	45	55
Q	59	43	51	4
R	74	4	71	65
S	72	76	4	68

Examine the table and answer questions 13 and 14

13. Which candidate has secured an in aggregate between 60% and 65%?

A. P B. Q C. R D. S

14. For which paper did the students achieve the highest average sores?

A. I B. II C. III D. IV

VI. Study the following table which shows the number of candidates belonging to different areas who appeared and passed a national competitive examination during the period 1990 – 1995 and answer the questions 15 to 17.

Year	Rural		Semi Urban		Capital City		Metropolis	
	Appeared	Passed	Appeared	Passed	Appeared	Passed	Appeared	Passed
1990	1652	208	7894	2513	5054	1468	9581	3214
1991	1839	317	8562	2933	7164	3248	10158	4018
1992	2153	932	8139	2468	8258	3159	9695	3038
1993	5032	1798	9432	3528	8529	3628	11247	5158
1994	4915	1658	9784	4015	9015	4311	12518	6328
1995	5628	2392	9969	4263	1725	4526	13624	6419

15. Which category of candidates who appeared and passed the competitive examinations registered a continuous increase over the period from 1990 to 1995?

A. Semi urban B. Capital city C. Capital & Rural D. None of these

16. In which year was the pass percentage of candidates from semi urban areas the lowest?

A. 1991 B. 1993 C. 1990 D. 1992

17. From 1991 to 1992. What was the percentage of reduction in the number of semi urban candidates who appeared in the examination from 1991 to 1992?

A. 5 B. 10 C. 15 D. 8

Note:

1991 figure : 8562

1992 figure : 8139

Reduction = 423

Percentage decrease = 423/8562 × 100 = 4.9 = 5 nearly

VII. Study the following table showing the various causes of death in different years from 1970 to 2002 and answer question 20.

Causes	1970	1980	1990	2000
Cancer	12.7%	16.5%	17.1%	18.00%
Cardio Vascular	36.2%	39.8%	42.3%	40.1%
Violence	8.7%	10.8%	12.1%	14.0%
Earth quakes	4.4%	4.9%	2.1%	1.1%
Accident	10.5%	8.00%	9.2%	8.2%
Floods	5.0%	5.00%	2.0%	1.0%
Others	22.5%	15.00%	15.2%	17.6%

18. Two inferences based on the data in the table are given. Which are of the following is true?

Statement: (1) Cancer shows the same trend as violence.

(ii) Earth quakes and floods have shown a decline.

A. Both (i) and (ii) are false

B. Statement (i) is true

C. Statement (ii) is true

D. Both (i) and (ii) are true

Answer keys

1.B	2.C	3.C	4.C	5.A	6.C	7.C	8.C	9.A	10.D
11.C	12.A	13.A	14.A	15.D	16.D	17.A	18.B		

Unit - VIII

INFORMATION AND COMMUNICATION TECHNOLOGY (ICT)

1. ICT: MEANING, ADVANTAGES, DISADVANTAGES AND USES
2. GENERAL ABBREVIATIONS AND TERMINOLOGY
3. BASICS OF INTERNET AND E-MAILING

Unit - VIII

INFORMATION AND COMMUNICATION TECHNOLOGY

1. ICT: MEANING, ADVANTAGES, DISADVANTAGES AND USES

a. Information and Communication Technology (ICT)

ICT, is well-accepted and has considerable role in modern educational practice. The use of ICT involves drafting and re-drafting, editing and selecting, making connections among what is known and generating new knowledge from the interaction with what is already known.

ICT can provide opportunities for simulated learning, meta-cognition stimulates higher order thinking and can develop a social basis for all forms of learning. It helps immensely in breaking subject boundaries and acts as the foundation for developing project-based, real-world ('authentic') learning. Student-centered learning and intrinsic motivation are also among the advantages of using ICT in education. The above described features of the ICT can be considered as a corollary for developing a constructivist approach to learning.

In the new learning context where neither the teacher nor the text book is the repository of all knowledge, the internet acts as a medium for the practice of constructivism in learning. This is because the ICT is an expanding store of accessible information and it requires students to evaluate and select relevant information and helps them to select their own pathways for learning. The internet questions the conventional notions of authority, validity and even the nature and ownership of knowledge. Internet knowledge is non-hierarchical. Student-centered learning is a natural consequence of the use of the internet where every learner has access to existing knowledge which can be accrued, stored, classified and recalled within short time. It gives greater control over learning by the learner.

b. Higher order thinking and ICT

The impact of ICT and the connected new technologies has shifted the emphasis from teaching to learning and from the product to the process of learning. Students will need to focus on how and where to acquire, store and utilise knowledge rather than on how to remember it in its totality. Effective teachers will be those who can scaffold learning experiences for students and support them in the navigation of their own learning.

Castro claims that using ICT in classrooms, particularly in the constructivist approach, has great potential to develop students' higher order cognitive skills. Similarly, Wishart reports that computer programs can act as cognitive tools which facilitate the construction of higher order schemata as well as the use of cognitive skills such as formal operational and abstract reasoning which were previously considered to be unattainable by younger children.

Project-based learning, involved in the learning through ICT, encourages students to make their own decisions about their own learning and to find out answers through exploratory processes. Many problems which appear in learning (what if questions and their answers) often require discussions, interactions and communication with others. The sum total of such interactions will lead to higher level learning with maximum economy of time and labour.

Modern education is facing several new problems. For example, the content of the curricula has increased several folds. The need to provide authentic, real-world learning experiences which would help to acquire the expected learning outcomes demands different strategies other than verbal transmission method. What is demanded is the need for active meaningful learning based on real-life tasks which will be multi disciplinary, project based, participatory ('minds-on' as well as 'hands-on') and collaborative. Collaborative work will require 'ad hoc' grouping of students, the pattern of which will have to be changed from time to time. All these demand a new system of pedagogies-active pedagogies.

c. ICT for Equal Opportunities

ICT helps the teachers to give equal opportunities for students, to suit their individual differences. Even the students with special educational needs and handicaps receive a better deal once ICT is employed. Students with special educational needs normally experience learning difficulties while put into conventional classrooms.

ICT can help the students with special educational needs in the following ways:

- giving special attention to learners who are dyslexic with the help of technological contrivances like voice-activated computers;
- providing learners with visual impairments technical supports like screen magnifier and talk-back facilities; and
- keeping learners with cerebral palsy with contrivances like light- weight laptops.

An important paper by Sandals under the title 'Computer Assisted Applications for Learning with Special Needs Children' advocates the view that there are many positive advantages for Computer Assisted Instruction for the handicapped children. This includes subjective, behavioural advantages to learners as demonstrated by the improved attitude of students and their peers.

The ICT is known to have a gender bias as pointed out by Laches. According to him, boys were found to be more confident than girls in using computers. Boys tended to make more effective use of computers than girls. Obviously, this finding suggests that the teacher must be vigilant to ensure equal or near-equal competency for both boys and girls in the use of the hardware of communication technologies.

d. ICT and Pedagogy

Since schools are the formal agencies created to promote student learning, ICT will have to be used in a systematic fashion to improve the quality of student learning the related pedagogy has to be different.

There is no doubt in that the ICT has successfully brought about many desirable changes in the conception and practice of pedagogy in several areas. Most important among these are the radical changes it has brought about in:

- pedagogic approaches to teaching and learning,
- changes in teaching and learning styles and instructional behaviour; and
- in redefining the whole context of teaching and in reconceptualizing the process of learning.

The major tendency in modern education is to move away from teacher-centred instruction towards the facilitation of self learning using ICT, particularly through group work and student-centred learning. Teachers and learners play different new roles. Instead of teachers designing the strategies for learning teachers and learners become active partners in the co-construction of knowledge. With ICT, the role and tasks of the teacher are still vital and add value to learning.

One claim of the ICT is that it can accommodate different learning styles – the characteristic or preferred ways in which particular learners learn and interact with the learning environment. A learner who depends more on visual memory gets the visual input needed; those who depend more on words will get this form of input, etc. For the ICT to be able to accommodate different learning styles teachers will have to be actually aware of how their students learn and how they would like to learn. These trends will have to be built into their planning for instruction.

e. Use of ICT for Student Assessment

Traditional assessment quite often degenerates into testing for recall, and ability to remember factual knowledge and procedures. Students often have to wait for several days or, in the case of common examinations, months for results since the data has to be processed by hand. Use of ICT, however, will speed up the processing Results can be declared within a few days once the ICT methods are used. The provision of diagnostic assessment of strengths, weaknesses, difficulties, achievements and ways of learning and thinking is enriched and facilitated by the ICT, not only in terms of speed, but also in terms of the efficiency and quality of the feedback.

Assessment, using ICT, acts as a spring board for learning; it can be used most effectively in formative evaluation. It helps to strengthen the links between assessment and learning.

Advantages of IT-based Assessment

The following are main advantages:

- Rapid feedback.
- Richer feedback; the computer can analyse the learner's performance in more detail and, sharper feedback is done than the feedback of conventional classroom teacher using traditional methods.

- Could help to assess higher order thinking and learning, often using real-world simultations.
- Longitudinal assessment possible through stored databases of each student, enabling progress to be tracked and presented easily.
- Multidisciplinary tasks are better assessed using ICT.
- Links between learning, diagnosis and assessment get strengthened; assessment is linked to learning.
- Helps Student self-assessment.
- Computer Adaptive Testing (CAT) enables assessment to be tailored to individual levels. (In CAT the question to come depends on his previous performance).
- Gap between learners and assessors is bridged; teachers, peers and individual students act both as learners and as assessors.
- Examination anxiety gets reduced.

  Computerised question banks improve the quality of testing and help in speeding up scoring using mechanical strategies.

f. ICT in Administration

Schools use the ICT for a variety of administrative functions. Teachers can use the ICT to streamline record keeping and related administrative tasks. With the ICT, reports become more reliable, updated, timely and easy to retrieve and read. ICT helps to provide guidelines for interpretation (percentiles, ranks, etc.) This results in a reduction in the need to sort out and do hand calculations of documents. Also, statistical and comparative analyses can be made immediately. Through the ICT, teachers and head teachers become more accountable, in terms of student achievements, dealing with complaints about teachers, deviation from curriculum planning and finding out time tables, etc. In short administration becomes more efficient and transparent.

The application of information systems in school management has its impact on accountability, evaluation of teaching and learning, super vision, record keeping (e.g. attendance, writing reports, assessment, writing of lesson plans, resources), feedback and reports of meetings, shared decision making, shared values, etc. It can help in continuous leadership development, with increased functional efficiency in all areas of school work.

Student teachers are advised to find out the school's practices in the use of ICT for lesson planning, preparation and recording, communication, time table setting and administrative work. They are also advised to observe and understand the e-mail practices for improving educational communication.

g. Simulation and Games

Simulation is a quantitative procedure which describes a process by developing a model of that process and then conducting a series of organised experiments to predict the behaviour of the process over time. Simulation is a powerful technique which exploits some of the unique features of the computer as an aid to learning. It enables the students to experiment with situations which would otherwise be too expensive, too time-consuming or highly dangerous. Simulation in nuclear engineering is an example. In the training of nuclear engineers it is desirable for the student to carry out various experiments on the behaviour of nuclear reactor under various conditions; A nuclear reactor is a very expensive piece of laboratory equipment and there is a limit to the number of students who can work on it simultaneously. So these experiments are sure to be very costly. Moreover some of the experiments might pose obvious damages that threaten the safety of the student. An experiment which is based upon an accurate computer simulation can demonstrate the desired effects at considerably lower cost and at less risk to the student or the environment.

Game is used as an instructional strategy and also as a powerful learning material. It promotes discovery learning expected in certain areas. Games and simulations have considerable acceptance among students as interesting pedagogical tools. Computer games and simulations, in general, can:

- improve the speed and quality of student learning and student performance;
- stimulate and develop motivation and curiosity;
- enhance learning through visualization, experimentation, prediction, manipulation and logical thinking.
- develop confidence and enable students to experience success and a sense of achievement.

h. Don'ts with the ICT

The National Council for Educational Technology gives practical advice for teaching and learning with the ICT, in terms of seven 'don'ts'. They are:

1. Don't assign pupils to computers before preparing them for the task they are expected to perform.
2. Don't devise a task which has no relevance to what is required/unrelated to their experience.
3. Don't let the pupils use computers while you are explaining.
4. Don't leave the pupils just working on their task for the whole of the lesson without some form of meaningfull intervention.
5. Occassionally remind the students of the educational purpose behind the task
6. Don't expect the pupils to print out their work at the end of every lesson; they should be given enough of opportunities to print out what is most relevant at the end of a session.
7. Don't end the lesson without drawing them together to consolidate the results and discuss what they have achieved.
8. Don't rely on the technology to run the lesson; use the lesson to decide the ideal technology.

i. Health issues related to the use of IT

It is now very common for students to work on computers continuously for hours. Some use it for improving the quality of work. Others use computers for fun. Experts point out that there are certain dangers in the prolonged use of computers.

Any task that involves staring at a computer screen, (no matter how exciting or interesting, the sight is), leads to physical fatigue. Even when you may feel quite happy to continue this activity, your body may find it difficult to tolerate the exertion. The most common physical complaints are eye strain and problems with vision (blurring and itching being typical problems). Headaches are also usual due to prolonged viewing of a computer screen. Remember to look away from the screen for a few moments when you don't need to use it. Check that the level of lighting is comfortable and that you are not dealing with screen-reflected glare from windows or light sources. Glare reducing screens are useful to reduce exhaution. If you experience repeated headaches due to computer viewing, you should consult your doctor and take his advice.

You should keep your head and back straight and the top of the monitor should be just below the eye level. If your monitor is to the left or right of your keyboard you are putting strain on your neck. Long periods of time at the computer often lead to pain in the lumbar region of the back. Neck and shoulder problems are often the result of poor seating and the unscientific arrangement of the equipment on the desk. Stretching for the telephone or files, side ways viewing, should all be avoided by properly arranging all your requirements before you start your work on the computer.

When the demands inflicted on a person are beyond his ability to deal with them effectively, the result will be 'stress'. The stress could be either physiological or psychological. A lot of stigma is still attached to stress despite stress is the most common reason for absenting from work/for inability to concentrate on one's work for a long period. Most people are fairly good at spotting the signs of stress in others, but not always are sensitive to their own feelings. Signs of stress are feeling irritated, feeling depressed, not sleeping properly, having digestive problems, backaches and headaches and an increase in blood pressure. Realizing that you are experiencing stress in a negative way (remember that stress is relative) is the first step in taking corrective action.

The following will help you and your students to recognize and avoid the most common problems:

1. The computer area

Keep your computer area systematically organized. Items that you have to use frequently should remain close to you so that you don't have to stretch your hand and body too much. Avoid stuffing things under the desk in such a way that you cannot stretch your legs, and causing difficulty in locating what you want.

2. Adopt a good posture

Sit up straight and try to keep your hips, shoulders and ears in a straight line. This will give you greater comfort while sitting position.

3. *Feet should touch the floor*

If your feet don't touch the ground where it has to rest, use a foot rester or use a low seat.

4. *Support the lumbar area*

Make sure that your lower back is supported in order to help you maintain the lumbar curve in an ideal position.

5. *Tip seat forward*

For additional help in maintaining the lumbar curve, adjust the seat angle forward or use a wedge cushion.

6. *Position monitor*

The monitor should be placed where the top of the screen is at the eye level and directly in front of you. The distance between you and your monitor should be between 40 cm and 75 cm. Use the length of your arm as a general guide.

7. *Use a document holder*

Using a document holder near the monitor will help you to keep your head in a neutral position and avoid harmful straining of the neck.

8. *Take breaks and shift your position*

Shifting around can take the stress and strain muscles off. Be careful not to shift yourself right out of a good sitting posture. Mini-breaks in the course of work, with gentle stretching and exercise can make a big difference in how you feel.

9. *Use wrist supports for the keyboard and the computer mouse*

Proper support of the wrists is important for avoiding excessive stress to the carpal region and wrist muscles. Those who ignore this principle develop what medical people describe as the Carpel Tunnel Syndrome. Make sure that the supports are comfortable and that there are no sharp edges. Arms should be relaxed and at about a 90^{0} angle. If the keyboard is too high, consider mounting an adjustable keyboard tray.

10. *Phone position*

If you have to use the phone quite often during the work, consider using a headset. Cradling the phone between your shoulder and neck is sure to cause strain on your neck.

j. Impact of ICT on behavioural patterns

The ICT has come to stay and has become a part and parcel of modern life in all societies. It is playing a dominant role in how human beings live and work, whether at home or in the workplace.

The main advantage of ICT is that it has liberated human beings from tedious mechanical tasks which formerly needed considerable physical effort. Development of ICT has reduced the extent of physical effort of humans for a number of tasks. However, a condition where no physical work is expected of human being is also not desirable. Too much expansion of internet facilities has a potential danger in that it can transform human beings out of the social context in which they live. Almost every human activity from dealings, medical assistance, preparation of food, childrens education, planning for journey, are all controlled and managed using computer networks. Development of ICT may thus reach a stage where barring a few unavoidable exceptions, all activities will be done using ICT channels. Experts believe that non centralization will reduce human to the level machines. We can understand the negative impacts of ICT where human beings have no physical tasks to perform. This will lead to inaction of the brain and body. Since these organs are genetically designed for physical work, thinking and feeling, their dysfunction is likely to have negative repurcussions on human life. Thus when natural functions are supressed, it will lead to the creation of dehumanised society. Lack of physical work and lack of opportunity to communicate emotion through a common language, will result in a condition called 'information over load'. It is necessary that we evolve proper corrective measures to deal with such developments.

2. GENERAL ABBREVIATIONS AND TERMINOLOGY USED IN ICT

A

1. *Algorithm:* A prescribed set of well defined rules or processes for the solution of a problem, as per a series of accepted steps and procedures.
2. *Alphanumeric Field:* A data field in which alphabetic, numeric and special characters are accepted.
3 *Analog Computers:* A computer that represents its data in the form of a measurement of an actual property.
4. *Arithmetic Logic Unit (ALU):* The component of a CPU responsible for the performance of arithmetic and logical operations.
5. *Artificial Intelligence (AI):* Stands for intelligence which is created artificially; with the help of the new technologies. It is a branch of computer science concerned with the study and creation of computer systems that exhibit some form of intelligence, a system capable of doing independent thinking.
6. *Assembler:* The translating program used to convert assembly language to machine language.
7. *Automation:* A self-moving machine or one that moves by concealed machinery; a human being acting mechanically.

B

8. *Binary:* The number representation system with a base of two usually using just two symbols 0 and 1 as digits and expressing all other numbers using these two symbols.
9. *Broadcast Television (Open Circuit Television):* It refers to the ordinary television broadcasting. Anyone can receive the broadcast using a television receiver when properly connected.
10. *Byte:* A contiguous set of binary digits (bits), usually comprising eight bits operated upon as a unit to store/retrieve information.

C

11. *Cassette:* A closed container of magnetic tape with supply and take-up reels. The cheapest and lowest way to store information.
12. *Central Processing Unit (CPU):* The unit of hardware in a computer system in which all instruction and data processing occur.
13. *Chip (Silicon):* A small electronic component usually made of silicon that contains microscopic circuits. Also called an integrated circuit.
14. *Chips:* Miniaturised integrated circuits.
15. *Closed Circuit Television (CCTV):* Used for the transmission of pictures and sound to a limited network connected by a cable or microwave system. The telecast cannot be received by other sets out side the network.
16. *Coaxial Cable (Coax):* Common transmission media used for digital and analog transmission.
17. *Compilers:* The translating program used to convert high-level language to machine language.
18. *Computer:* A machine that processes information. More specifically, a machine that accepts information, applies procedures defined by a program of instructions furnished in advance, and supplies the results of those procedures. Computers belong to three categories: 1. Micro Computers 2. Mini Computers 3. Main Frame Computers.
19. *Cathode Ray Tube (CRT):* Another name for a picture tube, monitor or video display terminal (VDT).
20. *Current Awareness Service (CAS):* A service in which newly generated information is brought to the notice of the user in the shortest possible time.

D

21. *Data Processing:* Execution of a systematic sequence of operations upon data. eg: computing, merging, sorting
22. *Database:* A collection of data constructed to facilitate the updating, once only of the data components, and the access and retrieval of individual items. A detabase is usually designed in such a way as not to restrict its use to a single application.

23. *Document:* A document is an object that provides information. It is an embodied thought.

E

24. *Editor:* A program that facilitates the creation and correction of texts.
25. *Educational Technology Cell (ETC):* It aims at qualitative improvement in education through the improved use of technological supports, contrivances and accessories, created for service to a state. The bigger organisation of this kind serving the whole country is called the Centre for Educational Technology (CET).
26. *Edusat (Education Satellite):* An artificial satellite created to meet the needs of the education sector in the country, which helps to telecast, educational broadcasts. It is meant mainly for providing connectivity to educational programmes meant for schools, colleges, and higher levels of education and also for supporting non-formal education.
27. *E-governance:* It means the delivery of government for services and information to the public using electronic means. It helps in identifying and accommodating the views of the general public in governmental administrations and increase the accountability and transparency of a government/governing system.
28. *E-mail (Electronic Mail):* A general term to describe the storage and delivering of text or images to different computers through the internet.

F

29. *Fibre optics:* It is an optical transmission medium, which accepts an electrical signal, converts and transmits in the form of light pulses, and then reconverts the outputs to an electrical signal at the receiving end.
30. *File:* File is a collection of similar records used for electronic transmission.
31. *Floppy Disk:* A device for storing and retrieving data. It is a rotating storage medium associated with microcomputers. A floppy disk is a flexible circle of magnetic material sealed inside an envelop. Standard diameters are 3a and 5d.
32. *Flow chart:* Graphical representation of the sequence in a computer program.

G

33. *Guided media:* Transmission media using wire or cables. eg: copper wire, fibre optic cables, etc.

H

34. *Hard copy:* A printed copy of machine output in a form in which it can be directly interpreted. eg. printed reports, listings, documents, pictures, etc.
35. *Hard disk:* A small high-capacity disk storage device for use with a microcomputer.
36. *Hardware:* The machine part of the computer system.
37. *Home page:* The first page of a website.
38. *HTML:* Hypertext markup language

39. *Hybrid Computers:* A type of computer that combines the best features of analog and digital computers.

I

40. *Indexed sequential (ISAM) File:* A type of direct access media file that combines random and sequential access of data in the file through an index.
41. *Information Highways:* A high speed global network capable of routing to subscribers a series of new interactive services, such as distance learning, data bank querying teleshopping, telemedicine, pay-per-view television picture phoning, etc.
42. *Information Technology (IT):* It deals with all the information activities including location, acquisition, processing, storage and communication of information.
43. *Instructional Television (ITV):* Conducting instruction programme through Television.
44. *Interactive Video:* Using video in an interactive manner. Computers are used for making interactivity. So, it is also called Video-based Computer Assisted Learning (V-CAL).
45. *Internet:* A vast collection of different networks that use certain common protocols and provide certain common services.
46. *Internet Explorer:* Means a web browser, where the term 'browser' stands for.... include this term under '8'.

J

47. *Joy stick:* A graphical input device. A stick set in two crossed grooves. The movements of the stick are sensed and translated into binary instructions.

K

48. *Key board:* It is the part of a computer similar to a typewriter key board, used for giving instructions.

L

49. *Laptop:* A low weight transportable computer, which can be placed on the lap or equivalent space and operated.
50. *Large Scale Integration (LSI):* It is a process creating high density integrated chips, usually thousand gates on a chip.
51. *Local Area Network (LAN):* A communication system linking a number of computers within a defined small area (office building, university, industrial site, etc.) for a common purpose.

M

52. *Magnetic Disk:* A current storage medium which lets the computer retain large amount of data/program for ready processing. (a direct access medium)
53. *Magnetic Tape:* A magnetic storage medium. It is essentially a serial storage medium.

54. *Main Frames:* Largest and most expensive class of computers with work stations and high storage facility.
55. *Management Information System (MIS):* A computer system that integrates equipment, procedures and organisation personnel to develop information for management decision - making.
56. *Megabyte (MB):* Measuring unit for expressing the capacity of a storage system used in computers, Approximately one million bytes or one thousand kilobytes. This is unusually used to measure disk, tape or larger computer storage capacity.
57. *Microcomputer:* A computer system which is being fabricated around microprocessor.
58. *Mini Computer:* A small-to-medium-size computer usually able to execute several programs concurrently. There is no clear-cut distinction between a large micro computer and a small one, except that the mini is expandable to a much greater extent than a micro.
59. *Microform:* A term used for all types of micro-documents whether they are transparent or opaque, or in roll or sheet form. Microfilm, microfiche, microcard and microprint are examples.
60. *Modem:* A device that converts data into impulses and transmits them over telephone lines from the terminal to the computer and vice versa. (modulator/ define them used in 'M' used 'D': demodulator).
61. *Monitor:* Video display that gives a higher quality picture than a TV set. Colour monitors picture than a composite colour (so-so for reading words and numbers, fine for graphics and games), or RGB (red-green-blue). Display quality depends heavily on quality of the computer signal.
62. *Mother Board:* The main circuit board in a computer.
63. *Multimedia:* The technology used to merge sound and images.
64. *Multiprocessing:* The simultaneous execution of two or more instructions employing two or more CPUs.

N

65. *Network:* A collection of connected computers.

O

66. *On-line Teaching:* It is one type of computer mediated learning. On-line internet connectivity and on-line teaching materials including interactive learning packages are used for this purpose. Materials can be delivered through website or from a central location.
67. *Operating system:* Refers to a type of software that controls the operation of a computer system.

P

68. *Peripherals:* The devices which are external to central processing unit of computer but can be controlled by the computer. Peripherals include input-output and backing store devices.

69. *Plotters:* An output device used for drawing graphs/pictures etc. and produce hard copies of graphs and designs.
70. *Program:* Step-by-step set of instructions that directs the computer to perform certain operations to solve a problem preparing for the execution.
71. *Programming Language:* A high-level language designed for precise description of computer programs with formal definition of statements.

R

72. *Random Access Memory (RAM):* Main memory of the computer that is fabricated on a semiconductor chip. Information can be read from, and written and introduced into the memory by the user and therefore, it is also called read/write memory.
73. *Read Only Memory (ROM):* Main memory of the computer that is fabricated on as the random access memory but the contents of the main memory are fixed during manufacturing and cannot be modified i.e. only the contents can be accessed.
74. *Reprography:* It includes all the various activities and techniques associated with the reproduction of documents. eg. photostat, offset printing, etc.
75. *Resource centers:* An information lodging and exchange centre. Resources centres offer self-learning opportunities to students, teachers and other members of the community.

S

76. *Satellite Instructional Television Experiment (SITE):* It is an instructional television programme using satellite inorder to extend the range of broadcasting. It can be used effectively for adult education, non-formal education, distant education, correspondence education and extension programmes for different purposes like agricultural extension.
77. *Secondary/Auxiliary Storage:* Device: A permanent storage device having a large capacity but slower access time than main memory. eg. hard disk, floppy disk, magnetic tape, etc.
78. *Selective Dissemination of Information (SDI):* It is a Current Awareness Service (CAS) using computers. It keeps its user abreast of the latest developments in the field of his interest, unlike in an individualised service.
79. *Simulation:* Investigation of the behaviour of a system by establishing and running a model of the system.
80. *Software:* The program which direct a hardware (computer) to perform a set of desired operations to accomplish a work.
81. *System:* Organized set of related components, established to perform a certain task.

T

82. *Taskbar:* It can be seen at the bottom of a program window. It displays the current status of the program or computer system (like capslock on/off, Number lock on/off, etc.)

83. *Teleconferencing:* Means of interacting with others at remote places using TV - communication specially created for the purpose; using this technology we can communicate and interact with group of learners at different campuses and in different organisations.
84. *Terminal:* The peripheral device used to enter or extract data from the computer. It is sometimes referred to as 'get workstation' or 'human interface'. It usually consists of a CRT and key board, called a monitor.
85. *Tool Bar:* Shortcuts for same commonly used menu items are included in toolbars. eg. Standard Tool Bar and Formattng Toolbar from MS Word.
86. *Twisted pair:* Oldest and most common transmission medium. It consists of two wires twisted together in a helical form, just like a DNA module, typically about 1mm thick.

V

87. *Virtual Memory:* A store management system in which a user uses the storage of the computer without being constrained by the limited size of main store.
88. *Visual Display Unit (VDU):* Most popular output device which looks like a television screen.

W

89. *Web Browser:* A software which helps to see the web pages.
90. *Web Pages:* Pages from world wide web (WWW).
91. *Wide Area Network (WAN):* A network covering a wide geographical area.
92. *Word Processing:* Computer based system for inputting, editing, storing and printing of documents.
93. *World Wide Web (WWW):* A huge collection of documents called webpages.

3. BASICS OF INTERNET AND E-MAILING

The Internet is a huge chain of computer networks that can communicate with each other. The word Internet is coined from the words 'Interconnection' and 'Network'. It refers to the services that can be reached using the interconnected networks. When you connect to the internet from office or home, your computer becomes a tiny part of this giant network. Each computer user can communicate and share common resources, such as printers and storage space, with other users.

a. World Wide Web (WWW)

The World Wide Web is a vast collection of documents stored on Internet Computers. The Web refers to a specific kind of internet interface. The Web documents contain 'links' that lead to other Web pages and they contain graphics, sound and so on which open up new possibilities for presenting information. To start with, internet consisted of text-only (characters only) on WebPages. But at present, with the help of WWW it offers sound, video and animation.

The Web was invented in early 1990s, by Tim-Berners-Lee and it is considered as one of the key milestones in Internet usage. The idea behind the development of Web was to provide easy access to information and to provide the capability to move freely on the Internet. The World Wide Web is a system of media-rich documents spread across the Internet, linked with each other through related topics. WWW documents can contain texts, pictures, sound, video and more.

Web Server: It is a mechanism in which a program and a computer are clubbed into one entity which responds to the requests from Web Browsers for Internet Resources.

Web Browser: It is a program that allows a user to display and interact with a hypertext document. Netscape Navigator and Internet Explorer are examples.

Homepage: Home page is the first hypertext document to be shown when a user follows a link to the Web Server.

b. Internet Education

Internet education includes and provides the following:

Passive/active interactivity: Passive/active interactivity introduces the new class of user called the 'viewser' (viewer-user). Passive/active interactivity is fast developing to a common place technology as the Net matures. Innovative Web Developers, multimedia producers and broadcasters are using passive/active interactivity to introduce a new and better profile with new interest and requirements.

Some of the functions served by the internet are:

Hypermedia: Audio visual information can be conceptually linked with other non-time based data types on the Web. This basic 'link-integration' is the first step towards conceptual hypermedia (text-to-audiovisual media link is an example).

Interactive multimedia: Using the internet, as an interactive multimedia training delivery medium, is an exciting possibility that has been promised for a long time. While it once consisted uniquely of 'text-only Web 'Pages', the Internet now offers sound, video, and animation.

Distribution of Information: The internet is being used increasingly as a means of distributing information. If the information includes text and/or small graphics, they can be successfully delivered over the Internet.

Disseminating information: The internet is being used now more than ever, as a means of disseminating information and facilitating learning. Search engines are good SDI tools.

Need-based Instruction: Unlike TV networks, computer networks are invariably two-way. TV networks send the same information to all the stations at the same time; in computer networks, each particular message is usually routed to a particular computer.

Electronic Mail (e-mail): Electronic mail is certainly the most widely used information exchange today. Using this facility it can exchange e-mail with millions of people all over the world.

Surfing: Surfing the net means checking out sites on the Web. The software used to navigate the Web is known as a *browser*. The most popular browsers today are *Netscape Navigator* and *Microsoft Internet Explorer*.

Search Engines: Search engines are special tools that help to search information on the Net. 'Yahoo!' and 'Google' are examples for search engines.

Electronic Commerce: It is a word for buying and selling stuff over the Net. Now softwares are available to help in sending credit card number over the Net with safety and security.

Internet education is the need of today, and achieving it will increase efficiency, effectiveness and competitiveness.

c. E-learning

E-learning does not have a universally accepted definition. It is an approach to facilitate and enhance learning using information and communication technology. It may include all types of technology-enhanced learning (TEL), where technology is used to support the learning process. It is 'pedagogy empowered by digital technology'.

E-learning covers a vide set of applications and processes such as web-based learning, computer-based learning, virtual class rooms and digital collaboration. It includes the delivery of content via internet, intranet, extranet and videotape, satellite broadcast, interactive TV, CD-ROM and more.

Benefits of E-learning

1. Provides self directed and self paced learning
2. Enhances computer and internet skills
3. Fosters greater student-instructor contact
4. Provides on-demand access of learning
5. Accommodates multiple learning styles
6. Has no geographical barriers
7. Facilitates greater student interaction and collaboration
8. Is based upon validated pedagogical principles
9. Provides remote access
10. Provides round - the - clock accessibility (day and night accessibility)

d. Distance Education via Internet

Modern educational systems make greater use of the internet for distance eduction. In 1997, the Department of Computer Science at James Madison University in USA started a remote distance master program with a concentration in information security. Experience with this program has taught us that it is possible to develop a new and 'almost lecture less' paradigm for adult education. This experiment has opened up new possibilities in the use of distance education.

The program is almost lecture less since the instructors of the course meet the students only twice, once in the beginning and then at the end of the programme. In an initial meeting, of the session, the instructor presents an overview of the course and introduces the operational arrangements of the program. In the final meeting at the end of the course the instructors 'wrap up' the course. The final meeting also includes a final examination. The remaining 'sessions' of the program are conducted via the internet. with heavy emphasis on the use of electronic mail.

Students are free to communicate with the instructor via telephone, fax or by any other means. The students access all the information through a web site which contains the course description and the activities that the student needs to perform such as readings, assignments and for reaching some ancillary material that might have been prepared by the instructor. Students are encouraged to participate in 'threaded discussion groups' with minimal participation of the instructor, although the instructor clarifies any point that has reached a plateau and cannot be resolved by the students.

The statistical analysis of the results of the new experiment indicate that there are no significant differences between the two methods - the conventional on-campus method and the remote distance group method. In the area of students' accomplishments, it has been found that the students of the internet programme performed better than their on-campus counterparts.

Learner attitude towards distance learning has been categorised into four for comparison: 1. attitude towards the technology, 2. attitude towards distance education teaching methods, 3. attitude towards student and teacher interaction, and 4. attitude towards being a remote student. Definitely these attitudes of the leaner must favourably affect the smooth functioning of 'Internet Distance Learning'.

Computer mediated learning involves many radical changes in communication patterns. Rather than numerous verbal and nonverbal cues available in face to face encounters, distance learning environments constrain contact to primary text. Typically, user acceptance of distance technology requires attitudinal changes in how one thinks, and in composing materials and in communicating. Researchers point out that often new learners appear to experience some form of 'culture shock' which dissipates with additional practice and experience with the system.

e. Interactive Distance Learning over the Internet

Interactive distance learning provides learning through interaction from a distance. The architecture for the application of technology to Interactive Distance Learning (IDL) requirement will involve two major efforts:

1. The implementation of computer-based training activities meant to provide learning guidance, to supply detailed data for analysis and to capture small group intermediate and final products; and
2. The implementation of distance learning technology to link the Small Group Instructors (SGIs) with the small group during and after the construction of the intermediate and final products.

Initially, the students attend large group instruction together. Then, the students disperse into groups; a Small Group Instructor (SGI) is assigned to each group. The small group is required to involve in the decision - making process to analyse tools detailed in the text and to produce intermediate 'products' used as input to the next phase of the process. Gates are closed until the student products are reviewed by the SGI. The SGI grades the product and opens the gate before the group moves to the next phase. There are four phases in all. They are:

1. Analysis

Task description: Develop proper concepts about the essential tasks that the unit has to perform in order to accomplish the expected objectives.

Input: Instructor's guidance is only the input in this phase.

Approach: Using the automated instruction lessons, the necessary data have to be derived for the purpose of monitoring the small group instruction towards the development of the products.

2. Course of Action (COA) development

Task description: Develop multiple COAs that would accomplish the objective assigned by the instructor.

Input: Planning, guidance and 'phase-one' product.

Approach: Using automated instruction lessons, derive the necessary data to facilitate small group interaction in the development of the CAO plans.

3. COA analysis and comparison

Task description: Utilise appropriate method of analysis to identify the COA with the greatest probability of success.

Input: Multiple COAs from phase two.

Approach: Using automated instruction lessons derive the necessary data to help in small group interaction in the analysis of the CAO plans.

4. Execution

Task description: Review the COA with the SGI to determine the probable outcome of the recommended COA.

Input: Recommended COA from phase three.

Approach: SGI or small group interaction leading to the recommended COA's probable outcomes.

The primary role of the instructor is to facilitate the tactical decision - making process, as students try to formulate effective courses of action (COAs). During the decision - making process, students are assigned one or two functional roles in the analysis of the information. Students are expected to submit two interim products as inputs to the next phase of the process and one final product. The instructor will review, score and provide feedback to the group for each submitted product. Two interim products and one final product will be scored and used as a measure of student achievement.

Interactive distance learning can act as an effective communication aid for even mentally retarded persons and for persons with speech and communication disorders. Those persons can communicate with their instructor and get help and guidance to follow the written texts (instead of hearing spoken language) or other learning materials that use pictures of symbols. Such learners can learn just like any normal person. That means, Interactive Distance Learning provides an Augmentative and Alternative Communication (AAC). AAC means an alternative to spoken language and an augmentation and complement to speech. Alternative communication is often based on graphic symbols ie, pictures and photographs, and is used in combination with technical aids.

f. Interactive Multimedia

Interactive multimedia technology is the computer-delivered electronic system that allows the user to control, combine, and manipulate different types of media such as text, sound, video, graphics, and animation. The user is required to activate, manipulate, and respond to the presentation of instructional material and to control the rate and the route taken through the interactive instructional module. Instructional system design is a systematic approach to the development of instructional materials in which the instructors, learners, and materials work together to create successful learning environments. This warrants that the concepts and theories related to instructional system design must be reviewed and used while developing interactive multimedia instructional packages, such as CD-ROM.

The development of an interactive multimedia project is a process that involves three major developmental phases (Kristof & Satran). They are: information design, interaction design and presentation design. Successful instructional design products can be developed only if proven instructional theories are applied from the very beginning till the end, in the process of product development.

Multimedia systems are very effective for training and education. This is due to three following reasons.

1. Possibility of multi-channel communication;
2. the possibility to cover a large quantity of learning material;
3. greater access facilities to the learning material.

Teaching and learning become effective when visualisation, motion, and text are synchronised into one source of knowledge and computing power is used to transform passive learning into interactive, dynamic learning. The most important benefit of this technique is that this gives the option to personalise the style of studying and to make it more appropriate and effective.

g. Desktop Video Conferencing

Desktop video conferencing is a strategy which offers on-line courses using Computer Mediated Communication (CMC) techniques. It can also provide many-to-many communication through CMC techniques.

Computer mediated communication happens in four ways. These are:

1. information retrieval or 'one-alone' technique.
2. e-mail or one-to-one technique.
3. bulletin boards or one-to-many technique.
4. computer conferencing or many-to-many technique.

One-alone techniques primarily focus on the development of 'Self-directed Learning'. One-to-one technique typically uses e-mail for learner-learner and learner-instructor interaction where communication is best accomplished by a written text. In addition, one-to-many text-based technique typically uses 'bulletin board systems', 'list-serves', and 'news groups'. These techniques are asynchronous in nature and are free from rigid time constraints. Alternatively, the many-to-many-techniques or synchronous CMC, includes project groups, video conferencing, and audio conferencing.

These techniques facilitate three types of interaction as described by Moore and Kearsley:

1. Learner-content interaction occurs when students must synthesize their own knowledge through the materials provided.
2. Learner-instructor interaction is regarded as vital to the learning process. Instructor presents content, motivates students and offer guidance. This two-way communication helps to facilitate learning.
3. Learner-learner interaction helps foster a sense of community feeling and is essential for the development of a peer-group of students that would provide them an opportunity to collaborate and learn from each other.

Desktop Video Conferencing is an educational strategy that uses CMC to combine distance education and face-to-face instruction.

Education using Desktop Video Conferencing essentially includes on-line teaching. There are four necessary conditions for successful on-line teaching:

1. *Pedagogical*, performing the duties of an on-line educational facilitator
2. *Social*, promoting human relationships and creating a positive environment
3. *Managerial*, setting the agenda, objectives and procedural rules; and
4. *Technical*, making participants comfortable with the system and software. The goal is to make the technology transparent to the leaner. The on-line instructor needs to be a flexible, patient individual who will take the steps necessary to build up confidence and competence in the learners.

h. Interactive Technical Documentation

Many institutions are trying to find alternative ways to work with technical documentation for the purpose of eliminating the difficulties involved in the operation and maintenance of huge volumes of paper manuals of a technical nature. Therefore, hypertext principles for management of information are of special importance in a technical context, because they allow to access large amounts of textual and visual data in an associative fashion

Many concepts for providing technical support are visual or structural and reasoning in these situations demands immediate access to visual information. Multimedia systems rely on a high degree of interactivity and also heavily exploit visual metaphors such as graphics and icons. Therefore, these features of multimedia systems provide technical support.

Multimedia presentation and hypermedia programs are now effectively used in interactive technical documentation because it permits:

1. greater flexibility in presenting and searching for information contained in the instructional manuals;
2. better interaction through electronic exchange of technical information;
3. reduction in training cost.

In this approach, the domain-specific knowledge is represented by a structured collection of knowledge objects. In the simplest form, a knowledge object consists of: a fact, a production rule, a written or spoken text, a digitalised sound clip, an image, a video clip, etc.

Complex knowledge objects are more or less dynamic structures of objects. Such objects are designed in such a way that they can be used as building blocks for the construction of various utilities such as: performance support system, multimedia presentation and video or hypermedia programs.

i. ERNET (Education and Research Network)

In this era of globalisation and hyper-competition, the concept of teaching has under gone radical changes. Learning and dissemination of information are becoming more important in the new global society. Internet-based education and e-learning are becoming popular in present-day education.

India has been one of the countries which is attempting to technologise education and communication. The first effort of its kind in the country, can be traced back to the efforts taken by the Department of Electronics of the Govt. of India to initiate a project 'ERNET' with the funding from UNDP. The objective of this project was to create expertise in Research and Development (R&D) and Education in the areas of networking and Internet in the country. ERNET is dedicated to the above mission.

Today ERNET is the largest nationwide terrestrial and satellite network with its subsidiary centres located at all premier educational and research institutions in the country. Focus of ERNET is not limited to just providing connectivity, but also to meet the entire educational and research needs of institutions. Research, Development and Training are integral parts of the activities of the ERNET.

This system acts as an independent network to connect and provide ISP Services to educational institutions all over India, in academic and research activities. ERNET pioneered the internet technology in India.

The ERNET vision mission

The mission of the ERNET is to provide large - scale benefit to education and research institutions through innovation, quality development, productivity, human development and growth - If strives for excellence within the framework of the policies and mandate given by the Ministry of Information Technology.

The network aspires to be recognised as one of the most prestigious organisations offering quality service to educational institutions and programmes through innovation, speed, combined with flexibility. It has helped to empower the employees in connected sectors. This vision is the guiding principle, a realistic dream with credible and achievable outcomes in focus.

The progress of the ERNET is based on the following values.

1. Passion for perfection
2. Being different and unique
3. Eye for details
4. Improved customer relationship
5. Achieving the impossible

ICT - PRACTICE EXERCISE

1. Internet is:

A. a local computer network

B. a worldwide network of computers

C. an interconnected network of computers

D. a worldwide interconnected network of computers which use a common protocol to communicate with one another

2. The facilities available in the internet are:

i. electronic mail

ii. remote login

iii. file transfer

iv. word processing

A. i, ii B. i, ii, iii

C. i, ii, iv D. ii, iii and iv

3. Internet requires:

A. an international agreement to connect computers

B. a local area network

C. a commonly agreed set of rules to communicate between computers

D. a World Wide Web

4. Each computer connected to the internet must:

A. be an IBM PC

B. have a unique IP address

C. be internet compatible
D. have a modem connection

5. **IP address is currently:**
A. 4 bytes long
B. available in plenty
C. 6 bytes long
D. not assigned as it is all used up

6. **IP addresses are converted to:**
A. a binary string
B. alphanumeric string
C. a hierarchy of domain names
D. a hexadecimal string

7. **Internet addresses must always have at least:**
i. a country name or organization type
ii. internet service provider's name
iii. name of organization
iv. name of individual
v. type of organization
A. i, ii, iii B. ii, iii, iv
C. i, iii D. ii, iii, iv, v

8. **Internet use:**
A. Packet switching
B. Circuit switching
C. Telephone switching
D. Telex switching

9. **Internet data is broken up as:**
A. fixed length packets
B. variable length packets
C. not packetized
D. 64 bytes packets

10. **Internet packet data structure consists of:**
i. source address
ii. destination address
iii. serial number of packets
iv. message bytes

v. Control bits for error checking
vi. Path identification bits
A. i, ii, iii
B. i, ii, iii, iv
C. i, ii, iii, iv, v
D. i, ii, iii, iv, v, vi

11. The packets of an internet message:
A. take a predetermined path
B. take a path based on packet priority
C. go along different paths based on path availability
D. take the shortest path from source to destination

12. The time taken by internet packets:
A. can be predetermined before transmission
B. may be different for different packets
C. is irrelevant for audio packets
D. not covered by any of the above statements

13. By an intranet we mean:
A. a LAN of an organization
B. a Wide Area Network connecting all branches of an organization
C. a corporate computer network
D. a network connecting all computers of an organization and using the internet protocol

14. By an extranet we mean:
A. an extra fast computer network
B. the intranets of two co-operating organizations interconnected via a secure leased line
C. an extra network used by an organization for higher reliability
D. an extra connection to internet provided to co-operating organizati

15. World Wide Web:
A. is another name for internet
B. worldwide connection for computers
C. a collection of linked information residing on computers connected by the internet
D. a collection of worldwide information

16. Among services available on the World Wide Web are:

i. Encryption
ii. HTTP
iii. HTML
iv. Firewalls

A. i and ii
B. ii and iii
C. iii and iv
D. i and iv

17. A world wide web contains web pages:

A. residing in many computers
B. created using HTML
C. with links to other web pages
D. residing in many computers linked together using HTML

18. A web page is located using a:

A. Universal Record Linking
B. Uniform Resource Locator
C. Universal Record Locator
D. Uniformly Reachable Links

19. A URL specifies the following:

i. protocol used
ii. domain name of server hosting web page
iii. name of folder with required information
iv. name of document formatted using HTML
v. the name of ISP

A. i, ii, iii, iv
B. ii, iii, iv, v
C. i, iii, iv
D. i, ii, iii, v

20. A search engine is a program to search:

A. for information
B. web pages
C. web pages for specified index terms
D. web pages for information using specified search terms

21. HTML stands for:

A. Hyper Text Making Links
B. Hyper Text Markup Language
C. Higher Textual Marking of Links
D. Hyper Text Mixer of Links

22. HTML is similar to a:

A. word processing language
B. screen editor
C. scripting language
D. search engine

23. Desirable properties of a website are:

i. a meaningful address
ii. Help and search facilities
iii. Links to related sites
iv. Features to allow users to give feedback
v. Hosting on a mainframe

A. i, ii, iii
B. i, ii, iii, iv
C. i, ii, iii, iv, v
D. i, ii, iii, v

24. HTML uses:

A. pre-specified tags
B. user defined tags
C. tags only for linking
D. fixed tags defined by the language

25. HTML tags define:

A. The data types of elements of document
B. Presentation of specified elements of a document
C. The contents of the document
D. The structure of the document

26. The tag used in HTML to link it with other URL's is:

A. <A> B. <H>
C. <U> D. <L>

27. The tags used for specifying fonts in HTML are:

i. <B>

ii. <I>

iii. <U>

iv. <L>

A. (i) and (ii) B. (i) and (iii)

C. (ii) and (iv) D. (i),(ii) and (iii)

28. It is possible to display pictures (i.e, images) in HTML specification by using thetag.

A. <GR src = Picture file>

B. <PIC src =Picture file>

C. <IMG src =Picture file>

D. <GIF src=Picture file

29. SGML stands for:

A. Standard Generalized Markup Language

B. Structured General Markup Language

C. Standard Graphics Mapping Language

D. Standard General Markup Link

30. HTML and XML are markup languages:

A. Specially developed for the web B. Are based on SGML

C. Are versions of SGML D. Independent of SGML

31. XML stands for:

A. Extra Markup Language

B. Excellent Markup Links

C. Extended Markup Language

D. Extended Marking Links

32. XML uses:

A. user define tags

B. pre-defined tags

C. both predefined and user-defined tags

D. Extended tags used in HTML and makes them powerful

33. In order to interpret XML documents one should:

A. Use standardized tags

B. Have a document type definition which defines the tags

C. Define the tags separately

D. Specify tag filename

34. The advantages of XML over HTML are:

i. It allows processing of data stored in web-pages
ii. It uses meaningful tags which aids in understanding the nature of a document
iii. Is simpler than HTML
iv. It separates presentation and structure of document

A. (i),(ii) and (iii) B. (i),(ii) and(iv)
C. (ii),(iii) and (iv) D. (i),(iii) and (iv)

35. XSL definition is used along with XML definition to specify:

A. The data types of the contents of XML document
B. The presentation of XML document
C. The links with other documents
D. The structure of XML document

36. XLL definition is used along with XML to specify:

A. The data types of the contents of XML document
B. The presentation of XML document
C. The links with other documents
D. The structure of XML document

37. DTD definition is used along with XML to specify:

A. The data types of the contents of XML document
B. The presentation of XML document
C. The links with other documents
D. The structure of XML document

38. Name the person who developed first time the model of a Personal Computer(PC)

A. Alan Kay
B. Charles Babbage
C. John von Neumann
D. Elk cloner

39. ROT means:

A. Read Only Terminal
B. Reverse Order Transmission
C. Reverse Order Transaction
D. Receive Only Terminal

40. One Kilobyte (KB) exactly equals to—————Bytes.

A. 1000 Bytes B. 2048 Bytes
C. 1024 Bytes D. 512 Bytes

41. Who developed Linux Kernel?

A. Microsoft B. Richard Matthew Stallman

C. Linus Torvalds D. Vinton Cerf

42. VIRUS stands for:

A. Virtual Information Resource Under Security

B. Virtual Interactive Resource Under Siege

C. Virtual Information Resource Under Siege

D. Virtual Interactive Resource Under Security

43. First Mini Computer Developed in India.

A. TDC-316(Trombay Digital Computer in 1970)

B. TDC-512

C. PARAM 1000

D. PARAM 2000

44. The process that takes place between computer switch on and ready to use is called.

A. Loading B. Booting

C. Login D. Linking

45. The Indian city hosts the International software fest (Free Software Society) in 2008.

A. Thiruvananthapuram B. Bangalore

C. New Delhi D. Hyderabad

46. What is the use of the software 'File roller'?

A. File Merging utility

B. PDF editor

C. File compression utility

D. File conversion utility

47. Expand GIMP

A. Gnu Image Manipulation Program

B. Graphic Image Manipulation Program

C. Global Image Manipulation Program

D. Generic Image Manipulation Program

48. While increasing the size of the figures prepared in X-paint, the clarity decreased. What is the reason?

A. Because X-paint images are 'Raster images'.

B. Because X-paint images are 'Vector images'.

C. Because X-paint images provides poor quality images.

D. None of the above.

49. First Computer Virus

A. Melissa Virus, 1999.

B. Amiga, Boot sector virus, 1989.

C. Trojan

D. Elk cloner, 1982

50. Most precious award in the computer world

A. Turing Award (in the name of Alen Turing – Artificial Intelligence)

B. Knuth Prize

C. Seymour Cray Computer Engineering Award

D. Information science awards

51. The sport item in which 'Deep Blue' game software is used.

A. Billiard

B. Chess

C. Snooker

D. Rugby

52. Who discovered Mouse?

A. Douglas Engelbart

B. Don Gilbertson

C. Elk cloner

D. Vinton Cerf

53. The facility used to control a remote computer using Internet.

A. Remote login
B. Skype
C. Telnet
D. Team viewer

54. The process that gains the details in a computer without the permission of its administrator.

A. Hacking
B. Phishing
C. Stalking
D. Bullying

55. What is the use of Gnome Backer?

A. File compression utility

B. CD Writer Software

C. PDF Editor

D. Telnet

56. The foot icon in 'IT School Gnu/Linux' Panel stands for

A. GNOME Desktop(Gnu Netword Object Model Environment)

B. CUI Desktop

C. Windows based Desktop
D. KDE plasma Desktop

57. The software Dr. Geo helps the learning of:
A. Mathematics B. Geography
C. Biology D. Physics

58. How many symbols can be represented using UNICODE?
A. 63356 B. 65636
C. 65536 D. 65356

59. The persons behind Integrated Circuits (IC)
A. Jack Kilby of Texas Instruments and Robert Noyce of Fairchild Semiconductor
B. Eric Bern of Texas Instruments and Richard Noyce of Fairchild Semiconductor
C. Jack Kilby of Fairchild Semiconductor and Robert Noyce of Texas Instruments
D. Eric Bern of Fairchild Semiconductor and Richard Noyce of Texas Instruments

60. Which computer generation has the property Artificial Intelligence?
A. Sixth
B. Fifth Generation
C. Fourth
D. None of these

61. Sub folder means:
A. a folder inside another folder
B. Folder siblings
C. Substitute folder
D. Duplicate folder

62. What is Gnu grub?
A. File roller
B. Compression utility
C. Linker utility
D. Boot Loader

63. Father of Internet:
A. Vinton Cerf B. Ray Tomlinson
C. Alan Kay D. Turing

64. Name the Three main menus in IT School Gnu/Linux
A. Applications, Places, Destop

B. Places, Accessories, Programmes
C. Accessories, Places, System
D. Applications, Accessories, Desktop

65. Who discovered e-mail?
A. Stallman
B. Alan Kay
C. Ray Tomlinson
D. Vinton Cerf

Answer keys

1.D	2.B	3.C	4.B	5.A	6.C	7.C	8.A	9.B	10.C
11.C	12.C	13.D	14.B	15.C	16.B	17.D	18.B	19.A	20.D
21.B	22.A	23.B	24.D	25.B	26.A	27.A	28.C	29.A	30.B
31.C	32.A	33.B	34.B	35.B	36.C	37.A	38.A	39.D	40.C
41.C	42.C	43.A	44.B	45.A	46.C	47.A	48.A	49.D	50.A
51.B	52.A	53.C	54.A	55.B	56.A	57.A	58.C	59.A	60.B
61.A	62.D	63.A	64.A	65.C					

Unit - IX

PEOPLE AND ENVIRONMENT

1. PEOPLE AND ENVIRONMENT INTERACTION
2. SOURCES OF POLLUTION, POLLUTANTS AND THEIR IMPACT ON HUMAN LIFE
3. EXPLOITATION OF NATURAL AND ENERGY RESOURCES
4. NATURAL HAZARDS AND MITIGATION

Unit - IX

PEOPLE AND ENVIRONMENT

1. PEOPLE AND ENVIRONMENT INTERACTION

Environment is the totality or the complex of natural, built and social components that impact on human life directly or indirectly. Natural components include all the physical and natural phenomena that exist in surrounding nature. Built components include all that is around us that are built by human beings to increase their comforts. Social components constitute a set of cultural, moral and personal values and principles and their interrelations which often control human behaviour.

a. Biosphere

Biosphere is that portion of earth that is alive or where life exists. It extends from the bottom of the ocean to several kilometers up in the atmosphere, which is suitable for the existence of living organisms. This includes air, water and soil. These three are the components of the three major sub-divisions of the biosphere viz, atmosphere, hydrosphere and lithosphere respectively. These media are not completely independent of each other. Some of the atmospheric gases are dissolved in all natural waters, and moisture is present almost everywhere in the atmosphere.

1. Atmosphere: The multilayered gaseous envelope surrounding the earth is called atmosphere. The atmosphere remains in contact with all the major types of environment on the earth, interacting with them. Such interactions greatly affect their ability to support life. It filters sunlight before reaching the earth, affects climate and acts as a reservoir of several elements essential for the maintenance of life. The atmosphere surrounding the earth consists of a series of layers - troposphere, stratosphere, mesosphere, heterosphere and exosphere. The gaseous mixture of the troposphere which we call air is utilized by most organisms in respiration which helps organisms to liberate energy from food through oxidation. Air has a relatively constant composition of gases, as shown below:

Nitrogen	78.09%
Oxygen	20.93%
Argon	0.93%
Carbondioxide	0.03%
Miscellaneous	0.02%

Besides these gases, air may carry suspensions of liquids such as water in clouds and solids such as dust from ground, smoke from fires or salt from ocean spray, etc.

2. Hydrosphere: About three-fourth of the earth's surface is covered by hydrosphere, the main component of which is water. Water is one of the most unusual natural compounds found on earth, and it is also one of the most important among various compounds. Scientists believe that life on earth began in the seas. Water in some form or other is absolutely essential for the maintenance of all forms of life. Water is one of the main agents of soil formation and is the medium for several different ecosystems. It permeates the atmosphere and the outer layers of the lithosphere and has uneven distribution on the earth. Further, water in its two forms, salt water and fresh water, are two chief aquatic environments - namely marine environment and fresh water environment of the earth. The available water is not often in a form useful for human consumption, as can be seen from the following data:

97% is not available for human use since it is saline

2% is frozen as ice caps and glaciers

1% is available as fresh water

This underlines the importance of fresh water to human existence and the need for maintaining a proper balance in the use of water.

3. Lithosphere: The earth is a near - spherical, solid planet of the solar system rotating on its axis and revolving around the sun along an orbit, at a certain constant distance from the sun which varies slightly during a one - year period. The solid part of the earth is called lithosphere. The lithosphere is multilayered, the important ones being the crust, the mantle and the outer and inner core. The *core* is the central fluid or vapourised sphere having a diameter of about 2500kms. It is possibly composed of nickel and iron. The *mantle* extends for about 2900kms above the core. This is in a molten state. The outermost solid zone of the earth is called *crust* which is about 8 to 40kms above the mantle. The crust is very complex and its surface is covered with soil supporting rich and varied biological communities. Soil provides the living organisms with an environment that gives food and shelter to most living things. It also provides concealment from predators for the lesser animals.

The earth is unique among the planets in the solar system, since it alone houses life. Biosphere is the totality of living things on earth with its interacting surroundings, material resources, forces and events that organises the solar system.

b. Gaia Hypothesis

Gaia Hypothesis was introduced by James Lovelock in 1969. Gaia is the Greek Goddess of Mother earth. The mother earth concept is not alien to Indians. We imbibed the concept from the concept of 'Vasudaivakutumbakam' from Upanishads. *Gaia Hypothesis speculates that all living organisms take in energy and matter and discard waste products and hence one must be able to detect the existence of life by analysing the chemical composition of planet's atmosphere.* This hypothesis argues that there is a tight interlocking between the planet's living parts and its non living parts. It looks at life in a synthetic way, bringing together geology, microbiology, atmospheric chemistry and other disciplines. Gaia Hypothesis asserts that the surface of the earth, which is the environment of life, is really a part of life. Life actually makes and forms and changes the environment to which it adapts. Then that environment reacts with life that is growing, acting and changing with it.

c. Energy Flow

Energy can be defined as the capacity to do work. There are two kinds of energy - potential and kinetic. *Potential energy* is energy at rest. It stands for the energy associated with a body because of its physical position. It is capable of and available for work. *Kinetic energy* is that energy, which emerges from motion. It is this energy that results in work.

The storage and expenditure of energy is described by two laws of thermodynamics. The first law of thermodynamics, called *law of conservation of energy* states that energy is neither created nor destroyed. It may change forms, pass from one place to another, or act upon matter in various ways, but regardless of what transfers and transformations take place, no gain or loss occurs in the total energy. This means that energy is simply transformed from one form to another or is transferred from one place to another. When wood is burnt, the potential energy present in the molecules of wood equals the kinetic energy released, and heat is transmitted to the surrounding environment. This is said to be an *exothermic reaction*. This means a reaction which releases energy. A reaction may sometime be endothermic. This means a reaction which absorbs energy into the system. In *endothermic reaction*, energy from the surrounding gets absorbed into a reaction. For example, in photosynthesis, the molecules of the products store more energy than the reactants. The extra energy is acquired from the sunlight, but even then there is no gain or loss in total energy. What is present in sunlight is transferred to the plant. Further, though the total amount of energy involved in any chemical reaction, such as burning of wood, does not increase or decrease, much of the potential energy stored in the substance undergoing reaction is degraded during the reaction into a form incapable of doing any further work. This energy ends up as heat that helps to disorganize or randomly disperse the molecules involved, thus making them useless for further work. This can be considered as a disorder. The measure of this relative disorder is named *entropy*.

The second law of thermodynamics states that whenever energy is transformed from one kind to another, there is an increase in entropy and a decrease in the amount of useful energy. Thus when coal is burnt in a boiler to produce steam, some of the energy creates steam that performs work, but part of the energy is dispersed as heat to the surrounding air. The same thing happens also to energy in the ecosystem. When energy is transformed from one organism to another in the form of food, a large part of that energy is degraded as heat and results in an increase in the disorder of energy. The remaining energy alone is stored in the living tissue.

Three sources of energy account for all the work of the ecosystem: gravitation, internal forces within the earth and solar radiation. The last is very significant for the ecosystem.

The solar radiations which originate from the sun is the source of energy required for life and life is what sets the ecosystem apart from other natural systems.

Organisms that are included in the food chain are classified under different levels on the basis of reception and transfer of energy. These levels are said to be trophical levels. Plants that exist by receiving energy directly from the sun are called producers and they belong to the first trophic level. Those organisms that survive by eating the plants belong to the second trophic level. The organisms that get food energy by eating these organisms are said to be in the third trophic level. Thus, at each step in the food chain, food energy is transferred from one trophic level to the next higher level. About 90% of energy is lost as heat due to disorder and about 10% is passed on to the next level of consumers. The total energy that falls on green plants per one square metre per day is about 3000 Kilo Calories (Kcal). Out of this, the energy absorbed by the green plants will be roughly only 1500cal. Out of this, the amount of energy fixed by green plants will be 15 cal. The rest is lost as heat in the process of transformation of light energy into potential energy of food. 15 cal represent net primary production (PN) at the first trophic level. This part of energy is passed on to the grass-eating creatures. About 1.5 cal will be incorporated as food energy by the second trophic level (P_2). A similar degradation of energy takes place when food energy is passed on from the second trophic level to the third trophic level (P_3).

This shows that only ten percent of the energy entering a particular trophic level is available for transfer to the next higher trophic level. This is known as the Ten Percent Law.

As we move further and further from green plants, the energy available to animals of successive food levels decreases. As food energy travels from one trophic level to the next trophic level, energy component of the ecosystem moves within the ecosystem in one direction only, as in one way traffic. This *unidirectional energy flow* is a *universal* phenomenon in all ecosystems. Because of this unidirectional flow of energy a constant external supply of energy is necessary to maintain an ecosystem. Sun acts as the inexhaustible source of this external supply of energy for the maintenance of life in the ecosystem. Since this energy transmission is through the green plants to start with, the population of green plants has to be increased in order to support the human population.

d. Ecological Awareness

During early days, man did not create any threat to the environment. He lived in harmony with nature. But the explosion of population coupled with ever increasing rate of consumption has resulted in the rapid degradation of nature. Industrialisation has resulted in the depletion of non-renewable resources and atmospheric pollution. The wide spread use of fertilisers and pesticides has degraded the soil. This is adversely affecting the balance of the ecosystem. When our environment deteriorates, our civilization declines. Man's manipulation of his environment causes an environmental imbalance. Our very existence is in peril once the balance is disturbed beyond a limit. Even highly educated people are not aware of the danger that we cause to nature, in the name of development. Most of the educated people in society are illiterate when it come to environmental issues. All these necessitate programmes for creating ecological awareness among the people. Many movements were organized for this purpose. Some of these are described below:

1. Rachel Carson: Rachel Carson is one of the most influential women in the history of science. With the publication of her book, *Silent Spring*, in 1962, she single-handedly launched the American and global environmental movements. A marine biologist by training, Carson and her writing taught human beings a new way of thinking about the earth.

Carson challenged the widely accepted notion that man was destined to control nature - using injurious chemicals to control pests. She questioned the right of human beings to use chemicals like chlorinated hydrocarbons such as the DDT, where effects cannot be reversed. Her critics accused her of being hysterical, challenged her credibility as a scientist and launched a negative propaganda campaign against her books. But she continued her propaganda. As a result of the book and its reception, the Environmental Protection Agency was established in 1970 and Pesticide Regulation and the Food Safety Inspection Service were created under its auspices and the use of DDT was completely banned in the U.S. This movement gradually spread to all parts of the world.

The most bitter irony about this movement was that Carson herself became a victim of environmental toxins. Two years after the publication of Silent Spring, Carson died of breast cancer. However, she could create a view that the balance of nature is a major force in the survival of man.

2. Stockholm Conference: Since 1970, there has been a increasing awareness about the need to give special attention to environmental problems through environmental education. The United Nations reflected the global nature of this awareness when, in 1972, it organised the first International Conference on Human Environment in Stockholm, Sweden. It was attended by representatives of 114 nations and many environmentalists and nature lovers. The conference revealed a widening interest in environment education and established the generality of environmental problems. It also exposed a lack of widespread experience in tackling the problems connected with environmental issues. Perhaps the most outstanding achievement of the conference was the establishment of the United Nations Environment Programme (UNEP) which together with the UNESCO, embarked upon an International Environment Programme in January, 1975. The conference declared that June 5 will be observed as the World Environment Day, every year.

3. Rio Conference: The United Nations arranged a Conference on Environment and Development at Rio de Janeiro in Brazil in 1992 and reaffirmed the Declaration of the Stockholm Conference on Human Environment. The conference was attended by 115 heads of states and about 1000 delegates from all over the world.

The preamble of the conference states the necessity for working towards international agreements which respect the interests of all and protect the integrity of the global environmental and developmental system. Recognising the integral and interdependent nature of earth, Rio Conference proclaimed the Declaration on environment and development.

4. State of Awareness in India: India is one of the countries of the world, where the constitution emphasises the need for the protection and careful use of natural resources.

Article 48 (A) states that the State shall endeavour to protect and improve the environment, to safeguard the forests and wild life in the country.

Article 51(g) states that it is the duty of every citizen of India "to protect and improve the natural environment including forests, lakes, rivers and wild life and to have compassion for living creatures."

The following are the major activities undertaken by India for dealing with environmental issues:

1. In 1972 the Government set up a National Committee on Environmental Planning and Co-ordination (NCEPC). This apex body at the national level identifies important problems in the area and works out their solutions, and reviews connected policies and programmes. It has also funded a number of research projects on environmental preservation and biosphere studies.
2. In 1974, the Government passed a law for the prevention and control of water pollution and set up a Central Water Pollution Control Board.
3. Environmental Boards have also been set up in every State with the Chief Minister as Chairman.
4. At the centre, an environmental information service has been set up to collect information related to environmental matters from all parts of the country.
5. A separate Department of Environment has been set up by the Government of India to co-ordinate the activities and advise the government on environmental matters.
6. The introduction of Environmental Education as a curricular component at under graduate and post graduate levels has become mandatory on the part of universities by a judgement of the Supreme Court of India on the case 'M.C. Mehta Vs Union Government'.
7. In the Central Ministry, we have a portfolio exclusively for environmental protection led by a cabinet minister (Now Jayanti Natarajan)

e. Ecosystems

The ecosystems are the basic functional ecological units which include both the organisms and the non-living environment, each influencing the properties of the other and both necessary for maintenance of life. They are complex self-sustaining natural systems which include all the interactions that bind their living and non-living components together into stable systems. These interactions are of three types (i) those between organisms, (ii) the relationship between organisms and the physical environment, and (iii) the interactions of various phases of the non-living environment which mould its own change. The major ecosystems in our country are described below:

1. Forest: The word forest is derived from Latin 'foris' meaning outside, the reference being to village boundary or fence, and must have included all uncultivated and uninhabited land. Today a forest is any land managed for the diverse purposes of forestry whether covered with trees, shrubs, climbers, etc. or not. The forest biomes include a complex assemblage of different kinds of biotic communities. Optimum conditions of temperature and ground moisture responsible for the growth of trees contribute greatly to the establishment of forest communities. In addition, 50 mm rainfall is a pre-requisite for the growth of trees. The nature of soil, wind and air currents determine the distribution of forest vegetation. Normally ecologists recognise among forest communities such features as their evergreen nature, whether they are deciduous or nondeciduous, as well as their shape, whether they are broad-leaved as in tropical forests or more needle-like as in the coniferous forest and temperate forest. On the basis of these features, the forest biomes of the world have been classified into the following categories: coniferous forest, tropical forest and temperate forest. All these forest biomes are generally arranged on a gradient from north to south or from high altitude to lower altitude.

2. Desert: Deserts are the biome formed in the driest of environments. Temperature may range from very hot as in hot deserts to very cold as in cold deserts. Major hot deserts of the world are situated near the tropics of cancer and capricon, with a rain fall less than 10 mm. The most important of all hot deserts of the world is the 'Sahara - Arabia - Gobi' desert complex extending from Africa to Central Asia where rainfall is highly irregular and very insignificant. Also humidity is very low due to excessive evaporation. Fairly extensive hot deserts occur in India, South America, North America and Australia also. The cold deserts occur at high elevations where the temperature is low and rainfall is scanty as the air loses its moisture content as it ascends higher and higher. Cold deserts occur in Ladakh regions of the Himalayas - Tibet and Bolivia in the Arctic region. The hot and cold deserts may also be distinguished by differences in plant population which are mostly of the succulent type like cactus. Desert plants which tend to be shrubs are adapted to drought conditions by reduced leaf size and the dropping of leaves in dry conditions. Both these phenomena help in reducing water loss via evaprotranspiration. The animals present in the desert are reptiles, insects and burrowing rodents. All these animals possess special morphological, physiological and ethological adaptations for deserts.

3. Marine: The marine environment involving seas and oceans is large, occupying 70 percent of the earth's surface. The volume of the marine environment lighted by the sun is small in comparison to the total volume of water involved. This and the dilute solutions of nutrients limit production in the marine. All the seas are interconnected by currents, dominated by waves, influenced by tides and characterised by saline water. The seashore and banks are the homes of many organisms. The open ocean, many hundreds of kilometers away from land too supports plant and animal communities of great diversity and complexity. In the marine environment, the most important physical factors which influence marine life are light, temperature, pressure, salinity, tides and currents.

4. Estuarine: Waters of all streams and rivers ultimately drain into the sea. The place where this fresh water joins the salt water is called the estuary. Estuaries are the transitional zones between the sea and rivers and are the sites of unique ecological properties possessing a characteristic biological make up. They are semi-enclosed coastal bodies of water that have a free connection with the open sea and within which sea water is measurably diluted with fresh water from rivers. Not all rivers open into estuaries; some simply discharge their runoff into the ocean. Estuaries differ in size, shape and volume of water flow, all influenced by the geology of the region in which they occur. As the river reaches the encroaching sea, sediments carried by the stream are dropped in the quiet water. This accumulates to form deltas in the upper reaches of the mouth and shortens the estuary. When silt and mud accumulations become high enough to be exposed at low tide, tidal flats develop, which divide and braid the original channel of the estuary. At the same time, ocean currents and tides erode the coast line and deposit material on the seaward side of the estuary, thereby shortening the mouth. If more materials are deposited than is carried away, then barrier beaches, islands, and brackish lagoons appear.

5. Fresh water: The fresh water has a low percentage of dissolved salts; also, is subjected to the influence of an array of physical and chemical factors. The rise and fall of these factors very frequently affect the fauna, altering their number and diversity. There are two kinds of fresh water ecosystems. They are lentic ecosystems and lotic ecosystems. Lentic ecosystems include all standing water habitats such as ponds, lakes, etc. The **pond** is a dynamic ecosystem since the boundaries are limited and water is retained in a trough lined by terrestrial regions. The nutrients enter through surface run offs and remain in the ecosystem. The accumulation of nutrients favours luxuriant growth of flora and fauna. Lotic ecosystems include all moving water habitats such as rivers, streams, etc. **Rivers** exhibit very high degrees of variability in many characteristics, such as size, nature of flow, etc. For example the size of rivers in India varies from the big Ganga to the trickle of a small spring. In the nature of the flow they vary from raging torrents and water falls to one that may be so smooth as to be almost unnoticeable. A given river varies considerably during the course of its long journey, as it changes from a mountain brook to a large river. This is more noticeable in the abiotic factors of the environment, but all features of the ecosystem are found to vary.

6. Man-made Ecosystems: As we are all aware, man has changed the environment to a greater extent than any other species. Such changes are referred to as man-made ecosystem or artificial ecosystem. They are of various stability and duration. Familiar examples are parks and gardens, dams and reservoirs, canals, fishery tanks, aquarium, crop lands, etc.

2. SOURCES OF POLLUTION, POLLUTANTS AND THEIR IMPACT ON HUMAN LIFE

Man and his environment are inseparable. Environment is all that surrounds man. Environment not only surrounds man but it also affects him and influences him. Good environment has positive and healthy influence while bad environment has negative and unhealthy influence. In this way, environment forms the eco-system which has, quite recently, become one of the most important concerns of man. *Pollution means the act of making dirty or the act of destroying the purity of something.* Pollution is an undesirable change in physical, chemical or biological characteristics of air, water and land that may or will adversely affect human life, living conditions and cultural assets. The pollutants are the residue of things we make, sublists we create when we throw away used things, etc. *Pollutant can be defined as "a constituent in the wrong amount, at the wrong place or at a wrong time."* Environmental pollution means altering the environment in such a manner that it is unable to play its role properly. A polluted environment is not going to maintain, nourish and sustain humanity. Rather it is going to become the cause of misery and agony to the humans in the area. The most common forms of environmental pollution are air pollution, water pollution, land pollution, sound pollution and radiation pollution.

a. Air Pollution

The atmosphere is a gaseous envelope which surrounds the earth. It is the most important component of this envelope, important element since it supports life in different forms for all types of life in the biosphere. One can survive for a few days without water and for a few weeks without food but cannot live even for a few minutes without air. This points to the need for keeping air free from contamination/pollution. Air pollution may be defined as the occurrence in air, of any foreign material or gas which are harmful to man, vegetation, animals or chemical materials used for buildings and other constructed structures. The contamination of air with dust, smoke and other harmful gases may be considered as air pollution. Air becomes polluted when its natural composition is disturbed either by natural or man-made sources or by both.

Causes of Air Pollution

1. Means of transport: The waste gases thrown out by internal combustion engines in automobiles in an important source of air pollution. During the period of technological development, there has been a rapid increase in the number of vehicles. It has raised the traffic density. The motor vehicles function mostly with the energy supplied by oil in the form of petrol and diesel. When these are subjected to chemical reaction within the internal combustion engines, they release a variety of gases which are highly poisonous. Take for example, a gas like carbon monoxide which is highly poisonous and hence dangerous to all forms of life.

2. Industrialization: There is rapid industrial development in our country. New factories are being opened almost every day. The dust, smoke and gases like hydrogen sulphide, sulphates, oxides, chlorides, etc. produced by these factories while burning fuel are released to the atmosphere, causing pollution in different forms.

3. Fuel: Various kinds of fuel (fire wood, unused portions of wood etc.) are consumed in large quantities for burning, cookery, etc. manufacture dangerous chemicals, harmful particles (like cotton particles in textile factories, poisonous chemicals, etc.) Burning of these fuels produce large quantities of carbon dioxide and other poisonous gases like carbon monoxide.

4. Use of Insecticides: Different kinds of insecticides readily available in the market are indiscreetly used to destroy insects. Many of them use in distinctive molecules which remain active for several decades. These get mixed with air and thus pollute it.

5. Deforestation: As a result of population explosion people destroy forests for cultivation and habitation. Consequently, the proportion of carbon dioxide in the atmosphere increases and thus air gets polluted.

6. Lack of proper disposal of garbage: Often adequate arrangements are not available for the proper disposal of public garbage in cities. Heaps of residual material (both organic and non organic) can be seen dumped in public places. They decay and pollute the surrounding air. This becomes a health hazard in most populous cities.

7. Use of refrigerators and Air conditioners emitting chlorofluro carbon.

Consequences of Air Pollution

1. Effect on climate: The disproportionate distribution of the constituents of air ultimately results in harmful climatic changes. For example, the amount of carbon dioxide is reported to have risen by 16% in the last 100 years. Such changes disturb the condition of temperature, humidity, etc. and this change the climate of different geographic areas.

2. Effect on visibility: Dust in the air and the smoke released from various sources affect proper visibility, especially of localities in industrial areas.

3. Effect on materials: Buildings are affected adversely due to air pollution. The coating on the building get faded or blackened. Even marble walls are affected. Other materials are also affected by air pollution in different forms.

4. Effect on agriculture: Productivity decreases and the quality of agriculture products deteriorates. One of the reasons for this is that air pollution affects the growth of plants and trees.

5. Effect on man: Breathing in of impure air causes different diseases, especially respiratory and allergy diseases. The impurities are carried to the future generations.

6. Effect on ozone layer: Air pollution causes apparent depletion of the ozone layer in the atmosphere, the balance of which is of immense significance in maintaining the balance of climatic conditions.

Attempts to control air pollution at source are made in two ways as:

i. By separating the pollutants from the gases being polluted.

ii. By converting the pollutants to harmless products before their release.

b. Water Pollution

Water is the most important natural resource that sustains life on earth. It is vital for the healthy maintenance of all forms of life, including that of vegetations. We depend on water for irrigation, industry, domestic needs, drinking purpose, sanitation and disposal of waste. Streams, rivers, tanks, wells, canals, ponds, lakes, sea and oceans are the major sources of water. All these have become polluted due to unplanned and unbalanced industrial policy, urbanization and adoption of unscientific life styles. The contamination of water with soluble sewage and industrial wastes is called water pollution. This menace is the one that affects the health of living organisms most dangerously. It is now well known that impure water is the root cause of many of the dangerous diseases.

Causes of Water Pollution

1. Bathing and washing: It is a normal practice to wash clothes and take bath in rivers, canals and ponds. Animals also are washed in revers and canals. This would certainly pollute water.

2. Sewage: The dirty water is carried into rivers sewage duets, canals and ponds and even to the sea, through sewage ducts. This is one of the major reasons for pollution of natural water. This form of pollution is much more in cities.

3. Industrial wastes: Dirty water and wastes released from cloth mills, paper mills and other industrial concerns dangerously pollute water.

4. Fertilizers and pesticides: Modern agriculture relies heavily on fertilizers and pesticides. To increase production, strong fertilizers are used. Chemicals used for killing pests are poisonous materials that make water unfit for drinking and also cause dangerous diseases.

5. Detergents: Different kinds of detergents are used for cleaning purposes and these ultimately get mixed with river water. These phosphates deposited in the water make it harmful for living creatures.

6. Dust particles: Dust particles deposited in water (in a great quantity), are another source for water pollution.

7. Hot water: Discharge of hot water from power plants and factories directly affect living organisms like plants, small creatures, etc.

Consequences of Water Pollution

1. Diseases: Water pollution causes diseases such as diarrhoea, cholera, jaundice, typhoid and cancer.

2. Land pollution: Water pollution leads to pollution of adjacent land areas.

3. Negative effect on vegetation and life: Water pollution adversely affects marine vegetation and affects the life of all aquatic creatures.

In order to reduce the extent of water pollution, the sewage and factory wastes have to be cleaned before they flow into water bodies. Industrial wastes can be recycled and used for manufacturing new commodities.

c. Land Pollution

Land pollution occurs in different ways. It is both a natural and a social hazard. Land has been considered by most cultures as 'mother' or 'as goddess', from very early days of history. This is because we have to depend upon land for food as well as shelter and for other comforts. Recently, increasing incidents of land pollution have been reported. The fertility of agricultural land is decreasing because of dust storms, floods and irrational use of irrigation, and chemical polution. Lands that were once fertile have been transformed almost to deserts. Soil-erosion and increasing salinity of the soil are factors which cause new concerns for human beings. Recent reports of landslides in the mountainous areas are alarming. They are indications of the calamities the human race has to face unless proper precautionary measures are adopted to correct them.

Causes of Land Pollution

Factors which cause land pollution are:

1. Over population: Because of over population, farmlands and grasslands are fast being converted into residential sites. Construction of houses and factories is causing decline in land fertility. All these lead to land pollution.

2. Deforestation: Deforestation is causing soil erosion. Soil erosion is seriously hampering agricultural and industrial activities as well as human life.

3. Excessive use of chemicals: Indisciminate use of chemicals and synthetic manures for increasing production lead to large - scale pollution. These chemicals are slowly damaging the vitality of land.

4. Nuclear explosions: Nuclear explosions have become a part of the nuclear power race between some of the powerful nations. Hydrogen bombs, experiments using atomic weapons and nuclear explosions are causing air as well as land pollution, the fall-outs of which often spread to other parts of the world.

5. Water logging: Water logging spoils land. Croplands are specially polluted due to this practice.

Consequences of Land Pollution

The following are the major consequences of land pollution:

1. Decrease of farmland
2. Shifting of cultivation
3. Decrease in fertility
4. Imbalance in the constitution of the atmosphere

d. Sound Pollution

Unwanted or injurious forms of sound is called *noise.* The intensity of noise (noise pollution) can be measured using the unit called *decibel.* The mildest sound that human ear can detect is called *threshold of hearing.* WHO has prescribed standard sound as 55 decibel during the day and 45 decibel at night. Sound pollution is a new hazard for the already polluted environment. The sweet and natural sounds of birds, rivers, house-hold wheel and the bullock cart have now been replaced by jarring sounds which has no end. The whole world is in the grip of sound pollution.

Causes of Sound Pollution

1. Vehicles for human transportation: Different types of vehicles like aeroplanes, trains run using steam engines, etc. produce a variety of unpleasant and jarring sounds. Such sound cause discomfort to the ear and could cause psychological disturbance and related diseases.

2. Loud speakers: These days loud speakers are used for various purposes mostly for propaganda. This not only disturbs the peaceful existence of humans but also stands in the way of people to conduct their day-to-day life activities (eg: learning, conversing, teaching, etc).

3. Mass media: Mass media played in high pitch - especially the TV and the tape recorders, etc. have become big hazards for people living in crowded cities.

4. Industries: Textile mills, printing presses, engineering establishments, and workshops, etc. all produce unbearable noise and thus cause sound pollution.

5. Defense equipment: Use of equipments like tanks, artillery, rocket launching activities, explosions, firing practice, supersonic planes, etc. produce extremely loud noise, leading to large-scale sound pollution.

Consequences of Sound Pollution

1. Deafness: Constant exposure to dangerously loud noise often cause problems to ears, thereby resulting in partial or total deafness.

2. Effect on pregnant women: Prenatal development of the child is adversely affected by sound pollution.

3. Effect on the nervous system: Blood pressure, mental tension, heart disease develop in many cases, as the after-effect of pressure on nervous system created by sound pollution. Patients suffering from hyper tension cannot withstand the stress of loud noise.

4. Efficiency of individuals: Efficiency in work gets decreased when sound increases. It is a common experience that works which need concentration cannot be done in the midst of distracting sounds.

e. Radiation Pollution

Radioactive substances are most toxic, as compared to organic poisons. Nuclear war materials, test explosions, working of power plants and the use of radio-isotopes in medicines, industry and research are the main sources of radioactive pollution that could threaten or degrade the quality of environment.

Causes of Radiation Pollution

1. Natural processes: Rocks and soil sources containing radium, uranium, thorium, potassium, carbon, etc. are affected by natural forces resulting in radiation. This is what is described as 'natural process'.

2. Human activities: Atomic explosions, nuclear reactors and other radiation sources, use of materials such as iodine, strontium, plutonium, cobalt, etc. are some of the other sources of radiation pollution created by human activities.

Consequences of Radiation Pollution

1. Active effects: These refer to the after effects that occur after radiation. Its severity will depend on the dose and type of radiation, size and type of tissue or organ exposed to radiation and the duration of the explosion. The basic damage that occurs is the damage to the DNA. This causes damage to the tissues of many internal organs like liver, reproductive system, etc.

2. Late effects: Late effects manifest months and years after the exposure. Carcinogenesis is one example of the late effect. Another one is the genetic damage.

Central and State Pollution Control Boards

In our country several legislative measures have been adopted to prevent and control different undesirable actions that might hamper the quality of the environment. The most important among these are:

1. The Water (Prevention and Control of Pollution) Act, 1974
2. The Air (Prevention and Control of Pollution) Act, 1981
3. The Environment (Protection) Act, 1986, and
4. The Motor Vehicles Act, 1988

These are implemented through the Central Pollution Control Board (CPCB). There are State Pollution Control Boards (SPCB) to advise respective state Governments on matters connected with environmental pollution.

Major Global Environmental Threats

Of the existing environmental threats the following are the major ones:

1. Depletion of Ozone Layer
2. Green House Effect and Global Warming
3. Deforestation, Soil erosion, Desertification and Drought
4. Pollution of Air, Water, Land and Sound

5. Acid Precipitation / Rain
6. Toxic Waste Disposal
7. Resource Depletion, in the following forms:
   i. Depletion of ground water
   ii. Depletion of biological diversity
   iii. Depletion of genetic variability
   iv. Depletion of ocean bed resources
   v. Depletion of non-renewable resources
8. Energy Crisis - Nuclear energy, Radiation and Synthetic Fuel.
9. Biological Weapon Research and Nuclear Arms Race
10. Conquering the Outer Space.

3. EXPLOITATION OF NATURAL AND ENERGY RESOURCES

Man, with his capacity to adapt himself to a wide variety of environments and environmental changes, has earned a dominant place in the biosphere. Today, he is occupying the top most position in the food chain of the earth's ecosystem. The successful survival of modern man in an ecosystem is made possible by his ability to establish and maintain homeostasis with the external environment.

For his existence man will have to utilize the resources of nature. Primitive man exploited nature in a moderate way to meet his basic needs. But the modern man is exploiting the natural resources on a large scale. As a result, there has been much disruption of the functioning of natural environment and depletion of natural resources. These disturbances have caused great concern to man. No man can survive without proper management of his environment. The effects of man's disturbances can be minimised through the understanding of the ecological principles.

a. Renewable and Non-renewable Resources

A resource has been defined as "any means of attaining given ends" or "a source of supply or support generally held in reserve." Natural resources include total natural environment, that is the entire surface layer of earth. So the natural resources are the components of atmosphere, hydrosphere and lithosphere.

It is universally accepted that human survival depends on resources which nature has bestowed on him. It is also increasingly realised that rapid population growth has resulted in increasing the pressure on natural resources.

Based on the abundance and availability, natural resources can be divided into two categories. They are renewable and non-renewable resources.

1. Renewable resources

These resources get naturally replaced after being used. For example, underground water drawn from wells may eventually be replenished by rainwaters or by extra flow from underground sources. When trees are cut down, new ones either come up or can be planted. These resources reappear by quick replacement, recycling and reproduction within a particular time. Some of these processes are described below:

1. Water: Access to water is a vital human need. Most of the early human settlements were founded close to rivers that would serve as a reliable source of water. As the populations of these settlements grew, the amount of water supplied by the streams often became insufficient. People then resorted to bringing water from a more distant source through canals, or digging wells to obtain water from underground sources.

A reliable water supply is critical not only for survival and health, but also for agriculture and industry. Globally, crop irrigation accounts for 73 percent of the demand for water, while it is 21 percent for industry and 6 percent for domestic use. These proportions may vary from one region to another. Demand in each of these sectors has been increasing due to population growth and improvements in the standard of living. Water resource management focuses on two major concerns: (1) how to preserve the *quality* of water resources, and (2) how to ensure that an adequate *quantity* of water will be available to meet present and future needs. Although water is, in principle, a renewable resource, the time it takes to replenish a particular water source can be much longer than a human lifetime in certain cases.

2. Biomass: Biomass, in the form of fuel wood, is the dominant source of energy. Biomass fuels - primarily fuel in the form of wood and animal dung are still widely used throughout the world. Not all biomass energy is obtained directly from the burning of plant matter. Charcoal is a form of biomass energy in which the wood is not burned directly in the stove or fireplace but is first transformed into a more convenient and longer lasting form of fuel. In regions where people rely heavily on charcoal, there will be significant chance of deforestation. Proposed energy and fuel-wood conservation schemes focus on more efficient charcoal - producing techniques and the development of more efficient stoves for domestic use.

Animal dung is a form of biomass energy in which plant matter is processed in the digestive tracts of animals before it is made available for use as a fuel. Methane (CH_4) gas can also be derived from decaying animal wastes, collected and used as a fuel, referred to as *biogas*.

Biomass is, in principle, a completely renewable form of energy. However, as mentioned earlier, all energy sources have some drawbacks and environmental impacts. As with all renewable resources, in regions where the rate of use exceeds the rate of replenishment, the resource becomes disproportionally depleted.

2. Non-renewable resources

There are resources which cannot be replenished within a small period. For example, it can take millions of years for the formation of fossil fuels or for deposits of valuable ores of metals. That is why, even though many of the geologic processes that once formed such deposits are still occurring, these are considered non renewable resources.

They are being renewed on a geologic time scale rather than a human time scale. Some of these are described below:

1. Fossil fuels: The fuels which are formed from fossils and from which energy can be made available for various purposes are called fossil fuels. It includes coal, petroleum, natural gas, oilshales and tar sands.

2. Ores of metals: The mineral deposits are not distributed uniformly all over the surface of the earth. They are concentrated only in certain parts. India is not self-sufficient in metal ores. Every year we are spending huge amounts for importing metals. At the same time, India occupies a very prominent position in the world market for the production of some minerals like manganese, mica, iron, aluminium, megnesium, titanium and thorium.

It is therefore very much desirable that natural resources are conserved carefully and managed wisely to avoid their wastage and depletion. The conservation and efficient utilisation of resources is vital for meeting the demands of the growing population.

b. Human Interaction with the Resources

The guiding principle in the management of both renewable and nonrenewable resources is *sustainability*, ie., cautious, planned utilization of earth resources to meet current needs without degradation of the viability of ecosystems or jeopardization of the future availability of those resources. Certain strategies leading to this end are discussed below:

1. Sustainable management of renewable resources

The primary concern in the sustainable management of renewable resources is to ensure that thc rate at which the resource is being utilized does not exceed the rate at which it is being replenished or regenerated. This means that water should not be withdrawn from wells at a faster rate than the rate at which rainwater or underground sources is replenish underground water storage. In the same way, the number of trees cut down should not exceed the number of new saplings planted.

2. Sustainable management of nonrenewable resources

The focus of nonrenewable resource management differs from that of renewable resource management. The salient feature of nonrenewable resources is that they can be depleted; the more we use, the less they remain. The Earth is essentially a *closed system*. The amount of matter in the Earth System is fixed. The existing solid earth resources are all that we have and probably all we will ever have.

c. Limits to Growth

The *carrying capacity* of an ecosystem is the maximum population of a given organism that the ecosystem can hold without being degraded. There is a carrying capacity for the biosphere, for each ecosystem and for each habitat at any given time. If the population increases beyond the carrying capacity of a habitat, the environment deteriorates and the population may decline sharply until a new equilibrium is reached.

It is too well-known the rapidly growing world population of the present is straining the earth's carrying capacity to sustain it. We are not only running out of non-renewable resources but are also faced with the danger of renewable resources failing to regenerate due to the increased rate of resource extraction.

d. Sustainable Development

Development that meets the needs of all people, improves the quality of their lives, sustains the existence of the diverse types of organisms and maintains the quality of the environment can be termed as *sustainable development.*

It is the process of social and economic betterment that satisfies the present needs and at the same time maintains future options and conserves natural resources and diversity. *Sustainable development is ecologically equitable, culturally durable and socially enjoyable.*

1. Goals of sustainable development

These are:

1. Survival and well being of human beings
2. Survival and well being of all other living species
3. Survival and well being of the physical surrounding of the environment, natural resources and all factors that support life on earth.

2. Conditions for achieving the goals of sustainable development

These are:

1. Planned utilization of resources and protection of natural wealth.
2. Change in attitudes and life styles of human beings and accepting ideal behavioural patterns based on environmental ethics.

3. Sincere love, care and consideration for all other living beings

The concept of sustainability has emerged as a key issue in developmental planning only very recent times. The Stockholm Conference on the Human Environment 1972 and the International Conference of Population held in 1984 at Mexico City reflected concern for sustainable development. The International Planned Parenthood Federation (IPPF) and the International Union for Conservation of Nature and Natural Resources (IUCN) have both stressed this new approach to development. The recent report of the World Commission on Environment and Development 1987, headed by the Norwegian Prime Minister Mrs. Brundtland has used sustainable development as a key concept in all the future developmental activities to be undertaken by world nations.

The need for sustainable development presupposes that the present development is not sustainable and hence it is urged to opt for a new approach to development. There is need to integrate population, environment and natural resource policies into national development strategies so as to ensure environmentally sound sustainable development. The major emphasis of this approach is on meeting the basic needs of the people and improving their quality of life without adversely affecting the viability of the environment. It demands new development strategies which anticipate environmental problems and the adoption of sound precautionary measures to avoid the resultant problems.

However, the goal of sustainable development is not likely to be attained unless the implications of inter-relationships among population, environment, resources and development are adequately understood and appreciated by the people in a country. There is a pressing need to create correct perceptions about the growing degeneration and degradation of the environment and critical resources in the context of rapid population growth and the adoption of lop-sided policies used for development. The correction lies in creating a general awareness and proper understanding of environmental problems and their possible solutions supported by legislative action and political will.

4. NATURAL HAZARDS AND MITIGATION

Environmental management is "the reduction or minimisation of the impact of human activities on environment; it should be a scientific policy to protect the overuse or misuse of environmental resources". Environmental management involves a fair balance of socio-economic development of the society on the one hand and maintenance of environmental quality on the other.

It is true that ecological balance and ecosystem stability are duly maintained by nature itself; but the craze for extending modern scientific, technological and industrial developments have disturbed the ecological balance and the ecosystem stability through rapid exploitation of natural resources and the adoption of improved means of transportation and heavy industrialization. Thus, human activities of modern man have disturbed the natural and harmonious relationship between man and his environment. Therefore, it is the need of the day to employ the concept of environmental management, with a view to maintain the ecological balance and stability of the ecosystem.

Environmental management is meant to harmonise the relationship between environment and man so that the quality of the environment and of human society may be improved. This objective can be achieved by checking the destructive activities of man as well as the use of conservation, protection, regulation and regeneration of nature. It is related to a rational adjustment of man with nature, which involves judicious exploitation and utilization of natural resources without disturbing ecological balances and ecosystem equilibrium. Environmental management is, therefore, a compromise between ecological balance, ecosystem stability and human socio-economic progress and thus it must take into account the ecological principles governing nature and the socio-economic needs of the society.

a. Environmental Impact Assessment (EIA)

EIA is an important aspect of environmental management, because under this aspect, plans, projects and programmes are assessed in order to evaluate or visualize their adverse effects on the quality of the environment. The impact of human activities involving the use of natural resources on the quality of the environment is known as *environmental impact*. Evaluation of this impact is called *environmental impact assessment*. It attempts to produce estimates of environmental consequences in terms of the probable adverse effects of the proposed projects. On the basis of this estimate, proposed plans and project actions are evaluated so as to check the adverse effects by making environmental changes accountable.

b. Methods Used for Environmental Impact Assessment

We have seen that the major objective of the EIA is to promote efforts towards the prevention of damages or adverse effects of human activities on the environment and to optimise the health conditions and welfare of man. Such assessments are based on scientific studies of the conditions of ecological balance and stability of the ecosystem of particular geographic domains, with reference to proposed plans or projects. The following steps are generally employed in the procedures used for impact assessment:

1. describe the present nature of environment
2. specify the details of the project and its needs and objectives
3. examine in detail the effects of the project on the environment
4. estimate the short term and long-term impacts of an environmental policy/action
5. propose and compare alternatives arising out of the project
6. present a projection of the future of the site with and without the project
7. suggest remedial measures for activities which will help to reduce the evils of the new project.

A variety of methodologies and procedures for EIA have been devised by scientific research organisations to suit the differences in the nature of the proposed plans and projects as well as in the environmental conditions of the proposed sites.

c. Environmental Impact Assessment Report

There are several standard methods and modalities used for the preparation of EIA Reports. The one that is generally used in India is the check list method. The evaluation authorities prepare appropriate check lists for the different types of projects. Normally such reports spell out the purpose of the project, description of the intended actions, justification/need of the project, present status of the project, time schedule of major activities, location of the project including important facilities in and near the area, characteristics of the population served by the project, overall cost and details of the environment prior to proposed action within an area of 20 km radius.

d. Disaster Management Plan (DMP)

The DMP is a 'loss control process' which reduces the risk at large following a disaster, in the most efficient manner possible, at minimum cost. The disasters such as flood and drought that are likely to cause risks to the project have to be assessed for this purpose. It involves the co-ordination of all the safety activities so that the most appropriate protection is provided in minimum time and at minimum cost.

e. Environment Management Plan (EMP)

The EMP is to be formulated after the assessment of the beneficial as well as the adverse environmental impacts of the project and recommending necessary measures for controlling and for reducing its adverse effects. It should include a scheme for resettlement of those who are to be evacuated from the project site and details of measures proposed for controlling the adverse effects caused by the project on the environment. It should invariably give details of relocation of roads, drainage, etc. affected by the project and the schemes envisaged for reducing and/or for avoiding or reducing the adverse effects of such changes on the environment.

Environment movements in India

As a result of the lethargic attitude of the Governments towards environmental problems, people's movements have come up in different parts of the country to find solutions to deal with the inadequacies. These movements have addressed the problems such as exploitation of natural resources, deforestation, environmental pollution and problems faced by the local inhabitants. The major movements that played very important roles in creating environmental awareness among the people are enumerated below:

a. The Bishnoi Movement

The Bishnoi Movement was started by Sage *Sambaji* in Western India about 400 years ago. When the villages were hit by a severe drought, he advised the people not to cut down trees and to maintain nature in its pristine form. This idea attracted the people and they established the Bishnoi villages which became green and prosperous. After three centuries when the ruler of the region ordered the cutting down of trees for building a palace for his use the people resisted. They ran to the groves and hugged the trees. The axe-men cut them into pieces and restarted the felling of trees. When the king heard about it, he ordered that cutting of trees be stopped and Bishnoi cult of tree worship was resumed with new vigour.

b. The Chipko Movement

The Chipko Movement was started in 1973 against deforestation in the Chameli District of Uttar Pradesh. The people resisted the attempt of Simud Company to fell trees with the permission of the Government. The company suspended the felling activity temporarily. Later when the forest department tried to cut trees, the people did not allow the axe-men even to enter the forest. The movement under the strong leadership of Sunderlal Bahuguna and Chandi Prasad Bhat spread to other parts of the country. It is this movement that is responsible for the enactment of the Forest Protection Act 1980 and the creation of a separate Ministry for Environment at the Centre.

c. The Narmada Bachao Andolan (NBA)

The Narmada Bachao Andolan in an important environmental movement led by the veteran Gandhian Baba Amte and Medha Patkar, for proper rehabilitation of over one lakh people evicted on account of the Narmada Valley Project. The ousted people, spread across Gujarath, Maharashtra and Madhya Pradesh, started a strong movement against constructing large dams. They opposed the efforts of the Government to move the people living in the area to some other place. The new ideological stance was centred on policies like questioning the development policies which cause impoverishment of a large section of people of the area concerned, for the benefit of people from other areas. The question of equity in the case of development was raised very strongly by the movement. The new attitude generated by the movement has spread to other parts of the country.

d. The Baliyapal Movement

The Government of India decided to setup a missile testing range at Baliyapal in Orissa. Baliyapal became a centre of controversy because the area intended to be taken over for the testing range was a very fertile area with a thick population. The protestors demanded that the project be located in a less densily populated and less developed areas. The Government could not implement its decision because of the strong resistance of the people.

e. The Silent Valley Movement

The silent valley movement was spearheaded by Kerala Sastra Sahitya Parished (KSSP) against the proposed Hydro Electric Project in the Kunthipuzha which is a tributary of Periyar. The objection to the project was that the project will cause irrevocable damage to the last remnants of tropical evergreen forests of the Western Ghats for generating 75 mega watts of power. As a result of the strong protest the then Prime Minister Smt. Indira Gandhi appointed a Committee headed by the famous agricultural scientist Dr. M.S. Swaminathan to examine the costs and benefits of the project. On the recommendation of the Committee, the Government dropped the project.

In a way, these movements have succeeded in drawing the attention of the public in this country to the tragedy that is going to fall on us once we follow unscientific policies for exploiting the environment. The importance of such movements should not be ridiculed or underrated. The lessons they provide should guide us in our new policy-making. What is required is to adopt positive steps to face the probable threats to nature and humanity alike.

People and Environment – PRACTICE EXERCISE

1. Biotic environment includes:

A. producers B. consumers
C. decomposers D. all the above

2. Decomposers include:

A. bacteria B. fungi
C. both bacteria and fungi D. animals

3. Abiotic environment does not include:

A. air B. water
C. soil D. plants

4. Vermicomposting is done by:

A. fungus B. bacteria
C. worms D. animals

5. The group of organisms which convert light into food are called

A. autotrophs B. heterotrophs
C. decomposers D. omnivores

6. Which one the following is not biodegradable?

A. vegetables B. fruits
C. earthworm D. aluminium foil

7. Animals which are active at night are:

A. Owl B. Rat
C. Cockroaches D. All the above

8. Animals that can tolerate the extreme heat of the desert are:

A. Rats B. Camels
C. Sheep D. Lion

9. Air pollution on a large scale is caused by:

A. Insecticides B. Sewage pollutants
C. Smoke D. Loud Speakers

10. Which one of the following diseases are spread by the contamination of drinking water?

A. Scurvy B. Typhoid
C. Malaria D. Anaemia

11. The Van Mahotsav Day is observed in India on:

A. Second of October B. First of December
C. Tenth of August D. First of July

12. Which of the following wastes will not get decomposed by the bacteria to form the compost?

A. Kitchen waste from food B. Plastic and polythene bags
C. Dead plants D. Bodies of insects living in the soil

13. Which of the following problems is not created by noise pollution ?

A. Diarrhoea B. Hypertension
C. Deafness D. Irritation

14. The green colour seen in plants is caused by a pigment called:

A. glucose B. nitrogen
C. chlorophyll D. oxygen

15. Air is composed of gases, water vapours and:

A. dust particles B. raindrops
C. fog D. smoke

16. Quinine used in the treatment of malaria, obtained from:

A. Eucalyptus plant B. Aconite plant
C. Cinchona plant D. Ginger plant

17. The major source of energy on the earth is:

A. electricity B. coal
C. sunlight D. valcanoes

18. When trees are cut, the amount of oxygen present in that area:

A. decreases B. increases
C. both (A) and (B) D. remains almost the same

19 The major natural process through which plants reproduce is called:

A. Hybridization B. Grafting
C. Pollination D. Tissue culturing

20. Nearly 71% of the earth surface is covered with:

A. land B. air C. water D. coal

21. A non-material source of energy is:

A. Solar Energy B. Mined Fuels from the depths of the earth
C. Nuclear Energy D. Natural fuels on the surface of the earth

22. An ideal way to dispose plant waste is:

A. Burning them
B. Composting
C. Dumping them in a water body
D. Use them for industrial purposes

23. An eco-friendly slogan which has a strong uppeal to human safety is:

A. 'Do or die'
B. 'Birds of the same feather fly together'
C. 'Say no to crackers'
D. 'Time and tide wait for none'

24. The term 'dead' with respect to a water body refers to:

A. The inability of a water body to sustain aquatic life
B. The ability of a water body to sustain aquatic life
C. The inability of a water body to flow
D. The heating or cooling of a water body

25. A water borne contagious disease:

A. Small pox
B. Meningitis
C. Diarrhea
D. Cholera

26. Water suitable for drinking is called:

A. Pure Water
B. Portable Water
C. Potable Water
D. Natural Water

27. The best household method to obtain potable water:

A. Filtration
B. Boiling
C. Chemical Treatment
D. Decantation

28. The specific aim of ecology is to study:

A. to study the distribution patterns of plants and animals on earth
B. to study how best we can preserve diversity of life on earth
C. to study the implications of atmospheric pollution
D. all the above.

29. Which among the following is not a contribution of the natural ecosystems?

A. Atmospheric gas regulation
B. Water supply
C. Nutrient cycling
D. Climate regulation

30. Which hypothesis, concerning the diversity of life on earth, states that "biodiversity and ecosystem function are not linked"?

A. idiosyncratic hypothesis
B. rivet hypothesis
C. redundancy hypothesis
D. diversity-stability hypothesis

31. A natural phenomenon that causes atmospheric pollution is:

A. global warming
B. polar melting
C. greenhouse effect
D. desertification

32. One of the best solutions to get rid of non-biodegradable wastes is:

A. burning
B. dumping
C. burying
D. recycling

33. Animal dung can be described as:

A. biodegradable waste
B. non-biodegradable waste
C. hazardous waste
D. toxic waste

34. Which of the following is biodegradable?

A. iron nails
B. plastic mugs
C. leather belts
D. silver foil

35. Which of the following is non-biodegradable?

A. animal bones
B. nylon
C. tea leaves
D. wool

36. Name the process in which a harmful chemical enters the food chain and gets concentrated at each level in the food chain.

A. Concentration
B. Biomagnification
C. Expansion
D. Pollution

37. Most of the trash your family throws away each day ends up getting.......

A. Recycled
B. Burned
C. Landfilled
D. Eaten

38. Which are of the following does not contain mercury?

A. Computer disks
B. Blinking lights in sneakers
C. Fluorescent light bulbs
D. Thermometers

39. Which items are recyclable?

A. Plastic milk jugs
B. Cereal boxes
C. Aluminum soda cans
D. All of the above

40. What is the environmentally friendly way to dispose of used tires?

A. Send them to a landfill
B. Recycle them into a playground matting
C. Dump them in a ditch along the roadway
D. Collect them and put them in a big pile for burning

41. What is groundwater?

A. Water that is spilled onto the ground

B. Water beneath the ground surface

C. The bottom part of a lake or river

D. Rainwater that lands on the ground

42. Which material do we use most and then throw a way?

A. Glass B. Paper

C. Aluminum D. Plastic

43. Used oil should be disposed of by:

A. Burning it in open air

B. Watering it down and spreading it as a fertilizer

C. Collecting it in a sealed container and selling it those who use it

D. Keeping in the garage for several years before throwing it away in the trash

44. Our waterways are polluted by:

A. Waste oil implied on the banks of water ways

B. Leaking of gasoline from storage tanks

C. Domestic waste carried to them by rain

D. All of the above

45. The effect of pollution is first and most marked on:

A. natural flora of a place B. natural balance of our environment

C. natural geochemical cycles D. all the above.

46. The major threat for human existence in present-day world is:

A. reduced agricultural land

B. higher levels of population increase and environmental pollution

C. deforestation D. high degree of population increase.

47. Maximum amount of air pollution is caused by:

A. use of household detergents and pesticides

B. automobile exhausts and chemicals from industries

C. sewage and pesticides spread through water

D. sewage and industrial effluents.

48. Which of the following groups contain only biodegradable items?

A. Grass, flowers, leather B. Grass, wood, plastic

C. Fruit peels, cakes, and oil D. Cake, wood, grass

49. Which of the following constitute a food chain?

A. Grass, wheat, mango
B. Grass, goat, human
C. Goat, cow, elephant
D. Grass, fish, goat

50. Which of the following are environment friendly practices?

A. Carrying cloth bags to put purchases in while shopping.
B. Switching off unnecessary lights and fans.
C. Walking to school instead of getting your mother to drop you in her scooter.
D. All the above.

51. Which of the following is an omnivorous animal?

A. Deer
B. Cat
C. Lion
D. Goat

52. Which of the following is not an abiotic component of an ecosystem?

A. Plants
B. Soil
C. Air
D. Sunlight

53. Which of the following is a man made ecosystem?

A. Pond
B. Aquarium
C. Lake
D. Forest

54. Producer represents the .... trophic level.

A. First
B. Second
C. Third
D. Fourth

55. The D.D.T. is:

A. non-degradable pollutant
B. degradable pollutant
C. green house gas
D. none of these

56. Which of the following acts as a main factor in water pollution?

A. Pesticides
B. Industrial wastes
C. Detergents
D. NH_3

57. Minamata disease is a pollution-related disease which results from:

A. release of human organic waste into drinking water
B. accumulation of arsenic into the atmosphere
C. release of industrial waste mercury into fishing water
D. oil spills into sea

58. The disease 'Minamata' is caused by .... poisoning.

A. Lead B. Zinc

C. Mercury D. Copper.

59. Ozone hole is largest over

A. Antarctica B. Europe

C. Africa D. India.

60. Phosphate pollution is brought about by:

A. Phosphate rocks

B. Fertilizers

C. Phosphate rocks and sewage

D. Fertilizers and sewage.

61. Most harmful environmental pollutants are:

A. Natural nutrients in excess

B. Human organic wastes

C. Non-biodegradable chemicals

D. Waste animal feed.

62. Thermal pollution is more common near

A. Hot water springs

B. Coal-based power plants

C. Tropical regions

D. Temperate regions.

63. Pollution indicator plants

A. Purify atmosphere

B. Resist pollution

C. Are sensitive to pollutants

D. Can indicate onset of rain.

64. Positive pollution of soil is due to:

A. Reduction in soil productivity

B. Addition of wastes on soil

C. Excess use of fertilizers

D. All of these.

65. Smog is a combination of:

A. Lava and steam

B. Smoke and fog

C. Water and smoke

D. Air and water.

66. The pollutants discharged by jet planes are:

A. Smoke B. Fog C. Smog D. Aerosols

67. Sound becomes a hazardous noise pollution if its level is above:

A. 30 dB B. 80 dB C. 120 dB D. 150 dB

68. Pollution of water is caused by:

A. Industrial effluents B. Sewage

C. Farm run off D. All of these

69. Which one among the following is an air pollutant?

A. aerosols B. sewage C. DDT D. fertilizers

70. Which of the following does not cause soil erosion?

A. wind B. overgrazing C. sun D. water

71. Acid rain is due to:

A. combustion of fossil fuels B. oil slick

C. oxides of sulphur D. nuclear wars

72. Among the most harmful non-biodegradable waste is:

A. cowdung B. plastics C. garbage D. radioactive waste

73. An example of a renewable resource is:

A. clay B. sand C. water D. fossil fuels

74. Which one of the following is a non-biodegradable waste?

A. manure B. cow durig C. plastics D. garbage

75. The main source of water is:

A. rivers B. rain C. ponds D. canals

76. Pollution is not caused by the use of:

A. solar energy B. wood

C. petrol D. unsaturated hydrocarbons

77. In water pollution, industries are said to be the:

A. line sources B. point sources

C. area sources D. none of these

78. Which one of the following is a non-renewable resource?

A. Coal B. Wate C.Forest D. Turtle

79. Which one of the following is biodegradable?

A. Cow dung B. Coke cans C. Polythene D. DDT

80. Maximum threat to the earth is from:

A. soil erorsian B. Ozone hole formation

C. Water pollution D. Soil erosion

81. A lake, in which fishes die in bulk, is described as a:

A. Oligotrophic Lake B. Eutrophic Lake

C. Organotrophic Lake D. None of these

82. A disease which commonly affect industrial workers is:

A. Silicosis B. Fluorosis

C. Asthma D. None of these

83. The concentration of DDT while it travels along the food chain:

A. Increases B. Stays constant

C. Decreases D. Fluctuates randomly

84. Greenhouse effect is caused by:

A. Green plants B. Infrared rays

C. UV rays D. Ultra violet rays

85. Which one of the following countries are responsible for maximum air pollution?

A. India B. USA C. Russia D. Britain

86. If the fertilizers are added to fresh water:

A. Plants will die

B. Eutrophication will occur

C. Fish population will decrease

D. Overall animal population will increase.

87. The part of the body most effected by fluoride pollution is:

A. Brain B. Teeth C. Heart D. Kidney

88. In almost all Indian metropolitan cities like Delhi, the major atmospheric pollutant(s) is/are:

A. Oxides of nitrate

B. Suspended particulate matter (SPM)

C. Carbon dioxide and carbon monoxide

D. Oxides of sulphur

89. Biological Oxygen Demand (BOD) is a measure of:

A. Amount of oxygen needed by green plants during night

B. Amount of carbon monoxide inseparably combined with haemoglobin

C. Industrial wastes poured into water bodies

D. Extent to which water is polluted with organic compounds

90. In 1984, the Bhopal gas tragedy took place because the chemical methyl isocyanate:

A. reacted with ammonia B. reacted with carbon dioxide

C. reacted with water D. reacted with carbon monoxide

91. Blood analysis of a patient reveals an usually high quantity of carboxyhemoglobin content Which of the following conclusions is most likely to be correct? The patient has been inhaling polluted air containing unusually high content of ______

A. Chloroform B. Carbondioxide

C. Carbon monoxide D. Carbon disulfide

92. The noise level of an average office is normally close to:

A. 20 db B. 30 db C. 40 db D. 60 db

93. A lake with an inflow of domestic sewage rich in organic waste is likely to develope into:

A. a dry lake very soon due to algal bloom

B. a lake where the number of fishes increase more profusely because of the availability of better nutrients

C. a lake in which fishes die in large numbers because of depletion of oxygen

D. a lake with more number of aquatic food web organisms.

94. The world environment day is celebrated each year on:

A. 6th of June B. 5th of June

C. 6th of August D. 5th of May

95. Which gas leakage was responsible for the Bhopal Gas Tragedy of 1984?

A. Hydrogen Cyanide
B. Ammonia
C. 2,4-Dichlorophenoxy Acetic Acid
D. Methyl Isocyanate

96. Which is the full form of the abbreviation BOD:

A. Biological Oxygen Demand
B. Biosynthetic Oxygen Demand
C. Biogeochemical Oxygen Destroyer
D. Biogeochemical Oxygen Dilution

97. The term 'Bio-magnification' refers to the:

A. growth of organisms due to increased food consumption
B. increase of population of living things in an environment
C. blowing up of environmental hazards by environmentalists
D. increase in concentration of non-degradable pollutants as they pass through food chain.

98. Which one of the following chemicals is not used for disinfection of drinking water?

A. Chlorine B. Ozone C. Chloramine D. Phenyl

99. Prolonged liberal irrigation of agricultural fields is likely to create the problem of:

A. acidity B. aridity C. salinity D. metal toxicity

100. In your opinion, which is the most effective way to conserve the plant diversity of an area?

A. By creating biosphere reserve
B. By creating botanical gardens
C. By developing seed bank
D. By greater use of tissue culture method

101. Which one of the following is a pair of endangered species?

A. Garden Lizard and Mexican Poppy
B. Rhesus Monkey and Sal Tree
C. Indian Peacock and Carrot Grass
D. Hornbill and Indian Aconite

102. If the Bengal Tiger becomes extinct, the result would be:

A. Hyaenas and Wolves will become scarce
B. The wild areas will be safe for man and domestic animals

C. The gene pool of the animal will be lost for ever

D. The population of beautiful animals like deers will get stabilized.

103. Which one of the following pairs of geographical areas show maximum biodiversity in our country?

A. Sunderbans and Rann of Kutch

B. Eastern Ghats and West Bengal

C. Eastern Himalayas and Western Ghats

D. Kerala and Punjab

104. Genetic diversity in agricultural crops is threatened by:

A. introduction of high yielding varieties

B. intensive use of fertilizers

C. extensive intercropping

D. intensive use of biopesticides

105. Which of the following is considered a hot-spot of biodiversity in India?

A. Aravali Hills B. Western Ghats

C. Indo-gangetic Plain D. Eastern Ghats

106. Which of the following pairs an animal plant combination represents endangered organisms in India?

A. banyan and black duck

B. Bentinckianscobarica and red panda

C. tamarind and rhesus monkey

D. cinchona and leopard

107. Which of the following represents a correctly - matched pair of an endangered animal and a national park?

A. Great Indian Bustard : Keoladeo National Park

B. Lion : Corbett National Park

C. Rhinoceros: Kaziranga National Park

D. Hamadryad: Pappinisseri Snake Park

108. What is the main cause for the extinction of some species in tropical forests?

A. Deforestation B. Afforestation

C. Pollution D. Forest Fire

109. In India, we find mangoes with different flavours, colours, fibre-content, sugar content and even shelf-life. The large variation is on account of:

A. species diversity B. induced mutations
C. genetic diversity D. hybridization

110. Biosphere reserves differ from national parks and wildlife sanctuaries because in the former:

A. human beings are not allowed to enter
B. human beings act as an integral part of the system
C. plants are given greater attention than animals
D. living organisms are brought from all over the world and preserved for posterity

111. Read the two statements 'X' and 'Y'

Statement 'X' : Diversity observed in the entire geographical area is called gamma diversity. **Statement 'Y'** : Biodiversity decreases from high altitude to low altitude.

Identify the correct choice from these given below:

A. statement 'X' is correct, but 'Y' is wrong
B. statement 'Y' is correct, but 'X' is wrong
C. both the statements 'X' and 'Y' are correct
D. both the statements 'X' and 'Y' are wrong

112. The world biodiversity day is celebrated annually on

A. 5th June B. 29th December
C. 22nd April D. 16th September

113. Which of the following two regions of our country are known for their rich biodiversity?

A. Western Ghats and Eastern Himalayas
B. Western Ghats and Deccan Plateau
C. Eastern Himalayas and Gangetic Plain
D. Trans Himalayas and Deccan Peninsula

114. Quinine is obtained from the:

A. bark of *Cinchona* B. root of *Cinchona*
C. wood of *Cinchona* D. leaves of *Cinchona*

115. Extinction of a species in a food chain is compensated by:

A. food chain B. ecological pyramid
C. food web D. none of these

116. More than 70% of world's fresh water is contained in:

A. Polar ice
B. Glaciers and mountains
C. Antarctica
D. Greenland

117. Which one of the following pairs is mismatched?

A. fossil fuel burning: release of CO_2
B. nuclear plant; radioactive wastes
C. solar energy: greenhouse effect
D. becomes burning: release of CO_2

118. Which one of the following statements pertaining to pollutants is correct?

A. DDT is a non-biodegradable pollutant
B. Excess fluoride in drinking water causes osteoporosis.
C. Excess cadmium in drinking water causes black foot disease.
D. Methyl mercury in water may cause 'Itai Itai' disease.

119. Montreal protocol which calls for appropriate action to protect the ozone layer from human activities was passed in the year:

A. 1985
B. 1986
C. 1987
D. 1988

120. The 'blue baby syndrome' results from:

A. excess of TDS (total dissolved solids)
B. excess of chloride
C. methaemoglobin
D. excess of dissolved oxygen

121. Photochemical smog pollution does not contain:

A. PAN (peroxy acyl nitrate)
B. ozone
C. nitrogen dioxide
D. carbon dioxide

122. Effect of pollution is observed first on:

A. microorganisms
B. food crop
C. green vegetable
D. herbivores

123. Pollution from animal excreta and organic waste from kitchen can be most profitably minimized by:

A. storing them in undeground storage tanks
B. using them for producing biogas

C. vermiculture

D. using them directly as biofertilizers

124. Which one of the following is an environment-related disorder, together with its main cause?

A. Block lung disease (pneumoconiosis) found mainly in workers in stone quarries and crushers.

B. Blue baby disease (methaemoglobinaemia) due to heavy use of nitrogenous fertilizers in the area.

C. Non-hodgkin's lymphoma found mainly in workers involved in manufacture of neem based pesticides

D. Skin cancer mainly in people exposed to benzene and methane

125. The Montreal Protocol refers to:

A. persistent organic pollutants

B. global warming and climatic change

C. substances that deplete the ozone layer

D. biosafety of genetically modified organisms

126. Increased asthmatic attacks in certain seasons are related to:

A. eating fruits preserved in tin containers

B. inhalation of-seasonal pollen

C. low temperature

D. hot and humid environment

127. Effect of pollution is first marked on:

A. microorganism

B. green vegetation of an area

C. food crops

D. none of these

128. Ozone hole or ozone depletion results in:

A. LTV radiation reaching the earth

B. Cataract

C. increase in skin cancer

D. all the above

129. Ultra violet radiation from sunlight causes a reaction that produces:

A. fluorides

B. carbon monoxide

C. sulphur dioxide
D. ozone

130. Which of the following metals cause harmful effects on the humans?

A. Lead B. Cobalt
C. Uranium D. All of these

131. Ozone is spread in the swimming pool because:

A. it acts as a disinfectant
B. it absorbs UV radiations
C. ozone can be created easily from O_2 (Oxygen)
D. all of the above

132. A study of the accidents at the Chernobyl Nuclear Power Plant in the Soviet Union and the severe air pollution in Mexico would lead to the conclusion that:

A. technology can cause its own problems throughout the world
B. international trade is more profitable than domestic commerce
C. modern science cannot solve most political problems
D. agricultural nations have caused major world environmental problems

133 A major environmental problem affecting Latin America, Sub-Saharan Africa, and Southeast Asia has been:

A. air pollution
B. Deforestation
C. disposal of nuclear waste
D. acid rain

134. Many scientists believe that 'greenhouse effect' is the result of:

A. overgrazing on land in developing nations
B. using large amounts of gasoline, oil, and coal in developed nations
C. testing nuclear weapons in violation of the Nuclear Test Ban Treaty
D. using natural fertilizers to increase crop production

135. The amount of carbon dioxide in the atmosphere has increased in recent years. Environmentalists suggest that this change is a direct result of the:

A. improper storage of solid and nuclear waste
B. overcutting of forests and the increased use of fossil fuels
C. dumping of inorganic material into lakes and rivers
D. use of herbicides and toxic substances such as asbestos and DDT

136. In developing countries, the use of wood, charcoal, and dung as major sources of energy has created an increase in:

A. economic dependence on industrialized nations

B. sales and profits for international oil corporations

C. deforestation and other environmental problems

D. nuclear waste products

137. A negative impact of the use of modern technology is that:

A. levels of air and water pollution increases to dangerous levels

B. economic opportunities are frequently limited

C. contacts with other cultures decrease

D. international trade is limited

138. In Latin America, the deforestation of the Amazon rain forest has led to:

A. the maintenance of a traditional way of life

B. the discovery of new medicines

C. overpopulation in rural regions

D. environmental dangers

Answer keys

1.D	2.C	3.D	4.C	5.A	6.D	7.D	8.B	9.C	10.B
11.D	12.B	13.A	14.C	15.A	16.C	17.C	18.D	19.C	20.C
21.A	22.B	23.C	24.A	25.D	26.C	27.B	28.A	29.B	30.A
31.C	32.D	33.A	34.C	35.B	36.B	37.C	38.A	39.D	40.B
41.B	42.B	43.C	44.D	45.B	46.B	47.B	48.C	49.B	50.D
51.B	52.A	53.B	54.A	55.A	56.A	57.C	58.C	59.A	60.D
61.D	62.B	63.B	64.D	65.B	66.D	67.B	68.D	69.A	70.C
71.C	72.D	73.C	74.C	75.B	76.A	77.A	78.A	79.A	80.B
81.B	82.A	83.A	84.B	85.B	86.B	87.B	88.C	89.D	90.C
91.C	92.D	93.C	94.B	95.D	96.A	97.D	98.D	99.C	100.A
101.D	102.C	103.C	104.C	105.B	106.B	107.C	108.A	109.C	110.B
111.A	112.B	113.A	114.A	115.C	116.A	117.C	118.A	119.C	120.C
121.D	122.A	123.B	124.B	125.C	126.B	127.B	128.D	129.D	130.D
131.A	132.A	133.B	134.B	135.B	136.C	137.A	138.D		

Unit - X

HIGHER EDUCATION SYSTEM: GOVERNANCE, POLITY AND ADMINISTRATION

STRUCTURE OF THE INSTITUTIONS FOR HIGHER LEARNING AND RESEARCH IN INDIA; FORMAL AND DISTANCE EDUCATION; PROFESSIONAL/TECHNICAL AND GENERAL EDUCATION; VALUE EDUCATION: GOVERNANCE, POLITY AND ADMINISTRATION; CONCEPT, INSTITUTIONS AND THEIR INTERACTIONS.

Unit - X

HIGHER EDUCATION SYSTEM: GOVERNANCE, POLITY AND ADMINISTRATION

It is essential for a teacher in higher education institution to know about its structure, functions and administrative set up if he has to function effectively within the system. A researcher is also expected to acquaint himself with the above details, and also the details of the facilities available in various institutions of higher learning and national level research centres. This section is meant for discussing and developing the most important notions about the structure and functions of the higher education system in India - its governance, the various aspects of its management, the different categories of higher education institutions in India and the leading centres of research in India, the facilities they provide, and a host of other such details. Without this knowledge a teacher in higher education as a researcher cannot guide his student for further studies and higher researches. The teacher himself can enhance the horizons of his knowledge, availing of the facilities offered by these institutions. The knowledge about the objectives and functions about the UGC also is essential. The UGC has included this component in the revised curriculum for NET/JRF Examinations for obvious reasons.

It may be noted that higher education institutions always aim at growing continuously and developing themselves to cope with the changing environment. Those who decide to enter into this field are expected to have a clear understanding about the different institutional components and its built-in structure.

The development of higher education in India has a chequered history in the post independent period. There were only about 21 universities and 495 colleges in India (with a total enrolment of about 2 lakhs students) at the time of independence. As of 1989 there were 174 universities including deemed universities, 10 Institutions of National Importance and 5646 colleges. It is estimated that at the time of independence about 5 million students were enrolled in these institutions and about two hundred and fifty thousand faculty members were working in these institutions. The numbers as of 2012 will be much more. This developmental profile shows unprecedented growth in the higher education system. As we advance through two more decades the growth and development of the institutions are likely to be far more than what it is even in developed countries. We have different categories of universities - Central Universities, State Universities, (affiliating and non affiliating), Federal Universities, Open Universities, (both national as well as state open universities), Deemed Universities (both gevernmental as well as private), Uni-faculty and Multi faculty Universities, etc. Open universities like IGNOU and Central Universities like Aligarh have established its study centres and community colleges through out in the length and breadth of the country. More and more Autonomous Colleges have come up in the recent past.

National level institutes like NITs, IITs and IIMs have also come up. More and more extensions have been made by the universities, establishing departments in new subject areas like e-commerce, population and demographic studies, bio-informatics, nano technology, oceanography, etc. etc.

Recently the Central Minister for Human Resource Development, Mr. Kapil Sibal has emphasized the need for qualitative and quantitative development of higher education institutions. We need to establish new universities, new departments in the existing universities, new research institutes, more and more institutes of technologies. Our existing facilities are woefully inadequate to meet the needs of the fast growing knowledge based economy of 21st century. The Knowledge Commission has recommended the need for achieving a higher target in higher education - around 1500 universities for the country to cater to its fast-changing developmental needs.

A democratic country like India cannot be satisfied with a uni-track system of higher education. Different institutions have defferent administrative and managerial structures. It is therefore essential that every teacher in higher education is well-acquainted with these structural, functional and managerial differences practised by the different institutions.

In the following pages we are presenting an over view of different facets of higher education in the country. This will provide the knowledge base for answering the questions relating to Indian higher education.

HIGHER EDUCATION IN INDIA

Our achievements in higher education in terms of quantity in impressive. But this is not true of quality. The resource crisis assumed alarming dimensions in the recent decades allthough the outlook in improving will go beyond our expectations. The neighbouring countries like China, Taiwan and Korea are investing much more in higher education than India. The demand for higher education has surged forward rapidly. Higher education is being looked upon as the means of entry into the dynamic world of growth and progress and the basis of enduring economic security. But we also have to note that less than 0.01 percent of the aspirants get admission to our National Level Institutes of Technology. The entrance examinations are attempted by millions of students; but a negligibly small percent alone qualify for selection.

We are aware that there is a decline in the land-based economy of the country shifting to the services and knowledge-based industries. Therefore the need for providing more resources, more infrastructure and more resourceful faculty members for the new areas has been recognized. It was in this context, the possibility of private investors in the higher education sector was explored by the central and state governments. Curretly we have several institutions of higher education run by private managements, trusts and societies as self-financing institutions.

It is very clear that higher education in India has been the single and most potent means of social mobility. From the lower strata of the society, if anyone has grown up to higher and respectable status, it is only through higher education. The challenge confronted by those in the lower economic and social strata is the tough competitive examinations that require intensive preparation. Despite scholarships and financial assistance, the avenues are still closed to the rural and economically less privileged aspirants.

History of Higher Education in India

India was one of the oldest of cultures to think of formal higher education which was open to scholars even from other countries. We had ancient centres of excellence attracting students from various parts of India and abroad. The two ancient Indian universities, Nalanda and Taxila, were reputed centres of learning and attracted foreign scholars like Fahien and Huen Tsang. Our superiority in subjects like astronomy, mathematics, philosophy, ayurveda, metallurgy and many other such branches of knowledge brought us international acceptance in the early AD's. Our 'Pathsalas', 'Vihars' and 'Madrasas' flourished at various points of history, in different parts of the country during the pre-British period. British Education in India was launched in a big way in 1835, with Lord Macaulay's minutes. He, in fact popularised Western education through the medium of English. The spread of English education paved the way for the establishment of schools, colleges and universities of the British type in the governmental and aided sectors, Missionaries played a key role in the spread of education by starting private institution with Government recognition. Universities of Bombay, Madras and Calcutta were established in 1857 following the recommendations of Woods Dispatch. Universities of Allahabad and Punjab were established in 1887. There were extremely inadequate facilities for higher education in the early years. In 1951, only one person per thousand had the opportunity to get admission to higher education institutions. The situation has changed dramatically during the past 60 years.

In the post independence period, the main thrust has been on education for the masses. Realizing that national development is possible only through human resource development, our leaders appointed the great scholar, philosopher and visionary Dr. S. Radhakrishnan as the Chairman of the first education commission to be set up in independent India. This Commission (the University Education Commission'), came out with several useful recommedation for giving a new shape and thrust to Indian higher education. The commission has a clear vision about products turned out by our universities. It hoped that the new generation graduates would dedicate their services to the upliftment of the downtrodden people of the country inhabiting its rural and backward areas. It was also envisaged that the democratic, secular and socialist values of our nation would be upheld by the beneficiaries of higher education, which will eventually be taken into the grass-root level.

In the Second Five Year Plan of the country gave a new life to Indian education as can be seen from its focal thrust areas:

- Basic education
- Expansion of elementary education

- Diversification of secondary education
- Improvement of standard of colleges and universities
- Implementation of social education and cultural development programmes

Consequently, Regional Engineering Colleges (RECs) and IITs were established in India. A large number of research and teaching institutions and universities were established covering disciplines like technology, sciences, social sciences, management studies and arts. By the year 1991, 5.8 persons per thousand were enrolled in Higher Education. This showed that we have advanced considerably in our ability to provide higher education. From 0.01 percent enrolment in higher education, to 5.8 percent is a significant improvement.

By 1988-89 the enrolment in higher education had increased to 7.5 per thousand. In 2004, there were 300 universities in the place of 21 universities in 1947. This included deemed universities, 18 medical universities and 40 agricultural universities. There were more than 15000 colleges and the enrolment rise was up to 10 millions. The present enrolment in higher education would be much higher due to the establishment of a number of open universities, self-financing colleges and several new generation colleges offering higher education in almost all modern disciplines.

EXISTING NATIONAL LEVEL RESEARCH AND TEACHING INSTITUTIONS

A large number of research institutions were established during the different five year plans. A good number of councils and organizations like the following were created for supporting research in important subject areas:

- Indian Council of Social Science Research (ICSSR)
- Indian Council of Historical Research (ICHR)
- Indian Council of Philosophical Research (ICPR)
- National Council of Rural Institute (NCRI)
- Department of Science and Technology (DST)
- Department of Biochemistry (DBT)
- Department of Oceanography (DO)
- Council of Scientific and Industrial Research (CSIR)
- Indian Council of Agricultural Research (ICAR)
- Indian Council of Medical Research (ICMR)
- Defence Research & Development Organization (DRDO)
- National Council for Teacher Education (NCTE)
- All India Council for Technical Education (AICTE)
- English & Foreign Language University (EFLU)
- National Institute of Mental Health and Neuro Sciences (NIMHNS)
- National Academy of Science (C.V. Raman Institute)
- National University of Educational Planning & Administration (NUEPA)

(The list is not exhaustive)

All these institutes and councils promote research in almost all the important subject areas by providing scholarships and other support facilities. The ICSSR supports 28 research institutes in different parts of the country in partnership with the state governments. It provides funds for research scholarships and awards and for supporting the infrastructural and academic facilities. The Institute of Economic Growth (IEG) provides training for Indian Economic Service (IES) probationers. Excellent faculties could be developed through these institutes for taking up the challenge of teaching post graduate students. Under the ICSSR, some institutions have undertaken commendable teaching and research programmes as Deemed Universities. Gokhale Institute of Politics and Economics (GIPE) at Pune and Indira Gandhi Institute of Development Research (IGIDR) at Mumbai, are examples.

The CSIR has a network of 40 laboratories and 80 field centres in various parts of the country to undertake fundamental and applied research in diverse areas of science and technology. These laboratories have been globally recognized for their excellence in infrastructure. Aero - space Engineering, Drugs and Pharmaceuticals, Bioscience and Biotechnology, Petrochemicals, Leather Processing, Geophysics and Radio physics are some of the subjects for which research facilities are provided by CSIR. M.Phil, Ph.D and Post Doctoral degree programmes are offered in many of the new generation universities, especially in the deemed universities.

Open and Distance Learning (ODL) centres also cater to the needs of about 30 percent of learners in higher education. Multimedia approach is adopted by distance learning centres to ascertain better interaction with the distant learners. The IGNOU with its several Regional Centres and study centres is the most prominent university functioning in the field of distance education.

The UGC has always been supporting research and learning facilities in various universities and colleges by sanctioning funds for improving infrastructural facilities and for operating research projects. The UGC also monitors and grants accreditation to the colleges and universities evaluating periodically the functional aspects of the institutions. The National Assessment and Accreditation Committee (NAAC) has been constituted for visiting institutions and awarding grades like A+, A, B+, B and so forth to institutions, taking into account the levels reached by them as per an accepted set of parameters and its ability to maintain quality. The major responsibility of the UGC is to maintain and strengthen higher education by improving standards of teaching and research.

UGC and its functions

The UGC was constituted in 1956 as a statutory body which was a landmark event in the development of higher education in India. Now the areas on which the UGC concentrates its attention are:

- setting up of autonomous colleges
- redesigning courses to meet the demands of the emerging new world scenario of higher education
- setting up State Councils for Higher Education
- developing and experimenting alternate models of managing universities and colleges
- conducting competitive examinations for recruiting teachers and research fellows
- providing training and orientation to teachers through Academic Staff Colleges
- accreditation of institutions based on the reports of NAAC visiting team of experts
- Allotment of funds for developing infrastructure and for organizing seminars, workshops, research projects and for Faculty Improvement Programmses (FIP) for encouraging teachers to conduct research for their professional enhancement

DIFFERENT TYPES OF INSTITUTIONS FUNCTIONING IN HIGHER EDUCATION

The present system of affiliating colleges to a university (what we refer to as the affiliating system of higher education) was introduced in 1857 when the first 3 universities were established in Madras, Bombay and Calcutta. This was in the pattern of the University of London, which at that time was functioning as an affiliating university. London university was the only affiliating university at the time. It discontinued this deal within the next two decades. But we in India, have stuck to this model for no obvious reason. At present we have higher education institutions managed in different ways.

a. Affiliated Institutions

Under this model, several colleges in a locality (termed the jurisdiction of a university) are affiliated to a university set up by the State. This at the time was beneficial for spreading education to remote areas rather than concentrating within the university campus. The colleges follow a common curriculum prescribed by the affiliating university. The examinations are conducted by the university and certification also is done by the university. Large number of students get access to higher education because colleges can be located in all convenient points in the jurisdictional area. The standards of the institutions under a university are likely to vary significantly. The universities to which these colleges are affiliated are not partners in the academic programmes of the colleges. Appointment of faculty members is done by the colleges themselves, but with the approval of the University.

b. Unitary Universities

Unitary universities are more or less residential in nature, and consist of a few colleges/schools directly controlled by the university. Students have to stay either in college hostel or within reach of the college, within the prescribed jurisdiction of the

University. Classes are organized in the campus. There are no affiliating colleges or institutions for these universities. Examples of this type of university are Aligarh, Banaras, Lucknow and Baroda Universities. medical, engineering colleges, and other colleges, various departments offering education science/social science and humanities are all functioning within the same campus. This assumption is no longer in vogue in universities like Aligarh. The Aligarh Muslim University has recently started its sub-centres even in such remote areas like Kerala. A typical university has several schools of faculties for academic and research purposes.

c. Federal University

A federal university shares is academic programmes and curriculum transaction activities with its constituent colleges. The University of Delhi is federal in its character. Such universities do not affiliate colleges, but they have constituent colleges. The academic and administrative functions are managed by the federating university. University controls course designs, selection of staff and conduct of exams. Teachers in constituent colleges have better representation in academic bodies of the University.

d. Affiliating University

Affiliating University campus will have its own departments of teaching and research within the campus. At the same time, many colleges in the jurisdiction of the university are affiliated to it. The major functions of affiliating university are to:

a. Decide the course of study, prepare curriculum (by the academic councils and board of studies constituted by the university)

b. Setting question papers, conducting examinations and evaluating answer books and

c. Issuing mark lists and certificates to the candidates.

These universities have no administrative or financial control over the colleges other than approval of appointment of teachers. University of Mysore, Kerala, Madras and Kolkata are examples.

e. Deemed University

Normally universities are statutory bodies established under either a state act/ central act promulgated by one of the State Assemblies or by the Parliament of India. Considering the technical difficulties implied in creating a statutary university, the UGC came out with an alternative model, where an institution is given the statutory power. But the UGC is empowered to declare it as a 'deemed university' with the power to describe courses and confer degrees. This is done taking into account its unique nature and functions and its academic reputation. Professional bodies like ICAR and ICMR function like universities, establishing institutions under their auspices and controlling professional education. The Gandhigram Institute of Rural Development and the Kerala Kalamandalam are examples of two 'deemed universities' performing in two unique areas. Deemed Universities generally function in specialized areas like law, engineering, medicine, ayurveda, etc.

f. Autonomous Colleges

A college that functions with considerable freedom in a number of academic functions, but functioning as an affiliated college in other respects is what is termed an autonomous college. These colleges have the autonomy to decide its curriculum, conduct examination, appoint faculty members, start courses etc. and award degrees and certificates signed by university authorities. Those colleges which have established academic reputation and adequate facilities are assessed by the UGC and conferred the status of autonomous colleges. The National Policy of Education 1986 has favoured the setting up of autonomous colleges and use this rationale for decentralizing the planning and management functions in higher education.

Higher Education - PRACTICE EXERCISE

1. What is the expansion of ICAR?

A. Indian Council of Aeronautic Research
B. Indian Council of Agricultural Research
C. Institute of Culture and Aesthetic Resources
D. Institute of Cochlear and Auditory Research

2. Match the institutions in column A with their locations in Column B

A	B
i) National Diary Research Institute	(a) – Mysore
ii) National Institute of Mental Health and Neuro-sciences	(b) – Hyderabad
iii) All India Institute of Speech and Hearing	(c) – Mumbai
iv) Central University of English and Foreign Languages	(d) – Karnal
v) Babha Atomic Research Centre	(e) – Bangalore
	(f) – New Delhi
	(g) – Madras

A. i) (g) ii) (f) iii) (b) iv) (a) v) (e)
B. i) (b) ii) (c) iii) (a) iv) (d) v) (f)
C. i) (c) ii) (a) iii) (b) iv) (g) v) (e)
D. i) (d) ii) (e) iii) (a) iv) (b) v) (c)

3. Which of the following is not a fundamental Right according to the Indian Constitution?

A. Right to property
B. Right to speech
C. Right to practice religion
D. Right to travel

4. An autonomous college is different from an affiliated college because:

A. the former has no syndicate and senate to regulate its functions

B. the later has control over a larger jurisdiction

C. the later has centralized system of curriculum and evaluation

D. the former has freedom for deciding curriculum, conducting examination and awarding degrees or diplomas.

5. Which of the following is not a function of the UGC?

A. Allocate and sanction funds for colleges and universities for development and research

B. Disseminate information pertaining to higher education

C. Appoint heads of institutions in colleges and universities, and nominate syndicate members

D. Decide standards and recommend measures for improvement.

6. Which of the following is a Central University?

A. Mumbai University B. Delhi University

C. Madras University D. Calcutta University.

7. The members of the Indian Cabinet are selected by:

A. The President of India B. The Prime Minister

C. The Lok Sabha D. The Lok Sabha and the Rajya Sabha

8. The Planning Commission in India is:

A. a Constitutional body B. an official body

C. a non-governmental body D. an Advisory body

9. The National Council for Teacher Education (NCTE) is a:

A. Statutory Body B. Advisory Committee

C. Regulatory Agency D. Supervisory Committee

10. The UGC started functioning following:

A. a resolution in the Parliament

B. a bill in the Parliament

C. the recommendation of the Education Commission

D. the recommendation of the Advising Committee of the Central Cabinet

11. Which of the following is known as 'the soul' of the Indian Constitution?

A. Preamble B. Fundamental Rights

C. Directive Principles D. Articles

12. Mother Teresa Women's University is situated in:

A. Chennai B. Pune
C. Kodaikanal D. Mumbai

13. Gandhigram Rural Institute functions at:

A. Dindigal B. Delhi
C. Bangalore D. Rajkot

14. National University of Educational Planning and Administration (NUEPA) is at:

A. Hyderabad B. Bangalore
C. Delhi D. Baroda

15. Inter University Centre of Astronomy and Astrophysics is situated in:

A. Bhubaneswar B. Pune
C. Calcutta D. Mysore

16. Match the Institutions in Column A with their locations in Column B.

A	B
i) Indian Academy of Science	(a) New Delhi
ii) Central Institute of Indian Languages	(b) Hyderabad
iii) National Institute of Research of Food and Nutrition	(c) Pune
iv) Centre for Cultural Resources and Training	(d) Mysore
v) National Film Institute	(e) Chennai
	(f) Bangalore

A. (i) (f) (ii) (a) (iii) (c) (iv) (b) (v) (e)
B. (i) (f) (ii) (d) (iii) (b) (iv) (a) (v) (c)
C. (i) (a) (ii) (c) (iii) (d) (iv) (e) (v) (b)
D. (i) (e) (ii) (f) (iii) (c) (iv) (b) (v) (a)

17. Which of the following is not a professional body functioning in Indian higher education?

A. ICAR B. ICMR
C. ICHR D. ICSE

18. The major difference between a Federal University and Unitary University is that:

A. Federal University has more autonomy
B. Unitary University has meagre infra-structural facilities

C. Federal University shares teaching activity with its constituent colleges

D. Unitary University has a higher status.

19. The authority to declare an institution as Deemed University is vested in:

A. The Central Government B. The Parliament

C. The NAAC D. The UGC

20. The National Literacy Mission launched in 1988 aimed at attaining at lest 75% literacy of children by:

A. 2004 B. 2005 C. 2006 D. 2008

21. 20th September 2004 is a day of importance to educators in that it was in this day the:

A. the programme called Ekalavya was started

B. the lap-top computer was introduced for the first time

C. Edusat was launched

D. Surveyor (American Satellite) sent photographs of planet Mercury.

22. Santhi Niketan in Kolkotta was established by:

A. Bankim Chandra Chatterji

B. Subhash Chandra Bose

C. Surendranath Banerjee

D. Rabindranath Tagore

23. A University without affiliated colleges, but having its own constituent colleges is known as a:

A. Central University B. Federal University

C. Unitary University D. Deemed University

24. Which among the following is not an agency for funding for the maintenance and quality of universities and colleges?

A. UGC B. ICAR C. ICMR D. NAAC

25. Which of the following is a Central University?

A. Mumbai University B. Delhi University

C. Madras University D. Kolkatta University

26. The Indian Parliament consists of:

A. Prime Minister, Cabinet and Speaker

B. MPs, Speaker, Deputy Speaker and Cabinet

C. President, Lok Sabha and Rajyasabha

D. President, Vice President and Cabinet

27. Where is the Netaji Subhash National Institute of Sports located?

A. Patiala B. Delhi

C. Bangalore D. Mumbai

28. National Defence Academy is at:

A. Delhi B. Khadakvasla

C. Mumbai D. Hyderabad

29. Match the items in column 'A' with those of column 'B'.

A	B
(a) Unitary University	(i) Bangalore University
(b) Deemed University	(ii) Gandhigram University
(c) Federal University	(iii) Aligarm Muslim University
(d) Affiliated University	(iv) IGNOU
(e) Open University	(v) Delhi University

A. (a) iii, (b) v, (c) ii, (d) i, (e) iv

B. (a) ii, (b) iii, (c) i, (d) iv, (e) v

C. (a) i, (b) ii, (c) v, (d) iii, (e) iv

D. (a) v, (b) iii, (c) iv, (d) ii, (e) i

30. AICTE is a statutory Committee with powers to regulate:

A. Centre for technological Education

B. Teacher Education

C. Technical Education

D. Commercial Education

31. The expanded form of NAAC is:

A. National Aeronautic and Applied Science College

B. National Agency of Aviation Courses

C. National Academy of Administrative Careers

D. National Assessment and Accreditation Council

32. The Chancellors of an affiliating state university will be:

A. The Education Minister of the State

B. The Governor of the State

C. A Senior educationist nominated by the state

D. A reputed person elected by the Syndicate of the university

33. Aligarh University and Benaras University are both:

A. Affiliating Universities
B. Federal Universities
C. Unitary Universities
D. Deemed Universities

34. What is the most important limitation of affiliating universities in India?

A. The college affiliated to a university are situated in remote areas
B. The university does not work as a partner in research and academic pursuits of the colleges
C. The curriculum is centralized
D. The university interferes with the administrative functions of the colleges.

35. Which one of the following is not time of an the affiliating University?

A. It prescribes the curriculum for conducting courses in affiliated universities
B. It is responsible for conducting examinations for certification of students in affiliated institutions
C. It has ownership over the buildings and properties of the college
D. It approves the appointment of teacher in affiliated institutions

36. The most important characteristic of a unitary University is that:

A. The academic activities are organized with in the campus and most of the students stay in the hostels or in the vicinity.
B. The teachers in the Unitary University are better qualified and paid.
C. The salary of the teachers is being paid by the Central Government.
D. Sophisticated facilities are provided in those universities.

37. Which one of the following is not a unitary university?

A. Aligarh Muslim University
B. Banaras Hindu University
C. Bangalore University
D. Lucknow University

38. Which is the most important feature of a federal university?

A. The departments in the university function autonomously.
B. The teaching work is shared by the university with its constituent colleges.
C. The Vice Chancellor of the university is appointed by the Central Government.
D. The university has no colleges affiliated to it and all the institutions are located within its campus.

39. The statutory body with the authority to declare an institution as 'Deemed University' is:

A. The Higher Education Council of the state
B. The National Assessment and Accreditation Council
C. The UGC
D. The Ministry of Human Resource Development, Govt. of India

40. The ICMR stands for:

A. Indian Council for Mineral Resources

B. Indian Council for Manpower Research

C. Indian National Council for Marine Resources

D. Indian Council for Medical Research

41. Autonomous colleges were established in the country following the recommendations of:

A. Kothari Commission

B. Indian Education Policy – Draft Report

C. University Education Commission

D. National Policy on Education 1986

42. In autonomous college qualifies for their status based on:

A. The quality of the teaching it provides

B. The standards and reputation it has maintained in the past

C. The examination results of the college

D. The ability of the college to comply with the conditions stipulated by the university.

43. 'Open Universities' differ from regular universities mainly in terms of:

A. its ability to cater to the learning needs of a large number of students.

B. There is no rigid time schedule attendance restrictions and entry qualifications in OU

C. O.U. is run entirely with the help of multimedia institutional packages.

D. O.U. admits students from various parts of the country and abroad

44. Match the items in column 'A' with that of in column 'B'.

A	B
(i) ICHR	(a) Indian Council of Medical Research
(ii) ICAR	(b) Indian Council of Scientific and Industrial Research
(iii) ICMR	(c) International Committee for Human Resource
(iv) CSIRD	(d) Indian Council of Agricultural Research
(v) ICSSR	(e) Institute of Commerce and Social Science Research
	(f) Indian Council for Social Science Research
	(g) Indian Council for Historical Research

A. i) (d), ii) (b), iii) (g), iv) (c), v) (a)
B. i) (g), ii) (d), iii) (a), iv) (b), v) (f)
C. i) (b), ii) (f), iii) (g), iv) (a), v) (e)
D. i) (e), ii) (b), iii) (c), iv) (a), v) (d)

45. Who is the Visitor of the different Central Universities of the country?

A. The President of India
B. The Prime Minister of India
C. The Central Minister for Human Resource Development
D. The Secretary of the Human Resource Ministry

46. One of the Universities in India has the Prime Minister as its Chancellor. Which is this University?

A. Delhi University B. Banaras Hindu University
C. Viswabharathy University D. Aligarh Muslim University

47. The Indian Statistical Institute is located in:

A. Kolkatta B. Mumbai
C. Delhi D. Chenai

48. The supreme governing body of the Universities which acts on behalf of its Court/Senate is:

A. The syndicate B. The Academic council
C. The Faculty D. The Board of Studies

49. The Inter University Centre for Astronomy and Astrophysics under the UGC is located at:

A. Mumbai B. Pune
C. Hyderabad D. Delhi

50. The Tata Institute of Fundamental Research is situated in:

A. Kolkotta B. Bangalore
C. Mumbai D. Hyderabad

51. The first Education Commission in Independent India to recommend measures for improving higher education was chaired by:

A. Dr. A. Lakshmanaswami Mudaliar
B. Dr. Kothari
C. Dr. S. Radhakrishnan
D. Dr. Zakir Hussain

52. The major problem that hindered the development of higher education in India during the post-independent period was:

A. the negligent attitude of those in power

B. the poor quality of human resources in the country

C. inadequate allocation of resources and funds for higher education

D. investing all the funds for the five-year plans

53. Universities of Bombay, Madras and Calcutta were established in the year:

A. 1857 B. 1902

C. 1910 D. 1912

54. The Gokhale Institute of Politics & Economics (GIPE) is situated in:

A. Mumbai B. Pune

C. Chennai D. Bhubaneswar

55. The Indira Gandhi Institute of Development Research (IGIDR) is located at:

A. Kolkatta B. Manipur

C. Mumbai D. Baroda

56. The Open and Distance Learning System (ODL) mainly aims at:

A. democratizing higher education

B. spreading universal education

C. extending the reach of higher education to aspiring student in remote rural areas

D. vocationalisation of courses in higher education

57. The University Education Commission in India was constituted in the academic year:

A. 1948-49 B. 1956-57

C. 1964-65 D. 1986-87

58. Which education commission recommended that at least 6% of the GDP is to be spent on education?

A. University Education Commission (1948-49)

B. Secondary Education Commission (1956-57)

C. Indian Education Commission (1964-66)

D. National Policy on Education (1986)

59. The system of affiliating colleges to a university was introduced in India in 1857, following the pattern followed at the time by the:

A. Harvard University B. University of London
C. Cambridge University D. Columbia University

60. The UGC was established following the recommendations of the:

A. Mudaliar Commission B. Kothari Commission
C. Radhakrishnan Commission D. National Policy on Education

61. The UGC constituted in:

A. 1948 B. 1956
C. 1964 D. 1986

62. The All India Council for Technical Education (AICTE) as a national expert body was set up in the year:

A. 1945 B. 1947
C. 1948 D. 1949

63. The All India Council for Technical Education (AICTE) was given statutory powers in the year:

A. 1964-65 B. 1980-81
C. 1987-88 D. 1990-91

64. Academic Staff Colleges were established by the UGC with a view to providing:

A. Research facilities to teachers in colleges
B. Linkage between colleges and universities.
C. Orientation Courses and Refresher Courses for teachers in higher education.
D. Monitoring the academic activities of higher education institutions.

65. The first Open University in India was established in 1982 at:

A. Madras B. Delhi
C. Mysore D. Andhra Pradesh

66. The IGNOU was established by an Act of Parliament in:

A. 1980 B. 1982
C. 1985 D. 1992

67. The UGC was constituted in 1945 in the British pattern as recommended in:

A. Woods Dispach B. Sargent Report
C. Macaulay's Minutes D. Radhakrishnan Commission

68. The UGC started functioning in the existing pattern following a bill passed in the Parliament in:

A. 1953 B. 1954
C. 1956 D. 1964

69. The Chief Executive and the chief Academic Head of a university in India is:

A. The Chancellor B. The Pro Chancellor
C. The Vice-Chancellor D. The Visitor

70. Match the items in column A with that of in column B.

A	B
(i) Kota Open University	(a) Nasik
(ii) Nalanda Open University	(b) New Delhi
(iii) Yaswanta Rao Chavan Maharashtra Open University	(c) Kolkatta
(iv) Indira Gandhi National Open University	(d) Bihar
	(e) Rajastan

A. (i) (a) (ii) (c) (iii) (b) (iv) (e)
B. (i) (b) (ii) (c) (iii) (d) (iv) (e)
C. (i) (c) (ii) (b) (iii) (d) (iv) (a)
D. (i) (e) (ii) (d) (iii) (a) (iv) (b)

Answer keys

1.B	2.D	3.A	4.D	5.C	6.B	7.B	8.D	9.A	10.B
11.A	12.C	13.A	14.C	15.B	16.B	17.D	18.C	19.D	20.B
21.C	22.D	23.B	24.D	25.B	26.C	27.A	28.B	29.A	30.C
31.D	32.B	33.C	34.B	35.C	36.A	37.C	38.B	39.C	40.D
41.D	42.B	43.B	44.B	45.A	46.C	47.A	48.A	49.B	50.C
51.C	52.C	53.A	54.B	55.C	56.C	57.A	58.C	59.B	60.C
61.B	62.A	63.C	64.C	65.D	66.C	67.B	68.C	69.C	70.D

Part – II

Previous Years
Solved Question Papers

Part - II

Previous Years Question Papers

UGC NET-JRF EXAMINATION DECEMBER 2004

SOLVED QUESTION PAPER

PAPER - I

Note : This paper contains **fifty** (50) multiple-choice questions, each question carrying **two** (2) marks. Attempt **all** of them.

1. **Discussion Method can be used when :**
   A. The topic is very difficult
   B. The topic is easy
   C. The topic is difficult
   D. All the above

2. **Which of the following is a teaching aid ?**
   A. Working Model of Wind Mill
   B. Tape Recorder
   C. 16 mm Film Projector
   D. All the above

3. **The main aim of teaching is :**
   A. To develop only reasoning
   B. To develop only thinking
   C. Both (A) and (B)
   D. To give information

4. **The quality of teaching is reflected :**
   A. By the attendance of students in the class
   B. By the pass percentage of students
   C. By the quality of questions asked by students
   D. By the duration of silence maintained in the class

5. **The present annual examination system :**
   A. promotes rote learning
   B. does not promote good study habits
   C. does not encourage students to be regular in class
   D. All the above

6. **A college wants to give training in use of Statistical Package for Social Sciences (SPSS) to researchers. For this the college should organise :**
   A. Conference
   B. Seminar
   C. Workshop
   D. Lecture

7. **Which of the following is NOT the characteristic of a research ?**
   A. Research is systematic
   B. Research is not a process
   C. Research is problem oriented
   D. Research is not passive

8. Which of the following statement is correct ?

A. Discoveries are researches

B. Researches lead to discovery

C. Invention and Research are related

D. None of the above

9. Which of the following statement is correct ?

A. In research, objectives can be worded in question form

B. In research, objectives can be worded in statement form

C. Objectives are to be stated in Chapter I of the Thesis

D. All the above

10. Match List A with List B and choose the correct answer from the code given below :

List A	List B
(a) Historical Method	(i) Past events
(b) Survey Method	(ii) Vision
(c) Philosophical Method	(iii) Present events
(d) Experimental Method	(iv) Exceptional cases
	(v) Future action

Code :

	(a)	(b)	(c)	(d)
A.	(i)	(iii)	(ii)	(v)
B.	(i)	(ii)	(iv)	(v)
C.	(i)	(iv)	(ii)	(v)
D.	(i)	(ii)	(iii)	(iv)

1. Read the following passage and answer the question numbers 11 to 15.

Each day at the Shantiniketan School starts with the Saraswati Vandana. When painting competitions are held in the school, images of Hindu gods and goddesses are most common. Sanskrit is a favourite subject of many a student. Nothing new about it except that the 1,200 - odd students studying in the Hindu - run school are Muslims.

In 1983, when Ranchodbhai Kiri started Shantiniketan in the all - Muslim Juhapura area of Ahmedabad in Gujarat, only 20 percent of the students were Muslims. But when riots involving the Muslims of Juhapura and the Hindus of nearby Jivrajpark - Vejalpur affected the locality, Hindus started migrating. Today, all the students are Muslims and the school is an unparalled example of harmony. In the 2002, when a section of inflamed Muslims wanted the school closed, the parents of the students stood like a wall behind it.

Shantiniketan's principal says, "We never thought of moving the school out of the area because of the love and affection of the local Muslims. Indeed they value the high standard of education which we have set." Such is the reputation of the school that some of the local Muslim strongmen accused of involvement in communal riots are willing to protect the school during the riots.

The parents of Shantiniketan's students believe that it's the best school when it comes to the quality of the teaching. A large number of students have gone for both graduation and post graduation studies. Significantly, the only Muslim teacher in the 40 - member teaching staff, Husena Mansuri, teaches Sanskrit. Infact, she is so happy at the school that she recently declined the principalship of another Muslim - run school.

Some of the students' entries in a recent school painting competition were truly moving. One drew a pciture of Bharat Mata with a mosque and temple, while another portrayed a boy tying rakhi to his sister. Trully, Shantiniketan is a beacon of hope that, despite the provocations from both communities, Hindus and Muslims can live side-by-side with mutual respect.

11. How the Shantiniketan school starts the day ?

A. National anthem B. Prayer

C. Saraswati Vandana D. Puja

12. Write the subject which is preferred by most of the students

A. Hindi B. English

C. Sanskrit D. Gujarati

13. Who protects the school during the riot times ?

A. Local Muslims B. Hindus

C. Politicians D. Christians

14. Who is the teacher of Sanskrit ?

A. Ranchodbhai Kiri B. Manisha Vakil

C. Husena Mansuri D. Husena Khatoon

15. What is the hope despite the communal riots ?

A. Hindus and Muslims cannot live side by side

B. Hindus and Muslims can live side by side

C. Only Hindus can live

D. Only Muslims can live

16. Match List I with List II and choose the correct answer using the codes given below :

List I	**List II**
(Distinguished Ladies)	(Area of work)
(a) Jhumpa Lahiri	(i) Journalist
(b) Barkha Dutt	(ii) Novelist
(c) Aparna Sen	(iii) Film Actress
(d) Smita Patil	(iv) Film Director

Code :

	(a)	(b)	(c)	(d)
A.	(iv)	(iii)	(ii)	(i)
B.	(ii)	(i)	(iv)	(iii)
C.	(iv)	(i)	(iii)	(ii)
D.	(ii)	(iii)	(iv)	(i)

17. Which of the following pair is not correctly matched ?

A. Aajtaak - 24 hours news channel

B. F.M. Stations - Radio

C. National Geography channel - Television

D. Vir Sanghvi - India Today

18. Which is the oldest soap opera telecasted in India ?

A. Kahani Ghar Ghar Ke B. Buniad

C. Humlog D. Saas bhi Kabhi Bahu Thee

19. Which satellite channel uses the adline, "Knowing is everything" ?

A. BBC World B. Star

C. Sony D. Zee

20. Which is the "First made in India" Kids channel of television ?

A. Cartoon Network

B. Walt Disney

C. United Home Entertainment's Hungama TV

D. Nick Jr.

21. The letters in the first set have certain relationships. On the basis of the relationship which is the right choice for the second set ?

BF : GK : : LP : ?

A. JK B. QW C. VW D. RQ

22. If the BLOOD is coded as 24113 and BRUST as 26078, then code for ROBUST is :

A. 620781 B. 612078 C. 678102 D. 610732

23. A bag contains an equal number of one rupee, 50 paise and 25 paise coins. If the total amount in the bag is ₹ 66666635, how many coins of each type are there ?

A. 15 B. 18 C. 20 D. 25

24. In the sequence of numbers

$\frac{2}{3}, \frac{4}{7} \times \frac{11}{21}, \frac{16}{31}$

the missing number X is :

A. $\frac{8}{10}$ B. $\frac{6}{10}$ C. $\frac{5}{10}$ D. $\frac{7}{10}$

25. If A stands for 5, B for 6, C for 7, D for 8, and so on, what do the following numbers stand for :

22, 25, 8, 22 and 5 ?

A. PRIYA B. NEEMA C. MEENA D. RUDRA

26. Which of the following statements are always true ?

(A) A wooden table is a table

(B) Now, it is raining or not raining

(C) The sun rises in the East every day

(D) A chicken comes out of a hen's egg

Choose the correct answer from the code given below :

Code :

A. (a) and (c) B. (a), (c) and (d)

C. (a) and (b) D. (b) and (c)

27. Which of the following statements are mutually inconsistent ?

(a) Mostly poets are not egoistic

(b) Mostly poets are humble

(c) Some poets are egoistic

(d) Some poets are not non-egoistic

Choose the correct answer from the code given below :

Code :

A. (a) and (d)	B. (b) and (c)
C. (a) and (c)	D. (c) and (d)

28. Which of the following statements is/are absolutely impossible ?

(a) A woman giving birth to her own grandchild

(b) A man attending his own funeral

(c) The Sun not rising in the East some day

(d) Cars running without petrol

Choose the correct answer from the code given below :

Code :

A. (a) and (b)	B. (c) and (d)
C. (b)	D. (a)

29. Which of the following are incorrect ways of arguing ?

(a) If horses are cows, and if cows are sheep, then all horses must be sheep.

(b) If top actors are famous, and Shah Rukh Khan is famous, then Shah Rukh Khan is a top actor

(c) Lata is the second sister of Raju, hence Raju is the second brother of Lata

(d) A is not equal to B, but B is equal to C, hence A is equal to C.

Choose the correct answer from the code given below :

Code :

A. (a), (b) and (c)	B. (a), (c) and (d)
C. (b), (c) and (d)	D. (a), (b) and (d)

30. Which of the following statements say the same thing ?

(a) "I am clever" (said by Rama)

(b) "I am clever" (said by Raju)

(c) "My son is clever" (said by Rama's father)

(d) "My brother is clever" (said by Rama's sister)

(e) "My brother is clever" (said by Rama's only sister)

(f) "My sole enemy is clever" (said by Rama's only enemy) Choose the correct answer from the code given below :

Code :

A. (a), (c), (d), (e) and (f)	B. (a) and (b)
C. (d) and (e)	D. (a) and (f)

2. Study the following graph and answer Question Numbers 31 to 33 :

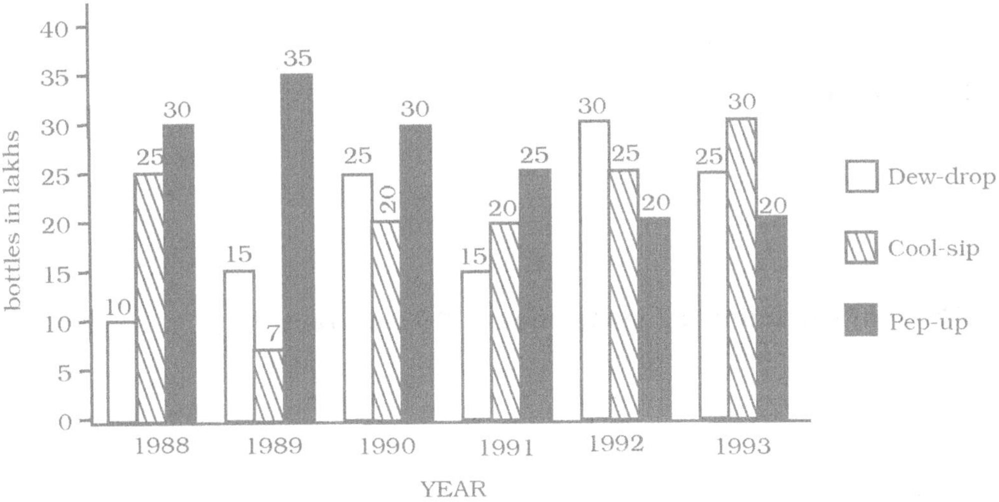

31. In which year was the sale of 'Pep-up' the maximum ?

A. 1990 B. 1992

C. 1993 D. None of the above

32. In the case of which soft drink was the average annual sale maximum during the period 1988-1993.

A. Pep-up only B. Cool-sip only

C. Cool-sip and Dew-drop D. Pep-up and Dew-drop

33. What was the approximate percent drop in the sale of Pep-up in 1990 over its sale in 1989 ?

A. 5 B. 12 C. 14 D. 20

34. The "Report on Currency and Finance" for each of the financial year in India is published by :

A. Reserve Bank of India B. Ministry of Finance

C. Planning Commission D. Central Statistical Organisation

35. The number of students in two classes A and B and the respective "mean" of the marks obtained by each of the class are given in the following table :

	Class A	**Class B**
Number of Students	20	80
Arithmatic Mean	10	20

The combined "mean" of the marks of the two classes will be :

A. 18 B. 15

C. 10 D. 20

36. ICT stands for :

A. International Communication Technology

B. Intera Common Terminology

C. Information and Communication Technology

D. Inter connected Terminals

37. Which of the following statement is NOT correct ?

A. Computer is capable of processing only digital signal

B. Computer is capable of analysing both quantitative and qualitative data

C. Appropriate software is required for processing the data

D. Computer is capable of processing digital as well as analog signals

38. Which of the following is the appropriate definition of Information Technology ?

A. Information Technology refers to the use of hardware and software for processing information

B. Information Technology refers to the use of hardware and software for distribution of useful information

C. Information Technology refers to the use of hardware and software for storage, retrieval, processing and distributing information of many kinds.

D. Information Technology refers to the use of principles of Physical sciences and Social sciences for processing of information of many kinds.

39. Which of the following statement is correct ?

A. Virus improves the speed of processing information through computer

B. Internet does not allow the virus to spread

C. Virus is a part of software

D. Virus is an operating system

40. Which of the following is correct statement ?

A. Computers can be used for diagnosing the difficulty of a student in learning a subject

B. Psychological testing can be done with the help of computer provided a software is available

C. A set of instructions is called a programme

D. All the above

41. Global warming during winter becomes more pronounced at the :

A. Equator B. Poles

C. Tropic of Cancer D. Tropic of Capricorn

42. In the study of man - environment interaction, the statement of Miss Semple that "the humans are solely the product of their environment", is :

A. An opinion B. A prejudice

C. A fact D. A widely accepted phenomenon

43. In analysis of man - environment relationship Pragmatic Possibilism implies that :

A. There is no limit for man to exploit resources of earth

B. There are limited possibilities to explore earth's resources

C. The man has to watch and assess the situation and then go ahead with resource utilization

D. The man has to keep in mind only his basic needs while planning to harness the potential of resourceful earth

44. Arrange Column II in proper sequence so as to match it with Column I and choose the correct answer from the code given below :

Column I	**Column II**
Activity	Noise level
(a) Hearing	(i) 30 dB
(b) Whispering	(ii) 1 dB
(c) Interference with sleep	(iii) 60 dB
(d) Normal talk	(iv) 30 - 50 dB

Code :

	(a)	(b)	(c)	(d)
A.	(i)	(ii)	(iii)	(iv)
B.	(ii)	(i)	(iv)	(iii)
C.	(iv)	(ii)	(iii)	(i)
D.	(iii)	(i)	(ii)	(iv)

45. The maximum loss of forest lands in India is caused by :

A. River valley projects B. Industries

C. Means of transportation D. Agriculture

46. In which year the University Grants Commission was established ?

A. 1948 B. 1944 C. 1953 D. 1960

47. Another name of Basic Education or Nai Talim is :

A. Compulsory Education B. New Education Policy

C. Wardha Education Plan D. Sarva Shikshya Abhiyan

48. The Idea of 'Democratic Decentralisation' in India was popularised by :

A. A.D. Gorwala Committee, 1951

B. Paul H. Appleby Committee, 1953

C. B.R. Mehta Committee, 1957

D. Ashok Mehta Committee, 1978

49. In India, a political party is recognised as a National or Regional Party by the :

A. President of India

B. Election Commission of India

C. Law ministry in consultation with the Law Commission of India

D. Union Parliament in consultation with the State Legislatures

50. Which of the following factors is/are responsible for the increase of the role of Government in Developing Countries ?

(a) Economic Planning (b) Rising expectation of People

(c) Privatisation (d) Emergence of the concept of Welfare State

Select the most appropriate answer from the code given below :

Code :

A. (a) and (d) B. (a), (b) and (d)

C. Only (c) D. Only (d)

Answer keys

1.C	2.D	3.C	4.C	5.D	6.C	7. B	8.B	9.C	10.A
11.C	12.C	13.A	14.C	15.B	16.B	17.D	18.C	19.A	20.C
21.B	22.B	23.C	24.D	25.D	26.B	27.C	28.A	29.B	30.A
31.D	32.A	33.C	34.A	35.B	36.C	37.A	38.C	39.C	40.D
41.D	42.D	43.C	44.B	45.D	46.C	47.C	48.C	49.B	50.A

UGC NET-JRF EXAMINATION JUNE 2005

SOLVED QUESTION PAPER

PAPER - I

Note : This paper contains **fifty** (50) multiple-choice questions, each question carrying **two** (2) marks. Attempt **all** of them.

1. **Which of the following is NOT true?**
   A. Teaching is an art
   B. Teachers can be trained
   C. Teachers are born not made
   D. Teachers are made

2. **The teacher, before concluding the lesson, should**
   A. motivate the students for the next lesson
   B. write down homework on the blackboard
   C. check up whether the students have learnt the lesson
   D. narrate some tit-bits.

3. **What is the real meaning of DISTANCE EDUCATION?**
   A. Education which is provided to villages situated in remote areas
   B. Education which is provided to those who cannot afford to go to regular schools/colleges.
   C. Education which is provided to those who are in service.
   D. Education which is provided through correspondence to those who have neither time nor any resource to join any educational institution.

4. **What should a teacher do to help slow learners?**
   A. Organise remedial teaching
   B. Give awards to such children
   C. Make the syllabus light for them
   D. Promise them financial assistance.

5. **In a row of children, Sheena is fifth from left and Beena is sixth from right. If they interchange their places, Sheena becomes thirteenth from left. In this condition, what place will be occupied by Beena from right?**
   A. 4th B. 14th C. 15th D. 18th

6. The memory of a computer is comm expressed in terms of kilobytes a megabytes. A byte is made up of:

A. 8 binary digits B. 8 decimal digits

C. 2 binary digits D. 2 decimal digits

Directions Q. 7 to 11: Read the passage given below to answer these questions on the basis of the contents of the passage, and what is stated and implied therein:

The amount of water in the world is limited. The human race, and the other species which share the planet, cannot expect an infinite supply. Water covers about two-thirds of the Earth's surface, admittedly. But most of it is too salty for use. Only 2.5% of the world's water is not salty, and two-thirds of that is looked up in icecaps and glaciers. Of what is left, about 20% is in remote areas. Humans have available less than 0.08% of all the Earth's water. Yet over the next two decades, our use is estimated to increase by about 40%. In 1999, the United Nations Environment Programme (UNEP) reported that 200 scientists in 50 countries had identified water shortage as one of the two most worrying problems for the new millennium (the other was global warming).

We use about 70% of the water that we have in agriculture. But the World Water Council believes that by 2020, we shall need 17% more water than is available if we are to feed the world. So, if we go on, millions more will go to bed hungry and thirsty each night than do so already. Today, one person out of five across the world has no access to safe drinking water and one out of two lakh to safe sanitation. Today, and every day, more than 30,000 children die before reaching their fifth birthdays, killed either by hunger or by easily preventable diseases. And adequate safe water is the key to good health and a proper diet.

There are several reasons for the water crisis. One is the rise in population and the desire of better living standards, in China, it takes thousands tonnes of water to produce one tonne of wheat. Another is the inefficiency of the way we use much of our water. Irrigation allows wastage on a prodigal scale, with the water trickling away or simply evaporating before it can do any good. And pollution is making more of the water that is available to us unfit for use. The Aral Sea in Central Asia is one of the starkest examples of what pollution can do, to the land as well as to the water. Increasingly, governments are seeking to solve their water problems by turning away from reliance on rainfall and surface water, and using subterranean supplies of groundwater, instead. But that is like making constant withdrawals from a bank account without ever paying anything into it. And using up irreplaceable groundwater does not simply mean the depletion of a once-and-for-all resource. Rivers, wetlands and lakes that depend on it can dry out. Saline seawater can flow in to replace the fresh water that has been pumped out. And the emptied underground aquifers can be compressed, causing surface subsidence — a problem familiar in Bangkok, Mexico City and Venice.

There are some ways to begin to tackle the problem. Irrigation systems which drip water directly onto plants are one. There will be scope to plant less water intensive crops, and perhaps desalination may play a part - though it is energy-hungry and leaves quantities of brine for disposal.

7. **According to the passage, scientists all over the world have identified two most worrying problems for the new millennium. Water shortage is one, the other being**

   A. Sanitation

   B. lack of adequate drinking water

   C. Waterborne diseases

   D. Global warming

8. **In the field of irrigation, according to the World Water Council, how much additional water would we require by 2020?**

   A. 0.08% B. 17% C. 20% D. 70%

9. **Besides depletion of an important water resource, other side effects of taking out underground water are brought out by the out in the passage?**

   A. Drying of dependent lakes

   B. Saline water ingress into vacated space

   C. Surface subsidence

   D. Release of locked-up gas

10. **What percentage of world population, according to the author, has no access to safe drinking water?**

    A. 2.5% B. 20% C. 0.08% D. 17%

11. **The author has given some reasons for water crisis. Which of the following is not a reason given by the author?**

    A. Population increase

    B. Inefficient way of use of water

    C. Irrigation-related wastage and pollution

    D. Climatic change bringing less rain to some regions & more to others

Directions: These questions are independent.

12. **If the price index for the year 2002 was 120 and for the year 2003, it is 130, then the rate of inflation would be:**

    A. 7.69% B. 10% C. 8.3% D. 13%

13. **Find the incorrect one:**

    A. Hertz is used to measure frequency

B. Kelvin is used to measure temperature

C. Bel is used to measure atmospheric pressure

D. Ohm is used to measure electrical resistance

14. One gram of fat gives

A. 30 g of energy

B. 7 KJ of energy

C. 9 Kcal of energy

D. 4 M J of energy

15. The embryo/foetus gets its food supply from

A. Arteries of the mother

B. The uterus

C. The placenta

D. The amniotic sac

16. Sucrose contains

A. Glucose and Galactose

B. Glucose and fructose

C. Fructose and Galactose

D. Glucose, Fructose and Galactose

17. Which chemical is mainly responsible for depletion of ozone layer in the atmosphere?

A. Sulphur dioxide

B. Chlorofluoro carbon

C. Carbon dioxide

D. Nitrus oxide

18. Which nutrient is digested first in the mouth?

A. Protein B. Carbohydrate

C. Fat D. Vitamin

19. Which chemical is used for purification of water?

A. Potassium sulphate

B. Potassium permanganate

C. Sulphuric Acid

D. Nitric acid

20. Find the incorrect statement:

A. Cosmic describes anything occurring or located in outer space

B. Lithosphere is the top crust of the Earth which includes the land surface and the ocean floors

C. Silicon constitutes the second most important element in the composition of the Earth

D. A tributary is a river which leaves the main river and flows separately

21. The constitution provides that no Vidhan Sabha can have less than 60 members. Which of the following State Assemblies is an exception to it?

A. Tripura B. Meghalaya

C. Sikkim D. Mizoram

22. Who will discharge the function of the President if for any reason both the offices of the President and the Vice President fall vacant?

A. Attorney General

B. Speaker of the Lok Sabha

C. Chief Justice of India

D. Chief Election Commissioner

23. The average depth of a river is 5ft. A person 5 ft 8 in tall, who doesn't know swimming, wants to cross it on foot. What should he do?

A. Walk across the river without fear

B. Compute standard deviation of the river and then decide

C. Find out extreme depths of the river and then decide

D. Learn swimming first

Directions Q. 24: In this question, a statement is given followed by two assumptions (I) and (II). You are to consider each statement and the assumptions that follow and decide which of the assumptions is implicit in the given Indicate your answer as:

a) If only I) is implicit

b) If only II) is implicit

c) If both I) and II) are implicit

d) If neither I) nor II) is implicit

Statement :

Education and economic advancement leads to n loss of hold of religion on mind.

Assumptions:

I) Education leads to economic devolopment

II) Religion can make priceless contribution to the society.

Directions (Q. 25 to 28): The graph below shows the distribution of funds by a state on various items. Study the diagram and answer the questions.

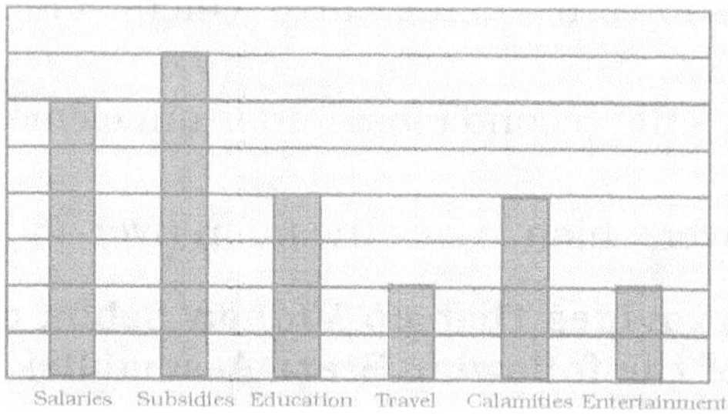

25. The expenditure on salaries and travel is equal to the expenditure on:

A. Education and natural calamities

B. Subsidies and entertainment

C. Education and entertainment

D. Subsidies and natural calamities

26. If the money spent on entertainment is used for natural calamities, then there will be equal expenditure on:

A. Subsidies and natural calamities

B. Salaries and natural calamities

C. Education and natural calamities

D. Travel and natural calamities

27. More than 50% of the expenditure is on:

A. Salarieses, travel and entertainment

B. Subsidies, natural calamities and travel

C. Education, salaries and entertainment

D. Natural calamities, education and travel

28. The expenditure made on Salaries and Education is:

A. less than that on natural calamities and entertainment

B. less than that on travel, entertainment and nalural calamities

C. more than that on entertainment, travel and natural calamities

D. more than that on subsidies and natural calamities

Directions: These questions are independent.

29. A person walks facing North 10m and then he turns left and walks 5m. He again turns left and walks 10m. How far is he from his original position and towards which direction?

A. 20m South B. 15m West

C. 10m East D. 5m West

30. Whose words are these: "Education has produced vast population able to read but unable distinguish what is worth reading"?

A. Edmund Burke B. Reinhold Neibubr

C. G.M. Trevelyn D. George Bernard Shaw

31. What general term describes the physical equipment of a computer system, such as video screen, keyboard and storage devices?

A. Hardware B. Software

C. Input devices D. Output devices

32. All of the following are examples databases EXCEPT?

A. collection of country music on CD

B. a CD-ROM encyclopaedia

C. computerised student information

D. an online catalogue

33. Compared with a traditional card catalogue, which of the following is NOT an advantage of an electronic card catalogue?

A. contains information on more books

B. less costly to install and operate

C. allows books to be shelved more quickly

D. allows sophisticated search strategies

34. When will the validity and reliability of research be doubtful?

A. The source of information is biased

B. The research was done long after the incident

C. The researcher cannot draw logical conclusions

D. all of the above

35. What are the things that a researcher must be careful about when he writes his research report?

A. not using numerical figures when beginning a sentence

B. arrange all data in logical or chronological order

C. compare the results with other studies

D. all of the above

36. What is the best method a researcher will use if he wants to study the future of a political party in India (such as BJP or Congress)?

A. Questionnaire
B. Survey
C. Trend Analysis
D. Regression

37. A survey would be best used when:

(a) learning the facts about an existing situation
(b) comparing present status with established norms
(c) critical analysis of an existing situation
(d) identifying means of improvement in the existing situation

A. a and b B. a, b and c
C. a, b, c and d D. b and c

Directions (Q 38): Read the statement and the reason given below and decide their relationship.

38. *Statement (A):*

The ozone layer at Antartica is very thin and has developed a hole.

Reason (R) :

On account of the severe cold in Antartica, the greenhouse gases are centralised there.

Select the correct answer from the following

A. (A) is true but (R) is false
B. (R) is true but (A) is false
C. Both (A) and (R) are true but (R) is correct explanation of (A)
D. Both (A) and (R) are true but (R) is not correct explanation of (A)

39. The climate of a place depends upon many factors. Four factors of them are given below. Which one of the following is the most important factor?

A. Distance from sea
B. Direction of wind
C. Latitude
D. Sea currents

40. If a person crosses the international date line from the western hemisphere on 9th April, what will be the date of his arrival in the eastern hemisphere?

A. 9th April B. 10th April
C. 8th April D. 11th April

41. If a map is magnified from

1 : 20,000 to 1 : 1,00, 000 then its area will be

A. Twenty five times of original area

B. Twenty times of original area

C. Ten times of original area

D. Five times of original area

42. The least number which when divided by 5, 6, 8 and 10 leaves the remainder 3, 4, 6 and 8 respectively, is:

A. 122 B. 120 C. 118 D. 116

43. What would come in the last term of the series: EGIMP : FILQU :: FHJL :?

A. GJMP B. GMJP C. JGPM D. HKNQ

44. If the two terms to the left bear the ihiiih relationship as the two terms to the right, limn find the missing term: 68 : 130 :: ... , 350

A. 240 B. 222 C. 216 D. 210

45. 108. In a certain code language, VICTORY is written as YLFWWRUB. In the same way 'FAILURE' is written in that code language as

A. IDLNXUH B. JDLOXUH

C. IDLOXVH D. IDLOXUH

46. A man is facing south. He turns 135 degrees in the anticlockwise direction and then 180 degrees in the clockwise direction. Which direction is he facing now?

A. North-east B. North-west

C. South-east D. South-west

47. "Life is a tale told by an idiot which is full of sound and fury signifying nothing." This is the ______ definition of life.

A. Universally accepted

B. Wrong

C. Narrow

D. Arbitrary

48. In which of the following types of communication methods can 'Audio conferencing' be classified?

A. One sided verbal B. Two sided verbal

C. One sided non-verbal D. Two sided non-verbal

49. Which one of the following is the last important in effective communication?

A. Full control on language

B. Good vocabulary

C. Attractive personality of messenger

D. Full control over communicablet subject

50. Any obstacle in communication process is known as:

A. Encroachment B. Hindrance

C. Noise D. Inner Process

Answer keys

1.C	2.A	3.D	4.A	5.B	6.A	7. D	8. B	9. D	10.B
11.D	12.C	13.C	14.C	15.C	16.B	17.B	18.B	19.B	20.D
21.D	22.C	23.C	24.D	25.A	26.B	27.B	28.C	29.D	30.C
31.A	32.A	33.C	34.D	35.D	36.C	37.B	38.D	39.C	40.A
41.A	42.C	43.A	44.B	45.D	46.D	47.A	48.B	49.C	50.C

UGC NET-JRF EXAMINATION DECEMBER 2005

SOLVED QUESTION PAPER

PAPER - I

Note : This paper contains **fifty** (50) multiple-choice questions, each question carrying **two** (2) marks. Attempt **all** of them.

1. **Team teaching has the potential to develop :**
   A. Competitive spirit
   B. Co-operation
   C. The habit of supplementing the teaching of each other
   D. Highlighting the gaps in each other's teaching

2. **Which of the following is the most important characteristic of Open Book Examination system ?**
   A. Students become serious
   B. It improves attendance in the classroom
   C. It reduces examination anxiety amongst students
   D. It compels students to think

3. **Which of the following methods of teaching encourages the use of maximum senses ?**
   A. Problem-solving method
   B. Laboratory method
   C. Self-study method
   D. Team teaching method

4. **Which of the following statement is correct ?**
   A. Communicator should have fine senses
   B. Communicator should have tolerance power
   C. Communicator should be soft spoken
   D. Communicator should have good personality

5. **An effective teacher is one who can :**
   A. control the class
   B. give more information in less time
   C. motivate students to learn
   D. correct the assignments carefully

6. One of the following is not a quality of researcher :

A. Unison with that of which he is in search

B. He must be of alert mind

C. Keenness in enquiry

D. His assertion to outstrip the evidence

7. A satisfactory statistical quantitative method should not possess one of the following qualities :

A. Appropriateness B. Measurability

C. Comparability D. Flexibility

8. Books and records are the primary sources of data in :

A. historical research

B. participatory research

C. clinical research

D. laboratory research

9. Which of the following statement is correct ?

A. objectives should be pin-pointed

B. objectives can be written in statement or question form

C. another word for problem is variable

D. all the above

10. The important pre-requisites of a researcher in sciences, social sciences and humanities are :

A. laboratory skills, records, supervisor, topic

B. Supervisor, topic, critical analysis, patience

C. archives, supervisor, topic, flexibility in thinking

D. topic, supervisor, good temperament, pre-conceived notions

1. Read the following passage and answer the questions 11 to 15 :

Knowledge creation in many cases requires creativity and idea generation. This is especially important in generating alternative decision support solutions. Some people believe that an individual's creative ability stems primarily from personality traits such as inventiveness, independence, individuality, enthusiasm, and flexibility. However, several studies have found that creativity is not so much a function of individual traits as was once believed, and that individual creativity can be learned and improved. This understanding has led innovative companies to recognise that the key to fostering creativity may be the development of an idea-nurturing work environment. Idea-generation methods and techniques, to be used by individuals or in groups, are consequently being developed. Manual methods for supporting idea generation, such as brainstorming in a group, can be very successful in certain situations. However, in other situations, such an approach is either not economically feasible or not possible. For example, manual methods in group creativity sessions will not work or will not be effective when : (1) there is no time to conduct a proper idea-generation session; (2) there is a poor facilitator (or no facilitator at all); (3) it is too expensive to conduct an idea-generation session; (4) the subject matter is too sensitive for a face-to-face session; or (5) there are not enough participants, the mix of participants is not optimal, or there is no climate for idea generation. In such cases, computerised idea-generation methods have been tried, with frequent success.

Idea-generation software is designed to help stimulate a single user or a group to produce new ideas, options and choices. The user does all the work, but the software encourages and pushes, something like a personal trainer. Although idea-generation software is still relatively new, there are several packages on the market. Various approaches are used by idea-generating software to increase the flow of ideas to the user. Idea Fisher, for example, has an associate lexicon of the English language that cross-references words and phrases. These associative links, based on analogies and metaphors, make it easy for the user to be fed words related to a given theme. Some software packages use questions to prompt the user towards new, unexplored patterns of thought. This helps users to break out of cyclical thinking patterns, conquer mental blocks, or deal with bouts of procrastination.

11. The author, in this passage has focussed on

A. knowledge creation
B. idea-generation
C. creativity
D. individual traits

12. Fostering creativity needs an environment of

A. decision support systems
B. idea-nurturing
C. decision support solutions
D. alternative individual factors

13. Manual methods for the support of idea-generation, in certain occasions,

A. are alternatively effective
B. can be less expensive
C. do not need a facilitator
D. require a mix of optimal participants

14. Idea-generation software works as if it is a :

A. stimulant
B. knowledge package
C. user-friendly trainer
D. climate creator

15. Mental blocks, bouts of procrastination and cyclical thinking patterns can be won when :

A. innovative companies employ electronic thinking methods
B. idea-generation software prompts questions
C. manual methods are removed
D. individuals acquire a neutral attitude towards the software

16. Level C of the effectiveness of communication is defined as :

A. channel noise B. semantic noise
C. psychological noise D. source noise

17. Recording a television programme on a VCR is an example of :

A. time-shifting B. content reference
C. mechanical clarity D. media synchronisation

18. A good communicator is the one who offers to his audience :

A. plentiful of information B. a good amount of statistics
C. concise proof D. repetition of facts

19. The largest number of newspapers in India is published from the state of:

A. Kerala B. Maharashtra
C. West Bengal D. Uttar Pradesh

20. Insert the missing number :

8 24 12 ? 18 54

A. 26 B. 24 C. 36 D. 32

21. January 1, 1995 was Sunday. What day of the week lies on January 1, 1996 ?

A. Sunday B. Monday
C. Saturday D. None of these

22. The sum of a positive number and its reciprocal is twice the difference of the number and its reciprocal. The number is :

A. $\sqrt{2}$ B. $\frac{1}{\sqrt{2}}$ C. $\sqrt{3}$ D. $\frac{1}{\sqrt{3}}$

23. In a certain code, ROUNDS is written as RONUDS. How will PLEASE will be written in the same code :

A. L PA E S E B. P L A E S E
C. L P A E E S D. P L A S E E

24. At what time between 5.30 and 6.00 will the hands of an clock be at right angles ?

A. 43 115 min. past 5 B. 43 117 min. past 5

C. 40 min. past 5 D. 45 min past 5

25. Statements : I All students are ambitious

II All ambitious persons are hard working

Conclusions : (i) All students are hard-working

(ii) All hardly working people are not ambitious

Which of the following is correct ?

A. Only (i) is correct B. Only (ii) is correct

C. Both (i) and (ii) are correct D. Neither (i) nor (ii) is correct

26. Statement : Most students are intelligent

Conclusions : (i) Some students are intelligent

(ii) All students are not intelligent

Which of the following is implied ?

A. Only (i) is implied B. Only (ii) is implied

C. Both (i) and (ii) are implied D. Neither (i) nor (ii) is implied

27. Statement : Most labourers are poor

Conclusions :

(i) Some labourers are poor

(ii)All labourers are not poor

Which of the following is implied ?

A. Only (i) is implied B. Only (ii) is implied

C. Both (i) and (ii) are implied D. Neither (i) nor (ii) is implied

28. Line access and avoidance of collision are the main functions of :

A. the CPU B. the monitor

C. network protocols D. wide area networks

29. In the hypermedia database, information bits are stored in the form of :

A. signals B. cubes

C. nodes D. symbols

30. Communications bandwidth that has the highest capacity and is used by microwave, cable and fibre optics lines is known as :

A. hyper-link B. broadband

C. bus width D. carrier wave

31. An electronic bill board that has a short text or graphical advertising message is referred to as :

A. bulletin B. strap
C. bridge line D. banner

32. Which of the following is not the characteristic of a computer ?

A. computer is an electrical machine
B. computer cannot think at its own
C. computer processes information error free
D. computer can hold data for any length of time

33. Bitumen is obtained from :

A. Forests and Plants B. Kerosene oil
C. Crude oil D. underground mines

34. Malaria is caused by :

A. bacterial infection B. viral infection
C. parasitic infection D. fungal infection

35. The cloudy nights are warmer compared to clear nights (without clouds) during winter days. This is because :

A. clouds radiate heat towards the earth
B. clouds prevent cold wave from the sky, descend on earth
C. clouds prevent escaping of the heat radiation from the earth
D. clouds being at great heights from earth absorb heat from the sun and send towards the earth

36. Largest soil group of India is :

A. Red soil B. Black soil
C. Sandy soil D. Mountain soil

37. Main pollutant of the Indian coastal water is :

A. oil spill B. municipal sewage
C. industrial effluents D. aerosols

38. Human ear is most sensitive to noise in the following frequency ranges:

A. 1-2 KHz B. 100-500 Hz
C. 10-12 KHz D. 13-16 KHz

39. Which species of chromium is toxic in water :

A. Cr + 2 B. Cr + 3
C. Cr + 6 D. Cr is non-toxic element

40. Match List - I (Dams) with List - II (River) in the following :

List - I (Dams)	List - II (River)
a. Bhakra	(i) Krishna
b. Nagarjunasagar	(ii) Damodar
c. Panchet	(iii) Sutlej
d. Hirakud	(iv) Bhagirathi
e. Tehri	(v) Mahanadi

	a	b	c	d	e
A.	v	iii	iv	ii	i
B.	iii	i	ii	v	iv
C.	i	ii	iv	iii	v
D.	ii	iii	iv	i	v

41. A negative reaction to a mediated communication is described as :

A. flak
B. fragmented feedback
C. passive response
D. non-conformity

42. The launch of satellite channel by IGNOU on 26th January 2003 for technological education for the growth and development of distance education is :

A. Eklavya channel
B. Gyandarshan channel
C. Rajrishi channel
D. None of these

43. Match List - I with List-II and select the correct answer from the code given below :

List - I (Institutions)	List - II (Locations)
(a) The Indian Council of Historical Reasearch (ICHR)	(i) Shimla
(b) The Indian Institute of Advanced Studies (IIAS)	(ii) New Delhi
(c) The Indian Council of Philosophical Research (ICPR)	(iii) Banglore
(d) The Central Institute of Coastal Engineering for fisheries	(iv) Lucknow

	a	b	c	d
A.	ii	i	iv	iii
B.	i	ii	iii	iv
C.	ii	iv	i	iii
D.	iv	iii	ii	i

44. Which of the following is not a Fundamental Right ?

A. Right to equality

B. Right against exploitation

C. Right to freedom of speech and expression

D. Right of free compulsory education of all children upto the age of 14

45. The Lok - Sabha can be dissolved before the expiry of its normal five year term by :

A. The Prime Minister

B. The Speaker of Lok Sabha

C. The President on the recommendation of the Prime Minister

D. None of the above

46 to 50 NOT FOR VISUALLY HANDICAPPED CANDIDATES

2. ***Study the following graph carefully and answer Q.No. 46 to 50 given below it :***

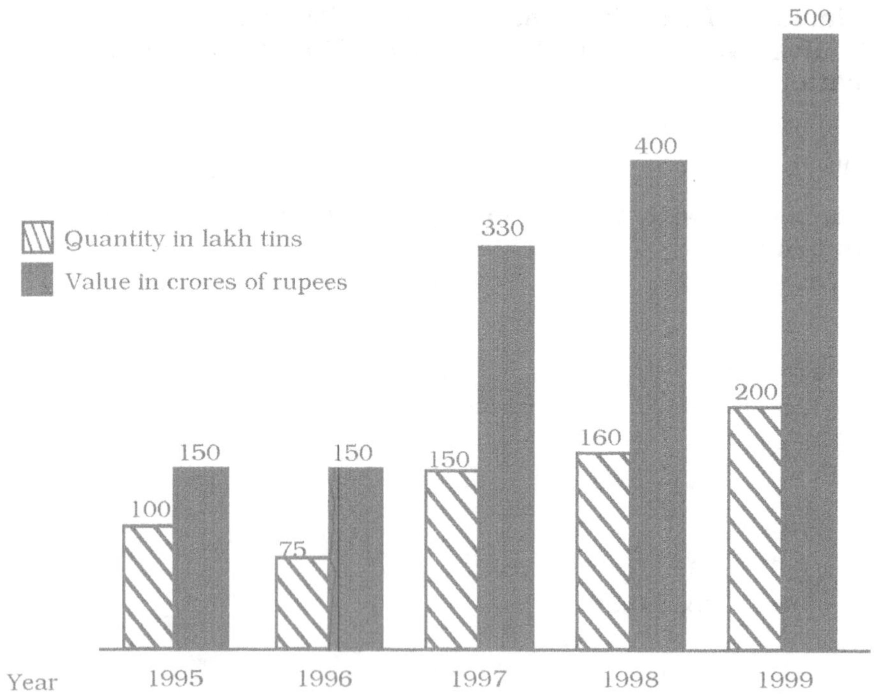

46. In which year the value per tin was minimum ?

A. 1995 B. 1996 C. 1998 D. 1999

47. What was the difference between the tins exported in 1997 and 1998 ?

A. 10 B. 1000 C. 100000 D. 1000000

48. What was the approximate percentage increase in export value from 1995 to 1999 ?

A. 350 B. 330.3 C. 433.3 D. None of these

49. What was the percentage drop in export quantity from 1995 to 1996 ?

A. 75 B. 50 C. 25 D. None of these

50. If in 1998, the tins were exported at the same rate per tin as that in 1997, what would be the value (in crores of rupees) of export in 1998 ?

A. 400 B. 375 C. 352 D. 330

Answer keys

1.C	2.C	3.B	4.A	5.C	6.D	7.D	8.A	9.A	10.B
11.A	12.B	13.A	14.A	15.B	16.A	17.D	18.A	19.D	20.C
21.B	22.C	23.B	24.B	25.A	26.C	27.C	28.C	29.A	30.B
31.A	32.A	33.C	34.C	35.C	36.C	37.B	38.A	39.C	40.B
41.C	42.A	43.A	44.D	45.C	46.A	47.D	48.D	49.C	50.C

UGC NET-JRF EXAMINATION JUNE 2006

SOLVED QUESTION PAPER

PAPER - I

Note : This paper contains **fifty** (50) multiple-choice questions, each question carrying **two** (2) marks. Attempt **all** of them.

1. **Which of the following comprise teaching skill?**

   A. Black Board writing B. Questioning

   C. Explaining D. All the above

2. **Which of the following statements is most appropriate?**

   A. Teachers can teach.

   B. Teachers help can create in a student a desire to learn.

   C. Lecture Method can be used for developing thinking.

   D. Teachers are born.

3. **The first Indian chronicler of Indian history was:**

   A. Megasthanese B. Fahiyan

   C. Huan Tsang D. Kalhan

4. **Which of the following statements is correct?**

   A. Syllabus is a part of curriculum.

   B. Syllabus is an annexure to curriculum.

   C. Curriculum is the same in all educational institutions affiliated to a particular university.

   D. Syllabus is not the same in all educational institutions affiliated to a particular university.

5. **Which of the two given options is of the level of understanding?**

   (I) Define noun.

   (II) Define noun in your own words.

   A. Only I B. Only II C. Both I and II D. Neither I nor II

6. **Which of the following options are the main tasks of research in modern society?**

   (I) to keep pace with the advancement in knowledge.

   (II) to discover new things.

(III) to write a critique on the earlier writings.

(IV) to systematically examine and critically analyse the investigations/sources with objectivity.

A. IV, II and I B. I, II and III C. I and III D. II, III and IV

7. Match List-I (Interviews) with List-II (Meaning) and select the correct answer from the code given below:

List - I (Interviews)	List - II (Meaning)
a. structured interviews	(i) greater flexibility approach
b. Unstructured interviews	(ii) attention on the questions to be answered
c. Focussed interviews	(iii) individual life experience
d. Clinical interviews	(iv) Pre determined question
	(v) non-directive

Code :

	a	b	c	d
A.	(iv)	(i)	(ii)	(iii)
B.	(ii)	(iv)	(i)	(iii)
C.	(v)	(ii)	(iv)	(i)
D.	(i)	(iii)	(v)	(iv)

8. What do you consider as the main aim of inter disciplinary research?

A. To bring out holistic approach to research

B. To reduce the emphasis of single subject in research domain

C. To over simplify the problem of research

D. To create a new trend in research methodology

9. One of the aims of the scientific method in research is to:

A. improve data interpretation B. eliminate spurious relations

C. confirm triangulation D. introduce new variables

10. The depth of any research can be judged by:

A. title of the research

B. objectives of the research

C. total expenditure on the research

D. duration of the research

1. Read the following passage and answer the questions 11 to 15:

The superintendence, direction and control of preparation of electoral rolls for, and the conduct of, elections to Parliament and State Legislatures and elections to the offices of the President and the Vice - President of India are vested in the Election Commission of India. It is an independent constitutional authority.

Independence of the Election Commission and its insulation from executive interference is ensured by a specific provision under Article 324 (5) of the constitution that the chief Election Commissioner shall not be removed from his office except in like manner and on like grounds as a Judge of the Supreme Court and conditions of his service shall not be varied to his disadvantage after his appointment.

In C.W.P. No. 4912 of 1998 (Kushra Bharat Vs. Union of India and others), the Delhi High Court directed that information relating to Government dues owed by the candidates to the departments dealing with Government accommodation, electricity, water, telephone and transport etc. and any other dues should be furnished by the candidates and this information should be published by the election authorities under the commission.

11. The text of the passage reflects or raises certain questions:

A. The authority of the commission can not be challenged.

B. This would help in stopping the criminalization of Indian politics.

C. This would reduce substantially the number of contesting candidates.

D. This would ensure fair and free elections.

12. According to the passage, the Election Commission is an independent constitutional authority. This is under Article No.:

A. 324 B. 356 C. 246 D. 161

13. Independence of the Commission means:

A. have a constitutional status. B. have legislative powers.

C. have judicial powers. D. have political powers.

14. Fair and free election means:

A. transparency B. to maintain law and order

C. regional considerations D. role for pressure groups

15. The Chief Election Commissioner can be removed from his office under Article:

A. 125 B. 352 C. 226 D. 324

16. The function of mass communication of supplying information regarding the processes, issues, events and societal developments is known as:

A. content supply B. surveillance

C. gratification D. correlation

17. The science of the study of feedback systems in humans, animals and machines is known as:

A. cybernetics B. reverse communication

C. selectivity study D. response analysis

18. Networked media exist in inter-connected:

A. social environments

B. economic environments

C. political environments

D. technological environments

19. The combination of computing, telecommunications and media in a digital atmosphere is referred to as:

A. online communication B. integrated media

C. digital combine D. convergence

20. A dialogue between a human-being and a computer programme that occurs simultaneously in various forms is described as:

A. man-machine speak B. binary chat

C. digital talk D. interactivity

21. Insert the missing number:

$\frac{16}{32}, \frac{15}{33}, \frac{17}{31}, \frac{14}{34}$?

A. $\frac{19}{35}$ B. $\frac{19}{30}$ C. $\frac{18}{35}$ D. $\frac{18}{30}$

22. Monday falls on 20th March 1995. What was the day on 3rd November 1994?

A. Thursday B. Sunday C. Tuesday D. Saturday

23. The average of four consecutive even numbers is 27. The largest of these numbers is:

A. 36 B. 32 C. 30 D. 28

24. In a certain code, FHQK means GIRL. How will WOMEN be written in the same code?

A. VNLDM B. FHQKN C. XPNFO D. VLNDM

25. At what time between 4 and 5 O'Clock will the hands of a watch point in opposite directions?

A. 45 min. past 4

B. 40 min. past 4

C. $50\frac{4}{11}$ min. past 4

D. $54\frac{6}{11}$ min. past 4

26. Which of the following conclusions is logically valid based on statement given below?

Statement : Most teachers are hard working.

Conclusions : (I) Some teachers are hard working.

(II) Some teachers are not hard working.

A. Only (I) is implied

B. Only (II) is implied

C. Both (I) and (II) are implied

D. Neither (I) nor (II) is implied

27. Who among the following can be asked to make a statement in Indian Parliament?

A. Any MLA

B. Chief of Army Staff

C. Solicitor General of India

D. Mayor of Delhi

28. Which of the following conclusions is logically valid based on statement given below?

Statement : Most of the Indian states existed before independence.

Conclusions : (I) Some Indian States existed before independence.

(II) All Indian States did not exist before independence.

A. only (I) is implied

B. only (II) is implied

C. Both (I) and (II) are implied

D. Neither (I) nor (II) is implied

29. Water is always involved with landslides. This is because it:

A. reduces the shear strength of rocks

B. increases the weight of the overburden

C. enhances chemical weathering

D. is a universal solvent

30. Direction for this question:

Given below are two statements (a) and (b) followed by two conclusions (i) and (ii). Considering the statements to be true, indicate which of the following conclusions logically follow from the given statements by selecting one of the four response alternatives given below the conclusion :

Statements : (a) all businessmen are wealthy.
(b) all wealthy people are hard working.

Conclusions : (i) All businessmen are hard working.
(ii) All hardly working people are not wealthy

A. Only (i) follows
B. Only (ii) follows
C. Only (i) and (ii) follows
D. Neither (i) nor (ii) follows

31. Using websites to pour out one's grievances is called:

A. cyberventing B. cyber ranting
C. web hate D. web plea

32. In web search, finding a large number of documents with very little relevant information is termed:

A. poor recall B. web crawl
C. poor precision rate D. poor web response

33. The concept of connect intelligence is derived from:

A. virtual reality B. fuzzy logic
C. bluetooth technology D. value added networks

34. Use of an ordinary telephone as an Internet applicance is called:

A. voicenet B. voice telephone
C. voice line D. voice portal

35. Video transmission over the Internet that looks like delayed livecasting is called:

A. virtual video B. direct broadcast
C. video shift D. real-time video

36. Which is the smallest North-east State in India?

A. Tripura B. Meghalaya
C. Mizoram D. Manipur

37. Tamilnadu coastal belt has drinking water shortage due to:

A. high evaporation

B. sea water flooding due to tsunami

C. over exploitation of ground water by tubewells

D. seepage of sea water

38. While all rivers of Peninsular India flow into the Bay of Bengal, Narmada and Tapti flow into the Arabian Sea because these two rivers:

A. Follow the slope of these rift valleys

B. The general slope of the Indian peninsula is from east to west

C. The Indian peninsula north of the Satpura ranges, is tilted towards the west

D. The Indian peninsula south of the satpura ranges is tilted towards east

39. Soils in the Mahanadi delta are less fertile than those in the Godavari delta because of:

A. erosion of top soils by annual floods

B. inundation of land by sea water

C. traditional agriculture practices

D. the derivation of alluvial soil from red-soil hinterland

40. Which of the following institutions in the field of education is set up by the MHRD Government of India?

A. Indian council of world Affair, New Delhi

B. Mythic Society, Bangalore

C. National Bal Bhawn, New Delhi

D. India International Centre, New Delhi

41. Assertion (A) : Aerosols have potential for modifying climate

Reason (R) : Aerosols interact with both short waves and radiation

A. Both (A) and (R) are true, and (R) is the correct explanation of (A)

B. Both (A) and (R) are true, but (R) is not the correct explanation of (A)

C. (A) is true, but (R) is false

D. (A) is false, but (R) is true

42. 'SITE' stands for:

A. System for International technology and Engineering

B. Satellite Instructional Television Experiment

C. South Indian Trade Estate

D. State Institute of Technology and Engineering

43. What is the name of the Research station established by the Indian Government for 'Conducting Research at Antarctic'?

A. Dakshin Gangotri

B. Yamunotri

C. Uttari Gangotri

D. None of the above

44. Ministry of Human Resource Development (HRD) includes:

A. Department of Elementary Education and Literacy

B. Department of Secondary Education and Higher Education

C. Department of Women and Child Development

D. All the above

45. Parliament can legislate on matters listed in the State list:

A. With the prior permission of the President.

B. Only after the constitution is amended suitably.

C. In case of inconsistency among State legislatures.

D. At the request of two or more States.

Question Number 46 to 50 Not for VISUALLY HANDICAPPED CANDIDATES.

The following pie chart indicates the expenditure of a country on various sports during a particular year. Study the pie chart and answer Question Number 46 to 50.

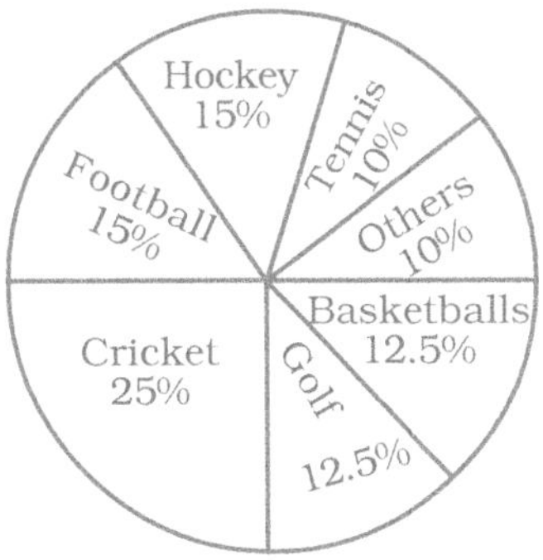

46. The ratio of the total expenditure on football to that of expenditure on hockey is:

A. 1 : 15 B. 1 : 1 C. 15 : 1 D. 3 : 20

47. If the total expenditure on sports during the year was Rs. 1,20,000,00 how much was spent on basket ball?

A. ₹ 9,50,000 B. ₹ 10,00,000

C. ₹ 12,00,000 D. ₹ 15,00,000

48. The chart shows that the most popular game of the country is:

A. Hockey B. Football

C. Cricket D. Tennis

49. Out of the following country's expenditure is the same on:

A. Hockey and Tennis B. Golf and Basket ball

C. Cricket and Football D. Hockey and Golf

50. If the total expenditure on sport during the year was ₹ 1,50,00,000 the expenditure on cricket and hockey together was:

A. ₹ 60,00,000 B. ₹ 50,00,000

C. ₹ 37,50,000 D. ₹ 25,00,000

Answer keys

1.D	2.B	3.D	4. A	5.B	6. A	7. A	8.A	9.B	10.B
11.A	12.A	13.A	14.B	15.D	16.B	17.A	18.D	19.D	20.D
21.D	22.A	23.C	24.A	25.D	26.B	27.C	28.B	29.D	30.A
31.A	32.A	33.D	34.C	35.D	36.C	37.D	38.B	39.A	40.C
41.A	42.B	43.A	44.D	45.D	46.B	47.D	48.C	49.B	50.A

UGC NET-JRF EXAMINATION DECEMBER 2006

SOLVED QUESTION PAPER

PAPER - I

Note : This paper contains **fifty** (50) multiple-choice questions, each question carrying **two** (2) marks. Attempt **all** of them.

1. **Which of the following is not instructional material?**

A. Over Head Projector B. Audio Cassette

C. Printed Material D. Transparency

2. **Which of the following statement is not correct?**

A. Lecture Method can develop reasoning

B. Lecture Method can develop knowledge

C. Lecture Method is one way process

D. During Lecture Method students are passive

3. **The main objective of teaching at Higher Education Level is:**

A. To prepare students to pass examination

B. To develop the capacity to take decisions

C. To give new information

D. To motivate students to ask questions during lecture

4. **Which of the following statement is correct?**

A. Reliability ensures validity

B. Validity ensures reliability

C. Reliability and validity are independent of each other

D. Reliability does not depend on objectivity

5. **Which of the following indicates evaluation?**

A. Ram got 45 marks out of 200

B. Mohan got 38 percent marks in English

C. Shyam got First Division in final examination

D. All the above

6. **Research can be conducted by a person who:**

A. has studied research methodology

B. holds a postgraduate degree

C. possesses thinking and reasoning ability

D. is a hard worker

7. Which of the following statements is correct?

A. Objectives of research are stated in first chapter of the thesis

B. Researcher must possess analytical ability

C. Variability is the source of problem

D. All the above

8. Which of the following is not the Method of Research?

A. Observation B. Historical

C. Survey D. Philosophical

9. Research can be classified as:

A. Basic, Applied and Action Research

B. Quantitative and Qualitative Research

C. Philosophical, Historical, Survey and Experimental Research

D. All the above

10. The first step of research is:

A. Selecting a problem B. Searching a problem

C. Finding a problem D. Identifying a problem

1. Read the following passage and answer the question nos. 11 to 15:

After almost three decades of contemplating Swarovski -encrusted navels on increasing flat abs, the Mumbai film industry is on a discovery of India and itself. With budgets of over 30 crore each, four soon to be released movies by premier directors are exploring the idea of who we are and redefining who the other is. It is a fundamental question which the bling-bling, glam-sham and disham-disham tends to avoid. It is also a question which binds an audience when the lights go dim and the projector rolls : as a nation, who are we ? As a people, where are we going ?

The Germans coined a word for it, zeitgeist, which perhaps Yash Chopra would not care to pronounce. But at 72, he remains the person who can best capture it. After being the first to project the diasporic Indian on screen in Lamhe in 1991, he has returned to his roots in a new movie. Veer Zaara, set in 1986, where Pakistan, the traditional other, the part that got away, is the lover and the saviour. In Subhas Ghai's Kisna, set in 1947, the other is the English woman. She is not a memsahib, but a mehbooba. In Ketan Mehta's The Rising, the East India Englishman is not the evil oppressor of countless cardboard characterisations, which span the spectrum from Jewel in the Crown to Kranti, but an honourable friend.

This is Manoj Kumar's Desh Ki dharti with a difference : there is culture, not contentious politics; balle balle, not bombs : no dooriyan (distance), only nazdeekiyan (closeness).

All four films are heralding a new hero and heroine. The new hero is fallible and vulnerable, committed to his dharma, but also not afraid of failure - less of a boy and more of a man. He even has a grown up name : Veer Pratap Singh in Veer-Zaara and Mohan Bhargav in Swades. The new heroine is not a babe, but often a bebe, dressed in traditional Punjabi clothes, often with the stereotypical body type as well, as in Bride and Prejudice of Gurinder Chadha.

11. Which word Yash Chopra would not be able to pronounce?

A. Bling + bling B. Zeitgeist
C. Montaz D. Dooriyan

12. Who made Lamhe in 1991?

A. Subhash Ghai B. Yash Chopra
C. Aditya Chopra D. Sakti Samanta

13. Which movie is associated with Manoj Kumar?

A. Jewel in the Crown B. Kisna
C. Zaara D. Desh Ki dharti

14. Which is the latest film by Yash Chopra?

A. Deewar B. Kabhi Kabhi
C. Dilwale Dulhaniya Le Jayenge D. Veer Zaara

15. Which is the dress of the heroine in Veer-Zaara?

A. Traditional Gujarati Clothes
B. Traditional Bengali Clothes
C. Traditional Punjabi Clothes
D. Traditional Madrasi Clothes

16. Which one of the following can be termed as verbal communication?

A. Prof. Sharma delivered the lecture in the class room.
B. Signal at the cross-road changed from green to orange.
C. The child was crying to attract the attention of the mother.
D. Dipak wrote a letter for leave application.

17. Which is the 24 hours English Business news channel in India?

A. Zee News B. NDTV 24×7
C. CNBC D. India News

18. Consider the following statements in communication:

(i) Hema Malini is the Chairperson of the Children's Film Society, India.

(ii) Yash Chopra is the Chairman of the Central Board of Film Certification of India.

(iii) Sharmila Tagore is the Chairperson of National Film Development Corporation.

(iv) Dilip Kumar, Raj Kapoor and Preeti Zinta have all been recipients of Dada Saheb Phalke Award.

Which of the statements given above is/are correct?

A. (i) and (iii) B. (ii) and (iii) C. (iv) only D. (iii) only

19. Which of the following pair is not correctly matched?

A. N. Ram : The Hindu

B. Barkha Dutt : Zee News

C. Pranay Roy : NDTV 24×7

D. Prabhu Chawla : Aaj taak

20. "Because you deserve to know" is the punchline used by:

A. The Times of India B. The Hindu

C. Indian Express D. Hindustan Times

21. In the sequence of numbers 8, 24, 12, X, 18, 54 the missing number X is:

A. 26 B. 24 C. 36 D. 32

22. If A stands for 5, B for 6, C for 7, D for 8 and so on, then the following numbers stand for 17, 19, 20, 9 and 8:

A. PLANE B. MOPED C. MOTOR D. TONGA

23. The letters in the first set have certain relationship. On the basis of this relationship what is the right choice for the second set?

AST : BRU : : NQV : ?

A. ORW B. MPU C. MRW D. OPW

24. In a certain code, PAN is written as 31 and PAR as 35. In this code PAT is written as:

A. 30 B. 37 C. 38 D. 39

25. The sides of a triangle are in the ratio of21 : 13 : 14 . If its perimeter is 52 cm, the length of the smallest side is:

A. 9 cm B. 10 cm C. 11 cm D. 12 cm

26. Which one of the following statements is completely non-sensical?

A. He was a bachelor, but he married recently.

B. He is a bachelor, but he married recently.

C. When he married, he was not a bachelor.

D. When he was a bachelor, he was not married.

27. Which of the following statements are mutually contradictory?

(i) All flowers are not fragrant.

(ii) Most flowers are not fragrant.

(iii) None of the flowers is fragrant.

(iv) Most flowers are fragrant.

Choose the correct answer from the code given below:

Code :

A. (i) and (ii) B. (i) and (iii)

C. (ii) and (iii) D. (iii) and (iv)

28. Which of the following statements say the same thing?

(i) "I am a teacher" (said by Arvind)

(ii) "I am a teacher" (said by Binod)

(iii) "My son is a teacher" (said by Binod's father)

(iv) "My brother is a teacher" (said by Binod's sister)

(v) "My brother is a teacher" (said by Binod's only sister)

(vi) "My sole enemy is a teacher" (said by Binod's only enemy) Choose the correct answer from the code given below :

Code :

A. (i) and (ii) B. (ii), (iii), (iv) and (v)

C. (ii) and (vi) D. (v) and (vi)

29. Which of the following are correct ways of arguing?

(i) There can be no second husband without a second wife.

(ii) Anil is a friend of Bob, Bob is a friend of Raj, hence Anil is a friend of Raj.

(iii) A is equal to B, B is equal to C, hence A is equal to C.

(iv) If everyone is a liar, then we cannot prove it.

Choose the correct answer from the code given below :

Code :

A. (iii) and (iv) B. (i), (iii) and (iv)

C. (ii), (iii) and (iv) D. (i), (ii), (iii) and (iv)

30. Which of the following statement/s are ALWAYS FALSE?

(i) The sun will not rise in the East some day.

(ii) A wooden table is not a table.

(iii) Delhi city will be drowned under water.

(iv) Cars run on water as fuel.

Choose the correct answer from the code given below:

Code :

A. (i), (iii) and (iv) B. Only (iii)

C. (i), (ii) and (iii) D. (ii) alone

2. Study the following graph and answer question numbers 31 to 33:

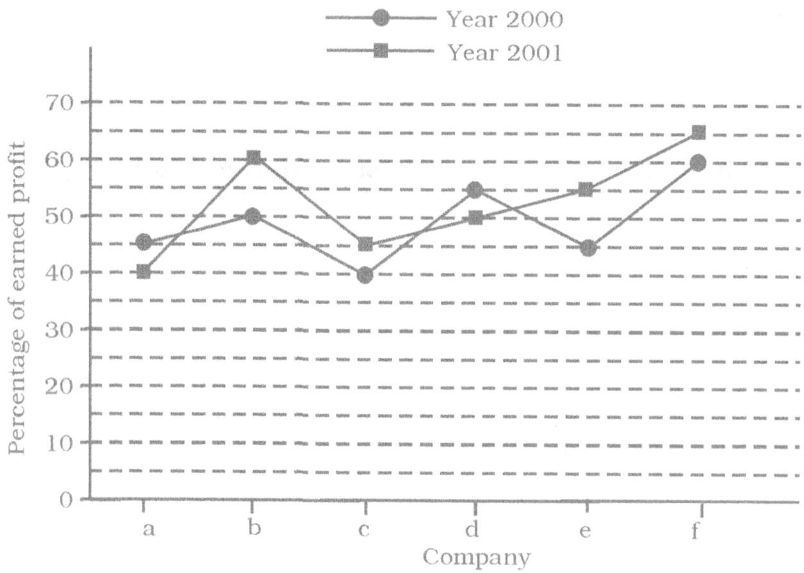

31. In the year 2000, which of the following Companies earned maximum percent profit?

A. a B. b C. D D. F

32. In the year 2001, which of the following Companies earned minimum percent profit?

A. a B. c C. d D. E

33. In the years 2000 and 2001, which of the following Companies earned maximum average percent profit?

A. f B. e C. d D. b

34. Human Development Report for 'each' of the year at global level has been published by:

A. UNDP B. WTO

C. IMF D. World Bank

35. The number of students in four classes A, B, C, D and their respective mean marks obtained by each of the class are given below:

	Class A	Class B	Class C	Class D
Number of students	10	40	30	20
Arithmetic mean	20	30	50	15

The combined mean of the marks of four classes together will be :

A. 32 B. 50 C. 20 D. 15

36. LAN stands for:

A. Local And National B. Local Area Network

C. Large Area Network D. Live Area Network

37. Which of the following statement is correct?

A. Modem is a software

B. Modem helps in stabilizing the voltage

C. Modem is the operating system

D. Modem converts the analog signal into digital signal and vice-versa

38. Which of the following is the appropriate definition of a computer?

A. Computer is a machine that can process information.

B. Computer is an electronic device that can store, retrieve and process both qualitative and quantitative data quickly and accurately.

C. Computer is an electronic device that can store, retrieve and quickly process only quantitative data.

D. Computer is a machine that can store, retrieve and process quickly and accurately only qualitative information

39. Information and Communication Technology includes:

A. On line learning B. Learning through the use of EDUSAT

C. Web Based Learning D. All the above

40. Which of the following is the appropriate format of URL of e-mail?

A. www_mail.com B. www@mail.com

C. WWW@mail.com D. www.mail.com

41. The most significant impact of volcanic erruption has been felt in the form of:

A. change in weather
B. sinking of islands
C. loss of vegetation
D. extinction of animals

42. With absorption and decomposition of CO_2 in ocean water beyond desired level, there will be:

A. decrease in temperature
B. increase in salinity
C. growth of phyto plankton
D. rise in sea level

43. Arrange column II in proper sequence so as to match it with column I and choose the correct answer from the code given below:

Column I Water Quality	Column II pH Value
A. Neutral	(i) 5
B. Moderately acidic	(ii) 7
C. Alkaline	(iii) 4
D. Injurious	(iv) 8

Code :

	(a)	(b)	(c)	(d)
A.	(ii)	(iii)	(i)	(iv)
B.	(i)	(iii)	(ii)	(iv)
C.	(ii)	(i)	(iv)	(iii)
D.	(iv)	(ii)	(iii)	(i)

44. The maximum emission of pollutants from fuel sources in India is caused by:

A. Coal
B. Firewood
C. Refuse burning
D. Vegetable waste product

45. The urbanisation process accounts for the wind in the urban centres during nights to remain:

A. faster than that in rural areas
B. slower than that in rural areas
C. the same as that in rural areas
D. cooler than that in rural areas

46. The University Grants Commission was constituted on the recommendation of:

A. Dr. Sarvapalli Radhakrishnan Commission

B. Mudaliar Commission

C. Sargent Commission

D. Kothari Commission

47. Which one of the following Articles of the Constitution of India safeguards the rights of Minorities to establish and run educational institutions of their own liking?

A. Article 19 B. Article 29 C. Article 30 D. Article 31

48. Match List - I (Institutions) with List - II (Functions) and select the correct answer by using the code given below:

List - I (Institutions)	List - II (Functions)
A. Parliament	(i) Formulation of Budget
B. C & A.G.	(ii) Enactment of Budget
C. Ministry of Finance	(iii) Implementation of Budget
D. Executing Departments	(iv) Legality of expenditure
	(v) Justification of Income

Code :

	(a)	(b)	(c)	d)
A.	(iii)	(iv)	(ii)	(i)
B.	(ii)	(iv)	(i)	(iii)
C.	(v)	(iii)	(iv)	(ii)
D.	(iv)	(ii)	(iii)	(v)

49. Foundation training to the newly recruited IAS (Probationers) is imparted by:

A. Indian Institute of Public Administration

B. Administrative Staff College of India

C. L.B.S. National Academy of Administration

D. Centre for Advanced Studies

50. Electoral disputes arising out of Presidential and Vice-Presidential Elections are settled by:

A. Election Commission of India

B. Joint Committee of Parliament

C. Supreme Court of India

D. Central Election Tribunal

Answer keys

1.D	2.A	3.B	4.B	5.D	6.C	7.D	8.A	9.D	10.D
11.B	12.B	13.D	14.D	15.C	16.A	17.C	18.D	19.B	20.D
21.C	22.B	23.D	24.B	25.D	26.B	27.D	28.B	29.A	30.D
31.D	32.A	33.A	34.A	35.A	36.B	37.D	38.B	39.D	40.D
41.A	42.C	43.C	44.B	45.B	46.C	47.C	48.B	49.C	50.C

UGC NET-JRF EXAMINATION JUNE 2007

SOLVED QUESTION PAPER

PAPER - I

Note : This paper contains **fifty** (50) multiple-choice questions, each question carrying **two** (2) marks. Attempt **all** of them.

1. **Teacher uses visual-aids to make learning:**

A. simple B. more knowledgeable
C. quicker D. interesting

2. **The teacher's role at the higher educational level is to:**

A. provide information to students
B. promote self-learning in students
C. encourage healthy competition among students
D. help students to solve their personal problems

3. **Which one of the following teachers would you like the most:**

A. punctual
B. having research aptitude
C. loving and having high idealistic philosophy
D. who often amuses his students

4. **Micro teaching is most effective for the student-teacher:**

A. during the practice-teaching
B. after the practice-teaching
C. before the practice-teaching
D. none of the above

5. **Which is the least important factor in teaching?**

A. punishing the students
B. maintaining discipline in the class
C. lecturing in impressive way
D. drawing sketches and diagrams on the black-board

6. **To test null hypothesis, a researcher uses:**

A. t test B. ANOVA
C. x2 D. factorial analysis

7. A research problem is feasible only when:

A. it has utility and relevance

B. it is researchable

C. it is new and adds something to knowledge

D. all the above

8. Bibliography given in a research report:

A. shows vast knowledge of the researcher

B. helps those interested in further research

C. has no relevance to research

D. all the above

9. Fundamental research reflects the ability to:

A. Synthesize new ideals

B. Expound new principles

C. Evaluate the existing material concerning research

D. Study the existing literature regarding various topics

10. The study in which the investigators attempt to trace an effect is known as:

A. Survey Research

B. 'Ex-post Facto' Research

C. Historical Research

D. Summative Research

1. Read the following passage and answer the questions 11 to 15:

All political systems need to mediate the relationship between private wealth and public power. Those that fail risk a dysfunctional government captured by wealthy interests. Corruption is one symptom of such failure with private willingness-to-pay trumping public goals. Private individuals and business firms pay to get routine services and to get to the head of the bureaucratic queue. They pay to limit their taxes, avoid costly regulations, obtain contracts at inflated prices and get concessions and privatised firms at low prices. If corruption is endemic, public officials - both bureaucrats and elected officials - may redesign programmes and propose public projects with few public benefits and many opportunities for private profit. Of course, corruption, in the sense of bribes, pay-offs and kickbacks, is only one type of government failure. Efforts to promote 'good governance' must be broader than anti-corruption campaigns. Governments may be honest but inefficient because no one has an incentive to work productively, and narrow elites may capture the state and exert excess influence on policy. Bribery may induce the lazy to work hard and permit those not in the inner circle of cronies to obtain benefits. However, even in such cases, corruption cannot be confined to 'functional' areas. It will be a temptation whenever private benefits are positive. It may be a reasonable response to a harsh reality but, over time, it can facilitate a spiral into an even worse situation.

11. The governments which fail to focus on the relationship between private wealth and public power are likely to become:

A. Functional B. Dysfunctional

C. Normal functioning D. Good governance

12. One important symptom of bad governance is:

A. Corruption

B. High taxes

C. Complicated rules and regulations

D. High prices

13. When corruption is rampant, public officials always aim at many opportunities for:

A. Public benefits B. Public profit

C. Private profit D. Corporate gains

14. Productivity linked incentives to public/private officials is one of the indicatives for:

A. Efficient government B. Bad governance

C. Inefficient government D. Corruption

15. The spiralling corruption can only be contained by promoting:

A. Private profit B. Anti-corruption campaign

C. Good governance D. Pay-offs and kick backs

16. Press Council of India is located at:

A. Chennai B. Mumbai

C. Kolkata D. Delhi

17. Adjusting the photo for publication by cutting is technically known as:

A. Photo cutting B. Photo bleeding

C. Photo cropping D. Photo adjustment

18. Feed-back of a message comes from:

A. Satellite B. Media

C. Audience D. Communicator

19. Collection of information in advance before designing communication strategy is known as:

A. Feed-back B. Feed-forward

C. Research study D. Opinion poll

20. The aspect ratio of TV screen is:

A. 4 : 3 B. 4 : 2

C. 3 : 5 D. 2 : 3

21. Which is the number that comes next in the sequence?

9, 8, 8, 8, 7, 8, 6, ______

A. 5 B. 6 C. 8 D. 4

22. If in a certain language TRIVANDRUM is coded as 2 5 9 5 3 5 4 7 5 8, how would MADRAS be coded?

A. 8 3 4 5 3 6 B. 8 3 4 5 3 8

C. 8 3 4 5 3 0 D. 8 3 4 5 3 9

23. The question to be answered by factorial analysis of the quantitative data does not explain one of the following :

A. Is 'X' related to 'Y'?

B. How is 'X' related to 'Y'?

C. How does 'X' affect the dependent variable 'Y' at different levels of another independent variable 'K' or 'M'?

D. How is 'X' by 'K' related to 'M'?

24. January 12, 1980 was Saturday, what day was January 12, 1979:

A. Saturday B. Friday

C. Sunday D. Thursday

25. How many Mondays are there in a particular month of a particular year, if the month ends on Wednesday?

A. 5 B. 4

C. 3 D. None of the above

26. From the given four statements, select the two which cannot be true but yet both can be false. Choose the right pair:

(i) All men are mortal

(ii) Some men are mortal

(iii) No man is mortal

(iv) Some men are not mortal

A. (i) and (ii)
B. (iii) and (iv)
C. (i) and (iii)
D. (ii) and (iv)

27. A Syllogism must have:

A. Three terms
B. Four terms
C. Six terms
D. Five terms

28. Copula is that part of proposition which denotes the relationship between:

A. Subject and predicate
B. Known and unknown
C. Major premise and minor premise
D. Subject and object

29. "E" denotes:

A. Universal Negative Proposition
B. Particular Affirmative Proposition
C. Universal Affirmative Proposition
D. Particular Negative Proposition

30. 'A' is the father of 'C', and 'D' is the son of 'B'. 'E' is the brother of 'A'. If 'C' is the sister of 'D', how is 'B' related to 'E'?

A. daughter
B. husband
C. sister-in-law
D. brother-in-law

31. Which of the following methods will you choose to prepare choropleth map of India showing urban density of population:

A. Quartiles
B. Quintiles
C. Mean and SD
D. Break-point

32. Which of the following methods is best suited to show on a map the types of crops being grown in a region:

A. Choropleth
B. Chorochromatic
C. Choroschematic
D. Isopleth

33. A ratio represents the relation between:

A. Part and Part
B. Part and Whole
C. Whole and Whole
D. All of the above

34. Out of four numbers, the average of the first three numbers is thrice the fourth number. If the average of the four numbers is 5, the fourth number is:

A. 4.5
B. 5
C. 2
D. 4

35. Circle graphs are used to show:

A. How various sections share in the whole

B. How various parts are related to the whole

C. How one whole is related to other wholes

D. How one part is related to other parts

36. On the keyboard of computer each character has an "ASCII" value which stands for:

A. American Stock Code for Information Interchange

B. American Standard Code for Information Interchange

C. African Standard Code for Information Interchange

D. Adaptable Standard Code for Information Change

37. Which part of the Central Processing Unit (CPU) performs calculation and makes decisions:

A. Arithematic Logic Unit
B. Alternating Logic Unit
C. Alternate Local Unit
D. American Logic Unit

38. "Dpi" stands for:

A. Dots per inch
B. Digits per unit
C. Dots pixel inch
D. Diagrams per inch

39. The process of laying out a document with text, graphics, headlines and photographs is involved in:

A. Deck Top Publishing
B. Desk Top Printing
C. Desk Top Publishing
D. Deck Top Printing

40. Transfer of data from one application to another line is known as:

A. Dynamic Disk Exchange
B. Dodgy Data Exchange
C. Dogmatic Data Exchange
D. Dynamic Data Exchange

41. Tsunami occurs due to:

A. Mild earthquakes and landslides in the oceans

B. Strong earthquakes and landslides in the oceans

C. Strong earthquakes and landslides in mountains

D. Strong earthquakes and landslides in deserts

42. Which of the natural hazards have big effect on Indian people each year?

A. Cyclones
B. Floods
C. Earthquakes
D. Landslides

43. Comparative Environment Impact Assessment study is to be conducted for:

A. the whole year
B. three seasons excluding monsoon
C. any three seasons
D. the worst season

44. Sea level rise results primarily due to:

A. Heavy rainfall
B. Melting of glaciers
C. Submarine volcanism
D. Seafloor spreading

45. The plume rise in a coal based power plant depends on:

(i) Buoyancy
(ii) Atmospheric stability
(iii) Momentum of exhaust gases

Identify the correct code:

A. (i) and (ii) only
B. (ii) and (iii) only
C. (i) and (iii) only
D. (i), (ii) and (iii)

46. Value education makes a student:

A. Good citizen
B. Successful businessman
C. Popular teacher
D. Efficient manager

47. Networking of libraries through electronic media is known as:

A. Inflibnet
B. Libinfnet
C. Internet
D. HTML

48. The University which telecasts interactive educational programmes through its own channel is:

A. B. R. Ambedkar Open University, Hyderabad
B. I. G. N. O. U.
C. University of Pune
D. Annamalai University

49. The Government established the University Grants Commission by an Act of Parliament in the year:

A. 1980
B. 1948
C. 1950
D. 1956

50. Universities having central campus for imparting education are called:

A. Central Universities
B. Deemed Universities
C. Residential Universities
D. Open Universities

Answer keys

1.D	2.B	3.B	4.A	5. A	6.B	7.D	8.A	9. B	10.B
1.B	12.A	13.C	14.A	15.C	16.D	17.C	18.C	19.D	20.A
21.C	22.A	23.D	24.B	25.B	26.D	27.A	28.A	29.A	30.C
31.A	32.A	33.D	34.C	35.B	36.B	37.A	38.A	39.C	40.D
41.B	42.B	43.A	44.B	45.B	46.A	47.A	48.B	49.D	50.A

UGC NET-JRF EXAMINATION DECEMBER 2007

SOLVED QUESTION PAPER

PAPER - I

Note : This paper contains **fifty** (50) multiple-choice questions, each question carrying **two** (2) marks. Attempt **all** of them.

1. **Verbal guidance is least effective in the learning of:**

A. Aptitudes B. Skills

C. Attitudes D. Relationship

2. **Which is the most important aspect of the teacher's role in learning?**

A. The development of insight into what constitutes an adequate performance

B. The development of insight into what constitutes the pitfalls and dangers to be avoided

C. The provision of encouragement and moral support

D. The provision of continuous diagnostic and remedial help

3. **The most appropriate purpose of learning is:**

A. personal adjustment

B. modification of behaviour

C. social and political awareness

D. preparing oneself for employment

4. **The students who keep on asking questions in the class should be:**

A. encouraged to find answer independently

B. advised to meet the teacher after the class

C. encouraged to continue questioning

D. advised not to disturb during the lecture

5. **Maximum participation of students is possible in teaching through :**

A. discussion method B. lecture method

C. audio-visual aids D. text book method

6. **Generalised conclusion on the basis of a sample is technically known as:**

A. Data analysis and interpretation B. Parameter inference

C. Statistical inference D. All of the above

7. The experimental study is based on:

A. The manipulation of variables
B. Conceptual parameters
C. Replication of research
D. Survey of literature

8. The main characteristic of scientific research is:

A. empirical
B. theoretical
C. experimental
D. all of the above

9. Authenticity of a research finding is its:

A. Originality
B. Validity
C. Objectivity
D. All of the above

10. Which technique is generally followed when the population is finite?

A. Area Sampling Technique
B. Purposive Sampling Technique
C. Systematic Sampling Technique
D. None of the above

1. Read the following passage and answer the questions 11 to 15:

Gandhi's overall social and environmental philosophy is based on what human beings need rather than what they want. His early introduction to the teachings of Jains, Theosophists, Christian sermons, Ruskin and Tolstoy, and most significantly the Bhagavad Gita, were to have profound impact on the development of Gandhi's holistic thinking on humanity, nature and their ecological interrelation. His deep concern for the disadvantaged, the poor and rural population created an ambience for an alternative social thinking that was at once far-sighted, local and immediate. For Gandhi was acutely aware that the demands generated by the need to feed and sustain human life, compounded by the growing industrialization of India, far outstripped the finite resources of nature. This might nowadays appear naïve or commonplace, but such pronouncements were as rare as they were heretical a century ago. Gandhi was also concerned about the destruction, under colonial and modernist designs, of the existing infrastructures which had more potential for keeping a community flourishing within ecologically-sensitive traditional patterns of subsistence, especially in the rural areas, than did the incoming Western alternatives based on nature-blind technology and the enslavement of human spirit and energies.

Perhaps the moral principle for which Gandhi is best known is that of active non-violence, derived from the traditional moral restraint of not injuring another being. The most refined expression of this value is in the great epic of the Mahabharata, (c. 100 BCE to 200 CE), where moral development proceeds through placing constraints on the liberties, desires and acquisitiveness endemic to human life. One's action is judged in terms of consequences and the impact it is likely to have on another. Jainas had generalized this principle to include all sentient creatures and biocommunities alike. Advanced Jaina monks and nuns will sweep their path to avoid harming insects and even bacteria. Non-injury is a non-negotiable universal prescription.

11. Which one of the following have a profound impact on the development of Gandhi's holistic thinking on humanity, nature and their ecological interrelations?

A. Jain teachings B. Christian sermons

C. Bhagavad Gita D. Ruskin and Tolstoy

12. Gandhi's overall social and environmental philosophy is based on human beings':

A. need B. desire C. wealth D. welfare

13. Gandhiji's deep concern for the disadvantaged, the poor and rural population created an ambience for an alternative:

A. rural policy B. social thinking

C. urban policy D. economic thinking

14. Colonial policy and modernisation led to the destruction of:

A. major industrial infrastructure

B. irrigation infrastructure

C. urban infrastructure

D. rural infrastructure

15. Gandhi's active non-violence is derived from:

A. Moral restraint of not injuring another being

B. Having liberties, desires and acquisitiveness

C. Freedom of action

D. Nature-blind technology and enslavement of human spirit and energies

16. DTH service was started in the year:

A. 2000 B. 2002 C. 2004 D. 2006

17. National Press day is celebrated on:

A. 16th November B. 19th November

C. 21st November D. 30th November

18. The total number of members in the Press Council of India are:

A. 28 B. 14 C. 17 D. 20

19. The right to impart and receive information is guaranteed in the Constitution of India by Article:

A. 19 (2)A. B. 19 (16)

C. 19 (2) D. 19 (1) (a)

20. Use of radio for higher education is based on the presumption of:

A. Enriching curriculum based instruction

B. Replacing teacher in the long run

C. Everybody having access to a radio set

D. Other means of instruction getting outdated

21. Find out the number which should come at the place of question mark which will complete the following series:

5, 4, 9, 17, 35, ?, 139

A. 149 B. 79 C. 49 D. 69

Questions 22 to 24 are based on the following diagram in which there are three interlocking circles I, S and P, where circle I stands for Indians, circle S for Scientists and circle P for Politicians.

Different regions in the figure are lettered from a to f.

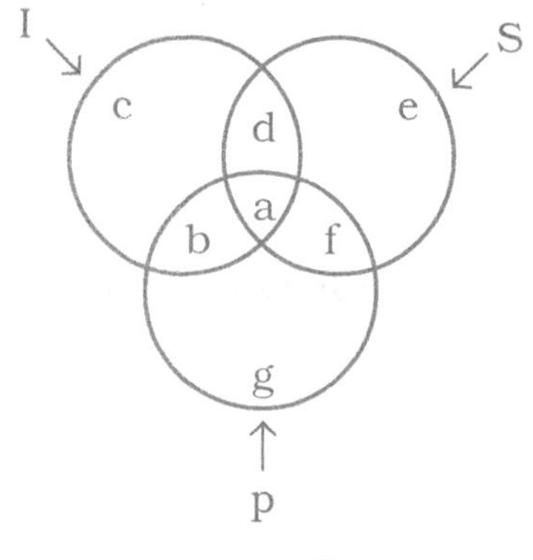

22. The region which represents Non-Indian Scientists who are Politicians:

A. f B. d C. a D. c

23. The region which represents Indians who are neither Scientists nor Politicians:

A. g B. c C. f D. a

24. The region which represents Politicians who are Indians as well as Scientists:

A. b B. c C. a D. d

25. Which number is missing in the following series? 2, 5, 10, 17, 26, 37, 50?

A. 63 B. 65 C. 67 D. 69

26. The function of measurement includes:

A. Prognosis B. Diagnosis
C. Prediction D. All of the above

27. Logical arguments are based on:

A. Scientific reasoning B. Customary reasoning
C. Mathematical reasoning D. Syllogistic reasoning

28. Insert the missing number:

4 : 17 : : 7 : ?

A. 48 B. 49 C. 50 D. 51

29. Choose the odd word:

A. Nun B. Knight C. Monk D. Priest

30. Choose the number which is different from others in the group:

A. 49 B. 63 C. 77 D. 81

31. Probability sampling implies:

A. Stratified Random Sampling
B. Systematic Random Sampling
C. Simple Random Sampling
D. All of the above

32. Insert the missing number:

$\frac{36}{62}, \frac{39}{63}, \frac{43}{61}, \frac{48}{64}, ?$

A. $\frac{51}{65}$ B. $\frac{56}{60}$ C. $\frac{54}{65}$ D. $\frac{33}{60}$

33. At what time between 3 and 4 O'clock will the hands of a watch point in opposite directions?

A. 40 minutes past three B. 45 minutes past three
C. 50 minutes past three D. 55 minutes past three

34. Mary has three children. What is the probability that none of the three children is a boy?

A. $\frac{1}{2}$ B. $\frac{1}{3}$ C. $\frac{3}{4}$ D. 1

35. If the radius of a circle is increased by 50 per cent. Its area is increased by:

A. 125 per cent B. 100 per cent
C. 75 per cent D. 50 per cent

36. CD ROM stands for:

A. Computer Disk Read Only Memory
B. Compact Disk Read Over Memory
C. Compact Disk Read Only Memory
D. Computer Disk Read Over Memory

37. The 'brain' of a computer which keeps peripherals under its control is called:

A. Common Power Unit B. Common Processing Unit
C. Central Power Unit D. Central Processing Unit

38. Data can be saved on backing storage medium known as:

A. Compact Disk Recordable B. Computer Disk Rewritable
C. Compact Disk Rewritable D. Computer Data Rewritable

39. RAM means :

A. Random Access Memory B. Rigid Access Memory
C. Rapid Access Memory D. Revolving Access Memory

40. www represents :

A. who what and where B. weird wide web
C. word wide web D. world wide web

41. Deforestation during the recent decades has led to:

A. Soil erosion B. Landslides
C. Loss of bio-diversity D. All the above

42. Which one of the following natural hazards is responsible for causing highest human disaster?

A. Earthquakes B. Volcanic eruptions
C. Snow-storms D. Tsunami

43. Which one of the following is appropriate for natural hazard mitigation?

A. International AID B. Timely Warning System
C. Rehabilitation D. Community Participation

44. Slums in metro-city are the result of:

A. Rural to urban migration
B. Poverty of the city-scape
C. Lack of urban infrastructure
D. Urban-governance

45. The great Indian Bustard bird is found in:

A. Thar Desert of India
B. Coastal regions of India
C. Temperate Forests in the Himalaya
D. Tarai zones of the Himalayan Foot

46. The first Indian Satellite for serving the educational sector is known as:

A. SATEDU
B. INSAT - B
C. EDUSAT
D. INSAT - C

47. Exclusive educational channel of IGNOU is known as:

A. Gyan Darshan
B. Gyan Vani
C. Door Darshan
D. Prasar Bharati

48. The head quarter of Mahatma Gandhi Antarrashtriya Hindi Vishwavidyalaya is situated in:

A. Sevagram
B. New Delhi
C. Wardha
D. Ahmedabad

49. Match List - I with List - II and select the correct answer using the codes given below:

List - I (Institutes)	**List - II (Locations)**
A. Central Institute of English and Foreign Languages	(i) Chitrakoot
B. Gramodaya Vishwavidyalaya	(ii) Hyderabad
C. Central Institute of Higher Tibetan Studies	(iii) New Delhi
D. IGNOU	(iv) Dharmasala

Codes:

	(a)	(b)	(c)	(d)
A.	(ii)	(i)	(iv)	(iii)
B.	(iv)	(iii)	(ii)	(i)
C.	(iii)	(iv)	(i)	(ii)
D.	(i)	(ii)	(iv)	(iii)

50. The aim of vocationalization of education is:

A. preparing students for a vocation along with knowledge

B. converting liberal education into vocational education

C. giving more importance to vocational than general education

D. making liberal education job-oriented

Answer keys

1.B	2.A	3.B	4.A	5.C	6.C	7.A	8.D	9.D	10.C
11.C	12.D	13.B	14.D	15.A	16.C	17.A	18.A	19.D	20.A
21.D	22.A	23.B	24.C	25.B	26.D	27.D	28.C	29.B	30.B
31.D	32.C	33.C	34.B	35.A	36.C	37.D	38.A	39.A	40. D
41.D	42.A	43.B	44.A	45.A	46.C	47.A	48.C	49.A	50.A

UGC NET-JRF EXAMINATION JUNE 2008
SOLVED QUESTION PAPER
PAPER - I

Note : This paper contains **fifty** (50) multiple-choice questions, each question carrying **two** (2) marks. Attempt **all** of them.

1. The teacher has been glorified by the phrase "Friend, philosopher and guide" because:

A. He has to play all vital roles in the context of society

B. He transmits the high value of humanity to students

C. He is the great reformer of the society

D. He is a great patriot

2. The most important cause of failure for teacher lies in the area of:

A. inter personal relationship

B. lack of command over the knowledge of the subject

C. verbal ability

D. strict handling of the students

3. A teacher can establish rapport with his students by:

A. becoming a figure of authority

B. impressing students with knowledge and skill

C. playing the role of a guide

D. becoming a friend to the students

4. Education is a powerful instrument of:

A. Social transformation B. Personal transformation

C. Cultural transformation D. All the above

5. A teacher's major contribution towards the maximum self-realization of the student is affected through:

A. Constant fulfillment of the students' needs

B. Strict control of class-room activities

C. Sensitivity to students' needs, goals and purposes

D. Strict reinforcement of academic standards

6. Research problem is selected from the stand point of:

A. Researcher's interest B. Financial support
C. Social relevance D. Availability of relevant literature

7. Which one is called non-probability sampling?

A. Cluster sampling B. Quota sampling
C. Systematic sampling D. Stratified random sampling

8. Formulation of hypothesis may NOT be required in:

A. Survey method B. Historical studies
C. Experimental studies D. Normative studies

9. Field-work based research is classified as:

A. Empirical B. Historical
C. Experimental D. Biographical

10. Which of the following sampling method is appropriate to study the prevalence of AIDS amongst male and female in India in 1976, 1986, 1996 and 2006?

A. Cluster sampling B. Systematic sampling
C. Quota sampling D. Stratified random sampling

1. Read the following passage and answer the questions 11 to 15:

The fundamental principle is that Article 14 forbids class legislation but permits reasonable classification for the purpose of legislation which classification must satisfy the twin tests of classification being founded on an intelligible differentia which distinguishes persons or things that are grouped together from those that are left out of the group and that differentia must have a rational nexus to the object sought to be achieved by the Statute in question. The thrust of Article 14 is that the citizen is entitled to equality before law and equal protection of laws. In the very nature of things the society being composed of unequals a welfare State will have to strive by both executive and legislative action to help the less fortunate in society to ameliorate their condition so that the social and economic inequality in the society may be bridged. This would necessitate a legislative application to a group of citizens otherwise unequal and amelioration of whose lot is the object of state affirmative action. In the absence of the doctrine of classification such legislation is likely to flounder on the bed rock of equality enshrined in Article 14. The Court realistically appraising the social and economic inequality and keeping in view the guidelines on which the State action must move as constitutionally laid down in Part IV of the Constitution evolved the doctrine of classification. The doctrine was evolved to sustain a legislation or State action designed to help weaker sections of the society or some such segments of the society in need of succour. Legislative and executive action may accordingly be sustained if it satisfies the twin tests of reasonable classification and the rational principle correlated to the object sought to be achieved.

The concept of equality before the law does not involve the idea of absolute equality among human beings which is a physical impossibility. All that Article 14 guarantees is a similarity of treatment contra-distinguished from identical treatment. Equality before law means that among equals the law should be equal and should be equally administered and that the likes should be treated alike. Equality before the law does not mean that things which are different shall be as though they are the same. It of course means denial of any special privilege by reason of birth, creed or the like. The legislation as well as the executive government, while dealing with diverse problems arising out of an infinite variety of human relations must of necessity have the power of making special laws, to attain any particular object and to achieve that object it must have the power of selection or classification of persons and things upon which such laws are to operate.

11. Right to equality, one of the fundamental rights, is enunciated in the constitution under Part III, Article:

A. 12 B. 13 C. 14 D. 15

12. The main thrust of Right to equality is that it permits:

A. class legislation

B. equality before law and equal protection under the law

C. absolute equality

D. special privilege by reason of birth

13. The social and economic inequality in the society can be bridged by:

A. executive and legislative action

B. universal suffrage

C. identical treatment

D. none of the above

14. The doctrine of classification is evolved to:

A. Help weaker sections of the society

B. Provide absolute equality

C. Provide identical treatment

D. None of the above

15. While dealing with diverse problems arising out of an infinite variety of human relations, the government:

A. must have the power of making special laws

B. must not have any power to make special laws

C. must have power to withdraw equal rights

D. none of the above

16. Communication with oneself is known as:

A. Group communication

B. Grapevine communication

C. Interpersonal communication

D. Intrapersonal communication

17. Which broadcasting system for TV is followed in India?

A. NTSE B. PAL

C. SECAM D. NTCS

18. All India Radio before 1936 was known as :

A. Indian Radio Broadcasting

B. Broadcasting Service of India

C. Indian Broadcasting Service

D. All India Broadcasting Service

19. The biggest news agency of India is:

A. PTI B. UNI C. NANAP D. Samachar Bharati

20. Prasar Bharati was launched in the year:

A. 1995 B. 1997 C. 1999 D. 2001

21. A statistical measure based upon the entire population is called parameter while measure based upon a sample is known as:

A. Sample parameter B. Inference

C. Statistics D. None of these

22. The importance of the correlation co-efficient lies in the fact that:

A. There is a linear relationship between the correlated variables.

B. It is one of the most valid measure of statistics.

C. It allows one to determine the degree or strength of the association between two variables.

D. It is a non-parametric method of statistical analysis.

23. The F-test :

A. is essentially a two tailed test.

B. is essentially a one tailed test.

C. can be one tailed as well as two tailed depending on the hypothesis.

D. can never be a one tailed test.

24. What will be the next letter in the following series : DCXW, FGVU, HGTS,

A. AKPO B. JBYZ C. JIRQ D. LMRS

25. The following question is based on the diagram given below. If the two small circles represent formal class-room education and distance education and the big circle stands for university system of education, which figure represents the university systems?

A. 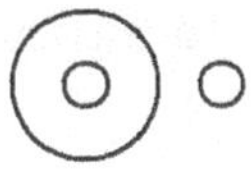

B. 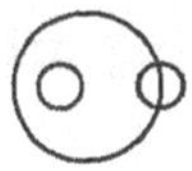

C. 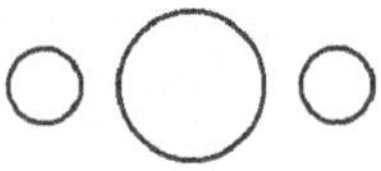

D. 

26. The statement, 'To be non-violent is good' is a :

A. Moral judgement B. Factual judgement

C. Religious judgement D. Value judgement

27. Assertion (A) : Man is a rational being. Reason (R) : Man is a social being.

A. Both (A) and (R) are true and (R) is the correct explanation of (A)

B. Both (A) and (R) are true but (R) is not the correct explanation of (A)

C. (A) is true but (R) is false

D. (A) is false but (R) is true

28. Value Judgements are:

A. Factual Judgements

B. Ordinary Judgements

C. Normative Judgements

D. Expression of public opinion

29. Deductive reasoning proceeds from:

A. general to particular

B. particular to general

C. one general conclusion to another general conclusion

D. one particular conclusion to another particular conclusion

30. AGARTALA is written in code as 14168171, the code for AGRA is:

A. 1641 B. 1416 C. 1441 D. 1461

31. Which one of the following is the most comprehensive source of population data?

A. National Family Health Surveys

B. National Sample Surveys

C. Census

D. Demographic Health Surveys

32. Which one of the following principles is not applicable to sampling?

A. Sample units must be clearly defined

B. Sample units must be dependent on each other

C. Same units of sample should be used throughout the study

D. Sample units must be chosen in a systematic and objective manner

33. If January 1st, 2007 is Monday, what was the day on 1st January 1995?

A. Sunday B. Monday

C. Friday D. Saturday

34. Insert the missing number in the following series:

4 16 8 64 ? 256

A. 16 B. 24 C. 32 D. 20

35. If an article is sold for ₹ 178 at a loss of 11%; what would be its selling price in order to earn a profit of 11%?

A. ₹ 222.50 B. ₹ 267 C. ₹ 222 D. ₹ 220

36. WYSIWYG - describes the display of a document on screen as it will actually print:

A. What you state is what you get

B. What you see is what you get

C. What you save is what you get

D. What you suggest is what you get

37. Which of the following is not a Computer language?

A. PASCAL B. UNIX C. FORTRAN D. COBOL

38. A key-board has at least:

A. 91 keys B. 101 keys C. 111 keys D. 121 keys

39. An E-mail address is composed of:

A. two parts B. three parts C. four parts D. five parts

40. Corel Draw is a popular:

A. Illustration programme B. Programming language

C. Text programme D. None of the above

41. Human ear is most sensitive to noise in which of the following ranges:

A. 1 - 2 KHz B. 100 - 500 Hz

C. 10 - 12 KHz D. 13 - 16 KHz

42. Which one of the following units is used to measure intensity of noise?

A. decible B. Hz C. Phon D. Watts/m^2

43. If the population growth follows a logistic curve, the maximum sustainable yield:

A. is equal to half the carrying capacity.

B. is equal to the carrying capacity.

C. depends on growth rates.

D. depends on the initial population.

44. Chemical weathering of rocks is largely dependent upon:

A. high temperature B. strong wind action

C. heavy rainfall D. Glaciations

45. Structure of earth's system consists of the following:

Match List-I with List-II and give the correct answer.

List-I (Zone)	List-II (Chemical Character)
A. Atmosphere	(i) Inert gases
B. Biosphere	(ii) Salt, fresh water, snow and ice
C. Hydrosphere	(iii) Organic substances, skeleton matter
D. Lithosphere	(iv) Light silicates

Codes :

	(a)	(b)	(c)	(d)
A.	(ii)	(iii)	(i)	(iv)
B.	(i)	(iii)	(ii)	(iv)
C.	(ii)	(i)	(iii)	(iv)
D.	(iii)	(i)	(ii)	(iv)

46. NAAC is an autonomous institution under the aegis of:

A. ICSSR B. CSIR C. AICTE D. UGC

47. National Council for Women's Education was established in:

A. 1958 B. 1976 C. 1989 D. 2000

48. Which one of the following is not situated in New Delhi?

A. Indian Council of Cultural Relations

B. Indian Council of Scientific Research

C. National Council of Educational Research and Training

D. Indian Institute of Advanced Studies

49. Autonomy in higher education implies freedom in:

A. Administration B. Policy-making

C. Finance D. Curriculum development

50. Match List-I with List-II and select the correct answer from the code given below:

List-I (Institutions)	*List-II (Locations)*
A. Dr. Hari Singh Gour University	(i) Mumbai
B. S.N.D.T. University	(ii) Baroda
C. M.S. University	(iii) Jodhpur
D. J.N. Vyas University	(iv) Sagar

Codes :

	(a)	(b)	(c)	(d)
A.	(iv)	(i)	(ii)	(iii)
B.	(i)	(ii)	(iii)	(iv)
C.	(iii)	(i)	(ii)	(iv)
D.	(ii)	(iv)	(i)	(iii)

Answer keys

1.A	2.A	3.D	4.D	5.C	6.C	7.B	8.B	9.A	10.D
11.C	12.B	13.A	14.C	15.A	16.D	17.B	18.C	19.A	20.B
21.A	22.C	23.A	24.C	25.B	26.D	27.B	28.C	29.A	30.D
31.C	32.B	33.A	34.A	35.C	36.B	37.B	38.B	39.A	40.A
41.A	42.A	43.B	44.C	45.B	46.D	47.A	48.D	49.A	50.A

UGC NET-JRF EXAMINATION DECEMBER 2008
SOLVED QUESTION PAPER
PAPER - I

Note : This paper contains **fifty** (50) multiple-choice questions, each question carrying **two** (2) marks. Attempt **all** of them.

1. According to Swami Vivekananda, teacher's success depends on:

A. His renunciation of personal gain and service to others

B. His professional training and creativity

C. His concentration on his work and duties with a spirit of obedience to God

D. His mastery on the subject and capacity in controlling the students

2. Which of the following teacher, will be liked most?

A. A teacher of high idealistic attitude

B. A loving teacher

C. A teacher who is disciplined

D. A teacher who often amuses his students

3. A teacher's most important challenge is:

A. To make students do their home work

B. To make teaching-learning process enjoyable

C. To maintain discipline in the classroom

D. To prepare the question paper

4. Value-education stands for:

A. making a student healthy

B. making a student to get a job

C. inculcation of virtues

D. all-round development of personality

5. When a normal student behaves in an erratic manner in the class, you would:

A. pull up the student then and there

B. talk to the student after the class

C. ask the student to leave the class

D. ignore the student

6. The research is always -

A. verifying the old knowledge

B. exploring new knowledge

C. filling the gap between knowledge

D. all of these

7. The research that applies the laws at the time of field study to draw more and more clear ideas about the problem is:

A. Applied research

B. Action research

C. Experimental research

D. None of these

8. When a research problem is related to heterogeneous population, the most suitable sampling method is:

A. Cluster Sampling

B. Stratified Sampling

C. Convenient Sampling

D. Lottery Method

9. The process not needed in experimental research is:

A. Observation

B. Manipulation and replication

C. Controlling

D. Reference collection

10. A research problem is not feasible only when:

A. it is researchable

B. it is new and adds something to knowledge

C. it consists of independent and dependent variables

D. it has utility and relevance

1. Read the following passage carefully and answer the questions 11 to 15:

Radically changing monsoon patterns, reduction in the winter rice harvest and a quantum increase in respiratory diseases all part of the environmental doomsday scenario which is reportedly playing out in South Asia. According to a United Nations Environment Programme report, a deadly three-kilometer deep blanket of pollution comprising a fearsome, cocktail of ash, acids, aerosols and other particles has enveloped in this region. For India, already struggling to cope with a drought, the implication of this are devastating and further crop failure will amount to a life and death question for many Indians. The increase in premature deaths will have adverse social and economic consequences and a rise in morbidities will place an unbearable burden on our crumbling health system. And there is no one to blame but ourselves. Both official and corporate India has always been allergic to any mention of clean technology. Most mechanical two wheelers roll of the assembly line without proper pollution control system. Little effort is made for R&D on simple technologies, which could make a vital difference to people's lives and the environment.

However, while there is no denying that South Asia must clean up its act, skeptics might question the timing of the haze report. The Kyoto meet on climate change is just two weeks away and the stage is set for the usual battle between the developing world and the West, particularly the Unites States of America. President Mr. Bush has adamantly refused to sign any protocol, which would mean a change in American consumption level. U.N. environment report will likely find a place in the U.S. arsenal as it plants an accusing finger towards controls like India and China. Yet the U.S.A. can hardly deny its own dubious role in the matter of erasing trading quotas.

Richer countries can simply buy up excess credits from poorer countries and continue to pollute. Rather than try to get the better of developing countries, who undoubtedly have taken up environmental shortcuts in their bid to catch up with the West, the USA should take a look at the environmental profigacy, which is going on within. From opening up virgin territories for oil exploration to relaxing the standards for drinking water, Mr. Bush's policies are not exactly beneficial, not even to America's interests. We realize that we are all in this together and that pollution anywhere should be a global concern otherwise there will only be more tunnels at the end of the tunnel.

11. Both official and corporate India is allergic to:

A. Failure of Monsoon

B. Poverty and Inequality

C. Slowdown in Industrial Production

D. Mention of Clean Technology

12. If the rate of premature death increases it will:

A. Exert added burden on the crumbling economy

B. Have adverse social and economic consequences

C. Make positive effect on our effort to control population

D. Have less job aspirants in the society

13. According to the passage, the two wheeler industry is not adequately concerned about:

A. Passenger safety on the roads

B. Life cover insurance of the vehicle owner

C. Pollution control system in the vehicle

D. Rising cost of the two wheelers

14. What could be the reason behind timing of the haze report just before the Kyoto meet?

A. United Nations is working hand-in-glove with U.S.A.

B. Organizers of the forthcoming meet to teach a lesson to the U.S.A.

C. Drawing attention of the world towards devastating effects of environment degradation.

D. U.S.A. wants to use it as a handle against the developing countries in the forthcoming meet

15. Which of the following is the indication of environmental degradation in South Asia?

A. Social and economic inequality

B. Crumbling health care system

C. Inadequate pollution control system

D. Radically changing monsoon pattern

16. Community Radio is a type of radio service that caters to the interest of:

A. Local audience
B. Education

C. Entertainment
D. News

17. Orkut is a part of:

A. Intra personal Communication

B. Mass Communication

C. Group Communication

D. Interpersonal Communication

18. Match List-I with List-II and select the correct answer using the codes given below:

List - I	*List - II*
(Artists)	*(Art)*
A. Amrita Shergill	(i) Flute
B. T. Swaminathan Pillai	(ii) Classical Song
C. Bhimsen Joshi	(iii) Painting
D. Padma Subramaniyam	(iv) Bharat Natyam

Codes :

	(a)	(b)	(c)	(d)
A.	(iii)	(i)	(ii)	(iv)
B.	(ii)	(iii)	(i)	(iv)
C.	(iv)	(ii)	(iii)	(i)
D.	(i)	(iv)	(ii)	(iii)

19. Which is not correct in latest communication award?

A. Salman Rushdie - Booker's Prize - July 20, 2008

B. Dilip Sanghavi - Business Standard CEO Award July 22, 2008

C. Tapan Sinha - Dada Saheb Falke Award, July 21, 2008
D. Gautam Ghosh - Osians Lifetime Achievement Award July 11, 2008

20. Firewalls are used to protect a communication network system against:

A. Unauthorized attacks B. Virus attacks
C. Data-driven attacks D. Fire-attacks

21. Insert the missing number in the following:

$\frac{2}{4}, \frac{4}{7}, ?, \frac{11}{21}, \frac{15}{31}$

A. $\frac{10}{8}$ B. $\frac{6}{10}$ C. $\frac{5}{10}$ D. $\frac{7}{13}$

22. In a certain code, GAMESMAN is written as AGMEMSAN. How would DISCLOSE be written in that code?

A. IDSCOLSE B. IDCSOLES
C. IDSCOLES D. IDSCLOSE

23. The letters in the first set have a certain relationship. On the basis of this relationship mark the right choice for the second set:

AST : BRU : : NQV : ?

A. ORW B. MPU C. MRW D. OPW

24. On what dates of April 1994 did SUNDAY fall?

A. 2, 9, 16, 23, 30 B. 3, 10, 17, 24
C. 4, 11, 18, 25 D. 1, 8, 15, 22, 29

25. Find out the wrong number in the sequence: 125, 127, 130, 135, 142, 153, 165

A. 130 B. 142 C. 153 D. 165

26. There are five books A,B,C,D and E. The book C lies above D, the book E is below A and B is below E. Which is at the bottom?

A. E B. B C. A D. C

27. Logical reasoning is based on:

A. Truth of involved propositions
B. Valid relation among the involved propositions
C. Employment of symbolic language
D. Employment of ordinary language

28. Two propositions with the same subject and predicate terms but different in quality are:

A. Contradictory B. Contrary

C. Subaltern D. Identical

29. The premises of a valid deductive argument:

A. Provide some evidence for its conclusion

B. Provide no evidence for its conclusion

C. Are irrelevant for its conclusion

D. Provide conclusive evidence for its conclusion

30. Syllogistic reasoning is :

A. Deductive B. Inductive

C. Experimental D. Hypothetical

1. Study the following Venn diagram and answer questions nos. 31 to 33.

Three circles representing GRADUATES, CLERKS and GOVERNMENT EMPLOYEES are intersecting. The intersections are marked A, B, C, e, f, g and h. Which part best represents the statements in questions 31 to 33 ?

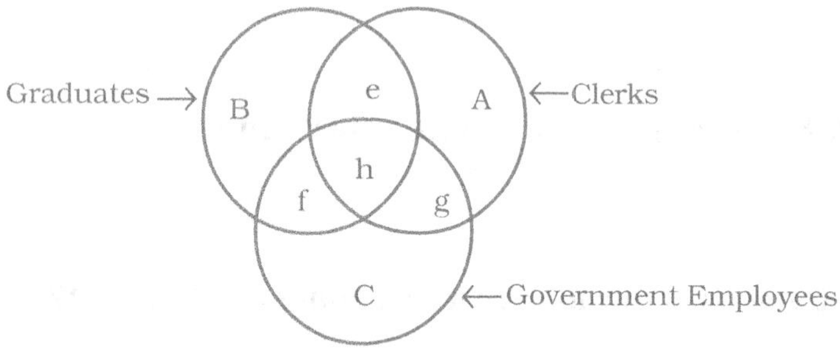

31. Some Graduates are Government employees but not as Clerks.

A. h B. g C. f D. e

32. Clerks who are graduates as well as government employees:

A. e B. f C. g D. h

33. Some graduates are Clerks but not Government employees.

A. f B. g C. h D. e

2. Study the following graph and answer questions numbered from 34 to 35:

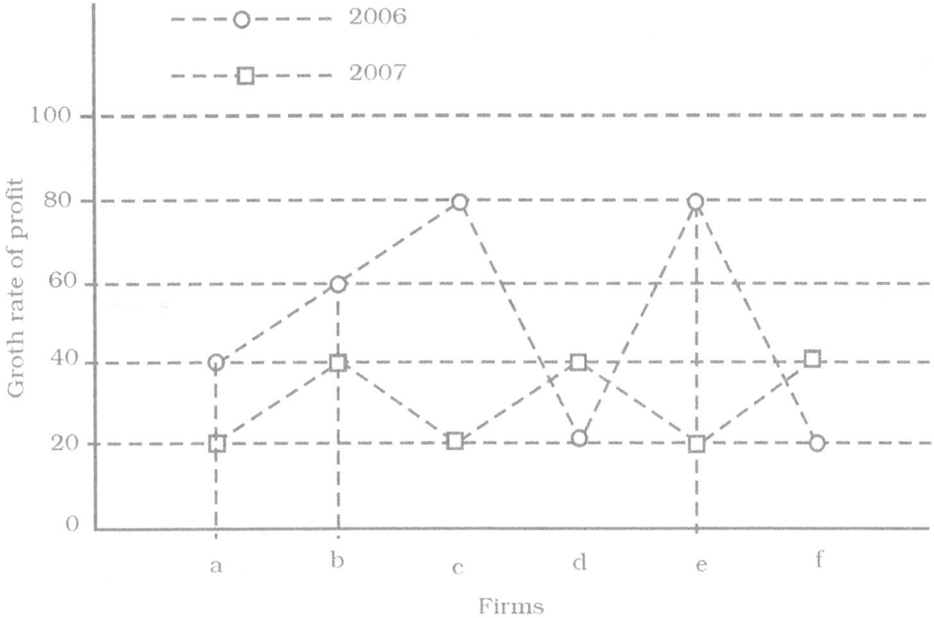

34. Which of the firms got maximum profit growth rate in the year 2006?

A. ab B. ce C. cd D. ef

35. Which of the firms got maximum profit growth rate in the year 2007?

A. bdf B. acf C. bcd D. ace

36. The companyTally Solutions is owned by:

A. Shiv Nadar B. TATA C. Narayan Moorthy D. Goenka

37. Errors in computer programmes are called:

A. Follies B. Mistakes C. Bugs D. Spam

38. HTML is basically used to design:

A. Web-page B. Web-site C. Graphics D. Tables and Frames

39. 'Micro Processing' is made for:

A. Computer B. Digital System

C. Calculator D. Electronic Goods

40. Information, a combination of graphics, text, sound, video and animation is called:

A. Multiprogramme B. Multifacet
C. Multimedia D. Multiprocess

41. Which of the following pairs regarding typical composition of hospital wastes is incorrect?

A. Plastic 9 - 12% B. Metals 1 - 2%
C. Ceramic 8 - 10% D. Biodegradable 35 - 40%

42. Fresh water achieves its greatest density at:

A. 248 C B. 08 C C. 48 C D. 22.58 C

43. Which one of the following is not associated with earthquakes?

A. Focus B. Epicenter
C. Seismograph D. Swells

44. The tallest trees in the world are found in the region:

A. Equatorial region B. Temperate region
C. Monsoon region D. Mediterranean region

45. Match List-I with List-II and select the correct answer from the codes given below :

List - I	*List - II*
(National Parks)	*(States)*
A. Periyar	(i) Orissa
B. Nandan Kanan	(ii) Kerala
C. Corbett National Park	(iii) Rajasthan
D. Sariska Tiger Reserve	(iv) Uttarakhand

Codes :

	(a)	(b)	(c)	(d)
A.	(ii)	(i)	(iv)	(iii)
B.	(i)	(ii)	(iv)	(iii)
C.	(iii)	(ii)	(i)	(iv)
D.	(i)	(ii)	(iii)	(iv)

46. According to Radhakrishnan Commission, the aim of Higher Education is:

A. To develop the democratic values, peace and harmony

B. To develop great personalities who can give their contributions in politics, administration, industry and commerce

C. Both (A) and (B)

D. None of these

47. The National Museum at New Delhi is attached to:

A. Delhi University

B. a Deemed University

C. a Subordinate Office of the JNU

D. Part of Ministry of Tourism and Culture

48. Match List-I with List-II and select the correct answer from the code given below:

List - I *(Institutions)*	*List - II* *(Locations)*
A. National Law Institute	(i) Shimla
B. Indian Institute of Advanced Studies	(ii) Bhopal
C. National Judicial Academy	(iii) Hyderabad
D. National Savings Institute	(iv) Nagpur

Codes :

	(a)	(b)	(c)	(d)
A.	(iii)	(ii)	(iv)	(i)
B.	(i)	(ii)	(iii)	(iv)
C.	(iv)	(iii)	(i)	(ii)
D.	(iii)	(i)	(ii)	(iv)

49. Election of Rural and Urban local bodies are conducted and ultimately supervised by:

A. Election Commission of India

B. State Election Commission

C. District Collector and District Magistrate

D. Concerned Returning Officer

50. Which opinion is not correct?

A. Education is a subject of concurrent list of VII schedule of Constitution of India

B. University Grants Commission is a statutory body

C. Patent, inventions, design, copyright and trade marks are the subject of concurrent list

D. Indian Council of Social Science Research is a statutory body related to research in social sciences

Answer keys

1.C	2.B	3.B	4.C	5.B	6.D	7.D	8.B	9.D	10.D
11.D	12.B	13.C	14.C	15.D	16.A	17.C	18.A	19.D	20.C
21.D	22.A	23.D	24.B	25.B	26.B	27.B	28.B	29.D	30.A
31.C	32.D	33.D	34.B	35.A	36.D	37.C	38.A	39.A	40.C
41.A	42.C	43.D	44.D	45.A	46.C	47.B	48.D	49.B	50.C

UGC NET-JRF EXAMINATION JUNE 2009

SOLVED QUESTION PAPER

PAPER - I

Note: This paper contains **fifty** (50) multiple-choice questions, each questions carrying **two** (2) marks. Attempt **all** of them.

1. **Which of the following comprises teaching skills?**
   A. Blackboard writing
   B. Questioning
   C. Explaining
   D. All of these

2. **The teacher, before concluding the lesson, should**
   A. motivate the students for the next lesson
   B. write down homework on the blackboard
   C. check up whether the students have learnt the lesson
   D. narrate some tit-bus.

3. **What is the real meaning of DISTANCE EDUCATION?**
   A. Education which is provided to villages situated in remote areas
   B. Education which is provided to those who cannot afford to go to regular schools/ colleges
   C. Education which is provided to those who are in service
   D. Education which is provided through correspondence to those who have neither time nor any resource to join any educational institution

4. **What should a teacher do to help slow learners?**
   A. Organise remedial teaching
   B. Give awards to such children
   C. Make the syllabus light for them
   D. Promise them financial assistance

5. **In a row of children, Sheena is fifth from left and Beena is sixth from right. If they interchange their places, Sheena becomes thirteenth from left. In this condition, what place will be occupied by Beena from right?**
   A. 4th B. 14th C. 15th D. 18th

6. **The memory of a computer is commonly expressed in terms of kilobytes and megabytes. A byte is made up of:**

   A. 8 binary digits

   B. 8 decimal digits

   C. 2 binary digits

   D. 2 decimal digits

Directions Q. 7 to 11:

Read the passage given below to answer these questions on the basis of the contents of the passage, and what is stated and implied therein:

The amount of water in the world is limited. The human race, and the other species which share the planet, cannot expect an infinite supply. Water covers about two-thirds of the Earth's surface, admittedly. But most of it is too salty for use. Only 2.5% of the world's water is not salty, and two-thirds of that is locked up in icecaps and glaciers. Of what is left, about 20% is in remote areas. Humans have available less than 0.08% of all the Earth's water. Yet over the next two decades, our use is estimated to increase by about 40%. In 1999, the United Nations Environment Programme (UNEP) reported that 200 scientists in 50 countries had identified water shortage as one of the two most worrying problems for the new millennium (the other was global warming).

We use about 70% of the water that we have in agriculture. But the World Water Council believes that by 2020, we shall need 17% more water than is available if we are to feed the world. So, if we go on, millions more will go to bed hungry and thirsty each night than do so already. Today, one person out of five across the world has no access to safe drinking water, and one out of two lakh to safe sanitation. Today, and every day, more than 30,000 children die before reaching their fifth birthdays, killed either by hunger or by easily preventable diseases. And adequate safe water is the key to good health and a proper diet.

There are several reasons for the water crisis. One is the rise in population and the desire of better living standards. In China, it takes 1,000 tonnes of water to produce one tonne of wheat. Another is the inefficiency of the way we use much of our water. Irrigation allows wastage on a prodigal scale, with the water trickling away or simply evaporating before it can do any good. And pollution is making more of the water that is available to us unfit for use. The Aral Sea in Central Asia is one of the starkest examples of what pollution can do, to the land as well as to the water. Increasingly, governments are seeking to solve their water problems by turning away from reliance on rainfall and surface water, and using subterranean supplies of groundwater, instead. But that is like making constant withdrawals from a bank account without ever paying anything into it. And using up irreplaceable groundwater does not simply mean the depletion of a once-and-for-all resource. Rivers, wetlands and lakes that depend on it can dry out. Saline seawater can flow in to replace the fresh water that has underground aquifers can be compressed, causing surface subsidence - a problem familiar in Bangkok, Mexico City and Venice.

There are some ways to begin to tackle the problem. Irrigation systems which drip water directly onto plants are one. There will be scope to plant less water intensive crops, and perhaps desalination may play a part — though it is energy-hungry and leaves quantities of brine for disposal.

7. **According to the passage, scientists all over the world have identified two most worrying problems for the new millennium. Water shortage is one, the other being**

   A. Sanitation

   B. lack of adequate drinking water

   C. Waterborne diseases

   D. Global warming

8. **In the field of irrigation, according to the World Water Council, how much additional water would we require by 2020?**

   A. 0.08% B. 17%

   C. 20% D. 70%

9. **Besides depletion of an important water resource, other side effects of taking out underground water are brought out by the author. Which of the following is not brought out in the passage?**

   A. Drying of dependent lakes

   B. Saline water ingress into vacated space

   C. Surface subsidence

   D. Release of locked-up gas

10. **What percentage of world population, according to the author, has no access to safe drinking water?**

    A. 2.5% B. 20%

    C. 0.08% D. 17%

11. **The author has given some reasons for water crisis. Which of the following is not a reason given by the author?**

    A. Population increase

    B. Inefficient way of use of water

    C. Irrigation-related wastage and pollution

    D. Climatic change bringing less rain to some regions & more to others

12. **Which of the following statements is most appropriate?**
A. Teachers can teach
B. Teachers can help create in a student a desire to learn
C. Lecture method can be used for developing thinking
D. Teachers are born

13. **Which of the following best defines an Ecosystem?**
A. A system that studies the volume, intensity and velocity of echos
B. A system that governs the radiation of energy from the sun
C. A system that classifies living organisms
D. The physical environment and the organisms that live therein

14. **Which of the following statements is correct?**
A. Syllabus is part of the curriculum
B. Syllabus is an annexure to the curriculum
C. Curriculum is the same in all educational institutes affiliated to a particular university
D. Syllabus is not the same in all educational institutes affiliated to a particular university

15. **Which of the two given options is of the level of understanding?**
(I) Define noun
(II) Define noun in your own words
A. Only (I)
B. Only (II)
C. Both I and II
D. Neither I nor II

16. **Sucrose contains**
A. Glucose and Galactose
B. Glucose and fructose
C. Fructose and Galactose
D. Glucose, Fructose and Galactose

17. **Which chemical is mainly responsible for depletion of ozone layer in the atmosphere?**
A. Sulphur dioxide
B. Chlorofluoro carbon
C. Carbon dioxide
D. Nitrus oxide

18. Which nutrient is digested first in the mouth?

A. Protein B. Carbohydrate

C. Fat D. Vitamin

19. Which chemical is used for purification of water?

A. Potassium sulphate

B. Potassium permanganate

C. Sulphuric Acid

D. Nitric acid

20. Find the incorrect statement:

A. Cosmic describes anything occurring or located in outer space

B. Lithosphere is the top crust of the Earth which includes the land surface and the ocean floors

C. Silicon constitutes the second most important element in the composition of the earth.

D. A tributary is a river which leaves the main river and flows separately

21. The constitution provides that no Vidhan Sabha can have less than 60 members. Which of the following State Assemblies is an exception to it?

A. Tripura B. Meghalaya

C. Sikkim D. Mizoram

22. Who will discharge the function of the President if for any reason both the offices-of the President and the Vice President fall vacant?

A. Attorney General

B. Speaker of the Lok Sabha

C. Chief Justice of India

D. Chief Election Commissioner

23. The average depth of a river is 5 ft. A person 5 ft 8 inches tall, who doesn't know swimming, wants to cross it on foot. What should he do?

A. Walk across the river without fear

B. Compute standard deviation of the river and then decide

C. Find out extreme depths of the river and then decide

D. Learn swimming first

Directions Q. 24: In this question, a statement is given followed by two assumptions (I) and (II). You are to consider each statement and the assumptions that follow and decide which of the assumptions is implicit in the given statement. Indicate your answer as:

A. If only I) is implicit

B. If only II) is implicit

C. If both I) and II) are implicit

D. If neither I) nor II) is implicit

Statement:

Education and economic advancement leads to a steady loss of hold of religion on people's mind.

Assumptions:

I) Education leads to economic development:

II) Religion can make priceless contribution to the society.

Directions (Q. 25 to 28) The graph below shows the distribution of funds by a state on various items. Study the diagram and answer the questions.

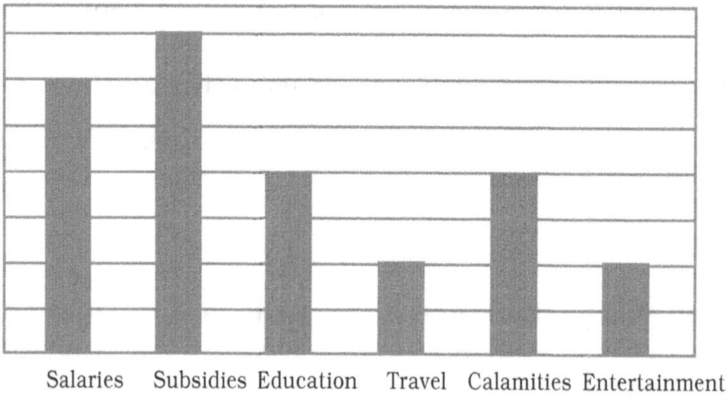

25. The expenditure on salaries and travel is equal to the expenditure on:

A. Education and natural calamities

B. Subsidies and entertainment

C. Education and entertainment

D. Subsidies and natural calamities

26. If the money spent on entertainment is used for natural calamities, then there will be equal expenditure on:

A. Subsidies and natural calamities

B. Salaries and natural calamities

C. Education and natural calamities

D. Travel and natural calamities

27. More than 50% of the expenditure is on:

A. Salaries, travel and entertainment

B. Subsidies, natural calamities and travel

C. Education, salaries and entertainment

D. Natural calamities, education and travel

28. The expenditure made on Salaries and Education is:

A. Less than that on natural calamities and entertainment

B. Less than that on travel, entertainment and natural calamities

C. More than that on entertainment, travel and natural calamities

D. More than that on subsidies and natural calamities

29. A person walks facing North 10 m and then he turns left and walks 5 m. He again turns left and walks 10m. How far is he from his original position and towards which direction?

A. 20m South B. 15m West

C. 10m East D. 5m West

30. Whose words are these: "Education has produced a vast population able to read but unable to distinguish what is worth reading"?

A. Edmund Burke

B. Reinhold Neibubr

C. G.M. Trevelyn

D. George Bernard Shaw

31. What general term describes the physical equipment of a computer system, such as video screen, keyboard and storage devices?

A. hardware B. software

C. input devices D. output devices

32. All of the following are examples of electronic databases EXCEPT?

A. collection of country music on CD

B. a CD-ROM encyclopaedia

C. computerised student information

D. an online catalogue

33. Compared with a traditional card catalogue, which of the following is NOT an advantage of an electronic card catalogue?

A. contains information on more books

B. less costly to install and operate

C. allows books to be shelved more quickly

D. allows sophisticated search strategies

34. When will the validity and reliability of research be doubtful?

A. The source of information is biased

B. The research was done long after the incident

C. The researcher cannot draw logical conclusions

D. all of the above

35. What are the things that a researcher must be careful about when he writes his research report?

A. not using numerical figures when beginning a sentence

B. arrange all data in logical or chronological order

C. compare the results with other studies

D. all of the above

36. What is the best method a researcher will use if he wants to study the future of a political party in India (such as BJP or Congress)?

A. Questionnaire B. Survey

C. Trend Analysis D. Regression

37. A survey would be best used when:

a) learning the facts about an existing situation

b) comparing present status with established norms

c) critical analysis of an existing situation

d) identifying means of improvement in the existing situation

A. A and B B. A, B and C

C. A, B, C and D D. B and C

Directions (Q 38): Read the statement and the reason given below and decide their relationship.

38. Statement A.: The ozone layer at Antarctica is very thin and has developed a hole.

Reason (R): On account of the severe cold in Antarctica, the greenhouse gases are centralised there. Select the correct answer from the following

A. (A) is true but (R) is false

B. (R) is true but (A) is false

C. Both A. and (R) are true but (R) is correct explanation of A.

D. Both A. and (R) are true but (R) is not correct explanation of A.

39. The climate of a place depends upon many factors. Four factors of them are given below. Which one of the following is the most important factor?

A. Distance from sea

B. Direction of wind

C. Latitude

D. Sea currents

40. If a person crosses the international date line from the western hemisphere on 9th April, what will be the date of his arrival in the eastern hemisphere?

A. 9th April   B. 10th April

C. 8th April   D. 11th April

41. If a map is magnified from 1 : 20,000 to 1 : 1 ,00, 000 then its area will be

A. Twenty five times of original area

B. Twenty times of original area

C. Ten times of original area

D. Five times of original area

42. The least number which when divided by 5, 6, 8 and 1 0 leaves the remainder 3, 4, 6 and 8 respectively, is:

A. 122   B. 120

C. 118   D. 116

43. What would come in the last term of the series: EGIMP : FILQU : : FHJL :?

A. GJMP   B. GMJP

C. JGPM   D. HKNQ

44. If the two terms to the left bear the same relationship as the two terms to the right, then find the missing term: 68 : 1 30 : : ... :350

A. 240   B. 222

C. 216   D. 210

45. 108. In a certain code language, VICTORY is written as YLFWRUB. In the same way 'FAILURE' is written in that code language as

A. IDLNXUH   B. JDLOXUH

C. IDLOXVH   D. IDLOXUH

46. A man is facing south. He turns 135 degrees in the anticlockwise direction and then 180 degrees in the clockwise direction. Which direction is he facing now?

A. North-east   B. North-west

C. South-east   D. South-west

47. "Life is a tale told by an idiot which is full of sound and fury signifying nothing." This is the ______ definition of life.

A. Universally accepted

B. Wrong

C. Narrow

D. Arbitrary

48. In which of the following types of communication methods can 'Audio conferencing' be classified?

A. One sided verbal

B. Two sided verbal

C. One sided non-verbal

D. Two sided non-verbal

49. Which one of the following is the least important in effective communication?

A. Full control on language

B. Good vocabulary

C. Attractive personality of messenger

D. Full control over communicable subject

50. Any obstacle in communication process is known as:

A. Encroachment B. Hindrance

C. Noise D. Inner Process

Answer keys

1.D	2.A	3.D	4.A	5.B	6.A	7.D	8.B	9.D	10.B
11.D	12.B	13.D	14.A	15.B	16.B	17.B	18.B	19.B	20.D
21.D	22.C	23.C	24.D	25.A	26.B	27.B	28.C	29.D	30.C
31.A	32.A	33.C	34.D	35.D	36.C	37.B	38.D	39.C	40.A
41.A	42.C	43.A	44.B	45.D	46.D	47.A	48.B	49.C	50.C

UGC NET-JRF EXAMINATION DECEMBER 2009

SOLVED QUESTION PAPER

PAPER - I

Note : This paper contains **sixty** (60) questions, each question carrying **two** (2) marks. Candidate is expected to answer any Fifty (50) questions. In case more than 50 questions are attempted, only the first 50 questions will be evaluated.

1. The University which telecasts interaction educational programmes through its own channel is

A. Osmania University

B. University of Pune

C. Annamalai University

D. Indira Gandhi National Open University (IGNOU)

2. Which of the following skills are needed for present day teacher to adjust effectively with the classroom teaching ?

1. Knowledge of technology
2. Use of technology in teaching learning
3. Knowledge of students' needs
4. Content mastery

A. 1 & 3 B. 2 & 3 C. 2, 3 & 4 D. 2 & 4

3. Who has signed an MOU for Accreditation of Teacher Education Institutions in India ?

A. NAAC and UGC B. NCTE and NAAC

C. UGC and NCTE D. NCTE and IGNOU

4. The primary duty of the teacher is to

A. raise the intellectual standard of the students

B. improve the physical standard of the students

C. help all round development of the students

D. imbibe value system in the students

5. Micro teaching is more effective

A. during the preparation for teaching-practice

B. during the teaching-practice

C. after the teaching-practice
D. always

6. What quality the students like the most in a teacher ?

A. Idealist philosophy
B. Compassion
C. Discipline
D. Entertaining

7. A null hypothesis is

A. when there is no difference between the variables
B. the same as research hypothesis
C. subjective in nature
D. when there is difference between the variables

8. The research which is exploring new facts through the study of the past is called

A. Philosophical research
B. Historical research
C. Mythological research
D. Content analysis

9. Action research is

A. An applied research
B. A research carried out to solve immediate problems
C. A longitudinal research
D. Simulative research

10. The process not needed in Experimental Researches is

A. Observation
B. Manipulation
C. Controlling
D. Content Analysis

11. Manipulation is always a part of

A. Historical research
B. Fundamental research
C. Descriptive research
D. Experimental research

12. Which correlation co-efficient best explains the relationship between creativity and intelligence ?

A. 1.00
B. 0.6
C. 0.5
D. 0.3

1. Read the following passage and answer the Question Nos. 13 to 18 :

The decisive shift in British Policy really came about under mass pressure in the autumn and winter of 1945 to 46 – the months which Perderel Moon while editing Wavell's Journal has perceptively described as 'The Edge of a Volcano'. Very foolishly, the British initially decided to hold public trials of several hundreds of the 20,000

I.N.A. prisoners (as well as dismissing from service and detaining without trial no less than 7,000). They compounded the folly by holding the first trial in the Red Fort, Delhi in November 1945, and putting on the dock together a Hindu, a Muslim and a Sikh (P.K. Sehgal, Shah Nawaz, Gurbaksh Singh Dhillon). Bhulabhai Desai, Tejbahadur Sapru and Nehru appeared for the defence (the latter putting on his barrister's gown after 25 years), and the Muslim League also joined the countrywide protest. On 20 November, an Intelligence Bureau note admitted that "there has seldom been a matter which has attracted so much Indian public interest and, it is safe to say, sympathy ... this particular brand of sympathy cuts across communal barriers." A journalist (B. Shiva Rao) visiting the Red Fort prisoners on the same day reported that 'There is not the slightest feeling among them of Hindu and Muslim ... A majority of the men now awaiting trial in the Red Fort is Muslim. Some of these men are bitter that Mr. Jinnah is keeping alive a controversy about Pakistan.' The British became extremely nervous about the I.N.A. spirit spreading to the Indian Army, and in January the Punjab Governor reported that a Lahore reception for released I.N.A. prisoners had been attended by Indian soldiers in uniform.

13. Which heading is more appropriate to assign to the above passage ?

A. Wavell's Journal B. Role of Muslim League

C. I.N.A. Trials D. Red Fort Prisoners

14. The trial of P.K. Sehgal, Shah Nawaz and Gurbaksh Singh Dhillon symbolises

A. communal harmony

B. threat to all religious persons

C. threat to persons fighting for the freedom

D. British reaction against the natives

15. I.N.A. stands for

A. Indian National Assembly

B. Indian National Association

C. Inter-national Association

D. Indian National Army

16. 'There has seldom been a matter which has attracted so much Indian Public Interest and, it is safe to say, sympathy ... this particular brand of sympathy cuts across communal barriers.'

Who sympathises to whom and against whom ?

A. Muslims sympathised with Shah Nawaz against the British

B. Hindus sympathised with P.K. Sehgal against the British

C. Sikhs sympathised with Gurbaksh Singh Dhillon against the British

D. Indians sympathised with the persons who were to be trialled

17. The majority of people waiting for trial outside the Red Fort and criticising Jinnah were the

A. Hindus
B. Muslims
C. Sikhs
D. Hindus and Muslims both

18. The sympathy of Indian soldiers in uniform with the released I.N.A. prisoners at Lahore indicates

A. Feeling of Nationalism and Fraternity
B. Rebellious nature of Indian soldiers
C. Simply to participate in the reception party
D. None of the above

19. The country which has the distinction of having the two largest circulated newspapers in the world is

A. Great Britain
B. The United States
C. Japan
D. China

20. The chronological order of non-verbal communication is

A. Signs, symbols, codes, colours
B. Symbols, codes, signs, colours
C. Colours, signs, codes, symbols
D. Codes, colours, symbols, signs

21. Which of the following statements is not connected with communication?

A. Medium is the message.
B. The world is an electronic cocoon.
C. Information is power.
D. Telepathy is technological.

22. Communication becomes circular when

A. the decoder becomes an encoder
B. the feedback is absent
C. the source is credible
D. the channel is clear

23. The site that played a major role during the terrorist attack on Mumbai (26/11) in 2008 was

A. Orkut
B. Facebook
C. Amazon.com
D. Twitter

24. **Assertion (A)** : For an effective classroom communication at times it is desirable to use the projection technology.

Reason (R) : Using the projection technology facilitates extensive coverage of course contents.

A. Both (A) and (R) are true, and (R) is the correct explanation.

B. Both (A) and (R) are true, but (R) is not the correct explanation.

C. (A) is true, but (R) is false.

D. (A) is false, but (R) is true.

25. **January 1, 1995 was a Sunday. What day of the week lies on January 1, 1996 ?**

A. Sunday B. Monday

C. Wednesday D. Saturday

26. **When an error of 1% is made in the length and breadth of a rectangle, the percentage error (%) in the area of a rectangle will be**

A. 0 B. 1 C. 2 D. 4

27. **The next number in the series 2, 5, 9, 19, 37, ? will be**

A. 74 B. 75 C. 76 D. None of the above

28. **There are 10 true-false questions in an examination. Then these questions can be answered in**

A. 20 ways B. 100 ways

C. 240 ways D. 1024 ways

29. **What will be the next term in the following ? DCXW, FEVU, HGTS ?**

A. AKPO B. ABYZ C. JIRQ D. LMRS

30. **Three individuals X, Y, Z hired a car on a sharing basis and paid ₹ 1,040. They used it for 7, 8, 11 hours, respectively. What are the charges paid by Y ?**

A. ₹ 290 B. ₹ 320 C. ₹ 360 D. ₹ 440

31. **Deductive argument involves**

A. sufficient evidence B. critical thinking

C. seeing logical relations D. repeated observation

32. **Inductive reasoning is based on or presupposes**

A. uniformity of nature B. God created the world

C. unity of nature D. laws of nature

33. To be critical, thinking must be

A. practical B. socially relevant
C. individually satisfying D. analytical

34. Which of the following is an analogous statement ?

A. Man is like God B. God is great
C. Gandhiji is the Father of the Nation D. Man is a rational being.

Questions from 35 – 36 are based on the following diagram in which there are three intersecting circles. H representing The Hindu, I representing Indian Express and T representing The Times of India. A total of 50 persons were surveyed and the number in the Venn diagram indicates the number of persons reading the newspapers.

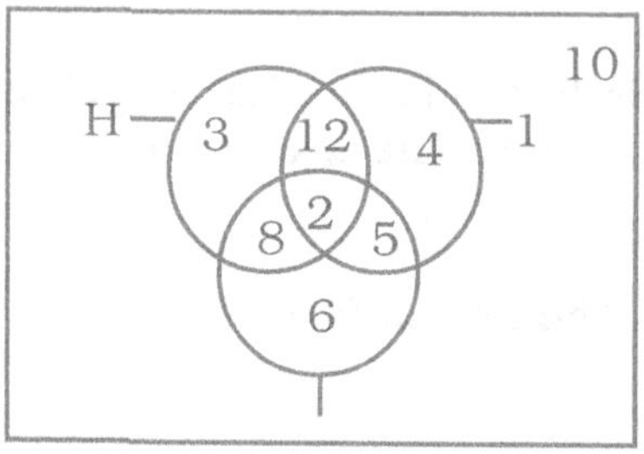

35. How many persons would be reading at least two newspapers ?

A. 23 B. 25 C. 27 D. 29

36. How many persons would be reading almost two newspapers ?

A. 23 B. 25 C. 27 D. 48

37. Which of the following graphs does not represent regular (periodic) behaviour of the variable f(t) ?

1. 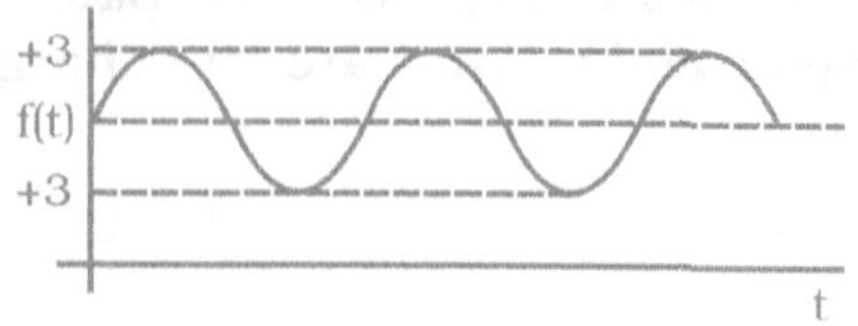

2. 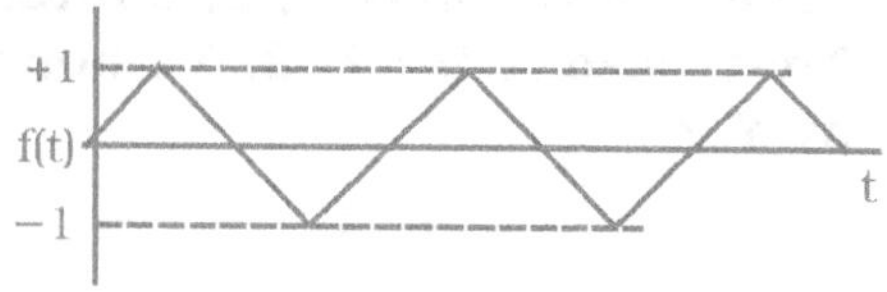

3. 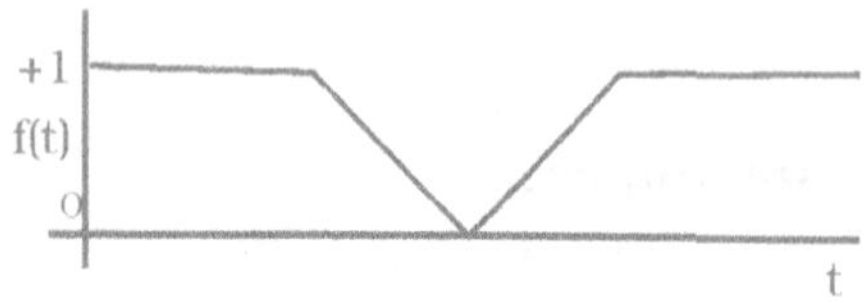

4. 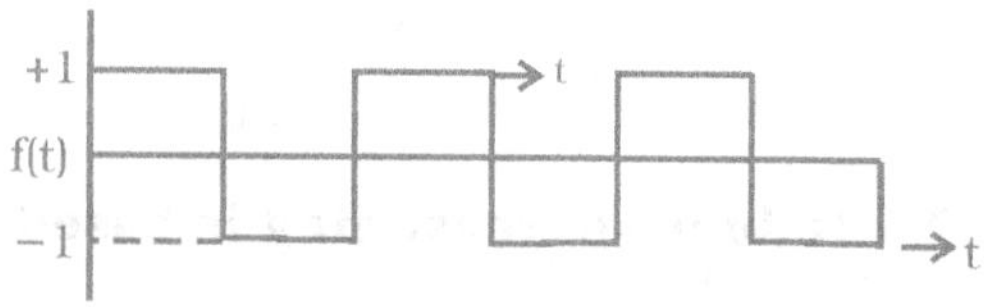

A. 1 B. 2 C. 3 D. 4

2. Study the following graph and answer the questions 38 to 40:

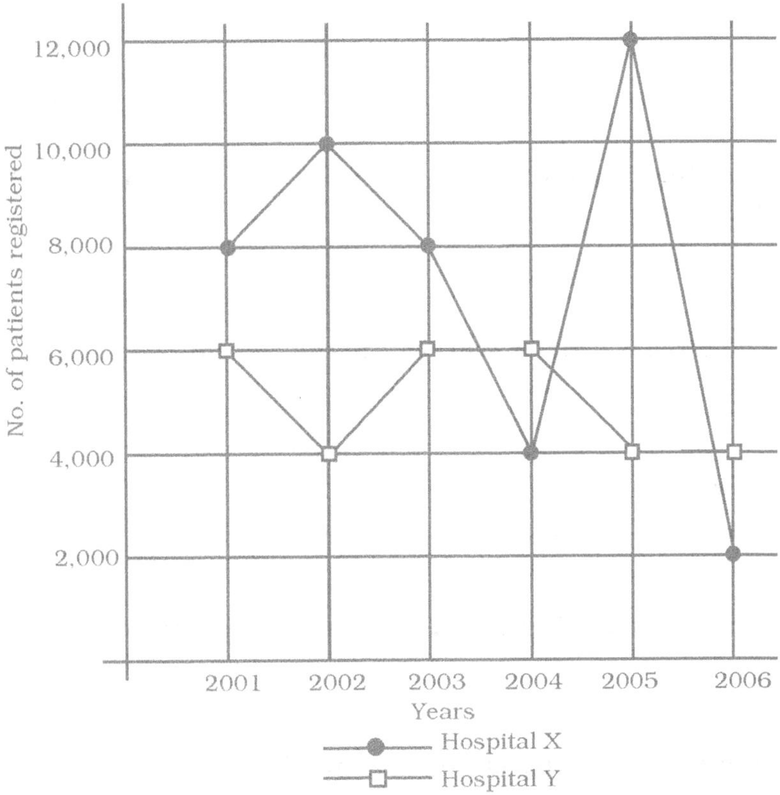

38. In which year total number of patients registered in hospital X and hospital Y was the maximum ?

A. 2003 B. 2004 C. 2005 D. 2006

39. What is the maximum dispersion in the registration of patients in the two hospitals in a year ?

A. 8000 B. 6000 C. 4000 D. 2000

40. In which year there was maximum decrease in registration of patients in hospital X ?

A. 2003 B. 2004 C. 2005 D. 2006

41. Which of the following sources of data is not based on primary data collection ?

A. Census of India B. National Sample Survey

C. Statistical Abstracts of India D. National Family Health Survey

42. Which of the four data sets have more dispersion ?

A.	88	91	90	92	89	91
B.	0	1	1	0	–1	–2
C.	3	5	2	4	1	5
D.	0	5	8	10	–2	–8

43. Which of the following is not related to information security on the Internet ?

A. Data Encryption B. Water marking
C. Data Hiding D. Information Retrieval

44. Which is the largest unit of storage among the following ?

A. Terabyte B. Megabyte
C. Kilobyte D. Gigabyte

45. bit stands for

A. binary information term B. binary digit
C. binary tree D. Bivariate Theory

46. Which one of the following is not a linear data structure ?

A. Array B. Binary Tree
C. Queue D. Stack

47. Which one of the following is not a network device ?

A. Router B. Switch
C. Hub D. CPU

48. A compiler is used to convert the following to object code which can be executed

A. High-level language B. Low-level language
C. Assembly language D. Natural language

49. The great Indian Bustard bird is found in

A. Thar Desert of Rajasthan B. Coastal regions of India
C. Malabar Coast D. Delta regions

50. The Sagarmanthan National Park has been established to preserve the eco-system of which mountain peak ?

A. Kanchenjunga B. Mount Everest
C. Annapurna D. Dhaulavira

51. Maximum soot is released from

A. Petrol vehicles
B. CNG vehicles
C. Diesel vehicles
D. Thermal Power Plants

52. Surface Ozone is produced from

A. Transport sector
B. Cement plants
C. Textile industry
D. Chemical industry

53. Which one of the following non-conventional energy sources can be exploited most economically ?

A. Solar
B. Wind
C. Geo-thermal
D. Ocean Thermal Energy Conversion (OTEC)

54. The most recurring natural hazard in India is

A. Earthquakes
B. Floods
C. Landslides
D. Volcanoes

55. The recommendation of National Knowledge Commission for the establishment of 1500 Universities is to

A. create more teaching jobs
B. ensure increase in student enrolment in higher education
C. replace or substitute the privately managed higher education institutions by public institutions
D. enable increased movement of students from rural areas to urban areas

56. According to Article 120 of the Constitution of India, the business in Parliament shall be transacted in

A. English only
B. Hindi only
C. English and Hindi both
D. All the languages included in Eighth Schedule of the Constitution

57. Which of the following is more interactive and student centric ?

A. Seminar
B. Workshop
C. Lecture
D. Group Discussion

58. The Parliament in India is composed of

A. Lok Sabha & Rajya Sabha

B. Lok Sabha, Rajya Sabha & Vice President

C. Lok Sabha, Rajya Sabha & President

D. Lok Sabha, Rajya Sabha with their Secretariats

59. The enrolment in higher education in India is contributed both by Formal System of Education and by System of Distance Education. Distance education contributes

A. 50% of formal system

B. 25% of formal system

C. 10% of the formal system

D. Distance education system's contribution is not taken into account while considering the figures of enrolment in higher education

60. Assertion (A) : The U.G.C. Academic Staff Colleges came into existence to improve the quality of teachers.

Reason (R) : University and college teachers have to undergo both orientation and refresher courses.

A. Both (A) and (R) are true and (R) is the correct explanation.

B. Both (A) and (R) are correct but (R) is not the correct explanation of (A).

C. (A) is correct and (R) is false.

D. (A) is false and (R) is correct.

Answer keys

1.D	2.C	3.B	4.C	5.A	6.B	7.A	8.B	9.B	10.D
11.D	12.B	13.C	14.A	15.D	16.D	17.B	18.A	19.D	20.A
21.D	22.A	23.A	24.B	25.B	26.B	27.B	28.A	29.C	30.B
31.C	32.A	33.D	34.A	35.C	36.C	37.C	38.C	39.A	40.D
41.C	42.D	43.B	44.A	45.B	46.B	47.B	48.A	49.A	50.B
51. D	52.D	53.A	54.B	55.B	56.B	57.D	58.A	59.B	60.A

UGC NET-JRF EXAMINATION JUNE 2010

SOLVED QUESTION PAPER

PAPER - I

Note :
- This paper contains **Sixty (60)** multiple choice questions, each question carrying **two (2)** marks.
- Candidate is expected to answer any **Fifty (50)** questions.
- In case more than **50** questions are attempted, only the first **50** questions will be evaluated.

1. Which one of the following is the most important quality of a good teacher?

A. Punctuality and sincerity

B. Content mastery

C. Content mastery and reactive

D. Content mastery and sociable

2. The primary responsibility for the teachers adjustment lies with:

A. The children

B. The principal

C. The teacher himself

D. The community

3. As per the NCTC norms, what should be the staff strength for a unit of 100 students at B.Ed level?

A. 1 + 7 B. 1 + 9 C. 1 + 10 D. 1 + 5

4. Research has shown that the most frequent symptom of nervous instability among teachers is:

A. Digestive upsets

B. Explosive behaviour

C. Fatigue

D. Worry

5. Which one of the following statements is correct?

A. Syllabus is an annexure to the curriculum

B. Curriculum is the same in all educational institutions

C. Curriculum includes both formal, and informal education

D. Curriculum does not include methods of evaluation

6. A successful teacher is one who is:

A. Compassionate and disciplinarian

B. Quiet and reactive

C. Tolerant and dominating

D. Passive and active

1. Read the following passage carefully and answer the questions 7 to 12.

The phrase "What is it like ?" stands for a fundamental thought process. How does one go about observing and reporting on things and events that occupy segments of earth space ? Of all the infinite variety of phenomena on the face of the earth, how does one decide what phenomena to observe ? There is no such thing as a complete description of the earth or any part of it, for every microscopic point on the earth's surface differs from every other such point. Experience shows that the things observed are already familiar, because they are like phenomena that occur at home or because they resemble the abstract images and models developed in the human mind.

How are abstract images formed? Humans alone among the animals possess language; their words symbolize not only specific things but also mental images of classes of things. People can remember what they have seen or experienced because they attach a word symbol to them.

During the long record of our efforts to gain more and more knowledge about the face of the earth as the human habitat, there has been a continuing interplay between things and events. The direct observation through the senses is described as a percept; the mental image is described as a concept. Percepts are what some people describe as reality, in contrast to mental images, which are theoretical, implying that they are not real.

The relation of Percept to Concept is not as simple as the definition implies. It is now quite clear that people of different cultures or even individuals in the same culture develop different mental images of reality and what they perceive is a reflection of these preconceptions. The direct observation of things and events on the face of the earth is so clearly a function of the mental images of the mind of the observer that the whole idea of reality must be reconsidered.

Concepts determine what the observer perceives, yet concepts are derived from the generalizations of previous percepts. What happens is that the educated observer is taught to accept a set of concepts and then sharpens or changes these concepts during a professional career. In any one field of scholarship, professional opinion at one time determines what concepts and procedures are acceptable, and these form a kind of model of scholarly behaviour.

7. **The problem raised in the passage reflects on:**
   A. thought process B. human behaviour
   C. cultural perceptions D. professional opinion

8. **According to the passage, human beings have mostly in mind:**
   A. Observation of things
   B. Preparation of mental images
   C. Expression through language
   D. To gain knowledge

9. **Concept means:**
   A. A mental image
   B. A reality
   C. An idea expressed in language form
   D. All the above

10. **The relation of Percept to Concept is:**
    A. Positive B. Negative C. Reflective D. Absolute

11. **In the passage, the earth is taken as:**
    A. The Globe B. The Human Habitat
    C. A Celestial Body D. A Planet

12. **Percept means:**
    A. Direct observation through the senses
    B. A conceived idea
    C. Ends of a spectrum
    D. An abstract image

13. **Action research means:**
    A. A longitudinal research
    B. An applied research
    C. A research initiated to solve an immediate problem
    D. A research with socio-economic objective

14. **Research is:**
    A. Searching again and again
    B. Finding solution to any problem
    C. Working in a scientific way to search for truth of any problem
    D. None of the above

15. A common test in research demands much priority on:

A. Reliability

B. Useability

C. Objectivity

D. All of the above

16. Which of the following is the first step in starting the research process?

A. Searching sources of information to locate problem

B. Survey of related literature

C. Identification of problem

D. Searching for solutions to the problem

17. If a researcher conducts a research on finding out which administrative style contributes more to institutional effectiveness? This will be an example of:

A. Basic Research

B. Action Research

C. Applied Research

D. None of the above

18. Normal Probability Curve should be:

A. Positively skewed

B. Negatively skewed

C. Leptokurtic skewed

D. Zero skewed

19. In communication, a major barrier to reception of messages is:

A. audience attitude

B. audience knowledge

C. audience education

D. audience income

20. Post-modernism is associated with:

A. newspapers B. magazines

C. radio D. television

21. Didactic communication is:

A. intra-personal

B. inter-personal

C. organisational
D. relational

22. In communication, the language is:
A. the non-verbal code
B. the verbal code
C. the symbolic code
D. the iconic code

23. Identify the correct sequence of the following:
A. Source, channel, message, receiver
B. Source, receiver, channel, message
C. Source, message, receiver, channel
D. Source, message, channel, receiver

24. Assertion (A) : Mass media promote a culture of violence in the society
Reason (R) : Because violence sells in the market as people themselves are violent in character
A. Both (A) and (R) are true and (R) is the correct explanation of (A)
B. Both (A) and (R) are true, but (R)is not the correct explanation of (A)
C. (A) is true, but (R) is false
D. Both (A) and (R) are false

25. When an error of 1% is made in the length of a square, the percentage error in the area of a square will be:
A. 0 B. ½ C. 1 D. 2

26. On January 12, 1980, it was a Saturday. The day of the week on January 12, 1979 was
A.Thursday B. Friday C. Saturday D. Sunday

27. If water is called food, food is called tree, tree is called earth, earth is called world, which of the following grows a fruit ?
A.Water B. Tree C. World D. Earth

28. E is the son of A, D is the son of B, E is married to C, C is the daughter of B. How is D related to E?
A. Brother B. Uncle C. Father-in-law D. Brother-in-law

29. If INSURANCE is coded as ECNARUSNI, how HINDRANCE will be coded?
A. CADNIHWCE B. HANODEINR
C. AELIRHDCN D. ECNARDNIH

30. Find the next number in the following series :

2, 5, 10, 17, 26, 37, 50, ?

A.63 B. 65

C. 67 D. 69

31. Which of the following is an example of circular arrangement?

A. God created man in his image and man created God in his own image

B. God is the source of scripture and the scripture is the source of our knowledge of God

C. Some of the Indians are great because India is great

D. Rama is great beacuse he is Rama

32. Lakshmana is a morally good person because:

A. he is religious

B. he is educated

C. he is rich

D. he is rational

33. Two statements I and II given below are followed by two conclusions (a) and (b). supposing the statements are true, which of the following conclusions can logically follow?

Statement:

I. Some religious people are morally good

II. Some religious people are rational

Conclusions:

(a) Rationally religious people are good morally

(b) Non rational religious persons are not morally good

A. only (a) follows

B. only (b) follows

C. both (a) and (b) follows

D. neither (a) nor (b) follows

34. Certainty is:

A. an objective fact

B. emotionally satisfying

C. logical

D. ontological

Questions from 35 to 36 are based on the following diagram in which there are three intersecting circles I, S and P where circle I stands for Indians, circle S stands for scientists and circle P for politicians. Different regions of the figure are lettered from a to g.

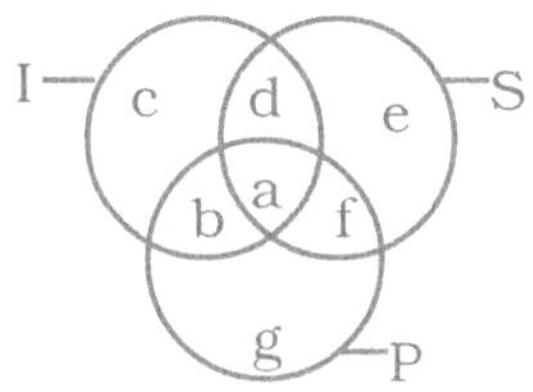

35. The region which represents non-Indian scientists who are politicians:

A. f B. d

C. a D. c

36. The region which represents politicians who are Indians as well as scientists:

A. b B. c

C. a D. d

37. The population of a city is plotted as a function of time (years) in graphic form below:

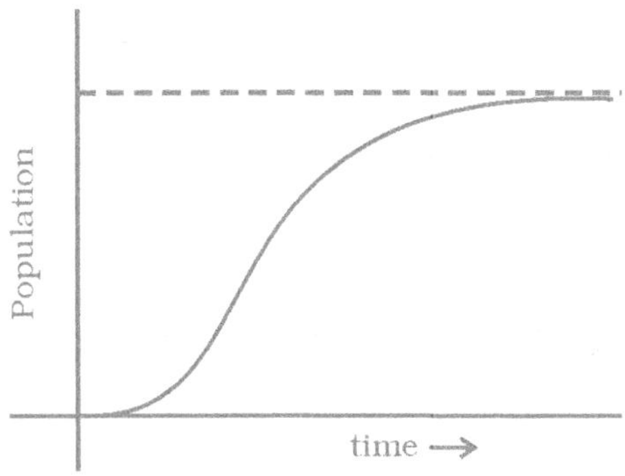

Which of the following inference can be drawn from above plot ?

A. The population increases exponentially

B. The population increases in parabolic fashion

C. The population initially increases in a linear fashion and then stabilizes

D. The population initially increases exponentially and then stabilizes

In the following chart, the price of logs is shown in per cubic metre and that of Plywood and Saw Timber in per tonnes. Study the chart and answer the following questions 38, 39 and 40.

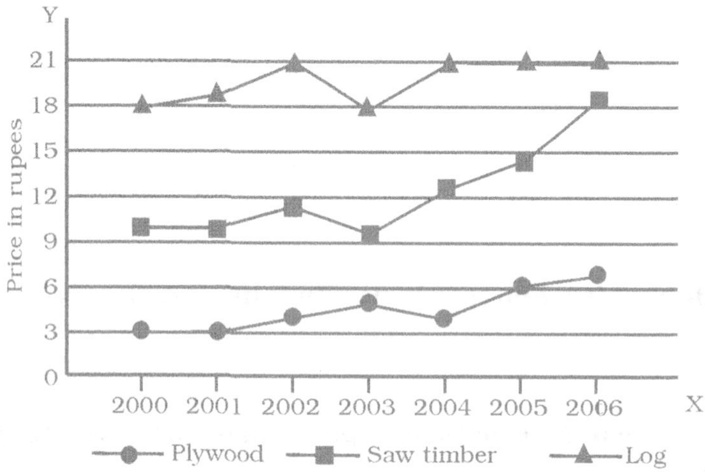

38. Which product shows the maximum percentage increase in price over the period?

A. Saw timber

B. Plywood

C. Log

D. None of the above

39. What is the maximum percentage increase in price per cubic metre of log?

A. 6 B. 12 C. 18 D. 20

40. In which year the prices of two products increased and that of the third increased ?

A. 2000 B. 2002 C. 2003 D. 2006

41. Which one of the following is the oldest Archival source of data in India?

A. National Sample Surveys

B. Agricultural Statistics

C. Census

D. Vital Statistics

42. In a large random data set following normal distribution, the ratio (%) of number of data points which are in the range of (mean ± standard deviation) to the total number of data points, is

A. ~ 50% B. ~ 67% C. ~ 97% D. ~ 47%

43. Which number system is usually followed in a typical 32-bit computer ?

A. 2 B. 8 C. 10 D. 16

44. Which one of the following is an example of Operating System ?

A. Microsoft Word
B. Microsoft Excel
C. Microsoft Access
D. Microsoft Windows

45. Which one of the following represent the binary equivalent of the decimal number 23 ?

A. 01011 B. 10111 C. 10011 D. None of the above

46. Which one of the following is different from other members ?

A. Google B. Windows C. Linux D. Mac

47. Where does a computer add and compare its data ?

A. CPU B. Memory C. Hard disk D. Floppy disk

48. Computers on an internet are identified by:

A. e-mail address B. street address
C. IP address D. None of the above

49. The Right to Information Act, 2005 makes the provision of:

A. Dissemination of all types of information by all Public authorities to any person.
B. Establishment of Central, State and District Level Information Commissions as an appellate body.
C. Transparency and accountability in Public authorities.
D. All of the above

50. Which type of natural hazards cause maximum damage to property and lives?

A. Hydrological B. Hydro-meteorological
C. Geological D. Geo-chemical

51. Dioxins are produced from:

A. Wastelands B. Power plants
C. Sugar factories D. Combustion of plastics

52. The slogan "A tree for each child" was coined for

A. Social forestry programme

B. Clean Air programme

C. Soil conservation programme

D. Environmental protection programme

53. The main constituents of biogas are:

A. Methane and Carbon di-oxide

B. Methane and Nitric oxide

C. Methane, Hydrogen and Nitric oxide

D. Methane and Sulphur di-oxide

54. Assertion (A) : In the world as a whole, the environment has degraded during past several decades.

Reason (R) : The population of the world has been growing significantly.

A. (A) is correct, (R) is correct and (R) is the correct explanation of (A).

B. (A) is correct, (R) is correct and (R) is not the correct explanation of (A).

C. (A) is correct, but (R) is false.

D. (A) is false, but (R) is correct.

55. Climate change has implications for:

1. soil moisture 2. forest fires

3. biodiversity 4. ground water

Identify the correct combination according to the code :

Codes :

A. 1 and 3

B. 1, 2 and 3

C. 1, 3 and 4

D. 1, 2, 3 and 4

56. The accreditation process by National Assessment and Accreditation Council (NAAC) differs from that of National Board of Accreditation (NBA) in terms of:

A. Disciplines covered by both being the same, there is duplication of efforts

B. One has institutional grading approach and the other has programme grading approach

C. Once get accredited by NBA or NAAC, the institution is free from renewal of grading, which is not a progressive decision

D. This accreditation amounts to approval of minimum standards in the quality of education in the institution concerned

57. Which option is not correct ?

A. Most of the educational institutions of National repute in scientific and technical sphere fall under 64th entry of Union list.

B. Education, in general, is the subject of concurrent list since 42nd Constitutional Amendment Act 1976.

C. Central Advisory Board on Education (CABE) was first established in 1920.

D. India had implemented the right to Free and Compulsory Primary Education in 2002 through 86th Constitutional Amendment.

58. Which statement is not correct about the "National Education Day" of India?

A. It is celebrated on 5th September every year

B. It is celebrated on 11th November every year

C. It is celebrated in the memory of India's first Union Minister of Education, Dr. Abul Kalam Azad

D. It is being celebrated since 2008

59. Match List-I with List-II and select the correct answer from the codes given below:

List – I (Articles of the Constitution)	*List – II (Institutions)*
(a) Article 280	(i) Administrative Tribunals
(b) Article 324	(ii) Election Commission of India
(c) Article 323	(iii) Finance Commission at Union level
(d) Article 315	(iv) Union Public Service Commission

Codes :

	(a)	(b)	(c)	(d)
A.	(i)	(ii)	(iii)	(iv)
B.	(iii)	(ii)	(i)	(iv)
C.	(ii)	(iii)	(iv)	(i)
D.	(ii)	(iv)	(iii)	(i)

60. Deemed Universities declared by UGC under Section 3 of the UGC Act 1956, are not permitted to

A. offer programmes in higher education and issue degrees.

B. give affiliation to any institute of higher education.

C. open off-campus and off-shore campus anywhere in the country and overseas respectively without the permission of the UGC.

D. offer distance education programmes without the approval of the Distance Education Council.

Answer keys

1.A	2.A	3.A	4.B	5.A	6.A	7.A	8.C	9.A	10.C
11.B	12.A	13.C	14.C	15.D	16.C	17.B	18.D	19.A	20.B
21.B	22.B	23.D	24.D	25.C	26.D	27.D	28.D	29.B	30.B
31.B	32.B	33.D	34.A	35.A	36.C	37.D	38.A	39.C	40.C
41.C	42.B	43.D	44.D	45.B	46.A	47.B	48.C	49.D	50.A
51.B	52.A	53.A	54.A	55.D	56.B	57.D	58.C	59.B	60.B

UGC NET-JRF EXAMINATION DECEMBER 2010

SOLVED QUESTION PAPER

PAPER - I

Note :
- This paper contains **Sixty (60)** multiple choice questions, each question carrying **two (2)** marks.
- Candidate is expected to answer any **Fifty (50)** questions.
- In case more than **Fifty (50)** questions are attempted, only the first **Fifty (50)** questions will be evaluated.

1. Which of the following variables cannot be expressed in quantitative terms ?

A. Socio-economic Status B. Marital Status

C. Numerical Aptitude D. Professional Attitude

2. A doctor studies the relative effectiveness of two drugs of dengue fever. His research would be classified as

A. Descriptive Survey B. Experimental Research

C. Case Study D. Ethnography

3. The term 'phenomenology' is associated with the process of

A. Qualitative Research B. Analysis of Variance

C. Correlational Study D. Probability Sampling

4. The 'Sociogram' technique is used to study

A. Vocational Interest B. Professional Competence

C. Human Relations D. Achievement Motivation

Read the following passage carefully and answer questions from 5 to 10 :

It should be remembered that the nationalist movement in India, like all nationalist movements, was essentially a bourgeois movement. It represented the natural historical stage of development, and to consider it or to criticise it as a working-class movement is wrong. Gandhi represented that movement and the Indian masses in relation to that movement to a supreme degree, and he became the voice of Indian people to that extent. The main contribution of Gandhi to India and the Indian masses has been through the powerful movements which he launched through the National Congress. Through nation-wide action he sought to mould the millions, and largely succeeded in doing so, and changing them from a demoralised, timid and hopeless mass, bullied and crushed by every dominant interest, and incapable of resistance, into a people with self-respect and self-reliance, resisting tyranny, and capable of united action and sacrifice for a larger cause.

Gandhi made people think of political and economic issues and every village and every bazaar hummed with argument and debate on the new ideas and hopes that filled the people. That was an amazing psychological change. The time was ripe for it, of course, and circumstances and world conditions worked for this change. But a great leader is necessary to take advantage of circumstances and conditions. Gandhi was that leader, and he released many of the bonds that imprisoned and disabled our minds, and none of us who experienced it can ever forget that great feeling of release and exhilaration that came over the Indian people.

Gandhi has played a revolutionary role in India of the greatest importance because he knew how to make the most of the objective conditions and could reach the heart of the masses, while groups with a more advanced ideology functioned largely in the air because they did not fit in with those conditions and could therefore not evoke any substantial response from the masses.

It is perfectly true that Gandhi, functioning in the nationalist plane, does not think in terms of the conflict of classes, and tries to compose their differences. But the action he has indulged and taught the people has inevitably raised mass consciousness tremendously and made social issues vital. Gandhi and the Congress must be judged by the policies they pursue and the action they indulge in. But behind this, personality counts and colours those policies and activities. In the case of very exceptional person like Gandhi the question of personality becomes especially important in order to understand and appraise him. To us he has represented the spirit and honour of India, the yearning of her sorrowing millions to be rid of their innumerable burdens, and an insult to him by the British Government or others has been an insult to India and her people.

5. Which one of the following is true of the given passage ?

A. The passage is a critique of Gandhi's role in Indian movement for independence.

B. The passage hails the role of Gandhi in India's freedom movement.

C. The author is neutral on Gandhi's role in India's freedom movement.

D. It is an account of Indian National Congress's support to the working-class movement.

6. The change that the Gandhian movement brought among the Indian masses was

A. Physical B. Cultural

C. Technological D. Psychological

7. To consider the nationalist movement or to criticise it as a working-class movement was wrong because it was a

A. historical movement B. voice of the Indian people
C. bourgeois movement D. movement represented by Gandhi

8. Gandhi played a revolutionary role in India because he could

A. preach morality B. reach the heart of Indians
C. see the conflict of classes D. lead the Indian National Congress

9. Groups with advanced ideology functioned in the air as they did not fit in with

A. objective conditions of masses B. the Gandhian ideology
C. the class consciousness of the people D. the differences among masses

10. The author concludes the passage by

A. criticising the Indian masses B. the Gandhian movement
C. pointing out the importance of the personality of Gandhi
D. identifying the sorrows of millions of Indians

11. Media that exist in an interconnected series of communication - points are referred to as

A. Networked media B. Connective media
C. Nodal media D. Multimedia

12. The information function of mass communication is described as

A. diffusion B. publicity
C. surveillance D. diversion

13. An example of asynchronous medium is

A. Radio B. Television
C. Film D. Newspaper

14. In communication, connotative words are

A. explicit B. abstract
C. simple D. cultural

15. A message beneath a message is labelled as

A. embedded text B. internal text
C. inter-text D. sub-text

16. In analog mass communication, stories are

A. static B. dynamic

C. interactive D. exploratory

17. Determine the relationship between the pair of words ALWAYS : NEVER and then select from the following pair of words which have a similar relationship :

A. often : rarely B. frequently : occasionally

C. constantly : frequently D. intermittently : casually

18. Find the wrong number in the sequence : 52, 51, 48, 43, 34, 27, 16

A. 27 B. 34 C. 43 D. 48

19. In a certain code, PAN is written as 31 and PAR as 35, then PAT is written in the same code as

A. 30 B. 37 C. 39 D. 41

20. The letters in the first set have certain relationship. On the basis of this relationship, make the right choice for the second set : AF : IK : : LQ : ?

A. MO B. NP C. OR D. TV

21. If 5472 = 9, 6342 = 6, 7584 = 6, what is 9236 ?

A. 2 B. 3 C. 4 D. 5

22. In an examination, 35% of the total students failed in Hindi, 45% failed in English and 20% in both. The percentage of those who passed in both subjects is

A. 10 B. 20 C. 30 D. 40

23. Two statements I and II given below are followed by two conclusions (a) and (b). Supposing the statements are true, which of the following conclusions can logically follow ?

Statements :

I. Some flowers are red.

II. Some flowers are blue.

Conclusions :

(a) Some flowers are neither red nor blue.

(b) Some flowers are both red and blue.

A. Only (a) follows B. Only (b) follows.

C. Both (a) and (b) follow. D. Neither (a) nor (b) follows.

24. If the statement 'all students are intelligent' is true, which of the following statements are false ?

(i) No students are intelligent.

(ii) Some students are intelligent.

(iii) Some students are not intelligent.

A. (i) and (ii) B. (i) and (iii) C. (ii) and (iii) D. (i) only

25. A reasoning where we start with certain particular statements and conclude with a universal statement is called

A. Deductive Reasoning B. Inductive Reasoning

C. Abnormal Reasoning D. Transcendental Reasoning

26. What is the smallest number of ducks that could swim in this formation– two ducks in front of a duck, two ducks behind a duck and a duck between two ducks ?

A. 5 B. 7 C. 4 D. 3

27. Mr. A, Miss B, Mr. C and Miss D are sitting around a table and discussing their trades.

(i) Mr. A sits opposite to the cook.

(ii) Miss B sits right to the barber

(iii)The washerman sits right to the barber

(iv) Miss D sits opposite to Mr. C

What are the trades of A and B ?

A. Tailor and barber B. Barber and cook

C. Tailor and cook D. Tailor and washerman

28. Which one of the following methods serve to measure correlation between two variables ?

A. Scatter Diagram B. Frequency Distribution

C. Two-way table D. Coefficient of Rank Correlation

29. Which one of the following is not an Internet Service Provider (ISP) ?

A. MTNL B. BSNL

C. ERNET India D. Infotech India Ltd.

30. The hexadecimal number system consists of the symbols

A. 0 – 7 B. 0 – 9 , A – F

C. 0 – 7, A – F D. None of these

31. The binary equivalent of (–15)10 is (2's complement system is used)

A. 11110001 B. 11110000

C. 10001111 D. None of these

32. 1 GB is equal to

A. 230 bits B. 230 bytes

C. 220 bits D. 220 bytes

33. The set of computer programs that manage the hardware/software of a computer is called

A. Compiler system B. Operation system

C. Operating system D. None of these

34. S/MIME in Internet technology stands for

A. Secure Multipurpose Internet Mail Extension

B. Secure Multimedia Internet Mail Extension

C. Simple Multipurpose Internet Mail Extension

D. Simple Multimedia Internet Mail Extension

35. Which of the following is not covered in 8 missions under the Climate Action Plan of Government of India ?

A. Solar power B. Waste to energy conversion

C. Afforestation D. Nuclear energy

36. The concentration of Total Dissolved Solids (TDS) in drinking water should not exceed

A. 500 mg/L B. 400 mg/L

C. 300 mg/L D. 200 mg/L

37. 'Chipko' movement was first started by

A. Arundhati Roy B. Medha Patkar

C. Ila Bhatt D. Sunderlal Bahuguna

38. The constituents of photochemical smog responsible for eye irritation are

A. SO_2 and O_3 B. SO_2 and NO_2

C. HCHO and PAN D. SO_2 and SPM

39. Assertion (A) : Some carbonaceous aerosols may be carcinogenic.

Reason (R) : They may contain polycyclic aromatic hydrocarbons (PAHs).

A. Both (A) and (R) are correct and (R) is the correct explanation of (A).

B. Both (A) and (R) are correct but (R) is not the correct explanation of (A).
C. (A) is correct, but (R) is false.
D. (A) is false, but (R) is correct.

40. Volcanic eruptions affect

A. atmosphere and hydrosphere
B. hydrosphere and biosphere
C. lithosphere, biosphere and atmosphere
D. lithosphere, hydrosphere and atmosphere

41. India's first Defence University is in the State of

A. Haryana
B. Andhra Pradesh
C. Uttar Pradesh
D. Punjab

42. Most of the Universities in India

A. conduct teaching and research only
B. affiliate colleges and conduct examinations
C. conduct teaching/research and examinations
D. promote research only

43. Which one of the following is not a Constitutional Body ?

A. Election Commission
B. Finance Commission
C. Union Public Service Commission
D. Planning Commission

44. Which one of the following statements is not correct ?

A. Indian Parliament is supreme.
B. The Supreme Court of India has the power of judicial review.
C. There is a division of powers between the Centre and the States.
D. There is a Council of Ministers to aid and advise the President.

45. Which one of the following statements reflects the republic character of Indian democracy ?

A. Written Constitution
B. No State religion
C. Devolution of power to local Government institutions
D. Elected President and directly or indirectly elected Parliament

46. Who among the following appointed by the Governor can be removed by only the President of India ?

A. Chief Minister of a State

B. A member of the State Public Service Commission

C. Advocate-General

D. Vice-Chancellor of a State University

47. If two small circles represent the class of the 'men' and the class of the 'plants' and the big circle represents 'mortality', which one of the following figures represent the proposition 'All men are mortal.' ?

A. 

B. 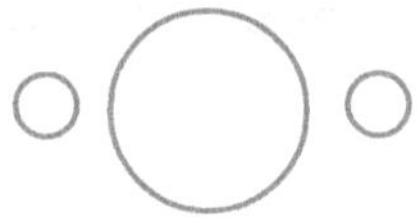

C. 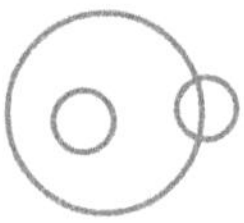

D. 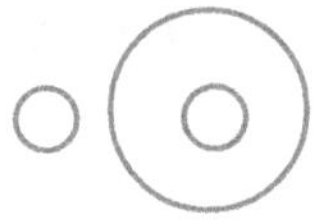

The following table presents the production of electronic items (TVs and LCDs) in a factory during the period from 2006 to 2010. Study the table carefully and answer the questions from 48 to 52 :

Year	2006	2007	2008	2009	2010
TVs	6000	9000	13000	11000	8000
LCDs	7000	9400	9000	10000	12000

48. In which year, the total production of electronic items is maximum?

A. 2006 B. 2007 C. 2008 D. 2010

49. What is the difference between averages of production of LCDs and TVs from 2006 to 2008?

A. 3000 B. 2867 C. 3015 D. 2400

50. What is the year in which production of TVs is half the production of LCDs in the year 2010 ?

A. 2007 B. 2006 C. 2009 D. 2008

51. What is the ratio of production of LCDs in the years 2008 and 2010 ?

A. 4 : 3 B. 3 : 4 C. 1 : 3 D. 2 : 3

52. What is the ratio of production of TVs in the years 2006 and 2007?

A. 6 : 7 B. 7 : 6 C. 2 : 3 D. 3 : 2

53. Some students in a class exhibit great curiosity for learning. It may be because such children

A. Are gifted B. Come from rich families

C. Show artificial behaviour D. Create indiscipline in the class

54. The most important quality of a good teacher is

A. Sound knowledge of subject matter B. Good communication skills

C. Concern for students' welfare D. Effective leadership qualities

55. Which one of the following is appropriate in respect of teacherstudent relationship ?

A. Very informal and intimate B. Limited to classroom only

C. Cordial and respectful D. Indifferent

56. The academic performance of students can be improved if parents are encouraged to

A. supervise the work of their wards

B. arrange for extra tuition

C. remain unconcerned about it

D. interact with teachers frequently

57. In a lively classroom situation, there is likely to be

A. occasional roars of laughter

B. complete silence

C. frequent teacher-student dialogue

D. loud discussion among students

58. If a parent approaches the teacher to do some favour to his/her ward in the examination, the teacher should

A. try to help him B. ask him not to talk in those terms

C. refuse politely and firmly D. ask him rudely to go away

59. Which of the following phrases is not relevant to describe the meaning of research as a process ?

A. Systematic Activity B. Objective Observation

C. Trial and Error D. Problem Solving

60. Which of the following is not an example of a continuous variable ?

A. Family size B. Intelligence

C. Height D. Attitude

Answer keys

1.B	2.B	3.A	4.C	5.B	6.D	7.C	8.B	9.A	10.C
11.A	12.B	13.B	14.A	15.D	16.A	17.A	18.B	19.B	20.C
21.A	22.D	23.A	24.B	25.B	26.D	27.B	28.D	29.D	30.B
31.A	32.B	33.C	34.A	35.D	36.A	37.D	38.C	39.A	40.D
41.A	42.C	43.D	44.D	45.A	46.B	47.B	48.C	49.	50.B
51.B	52.C	53.A	54.C	55.C	56.D	57.C	58.C	59.C	60.A

UGC NET-JRF EXAMINATION JUNE 2011

SOLVED QUESTION PAPER

PAPER - I

Note :
- This paper contains **Sixty (60)** multiple choice questions, each question carrying **two (2)** marks.
- Candidate is expected to answer any **Fifty (50)** questions.
- In case more than **50** questions are attempted, only the first **50** questions will be evaluated.

1 A research paper is a brief report of research work based on

A. Primary Data only B. Secondary Data only

C. Both Primary and Secondary Data D. None of the above

2. Newton gave three basic laws of motion. This research is categorized as

A. Descriptive Research B. Sample Survey

C. Fundamental Research D. Applied Research

3. A group of experts in a specific area of knowledge assembled at a place and prepared a syllabus for a new course. The process may be termed as

A. Seminar B. Workshop

C. Conference D. Symposium

4. In the process of conducting research 'Formulation of Hypothesis" is followed by

A. Statement of Objectives B. Analysis of Data

C. Selection of Research Tools D. Collection of Data

Read the following passage carefully and answer questions 5 to 10 :

All historians are interpreters of text if they be private letters, Government records or parish birthlists or whatever. For most kinds of historians, these are only the necessary means to understanding something other than the texts themselves, such as a political action or a historical trend, whereas for the intellectual historian, a full understanding of his chosen texts is itself the aim of his enquiries. Of course, the intellectual history is particularly prone to draw on the focus of other disciplines that are habitually interpreting texts for purposes of their own, probing the reasoning that ostensibly connects premises and conclusions. Furthermore, the boundaries with adjacent subdisciplines are shifting and indistinct : the history of art and the history of science both claim a certain autonomy, partly just because they require specialised technical skills, but both can also be seen as part of a wider intellectual history, as is evident when one considers, for example, the common stock of knowledge about cosmological beliefs or moral ideals of a period. Like all historians, the intellectual historian is a consumer rather than a producer of 'methods'. His distinctiveness lies in which aspect of the past he is trying to illuminate, not in having exclusive possession of either a corpus of evidence or a body of techniques. That being said, it does seem that the label 'intellectual history' attracts a disproportionate share of misunderstanding. It is alleged that intellectual history is the history of something that never really mattered. The long dominance of the historical profession by political historians bred a kind of philistinism, an unspoken belief that power and its exercise was 'what mattered'. The prejudice was reinforced by the assertion that political action was never really the outcome of principles or ideas that were 'more flapdoodle'. The legacy of this precept is still discernible in the tendency to require ideas to have 'licensed' the political class before they can be deemed worthy of intellectual attention, as if there were some reasons why the history of art or science, of philosophy or literature, were somehow of interest and significance than the history of Parties or Parliaments. Perhaps in recent years the mirror-image of this philistinism has been more common in the claim that ideas of any one is of systematic expression or sophistication do not matter, as if they were only held by a minority. Answer the following questions :

5. An intellectual historian aims to fully understand

A. the chosen texts of his own   B. political actions

C. historical trends   D. his enquiries

6. Intellectual historians do not claim exclusive possession of

A. conclusions   B. any corpus of evidence

C. distinctiveness   D. habitual interpretation

7. The misconceptions about intellectual history stem from

A. a body of techniques

B. the common stock of knowledge

C. the dominance of political historians

D. cosmological beliefs

8. What is philistinism?

A. Reinforcement of prejudice

B. Fabrication of reasons

C. The hold of land-owning classes

D. Belief that power and its exercise matter

9. **Knowledge of cosmological beliefs or moral ideas of a period can be drawn as part of**
   A. literary criticism B. history of science
   C. history of philosophy D. intellectual history

10. **The claim that ideas of any one is of systematic expression do not matter, as if they were held by a minority, is**
    A. to have a licensed political class
    B. a political action
    C. a philosophy of literature
    D. the mirror-image of philistinism

11. **Public communication tends to occur within a more**
    A. complex structure B. political structure
    C. convenient structure D. formal structure

12. **Transforming thoughts, ideas and messages into verbal and non-verbal signs is referred to as**
    A. channelisation B. mediation
    C. encoding D. decoding

13. **Effective communication needs a supportive**
    A. economic environment B. political environment
    C. social environment D. multi-cultural environment

14. **A major barrier in the transmission of cognitive data in the process of communication is an individual's**
    A. personality B. expectation
    C. social status D. coding ability

15. **When communicated, institutionalised stereotypes become**
    A. myths B. reasons
    C. experiences D. convictions

16. **In mass communication, selective perception is dependent on the receiver's**
    A. competence B. pre-disposition
    C. receptivity D. ethnicity

17. **Determine the relationship between the pair of words NUMERATOR : DENOMINATOR and then select the pair of words from the following which have a similar relationship:**

A. fraction : decimal B. divisor : quotient
C. top : bottom D. dividend : divisor

18. Find the wrong number in the sequence 125, 127, 130, 135, 142, 153, 165

A. 130 B. 142 C. 153 D. 165

19. If HOBBY is coded as IOBY and LOBBY is coded as MOBY; then BOBBY is coded as

A. BOBY B. COBY C. DOBY D. OOBY

20. The letters in the first set have certain relationship. On the basis of this relationship, make the right choice for the second set: K/T : 11/20 :: J/R:?

A. 10/8 B. 10/18 C. 11/19 D. 10/19

21. If A = 5, B = 6, C = 7, D = 8 and so on, what do the following numbers stand for? 17, 19, 20, 9, 8

A. Plane B. Moped C. Motor D. Tonga

22. The price of oil is increased by 25%. If the expenditure is not allowed to increase, the ratio between the reduction in consumption and the original consumption is

A. 1 : 3 B. 1 : 4 C. 1 : 5 D. 1 : 6

23. How many 8's are there in the following sequence which are preceded by 5 but not immediately followed by 3?

5 8 3 7 5 8 6 3 8 5 4 5 8 4 7 6

5 5 8 3 5 8 7 5 8 2 8 5

A. 4 B. 5 C. 7 D. 3

24. If a rectangle were called a circle, a circle a point, a point a triangle and a triangle a square, the shape of a wheel is

A. Rectangle B. Circle
C. Point D. Triangle

25. Which one of the following methods is best suited for mapping the distribution of different crops as provided in the standard classification of crops in India?

A. Pie diagram B. Chorochromatic technique
C. Isopleth technique D. Dot method

26. Which one of the following does not come under the methods of data classification?

A. Qualitative B. Normative

C. Spatial D. Quantitative

27. Which one of the following is not a source of data?

A. Administrative records B. Population census

C. GIS D. Sample survey

28. If the statement 'some men are cruel' is false, which of the following statements/statement are/is true?

(i) All men are cruel.

(ii) No men are cruel.

(iii) Some men are not cruel.

A. (i) and (iii) B. (i) and (ii)

C. (ii) and (iii) D. (iii) only

29. The octal number system consists of the following symbols:

A. 0 – 7 B. 0 – 9

C. 0 – 9, A – F D. None of the above

30. The binary equivalent of (–19)10 in signed magnitude system is

A. 11101100 B. 11101101

C. 10010011 D. None of these

31. DNS in internet technology stands for

A. Dynamic Name System B. Domain Name System

C. Distributed Name System D. None of these

32. HTML stands for

A. Hyper Text Markup Language

B. Hyper Text Manipulation Language

C. Hyper Text Managing Links

D. Hyper Text Manipulating Links

33. Which of the following is type of LAN?

A. Ethernet B. Token Ring

C. FDDI D. All of the above

34. Which of the following statements is true?

A. Smart cards do not require an operating system.

B. Smart cards and PCs use some operating system.

C. COS is smart card operating system.

D. The communication between reader and card is in full duplex mode.

35. The Ganga Action Plan was initiated during the year

A. 1986 B. 1988 C. 1990 D. 1992

36. Identify the correct sequence of energy sources in order of their share in the power sector in India:

A. Thermal > nuclear > hydro > wind

B. Thermal > hydro > nuclear > wind

C. Hydro > nuclear > thermal > wind

D. Nuclear > hydro > wind > thermal

37. Chromium as a contaminant in drinking water in excess of permissible levels, causes

A. Skeletal damage B. Gastrointestinal problem

C. Dermal and nervous problems D. Liver/Kidney problems

38. The main precursors of winter smog are

A. N_2O and hydrocarbons B. NOx and hydrocarbons

C. SO_2 and hydrocarbons D. SO_2 and ozone

39. Flash floods are caused when

A. the atmosphere is convectively unstable and there is considerable vertical wind shear

B. the atmosphere is stable

C. the atmosphere is convectively unstable with no vertical windshear

D. winds are catabatic

40. In mega cities of India, the dominant source of air pollution is

A. transport sector B. thermal power

C. municipal waste D. commercial sector

41. The first Open University in India was set up in the State of

A. Andhra Pradesh B. Delhi

C. Himachal Pradesh D. Tamil Nadu

42. Most of the Universities in India are funded by

A. the Central Government
B. the State Governments
C. the University Grants Commission
D. Private bodies and Individuals

43. Which of the following organizations looks after the quality of Technical and Management education in India?

A. NCTE B. MCI C. AICTE D. CSIR

44. Consider the following statements: Identify the statement which implies natural justice.

A. The principle of natural justice is followed by the Courts.
B. Justice delayed is justice denied.
C. Natural justice is an inalienable right of a citizen
D. A reasonable opportunity of being heard must be given.

45. The President of India is

A. the Head of State
B. the Head of Government
C. both Head of the State and the Head of the Government
D. None of the above

46. Who among the following holds office during the pleasure of the President of India?

A. Chief Election Commissioner
B. Comptroller and Auditor General of India
C. Chairman of the Union Public Service Commission
D. Governor of a State

Questions 47 to 49 are based upon the following diagram in which there are three interlocking circles A, P and S where A stands for Artists, circle P for Professors and circle S for Sportspersons. Different regions in the figure are lettered from a to f:

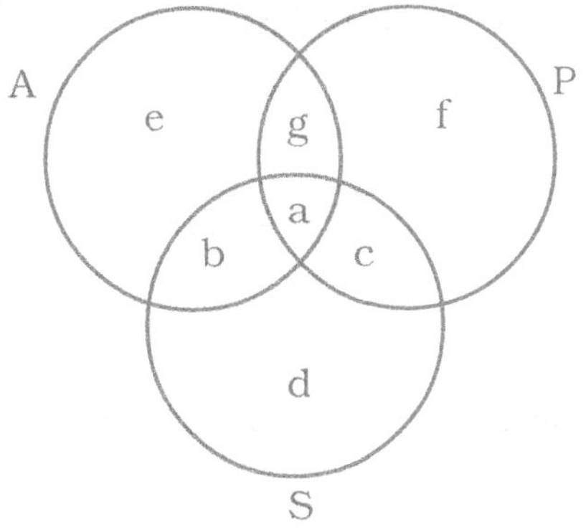

47. The region which represents artists who are neither sportsmen nor professors.

A. d B. e C. b D. g

48. The region which represents professors, who are both artists and sportspersons.

A. a B. c C. d D. g

49. The region which represents professors, who are also sportspersons, but not artists.

A. e B. f C. c D. g

63, 61, 66, 65, 70, 68

63, 62, 64, 69, 65, 64, 66, 67, 66, 64

50. The value of X, which is exceeded 10% of the time in the duration of measurement, is

A 69 B. 68 C. 67 D. 66

51. The value of X, which is exceeded 90% of the time in the duration of measurement, is

A. 63 B. 62 C. 61 D. 60

52. The value of X, which is exceeded 50% of the time in the duration of measurement, is

A. 66 B. 65 C. 64 D. 63

53. For maintaining an effective discipline in the class, the teacher should

A. Allow students to do what they like.

B. Deal with the students strictly.

C. Give the students some problem to solve.

D. Deal with them politely and firmly.

54. An effective teaching aid is one which

A. is colourful and good looking B. activates all faculties

C. is visible to all students D. easy to prepare and use

55. Those teachers are popular among students who

A. develop intimacy with them B. help them solve their problems

C. award good grades D. take classes on extra tuition fee

56. The essence of an effective classroom environment is

A. a variety of teaching aids

B. lively student-teacher interaction
C. pin-drop silence
D. strict discipline

57. On the first day of his class, if a teacher is asked by the students to introduce himself, he should
A. ask them to meet after the class
B. tell them about himself in brief
C. ignore the demand and start teaching
D. scold the student for this unwanted demand

58. Moral values can be effectively inculcated among the students when the teacher
A. frequently talks about values
B. himself practices them
C. tells stories of great persons
D. talks of Gods and Goddesses

59. The essential qualities of a researcher are
A. spirit of free enquiry
B. reliance on observation and evidence
C. systematization or theorizing of knowledge
D. all the above

60. Research is conducted to
I. Generate new knowledge
II. Not to develop a theory
III. Obtain research degree
IV. Reinterpret existing knowledge
Which of the above are correct ?
A. I, III & II B. III, II & IV
C. II, I & III D. I, III & IV

Answer keys

1.C	2.C	3.B	4.A	5.A	6.B	7.C	8.A	9.D	10.D
11.D	12.C	13.C	14.D	15.A	16.B	17.D	18.C	19.C	20.B
21.B	22.C	23.A	24.C	25.B	26.C	27.C	28.D	29.A	30.C
31.B	32.A	33.D	34.A	35.A	36.B	37.D	38.C	39.A	40.A
41.A	42.C	43.C	44.C	45.C	46.D	47.B	48.A	49.C	50.
51.	52.	53.	54.D	55.B	56.B	57.B	56.B	59.D	60.D

UGC NET-JRF EXAMINATION DECEMBER 2011

SOLVED QUESTION PAPER

PAPER - I

Note :
- This paper contains **Sixty (60)** multiple choice questions, each question carrying **two (2)**marks.
- Candidate is expected to answer any **Fifty (50)** questions.
- In case more than **Fifty (50)** questions are attempted, only the first **Fifty (50)** questions will be evaluated.

1. Photo bleeding means

A. Photo cropping B. Photo placement
C. Photo cutting D. Photo colour adjustment

2. While designing communication strategy feed-forward studies are conducted by

A. Audience B. Communicator
C. Satellite D. Media

3. In which language the newspapers have highest circulation ?

A. English B. Hindi
C. Bengali D. Tamil

4. Aspect ratio of TV Screen is

A. 4 : 3 B. 3 : 4 C. 2 : 3 D. 2 : 4

5. Communication with oneself is known as

A. Organisational Communication
B. Grapewine Communication
C. Interpersonal Communication
D. Intrapersonal Communication

6. The term 'SITE' stands for

A. Satellite Indian Television Experiment
B. Satellite International Television Experiment
C. Satellite Instructional Television Experiment
D. Satellite Instructional Teachers Education

7. What is the number that comes next in the sequence ? 2, 5, 9, 19, 37, ___

A. 76 B. 74 C. 75 D. 50

8. Find the next letter for the series MPSV.....

A. X B. Y C. Z D. A

9. If '367' means 'I am happy'; '748' means 'you are sad' and '469' means 'happy and sad' in a given code, then which of the following represents 'and' in that code?

A. 3 B. 6 C. 9 D. 4

10. The basis of the following classification is 'animal', 'man', 'house', 'book', and 'student' :

A. Definite descriptions B. Proper names

C. Descriptive phrases D. Common names

11. Assertion (A) : The coin when flipped next time will come up tails.

Reason (R) : Because the coin was flipped five times in a row, and each time it came up heads.

Choose the correct answer from below :

A. Both (A) and (R) are true, and (R) is the correct explanation of (A).

B. Both (A) and (R) are false, and (R) is the correct explanation of (A).

C. (A) is doubtful, (R) is true, and (R) is not the correct explanation of (A).

D. (A) is doubtful, (R) is false, and (R) is the correct explanation of (A).

12. The relation 'is a sister of ' is

A. non-symmetrical B. symmetrical

C. asymmetrical D. transitive

13. If the proposition "Vegetarians are not meat eaters" is false, then which of the following inferences is correct ? Choose from the codes given below:

1. "Some vegetarians are meat eaters" is true.
2. "All vegetarians are meat eaters" is doubtful.
3. "Some vegetarians are not meat eaters" is true.
4. "Some vegetarians are not meat eaters" is doubtful.

Codes :

A. 1, 2 and 3 B. 2, 3 and 4

C. 1, 3 and 4 D. 1, 2 and 4

14. Determine the nature of the following definition : 'Poor' means having an annual income of ₹ 10,000.

A. persuasive B. precising
C. lexical D. stipulative

15. Which one of the following is not an argument ?

A. If today is Tuesday, tomorrow will be Wednesday.
B. Since today is Tuesday, tomorrow will be Wednesday.
C. Ram insulted me so I punched him in the nose.
D. Ram is not at home, so he must have gone to town.

16. Venn diagram is a kind of diagram to

A. represent and assess the truth of elementary inferences with the help of Boolean Algebra of classes.
B. represent and assess the validity of elementary inferences with the help of Boolean Algebra of classes.
C. represent but not assess the validity of elementary inferences with the help of Boolean Algebra of classes.
D. assess but not represent the validity of elementary inferences with the help of Boolean Algebra of classes.

17. Inductive logic studies the way in which a premise may

A. support and entail a conclusion
B. not support but entail a conclusion
C. neither support nor entail a conclusion
D. support a conclusion without entailing it

18. Which of the following statements are true ? Choose from the codes given below.

1. Some arguments, while not completely valid, are almost valid.
2. A sound argument may be invalid.
3. A cogent argument may have a probably false conclusion.
4. A statement may be true or false.

Codes :

A. 1 and 2 B. 1, 3 and 4 C. 4 alone D. 3 and 4

19. If the side of the square increases by 40%, then the area of the square increases by

A. 60% B. 40% C. 196% D. 96%

20. There are 10 lamps in a hall. Each one of them can be switched on independently. The number of ways in which hall can be illuminated is

A. 10^2 B. 1023 C. 2^{10} D. 10 !

21. How many numbers between 100 and 300 begin or end with 2?

A. 100 B. 110 C. 120 D. 180

22. In a college having 300 students, every student reads 5 newspapers and every newspaper is read by 60 students. The number of newspapers required is

A. at least 30 B. at most 20

C. exactly 25 D. exactly 5

The total CO_2 emissions from various sectors are 5 mmt. In the Pie Chart given below, the percentage contribution to CO_2 emissions from various sectors is indicated.

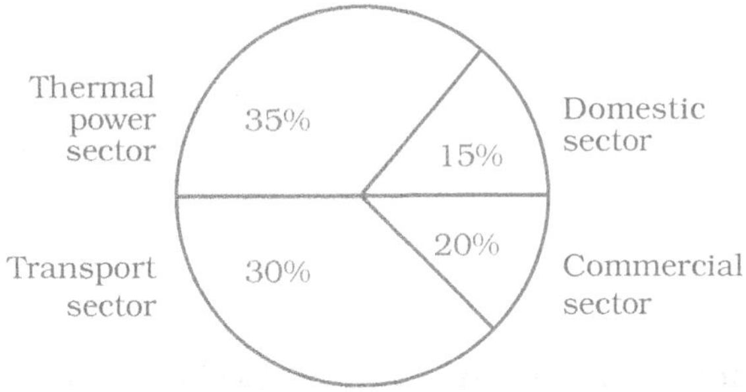

23. What is the absolute CO_2 emission from domestic sector ?

A. 1.5 mmt B. 2.5 mmt

C. 1.75 mmt D. 0.75 mmt

24. What is the absolute CO_2 emission for combined thermal power and transport sectors ?

A. 3.25 mmt B. 1.5 mmt

C. 2.5 mmt D. 4 mmt

25. Which of the following operating system is used on mobile phones ?

A. Windows Vista B. Android

C. Windows XP D. All of the above

26. If (y)*x* represents a number y in base *x*, then which of the following numbers is smallest of all ?

A. (1111)2 B. (1111)8

C. (1111)10 D. (1111)16

27. High level programming language can be converted to machine language using which of the following ?

A. Oracle
B. Compiler
C. Mat lab
D. Assembler

28. HTML is used to create

A. machine language program
B. high level program
C. web page
D. web server

29. The term DNS stands for

A. Domain Name System
B. Defense Nuclear System
C. Downloadable New Software
D. Dependent Name Server

30. IPv4 and IPv6 are addresses used to identify computers on the internet. Find the correct statement out of the following:

A. Number of bits required for IPv4 address is more than number of bits required for IPv6 address.
B. Number of bits required for IPv4 address is same as number of bits required for IPv6 address.
C. Number of bits required for IPv4 address is less than number of bits required for IPv6 address.
D. Number of bits required for IPv4 address is 64.

31. Which of the following pollutants affects the respiratory tract in humans?

A. Carbon monoxide
B. Nitric oxide
C. Sulphur di-oxide
D. Aerosols

32. Which of the following pollutants is not emitted from the transport sector?

A. Oxides of nitrogen
B. Chlorofluorocarbons
C. Carbon monoxide
D. Poly aromatic hydrocarbons

33. Which of the following sources of energy has the maximum potential in India?

A. Solar energy
B. Wind energy
C. Ocean thermal energy
D. Tidal energy

34. Which of the following is not a source of pollution in soil ?

A. Transport sector
B. Agriculture sector
C. Thermal power plants
D. Hydropower plants

35. Which of the following is not a natural hazard ?

A. Earthquake B. Tsunami

C. Flash floods D. Nuclear accident

36. Ecological footprint represents

A. area of productive land and water to meet the resources requirement

B. energy consumption

C. CO_2 emissions per person

D. forest cover

37. The aim of value education to inculcate in students is

A. the moral values B. the social values

C. the political values D. the economic values

38. Indicate the number of Regional Offices of University Grants Commission of India.

A. 10 B. 07 C. 08 D. 09

39. One-rupee currency note in India bears the signature of

A. The President of India

B. Finance Minister of India

C. Governor, Reserve Bank of India

D. Finance Secretary of Government of India

40. Match the List – I with the List – II and select the correct answer from the codes given below:

List – I (Commissions and Committees)	List – II (Year)
(a) First Administrative Reforms Commission	(i) 2005
(b) Paul H. Appleby Committee I	(ii) 1962
(c) K. Santhanam Committee	(iii) 1966
(d) Second Administrative Reforms Commission	(iv) 1953

Codes :

(a) (b) (c) (d)

A. (i) (iii) (ii) (iv) B. (iii) (iv) (ii) (i)

C. (iv) (ii) (iii) (i) D. (ii) (i) (iv) (iii)

41. Constitutionally the registration and recognition of political parties is the function performed by

A. The State Election Commission of respective States

B. The Law Ministry of Government of India

C. The Election Commission of India

D. Election Department of the State Governments

42. The members of Gram Sabha are

A. Sarpanch, Upsarpanch and all elected Panchas

B. Sarpanch, Upsarpanch and Village level worker

C. Sarpanch, Gram Sevak and elected Panchas

D. Registered voters of Village Panchayat

43. By which of the following methods the true evaluation of the students is possible ?

A. Evaluation at the end of the course. B. Evaluation twice in a year.

C. Continuous evaluation. D. Formative evaluation.

44. Suppose a student wants to share his problems with his teacher and he visits the teacher's house for the purpose, the teacher should

A. contact the student's parents and solve his problem.

B. suggest him that he should never visit his house.

C. suggest him to meet the principal and solve the problem.

D. extend reasonable help and boost his morale.

45. When some students are deliberately attempting to disturb the discipline of the class by making mischief, what will be your role as a teacher ?

A. Expelling those students.

B. Isolate those students.

C. Reform the group with your authority.

D. Giving them an opportunity for introspection and improve their behaviour.

46. Which of the following belongs to a projected aid ?

A. Blackboard B. Diorama

C. Epidiascope D. Globe

47. A teacher is said to be fluent in asking questions, if he can ask

A. meaningful questions

B. as many questions as possible

C. maximum number of questions in a fixed time

D. many meaningful questions in a fixed time

48. Which of the following qualities is most essential for a teacher ?

A. He should be a learned person.

B. He should be a well dressed person.

C. He should have patience.

D. He should be an expert in his subject.

49. A hypothesis is a

A. law B. canon

C. postulate D. supposition

50. Suppose you want to investigate the working efficiency of nationalised bank in India, which one of the following would you follow?

A. Area Sampling B. Multi-stage Sampling

C. Sequential Sampling D. Quota Sampling

51. Controlled group condition is applied in

A. Survey Research B. Historical Research

C. Experimental Research D. Descriptive Research

52. Workshops are meant for

A. giving lectures B. multiple target groups

C. showcase new theories D. hands on training/experience

53. Which one of the following is a research tool?

A. Graph B. Illustration

C. Questionnaire D. Diagram

54. Research is not considered ethical if it

A. tries to prove a particular point.

B. does not ensure privacy and anonymity of the respondent.

C. does not investigate the data scientifically.

D. is not of a very high standard.

Read the following passage carefully and answer the questions (Qn. Nos. 55 to 60):

The catalytic fact of the twentieth century is uncontrollable development, consumerist society, political materialism, and spiritual devaluation. This inordinate development has led to the transcendental 'second reality' of sacred perception that biologically transcendence is a part of human life. As the century closes, it dawns with imperative vigour that the 'first reality' of enlightened rationalism and the 'second reality' of the Beyond have to be harmonised in a worthy state of man. The *de facto* values describe what we are, they portray the 'is' of our ethic, they are *est* values (Latin *est* means is). The ideal values tell us what we ought to be, they are *esto* values (Latin *esto* 'ought to be').

Both have to be in the ebb and flow of consciousness. The ever new science and technology and the ever-perennial faith are two modes of one certainty, that is the wholeness of man, his courage to be, his share in Being. The materialistic foundations of science have crumbled down. Science itself has proved that matter is energy, processes are as valid as facts, and affirmed the non-materiality of the universe. The encounter of the 'two cultures', the scientific and the humane, will restore the normal vision, and will be the bedrock of a 'science of understanding' in the new century. It will give new meaning to the ancient perception that quantity (measure) and quality (value) coexist at the root of nature. Human endeavours cannot afford to be humanistically irresponsible.

55. The problem raised in the passage reflects overall on

A. Consumerism B. Materialism
C. Spiritual devaluation D. Inordinate development

56. The '*de facto*' values in the passage means

A. What is B. What ought to be
C. What can be D. Where it is

57. According to the passage, the 'first reality' constitutes

A. Economic prosperity B. Political development
C. Sacred perception of life D. Enlightened rationalism

58. Encounter of the 'two cultures', the scientific and the human implies

A. Restoration of normal vision
B. Universe is both material and non-material
C. Man is superior to nature
D. Co-existence of quantity and quality in nature

59. The contents of the passage are

A. Descriptive B. Prescriptive
C. Axiomatic D. Optional

60. The passage indicates that science has proved that

A. universe is material B. matter is energy
C. nature has abundance D. humans are

Answer keys

1.D	2.B	3.B	4.A	5.D	6.C	7. C	8.B	9.C	10.D
11.C	12.B	13.C	14.D	15.D	16.C	17.A	18.C	19.D	20.A
21.B	22.D	23.D	24.C	25.B	26.A	27.B	28.C	29.A	30.C
31.C	32.B	33.B	34.D	35.D	36.A	37.A	38.	39.	40.
41.C	42.	43.C	44.D	45.D	46.C	47.D	48.D	49.D	50.B
51.C	52.D	53.C	54.B	55.D	56.A	57.D	58.D	59.A	60.B

UGC NET-JRF EXAMINATION JUNE 2012

SOLVED QUESTION PAPER

PAPER - I

Note :
- This paper contains **Sixty (60)** multiple choice questions, each question carrying **two (2)** marks.
- Candidate is expected to answer any **Fifty (50)** questions.
- In case more than **Fifty (50)** questions are attempted, only the first **Fifty (50)** questions will be evaluated.

1. Video-Conferencing can be classified as one of the following types of communication :

A. Visual one way B. Audio-Visual one way

C. Audio-Visual two way D. Visual two way

2. MC National University of Journalism and Communication is located at

A. Lucknow B. Bhopal

C. Chennai D. Mumbai

3. All India Radio (A.I.R.) for broadcasting was named in the year

A. 1926 B. 1936 C. 1946 D. 1956

4. In India for broadcasting TV programmes which system is followed ?

A. NTCS B. PAL C. NTSE D. SECAM

5. The term 'DAVP' stands for

A. Directorate of Advertising & Vocal Publicity

B. Division of Audio-Visual Publicity

C. Department of Audio-Visual Publicity

D. Directorate of Advertising & Visual Publicity

6. The term "TRP" is associated with TV shows stands for

A. Total Rating Points B. Time Rating Points

C. Thematic Rating Points D. Television Rating Points

7. Which is the number that comes next in the following sequence ?

2, 6, 12, 20, 30, 42, 56, _____

A. 60 B. 64 C. 72 D. 70

8. Find the next letter for the series

YVSP ....

A. N　　B. M　　C. O　　D. L

9. Given that in a code language, '645' means 'day is warm'; '42' means 'warm spring' and '634' means 'spring is sunny'; which digit represents 'sunny' ?

A. 3　　B. 2　　C. 4　　D. 5

10. The basis of the following classification is : 'first President of India' 'author of *Godan*' 'books in my library', 'blue things' and 'students who work hard'

A. Common names　　B. Proper names

C. Descriptive phrases　　D. Indefinite description

11. In the expression 'Nothing is larger than itself' the relation 'is larger than' is

A. antisymmetric　　B. asymmetrical

C. intransitive　　D. irreflexive

12. Assertion (A) : There are more laws on the books today than ever before, and more crimes being committed than ever before.

Reason (R) : Because to reduce crime we must eliminate the laws.

Choose the correct answer from below :

A. (A) is true, (R) is doubtful and (R) is not the correct explanation of (A).

B. (A) is false, (R) is true and (R) is the correct explanation of (A).

C. (A) is doubtful, (R) is doubtful and (R) is not the correct explanation of (A).

D. (A) is doubtful, (R) is true and (R) is not the correct explanation of (A).

13. If the proposition "All men are not mortal" is true then which of the following inferences is correct ? Choose from the code given below :

1. "All men are mortal" is true.
2. "Some men are mortal" is false.
3. "No men are mortal" is doubtful.
4. "All men are mortal" is false.

Code :

A. 1, 2 and 3　　B. 2, 3 and 4

C. 1, 3 and 4　　D. 1 and 3

14. Determine the nature of the following definition : "Abortion" means the ruthless murdering of innocent beings.

A. Lexical B. Persuasive
C. Stipulative D. Theoretical

15. Which one of the following is not an argument ?

A. Devadutt does not eat in the day so he must be eating at night.
B. If Devadutt is growing fat and if he does not eat during the day, he will be eating at night.
C. Devadutt eats in the night so he does not eat during the day.
D. Since Devadutt does not eat in the day, he must be eating in the night.

16. Venn diagram is a kind of diagram to

A. represent and assess the validity of elementary inferences of syllogistic form.
B. represent but not assess the validity of elementary inferences of syllogistic form.
C. represent and assess the truth of elementary inferences of syllogistic form.
D. assess but not represent the truth of elementary inferences of syllogistic form.

17. Reasoning by analogy leads to

A. certainty B. definite conclusion
C. predictive conjecture D. surety

18. Which of the following statements are false? Choose from the code given below :

1. Inductive arguments always proceed from the particular to the general.
2. A cogent argument must be inductively strong.
3. A valid argument may have a false premise and a false conclusion.
4. An argument may legitimately be spoken of as 'true' or 'false'.

Code :

A. 2, 3 and 4 B. 1 and 3
C. 2 and 4 D. 1 and 2

19. Six persons A, B, C, D, E and F are standing in a circle. B is between F and C, A is between E and D, F is to the left of D. Who is between A and F ?

A. B B. C C. D D. E

20. The price of petrol increases by 25%. By what percentage must a customer reduce the consumption so that the earlier bill on the petrol does not alter ?

A. 20% B. 25% C. 30% D. 33.33%

21. If Ram knows that y is an integer greater than 2 and less than 7 and Hari knows that y is an integer greater than 5 and less than 10, then they may correctly conclude that

A. y can be exactly determined

B. y may be either of two values

C. y may be any of three values

D. there is no value of y satisfying these conditions

22. Four pipes can fill a reservoir in 15, 20, 30 and 60 hours respectively. The first one was opened at 6 AM, second at 7 AM, third at 8 AM and the fourth at 9 AM. When will the reservoir be filled ?

A. 11 AM B. 12 Noon C. 1 PM D. 1:30 PM

The total electricity generation in a country is 97 GW. The contribution of various energy sources is indicated in percentage terms in the Pie Chart given below ;

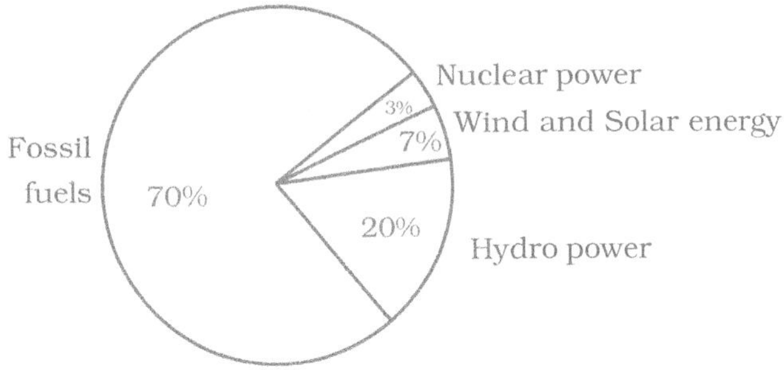

23. What is the contribution of wind and solar power in absolute terms in the electricity generation ?

A. 6.79 GW B. 19.4 GW C. 9.7 GW D. 29.1 GW

24. What is the contribution of renewable energy sources in absolute terms in the electricity generation ?

A. 29.1 GW B. 26.19 GW C. 67.9 GW D. 97 GW

25. TCP/IP is necessary if one is to connect to the

A. Phone lines B. LAN

C. Internet D. a Server

26. Each character on the keyboard of computer has an ASCII value which stands for

A. American Stock Code for Information Interchange

B. American Standard Code for Information Interchange

C. African Standard Code for Information Interchange
D. Adaptable Standard Code for Information Change

27. Which of the following is not a programming language ?

A. Pascal B. Microsoft Office
C. Java D. C++

28. Minimum number of bits required to store any 3 digit decimal number is equal to

A. 3 B. 5 C. 8 D. 10

29. Internet explorer is a type of

A. Operating System B. Compiler
C. Browser D. IP address

30. POP3 and IMAP are e-mail accounts in which

A. One automatically gets one's mail everyday
B. One has to be connected to the server to read or write one's mail
C. One only has to be connected to the server to send and receive email
D. One does not need any telephone lines

31. Irritation in eyes is caused by the pollutant

A. Sulphur di-oxide B. Ozone
C. PAN D. Nitrous oxide

32. Which is the source of chlorofluorocarbons ?

A. Thermal power plants
B. Automobiles
C. Refrigeration and Airconditioning
D. Fertilizers

33. Which of the following is not a renewable natural resource ?

A. Clean air B. Fertile soil
C. Fresh water D. Salt

34. Which of the following parameters is not used as a pollution indicator in water ?

A. Total dissolved solids B. Coliform count
C. Dissolved oxygen D. Density

35. S and P waves are associated with

A. floods B. wind energy

C. earthquakes D. tidal energy

36. Match Lists I and II and select the correct answer from the codes given below :

List – I	List – II
(i) Ozone hole	(a) Tsunami
(ii) Greenhouse effect	(b) UV radiations
(iii) Natural hazards	(c) Methane
(iv) Sustainable development	(d) Eco-centrism

Codes :

(i) (ii) (iii) (iv)

A. (b) (c) (a) (d) B. (c) (b) (a) (d)

C. (d) (c) (a) (b) D. (d) (b) (c) (a)

37. Indian Institute of Advanced Study is located at

A. Dharmshala B. Shimla

C. Solan D. Chandigarh

38. Indicate the number of Regional Offices of National Council of Teacher Education.

A. 04 B. 05 C. 06 D. 08

39. Which of the following rights was considered the "Heart and Soul" of the Indian Constitution by Dr. B.R. Ambedkar ?

A. Freedom of Speech B. Right to Equality

C. Right to Freedom of Religion D. Right to Constitutional Remedies

40. Who among the following created the office of the District Collector in India ?

A. Lord Cornwallis B. Warren Hastings

C. The Royal Commission on Decentralisation D. Sir Charles Metcalfe

41. The Fundamental Duties of a citizen include

1. Respect for the Constitution, the National Flag and the National Anthem
2. To develop the scientific temper.
3. Respect for the Government.
4. To protect Wildlife.

Choose the correct answer from the codes given below :

Codes :

A. 1, 2 and 3 B. 1, 2 and 4

C. 2, 3 and 4 D. 1, 3, 4 and 2

42. The President of India takes oath

A. to uphold the sovereignty and integrity of India.

B. to bear true faith and allegiance to the Constitution of India.

C. to uphold the Constitution and Laws of the country.

D. to preserve, protect and defend the Constitution and the law of the country.

43. If you get an opportunity to teach a visually challenged student along with normal students, what type of treatment would you like to give him in the class ?

A. Not giving extra attention because majority may suffer.

B. Take care of him sympathetically in the class- room.

C. You will think that blindness is his destiny and hence you cannot do anything.

D. Arrange a seat in the front row and try to teach at a pace convenient to him.

44. Which of the following is not a characteristic of a good achievement test?

A. Reliability B. Objectivity

C. Ambiguity D. Validity

45. Which of the following does not belong to a projected aid ?

A. Overhead projector B. Blackboard

C. Epidiascope D. Slide projector

46. For a teacher, which of the following methods would be correct for writing on the blackboard ?

A. Writing fast and as clearly as possible.

B. Writing the matter first and then asking students to read it.

C. Asking a question to students and then writing the answer as stated by them.

D. Writing the important points as clearly as possible.

47. A teacher can be successful if he/she

A. helps students in becoming better citizens

B. imparts subject knowledge to students

C. prepares students to pass the examination

D. presents the subject matter in a well organized manner

48. Dynamic approach to teaching means

A. Teaching should be forceful and effective

B. Teachers should be energetic and dynamic

C. The topics of teaching should not be static, but dynamic

D. The students should be required to learn through activities

49. The research that aims at immediate application is

A. Action Research B. Empirical Research

C. Conceptual Research D. Fundamental Research

50. When two or more successive footnotes refer to the same work which one of the following expressions is used ?

A. ibid B. et.al C. op.cit : D. loc.cit.

51. Nine year olds are taller than seven year olds. This is an example of a reference drawn from

A. Vertical study B. Cross-sectional study

C. Time series study D. Experimental study

52. Conferences are meant for

A. Multiple target groups

B. Group discussions

C. Show-casing new Research

D. All the above

53. Ex Post Facto research means

A. The research is carried out after the incident

B. The research is carried out prior to the incident

C. The research is carried out along with the happening of an incident.

D. The research is carried out keeping in mind the possibilities of an incident.

54. Research ethics do not include

A. Honesty B. Subjectivity

C. Integrity D. Objectivity

Read the following passage carefully and answer the questions 55 to 60 :

James Madison said, "A people who mean to be their own governors must arm themselves with power that knowledge gives." In India, the Official Secrets Act, 1923 was a convenient smokescreen to deny members of the public access to information. Public functioning has traditionally been shrouded in secrecy. But in a democracy in which people govern themselves, it is necessary to have more openness. In the maturing of our democracy, right to information is a major step forward; it enables citizens to participate fully in the decision-making process that affects their lives so profoundly. It is in this context that the address of the Prime Minister in the Lok Sabha is significant. He said, "I would only like to see that everyone, particularly our civil servants, should see the Bill in a positive spirit; not as a draconian law for paralyzing Government, but as an instrument for improving Government-Citizen interface resulting in a friendly, caring and effective Government functioning for the good of our People." He further said, "This is an innovative Bill, where there will be scope to review its functioning as we gain experience. Therefore, this is a piece of legislation, whose working will be kept under constant reviews."

The Commission, in its Report, has dealt with the application of the Right to Information in Executive, Legislature and Judiciary. The judiciary could be a pioneer in implementing the Act in letter and spirit because much of the work that the Judiciary does is open to public scrutiny, Government of India has sanctioned an e-governance project in the Judiciary for about 700 crores which would bring about systematic classification, standardization and categorization of records. This would help the judiciary to fulfil its mandate under the Act. Similar capacity building would be required in all other public authorities. The transformation from nontransparency to transparency and public accountability is the responsibility of all three organs of State.

55. A person gets power

A. by acquiring knowledge B. from the Official Secrets Act, 1923

C. through openings D. by denying public information

56. Right to Information is a major step forward to

A. enable citizens to participate fully in the decision making process

B. to make the people aware of the Act

C. to gain knowledge of administration

D. to make the people Government friendly

57. The Prime Minister considered the Bill

A. to provide power to the civil servants

B. as an instrument for improving Government-citizen interface resulting in a friendly, caring and effective Government

C. a draconian law against the officials

D. to check the harassment of the people

58. The Commission made the Bill effective by

A. extending power to the executive authorities

B. combining the executive and legislative power

C. recognizing Judiciary a pioneer in implementing the act in letter and spirit

D. educating the people before its implementation

59. The Prime Minister considered the Bill innovative and hoped that

A. It could be reviewed based on the experience gained on its functioning.

B. The civil servants would see the Bill in a positive spirit.

C. It would not be considered as a draconian law for paralyzing Government

D. All the above

60. The transparency and public accountability is the responsibility of three organs of the State.

These three organs are

A. Lok Sabha, Rajya Sabha and Judiciary

B. Lok Sabha, Rajya Sabha and Executive

C. Judiciary, Legislature and the Commission

D. Legislature, Executive and Judiciary

Answer keys

1.C	2.B	3.B	4.B	5.D	6.D	7.C	8.B	9.A	10.C
11.B	12.A	13.B	14.B	15.C	16.B	17.B	18.A	19.C	20.
21.A	22.C	23.A	24.C	25.C	26.B	27.B	28.D	29.C	30.C
31.C	32.C	33.D	34.D	35.C	36.A	37.B	38.A	39.D	40.B
41.B	42.D	43.D	44.C	45.B	46.D	47.A	48.A	49.A	50.A
51.B	52.D	53.A	54.B	55.A	56.A	57.B	58.C	59.A	60.C

UGC NET-JRF EXAMINATION DECEMBER 2012
SOLVED QUESTION PAPER
PAPER - I

Note :
- This paper contains **Sixty (60)** multiple choice questions, each question carrying **two (2)** marks.
- Candidate is expected to answer any **Fifty (50)** questions.
- In case more than **Fifty (50)** questions are attempted, only the first **Fifty (50)** questions will be evaluated.

1. **The English word 'Communication' is derived from the words**
   A. Communis and Communicare
   B. Communist and Commune
   C. Communism and Communalism
   D. Communion and Common sense

2. **Chinese Cultural Revolution leader Mao Zedong used a type of communication to talk to the masses is known as**
   A. Mass line communication
   B. Group communication
   C. Participatory communication
   D. Dialogue communication

3. **Conversing with the spirits and ancestors is termed as**
   A. Transpersonal communication
   B. Intrapersonal communication
   C. Interpersonal communication
   D. Face-to-face communication

4. **The largest circulated daily newspaper among the following is**
   A. The Times of India
   B. The Indian Express
   C. The Hindu
   D. The Deccan Herald

5. **The pioneer of the silent feature film in India was**
   A. K.A. Abbas
   B. Satyajit Ray
   C. B.R. Chopra
   D. Dada Sahib Phalke

6. **Classroom communication of a teacher rests on the principle of**
   A. Infotainment
   B. Edutainment
   C. Entertainment
   D. Power equation

7. The missing number in the series : 0, 6, 24, 60, 120, ?, 336, is

A. 240 B. 220 C. 280 D. 210

8. A group of 7 members having a majority of boys is to be formed out of 6 boys and 4 girls. The number of ways the group can be formed is

A. 80 B. 100 C. 90 D. 110

9. The number of observations in a group is 40. The average of the first 10 members is 4.5 and the average of the remaining 30 members is 3.5. The average of the whole group is

A. 4 B. 15/2 C. 15/4 D. 6

10. If MOHAN is represented by the code KMFYL, then COUNT will be represented by

A. AMSLR B. MSLAR C. MASRL D. SAMLR

11. The sum of the ages of two persons A and B is 50. 5 years ago, the ratio of their ages was 5/3. The present age of A and B are

A. 30, 20 B. 35, 15 C. 38. 12 D. 40, 10

12. Let a means minus (–), b means multiplied by („e), C means divided by („i) and D means plus (+). The value of 90 D 9 a 29 C 10 b 2 is

A. 8 B. 10 C. 12 D. 14

13. Consider the Assertion–I and Assertion–II and select the right code given below:

Assertion–I : Even Bank-lockers are not safe. Thieves can break them and take away your wealth. But thieves can not go to heaven. So you should keep your wealth in heaven.

Assertion–II : The difference of skincolour of beings is because of the distance from the sun and not because of some permanent traits. Skin-colour is the result of body's reaction to the sun and its rays.

Codes :

A. Both the assertions-I and II are forms of argument.

B. The assertion-I is an argument but the assertion-II is not.

C. The assertion-II is an argument but the assertion-I is not.

D. Both the assertions are explanations of facts.

14. By which of the following proposition, the proposition 'some men are not honest' is contradicted ?

A. All men are honest. B. Some men are honest.

C. No men are honest. D. All of the above.

15. A stipulative definition is

A. always true
B. always false
C. sometimes true sometimes false
D. neither true nor false

16. Choose the appropriate alternative given in the codes to replace the question mark.

Examiner – Examinee, Pleader – Client,

Preceptor – ?

A. Customer
B. Path-finder
C. Perceiver
D. Disciple

17. If the statement 'most of the students are obedient' is taken to be true, which one of the following pair of statements can be claimed to be true?

I. All obedient persons are students.

II. All students are obedient.

III. Some students are obedient.

IV. Some students are not disobedient.

Codes :

A. I & II
B. II & III
C. III & IV
D. II & IV

18. Choose the right code : A deductive argument claims that :

I. The conclusion does not claim something more than that which is contained in the premises.

II. The conclusion is supported by the premise/premises conclusively.

III. If the conclusion is false, then premise/premises may be either true or false.

IV. If premise/combination of premises is true, then conclusion must be true.

Codes :

A. I and II
B. I and III
C. II and III
D. All the above

On the basis of the data given in the following table, give answers to questions from 19 to 24 :

Government Expenditures on Social Services
(As percent of total expenditure)

Sl. No.	Items	2007-08	2008-09	2009-10	2010-11
	Social Services	11.06	12.94	13.06	14.02
(a)	Education, sports & youth affairs	4.02	4.04	3.96	4.46

(b)	Health & family welfare	2.05	1.91	1.90	2.03
(c)	Water supply, housing, etc.	2.02	2.31	2.20	2.27
(d)	Information & broadcasting	0.22	0.22	0.20	0.22
(e)	Welfare to SC/ST & OBC	0.36	0.35	0.41	0.63
(f)	Labour and employment	0.27	0.27	0.22	0.25
(g)	Social welfare & nutrition	0.82	0.72	0.79	1.06
(h)	North-eastern areas	0.00	1.56	1.50	1.75
(i)	Other social services	1.29	1.55	1.87	1.34
	Total Government expenditure	100.00	100.00	100.00	100.00

19. How many activities in the social services are there where the expenditure has been less than 5 percent of the total expenditures incurred on the social services in 2008-09 ?

A. One B. Three

C. Five D. All the above

20. In which year, the expenditures on the social services have increased at the highest rate ?

A. 2007-08 B. 2008-09 C. 2009-10 D. 2010-11

21. Which of the following activities remains almost stagnant in terms of share of expenditures ?

A. North-eastern areas B. Welfare to SC/ST & OBC

C. Information & broadcasting D. Social welfare and nutrition

22. Which of the following item's expenditure share is almost equal to the remaining three items in the given years ?

A. Information & broadcasting B. Welfare to SC/ST and OBC

C. Labour and employment D. Social welfare & nutrition

23. Which of the following items of social services has registered the highest rate of increase in expenditures during 2007-08 to 2010-11 ?

A. Education, sports & youth affairs B. Welfare to SC/ST & OBC

C. Social welfare & nutrition D. Overall social services

24. Which of the following items has registered the highest rate of decline in terms of expenditure during 2007-08 to 2009-10 ?

A. Labour and employment
B. Health & family welfare
C. Social welfare & nutrition
D. Education, sports & youth affairs

25. ALU stands for

A. American Logic Unit
B. Alternate Local Unit
C. Alternating Logic Unit
D. Arithmetic Logic Unit

26. A Personal Computer uses a number of chips mounted on a circuit board called

A. Microprocessor
B. System Board
C. Daughter Board
D. Mother Board

27. Computer Virus is a

A. Hardware
B. Bacteria
C. Software
D. None of these

28. Which one of the following is correct?

A. (17)10 = (17)16
B. (17)10 = (17)8
C. (17)10 = (10111)2
D. (17)10 = (10001)2

29. The file extension of MS-Word document in Office 2007 is ______.

A. pdf
B. doc
C. docx
D. txt

30. ______ is a protocol used by e-mail clients to download e-mails to your computer.

A. TCP
B. FTP
C. SMTP
D. POP

31. Which of the following is a source of methane ?

A. Wetlands
B. Foam Industry
C. Thermal Power Plants
D. Cement Industry

32. 'Minamata disaster' in Japan was caused by pollution due to

A. Lead
B. Mercury
C. Cadmium
D. Zinc

33. Biomagnification means increase in the

A. concentration of pollutants in living organisms

B. number of species

C. size of living organisms

D. biomass

34. Nagoya Protocol is related to

A. Climate change B. Ozone depletion

C. Hazardous waste D. Biodiversity

35. The second most important source after fossil fuels contributing to India's energy needs is

A. Solar energy B. Nuclear energy

C. Hydropower D. Wind energy

36. In case of earthquakes, an increase of magnitude 1 on Richter Scale implies

A. a ten-fold increase in the amplitude of seismic waves.

B. a ten-fold increase in the energy of the seismic waves.

C. two-fold increase in the amplitude of seismic waves.

D. two-fold increase in the energy of seismic waves.

37. Which of the following is not a measure of Human Development Index ?

A. Literacy Rate B. Gross Enrolment

C. Sex Ratio D. Life Expectancy

38. India has the highest number of students in colleges after

A. the U.K. B. the U.S.A.

C. Australia D. Canada

39. Which of the following statement(s) is/are not correct about the Attorney General of India ?

1. The President appoints a person, who is qualified to be a Judge of a High Court, to be the Attorney General of India.
2. He has the right of audience in all the Courts of the country.
3. He has the right to take part in the proceedings of the Lok Sabha and the Rajya Sabha.
4. He has a fixed tenure. Select the correct answer from the codes given below:

Codes :

A. 1 and 4 B. 2, 3 and 4

C. 3 and 4 D. 3 only

40. Which of the following prefix President Pranab Mukherjee desires to be discontinued while interacting with Indian dignitaries as well as in official nothings ?

1. His Excellency
2. Mahamahim
3. Hon'ble
4. Shri/Smt.

Select the correct answer from the codes given below :

Codes :

A. 1 and 3 B. 2 and 3

C. 1 and 2 D. 1, 2 and 3

41. Which of the following can be done under conditions of financial emergency ?

1. State Legislative Assemblies can be abolished.
2. Central Government can acquire control over the budget and expenditure of States.
3. Salaries of the Judges of the High Courts and the Supreme Court can be reduced.
4. Right to Constitutional Remedies can be suspended. Select the correct answer from the codes given below :

Codes :

A. 1, 2 and 3 B. 2, 3 and 4

C. 1 and 2 D. 2 and 3

42. Match List – I with List – II and select the correct answer from the codes given below :

List – I	List – II
(a) Poverty Reduction Programme	(i) Mid-day Meals
(b) Human Development Scheme	(ii) Indira Awas Yojana (IAY)
(c) Social Assistance Scheme	(iii) National Old Age Pension (NOAP)
(d) Minimum Need Scheme	(iv) MNREGA

Codes : (a) (b) (c) (d)

A. (iv) (i) (iii) (ii) B. (ii) (iii) (iv) (i)

C. (iii) (iv) (i) (ii) D. (iv) (iii) (ii) (i)

43. For an efficient and durable learning, learner should have

A. ability to learn only
B. requisite level of motivation only
C. opportunities to learn only
D. desired level of ability and motivation

44. Classroom communication must be

A. Teacher centric
B. Student centric
C. General centric
D. Textbook centric

45. The best method of teaching is to

A. impart information
B. ask students to read books
C. suggest good reference material
D. initiate a discussion and participate in it

46. Interaction inside the classroom should generate

A. Argument
B. Information
C. Ideas
D. Controversy

47. "Spare the rod and spoil the child", gives the message that

A. punishment in the class should be banned.
B. corporal punishment is not acceptable.
C. undesirable behaviour must be punished.
D. children should be beaten with rods.

48. The type of communication that the teacher has in the classroom, is termed as

A. Interpersonal
B. Mass communication
C. Group communication
D. Face-to-face communication

49. Which one of the following is an indication of the quality of a research journal ?

A. Impact factor
B. h-index
C. g-index
D. i10-index

50. Good 'research ethics' means

A. Not disclosing the holdings of shares/stocks in a company that sponsors your research.
B. Assigning a particular research problem to one Ph.D./research student only.
C. Discussing with your colleagues confidential data from a research paper that you are reviewing for an academic journal.
D. Submitting the same research manuscript for publishing in more than one journal.

51. Which of the following sampling methods is based on probability?

A. Convenience sampling B. Quota sampling
C. Judgement sampling D. Stratified sampling

52. Which one of the following references is written according to American Psychological Association (APA) format?

A. Sharma, V. (2010). Fundamentals of Computer Science. New Delhi: Tata McGraw Hill

B. Sharma, V. 2010. Fundamentals of Computer Science. New Delhi: Tata McGraw Hill

C. Sharma.V. 2010. Fundamentals of Computer Science, New Delhi: Tata McGraw Hill

D. Sharma, V. (2010), Fundamentals of Computer Science, New Delhi: Tata McGraw Hill

53. Arrange the following steps of research in correct sequence :

1. Identification of research problem
2. Listing of research objectives
3. Collection of data
4. Methodology
5. Data analysis
6. Results and discussion

A. 1 – 2 – 3 – 4 – 5 – 6 B. 1 – 2 – 4 – 3 – 5 – 6
C. 2 – 1 – 3 – 4 – 5 – 6 D. 2 – 1 – 4 – 3 – 5 – 6

54. Identify the incorrect statement:

A. A hypothesis is made on the basis of limited evidence as a starting point for further investigations.

B. A hypothesis is a basis for reasoning without any assumption of its truth.

C. Hypothesis is a proposed explanation for a phenomenon.

D. Scientific hypothesis is a scientific theory.

Read the following passage carefully and answer the questions (55 to 60) :

The popular view of towns and cities in developing countries and of urbanization process is that despite the benefits and comforts it brings, the emergence of such cities connotes environmental degradation, generation of slums and squatters, urban poverty, unemployment, crimes, lawlessness, traffic chaos etc. But what is the reality ? Given the unprecedental increase in urban population over the last 50 years from 300 million in 1950 to 2 billion in 2000 in developing countries, the wonder really is how well the world has coped, and not how badly. In general, the urban quality of life has improved in terms of availability of water and sanitation, power, health and education, communication and transport. By way of illustration, a large number of urban residents have been provided with improved water in urban areas in Asia's largest countries such as China, India, Indonesia and Philippines. Despite that, the access to improved water in terms of percentage of total urban population seems to have declined during the last decade of 20th century, though in absolute numbers, millions of additional urbanites, have been provided improved services. These countries have made significant progress in the provision of sanitation services too, together, providing for an additional population of more than 293 million citizens within a decade (1990-2000). These improvements must be viewed against the backdrop of rapidly increasing urban population, fiscal crunch and strained human resources and efficient and quality-oriented public management.

55. The popular view about the process of urbanization in developing countries is

A. Positive B. Negative

C. Neutral D. Unspecified

56. The average annual increase in the number of urbanites in developing countries, from 1950 to 2000 A.D. was close to

A. 30 million B. 40 million

C. 50 million D. 60 million

57. The reality of urbanization is reflected in

A. How well the situation has been managed.

B. How badly the situation has gone out of control.

C. How fast has been the tempo of urbanization.

D. How fast the environment has degraded.

58. Which one of the following is not considered as an indicator of urban quality of life ?

A. Tempo of urbanization B. Provision of basic services

C. Access to social amenities D. All the above

59. The author in this passage has tried to focus on

A. Extension of Knowledge

B. Generation of Environmental Consciousness

C. Analytical Reasoning

D. Descriptive Statement

60. In the above passage, the author intends to state

A. The hazards of the urban life
B. The sufferings of the urban life
C. The awareness of human progress
D. The limits to growth

Answer keys

1.A	2.A	3.A	4.A	5.D	6.B	7.D	8.B	9.A	10.A
11.A	12.D	13.A	14.A	15.A	16.C	17.C	18.A	19.C	20.D
21.C	22.D	23.D	24.D	25.D	26.D	27.C	28.D	29.C	30.C
31.A	32.B	33.A	34.D	35.C	36.A	37.C	38.B	39.A	40.C
41.C	42.A	43.D	44.B	45.D	46.C	47.C	48.A	49.A	50.A
51.D	52.A	53.B	54.B	55.B	56.D	57.A	58.A	59.B	60.A

UGC NET-JRF EXAMINATION JUNE 2013

SOLVED QUESTION PAPER

PAPER - I

Note :
- This paper contains **Sixty (60)** multiple choice questions, each question carrying **two (2)** marks.
- Candidate is expected to answer any **Fifty (50)** questions.
- In case more than **Fifty (50)** questions are attempted, only the first **Fifty (50)** questions will be evaluated.

1. The percentage share of renewable energy sources in the power production in India is around

A. 2–3% B. 22–25% C. 10–12% D. <1%

2. In which of the following categories the enrolment of students in higher education in 2010-11 was beyond the percentage of seats reserved ?

A. OBC students

B. SC students

C. ST students

D. Woman students

3. Which one of the following statements is not correct about the University Grants Commission (UGC) ?

A. It was established in 1956 by an Act of Parliament.

B. It is tasked with promoting and coordinating higher education.

C. It receives Plan and Non-Plan funds from the Central Government.

D. It receives funds from State Governments in respect of State Universities.

4. Consider the statement which is followed by two arguments (I) and (II):

Statement : Should India switch over to a two party system ?

Arguments: (I) Yes, it will lead to stability of Government.

(II) No, it will limit the choice of voters.

A. Only argument (I) is strong.

B. Only argument (II) is strong.

C. Both the arguments are strong.

D. Neither of the arguments is strong.

5. Consider the statement which is followed by two arguments (I) and (II) :

Statement: Should persons with criminal background be banned from contesting elections ?

Arguments: (I) Yes, it will decriminalise politics.

(II) No, it will encourage the ruling party to file frivolous cases against their political opponents.

A. Only argument (I) is strong.

B. Only argument (II) is strong.

C. Both the arguments are strong.

D. Neither of the arguments is strong.

6. Which of the following statement(s) is/are correct about a Judge of the Supreme Court of India ?

1. A Judge of the Supreme Court is appointed by the President of India.
2. He holds office during the pleasure of the President.
3. He can be suspended, pending an inquiry.
4. He can be removed for proven misbehaviour or incapacity.

Select the correct answer from the codes given below :

Codes :

A. 1, 2 and 3 B. 1, 3 and 4

C. 1 and 3 D. 1 and 4

7. In the warrant of precedence, the Speaker of the Lok Sabha comes next only to

A. The President B. The Vice-President

C. The Prime Minister D. The Cabinet Ministers

8. The black-board can be utilised best by a teacher for

A. putting the matter of teaching in black and white

B. making the students attentive

C. writing the important and notable points

D. highlighting the teacher himself

9. Nowadays the most effective mode of learning is

A. self study B. face-to-face learning

C. e-learning D. blended learning

10. At the primary school stage, most of the teachers should be women because they

A. can teach children better than men.
B. know basic content better than men.
C. are available on lower salaries.
D. can deal with children with love and affection.

11. Which one is the highest order of learning ?
A. Chain learning
B. Problem-solving learning
C. Stimulus-response learning
D. Conditioned-reflex learning

12. A person can enjoy teaching as a profession when he
A. has control over students.
B. commands respect from students.
C. is more qualified than his colleagues.
D. is very close to higher authorities.

13. "A diagram speaks more than 1000 words." The statement means that the teacher should
A. use diagrams in teaching.
B. speak more and more in the class.
C. use teaching aids in the class.
D. not speak too much in the class.

14. A research paper
A. is a compilation of information on a topic.
B. contains original research as deemed by the author.
C. contains peer-reviewed original research or evaluation of research conducted by others.
D. can be published in more than one journal.

15. Which one of the following belongs to the category of good 'research ethics' ?
A. Publishing the same paper in two research journals without telling the editors.
B. Conducting a review of the literature that acknowledges the contributions of other people in the relevant field or relevant prior work.
C. Trimming outliers from a data set without discussing your reasons in a research paper.
D. Including a colleague as an author on a research paper in return for a favour even though the colleague did not make a serious contribution to the paper.

16. Which of the following sampling methods is not based on probability?

A. Simple Random Sampling

B. Stratified Sampling

C. Quota Sampling

D. Cluster Sampling

17. Which one of the following references is written as per Modern Language Association (MLA) format ?

A. Hall, Donald. Fundamentals of Electronics,
New Delhi : Prentice Hall of India, 2005

B. Hall, Donald, Fundamentals of Electronics,
New Delhi : Prentice Hall of India, 2005

C. Hall, Donald, Fundamentals of Electronics,
New Delhi - Prentice Hall of India, 2005

D. Hall, Donald. Fundamentals of Electronics.
New Delhi : Prentice Hall of India, 2005

18. A workshop is

A. a conference for discussion on a topic.

B. a meeting for discussion on a topic.

C. a class at a college or a university in which a teacher and the students discuss a topic.

D. a brief intensive course for a small group emphasizing the development of a skill or technique for solving a specific problem.

19. A working hypothesis is

A. a proven hypothesis for an argument.

B. not required to be tested.

C. a provisionally accepted hypothesis for further research.

D. a scientific theory.

Read the following passage carefully and answer the questions (20 to 25) :

The Taj Mahal has become one of the world's best known monuments. This domed white marble structure is situated on a high plinth at the southern end of a four-quartered garden, evoking the gardens of paradise, enclosed within walls measuring 305 by 549 metres. Outside the walls, in an area known as Mumtazabad, were living quarters for attendants, markets, serais and other structures built by local merchants and nobles. The tomb complex and the other imperial structures of Mumtazabad were maintained by the income of thirty villages given specifically for the tomb's support. The name Taj Mahal is unknown in Mughal chronicles, but it is used by contemporary Europeans in India, suggesting that this was the tomb's popular name. In contemporary texts. It is generally called simply the Illuminated Tomb (Rauza-i-Munavvara).

Mumtaz Mahal died shortly after delivering her fourteenth child in 1631. The Mughal court was then residing in Burhanpur. Her remains were temporarily buried by the grief-stricken emperor in a spacious garden known as Zainabad on the bank of the river Tapti. Six months later her body was transported to Agra, where it was interred in land chosen for the mausoleum. This land, situated south of the Mughal city on the bank of the Jamuna, had belonged to the Kachhwaha rajas since the time of Raja Man Singh and was purchased from the then current raja, Jai Singh. Although contemporary chronicles indicate Jai Singh's willing cooperation in this exchange, extant *farmans* (imperial commands) indicate that the final price was not settled until almost two years-after the mausoleum's commencement. Jai Singh's further cooperation was insured by imperial orders issued between 1632 and 1637 demanding that he provide stone masons and carts to transport marble from the mines at Makrana, within his "ancestral domain", to Agra where both the Taj Mahal and Shah Jahan's additions to the Agra fort were constructed concurrently.

Work on the mausoleum was commenced early in 1632. Inscriptional evidence indicates much of the tomb was completed by 1636. By 1643, when Shah Jahan most lavishly celebrated the 'Urs ceremony for Mumtaz Mahal', the entire complex was virtually complete.

20. Marble stone used for the construction of the Taj Mahal was brought from the ancestral domain of Raja Jai Singh. The name of the place where mines of marble is

A. Burhanpur B. Makrana

C. Amber D. Jaipur

21. The popular name Taj Mahal was given by

A. Shah Jahan B. Tourists

C. Public D. European travellers

22. Point out the true statement from the following :

A. Marble was not used for the construction of the Taj Mahal.

B. Red sand stone is non-visible in the Taj Mahal complex.

C. The Taj Mahal is surrounded by a four-quartered garden known as Chahr Bagh.

D. The Taj Mahal was constructed to celebrate the 'Urs ceremony for Mumtaz Mahal'.

23. In the contemporary texts the Taj Mahal is known

A. Mumtazabad B. Mumtaz Mahal
C. Zainabad D. Rauza-i-Munavvara

24. The construction of the Taj Mahal was completed between the period

A. 1632- 1636 A.D B. 1630-1643 A.D.
C. 1632-1643 A.D. D. 1636-1643 A.D.

25. The documents indicating the ownership of land, where the Taj Mahal was built, known as

A. Farman B. Sale Deed
C. Sale-Purchase Deed D. None of the above

26. In the process of communication, which one of the following is in the chronological order ?

A. Communicator, Medium, Receiver, Effect, Message
B. Medium, Communicator, Message, Receiver, Effect
C. Communicator, Message, Medium, Receiver, Effect
D. Message, Communicator, Medium, Receiver, Effect

27. Bengal Gazette, the first Newspaper in India was started in 1780 by

A. Dr. Annie Besant B. James Augustus Hicky
C. Lord Cripson D. A.O. Hume

28. Press censorship in India was imposed during the tenure of the Prime Minister

A. Rajeev Gandhi B. Narasimha Rao
C. Indira Gandhi D. Deve Gowda

29. Communication via New media such as computers, teleshopping, internet and mobile telephony is termed as

A. Entertainment
B. Interactive communication
C. Developmental communication
D. Communitarian

30. Classroom communication of a teacher rests on the principle of

A. Infotainment B. Edutainment
C. Entertainment D. Enlightenment

31. _____ is important when a teacher communicates with his/her student.

A. Sympathy B. Empathy
C. Apathy D. Antipathy

32. In a certain code GALIB is represented by HBMJC. TIGER will be represented by

A. UJHFS B. UHJSF C. JHUSF D. HUJSF

33. In a certain cricket tournament 45 matches were played. Each team played once against each of the other teams. The number of teams participated in the tournament is

A. 8 B. 10 C. 12 D. 14

34. The missing number in the series 40, 120, 60, 180, 90, ?, 135 is

A. 110 B. 270 C. 105 D. 210

35. The odd numbers from 1 to 45 which are exactly divisible by 3 are arranged in an ascending order. The number at 6th position is

A. 18 B. 24 C. 33 D. 36

36. The mean of four numbers a, b, c, d is 100. If c = 70, then the mean of the remaining numbers is

A. 30 B. $\frac{85}{2}$ C. $\frac{170}{3}$ D. 110

37. If the radius of a circle is increased by 50%, the perimeter of the circle will increase by

A. 20% B. 30% C. 40% D. 50%

38. If the statement 'some men are honest' is false, which among the following statements will be true. Choose the correct code given below :

(i) All men are honest.

(ii) No men are honest.

(iii) Some men are not honest

(iv) All men are dishonest.

Codes :

A. (i), (ii) and (iii) B. (ii), (iii) and (iv)
C. (i), (iii) and (iv) D. (ii), (i) and (iv)

39. Choose the proper alternative given in the codes to replace the question mark.

Bee - Honey, Cow - Milk, Teacher - ?

A. Intelligence B.Marks C. Lessons D. Wisdom

40. P is the father of R and S is the son of Q and T is the brother of P. If R is the sister of S, how is Q related to T ?

A. Wife B. Sister-in-law

C. Brother-in-law D. Daughter-in-law

41. A definition put forward to resolve a dispute by influencing attitudes or stirring emotions is called

A. Lexical B. Persuasive C. Stipulative D. Precisions

42. Which of the codes given below contains only the correct statements?

Statements :

(i) Venn diagram is a clear method of notation.

(ii) Venn diagram is the most direct method of testing the validity of categorical syllogisms.

(iii) In Venn diagram method the premises and the conclusion of a categorical syllogism is diagrammed.

(iv) In Venn diagram method the three overlapping circles are drawn for testing a categorical syllogism.

Codes :

A. (i), (ii) & (iii) B. (i), (ii) & (iv) C. (ii), (iii) & (iv) D. (i), (iii) & (iv)

43. Inductive reasoning presupposes

A. unity in human nature B. integrity in human nature

C. uniformity in human nature D. harmony in human nature

Read the table below and based on this table answer questions from 44 to 49 : Area under Major Horticulture Crops

(in lakh hectares)

Year	Fruits	Vegetables	Flowers	Total Horticulture Area
2005-06	53	72	1	187
2006-07	56	75	1	194
2007-08	58	78	2	202
2008-09	61	79	2	207
2009-10	63	79	2	209

44. Which of the following two years have recorded the highest rate of increase in area under the total horticulture ?

A. 2005-06 & 2006-07 B. 2006-07 & 2008-09

C. 2007-08 & 2008-09 D. 2006-07 & 2007-08

45. Shares of the area under flowers, vegetables and fruits in the area under total horticulture are respectively :

A. 1, 38 and 30 percent B. 30, 38 and 1 percent

C. 38, 30 and 1 percent D. 35, 36 and 2 percent

46. Which of the following has recorded the highest rate of increase in area during 2005-06 to 2009-10 ?

A. Fruits B. Vegetables

C. Flowers D. Total horticulture

47. Find out the horticultural crop that has recorded an increase of area by around 10 percent from 2005-06 to 2009-10

A. Fruits B. Vegetables

C. Flowers D. Total horticulture

48. What has been the share of area under fruits, vegetables and flowers in the area under total horticulture in 2007- 08 ?

A. 53 percent B. 68 percent

C. 79 percent D. 100 percent

49. In which year, area under fruits has recorded the highest rate of increase?

A. 2006-07 B. 2007-08 C. 2008-09 D. 2009-10

50. 'www' stands for

A. work with web B. word wide web

C. world wide web D. worth while web

51. A hard disk is divided into tracks which is further subdivided into

A. Clusters B. Sectors C. Vectors D. Heads

52. A computer program that translates a program statement by statement into machine language is called a/an

A. Compiler B. Simulator C. Translator D. Interpreter

53. A Gigabyte is equal to

A. 1024 Megabytes B. 1024 Kilobytes

C. 1024 Terabytes D. 1024 Bytes

54. A Compiler is a software which converts

A. characters to bits

B. high level language to machine language

C. machine language to high level language

D. words to bits

55. Virtual memory is

A. an extremely large main memory.

B. an extremely large secondary memory.

C. an illusion of extremely large main memory.

D. a type of memory used in super computers.

56. The phrase 'tragedy of commons' is in the context of

A. tragic event related to damage caused by release of poisonous gases.

B. tragic conditions of poor people.

C. degradation of renewable free access resources.

D. climate change.

57. Kyoto Protocol is related to

A. Ozone depletion B. Hazardous waste

C. Climate change D. Nuclear energy

58. Which of the following is a source of emissions leading to the eventual formation of surface ozone as a pollutant ?

A. Transport sector

B. Refrigeration and Airconditioning

C. Wetlands

D. Fertilizers

59. The smog in cities in India mainly consists of

A. Oxides of sulphur

B. Oxides of nitrogen and unburnt hydrocarbons

C. Carbon monoxide and SPM

D. Oxides of sulphur and ozone

60. Which of the following types of natural hazards have the highest potential to cause damage to humans ?

A. Earthquakes B. Forest fires

C. Volcanic eruptions D. Droughts and Floods

Answer keys

1.	2.	3.D	4.	5.A	6.	7.	8.C	9.D	10.D
11.B	12.B	13.C	14.C	15.B	16.	17.	18.D	19.C	20.B
21.D	22.C	23.D	24.D	25.A	26.C	27.	28.C	29.B	30.B
31.B	32.A	33.B	34.B	35.C	36.D	37.	38.	39.D	40.B
41.B	42.	43.C	44.D	45.A	46.	47.A	48.B	49.C	50.C
51.B	52.D	53.A	54.B	55.C	56.C	57.C	58.A	59.B	60.D

UGC NET-JRF EXAMINATION DECEMBER 2013

SOLVED QUESTION PAPER

PAPER - I

Note :
- This paper contains **Sixty (60)** multiple choice questions, each question carrying **two (2)** marks.
- Candidate is expected to answer any **Fifty (50)** questions.
- In case more than **Fifty (50)** questions are attempted, only the first **Fifty (50)** questions will be evaluated.

1. The post-industrial society is designated as

A. Information Society B. Technology society
C. Mediated society D. Non-agricultural society

2. The initial efforts for internet based communication was for

A. Commercial communication
B. Military purposes
C. Personal interaction
D. Political campaigns

3. Internal communication within institutions is done through

A. LAN B. WAN C. EBB D. MMS

4. Virtual reality provides

A. Sharp pictures B. Individual audio
C. Participatory experience D. Preview of new films

5. The first virtual university of India came up in

A. Andhra Pradesh B. Maharashtra
C. Uttar Pradesh D. Tamil Nadu

6. Arrange the following books in chronological order in which they appeared. Use the code given below:

(i) Limits of Growth
(ii) Silent Spring
(iii) Our Common Future
(iv) Resourceful Earth

A. (i), (iii), (iv), (ii) B. (ii), (iii), (i), (iv)

C. (ii), (i), (iii), (iv) D. (i), (ii), (iii), (iv)

7. Which one of the following continents is at a greater risk of desertification?

A. Africa B. Asia

C. South America D. North America

8. "Women are closer to nature than men." What kind of perspective is this?

A. Realist B. Essentialist

C. Feminist D. Deep ecology

9. Which one of the following is not a matter of global concern in the removal of tropical forests?

A. Their ability to absorb the chemicals that contribute to depletion of ozone layer.

B. Their role in maintaining the oxygen and carbon balance of the earth.

C. Their ability to regulate surface and air temperatures, moisture content and reflectivity.

D. Their contribution to the biological diversity of the planet.

10. The most comprehensive approach to address the problems of man-environment interaction is one of the following:

A. Natural Resource Conservation Approach

B. Urban-industrial Growth Oriented Approach

C. Rural-agricultural Growth Oriented Approach

D. Watershed Development Approach

11. The major source of the pollutant gas, carbon mono-oxide (CO), in urban areas is

A. Thermal power sector B. Transport sector

C. Industrial sector D. Domestic sector

12. In a fuel cell driven vehicle, the energy is obtained from the combustion of

A. Methane B. Hydrogen C. LPG D. CNG

13. Which one of the following Councils has been disbanded in 2013?

A. Distance Education Council (DEC)

B. National Council for Teacher Education (NCTE)

C. National Council of Educational Research and Training (NCERT)

D. National Assessment and Accreditation Council (NAAC)

14. Which of the following statements are correct about the National Assessment and Accreditation Council?

1. It is an autonomous institution.
2. It is tasked with the responsibility of assessing and accrediting institutions of higher education.
3. It is located in Delhi
4. It has regional offices.

Select the correct answer from the codes given below:

A. 1 and 3 B. 1 and 2 C. 1, 2 and 4 D. 2, 3 and 4

15. The power of the Supreme Court of India to decide disputes between two or more States falls under its

A. Advisory Jurisdiction B. Appellate Jurisdiction

C. Original Jurisdiction D. Writ Jurisdiction

16. Which of the following statements are correct?

1. There are seven Union Territories in India.
2. Two Union Territories have Legislative Assemblies.
3. One Union Territory has a High Court.
4. One Union Territory is the capital of two States.

Select the correct answer from the codes given below:

A. 1 and 3 only B. 2 and 4 only

C. 2, 3 and 4 only D. 1, 2, 3 and 4

17. Which of the following statements are correct about the Central Information Commission?

1. The Central Information Commission is a statutory body.
2. The Chief Information Commissioner and other Information Commissioners are appointed by the President of India.
3. The Commission can impose a penalty upto a maximum of Rs.25,000/-.
4. It can punish an errant officer.

Select the correct answer from the codes given below:

A. 1 and 2 only B. 1, 2 and 4

C. 1, 2 and 3 D. 2, 3 and 4

18. Who among the following conducted the CNN-IBN - The Hindu 2013 Election Tracker Survey across 267 constituencies in 18 States?

A. The Centre for the Study of Developing Societies (CSDS)

B. The Association for Democratic Reforms (ADR)

C. CNN and IBN

D. CNN, IBN and The Hindu

19. In certain code TEACHER is written as VGCEJGT. The code of CHILDREN will be

A. EKNJFTGP B. EJKNFTGP

C. KNJFGTP D. None of these

20. A person has to buy both apples and mangoes. The cost of one apple is ₹ 7/- whereas that of a mango is ₹ 5/-. If the person has ₹ 38, the number of apples he can buy is

A. 1 B. 2 C. 3 D. 4

21. A man pointing to a lady said, "The son of her only brother is the brother of my wife". The lady is related to the man as

A. Mother's sister B. Grand mother

C. Mother-in-law D. Sister of Father-in-law

22. In this series 6,4,1,2,2,8,7,4,2,1,5,3,8,6,2,2,7,1,4,1,3,5,8,6, how many pairs of successive numbers have a difference of 2 each?

A. 4 B. 5 C. 6 D. 8

23. The mean marks obtained by a class of 40 students is 65. The mean marks of half of the students is found to be 45. The mean marks of the remaining students is

A. 85 B. 60 C. 70 D. 65

24. Anil is twice as old as Sunita. Three years ago, he was three times as old as Sunita. The present age of Anil is

A. 6 years B. 8 years C. 12 years D. 16 years

25. Which of the following is a social network?

A. amazon.com B. eBay

C. gmail.com D. Twitter

26. The population information is called parameter while the corresponding sample information is known as

A. Universe B. Inference

C. Sampling design D. Statistics

Read the following passage carefully and answer questions 27 to 32:

Heritage conservation practices improved worldwide after the International Centre for the Study of the Preservation and Restoration of Cultural Property (ICCROM) was established with UNESCO's assistance in 1959. The inter-governmental organization with 126 member states has done a commendable job by training more than 4,000 professionals, providing practice standards, and sharing technical expertise. In this golden jubilee year, as we acknowledge its key role in global conservation, an assessment of international practices would be meaningful to the Indian conservation movement. Consistent investment, rigorous attention, and dedicated research and dissemination are some of the positive lessons to imbibe. Countries such as Italy have demonstrated that prioritising heritage with significant budget provision pays. On the other hand, India, which is no less endowed in terms of cultural capital, has a long way to go. Surveys indicate that in addition to the 6,600 protected monuments, there are over 60,000 equally valuable heritage structures that await attention. Besides the small group in the service of archeological Survey of India, there are only about 150 trained conservation professionals. Inorder to overcome the severe shortage the emphasis has been on setting up dedicated labs and training institutions. It could make much better sense for conservation to be made part of main stream research and engineering institutes, as has been done in Europe.

Increasing funding and building institutions are the relatively easy part. The real challenge is to redefine international approaches to address local contexts. Conservation cannot limit itself to enhancing the art-historical value of the heritage structures, which international charters perhaps over emphasise. The effort has to be broad based: it must also serve as a means to improving the quality of life in the area where the heritage structures are located. The first task therefore is to integrate conservation efforts with second development plans that take care of people living in the heritage vicinity. Unlike in western countries, many traditional building crafts survive in India, and conservation practices offer an avenue to support them. This has been acknowledged by the Indian National Trust for Art and Cultural Heritage charter for conservation but is yet to receive substantial state support. More strength for heritage conservation can be mobilized by aligning it with the green building movement. Heritage structures are essentially eco-friendly and conservation could become a vital part of the sustainable building practices campaign in future.

27. The outlook for conservation heritage changed

A. after the establishment of the International Centre for the Study of the Preservation and Restoration of Cultural Property.

B. after training the specialists in the filed

C. after extending UNESCO's assistance to the educational institutions

D. after ASI's measures to protect the monuments

28. The inter-government organization was appreciated because of

A. increasing number of the members to 126

B. imparting training to professionals and sharing technical expertise

C. consistent investment in conservation

D. its proactive role in renovation and restoration

29. Indian conservation movement will be successful if there would be

A. Financial support from the Government of India

B. Non-governmental organizations role and participation in the conservation movement

C. consistent investment, rigorous attention, and dedicated research and dissemination of awareness for conservation.

D. Archaeological Survey of India's meaningful assistance

30. As per the surveys of historical monuments in India, there is very small number of protected monuments. As per given the total number of monuments and enlisted number of protected Monuments, percentage comes to

A. 10 percent B. 11 percent

C. 12 percent D. 13 percent

31. What should India learn from Europe to conserve our cultural heritage?

(i) There should be significant budget provision to conserve our cultural heritage

(ii) Establish dedicated labs and training institutions

(iii)Force the government to provide sufficient funds

(iv)Conservation should be made part of mainstream research and engineering institutes.

Chose correct answer from the codes given below:

A. (i), (ii), (iii), (iv) B. (i), (ii), (iv)

C. (i), (ii) D. (i), (iii), (iv)

32. INTACH is known for its contribution for conservation of our cultural heritage. The full form of INTACH is

A. International Trust for Art and Cultural Heritage

B. Intra-national Trust for Art and Cultural Heritage

C. Integrated Trust for Art and Cultural Heritage

D. Indian National Trust for Art and Cultural Heritage

33. While delivering lecture if there is some disturbance in the class, a teacher should

A. keep quiet for a while and then continue

B. punish those causing disturbance

C. motivate to teach those causing disturbance

D. not bother of what is happening in the class

34. Effective teaching is a function of

A. Teacher's satisfaction

B. Teacher's honesty and commitment

C. Teacher's making students learn and understand

D. Teacher's liking for professional excellence

35. The most appropriate meaning of learning is

A. Acquisition of skills B. Modification of behaviour

C. Personal adjustment D. Inclusion of knowledge

36. Arrange the following teaching process in order:

(i) Relate the present knowledge with previous one

(ii) Evaluation

(iii)Reteaching

(iv)Formulation instructional objectives

(v) Presentation of instructional materials

A. (i), (ii), (iii), (iv), (v) B. (ii), (i), (iii), (iv), (v)

C. (v), (iv), (iii), (i), (ii) D. (iv), (i), (v), (ii), (iii)

37. CIET stand for

A. Centre for Integrated Education and Technology

B. Central Institute for Engineering and Technology

C. Central Institute for Education Technology

D. Centre for Integrated Evaluation Techniques

38. Teacher's role at higher education level is to

A. provide information to students

B. promote self learning in students

C. encourage healthy competition among students

D. help students to solve their problems

39. The Verstehen School of Understanding was popularized by

A. German Social Scientists B. American Philosophers

C. British Academicians D. Italian Political Analysts

40. The sequential operations in scientific research are

A. Co-variation, Elimination of Spurious Relations, Generalization, Theorization

B. Generalization, Co-variation, Theorization, Elimination of Spurious Relations

C. Theorization, Generalization, Elimination of Spurious Relations, Co-variation

D. Elimination of Spurious Relations, Theorization, Generalization, Co-variation

41. In sampling, the lottery method is used for

A. Interpretation B. Theorization

C. Conceptualization D. Randomization

42. Which is the main objective of research?

A. To review the literature

B. To summarize what is already known

C. To get an academic degree

D. To discover new facts or to make fresh interpretation of known facts

43. Sampling error decreases with the

A. Decrease in sample size B. Increase in sample size

C. Process of randomization D. Process of analysis

44. The principles of fundamental research are used in

A. Action research B. Applied research

C. Philosophical research D. Historical research

45. Users who use media for their own ends are identified as

A. Passive audience B. Active audience

C. Positive audience D. Negative audience

46. Classroom communication can be described as

A. Exploration B. Institutionalisation

C. Unsignified narration D. Discourse

47. Ideological codes shape our collective

A. Productions B. Perceptions

C. Consumptions D. Creations

48. In communication, myths have power, but are

A. uncultural B. insignificant

C. imprecise D. unpreferred

49. The first multi-lingual news agency of India was

A. Samachar B. API
C. Hindustan Samachar D. Samachar Bharati

50. Organisational communication can also be equated with

A. intra-personal communication B. inter-personal communication
C. group communication D. mass communication

51. If two propositions having the same subject and predicate terms are such that one is the denial of the other, the relationship between them is called

A. Contradictory B. Contrary
C. Sub-contrary D. Sub-alternation

52. Ananya and Krishna can speak and follow English. Bulbul can write and speak Hindi as Archana does. Archana talks with Ananya also in Bengali. Krishna can not follow Bengali. Bulbul talks with Ananya in Hindi. Who can speak and follow English, Hindi and Bengali?

A. Archana B. Bulbul
C. Ananya D. Krishna

53. A stipulative definition may be said to be

A. Always true B. Always false
C. Sometimes true, sometimes false D. Neither true nor false

54. When the conclusion of an argument follows from its premise/premises conclusively, the argument is called

A. Circular argument B. Inductive argument
C. Deductive argument D. Analogical argument

55. Saturn and Mars are planets like the Earth. They borrow light from the Sun and moves around the Sun as the Earth does. So those planets are inhabited by various orders of creatures as the earth is. What type of argument is contained in the above passage?

A. Deductive B. Astrological
C. Analogical D. mathematical

56. Given below are two premises. Four conclusions are drawn from those two premises in four codes. Select the code that states the conclusion validly drawn.

Premises:

(i) All saints are religious (major)

(ii) Some honest persons are saints (minor)

Codes:

A. All saints are honest

B. Some saints are honest

C. Some honest persons are religious

D. All religious persons are honest

Following table provides details about the Foreign Tourist Arrivals (FTAs) in India from different regions of the world in different years. Study the table carefully and answer questions from 57 to 60 bases on this table.

Region	Number of Foreign Tourist Arrivals		
	2007	2008	2009
Western Europe	1686083	1799525	1610086
North America	1007276	1027297	1024469
South Asia	982428	1051846	982633
South East Asia	303475	332925	348495
East Asia	352037	355230	318292
West Asia	171661	215542	201110
Total FTAs in India	5081504	5282603	5108579

57. Find out the region that contributed around 20 percent of the total foreign tourist arrivals in India in 2009.

A. West Europe

B. North America

C. South Asia

D. South East Asia

58. Which of the following regions has recorded the highest negative growth rate of foreign tourist arrivals in India in 2009?

A. Western Europe

B. North America

C. South Asia

D. West Asia

59. Find out the region that has been showing declining trend in terms of share of foreign tourist arrivals in India in 2008 and 2009.

A. Western Europe

B. South East Asia

C. East Asia

D. West Asia

60. Identify the region that has shown hyper growth rate of foreign tourist arrivals than the growth rate of the total FTAs in India in 2008.

A. Western Europe

B. North America

C. South Asia

D. East Asia

Answer keys

1.A	2.B	3.A	4.C	5.D	6.D	7.A	8.C	9.D	10.A
11.B	12.B	13.A	14.B	15.A	16.D	17.C	18.A	19.B	20.D
21.C	22.C	23.A	24.C	25.D	26.D	27.A	28.C	29.B	30.D
31.C	32.D	33.A	34.C	35.B	36.C	37.C	38.B	39.A	40.C
41.D	42.D	43.B	44.B	45.D	46.B	47.B	48.B	49.A	50.B
51.B	52.C	53.C	54.B	55.C	56.B	57.B	58.A	59.A	60.A

Part – III

Model Question Papers for Practice Test

Part - III

Model Question Papers for Practice Test

MODEL QUESTION PAPER - 1

Note : This paper contains **sixty** (60) multiple choice questions, each carrying **two** (2) marks. Answer any **fifty** (50) questions. The total time for answering the paper is 75 minutes and the total marks for the paper is 100.

1. **ABCDE and F are sitting in a row. C is between A and B and is fourth from the right. D is fifth from the left. E is to the right of D. Who is seated on the left side of D?**

   A. A B. B C. C D. E

2. **Among four friends PQR and S, Q is taller than S only. R is taller than P. Who among them is the tallest?**

   A. P B. Q C. R D. S

3. **The total age of nine friends is 243 years. What will be the average age of these friends after 4 years?**

   A. 27 B. 25 C. 31 D. 21

4. **The word AMERICA is coded as IUMZQKI. What will be the code for BLACK?**

   A. JTIKS B. TJISK
   C. JWXZT D. JTSKI

5. **BADC: FEHG:: JILK:....?**

   A. IJKL B. MNOP C. NMPO D. KLMN

6. **What is the fourth term of the series 8712, 7623, 6534, ..., 4356, ...**

   A. 7623 B. 5445 C. 6512 D. 4358

7. **There is a group of persons consisting of Doctors, Engineers and Teachers in Medical and Engineering Colleges. Which diagram represents the group?**

A. 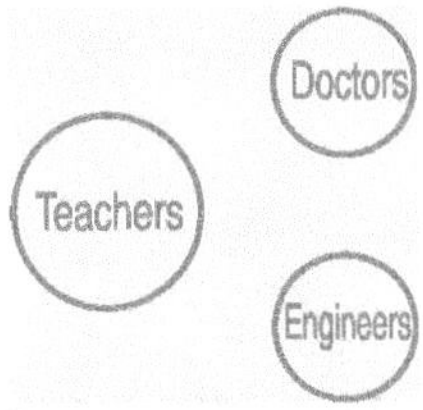

B. 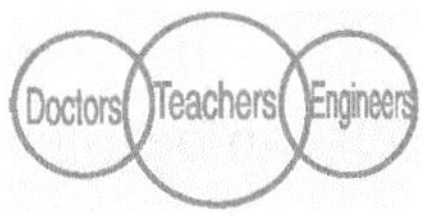

C. 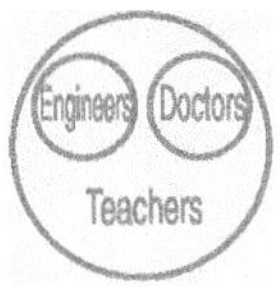

D. 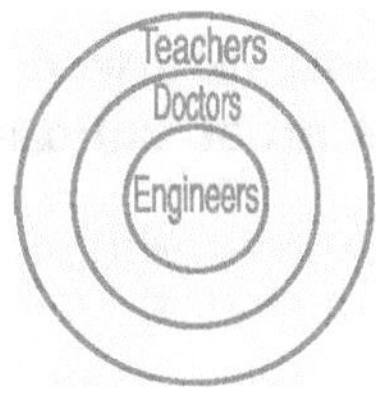

8. Read the following statements and choose the correct inference based on them

Statements:

A. All cadets in a school are boys

B. No cadet is dull

Inferences:

I. There are no girls in the school

II. Every boy in the school is a cadet

A. Inference I alone is true

B. Inference I, II are true

C. Both I and II are false

D. Inference II alone is true

9. A. All cats are mammals

B. All mammals have their own language for communication

I. All cats can communicate with other cats

II. All mammals speak a common language

A. I only

B. II only

C. Both I & II

D. Neither I nor II

10. A. All birds, with the exception of a few, feed their young ones

B. Cuckoo does not feed its young ones.

Interference:

I. Cuckoo is not a bird.

II. Cuckoo is a mammal.

A. Only I can be inferred

B. Only II can be inferred

C. Both I & II can be inferred

D. Neither I nor II can be inferred

11. A statement followed by two assumptions is given. Which of the answer choices is most valid as per the statement?

Statement:

The present system of education needs a thorough overhauling.

Assumptions:

I: Overhauling will help to improve the system.

II: The present educational system is outdated.

A. Only I is implied

B. Only II is implied

C. Both I & II are implied

D. Neither I nor II is implied

12. Read the following statements and choose the correct classification among the given choices.

A. Accumulation of carbon dioxide in the atmosphere causes green house effect & global warming.

B. All educational concessions should be denied to families which have more than two children.

C. Politicians cannot be trusted because they have no interest in the welfare of others.

D. Both her parents are rank holders in University examination; so she will also be good in her studies. She also must be very intelligent.

E. Don't tell others what you are going to do; just do it.

	Opinion	Advice	Prejudice	Fact	Assumption
a)	A	C	B	D	E
b)	C	B	D	E	A
c)	B	E	C	A	D
d)	A	C	E	D	B

1. Read the following passage carefully and answer questions 13 to 18.

Amnesty international's charge that tens of thousands of political prisoners including prisoners of conscience are languishing in Indian jails and that prisoners are routinely tortured in this country, has to be seen in a much wider context than the organisation's annual report cares to do. In its overall appraisal of 151 countries. Amnesty has accused that there are 112 reports of torturing prisoners, 63 of harboring prisoners of conscience, 61 of resorting to political killings and 53 of detaining people, without trial of these apparently overlapping categories. India seems to have been excluded from the list of 61 which undertake political killings. The report has, however, pointed out that, scores of people in India die of torture in police and military custody and that many also simply disappear. Clearly only a thin line separates the 61 charged with political murder from the rest. Before coming to such conclusions, however, it may also be necessary to classify the various countries according to their political systems. Torture by the security forces and killing at the behest of government makes no difference to the victims whether they are in a democratic country or a totalitarian one. It is also nobody's case that a democratic country is less culpable than a dictatorship in the event of human right violations. But the point perhaps still needs to be made that torture or disappearances represent a failure of the system in a democracy in contrast to being an integral part of state policy in a country ruled by an autocrat who is answerable to no one.

India may be guilty of keeping tens of thousands behind bars and of the other human right abuses mentioned by Amnesty. But it still remains a qualitatively different place from a totalitarian country. It is in this respect that Amnesty has been less than fair. It has chosen to ignore the distinctions between the good, the bad and the ugly. The openness of Indian society will be evident to anyone who spends half an hour in one of its chaotic market places or visits the law-courts or watches a political rally or reads a newspaper or strikes up a conversation with any person on the road. There is no sense of fear in India as in a dictatorship. There is also scope for securing relief from the high-handed behavior of the authorities. Unless such points are recognised, Amnesty's assessment will seem to be a dry recital of statistics which may pillory India simply because of its larger population. Mercifully, Amnesty now a days, at least, notes that the terrorists also indulge in human right violations. True, there is much that is wrong in India's prison system and with the way the terrorist challenge is somewhere met but the stress should be on activating the self correcting mechanism within a democracy and not merely on painting a grim, even biased picture of events.

13. The author suggests classification of various countries on one additional dimension. Which of the following is that new dimension?

A. economic progress

B. industrial progress

C. openness of a society

D. number of human right violations

14. What is the source of the information used by Amnesty International to accuse India of many human right violations?

A. from the data which it collected during its international meet

B. from Annual Report

C. its Seminar on Human Rights

D. its regional meet

15. The author of the passage:

A. agrees with the major findings of the report

B. disagrees with the major findings of the report

C. disagrees with the finding that the conditions of Indian prisons is totally bad

D. supports the totalitarian approach

16. The number of countries from which its Amnesty International has prepared its report is:

A. 112 B. 63 C. 131 D. 151

17. From which of the following categories of violating human rights violations have India been excluded in the report of the Amnesty International?

A. political killings

B. torturing of prisoners

C. detaining prisoners without trial

D. harboring prisoners of conscience

18. According to the author, the Amnesty International's report about India does not consider some of the major factors like:

A. progressive political policies adopted by democracies

B. the virtues of the autocratic rule

C. openness of society and the scope for correcting high-handed actions

D. failure of system to curtail crimes in prisons

2. ***The following table shows value of exports of a country A to some selected countries, for the period from 1979-80 to 1982-83. Study the details presented in the table and answer questions 19 & 20.***

Country	1979-80	1980-81	1981-82	1982-83
EEC	10-02	9-82	12-38	22-17
UK	16-42	17-00	16-81	17-19
Japan	17-93	20-21	18-17	21-67
Slovakia	3-00	2-94	3-04	4-67
Hungary	0-94	0-14	1-55	1-22
Switzerland	0-75	0-72	0-75	0-79
USSR	17-62	20-98	20-87	30-47
USA	23-76	20-68	26-28	27-54

19. The number of countries which have shown a continuous growth in exports over these years is:

A. 1 B. 2 C. 3 D. None

20. Which among the eight countries do we find the exports are lower from country A?

A. Hungary B. EEC C. Japan D. Switzerland

3. *Study the following figure that shows number of road accident deaths during the rainy season; and answer questions 21, 22 and 23.*

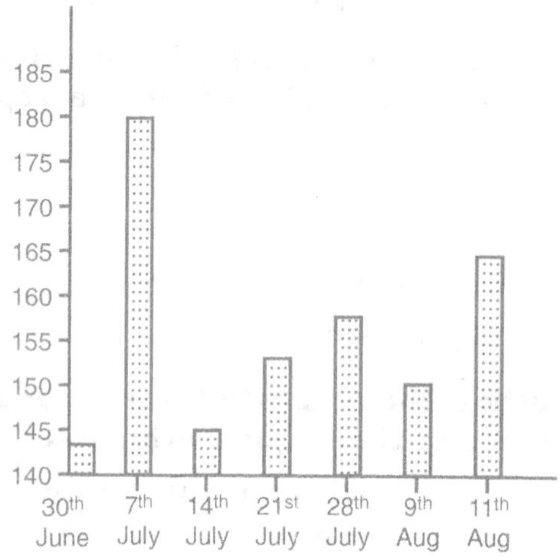

21. Between which two consecutive weekends was the rise in the number of deaths by road accident greatest:

A. 14th to 21st, July

B. 30th June to 7th July

C. 4th August to 11th August

D. 21st. July to 28th July

22. In how many weeks during the period do we have more that 150 road accident deaths?

A. 1 B. 2 C. 3 D. 4

23. In how many weeks were there less that 150 deaths by road accidents?

A. 0 B. 1 C. 2 D. 3

Study the diagram and answer the question 24 below:

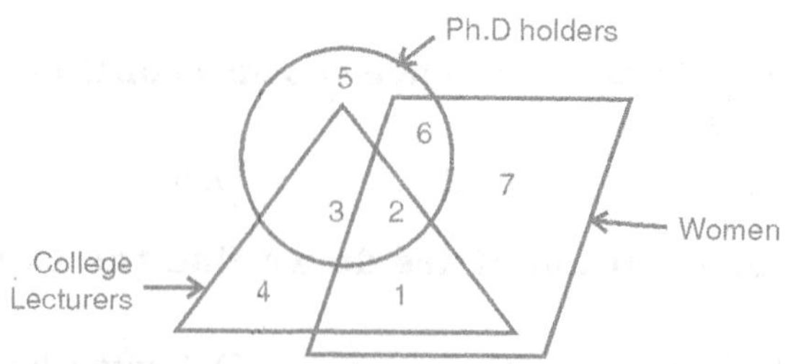

24. Which number indicate (s), women lectures who are Ph.D holders?

A. 2 B. 3 C. 2 & 6 D. 2 & 3

25. Information communication within the campus of an institution is known as:

A. interpersonal communication

B. mass communication

C. intra personal communication

D. grapevine communication

26. Feedback in a communication system is essential for:

A. improving the message content

B. making modifications in the process of communication

C. evaluating whether the message reached the receivers

D. to avoid distortion in communication

27. Which of the following will be a most effective method of communication in education?

A. Frequent questioning

B. Extempore lectures

C. Lectures with illustrations

D. Adopting greater interaction with learners

28. Multimedia approach is adopted for communication in distance education so as to:

A. provide learners more colourful learning experiences

B. enable learners to interact with the materials

C. compensate the deficiency of direct class-room student - teacher interaction

D. to expose the learner to original sources of information

29. Which of the following media is most effective for large-group communication?

A. Printed materials

B. Radio

C. Electronic media like TV

D. Cartoons & posters

30. Motivation, attitude, interest and receptibility are usually classified as:

A. source variables

B. message variables

C. receiver variables

D. feedback variables

31. Students in higher education will be benefited more if the teacher adopts which one of the following instructional approaches:

A. note dictation based on the topic to

B. suggests proper references for consultation

C. explains every small detail meticulously

D. motivates the students to adopt need-based exploration of the subject area

32. I prefer to be teacher because:

A. This profession helps me to enhance my personal capabilities and is a rewarding job

B. It gives lots of leisure time, attractive salary and scope for taking up private job

C. Interacting with the youth and working with them is an exciting experience for one

D. I was not able to land up in professions like medicine and engineering.

33. When you notice that a few of your students are troublesome in your class, the best way to deal with them is:

A. to ask them politely to leave the class

B. to report the matter to the Principal for official action

C. to talk to them confidentially after make them correct their behaviour

D. to ignore them and proceed with the class

34. Which one of the following is least important for a teacher in higher education?

A. guiding the research projects of one's students

B. organizing co-curricular activities in a big way

C. helping students to solve their personal academic and emotional problems

D. assisting the college authorities in performing their administrative functions

35. Which of the following combination of activities would make the class more effective?

A. illustrating, explaining, evaluating, scolding

B. questioning, illustrating, reinforcing, reversing

C. punishing, dictating, quoting humourous incidents, asking questions

D. motivating, interacting, empowering, facilitating

36. Which of the following would you endorse as the major professional responsibility of a teacher?

A. A teacher should be strict and matter of fact

B. A teacher should be flexible and friendly

C. A teacher has to keep some distance from the students

D. A teacher has enforce discipline

37. The term research as used in education stands for:

A. an attempt to discover hidden truths about education

B. an endeavour to test the validity of existing educational theories

C. a systematic and scientific process used for finding solutions to problems faced by professionals in education

D. a process to be adopted for completing a research project by a research guide

38. A research hypothesis can best be defined as:

A. a hunch which dawned on the investigator while doing research

B. an intelligent guess deduced from an established theory or from professional experience or from the researches done by other researchers

C. a hypothetical cause of the problem

D. an answer formulated to suit the researcher's objectives of the study

39. Which is the first and most important step in conducting formal research?

A. A well-formulated and defined problem

B. Identification of an experienced research supervisor

C. Locating appropriate tools for data collection

D. Deciding the samples upon which the study can be conducted.

40. Which of the following statements about research would you accept as valid?

A. A researcher should study everything about the area of research.

B. A researcher should penetrate deeper and deeper to some specific sub - areas within a major problem area

C. A researcher should continue data collection until his hypothesis is validated

D. A researcher should not hasten to reach a conclusion until his hypothesis is proved

41. Even though research endeavors are undertaken in thousands worth while new findings are very rare. This is because:

A. the new generation researchers are impatient

B. sophisticated facilities are not available

C. sustained efforts and resources are not often adequate
D. the researcher uses convergent thinking approaches to the exclusion of divergent thinking approaches

42. Which of the following sequence is most appropriate in research process?

i) Formulating a research hypothesis
ii) Setting objectives for the study
iii) Selecting a worthwhile problem for study and defining it scientifically
iv) Collecting data for hypothesis testing
v) Arriving at conclusions
vi) Analysing data

A. (iii)	(iv)	(i)	(ii)	(v)	(vi)
B. (iii)	(ii)	(i)	(iv)	(vi)	(v)
C. (ii)	(iii)	(i)	(iv)	(v)	(vi)
D. (i)	(ii)	(iii)	(iv)	(vi)	(v)

43. Where is 'Tidal Park' located?

A. Delhi B. Kolkata C. Chennai D. Mumbai

44. The micro processor is the part of computer which:

A. controls the flow and processing of all data
B. stores large amount of data to the computer
C. reads information from portable discs
D. reads information from discs and displays data

45. Modem is a device used in ICT which helps to convert:

A. digital information to analog information and vice-versa
B. sound signals into digital signals
C. images to digital data and vice-versa
D. graphic data into computer signals and vice-versa

46. The most important technic contrivance used for satellite telecasts is:

A. Radar B. Transponders
C. Transmitted sound D. Electro magnetic wares

47. The ISRO used its own version of Google Earth to provide sharper pictures of Indian Terrain. This 3D web-based tool is called:

A. Nethra B. Full Map C. India Map D. Bhuvan

48. The science and engineering of making intelligent machines or intelligent computer programes is called:

A. Robotics B. Artificial Intelligence
C. Nano Technology D. Typosquatting

49. Which is the most important feature of a Federal University?

A. The departments in the university function with full autonomy

B. The teaching work is shared by the university with its constituent colleges

C. The Vice-Chancellor of the university is appointed by the Central Government

D. The university has colleges affiliated to it, but all the institutions function within the campus

50. Which of the following is the statutory body to declare an institution as a Deemed University?

A. Higher Education Council of the state

B. National Assessment and Accreditation Council

C. The University Grants Commission

D. Ministry of Human Resources

51. The autonomous colleges were established following the recommendations of:

A. Kothari Commission

B. Draft Policy of Indian Education

C. University Education Commission

D. National Policy of Education 1986

52. Match the items in column A with the correct expansion of them from column B.

A

(i) ICHR (ii) ICAR (iii) ICMR

(iv) CSIR (v) ICSSR

B

a. Indian Council of Medical Research

b. Council for Scientific and Industrial Research

c. Inter University Council for Human Resources

d. Indian Council for Agricultural Research

e. Institute of Commerce and Social Science Research

f. Indian Council for Social Science Research

g. Indian Council for Historical Research

A. (i)-d (ii)-b (iii)-f (iv)-c (v)-a
B. (i)-g (ii)-d (iii)-a (iv)-b (v)-f
C. (i)-f (ii)-g (iii)-a (iv)-b (v)-e
D. (i)-d (ii)-c (iii)-e (iv)-b (v)-a

53. Who is the visitor of all the Central Universities in the country?

A. The President of India
B. The Prime Minister of India
C. The Central Minister for Human Resources Development
D. Secretary, of HRD Ministry, Govt. of India

54. One of the Universities in India has the Prime Minister as its visitor and Chancellor. Which is the University?

A. Delhi University
B. Benares University
C. Viswa Bharathy University
D. Jawahar Lal Nehru University

55. The Air (Prevention & Control of Pollution) Act was implemented in the year.

A. 1980 B. 1981 C. 1986 D. 1990

56. The region with high species diversity facing high threat from human beings is called:

A. Bio diversity hot spot B. Bio diversity zone
C. Endangered species region D. Red endemic spot

57. World Bio-diversity Day is observed on:

A. 8th December B. 5th July
C. 5th June D. 22nd May

58. Climatic variation and extinction of species are caused mainly by:

A. Water Pollution B. Deforestation
C. Toxic dumping D. Air Pollution

59. What is meant by 'Red Data Book'?

A. book on species that face the danger of extinction
B. book that explains the consequences of pollution
C. book on environmental protection
D. book on infra-red rays and its impact

60. World environment day is observed on:

A. 22nd March B. 22nd April C. 5th June D. 5th July

Answer keys

1.B (FACBDE) 2.C 3.C 4.A 5.C 6.B 7.B 8.C 9.A
10.D 11.C 12.C 13.D 14.B 15.B 16.D 17.A 18.D 19.D
20.D 21.B 22.D 23.B 24.A 25.D 26.B 27.D 28.C 29.C
30.C 31.D 32.A 33.C 34.D 35.D 36.B 37.C 38.B 39.A
40.B 41.D 42.B 43.C 44.A 45.A 46.B 47.D 48.B 49.B
50.C 51.D 52.B 53.A 54.C 55.B 56.A 57.D 58.B 59.A
60.C

MODEL QUESTION PAPER - 2

Note : This paper contains **sixty** (60) multiple choice questions, each carrying **two** (2) marks. Answer any **fifty** (50) questions. The total time for completing the paper is 75 minutes and the total marks for the paper is 100.

1. An effective teacher is one who can:

A. extract implicit obedience from all students

B. give more information to students in less time

C. motivate students to learn on their own

D. interact with students in equal terms

2. The test on the basis of which a teacher takes decisions about the learning inadequacies of his students is called:

A. standardized test

B. class test

C. Diagnostic test

D. Activity test

3. A teaching model is one which will help in:

A. bringing out the best in his students

B. in achieving some specific objectives using validated methods for optimising learning under given conditions

C. in achieving fast educational development in the part of his learners

D. none of these

4. Which one of the following models is based on information processing theory?

A. Jurisprudential Model

B. Class room Model

C. Inductive Model

D. Operant Conditioning Model

5. Continuous and comprehensive evaluation stands for:

A. a model of evaluation which helps to evaluate all expected outcomes using differing models of evaluation spread over a period of time.

B. a concept of evaluation which believes in giving several test papers to replace a long terminal examination

C. concept of evaluation which uses grading instead of marks

D. evaluation where a single teacher combines the evaluation done by different teachers for final grading

6. **Which of the following methods is most useful for teaching in higher education?**

   A. seminar presentation
   B. teacher-centered teaching
   C. Teaching in the natural environment
   D. computer assisted teaching

7. **Which branch of research treats research as part of a teacher's professional performance?**

   A. participant research
   B. applied research
   C. action research
   D. descriptive research

8. **A research finding in education is accepted by professionals because:**

   A. it has been conducted by expert
   B. it has been published in research journal
   C. it is based on a study conducted using the scientific method
   D. it is based on the use of the latest knowledge in the area

9. **Who developed the idea of t-test?**

   A. Karl Pearson
   B. William S. Gosset
   C. James. L. Murphy
   D. G.H. Garnelt

10. **Which sampling procedure gives each item an equal probability of being selected?**

    A. Systematic sampling
    B. Simple random sampling
    C. Quota sampling
    D. Stratified sampling

11. **The other name for the independent variable used in experimental research is**

    A. Treatment Variable
    B. Experimental Variable
    C. Manipulated Variable
    D. All the above

12. **The development of a hypothesis is essential in an experiment study because:**

A. it helps in defining the procedures to be adopted for conducting the study

B. it adds to the respectivility of the study

C. it helps to replicate the study

D. it helps in finalizing the title of he study

***Directions:* Read the following passage and answer questions 13 to 17**

Ocean water plays an indispensable role in supporting life. The great ocean basins hold about 300 million cubic miles of water. From this vast amount, about 80,000 cubic miles of water is sucked into the atmosphere each year by evaporation and returned by precipitation and drainage to the ocean. More than 24,000 cubic miles of rain descend annually upon the continents. This vast amount is required to replenish the lakes and streams, springs and water tables on which all flora and fauna are dependent. Thus, the hydrosphere permits organic existence.

The hydrosphere has strange characteristics because water has properties unlike those of other liquids. One anomaly is that water upon freezing expands by about 9 per cent, whereas most liquids contract on cooling. For this reason, ice floats on water bodies instead of sinking to the bottom. If the ice sank, the hydrosphere would soon be frozen solidly, except for a thin layer of surface-melt water during the summer season. Thus, all aquatic life would be destroyed and the interchange of warm and cold currents, which moderates climate would be notably absent.

Another outstanding characteristic of water is that water has a heat capacity which is the highest of all liquids and solids, except ammonia. This characteristic enables the oceans to absorb and store vast quantities of heat, thereby often preventing climatic extremes. In addition, water dissolves more substances than any other liquid. It is this characteristic which helps make oceans a great storehouse for minerals which have been washed down from the continents. In several areas of the world, these minerals are being commercially exploited. Solar evaporation of salt is widely practised, Potash is extracted from the Dead Sea, and magnesium is produced from sea water along the American Gulf Coast.

13. Ocean water plays an indispensable role in life because:

A. it is a source of pure water

B. helps to collect water flowing down the rivers

C. supports agriculture

D. it sustains organic existence

14. The term 'hydrosphere' stands for:

A. Water-bodies in the air

B. The property of water to expand on freezing

C. Seas, lakes and all the water available on earth defined collectively

D. The surface of the ocean

15. The high heat capacity of water:

A. prevents climatic extremes and creates a congenial weather for the sustenance of life

B. Prevents extreme heating of land

C. Prevents climatic extremes and sustains aquatic life

D. Prevents the function of icebergs all over the ocean

16. The author, calls oceans 'a great storehouse of minerals' because:

A. the rocks found under the ocean are rich in minerals

B. the oceans contain several salts in different forms

C. of its ability to dissolve different substances

D. The high amount of minerals it contains

17. Commercial explanation of minerals is used to stand for:

A. more use of minerals by human beings

B. devising without methods for extracting minerals under the sea for the one of human beings

C. more one of minerals in industries

D. using minerals under the sea for promoting trade

18. Which one of the following programmes is interested to connect 60,000 government and aided schools of the country through the internet?

A. Gyan Vahini B. Sankhya Vahini

C. Vidya Vahini D. None of these

19. If your fellow teacher overhears you committing a mistake while teaching, and points this out to you, what will be your reaction?

A. Request him not to report this to anybody else

B. Protest against his interfering in such personals matters

C. Discuss the issue with him and if convinced, accept the correction, and correct the error in next class

D. Defend yourself and take him should that your stand is correct

20. Which one of the following in the description of the ideal style you would use to deal with your students?

A. Accepting

B. Dominating

C. Threatening

D. Controlling

21. The most critical factor that determines the professional status of a teacher is his:

A. Instructional competency

B. Ability to mix with other teachers

C. Linguistic ability

D. Family background

22. The main function of educational psychology in a teacher-education curriculum is to provide prospective teachers:

A. a background of the research studies in developmental psychology which will help him to select ideal procedures for adoption

B. a picture of the needs, problems and styles connected with teacher behaviour

C. an insight into a various practices in modern education

D. a perspective of the practices for dealing with every day classroom problems

23. Which of the following is the largest public sector publishing house in India, for school related behaviour of students?

A. Publication Division, Govt. of India

B. Tata McGraw Hill

C. NCERT

D. None of these

24. X and Y are two children in Z's family. Z is the father of X but Y is not the son of Z. How are Y and Z related to each other ?

A. daughter and father

B. sister and brother

C. niece and uncle

D. niece and maternal uncle

25. If GUN is coded as HVO, what will be the word which in code language is UFBDI?

A. CATCH B. VGCEJ

C. TEACH D. LEARN

26. Which of the given options will complete the series?

B D F H J ?

A. L B. O C. M D. K

27. Find the odd one out:

A. Boy B. School C. Book D. Star

28. Find out the missing number in the following series:

21, 34, 47, 510, 613, ______?

A. 710 B. 713 C. 614 D. 716

29. A coin is tossed 5 times. What is the probability that head appears on odd number of times?

A. $\frac{2}{5}$ B. $\frac{1}{5}$ C. $\frac{1}{2}$ D. $\frac{4}{25}$

30. How many times would the angle between the two hands of a clock attain a maximum angle (180°) during the day-time (6 a.m. to 6 p.m.)

A. 24 times B. 6 times C. 12 times D. once

Directions: *Assume the following statement to be absolute truth when one of the following conclusions is:*

31. *Statement:* Every student of this university is an employee.

Conclusion: No student of this university is other than those who are employed.

A. True B. False

C. Can't say D. Either A. or B.

Directions: *In the questions (32-34) given below, an assumption A is followed by two reasons 1 and II Tick mark your-answers.*

A. If only I is the reason for A.

B. If only II is the reason for A.

C. If both I and II are reasons for A.

D. If either I or II is the reason for A.

32. A. In spite of their best efforts, the doctors sometimes could not save the patients who are suffering from meningitis

I. The patient is not brought to hospital in time.

II. Meningitis is too dangerous disease and hence nothing much can be done about it.

33. A. Many girls want to act in films which may or may not become box-office hits

I. Many girls want to prove their potential for acting.

II. Some girls simply want to act in the films

34. A. Mr. X left his political party and joined the opposition.

I. The objectives of the rival party appealed to him more.

II. The rival party promised better political prospects for him.

Directions: ***(Q. 35-36): Find which of the two arguments following the statement below is forceful? Give answers as per the following codes.***

A. Only 1 is strong B. Only II is strong

C. Both I and II are strong D. Neither I nor II is strong

35. ***Statement*** **: Should Bollywood stars and Pakistani actors involve in the India-Pakistan peace efforts?**

Arguments :

I. No, the peace talks are purely political, so no one else except the ruling politicians should be involved.

II. Yes, as these people have larger impact on masses than politicians, they can help in the peace efforts.

A. only argument I is strong

B. only argument II is strong

C. either I or II is strong

D. neither I nor II is strong

36. ***Statement :***

Should telecasting feature films be stopped ?

Arguments :

I. Yes. Young children are likely to be misguided by the feature films.

II. No. This is the only way to educate the masses.

A. only argument I is strong

B. only argument II is strong

C. either I or II is strong

D. neither I nor II is strong

Directions: ***Questions 37 are based on following: In a class of five students, ages are computed only in whole numbers and no two students in the group are of the same age. We also know that:***

1. Mohan is a year older than Madan
2. Madan is two years older than Jaipal
3. Jaipal is one year younger to Sushil
4. Sushil is two years younger to Mohan
5. Ahmed is two years younger to Jaipal.

37. Which one of the following given order is the oldest to the youngest?

A. Mohan, Madan, Jaipal, Sushil, Ahmed

B. Mohan, Madan, Sushil, Ahmed, Jaipal

C. Mohan, Madan, Sushil, Jaipal, Ahmed

D. Mohan, Jaipal, Madan, Ahmed, Sushil

Direction : Questions 38–39 are based on the following:

1. A cube has six sides each of a different colour
2. The red side is opposite the black
3. The green side is between the red side and the black side
4. The white side is adjacent to brown side
5. The brown side is adjacent to the blue side
6. The red side is facing down

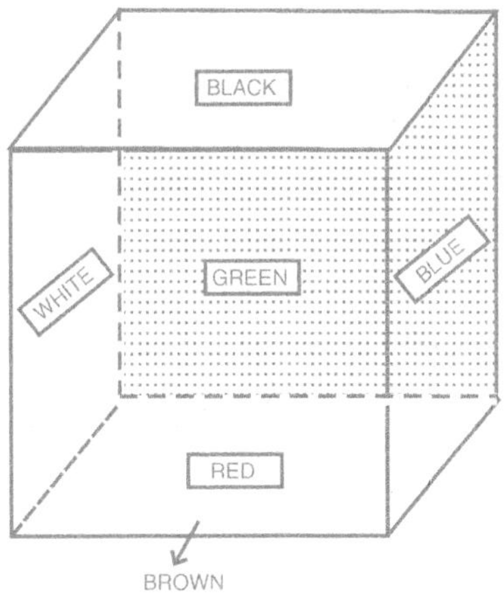

38. The side opposite to the brown side is:

A. Red B. Black C. White D. Green

39. The side opposite to the white side is

A. Black B. Brown C. Blue D. White

40.

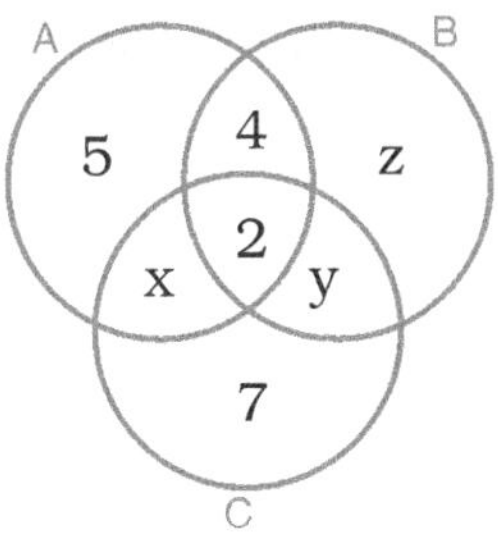

If n A. = 15, n B. = 20, and n C. = 25 and the values of x, y, and z respectively are

A. 4, 10 and 9

B. 10, 9 and 4

C. 4, 9 and 10

D. None of the above

41. Which of the following actions should be undertaken when a file retention date expires?

A. The storage medium on which the file resides should be retired from use

B. The file should be purged

C. The file retention date should be extended

D. The file should be retrieved from back up storage

42. A warm site is:

A. Partially equipped site where the computer environment consists of few equipment without the main computer.

B. Fully equipped computer centre in a ready state for continuing operations within hours.

C. A site where the computer environment is maintained without any equipment.

D. Dedicated, self developed recovery site that can backup critical applications

43. Which of the following is not a desirable control feature in a modem?

A. Attenuation amplification

B. Dynamic equalization

C. Automatic dial-up capabilities

D. Multiple transmission speeds

44. Which of the following is true regarding software testing?

A. Debugging is same as software testing.

B. For better results, software testing is done after implementation of the software.

C. Irrespective of the size of software, the documentation must be of fixed size.

D. Tests are designed after each level of software specification has been written.

45. MSAU is a :

A. Token

B. Network Architecture

C. Hub

D. None of these

46. PAGING provides:

A. paper leaves for noting down memories

B. small note-book of computers
C. one way wireless communication to the wandering users
D. none of these

47. Which one of the following country hosted the "World Earth Summit, June 1992" for discussing global environmental issues?

A. Japan B. USA C. Brazil D. India

48. Today concentration of greenhouse gases is high because of:

A. Increased combustion of fossil fuel
B. Deforestation
C. Industrial pollution
D. All the above

49. Most abundant pollutant in the atmosphere among the hydrocarbons is:

A. Methane B. Benzpyrene
C. Propane D. Ethane

50. Classical smog is:

A. Smog with secondary pollutants
B. Los Angeles smog
C. Yellow brown in colour
D. Dark brown in colour

51. Taj Mahal at Agra, is being damaged by:

A. Mathura refinery (air pollution)
B. Road constructions at Agra
C. Yamuna flood
D. Nuclear pollution and railway yard

52. Second largest contributor to green house effect on earth is :

A. CH_4 B. CO_2 C. N_2O D. CFCs.

53. The University Grants Commission (UGC) was established in :

A. 1956 B. 1957
C. 1989 D. 1987

54. Which organisation among the following is responsible for the maintenance of Central Universities ?

A. Union Ministry of Education
B. Finance Ministry

C. The Home Ministry

D. None of the above

55. Which one of the following, the Higher Education Information System Project has not designed?

A. University and College Administration System

B. University and College Admission System

C. Reorganisation Management System

D. Research Project Management System

56. Which organisation among the following was created for the co-ordination and maintenance of standards in higher education ?

A. UGC

B. NCERT

C. SCERT

D. HE1S Project

57. Which body controls the National Assessment and Accreditation Council?

A. ICSSR

B. UGC

C. MHRD

D. None of the above

58. The Lok-Sabha can be dissolved before the expiry of its normal five year term by:

A. the Prime Minister in the recommendation of the Parliament

B. the President on the recommendation of Prime Minister

C. the Speaker of Lok-Sabha

D. none of the above

59. What is the expansion of ICAR?

A. Indian Council for Aeronautic Research

B. International Committee for Atomic Research

C. Indian Council for Aesthetics and Recreation

D. Indian Council for Agricultural Research

60. Which of the following is established for imparting distance education?

A. IGNOU B. EFLU C. NCERT D. NUEPA

Answer keys

1.C	2.C	3.B	4.B	5.A	6.A	7.C	8.C	9.B	10.B
11.D	12.A	13.D	14.C	15.A	16.D	17.B	18.C	19.C	20.A
21.A	22.D	23.A	24.A	25.C	26.A	27.B	28.D	29.C	30.C
31.A	32.B	33.C	34.C	35.A	36.D	37.C	38.D	39.C	40.C
41.B	42.A	43.A	44.D	45.C	46.C	47.C	48.D	49.A	50.D
51.A	52.D	53.A	54.A	55.D	56.A	57.B	58.B	59.D	60.A

MODEL QUESTION PAPER - 3

Note : This paper contains **sixty** (60) multiple choice questions, each carrying **two** (2) marks. Answer any **fifty** (50) questions. The total time for completing the paper is 75 minutes and the total marks for the paper is 100.

1. **Find out the missing item.**

   Red, Blue..... Yellow.

   A. Black B. Red C. Orange D. Blue

2. **Find out the missing number.**

   36, 49, 64, 81, ..., 121.

   A. 91 B. 97 C. 99 D. 100

3. **The numbers entered in each of the seven sectors of the given circle are formed according to a common principle, the number to be entered in the eighth sector is missing. Find out the missing number.**

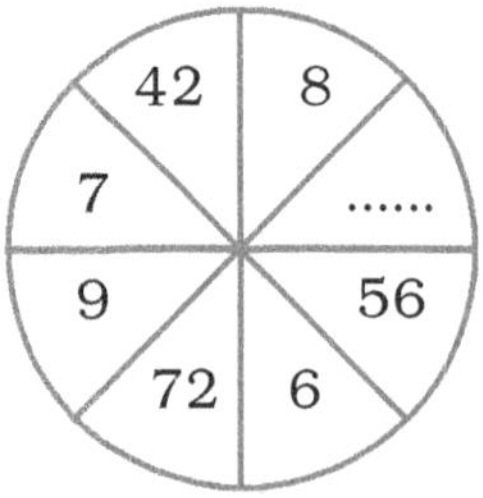

   A. 81 B.90 C.96 D.100

4. **If 'disease' is coded as 'illness' and 'Hospital' is coded as 'Medicine' - What will be the code for 'Doctor'?**

   A. Relief B. Injection C. Stethoscope D. Patient

5. **If XVU:CEF::YWV:.........?**

   A. XWU B. BDE C.DBE D. XUV

6. **If the third Saturday of a month is 19th. What will be the date on the 4th Sunday of the next month?**

   A. 24 B.23 C.22 D. 21

7. **Read the following statements and classify them in terms of facts, advice, assumption, opinion and prejudice.**

Statements:

(a) Don't overstrain even during examination times.

(b) Smoking is one of the major reasons for lung Cancer.

(c) Israelees are shrewd and unreliable.

(d) Production of electricity should never affect environment and ecological balance.

(e) The ruling party is facing a dilemma hence there will be a fall in the stock market.

	Fact	Advice	Assumption	Opinion	Prejudice
A.	(e)	(c)	(a)	(d)	(b)
B.	(b)	(a)	(e)	(d)	(c)
C.	(a)	(e)	(b)	(c)	(d)
D.	(c)	(b)	(d)	(a)	(e)

8. **The three words given below are related in some way. Which of the following alternatives has the same relationship?**

Student... Cadet..... Athlete

A. table, chair, furniture

B. wood, steel, shelf

C. doctor, patient, nurse

D. teacher, army, playground

9. **A school teacher wants to convince the parents about the merits of periodic tests as against annual examinations. "If students are repeatedly under the pressure of tests, they will lose their interest in school subjects". The above sentence is:**

A. in directly supporting the teacher's idea

B. supports the teacher's position indirectly

C. contradicts the teacher's stand

D. irrelevant to the main argument

10. **The forefathers of many successful industrialists in Poone are from Haryana. Mr. Sharma, a resident of Poone, came from Haryana. Therefore Mr. Sharma will be a successful industrialist. This inference is:**

A. not correct because all from Haryana are not industrialists

B. correct because one follows from the other

C. not correct because all industrialists in Poone are not from Haryana.

D. not correct because Mr. Sharma may or may not be from industrialists family.

11. Considering that the given proposition is true, which conclusion can be validly drawn from it? Proposition: Teachers seldom enjoy class room teaching. *Conclusions:*

A. Teachers frequently enjoy class room teaching

B. Teachers always enjoy classroom teaching

C. Teachers do not enjoy classroom teaching

D. Many teachers enjoy class room teaching.

12. All birds can fly:

The Penguin is a bird

Therefore the Penguin can fly

This inference is

A. Valid B. Invalid C. illogical D. long drawn

13. Which one of the following is not a bio-indicator of water pollution?

A. Blood worms

B. Stone flies

C. Sewage fungus

D. Sleedge worms

14. Fluoride pollution generally affects:

A. the brain B. the heart

C. the teeth D. the kidney

15. Effect of pollution is first marked on:

A. micro organisms

B. food crops

C. mushrooms

D. green vegetation

16. Ultra violet radiation from sunlight causes a reaction that produces:

A. Flourides B. Carbon monoxide

C. Sulphur dioxide D. Ozone

17. The pigment that protects plants from damage by ultra violet radiation:

A. Chlorophyll B. Xanthophyll

C. Caroteroids D. Phycocyamin

18. The 'blue baby syndrome' results from:

A. Excess of total dissolved solids

B. Excess of chloride
C. Methemoglobin
D. Excess of dissolved oxygen

1. *Read the following passage and answer question Nos. 19 to 24.*

The Bible has said that he who lives by the word shall perish by the word. It is one of the tragedies of history that the greatest exponents of non-violence, the most powerful opponents of the cult of the sword have died as a result of the sword succeeding over the principle of ahimsa. Christ died on the cross, Gandhiji was assassinated and the latest instance is the death of Dr. Martin Luther King. Is non-violence then an empty dream?; a mere dialectic in philosophy which seeks to conceal the seething passions which sway both the individual and the nation?

That is not true. Caesar dead is more powerful than Caesar alive. The crucification of Christ resulted in a great religion coming to birth which has moulded the thoughts and ideas of millions of people. The death of Gandhiji has brought into existence a philosophy which is not only the basis of statecraft in our own country but has influenced people all over the world and for ought we know the murder of Dr. King may hasten the removal of blot of apartheid from the face of the world.

There is always one great danger every prophet runs - his sayings and his message taking on the fixed mould of immutability. A prophet must be judged in the context of the time he lived and the problems that he had to face. Times change and old problems get solved and new ones present their challenge. But we refuse to give dynamism to the prophet's thoughts. We convert his preaching to empty slogans and refuse to permit any 'deviation' from what he wanted his followers to do, however meaningless such an action might have become and however divorced might be from the true essence of his philosophy.

Gandhiji has suffered and is suffering the same fate. There is hardly a platform where his name is not uttered and I am afraid, very often in vain. The most dishonest, the most defamed and the most corrupt politicians capitalise on his name and every day he is being assassinated again not in the body but in spirit.

Undoubtedly, Gandhiji's great contribution to political philosophy is his doctrine of non-violence. But it is a mistake to think that he merely preached physical non-violence. It has become abundantly clear now that unless the minds and spirits of men are cleansed war will not be abolished and the menace of retribution will hang dangerously over the head of mankind. But the threat of physical violence is no less. In South Africa, in Rhodesia, in the USA, racial arrogance and racial divisiveness is getting more and more marked. In our own country, the upsurge of regionalism and communalism emphasizes spiritual intolerance. Even in government there is a marked tendency towards a monolithic society. Independent and autonomous organs are under constant attack and non conformity can only be practised at the risk of political and even social ostracism. The age old tradition of our society has been tolerance and compassion. The great Buddha preached it and Gandhiji worked on it to make it a world creed and to give it a name and a flag. The second great contribution of Gandhiji was the application of the doctrine of the dignity of man to Indian society. For centuries, we have treated a large section of our fellow citizens as sub-human denying them elementary human rights. No one did more than Gandhiji to wipe out his blot from our society. If our constitution proudly proclaims the abolition of untouchability it is largely due to the awakening that Gandhiji brought about in the mind of upper caste Hindus. He himself performed all kinds of labour in order to prove that no shame is attached to any kind of work however menial.

19. Gandhiji worked to remove untouchability because:

A. he believed that menial work is no shame

B. he wanted the Indian constitution to abolish it

C. he wanted to change the minds of the upper caste Hindus

D. he wanted the dignity of man to be restored

20. Preaching of a prophet becomes empty slogans because?

A. We take it in its letter, not in spirit

B. We do not find it very relevant to the present way of life

C. We use it for achieving our selfish motive

D. We think that the preaching is for others to follow and not for us

21. Martin Luther King's name is associated with:

A. removal of social inequality

B. removal of apartheid

C. removal of poverty

D. removal of illiteracy

22. Non-violence implies:

A. merely physical non-violence

B. conformity and dependence

C. tolerance and compassion

D. upholding the dignity of man

23. The examples of Christ, Gandhiji and Martin Luther King are quoted in this passage to show that:

A. non-violence will always subdue violence

B. violence will pervade always

C. the cult of the sword, end with the sword

D. the opponents of violence themselves become victims of violence, but their death gives greater force to non voilence

24. "Caesar dead is more powerful than Caesar alive" this statement indicates that:

A. Martyrdom is desirable

B. Christianity originated from crucification

C. The great ideologies remain even though its exponents are extinguished

D. Apartheid could be eliminated by Martin Luther King's assassination

25. Some essential competencies of the effectiveness of a teacher are given below. Which combination of these competencies is most essential?

(i) Motivating the students

(ii) Organizing co-curricular programmes

(iii) Helping in college administration

(iv) Insisting on strict discipline

(v) adapting to new challenges

A. (i), (ii) and (iii) B. (iii), (iv) and (v)

C. (i), (ii) and (v) D. (ii), (iii), and (iv)

26. In a class of heterogeneous students, it is better for the teacher to:

(i) focus attention on the majority of students who are average

(ii) give special attention to the bright students in the class

(iii) conduct special classes for the benefit of slow learners

(iv) arrange remedial teaching sessions for the poor achievers

(v) Plan enrichment programmes for the bright learners

A. (i), (ii) and (iii) B. (ii), (iii) and (iv)

C. (i), (iii) and (v) D. (i), (iv) and (v)

27. When a teacher finds that most of the students in the class score poor marks in a test paper in his subject, which is the best strategy to be adopted?

A. Adopting strict and punitive measures to ensure that all students prepare well for the examinations.

B. Re-teach the entire portions so that everyone understands the topics included in the test paper ?

C. Provide more effective learning experiences and adopt remedial measures for the topics

D. Use different teaching aids and give more explanations for the topics in question

28. Indiscipline in the class is mainly due to:

A. the lack of interest of students in the subject

B. the monotonous nature of the subject and the inclusion of topics which are not intellectually challenging

C. the facilities available in the class-room are inadequate

D. the presentation strategy adopted by the teacher is neither sequential nor effctive

29. Which of the following is the best feedback for a teacher in higher classes?

A. The answer scripts of the students and the acceptance of the teacher given by students

B. The comments made by the school principal

C. The appreciation given by higher authorities

D. The everlasting influence of the teacher on the personality of the students

30. One of the following does not relate to the introductory phase of a lesson. Identify this phase from the given alternatives:

A. Motivating students

B. Testing their previous knowledge

C. Giving assignments and references sources

D. Presenting an overall picture of the topic

31. Match the items in column A with the items in column B.

a. Unitary University	(i) Bangalore University
b. Federal University	(ii) Gandhigram University
c. Deemed University	(iii) Aligarh Muslim University
d. Affiliated University	(iv) IGNOU
e. Open University	(v) Delhi University

A. a(iii) b(v) c(ii) d(i) e(iv)

B. b(ii) b(iii) c(i) d(iv) e(v)

C. c(i) b(ii) c(iv) d(v) e(iii)

D. a(iv) b(i) c(v) d(ii) e(iii)

32. AICTE is a regulatory committee and a statutory body for controlling:

A. Medical Education

B. Higher Education

C. Technical Education

D. Agricultural Education

33. What is the full form of NAAC?

A. National Aeronautic and Applied Courses

B. National Assessment and Accreditation Council

C. National Agency for Aviation Courses

D. National Academy for Administrative Careers

34. Central University of English and Foreign Languages (CUEFL) is located in:

A. Delhi B. Hyderabad

C. Mumbai D. Kolkotta

35. The Chancellor of a state affiliating University is:

A. The Governor of the State

B. The Education Minister of the state

C. An elected dignitary

D. The Chief Minister of the State

36. An Autonomous College is different from an Affiliated College under university in the following respect:

A. The former has no senate or syndicate to regulate its functions

B. The latter has control over a large jurisdiction

C. The latter has a centralised system of curriculum and evaluation.

D. The former has freedom for deciding curriculum, conducting evaluation and awarding degrees

37. The brain of the computer is called:

A. RAM B. ROM

C. CPU D. BIOS

38. What is the smallest unit of data in a computer?

A. Bit B. Byte

C. Exobit D. MB

39. What is the name of the unit of a computer where the operating system and data in current use are stored?

A. Microprocessor B. RAM

C. ROM D. System tray

40. A computer port is used to:

A. communicate with other computer peripherals

B. download files from the web

C. communicate with all hard drives

D. connect computers together

41. Which one works as an output and input device in a computer?

A. Modem B. Scanner C. Mouse D. Monitor

42. HTML is:

A. a computer software package

B. a programming language

C. an input device

D. a storage device

The following graph gives the ratio of the amounts of imports by a company to its amount of exports over a period from 1995 to 2001.

Graph of the Ratio Value of Imports to Exports of company X from 1995-2001

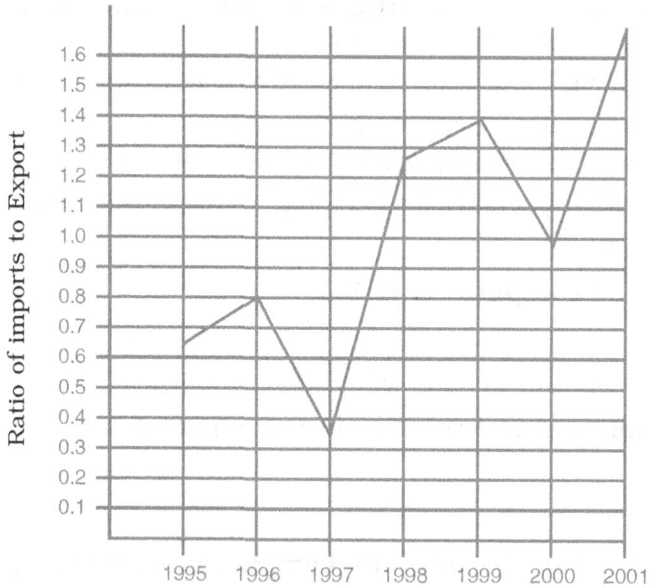

43. In how many of the given years were exports more than imports?

A. 1 B. 2 C. 3 D. 4

44. The ratio of the exports to imports was least during the year:

A. 1995 B. 1996 C. 1997 D. 2000

Study the pi-diagram given below and answer the questions 45 and 46.

Distribution of graduates in 10 optimal subjects offered in a college

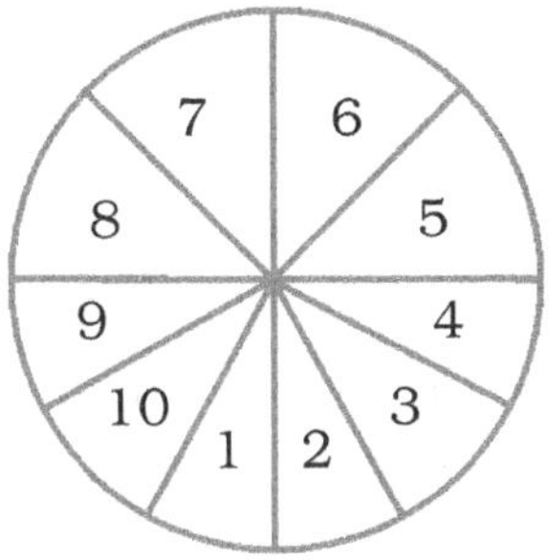

1. Physics
2. Chemistry
3. Biology
4. Mathematics
5. Commerce
6. Psychology
7. English
8. History
9. Microbiology
10. Economics

45. If the total number of graduates is 2500, how many are studying History and English put together?

A. 360 B. 478

C. 625 D. 600

Note: Number is proportion to the central Angles for region 5, 6, 7, 8 one 45° each. Angles for regions 9, 10,1, 2, 3, 4 are each 30°. Total angle at the unit = 360°.

46. Which of the following statements is correct if the total number of graduates is 1250?

A. Total students enrolled in Physics, Commerce and Psychology are 625.

B. In Physics, Chemistry and Biology there are more students when compared to Mathematics, Commerce and Psychology.

C. Equal number of students have been enrolled in Psychology and Commerce.

D. Total number of students in English, Maths and Microbiology are 400.

The table below shows the number of candidates appearing and passing in competitive examination from various categories of localities during the years 1990-95. Study the table and answer questions 47 and 48.

Year	Rural		Semi Urban		State Capital		Metropolis	
	Appeared	Passed	Appeared	Passed	Appeared	Passed	Appeared	Passed
1990	1652	208	7894	2513	5054	1468	9581	3214
1991	1839	317	8562	2933	7164	3248	10,158	4018
1992	2153	932	8139	2468	8258	3159	9695	3038
1993	5032	1798	9432	3528	8529	3628	11,247	5158
1994	4915	1658	9784	4015	9015	4311	12,518	6328
1995	5628	2392	9969	4263	1725	4526	13,624	6419

47. From which area did the candidates register a continuous, increase in both appearing for the examination and passing in the same examination?

A. Semi urban

B. State Capital

C. State capital and rural

D. None of the above

48. In which year was the percentage of candidates from semi urban areas the lowest?

A. 1991

B. 1993

C. 1990

D. 1992

49. In any research endeavour, a researcher should:

A. try to know everything in the area without going into the details relating to the sub-areas coming under it

B. try to penetrate deeper and deeper in to a specific sub-area identified for study

C. not to jump into conclusions until he collects enough data to support his hypothesis

D. refute his findings if they do not substantiate the hypothesis he has set

50. The 'Sine qua non' of a good research is:

A. A well defined problem

B. A properly stated hypothesis

C. clearly stated objectives

D. An expert superwising teacher

51. Which of the following statements describes the research process?

A. a process of problem solving

B. an enquiry to find out the truth

C. a hypothetico-deductive scientific approach for generating new knowledge

D. an objective attempt to study all relevant aspects a phenomenon systematically

52. What do you think is the most essential requirement for conducting research?

A. A good library

B. A researcher with an analytical mind

C. An experienced research supervisor

D. A research centre with a good research library of facilities

53. The most important characteristic of a good research is:

A. expertise of the research guide

B. use of sophisticated methodology

C. systematically prepared research report

D. knowledge of research procedures and the scientific attitude possessed by the researcher

54. A researcher should:

A. collect data to prove his hypothesis

B. collect as much data as possible relating to his research topic

C. collect data that will help to widen his knowledge about the problem

D. collect data to use advanced statistical designs

55. Under which category of communication would you include the 'facial expression' of your students while teaching?

A. Source

B. Feedback

C. Message

D. Media

56. In modern distance education, the curricular programmes are often communicated using:

A. radio B. printmedia

C. Multimedia D. Telecasts

57. Which one of the following is the most desirable practice for teaching in higher education institutions?

A. deliver carefully prepared lecture

B. deliver lectures along with LCD presentations

C. dictate notes on topics relevant for the final examinations

D. students are made to refer to original sources and led to first-hand experiences through projects, seminars and discussions.

58. Which one of the following is the most efficient as a communication booster for teaching in colleges?

A. Over head Projector B. Slide Projector

C. L.C.D. Projector D. Film Projector

59. Which one of the following aspects of communication is not desirable while teaching in college?

A. Reversing B. Illustrating

C. Focussing D. Narrating

60. Among the alternative strategies given below, which is the most effective for class room communication?

A. Teacher providing the global view of the content and relates it to past experience before the delivery of the content.

B. Teacher writes the caption on the blackboard and starts explaining the content

C. Giving indications regarding future references of the content being taught.

D. Relying on the prescribed text and clarifying and supplementing it with teacher's expansions.

Answer keys

1.C	2.D	3.B	4.A	5.B	6.A	7.B	8.D	9.C	10.D
11.C	12.D	13.B	14.C	15.D	16.D	17.C	18.C	19.C	20.A
21.B	22.C	23.D	24.C	25.C	26.D	27.C	28.D	29.D	30.C
31.A	32.C	33.B	34.B	35.A	36.D	37.C	38.A	39.B	40.A
41.A	42.B	43.D	44.C	45.C	46.C	47.D	48.D	49.B	50.A
51.C	52.B	53.D	54.C	55.B	56.C	57.D	58.C	59.A	60.A

MODEL QUESTION PAPER - 4

Note : This paper contains **sixty** (60) multiple choice questions, each carrying **two** (2) marks. Answer any **fifty** (50) questions. The total time for completing the paper is 75 minutes and the total marks for the paper is 100.

1. **Which one of the following statements about teachers do you accept as the most valid?**

   A. Good teachers are born and not made

   B. Any one can become a good teacher

   C. Both training and inherent qualities combine to make a good teacher

   D. Quality teacher-training can make a good teacher

2. **Which of the following is most important agency in the education of students of higher education**

   A. Family B. Parents

   C. Media D. Libraries and Websites

3. **Which factor is to be treated as the most important factor to be considered in framing a curriculum ?**

   A. Teacher's potentialities

   B. Student's capabilities and needs

   C. National ideologies

   D. Social and cultural ideals

4. **Education makes a human being to become:**

   A. Refined B. Socially efficient

   C. Critical D. All these

5. **Which one of the following facilities to be given least priority in higher education?**

   A. provision for drinking water B. facility for changing dress

   C. toilet facilities D. rest rooms

6. **An investigation of a single individual, group, or institution, or culture is called a:**

   A. Survey Research

   B. Construction Research

   C. Case study

   D. Ethnographic Research

7. The Research process takes definite shape only after:

A. data collection

B. formulation

C. report preparation

D. statistical analysis of data

8. In research study where data is to be collected using a questionnaire, the main factors to be considered are:

A. relating the items to the objectives of the study

B. determining which aspects of the data can be collected using the questionnaire

C. including items for which dependable responses can be obtained through questions

D. All of these

9. Which of the following is not a term used in historical research in education?

A. Internal criticism

B. Oral testimony

C. Secondary sources

D. Sampling designs

10. Four different definitions of educational research by experts define research as:

A. Manipulation of select variables to study their impact on another significant variable

B. Developing procedures for running the system of education using scientific methods

C. Developing verified knowledge for adoption by professionals in education

D. Creation of scientific new knowledge in education to add to the theory of education or for creating new practices in education

Read the following passage and answer the questions 11 to 15

The educational value of providing learning experiences which appeal to the eye as well as to the ears is well accepted. The inability of education to appeal to the eye is now accepted as a handicap to providing quality education. The system is now attempting to correct these drawbacks. Exhibitions are important ways for visual education that has gained great popularity in recent years. Exhibitions of collections of artistic and historical relevance like those in the world famous Victoria and Albert Museum in London provide valuable experiences. A natural focus for this particular form of education through the eye is the local museum. Museums and galleries play an increasingly important part in the educational life of their localities full stop. Possibly their greatest contribution is in the field of adult education. If they are valuable as a base for the display of material supplied from outside sources, they have a more important function of fostering local distinctions and tradition of all kinds. This they can do by their permanent collections, by special exhibitions circulated to other centres in the locality, for example, to colleges of further education or to community centres. An outstanding value of the exhibition method is that it does not provide instruction only, but by the display of works of craftsmanship and art it gives a training in appreciation, a sense of quality and individual character.

Another most important medium for visual education is the cine-film and at the present time the supply of specially produced educational films is being rapidly increased. The film, like the exhibition, is well adapted for demonstration of practical activities and skills of all kinds, and to the communication of cultural ideas and values. But it has a further distinctive contribution of particular importance in education. Owing to the exceptionally strong emotional impact of the cinema, films dealing with controversial topics-as, for example, the whole range upon to provoke discussion and arouse interest in current problems. There are now a number of sources for educational films.

Mention should also be made of the humbler filmstrip, which consists of a series of pictures printed on lengths of cine film and projected like miniature lantern slides. Being cheap and easily handled, they are an ideal means for illustrating informal demonstrations and lectures. These are already obtainable for a wide range of subjects from several commercial producers, and are likely to be supplied in increasing number from public sources. For those who still prefer the ordinary lantern slide, the largest and most accessible public collection, is that of the accessible Victoria and Albert Museum.

11. Exhibition have become a popular medium for education because:

A. it helps to increase the effectiveness of teaching by making learning more concrete

B. it appears to the sense of sight

C. it has become popular in all advanced educational systems

D. it is the most economic and practical way to teach

12. The educational potential of museums and galleries, in the opinion of the writer, is to be attributed to:

A. their entertainment value

B. their educational impact

C. their capacity to draw the people closer to reality

D. their capacity to cater to a wide array of learners

13. The author considers the exhibition method as outstanding:

A. because it blends fun with education

B. because it can be conducted in localities where it is in most demand

C. because it will increase popular interaction

D. because it comes closest to first-hand practical training

14. The author of the passage is of the opinion that the cinefilm is another most important visual education; because

A. it displays different practical activities against the background of differing cultural contexts

B. it appeals it our emotional faculty, creating a long-lasting impact

C. it is welcomed as the most convenient medium to educate people

D. people have natural inclination to watch the attractive display

15. The Visual education, in the opinion of the writer:

A. is the only answer to educate people

B. can make an impact only on the urban people

C. is likely to become an effective medium to educate the poor villagers

D. demands a huge investment for operation

16. Which of the following media, according to you, would be an ideal method for pushing the sales of chocolates among children, in a locality?

A. TV (advertisements) B. Radio

C. Newspapers D. Cinema

17. Which of the following is not a traditional medium for publicity?

A. Music B. TV

C. Literature D. Painting

18. "Cultivation of the dominant image patterns" was very similar to his mass communication theory. The name of this person is:

A. Donald L. Shaw B. Maxwell Mc Combs

C. George Gerber D. Davidson

19. Which of the following does not provide entertainment to the targeted audience?

A. Leaflets B. TV programmes

C. Magazines D. Newspaper, features

20. Telecasting TV educational programmes is useful because:

A. It affords the opportunity for large audience in the same auditorium or in different locations, to view the programme clearly

B. It can magnify the microscopic forms of life presented through the TV

C. It can present the natural phenomenon of the world in a natural form

D. All these

21. Pointing to a woman in a photograph Ajay says, "She is the daughter of the daughter of the only son of my grandfather". How is the lady related to Ajay?

A. Sister B. Maternal Aunt

C. Niece D. Mother

22. Identify the most suitable answer from among the given choices. People wear goggles because:

A. They protect their eyes from dazzling light

B. They conceal their eyes

C. They look handsome with them

D. They see better with their help

Direction (Q 23-25): Each questions contains two statements followed by four conclusions. Read the conclusions carefully and decide which of them logically follows from the given statements.

Mark answer A. if I follows from the statements

Mark answer B. if I, II and III follow from the statements

Mark answer C. if II and III follow from the statements

Mark answer D. if all the statements I to IV follows from the statements

23. Statements:

(a) All microprocessors are computers

(b) All computers are modems

Conclusions:

I. All microprocessors are modems.

II. All modems are micro-computers

III. All modems are computers.

IV. None of these

24. Statements:

(a) All worms are mosquitoes.

(b) All mosquitos are birds.

Conclusions:

I. All mosquitoes are worms.

II. All worms are birds.

III. All birds are mosquitoes.

IV. None of these

25. Statements:

(a) All sauces are pickles

(b) Some sauces are ketchup.

Conclusions:

I. All ketchup are sauces

II. All pickles are ketchup

III. All sauces are ketchup

IV. None of these.

Directions: Assuming that the first proposition is false, how will you treat the following propositions?

26. Only atheists are communists.

I. Whoever is not an atheist is other than a communist.

II. Anyone who is not a communist fails to be an atheist.

A. I is false B. II is false C. Both are false D. Both are correct

27. Which of the following Venn diagrams represents Frame, Model, Painting?

A. 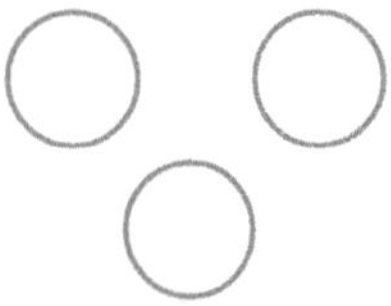

B. 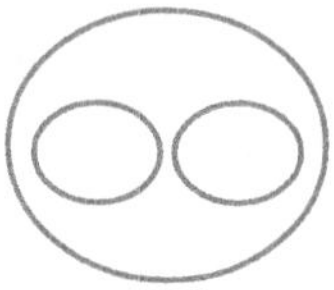

C. 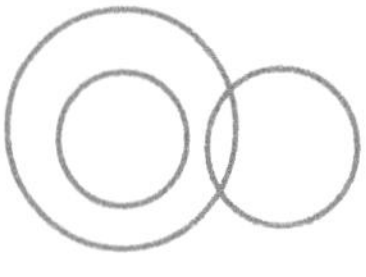

D. 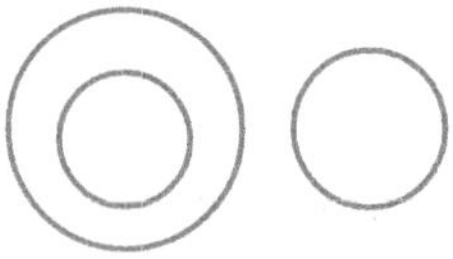

28. Hunt the odd man out:

A. Manmohan Singh B. Zail Singh C. Atal Bihari Vajpeyi D. Rajiv Gandhi

29. From the following statement, which argument is forceful?

Statement:

Do you think Indira Gandhi International Airport is safe for luggages?

Argument:

I. Yes, Of course, Returning of G.Q. Sheikh's bag with ₹ 18,500 cash and Jaan Muhammad's luggage with ₹ 5000 pounds evidence the honesty of the staff.

II. No, many people never get back luggages they lose.

A. Both I and II B. None of I and II

C. Only I D. Only II

30. Which of the following arguments is forceful?

Statement

If water pollution continues at this rate, it will eventually make oxygen molecules unavailable to water plants.

Assumptions :

I. Water pollution affects the growth of water plants.

II. Water pollution reduces the availability of oxygen in water.

A. Only I B. Only II

C. Both I and II D. None of I and II

Directions: Questions (31 to 35) are based on the following diagram of World Population. Study this diagram carefully and select one of the choices which appears to you as the answers:

World Population 1980-81

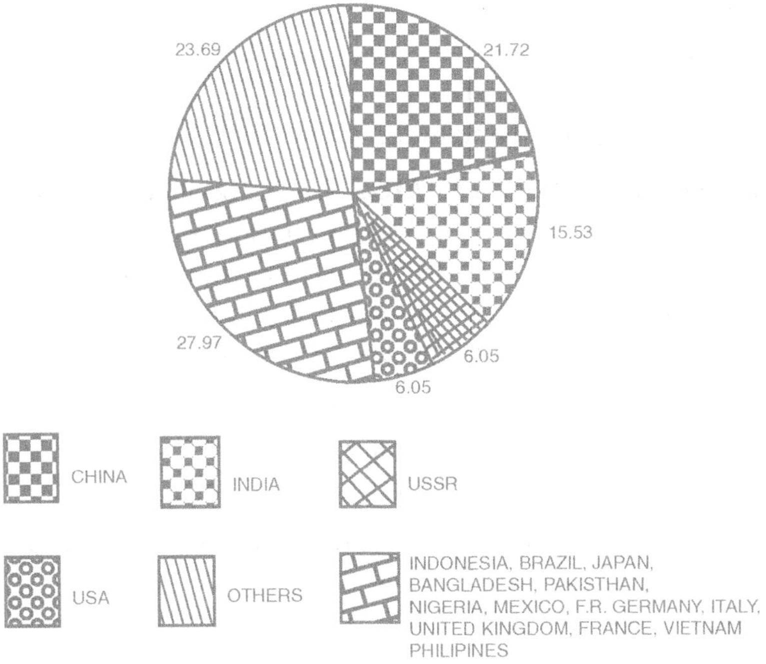

31. Which of the following statements is correct about the population of different countries?

A. India is among the four countries with the highest population in the world

B. India is among the three countries with the highest population in the world.

C. India is among the two countries with the highest population in the world.

D. India is the country with the highest population in the world

32. Among the countries which constitute 27.97% of the world population, which of following five countries are given in the descending order of their population

A. Indonesia, Brazil, Japan, Bangladesh and Pakistan

B. Nigeria, Mexico, Federal Republic of Germany, Italy and U.K.

C. France, Vietnam, Philippines, Indonesia and Brazil.

D. Cannot be ascertained on the basis of the given data.

33. India's population is higher than that of the combined population of U.S.S.R. and U.S.A. by:

A. 8.48 B. 10.49

C. 3.43 D. 6.05

34. The first four major countries of the world with the highest population, arranged in the descending order of magnitude are:

A. India, China, U.S.S.R. and U.S.A.

B. China, India, U.S.S.R. and U.S.A.

C. U.S.A., U.S.S.R., India and China

D. U.S.S.R., U.S.A., China and India

35. The aggregate population of China and India accounts for:

A. less than one quarter of the world population in 1980-81

B. less than the population of USA as per the estimate for 1980-81

C. less than 30 percent of the world population during the year 1980-81

D. over 37 percent of the world population during the year 1980-81

36. Internet Message Access Protocol persuits __________ mode of email access

A. Online B. Offline

C. Global D. None of the above

37. Security problem(s) that a PC can create in a Local Area Network are:

A. Multiplication Factor

B. Channel Factor

C. Both Multiplication and Channel Factors

D. Division Factor

38. Of the following, which is not an advantage of distributed processing over centralized processing?

A. If a disaster occurs at one site, processing can be continued in another site

B. It is easier to implement security controls in distributed processing than in a centralized processing arrangement

C. Investment is not huge and made one time, the system can be allowed to grow gradually

D. The cost of a communication subsystem is lower than that of a centralized system

39. The class of control used to overcome problems in communication system before they multiply is called:

A. Preventive B. Detective

C. Corrective D. Suggestive

40. The IT programme initiated by Government of India to create an IT infrastructure within all higher education institutes is known as:

A. Gyan Vahini

B. Sankhya Vahini

C. Vidya Vahini

D. None of these

41. On which region on the globe is the atmospheric pressure highest

A. At the South Pole

B. At the North Pole

C. At the Equator

D. Is the region between the two ( ) 30N and 30S

42. Which is the zone of the earth where the sun never appears at its zenith?

A. Sub-Arctic Zone

B. The Torrid Zone

C. The Temperate Zone

D. All the above

43. Which one of the following strategies will help to reduce the effects of global-warming?

A. Forest conservation

B. Energy conservation

C. Water conservation

D. Soil conservation

44. Which one of the following source of energy is rarely used by human beings?

A. Wind energy

B. Geo-thermal energy

C. Solar energy

D. Nuclear Energy

45. VOC stands for

A. Voice of Congo

B. Volatile Organic Chemical

C. Voluntary Organisation conservationists

D. Voice of Conscience

46. Extension Education as used in the country stands for:

A. Nonformal education intended to spread knowledge about new practices useful for development among villagers

B. A programme for educating the farmers

C. Extending educational opportunities to the socially deprived

D. Extending new knowledge to the doorstep of those who need it

47. A redistic approach towards education should be to define it as:

A. preparation for employment

B. a divine calling for disseminating knowledge

C. a formal process which will help human resource development

D. a system which helps to acquire educational qualifications

48. Which one of the following stands for "equal educational opportunity"?

A. Ensuring admission to all who desire to set a particular type of education

B. Providing opportunity for all to get education at any level

C. Provision of the same type of education for all who join schools

D. Providing equal opportunity to share the type of education for which one is most suited.

49. The most important factor to be taken into account by teachers in higher education institution is:

A. lead students to achieve high scores in the examination

B. lead students to the sources of information and use them for creating new knowledge

C. prepare students for the prestigious competitive examinations

D. providing the relevant information to students which help them to get high scores in the university examinations

50. The most important difference between informal education and non-formal education is that

A. The former is subjective, while the latter is objective

B. The former occurs within formal institutions, while the latter occurs outside such institution

C. The former is not organised, while the latter is organised

D. All of the above

51. Which of the following states had a central University before 11th five year plan?

A. Himachal Pradesh B. Kerala

C. Tamil Nadu D. Andhra Pradesh

52. Shiv Nadar is the head of:

A. HCL B. Infosys

C. Hotmail D. None of these

53. The levels of DDT in the bone tissue is highest among the:

A. Canadians B. Americans

C. Indians D. Chinese

54. The legislative functions of the Council of Ministers of the Union Government in India include the right to:

A. summon and prorogue the two Houses of Parliament

B. nominate two Anglo-Indian members to the Lok Sabha

C. nominate six members to the Rajya Sabha

D. introduce important legislative resolutions in the Parliament and convert them into laws of the country

55. In a group, 25 read HT, 35 read TOI, 5 read both, 2 don't read any of the above. The number of persons in the group is:

A. 59 B. 53

C. 55 D. 57

56. The most popular parametric test used by statisticians is based on:

A. the F-distribution B. the student -r distribution

C. the normal distribution D. none of these

57. Which of the following doesn't provide DTH Service in India?

A. Airtel B. Videocon

C. Sun D. Vodafone Essar

58. Five persons A,B,C,D and E occupy seat in a row such that A and B sit next to each other. In how many possible ways can these five people sit?

A. 24 B. 48

C. 72 D. 96

59. Examine the statement below and some of the conclusions drawn from it. Identify the correct conclusion. Statement : Smoking is injurious to health

Conclusions

I : All cigarettes are injurious to health.

II : Some smokers have proper health.

A. Only I follows

B. Only II follows

C. Both I and II are follow

D. None of these

60. In a certain code, ROUNDS is written as RONUDS. How will PLEASE be written in the same code?

A. PLAESE B. PLAESE

C. LPAEES D. PLASEE

Answer keys

1.C	2.D	3.B	4.D	5.B	6.C	7.B	8.D	9.D	10.D
11.A	12.D	13.D	14.B	15.C	16.A	17.B	18.B	19.A	20.D
21.C	22.A	23.A	24.B	25.A	26.C	27.C	28.B	29.B	30.B
31.C	32.D	33.C	34.B	35.D	36.A	37.C	38.B	39.A	40.B
41.D	42.C	43.A	44.D	45.B	46.A	47.C	48.D	49.B	50.C
51.D	52.A	53.C	54.D	55.B	56.B	57.D	58.B	59.A	60.B

MODEL QUESTION PAPER - 5

Note : This paper contains **sixty** (60) multiple choice questions, each carrying **two** (2) marks. Answer any **fifty** (50) questions. The total time for completing this paper is 75 minutes and the total marks for the paper is 100.

1. **Which one of the following stands for secret entry into a place with dishonest institutions?**

   A. elusive B. slink C. sneak D. cipher

2. **Loss and compensation have the same relationship as:**

   A. success and failure
   B. disease and prevention
   C. profit and loss
   D. damage and repair

3. **Read the following statements and choose the correct term to be used for the classification of each of three statements**

   (i) Candidates from afluent families cannot become good soldiers.
   (ii) He is the son of our chief justice. He must be a very brilliant boy.
   (iii) Obesity is closely related to cardiac complaints.
   (iv) Have proper sleep, even during your examination time.
   (v) Ruling parties will always lose the next election.

	Fact	opinion	prejudice	assumption	advice
A.	(i)	(ii)	(v)	(iv)	(iii)
B.	(v)	(i)	(ii)	(iii)	(iv)
C.	(iii)	(v)	(i)	(ii)	(iv)
D.	(ii)	(i)	(v)	(iii)	(iv)

4. **Farmers become more fatalists when they have to depend upon the weather over which they have no control. Modern technology introduced in Japan made its farmers independent of the weather. Therefore the farmers in Japan are much less fatalists when compared to their counterparts in India. This inference is:**

   A. correct
   B. not correct because all farmers in India are not fatalists
   C. not correct because some farmers in Japan are fatalists
   D. not correct because age-old beliefs will not change.

5. **The World Trade Organisation believes in Intellectual Property and Liberalised Trade Regime. This is based on the assumption that:**

A. modern economy bestows equal benefits
B. knowledge based economy and globalisation is a reality
C. all countries are well suited for modern trade
D. rich countries will always help the poor countries

Study the table given below and answer questions 6 and 7

Rice production in different Indian states during period 1960-61 to 1975-76

STATES	1960-61	1965-66	1970-71	1975-76
Andhra Pradesh	281.8	301.9	392.1	855.2
West Bengal	471.4	461.9	495.3	901.1
Gujarat	381.0	409.7	580.3	1100.2
Kerala	398.4	489.4	585.4	1236.3
Maharashtra	412.4	455.3	590.2	1413.4
Punjab	510.7	390.2	599.0	1500.1
Rajastan	286.8	313.2	420.0	1001.1
Orissa	303.9	326.2	393.0	1009.3

6. **Which state has registered the maximum decline in rank from 1960-61 to 1975-76.**
A. West Bengal B. Andhra Pradesh
C. Rajastan D. Orissa

7. **The top ranking rice producer in India during 1970-71 was:**
A. Punjab and Maharashtra B. Kerala and Gujarat
C. West Bengal and Kerala D. Punjab and Gujarat

Study the graph given below and answer the question based on it

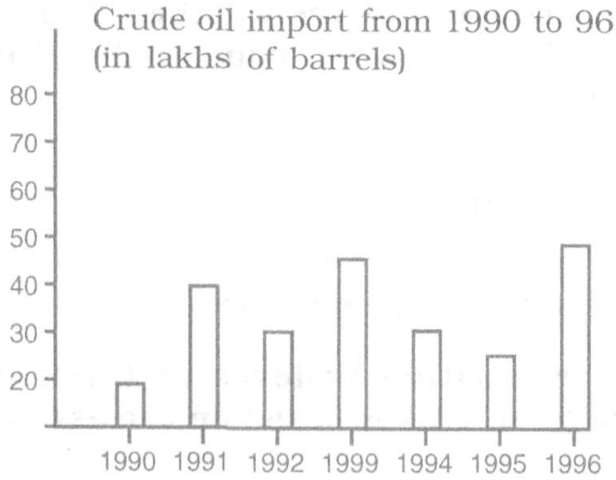

8. If the rate of one barrel of crude oil was ₹ 25 in 1994, what was the total value of import in that year?

A. ₹ 64.00 crores B. ₹ 220.00 lakhs

C. ₹ 2.25 crores D. ₹ 8.2 crores

Study the following diagram and answer question 9.

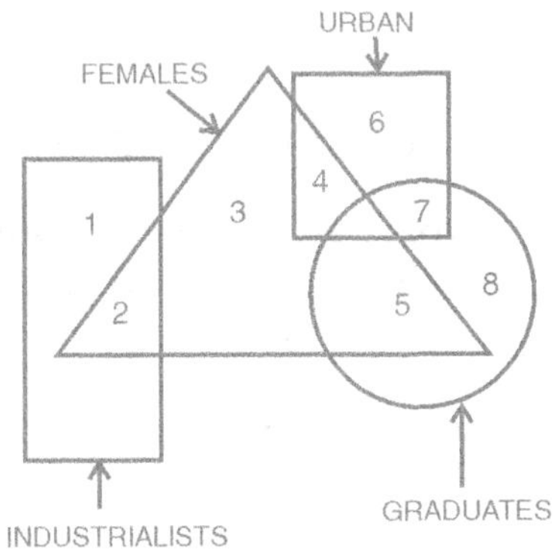

9. The graduate females are represented by the area in the diagram numbered.

A. 4 B. 5 C. 6 D. 7

Study the pi-diagram given below (which represents the average annual expenditure of a family on different items. Answer question 10 based on this diagram.

10. The percentage expenditure of the family on education and clothes is:

A. 37.5 B. 33.5 C. 25.0 D. 27.3

11. Find the correct answer using the following code. 97#67=3; 65#38=0; 90#43=2. If so, what is 87#41?

A. 10 B. 11 C. 9 D. 2

12. COLD : DQOI:: HEAT:..........?

A. IHFX B. IGEY C. JGFY D. IFCX

13. Find the missing number in the following figure:

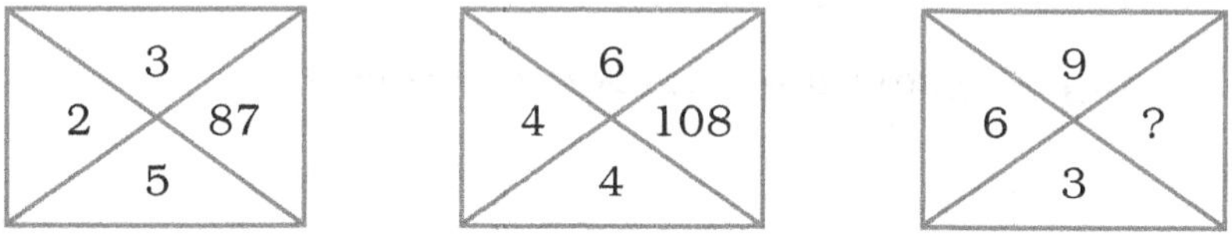

A. 180 B. 141 C. 129 D. 21

14. In a code language, the word 'BOLD' gets coded as 'DQNF' what is the world in the code language is expressed as 'JQPGUV'?

A. FOREST B. PORTEL C. HONEST D. LSRIWY

15. If the Second Saturday of a month is 8th, what will be the 4th Wednesday of that month?

A. 19 B. 21 C. 26 D. 25

16. Which of the following is the most important objective of teaching in higher education?

A. to provide guidance to the students in which they had to learn

B. prepare students for some of the vocations in high social demand

C. to enable students to score good marks in examinations and ensure them a respectable job

D. develop to the full potentialities of students including their personal and social competencies for this 21st century scenario

17. A tool for evaluating students performance will be reliable if:

A. it measures what is aims to measure

B. it yields the same scores to the same group of students irrespective of the time and place of administration

C. it objectively measures the performance it is expected to measure

D. it provides quantifiable scores for student assessment

18. In higher education institutions I would prefer a model of teaching which will help me to present through

A. Lectures to be followed by notes which will help them to remember the facts presented

B. Seminars and projects

C. Lecture followed by assignments

D. Dictation of notes followed by periodical tests

19. Which of the following activity is not related to the development phase of a lesson in the class room?

A. Testing the previous knowledge

B. Using illustrations

C. Progressive differentiation of the concept with the previously learned ones

D. Asking question involving intellectual challenges

20. If a student is found to be gloomy and lethargic in the class room, it is better to:

A. ignore him and continue the lesson

B. send him out of the class

C. enquire the reasons for his behavior privately

D. scold him for his lack of interest in learning

21. The research endeavour is:

A. a process which will help to improve teaching

B. one scientific method for solving problem connected with the theory/practice of education

C. a process of enquiry prescribed by the research supervisor

D. an academic exercise to refute the existing theories and practices in education

22. "Research projects very rarely lead to discoveries." This is because:

A. quality research is not easy to be practised

B. most researchers do not have the depth of knowledge to do quality research

C. the freedom of the researchers to curtailed often by their research supervisors

D. path-breathing discoveries are the results of divergent thinking which is often not present is most researchers

23. A research hypothesis is:

A. one suggested by experts in the area

B. deduced from the existing theories and experiences of the researches

C. what emerged from the review of related literature by the researcher

D. what one gets at while analysing the collected data

24. If a researcher wants to test the effectiveness of two different strategies, the most appropriate method of research will be:

A. survey method of research

B. ex-post facto research
C. experimental research
D. causal-comparative research

25. A good researcher should try to:
A. understand everything in his area of research in a very global perspective
B. concentrate on specific areas and delve deeply into that area
C. collect as much data as possible so as to make the study comprehensive
D. ignore the part of the data that is likely to disprove his hypothesis

Read the following passage and answer questions 26 to 30

The current views of morality are not of a very high order; some believe that morality is not something that needs to be studied by scholars and researchers. Some others think that morality is not related to religion. But an examination of the world's religions would show that without morality, religions cannot subsist. True morality covers religions for the most part. Anyone who observes the laws of morality for his own sake and not for any selfish end can be regarded as religious. There are groups in Russia who have come forward to dedicate their lives to the good of their country. Such men are truly moral. A man like the social activist J. Bentham, who discovered many good principles for English legislation and, tried very hard to spread education among the English and took a prominent part in improving the condition of the prisoners, such people may be regarded as truly moral.

Besides, it is a rule of ideal morality that it is not enough to follow the trodden path. We ought to follow the path which we know to be true, whether it is familiar or unfamiliar to us. In other words, when we know a particular path to be the right one we should set out on it without fear. We can progress only if we observe the laws of morality in this way. That is why true morality, true civilization and true progress are always to be found together.

If we examine our desires, we shall see that we do not wish for what we already have. We always value more that which we do not have. But desires are of two kinds. One is the pursuit of mere self-interest To attempt to fulfil this kind of desire, is immoral. The other impels us constantly to improve ourselves and to do good to others. We should never become overweening with any amount to good that we actually are longing to achieve do more good. True morality consists in our effort to realize such longing.

If we have no home or family of our own, that is nothing to be ashamed of. But if we have a home and abuse it, or own a business and practise fraud, we stray, from the path of morality. Morality consists in doing what we ought to do. We can prove the need for morality with a few Illustrations. Destruction has been the lot of peoples or families in which the seeds of immorality, such as disunity and untruth were permitted to be practised. To take an example from trade and business, we do not come across a single person who will say that truth should not be followed. The effect of justice and goodness is not to be imposed from outside. These qualities are inherent in us and should come from within.

Four hundred years ago, much injustice and untruth prevailed in Europe, so that people could not rest in peace even for a moment. The cause of this state of affairs was that the people had no sense of morality. We find that the attempt to do good to mankind is the highest level of morality. If we open the treasure-house of morality with this key, we shall find in it all the other principles.

26. According to the author of this passage, we should follow:

A. The trodden path

B. The universal religion

C. The unfamiliar path

D. The path of truth

27. Desire according to the author is immoral if it is:

A. a longing for something that one has

B. a longing for what one aspires for

C. a pursuit of self interest

D. a longing accompanied by lack of self control

28. The most appropriate title for the passage is:

A. Morality and Immorality

B. The ideal way to live

C. Good and Evil

D. Morality in life

29. The author says that:

A. The good we do is not be measured by us

B. We should not even think of doing evil deeds

C. We should give up our efforts after certain stage

D. We should do as per one mind's dictates

30. What according to the author is the key to open the treasure house of morality?

A. Attempt to do good to mankind is the highest morality

B. Being religious is the path to morality

C. Keeping away from disunity and untruth in all are personal and social activities

D. Fulfil the desires in congruence with the interests of others

31. What according to the author do we desire most?

A. The things that we liked ever since our childhood

B. The things that we had earlier, but which we lost later

C. The things that we do not have

D. The things that others have and we feel we should also have

32. Match the items in column 'I' with those in column 'II'

Column I	Column II
(i) Unitary University	(a) Bangalore and Madras Universities
(ii) Federal University	(b) Gandhigram University
(iii) Deemed University	(c) Aligarh and Benaras Universities
(iv) Affiliating University	(d) NCTE & AICTE
(v) Statutory Body	(e) IGNOU
(vi) Open University	(f) Delhi University

A. (i) & (b) ; (ii) & (c) ; (iii) & (a) ; (iv) & (d) ; (v) & (e) ; (vi) and (f)

B. (i) & (a); (ii) & (c) ; (iii) & (b) ; (iv) & (e) ; (v) & (f) ; (vi) and (d)

C. (i) & (f) ; (ii) & (b) ; (iii) & (c) ; (iv) & (a) ; (v) and (d) ; (vi) and (e)

D. (i) & (f) ; (ii) & (c) ; (iii) & (b) ; (iv) & (a) ; (v) & (d) ; (vi) & (e)

33. Which among the following is not an agency to sanction funds for the development, maintenance and quality improvement of universities?

A. UGC B. ICAR C. ICHR D. NAAC

34. Match the institutions listed in column A with their correct locations in column B

Column A.

1. Central Institute of Cultural Resources and Training
2. Indian Veterinary Research Institute
3. Indian Institute of Science
4. Inter University Centre of Astronomy and Astrophysics

Column B.

(a) Izath Nagar (b) Poone

(c) Delhi (d) Hyderabad

(e) Madras (f) Bangalore

A. (1) (a) ; (2) (c) ; (3) (e) ; (4) (f)

B. (1) (b) ; (2) (d) ; (3) (c) ; (4) (a)

C. (1) (c) ; (2) (a) ; (3) (f) ; (4) (b)

D. (1) (c) ; (2) (b) ; (3) (e) ; (4) (d)

35. Which of the following is not considered as part of technical education in India?

A. Physiotherapy B. Social work
C. Pharmacy D. Management

36. The power to appoint Governors of the states in India is vested in:
A. The Parliament
B. The Central Cabinet
C. The Loksabha & The Rajyasabha
D. The President of India

37. Nagarjun Sagar Project is in the river:
A. Godavari at Orissa
B. Krishna at Andhrapradesh
C. Kaveri at Tamil Nadu
D. Mahanadi at Orissa

38. The percentage of Nitrogen in the atmosphere is close to:
A. 78.1 B. 38.4
C. 71.8 D. 20.9

39. 'Karman Line' is the hypothetical boarder between the:
A. atmosphere and the ionosphere
B. ionosphere and the stratosphere
C. troposphere and the thermosphere
D. atmosphere and the stratosphere

40. The 'Green House Effect' is caused mainly by:
A. water pollution
B. decay of green vegetation on the earth's surface
C. deforestation
D. dissipation of heat blocked by concentration of carbon-di-oxide

41. The 'Red Data Book' stands for:
A. The book that classifies the species facing extinction
B. The book that explains the danger of atmospheric pollution
C. The book which deals will the environment and ecology
D. The book dedicated to environmentalists.

42. Teacher communication in the class room will be more effective only if the teacher:

A. uses instructional aids
B. supplements the textual materials with first hand concrete experiences
C. motivates the students and understands their needs
D. uses the accepted scientific methods for teaching

43. Which one of the following is the best feedback for a university teacher which will help him to understand the efficiency of his instructional strategies?

A. evaluation of students answer sheets and opening the marks scored by students
B. Comments made by students in his group to other students about the teacher's performance competence
C. Appreciation from co workers and authorities
D. The level of student involvement and enthusiasm in attending her class

44. The doubts raised by the students in a class relate to one element of communication Niz:

A. Message B. Feedback C. Receiver D. Source

45. The most important barrier in class room communication is:

A. lack of interest of students in the subject taught
B. interest ( ) by students in what is happening outside the class
C. noise outside the classroom which stands between the teacher and his students
D. teacher's lack of proficiency in communicating

46. Which one of the following strategies provides the maximum interpersonal communication in a class?

A. Lecture presentation
B. Group participation in learning
C. Seminar presentation
D. Brainstorming sessions organised by the teacher

47. Which city in India is known as 'The high-tech city' of the country?

A. Surat B. Pune C. Kolkotta D. Hyderabad.

48. Which are the two major categories of computers?

A. Analog Computers and Digital Computers
B. Mini and Micro Computers
C. Super and Mainframe Computers
D. General and Special Computers

49. What are the popular and most widely used output devices in a computer?

A. VDU and Printers
B. Floppy and Magnetic Tapes
C. CD's and Floppies
D. Hard Disc and Optical Disc

50. The term ERIC as used in ICT stands for:

A. A textual data base
B. The dictionary data base
C. The bibliographic data base
D. None of the above

51. The term 'back bones' as used in ICT stands for:

A. the largest computers on the net, connected by links
B. the central processing unit
C. the data base
D. the satellite transponders

52. Read the following proposition and categorise the inference into one of the four groups listed: "Anything that goes up, will definitely fall down".

Inference: The helicopter goes up; hence
the helicopter will definitely fall down".
This inference is:

A. a valid inference   B. an invalid inference
C. a long drawn inference   D. a probably correct inference

53. Study the graph of the price of three vegetables during a week. Which of the following is a correct inference from the data presented in the graph?

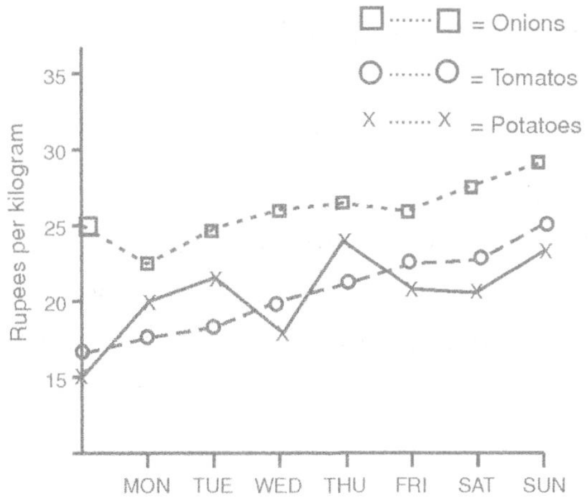

A. The price of all the three items were minimum on Monday

B. The price of potato and onion was maximum on Thursday

C. Among the three vegetables, the price of potatoes uses least on Monday

D. The price of onions was higher than that of tomatos and potatoes throughout the week

54. Pointing to A, B says "Her mothers younger son is my daughter's maternal uncle". What is the relation A with B

A. Mother B. Sister

C. Wife D. Daughter

55. Which one of the following Models of Teaching is most appropriate for making a lecture presentation more effective?

A. Jurisprudential Model

B. Advance Organizer Model

C. Concept Attainment Model

D. Inductive-thinking Model.

56. The validity and quality of a research can be determined by:

A. its acceptability by scholars

B. its publication in a reputed research Journal

C. the representation of the researcher

D. the consistency of its findings with the finding of other reputed researches

57. The status of an institution as a Deemed University is based on a declaration made by:

A. the Chancellor of the University

B. the Human Resource Minister of the country

C. the UGC

D. the Higher Education Council of a state

58. 'Bio-magnification' means:

A. the magnitude of temperature in the bio-sphere

B. the concentration of carbondioxide in the atmosphere

C. the magnified effect of pollution caused by increase in population

D. the accumulation of toxic substances in our body cells

59. Which one of the following doesnot belong to the common group?

A. Interpersonal Communication

B. Intra personal Communication

C. Grape-vine Communication

D. Classroom Communication

60. What does the term 'Parampadma' stand for?

A. The super computer developed by India

B. The software developed to facilitate e-governance

C. The name of the satellite launched by India

D. The name of a website used in computer communication

Answer keys

1.C	2.D	3.C	4.A	5.B	6.A	7.C	8.C	9.B	10.C
11.A	12.B	13.C	14.C	15.C	16.D	17.C	18.B	19.A	20.C
21.B	22.D	23.B	24.C	25.B	26.D	27.C	28.B	29.B	30.A
31.C	32.D	33.C	34.C	35.D	36.B	37.B	38.D	39.D	40.A
41.C	42.D	43.B	44.D	45.C	46.B	47.A	48.A	49.A	50.B
51.B	52.C	53.D	54.C	55.B	56.D	57.C	58.D	59.B	60.A

MODEL QUESTION PAPER - 6

Note : This paper contains **sixty** (60) multiple choice questions, each carrying **two** (2) marks. Answer any **fifty** (50) questions. The total time for completing the paper is 75 minutes and the total marks for the paper is 100.

1. I like teaching profession because:

A. this profession enjoys a high social status

B. it does not demand any hardwork

C. the profession brings you into contact with the young generation

D. this profession is one which places an important social responsibility of moulding the future generation.

2. The most valuable reward for teaching profession is:

A. Job scientification B. Good salary

C. Social approval D. The importance given to it by the Students

3. A teacher should not demand something which is beyond the stage of growth of students if they do so, it is likely to cause:

A. frustration among the pupils

B. make students maladjusted

C. encourage students to learn more earnestly

D. none of these

4. Ancient Indian teachers applied some of the modern psychological principles in educating the young children; an illustrative example is: They recognised the role of :

A. all students taught under the close supervision of the teacher

B. individualized teaching

C. the use of the 'Gurukul' type of schooling

D. reasonable use of punishment to facilitate learning

5. A new generation teacher must have sound knowledge of educational research because :

A. teacher with research qualification will be receiving higher salaries

B. teacher with research training will be more qualified

C. modern education functions using knowledge validated through research

D. those with research training will combine their research with teaching

6. **According to Plato, the main role of education is:**
   A. to develop the power of reasoning of the learners
   B. to create educated citizen
   C. the wholesome development of the of personality of each student
   D. to develop disciplined behaviour

7. **The word 'research' is derived from:**
   A. French B. Spanish
   C. Latin D. Greek

8. **A researcher wants to study the problems faced by school managers in running their schools. Which one of the following tools is most appropriate for him, if he wants to cover a large number of managers in his study?**
   A. Interview Schedule B. Schedule
   C. Mailed Questionnaire D. Rating Scale

9. **Which one of the following statement is not a correct description of educational research?**
   A. A systematic study of problems in education
   B. Use of scientific processes for solving problem facing education
   C. Problem solving for arriving at new generalization about educational practice
   D. An attempt to publish a scholarly work on education

10. **Which one of the following is not a step in educational research?**
   A. Selecting a problem and defining it using scientific terminology
   B. Framing the research questions to be answered
   C. Surveying the research studies conducted in the areas
   D. Rejecting data which disagrees with the stated hypothesis.

11. **The aim of any good research in education is to:**
   A. create acceptable new knowledge relating to either the theory of practice of education.
   B. obtain a doctoral degree which will improve one's job prospects
   C. develop a theme for publishing research papers which will improve one's employment prospects
   D. create a better impression about ourself as a teacher and as a scholar

12. **Ex post facto studies is another name of:**
   A. Analytical Research
   B. Descriptive Research
   C. Fundamental Research
   D. Experimental Research

1. Read the following passage carefully and answer the questions 13 to 17:

In the development of renaissance literature, we are taken much further afield. While Italy was the home of the most famous literary figures of the ``renaissance period, a literature typical of that period was popular in France, England, Germany, and Spain. The evolution of literature from a type dictated by churchmen and scholastics to one embodying secularism and individualism was very similar to the developments taking place in this field of fine arts. Renaissance literature has a strong dose of individualism and specific experience, a widening contact between the writer and everything connected with man. Interest in the scientific study of composition were results of classical influences. Scientific dictionaries for Netherlandish, Italian, German, French, and Spanish were prepared in the 16th century. Von Gesner published (1553) in Latin an analysis of more than 1000 spoken languages, which was the first step towards comparative philology.

Literary criticism had begun by the middle of the 16th century. A group in France with Ronsard as their head, organized a society to reform the French language. That a similar movement was under way in England is shown in a famous work by Sir Philip Sidney, Apologie for Poetrie. While most of these works were efforts to revive the classical spirit, if not the classical language, it is evident that all over Europe vernacular prose was gradually being raised to a position of literary dignity.

13. Prior to the renaissance period:

A. the influence of scholars was dominant in literature

B. the influence of religion was dominant in literature

C. the influence of art was dominant in literature

D. the influence of nationality was dominant in literature

14. The evolution of literature during the renaissance period was:

A. more or less same as development of fine arts during that period

B. totally different from what happened in the field of fine art of that period

C. in some respects dictated by churchmen and scholastics

D. appeared to secularism

15. The chief characteristic of renaissance literature was:

A. renewed interest in the publication of dictionaries

B. shift in literature from secularism to literary pursuits

C. widening contract between the writer and the actual life of the people around

D. preparing a dictionary of 100 spoken languages of Europe.

16. The Renaissance period witnessed:

A. The development of language through the development of literary criticism.

B. The development of language as a method of encouraging the study of science
C. The development of literature as part of a higher attempt to enrich the study of languages
D. The development of a scientific approach in the study of languages.

17. The most famous literary figures of the renaissance period first made their appearance in
A. Italy
B. England
C. Spain
D. Germany

18. When was Education TV first introduced in India?
A. 1954 B. 1958
C. 1959 D. 1970

19. Which one of the following is also referred to as cross-cultural communication?
A. Intra-cultural communication B. Intercultural communication
C. Intrapersonal communication D. Non-verbal communication

20. Experimental studies of communication attempt to analyse:
A. the ways the information processes work and their output
B. use a terminology similar to what is used in computer science
C. use the techniques used for describing a complex concept
D. use a terminology similar to that used in mathematics and engineering

21. Which one of the following teacher behaviours is appropriate if a teacher has to maximise his communication efficiency?
A. preferred treatment to students belonging to particular culture groups
B. derogatory reference to particular castes/communities likely to be present in the class
C. giving full acceptance to every student, ignoring their drawbacks
D. addressing your questions to the better students in the class

22. Which of the following is the most effective method of classroom communication?
A. lecture + Pictures
B. lectures with multimedia methods
C. Presenting written material along with film projections
D. Presenting written material in the form of slides

23. Which of the following works as watchdog of the press in India?

A. Press Trust of India

B. Press Council of India

C. Prasar Bharati

D. Ministry of Information and Broadcasting

24. Find out the odd item among the following:

A. PLENTY : LEPTYN

B. COWARD : OWCRAD

C. ALWINS : LWANIS

D. LOCATE : OCULTAU

25. In a certain code MINJUR is coded as 312574 and TADA as 6898, how can MADURAI be coded in the same pattern?

A. 3498178 B. 3894871

C. 3849781 D. 3897481

26. Insert the missing number.

8 24 12 ? 18 54

A. 26 B. 24 C. 36 D. 32

27. A group of 1200 persons including captains and soldiers is travelling in a train. For every 15 soldiers there is one captain. What is the number of captains in the group?

A. 85 B. 80 C. 75 D. 70

28. R is the brother of P, Q is the daughter of P, S is the sister of R while S is the brother of Q. Who is the uncle of S?

A. P B. Q C. R D. T

29. Two dice are tossed. The probability that total score is a prime number is?

A. $\frac{1}{6}$ B. $\frac{5}{12}$ C. $\frac{1}{2}$ D. $\frac{7}{9}$

30. If today is Sunday, what will be the day of the week on the 10th day from today?

A. Monday B. Tuesday

C. Wednesday D. None of these

For following statements, find which argument (s) is (are) forceful

31. Statement: Is it proper for ailing Pope John Paul to have missed the "Mass of Christ" at Vatican?

Arguments :

I. Yes, because he was sick and weak.

II. No, because this was 1st time he missed the Mass in his 26-year pontificate

A. Only I B. Only II C. Both D. None

32. Statement : Is the "Killer in custody" tag by attached to the Delhi Police justifiable?

Arguments :

I. Yes, the latest death of jeweller Parmeshwar Dayal in the custody points to the same.

II. No, they were suicides; what has the Delhi Police got to do with this ?

A. Only I B. Only II C. Both D. None

33. What inference is drawn from the argument ?

Argument :

Anything that goes up will definitely fall down.

Helicopter goes up.

Inference :

So, the helicopter will definitely fall down.

A. Valid B. Invalid

C. Doubtful D. Long drawn one.

34. Of the following statements, there are two of them, which cannot be true at the same time, but both can be false. Which are these two statements?

I. All machines make noise

II. Some machines make noise

III. No machine makes noise

IV. Some machines are not noisy

A. I and II B. III and IV

C. I and III D. II and IV

35. Which one of the following alternatives can be inferred from the argument given below:

The devil is dangerous because it deceives the people

A. Those who deceive the people are dangerous

B. All those who deceive the people are devils

C. All dangerous people deceive others

D. Some dangerous people deceive others

36. Statement:

Should a total ban be put on trapping wild animals ?

Arguments

I. Yes. trappers are making a lot of money.

II. No. bans on hunting and trapping will not be effective.

A. Argument 1 alone is strong

B. Argument II alone is strong

C. Either I or II is strong

D. Neither I nor II is strong

37. In a group, 40 people take tea, 35 take coffee, 7 take both tea and coffee. Also 20% of the members in the group do not take either tea or coffee. The number of persons in the group is

A. 68 B. 82

C. 85 D. None of the above

Directions (Qs. 38- 42) : Study the following graph of the sales of a company (domestic and foreign) during the four years period from 1998-1999 to 2002-2003 answer the questions below:

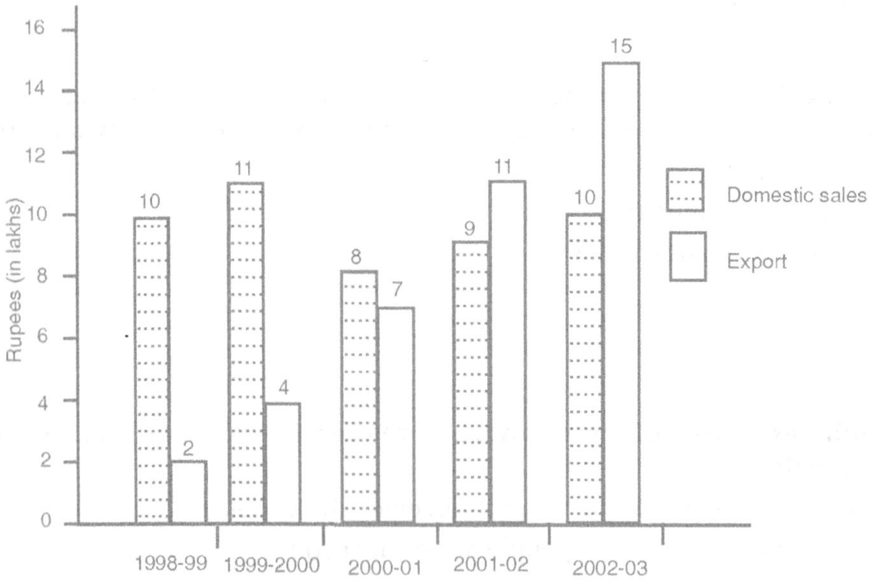

38. During which years did the annual total turnover of the company exceed ₹ 15 lakhs?

A. 1999-2000 and 2001-02

B. 2000-2001 and 2001-02

C. 2001-2002 and 2002-03

D. 1998-1999 and 2002-03

39. The two years between which of these was a maximum decline in exports during the five-year period:

A. between 1998-1999 and 1999-2000

B. between 1999-2000 and 2000-2001

C. between 2000-2001 and 2001-2002

D. between 2001-2002 and 2002-2003

40. The ratio of export to domestic sale for the year 2002-03 was:

A. 2:1 B. 2:3 C. 3:2 D. None of these

41. In which year was the total production least?

A. 1998-99 B. 2000-01

C. 1999-2000 D. None of these

42. Which of the following statements is always true?

A. If the numerator and the denominator of a fraction are increased or decreased by adding the same amount, the value of the fraction remains unchanged.

B. If the numerator and the denominator of a fraction are squared, the value of the fraction is unchanged.

C. The value of any fraction is less than one

D. The square of any integer is greater than 1, is greater than that number.

43. Which of the following is a browser?

A. IE B. Netscape

C. Google Chrome D. All of these

44. Which of the following is not a feature of WWW?

A. Retrieving of information

B. Enabling viewing of multimedia

C. Bulletin hypertext capability

D. All the above are features of www

45. Which one of the following is not associated with a computer?

A. Ability to think on its own

B. Accuracy in calculation

C. Speed in locating information

D. Capacity to store large amounts of information

46. A peripheral is :

A. a software inscribed in a hardware

B. a hardware inscribed in a software

C. the hardware part of a computer

D. the software part of computer

47. Which of the following is not true about a software?

A. software can be used to manipulate computer

B. a software includes programmes, instructions etc.

C. a software cannot be touched

D. a software can be touched

48. CD-ROM stand for :

A. compact Disc Research Organization Method

B. Circuit Design Research Orientated Memory

C. Compact Disc Read Only Memory

D. Carrier Drive Received and operated Memory

49. Where is Kodaikkanal situated ?

A. Cardamom Hills

B. Nilgiri Mountain

C. Annamalai Mountain

D. Palni Hills

50. What is Freon?

A. A gas used in a refrigerator

B. A natural gas like oxygen

C. A gas used for welding iron

D. A gas used as fuel in a bus

51. Nunataks are found in which one of the following countries?

A. Canada B. South America

C. Australia D. Greenland

52. Which soil is most unsuited for cultivation?

A. Sandy B. Black

C. Red D. Alluvial

53. The marble used for building Taj Mahal is chemically eroded by the action of:

A. Carbondioxide B. Nitrogen

C. Sulphurdioxide D. Oxygen

54. The Biotic, Physical and Meteorological components together are described as the:

A. Stratosphere B. Atmosphere

C. Environment D. Ionosphere

55. The Birla Institute of Technology is situated at:

A. Ranchi B. Jaipur C. Delhi D. Mumbai

56. How many Indian Institutes of Technology (IIT) are there in India?

A. Fifteen B. Six C. Four D. Ten

57. The Indian School of Mines is situated at:

A. Dhanbad (Jharkhand) B. Patna (Bihar)

C. Guwahati (Assam) D. Hyderabad (A.P.)

58. Environmental education as part of school education needs to be:

A. encouraged because the future of human beings will be decided by the awareness that they have about environmental issues.

B. discouraged because it will only add to the heavy curriculum

C. encouraged because it will help students to get high marks without having to learn difficult content

D. discouraged because it will only help to add to the work of the pupils

59. Institute of Nuclear Medicine and Allied Sciences is located at:

A. Delhi B. Chennai C. Mumbai D. Kolkata

60. Which of the following is not a Fundamental Right in this Indian constitution?

A. Right to equality

B. Right against exploitation

C. Right to freedom of speech and expression

D. Right of freedom for compulsory education of all children up to the age of 18

Answer keys

1.C	2.D	3.B	4.B	5.C	6.A	7.C	8.C	9.D	10.D
11.A	12.B	13.B	14.A	15.C	16.D	17.A	18.C	19.B	20.A
21.C	22.B	23.B	24.D	25.D	26.C	27.C	28.C	29.B	30.C
31.A	32.D	33.D	34.C	35.A	36.D	37.C	38.C	39.B	40.C
41.A	42.D	43.D	44.D	45.A	46.C	47.D	48.C	49.D	50.A
51.D	52.B	53.C	54.C	55.A	56.D	57.A	58.A	59.A	60.D

MODEL QUESTION PAPER - 7

Note : This paper contains **sixty** (60) multiple choice questions, each carrying **two** (2) marks. Answer any **fifty** (50) questions. The total time for completing this paper is 75 minutes and the total marks for the paper is 100.

1. Teaching will be very effective if the teacher:

A. has sufficient experience in teaching the subject

B. uses the scientific principles for instruction

C. uses proper instructional aids for teaching

D. motivates the students to learn the subject

2. I will give greater acceptance to a college teacher who:

A. organizes his teaching around self learning by students

B. understands the psychology of his students and takes steps to satisfy their needs

C. asks questions in between teaching to assess the effectiveness of his teaching

D. has perfect rapport with his students

3. Which of the following is not related to the development phase of the lecture?

A. Illustrating

B. Elucidating

C. Testing previous knowledge

D. Asking probing questions

4. Validity of a tool used for student evaluation is mainly dependent upon:

A. the coverage of the subject content prescribed

B. use of objective-type items for testing

C. the difficulty level of the items used in the test

D. the ability of the teacher to sample all the major instructional objectives he has set for this class

5. Which is the most desirable outcome of teaching in higher education?

A. high percentage of distinctions in the university examinations

B. increase in the number of students opting for the subject

C. ability to create new knowledge /develop new ways of doing things

D. developing of students' ability to deal with others

6. **The quality of a research supervisor is dependent upon:**
   A. the expertise of the research supervisor
   B. the availability of advanced facilities provided by the research centre
   C. the relevance and depth of the research problem
   D. the originality of the research problem and its likely impact on educational practice

7. **Examine the following statements about research and choose the correct answer from the four choices given.**
   (i) Research aims at developing new knowledge in any discipline
   (ii) Researcher is expected to go deep into specialized areas in his/her discipline
   (iii) Researcher collects as much data as possible relating to the problem selected
   (iv) Researcher is expected to validate/revalidate the existing principles and theories in one's discipline
   (v) Research is often the result of collective scholarship

   Which combination of the above statements is, according to you, the most valid generalization about the nature of research?

   A. (i), (ii) and (iii) B. (ii), (iii) and (iv)
   C. (i), (ii) and (iv) D. all this above

8. **A researcher often attempts to find out the effectiveness of a new method of teaching over the existing methods of teaching. The research procedure most suitable for this purpose is:**
   A. Experimental Method B. Survey Method
   C. Case study Method D. Discovery Method

9. **An academic discussion session in a college which permits full freedom to come out with highly unusual or even out of the way suggestions is called:**
   A. constructive workshop B. conferencing
   C. seminar discussions D. brain storming

10. **Which one of the following is not desirable in reporting educational research?**
    A. statement of objectives of the study
    B. statement of hypothesis of the study
    C. the non-technical languages for presentation
    D. Interpretation of the findings

11. Which number will replace the question mark in the following diagram?

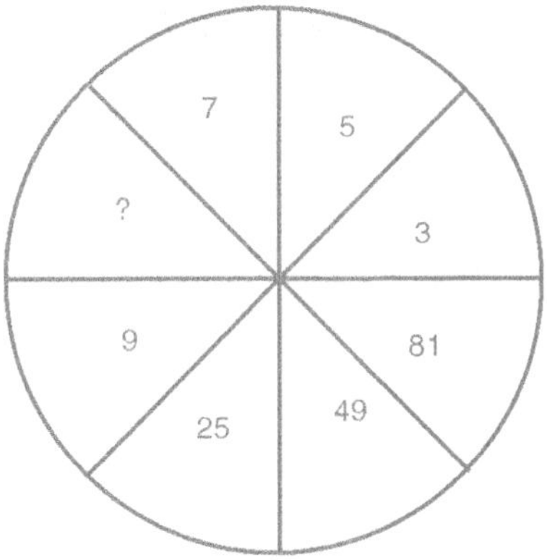

A. 3 B. 9 C. 6 D. 18

12. In a certain code, 123 means "success through hardwork", 345 means "hardwork brings triumph", 462 means "success always triumph", Using this data what is the code for 'success'?

A. 2 B. 3 C. 4 D. 5

13. Which of the following diagrams represents the overlap among the three categories students (S), cadets (C), athlete (A).

A. 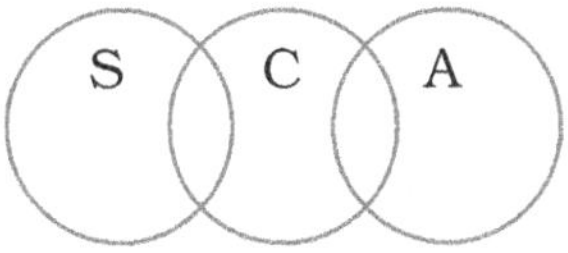

B. 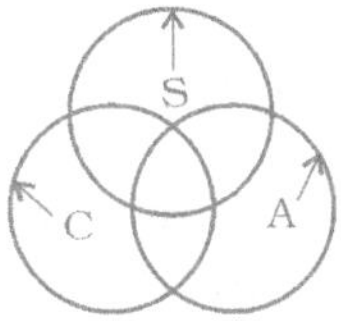

C. 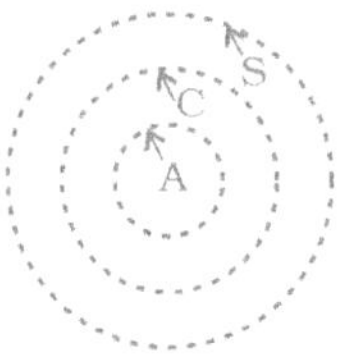

D. 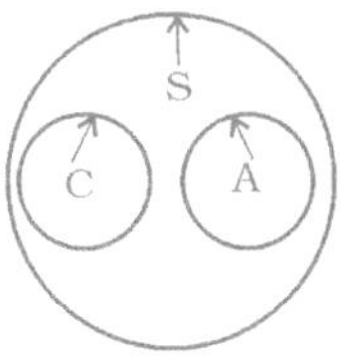

14. The difference between the age of A and B is 6 years and the ratio of their present ages is 2:3. What is A's age?

A. 12 B. 8 C. 18 D. 16

15. Complete the following series. 4,4,9,3,16,2, ______ ,1,36

A. 12 B. 32 C. 25 D. 18

Study the pi-diagram below representing the areas of farm land utilized by a farmer for cultivating various crops and answer question 16 and 17

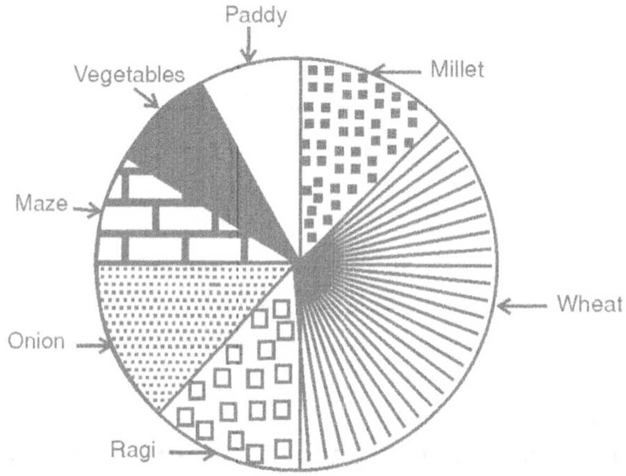

16. The area used for cultivating wheat is equal to the combined area used for cultivating:

A. ragi, onion and maze
B. paddy, vegetables, millet and ragi
C. maze, vegetables, paddy and ragi
D. millet, onion and maze

17. The total percentage of land which the farmer was men for cultivating wheat, ragi and onion is:

A. 75% B. 62.5% C. 45% D. 36.5%

The following table shows the causes of death among human beings in different parts of the world during the years 1950-1980. Study the table and answer the questions 18 and 19.

Causes	1950	1960	1970	1980
Cancer	12.7%	16.5%	17.1%	18.0%
Cardiovascular	36.2%	39.8%	42.3%	40.1%
Violence	8.7%	10.8%	12.1%	14.0%
Earthquakes	4.4%	4.9%	2.1%	1.1%
Accident	10.5%	8.0%	9.2%	8.2%
Flood	5.0%	5.0%	2.0%	1.0%
Others	22.5%	15.0%	15.2%	17.6%

18. Two inferences based on the data are given; decide which one is true?

Inferences (i) Incidence of cancer and violence have both increased during the period 1950-1980

(ii) Earthquakes and floods have both declined during period 1950-1980

A. Both (i) and (ii) are false
B. Only (i) is true
C. Only (ii) is true
D. Both (i) and (ii) are true

19. The death rate in 1960 due to natural calamities is approximately equal to:

A. cancer deaths in 1950
B. accident deaths in 1970
C. violence deaths in 1960
D. accident deaths in 1980

Study the following graph which represents to temperature of two cities during a selected week and answer questions 20 and 21.

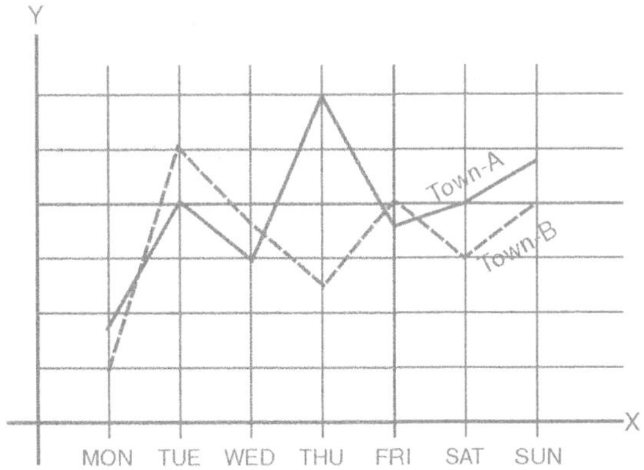

20. In which town the fluctuation in temperature is the highest, and between which days.

A. Town Y - Monday and Tuesday
B. Town X - Wednesday and Thursday
C. Town Y - Thursday and Friday
D. Town X - Thursday and Friday

21. On which day was the temperature of Town Y is closest to the temperature of Town X?

A. Saturday
B. Friday
C. Wednesday
D. Tuesday

22. What is meant by an ecological pyramid?

A. The pyramid of food grains stored for use in an emergency

B. The representation of inter-relationship between organisms and their food sources

C. The hierarchical representation of food habits of organisms

D. The graphic representation of the number, biomas and energy at successive trophic levels of an eco system

23. The increased threat to the environment due to Chloro Fluro Carbons (CFCS) is mainly due to:

A. Deforestation B. Automobiles

C. Air-conditioners & Refrigerators D. Water pollution

24. Which the following statements is true with respect to the composition of air?

A. 78% of Oxygen and 21 percent of Nitrogen

B. 21% of Oxygen and 0.9 percent of Carbon dioxide

C. 0.03% of Carbon dioxide and 21 percent of Argon

D. 78% of Nitrogen and 21 percent of Oxygen

25. The ozone layer surroundings the earth is located in:

A. The stratosphere B. The troposphere

C. The thermosphere D. The ionosphere

26. The bird sanctuary in the name of famous Ornithologist Salim Ali, is located in:

A. Assam B. Orissa

C. Rajastan D. Goa

Read the following passage and answer questions 27 to 32.

It is time we looked at our country from a new perspective. Where does the strength of India lie? Not in numbers, not necessarily in the moral stands that we take on some of the important international issues. In modern times the strength of a nation lies on its achievements in science and technology. This is not to say that other fields do not count.

In the five decades after independence, we have yet to demonstrate our originality in applied science and technology. Though Japan also started like us, by cultivating the technology of the West, the Japanese adopted, improved and displayed originality in several areas of science and technology. The generation which is at the helm of affairs in science and technology in our country after independence, mostly consisted of self-seekers. Barring a few exceptions, the science and technology managers in India concentrated in gaining politics power and influence. They loved publicity. Most of them stopped doing science while they managed science. Things would have been better had they been humble enough to acknowledge the difference between doing and managing science. Instead, they claimed they were the foremost in science and technology simply because they were at the helm of affairs. As a result they ceased to inspire the younger lot. India continues to be a borrower of science and technology, even though its potential for originality is substantial.

Our achievements in nuclear science and technology may be dazzling to our people, but, in worth and originality they are ordinary and routine. While our own people remain 'ignorant, the people of other countries know all about the pretention to knowledge of our nuclear science and technology managers. One subtle way of sabotaging our nuclear goals is to help hollow persons reach and remain at the helm of affairs. International bodies come in as handy tools in that subtle process. The veil of secrecy effectively protects the mismanagement in our nuclear establishments. The talk of national security comes as an easy weapon to prevent any probe into mismanagement of anything that happens in out nuclear science activities.

On nuclear science matters the media in our country, by and large, avoid the investigative approach. As a result, the mismatch between promise and performance in the nuclear field does not get exposed as much as mismanagement in other fields.

27. What does the author of this passage mean by 'doing science'?

A. projecting sub-standard performance as an outstanding achievement

B. managing effectively the administrative functions relating to science and technology

C. conducting routine research with has little impact on this way science is practised

D. scientific research/technological practices which make a real impact on the world of science

28. 'Doing science' and 'managing science' according to the author is analogous to:

A. setting a target and achieving it

B. a 'real achievement' and ' false claim'

C. 'original discovery' and 'running research establishments'

D. low-level scientific inventions, and by senior decision makers in science and seeking credit for it.

29. The main stand taken by the author of the passage is that:

A. The technocrats in the country are more concerned with political power than in advancing science

B. The Japanese scientists are superior to Indian scientists

C. The Indian scientists of the past generation showed great commitment to science than the present generation scientists

D. Indian politicians, by and large, are self-seekers.

30. Which one of the following statements is to be treated as a correct assessment of India's post independence nuclear & scientific advancement?

A. Scientists and technologists of post-independent India have displayed considerable originality

B. Indias achievement in nuclear science and technology is dazzling

C. The country's achievement in nuclear science and technology is dazzling only to our people

D. Our scientists have done full justice to the nuclear needs of this country

31. The author of the passage is fully convinced that:

A. most of the managers of science are not doing their work, but are interested in projecting their greatness

B. India's strength lies in the moral stands it takes on international issues

C. India's potential for originality in science and technology is utilized fully

D. our scientists are recognized abroad, though they are criticized in India

32. Why doesn't media hesitate to investigate into nuclear matters?

A. The wall of secrecy effectively helps the inefficient nuclear managers to misuse the funds for investigation

B. National security is an effective weapon to prevent anyone probing into the way nuclear projects and operated

C. The mismatch between promise and performance in our nuclear policy is not an area that is to be taken up by the media

D. The media is more interested in sensational issues like corruption, scandals and election fights

33. Five statements are given below.

Read them and classify them in terms of Facts, Opinion, Prejudice, Assumption and Advice:

(i) No political party should be in power for more than five years are a time

(ii) It is better to do what you can do, rather than telling others what you would do.

(iii) Gandhiji was an apostle of non-violence.

(iv) Those who educate their children in boarding schools are rich people.

(v) All Indians are ritualistic, pessimistic and superstitious.

	Opinion	Fact	Prejudice	Assumption	Advice.
A.	(iii)	(i)	(ii)	(v)	(iv)
B.	(i)	(iii)	(v)	(iv)	(ii)
C.	(iv)	(v)	(i)	(iii)	(ii)
D.	(v)	(iv)	(i)	(iii)	(ii)

34. What is the best inference that can be drawn from the following statements?

Statements: "All teachers are doctors", "some doctors are scholars"

A. All teachers arc scholars

B. Some doctors who are scholars are teachers

C. All scholars are doctors

D. All doctors are scholars and are teachers

35. Read the following four statements of which there are two statements both of which cannot be true at the same time; but, both can be false. Which are these two statements?

(i) All birds can fly.

(ii) Some birds fly

(iii) No bird can fly.

(iv) Some birds do not fly

A. (i) and (ii) B. (iii) and (iv)

C. (i) and (iii) D. (ii) and (iv)

36. A question followed by two arguments is given below. Read them and choose the most forceful argument.

Should political parties be banned?

(i) Yes, it is necessary to teach the politicians a lesson

(ii) No, it will lead to the end of democracy

A. (i) is forceful

B. (ii) is forceful

C. (i) and (ii) are both forceful

D. Neither (i) nor (ii) is forceful

37. "Listening is a mental activity. It begins with concentration". This statement implies that:

A. Listening improves concentration

B. Listening is followed by concentration

C. Listening starts with concentration

D. Sometimes it is possible to listen without concentration

38. The internet facility for searching about a specific subject is referred to as:

A. A Database B. A Search Engine

C. A Software D. A Website

39. Where is the IT park called 'Tidal Park' situated?

A. At Delhi B. At Kolkatha C. At Chennai D. At Mumbai

40. Which is the largest IT company in India?

A. Sathiam B. Wipro

C. T.C.S D. Intel

41. Who is known as the father of artificial intelligence?

A. Allen Turing

B. Sakuntaladevi

C. Viswanathan Anand

D. Ted Nelson

42. Communication in distance education using satellites like edusat is made possible through:

A. the Radar B. the Transponder

C. the Receptor D. the Transmitter

43. Planning Commission is:

A. a constitutional body

B. an official body

C. a non Governmental body

D. an advisory body

44. Which among the following is known as the 'soul of the Indian constitution'?

A. Preamble

B. Fundamental Rights

C. Directive Principles

D. Articles

45. Indian Parliament consists of:

A. Prime Minister, Cabinet and Speaker

B. MPs, Speaker, Deputy Speaker and cabinet

C. President, Lok Sabha and Rajyasabha

D. President, Vice President and Cabinet

46. Who is empowered to summon and adjourn the Indian Parliament?

A. The Speaker
B. The President of India
C. The Prime Minister
D. The Vice President of India

47. Match the items in list I with appropriate items in the list II and use this to select the correct answer from the given alternatives.

List I

1. National Institute of Mental Health and Neuro Sciences
2. National Council of Educational Research and Training
3. Netaji Subhash National Institute of Sports
4. National Defence Academy
5. Tata Institute of Fundamental Research

List II

(i) Patiala
(ii) Delhi
(iii) Khadakvasla
(iv) Mumbai
(v) Banglaore

A. 1. (v), 2. (ii), 3. (i), 4. (iii), 5. (iv)
B. 1. (iv), 2. (v), 3. (ii), 4. (iii), 5. (i)
C. 1. (iii), 2. (iv), 3. (i), 4. (ii), 5. (v)
D. 1. (ii), 2. (i), 3. (iii), 4. (v), 5. (iv)

48. Which one among the following is different from the others?

A. Interpersonal communication
B. Group communication
C. Intra-personal communication
D. Grapevine communication

49. Communication will be effective if:

A. the source is authoritative in communicating
B. the source is using multi media
C. the need and nature of receivers are taken into consideration
D. the medium of communication is the mothertongue

50. Attention, retention and recall are:

A. source variables

B. message variables

C. receiver variables

D. process variables

51. 'Ekalavya' is the T.V. Channel meant for telecasting:

A. Sports Events

B. Engineering & Technology Topics

C. UGC Programmes

D. IGNOU Education Programme

52. Which among the following is the major cause for distortion of communication in the classroom?

A. confusion on the part of the teacher

B. Noise inside the classroom

C. Noise outside the classroom

D. Student's inability to grasp the meaning

53. Which of the following models of teaching can be best used for developing the creativity of students?

A. Inquiry Training Model

B. Advance Organizer Model

C. Synectic Model

D. Inductive Thinking Model

54. The most important quality of a researcher is:

A. In-depth knowledge of the area

B. Deep knowledge of research methodology

C. An Analytical and penetrating mind

D. Ability to conform to conventional rules prescribed for researchers

55. Which one of the following number does not belong to the group?

A. 2325 B. 4349

C. 6267 D. 5482

56. The green house effect is caused mainly by:

A. Air pollution

B. Toxic biocides in this atmosphere

C. Dissipation of heat due to concentration of carbondioxide

D. Pesticide particles absorbed by the air

57. Read the following propositions and judge which inference is correct?

Statement

I. All birds can fly,

II. Penguin is a bird

Inference:

Therefore the penguin can fly

The above inference is a:

A. Valid inference

B. Invalid inference

C. Illogical inference

D. Long-drawn inference

58. Which of the following is an example for verbal communication?

A. Anu recites a poem to learn it by heart

B. The postman reads out the letter to the illiterate old woman

C. The baby cries when it is hungry

D, A cartoon in the daily ridiculing a government policy

59. What is the expansion of ICAR?

A. Indian Council for Aeronautic Research

B. International Committee for of Atomic Research

C. Indian Council of Aesthetics and Recreation

D. Indian Council of Agricultural Research

60. A Textual Data Base in ICT is known as:

A. ERIC B. VDU C. CPU D. Modem

Answer keys

1.B	2.A	3.D	4.D	5.C	6.D	7.D	8.A	9.D	10.C
11.B	12.A	13.B	14.A	15.C	16.A	17.B	18.D	19.B	20.A
21.C	22.D	23.C	24.D	25.A	26.D	27.D	28.C	29.A	30.C
31.A	32.B	33.B	34.B	35.C	36.B	37.B	38.B	39.C	40.C
41.A	42.B	43.D	44.A	45.C	46.B	47.A	48.C	49.C	50.C
51.B	52.A	53.C	54.C	55.D	56.C	57.D	58.B	59.D	60.A

MODEL QUESTION PAPER - 8

Note : This paper contains **sixty** (60) multiple choice questions, each carrying **two** (2) marks. Answer any **fifty** (50) questions. The total time for completing this paper is 75 minutes and the total marks for the paper is 100.

1. **Cognition is related to:**
   A. feeling
   B. thinking
   C. doing
   D. affecting

2. **A great teacher is one who:**
   A. inspires
   B. demonstrates
   C. help in learning to learn
   D. does all these

3. **The skill of achieving closure helps a teacher to:**
   A. recapitulate the teaching points covered in the class
   B. combine the parts learnt into meaningful whole
   C. summarize the steps for completing an assignment in a few words
   D. All the above

4. **Micro teaching is a:**
   A. scaled-down teaching arrangement for teaching a selected skill using a small class within a short time
   B. a teacher education technique allowing teachers to develop clearly defined teaching skills in a comfortable teaching situation
   C. a focussed attempt to develop teaching skills with the help of senior teaching members
   D. All the above

5. **In the video-recording technique, the sources of feedback are:**
   A. self, resource persons, and peer group members
   B. video tape, LCD and observation schedule
   C. both A and B
   D. none of these

6. **What is a primary source of data in historical research?**
   A. Oral testimony of traditions and customs

B. Official records - governments' documents, information preserved by society - religious organizations, etc.

C. Personal records, letters, diaries, autobiographies, wills, etc.

D. All the above, if they provide original first-hand accounts of events or experiences under study

7. What is a recorded sources of data?

A. Books

B. Journals

C. Internet clippings

D. All the above

8. Which of the following is an example of scientific knowledge?

A. knowledge created through scientific experimentation, capable of replication

B. knowledge contained in religious scriptures accepted by scholars

C. what is accepted as true knowledge by social and religious leaders

D. what is accepted as true by holy leaders of different religions

9. How do we decide whether a research hypothesis has been properly defined?

A. It should be precise, specific and consistent with most known facts

B. It should be formulated in such a way that it can be tested using objective data

C. It should be stated using scientific terminology

D. All the above

10. Which of the following are the examples of qualitative variable?

A. Caste

B. Gender

C. Both A and B

D. None of the above

Read the following passage and answer the questions 11-14:

Socrates taught that 'the man who is master of himself is truly free'. By being master of oneself, he meant, first knowing oneself, one's faults, weaknesses and one's good points without making any pretence and then being able to control oneself. This knowledge of himself is what helps a man to be courageous and the courageous man has a very important sort of freedom from fear. Socrates himself, because he was not afraid of the consequences, always felt free to teach what he thought was right. No wonder, all his pupils loved him very much. But he made some dangerous enemies by his strange ways of teaching and asking questions. Some of the rulers in Athens did not like people to be encouraged to ask questions, because they thought that people would begin to ask questions about what their rulers were doing. Therefore, they accused Socrates of teaching young men wicked things and leading them to throw off their religion. Finally, the great teacher Socrates was given death sentence. He was compelled to drink hemlock and pass away. However, his maxim 'know thyself' still offers us the light of knowledge of ourselves.

11. The phrase 'master of oneself' was used by Socrates to mean:

A. master of one's destiny

B. an enlightened person with the knowledge of oneself

C. one who defies another persons dominance over himself

D. one who is confident about one's strong points

12. Socrates was courageous in the sense:

A. he was not afraid of danger

B. he was not afraid of his enemies, however powerful

C. he was not afraid of the outcome of his actions

D. he was bold in expressing what he felt would help him to get public acceptance

13. The accusation against Socrates was:

A. blasphemy

B. teaching young men wicked things and opposing religion

C. Inciting the youth to question the authority of the rulers

D. encouraging rebellion against the rulers in the country

14. Hemlock is:

A. A deadly poison B. A life saving medicine

C. A kind of liquor D. A broth used by common people

15. Which one of the following persons is known as the 'Father of Indian Cinema'?

A. Santaram

B. Sathyajith Ray

C. Dada Saheb Phalke

D. GuruDutt

16. Informal communication network within an organization is known as:

A. Grapevine Communication B. Maps Communication

C. Intrapersonal Communication D. Intra-personal Communication

17. Which is the method used for receiving information in the market-based feedback system?

A. Audience - decision making

B. Media review

C. Direct feedback

D. All these

18. The competency of an effective communicator can be judged on the basis of the

A. personality of communicator

B. ability of the communicator to answer the needs of the target audience

C. experience of communicator in his select field

D. ability of communicator to interact properly with his target audience

19. Microphone is a hi-fi instrument. Here 'fi' means

A. field-worthy B. fidelity C. ft D. none of these

20. Find the missing letters in the following series:

AHQ, DJR, GLS, JNT, ???

A. KOU B. MQU C. MPU D. MPV

21. Out of four alternatives given below, one does not belong to the group of the other three; spot it.

A. Tenant B. Tattoo C. Talent D. Tavern

22. The two words given in the question are related in a certain way. Find out this relationship and identify this pair which bears the same relationship from among the four alternatives pairs

Clay : Cup

A. Iron : Chain B. Fibre : Plastic

C. Coin : Money D. Teacher : Classroom

23. If the BEGAN is coded as 257114 and CHILL AS 3891212, then code for CHILD is:

A. 37912 B. 389124 C. 38912 D. 398142

24. If Ajit is the brother of the son of Sethi's son, what is the relation between Ajit and Sethi?

A. Cousin B. Brother

C. Nephew D. Grandson

Directions (Q. 25-27): Each question below has two statements and an inference drawn from them. You have to determine whether the inference can necessarily be drawn from the statement including the alternative possibilities.

25. *Statements :* (i) A body which is propelled, moves.

(ii) Body 'x' moves.

Inference : **Body 'x' is propelled.**

A. True B. Probably True

C. False D. Can't say

26. *Statements :* The jury held him guilty.

He is not a member of the jury.

Inference : **The jury has no right to judge him as guilty**

A. True B. Probably True

C. False D. Probably false

27. *Statements :* All educated men are intelligent.

He is not an educated man.

Inference : **He is not intelligent.**

A. True B. Probably True

C. False D. Probably false

Directions (Q. 28-29): Each question below is followed by two arguments numbered I and II. You have to decide which of the arguments is a 'strong' argument and which is a 'weak' argument.

28. Should the admission to engineering courses be given only on merit without any concession to any particular group of students ?

Arguments : I. Yes, this will improve the quality of the engineers as they will be able to complete the courses successfully.

II. No, this will keep large number of socially and economically backward students out of the reach of the engineering courses.

A. Only 1 B. Only II C. Both D. None

29. Given below is a statement followed by 2 assumptions, Either one of these / or both these assumptions are correct or none of their assumption could be correct. You have to decide by selecting the appropriate choice.

Statement : Seeing the poor performance of Indian Cricket team, I think this team should be given a good coach.

Assumption :

I. A better coach can enhance the performance of the team

II. Performance of a team depends mainly upon the coach

A. Only I is implicit B. Both are implicit C. None D. Either one or two

Directions : Answer the questions (No. 30-34) with reference to the graph given below:

Rice Production in five states in India during the three-year period (2002-03 to 2004-05)

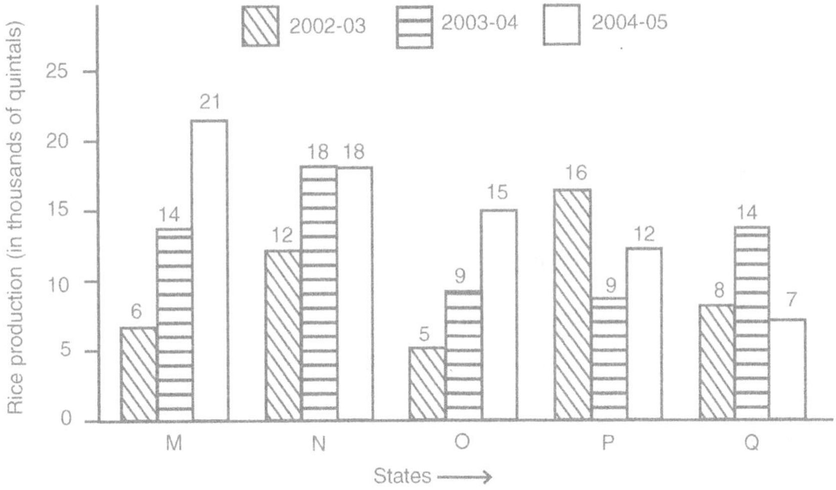

30. What is the difference between the rice production of state M and state Q during the three-year period?

A. 2000 quintals B. 12,000 quintals C. 14,000 quintals D. no difference

31. Which of the States registered a steady increase in the production of rice during the three-year period?

A. M and N B. M and O C. N only D. P and Q

32. How many quintals of rice were produced by State Q during the three-year period?

A. 29 B. 29000 C. 2900 D. 2900000

33. Which are the two states registered a rice production which is just one-third of what it is for the other states in 2004-05?

A. M and O B. M and Q C. N and Q D. N and P

34. Which of the following statements about rice production among the four states for the three-year period is false?

A. States M and O showed the same production in 2003-2004

B. There was no improvement in the production of rice in State N during the two year period from 2003-2005

C. Rice production among the five states during the period was maximum for State M

D. The total rice Production for States O and P in 2003-04 is less than the total production of rice of M & Q for the same year

35. The reciprocal of the fraction $\frac{11}{2}$ is:

A. $\frac{22}{4}$ B. $\frac{2}{11}$ C. $5\frac{1}{2}$ D. 5.5

36. Function of putting data on the stack is called:

A. Poping B. Pushing

D. Setting D. Storing

37. Mark which of the following is false:

A. To a 16-bit microprocessor a 32-bit bus can be connected

B. New data cannot be stored in RAM during program execution

C. Both the above

D. None of the above

38. Pick the odd one out:

A. Orkut B. Facebook

C. Gmail D. Twitter

39. Which of the following combine both GSM and CDMA technologies?

A. Tata Teleservices B. Aircel services

C. Airtel services D. Idea

40. Which of the following does not manufacture laptops?

A. Sony B. HCL

C. IBM D. Dell

41. Which region of earth's covering helps to establish long-distance wireless communication?

A. Stratosphere B. Ionosphere

C. Biosphere D. Atmosphere

42. Any living or non-living element or any physical agent which has an undesirable impact on the environment is called:

A. a change agent

B. a biomechanism

C. a poisonous gas

D. a pollutant

43. What is geo-thermal energy?

A. Energy derived from flowing water

B. Energy derived from coal mined from earth's surface

C. Energy absorbed by the water stored in dams

D. Energy contained in hot-water deposits within the earth's crust

44. Which of the following does not form part of a non-point pollution source?

A. evaporation
B. wastes disposal
C. dumping
D. sedimentation

45. Which are the two most populated countries of the world?

A. China and Russia
B. China and Japan
C. India and Russia
D. China and India

46. Indian Institute of Science (IISc) is situated in:

A. Bangalore
B. Kolkata
C. Mumbai
D. Chennai

47. The Union Territories in India are administered by:

A. The President of India through the Administrators appointed by him

B. The Prime Minister of India through administrators appointed by him

C. The Law Minister, Government of India

D. The Attorney-General of India

48. Directive Principles of State Policy as per the Indian constitution:

A. give freedom to citizen to move to other parts of the country

B. are classes meant to protect the depressed classes

C. provide for state actions which cannot be enforced by the courts

D. include clauses meant to give general directions for courts

49. Which of the following is not rightly matched?

A. Tata Institute of Social Sciences - Mumbai

B. Electro chemical Research Institute, Karaikudi

C. Sri Ram College of Commerce — Delhi
D. Indian Institute of Immunology — Bangaluru

50. In which year was the Jawaharlal Nehru University in Delhi established?

A. 1962 B. 1979 C. 1969 D. 1987

51. One of the most famous Indian Universities of the early AD's destroyed by foreign invaders is being recreated recently by a committee headed by:

A. Prof. Yespal B. Prof. Amartya Sen
C. Mr. Sam Petroda D. Prof. M.G.S. Narayanan

52. Video Conferencing is also known as :

A. Physical Conferencing
B. Remote Conferencing
C. Electronic Conferencing
D. None of these

53. The octane rating of any fuel increases by the addition of:

A. Carbon B. Methane C. Lead D. Sulphur

54. The full form of the ISRO is:

A. Indian Science Research Organization
B. International Social Research Organization
C. Imperial Science Research Operation
D. Indian Space Research Organizations

55. In a group of 60 people who take tea, 40 take coffee and 10 take both tea and coffee. If each person in the group takes at least one of the two drinks then the number of persons in the group is

A. 110 B. 100 C. 90 D. 120

56. Which one of the following tests could be classified as a non-parametric test?

A. t-test for comparison of two means
B. ANOVA for comparison of more than two means
C. ANCOVA for comparison of more than two adjusted means
D. test for goodness of fit

57. Approximately how many news channels are operating in India?

A. 249 B. 263 C. 275 D. 182

58. The time between 7 and 8 O'clock at which the hands of a clock be in straight line hands in opposite directions is:

A. $54\frac{6}{11}$ minutes past 7 B. $10\frac{10}{11}$ minutes past 7

C. $5\frac{5}{11}$ minutes past 7 D. 7:50

59. Read carefully the two statements given below. Assuming the two to be true, which of the conclusions is true?

Statements

(a) All green is grass; (b) No grass is red

Conclusions

I : No green is red

II : No red is green

A. Only I is correct

B. Only II is correct

C. Both I and II are correct

D. None of these

60. Pointing to a gentleman, Deepak said, "His only brother is the father of my daughter's father". How is the gentleman related to Deepak?

A. Father B. Brother-in-law

C. Uncle D. Father-in-law

Answer keys

1.B	2.D	3.D	4.D	5.C	6.D	7.D	8.A	9.D	10.C
11.B	12.C	13.B	14.A	15.C	16.A	17.D	18.B	19.B	20.C
21.C	22.A	23.B	24.D	25.C	26.C	27.C	28.A	29.B	30.B
31.B	32.B	33.B	34.A	35.B	36.B	37.C	38.C	39.A	40.C
41.B	42.D	43.D	44.C	45.D	46.A	47.A	48.C	49.D	50.C
51.B	52.C	53.C	54.D	55.C	56.D	57.A	58.C	59.A	60.C

MODEL QUESTION PAPER - 9

Note : This paper contains **sixty** (60) multiple choice questions, each carrying **two** (2) marks. Answer any **fifty** (50) questions. The total time for completing the paper is 75 minutes and the total marks for the paper is 100.

1. Disease and recovery have the same relationship as:

A. failure and success

B. sorrow and happiness

C. profit and loss

D. damage and repair

2. Students, schools, headmaster have the same relationship as:

A. furniture. steel, wood

B. books, magazines, periodicals

C. agriculturist, farmer, coolie

D. clients, courts, judges

3. Classify the following sentences into fact, advice, prejudice, assumption and opinion.

(i) Increased use of refrigerators and air-conditioners cause emission of chloro fluro carbons.

(ii) Dr. Sam is a leading cardiologist. so his daughter also must be a successful doctor.

(iii) Jews by birth are very shrewd.

(iv) Don't accept any eatables from fellow passengers

(v) He is a Kashmiri, he cannot be trusted.

	Fact	Advice	Prejudice	Assumption	Opinion
A.	(iii)	(v)	(ii)	(i)	(iv)
B.	(i)	(iv)	(v)	(ii)	(iii)
C.	(ii)	(iii)	(iv)	(i)	(v)
D.	(iv)	(ii)	(iii)	(v)	(i)

4. Farmers become more fatalists when they have to depend upon the weather upon which they have no control. Modern technology introduced in Japan made farmers independent of the weather. Therefore the farmers in Japan are much less fatalists when compared to their counterparts in other Asian countries. This inference is:

A. correct

B. not correct because all farmers in Asia are not fatalists

C. not correct because some farmers in Japan are fatalists

D. not correct because age-old beliefs will not change

5. A question followed by two arguments is given below. Question: "Should we prefer vegetarian food to non-vegetarian food?"

Argument: A: Yes, it is always good for health

B: No, because non-vegetarian food is rich in proteins

A. A is forceful

B. B is forceful

C. Both are forceful

D. Neither is foreceful

6. During the first week of June 20% of the students left a college as they were selected to professional courses, 250 students were newly admitted in the second week. Now the college has 1530 students. How many were there during the first week?

A. 1200 B. 1500

C. 1536 D. 1600

7. Out of the four numbers which share a common property, 3 of them have another common property also- Identify the one without the second property.

A. 6787 B. 4345

C. 5546 D. 3124

8. Complete the following series 5, 20, 80, ..., 1280

A. 360 B. 320

C. 1200 D. 960

9. In a secret code ABSTAIN is written as CDQRCKP. How will SAINT be written using this code?

A. CDRHL B. QCKPR

C. DEBJO D. AQZHM

10. The numbers in the different cells follow a certain rule. Find out the missing number in the bottom corner cell, using this rule

1	3	5	7
4	6	8	10
7	9	11	13
10	12	14	?

A. 15　　B. 16　　C. 10　　D. 7

The graph given below shows rainfall in the cities E,F,G and H for the year 1991 to 1995. Study the graph and answer the questions 11 and 12.

Graph showing the annual rainfall of 4 Indian cities during the 5 years from 1991 - 1996

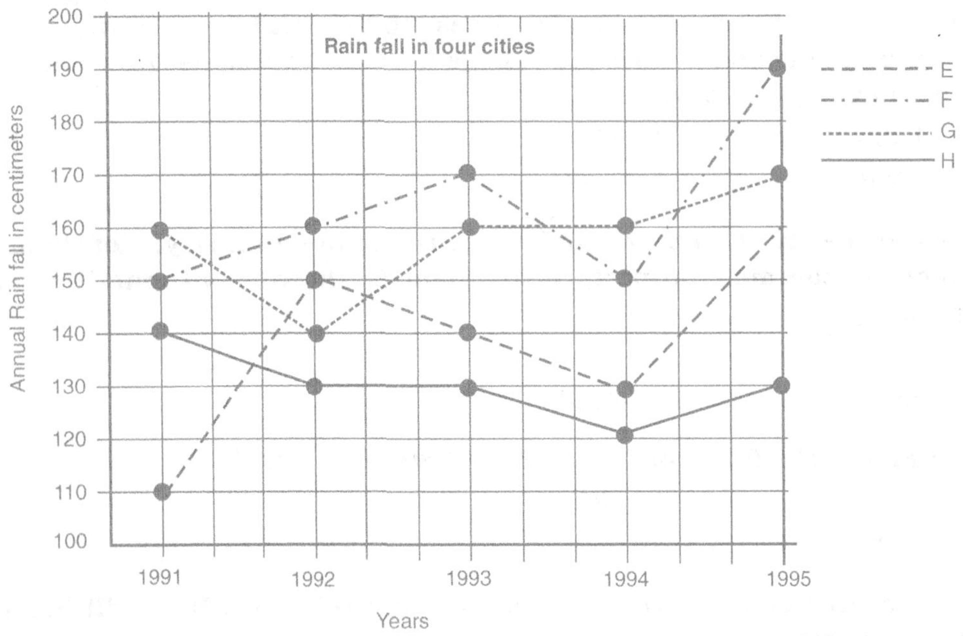

11. Which city has recorded the maximum average rainfall during the five-year period ?

A. E　　B. F

C. G　　D. H

12. Which city had the lowest rainfall in 1991, but had the second highest rainfall in 1995?

A. E B. F C. G D. H

Study the following table and answer the questions 13 & 14 given below:

DATA RELATING TO POPULATION AND LITERACY LEVELS OF DIFFERENT INDIAN STATES AND THE WHOLE COUNTRY AS OF 1991

Sl.No.	State	1	2
1	Rajastan	44	38.55
2	Madhya Pradesh	66.1	44.20
3	Orissa	31.6	49.09
4	Assam	22.4	52.89
5	West Bengal	68.1	57.70
6	Utter Pradesh	139.1	41.60
7	Bihar	86.4	38.48
8	Delhi	9.4	75.29
9	Haryana	16.5	65.85
10	Himachal Pradesh	5.2	63.86
11	Punjab	20.3	58.51
12	Andhra Pradesh	66.5	44.09
13	Tamil Nadu	55.8	62.66
14	Karnataka	45.0	56.04
15	Kerala	29.1	89.81
16	Gujarat	41.3	61.29
17	Maharashtra	78.9	64.87
18	Others	20.6	52.21
19	India	846.3	52.21

Note: 1 - Population in millions
2 - Literary level (percentage)

13. Compared to the total population of India, the population of UP and Bihar together is:

A. less than 1/4 B. equal to 1/4
C. more than 1/4 D. about 2/3 of it

14. Which one of the following statements in correct?

A. Literate population in Andhra Pradesh is more than that in most other states
B. The literacy level of Kerala compares favourably with that of Orissa
C. U.P. and Bihar account for about 25% of India's Literate population
D. Literacy rate of Bihar is close to half of what it is for Delhi

Study the pi-diagram & answer the question given below:

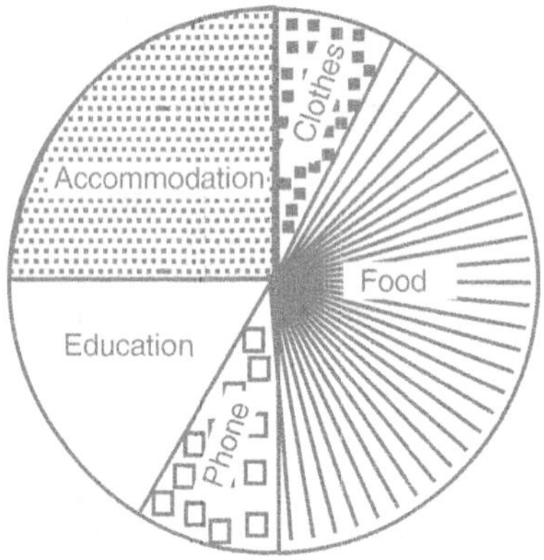

15. What is the percentage of combined expenditure incurred by the family on food, clothes and accommodation?

A. 37.5 B. 725 C. 75 D. 85

16. If a student gives a wrong answer to a question in the classroom, the appropriate action to this by a teacher would be to:

A. ignore the wrong answer and select another better student who can answer correctly
B. reword the question and address this to the same student
C. explain to the student why his answer is wrong and try to elicit the correct answer
D. scold the student for taking the question lightly

17. Who would you prefer to recruit as a teacher, from among the following candidates?

A. one with outstanding academic records but has poor communication skills
B. one with good communication skills but with average knowledge of the subject
C. one who has dedication to the profession and can motivate students
D. one with a long experience in teaching, irrespective of the other qualities

18. An effective teacher is the one who

A. is concerned more with preparing students for the common examination, rather than developing their personality

B. is friendly to the students and can get them to follow him

C. is pleasant and promises that he can help them to get jobs

D. acts as an inspiring teacher to all his students and motivates them to undertake deep level learning of his subject

19. Which one should be the stand taken by a teacher in higher education to his students?

A. All students are dignified, and responsible, and capable of self-learning

B. Most students are easy-go-lucky type, and hence they don't deserve serious teaching

C. A few students are hard-working and serious and can learn by themselves and it is better to give special attention to these students

D. Most students can be pressured to learn using insulting terms

20. Classroom teaching will be more effective if:

A. the teacher asks a few questions in between his lectures

B. the teacher explains using teaching aids

C. the teacher uses appropriate illustrations to the point

D. the teacher connects new information to their previous learning

Direction: Study the passage and answer the questions (21-26) given below:

Some religious leaders have projected the view their that man is made up of a body and a soul; but they are silent about the intellect. Their followers try to feed the body on earth and to save soul from perdition after death. But they neglect the claims of the mind. Bread for the body and virtue for the soul: these are regarded as the indispensable requistes of human welfare here and hereafter. Nothing is said about knowledge and education. Thus Jesus Christ spoke much of feeding the hungry. Healing the sick, and converting the sinners. But he never supported the need used for teaching the ignorant and increasing scientific knowledge which will make them better human beings. He himself was not a well educated man, and intellectual pursuits were beyond his horizon. Gautam Buddha also laid stress on morality, meditation and asceticism, but he did not attach great importance to history, science, art or literature. St. Ambrose deprecated scientific studies and wrote. "To discuss the nature and position of the earth does not help us in our hope for life to come". St. Basil said very frankly and foolishly. "It is not a matter of interest for us whether the earth is a sphere or a cylinder or a disc". Thomas Carlyle also followed the Christian tradition and when he declared that he honoured only two men (and no third man) the manual labourer and the religious teacher. He forgot the scientist, the scholar and the artist. The cynics of Grece despised education?

21. What have the religious leaders of the past taught about the body and the soul?

A. The man is made up of the body only

B. That man is made up of soul only

C. That the body has to be fed to keep it alive

D. That man is made up of a body and a soul together

22. What serves as the essential requisites for human welfare in this world and the other world?

A. Bread for the soul

B. Virtue for this soul

C. Knowledge for the soul

D. Scientific knowledge for man

23. Who are the religious leaders quoted by the author as deprecating scientist's studies?

I. St. Ambrose
II. St. Basil
III. Thomas Carlyle
IV. Gautam Budha
V. St. Basil

A. II and IV
B. I & IV
C. I & II
D. I & IV

24. Thomas Carlyle followed the Christian tradition when he asserted that:

A. he honoured only the manual labourer and the religious teachers

B. he honoured only the scientists and the scholars

C. the shape of the earth is not important for man

D. morality, meditation and asceticism are important

25. An ideal title for passage is:

A. The importance of science for Human Welfare

B. Philosophy and Morality

C. Approach to Philosophy Needed

D. Feeding the Hungry

26. What does the author emphasize through this passage?

A. Man's life on earth is incomplete if only body and spirit are developed

B. History, science, art and literature are all to be taught for intellectual growth of human beings

C. None of the great thinkers of the early years realised the importance of science and educating man

D. All the above

27. Which of the following is the best explanation for a research hypothesis?

A. A hypothesis is an intelligent guess deduced from existing theories or from first hand experience in a field

B. A hypothesis is an assumption derived from the review of related literature

C. A hypothesis means a possible solution to a problem, accepted as valid

D. A hypothesis is a solution of a problem, suggested by his expert research guide.

28. Which of the following is not a purpose of research?

A. Refuting an existing theory

B. Verifying an existing theory

C. Expanding the store of knowledge

D. Explaining a new phenomenon using the scientific method

29. The type of research where the variables are studied in retrospect in search of passive effects and relationship is called:

A. Longitudinal study B. Ex-post facto study

C. Trend study D. Cross-sectional study

30. Which one of the following statements about research would you accept as valid?

A. A research study should attempt to cover everything related to the area of research

B. A research study should attempt an indepth investigation of a specific area

C. A research study should rely mainly upon what other researches have done

D. A research study should be based on all exisiting data pertaining to the topic of study

31. Though several research projects in education are being conducted by discoveries are very rare. This is because:

A. many researchers do not have indepth knowledge of the research procedures

B. most researchers have no commitment to educational research

C. sophisticated facilities are not made available to most researchers

D. most researchers begin research with convergent thinking patterns wrong perception of educational research

32. Bio-magnification means:

A. accumulation of toxic biocides in living cells

B. the magnified effect of insecticides

C. large increase in the size of human population

D. swelling of certain parts of the body due to viral infections

33. 'Karman Line' is the hypothetical boarder between:

A. the atmosphere and the ionosphere

B. the ionosphere and the troposphere

C. the troposphere and the thermosphere

D. the atmosphere and the stratosphere

34. The green house effect is caused mainly by:

A. change of colour of such surfaces due to the growth of green moss

B. water pollution which turns the colour of stagnant water

C. dissipation of heat blocked by concentration of carbon-dioxide

D. none of the above

35. What is meant by 'Red Data Book'?

A. A document meant to educate the environmental workers

B. A Scientific document which lists and classifies the species facing extinction

C. A document which explains the danger of population explosion

D. A document which describes the threats to ecological balance on the globe

36. The oldest fungicide used for the management of plant diseases is:

A. Sulphur B. Copper

C. Mercury D. Nickel

37. Which one of the following is the major function to be performed by the UGC?

A. Controlling the working of the NAAC

B. Funding the payment of salaries to teachers in higher education

C. Maintenance of standards in higher education

D. Helping state universities in conducting research projects

38. As per Article 79 of the Indian constitution, the Indian Parliament includes:

A. The President of India, Vice President of India and the MPs

B. The central Cabinet, the Prime Minister of India and the and MPs

C. The President, The Lok Sabha and The RajyaSabha

D. The Speaker of the Loksabha, Deputy Speaker of the Loksabha and MPs

39. An autonomous college is different from a regular and affiliated college in respect of:

A. the levels in maintaining standards

B. the mode of selection and appointment of staff

C. the degree of control of the universities on the college

D. the freedom it has in conducting curricular programmes, student evaluations and award of degrees

40. Match the Institutions in column 'I' with those in column 'II'

Column I		Column II
(i) National Dairy Research Institute	-	(a) Hyderabad
(ii) Babha Atomic Research Centre	-	(b) Banglore
(iii) National Institute of Food and Nutrition	-	(c) Mumbai
(iv) Indian Institute of Science	-	(d) Karnal
(v) Central Institute of Indian Languages	-	(e) Mysore

A. (i) (a) (ii) (b) (iii) (d) (iv) (c) (v) (e)

B. (i) (d) (ii) (c) (iii) (a) (iv) (b) (v) (e)

C. (i) (e) (ii) (d) (iii) (b) (iv) (a) (v) (c)

D. (i) (e) (ii) (e) (iii) (b) (iv) (d) (v) (a)

41. Which of the following is not a fundamental right guaranteed in the Indian Constitution?

A. Right to property

B. Right to speech

C. Right to practice religion

D. Right to travel

42. What is meant by 'embedded computers'?

A. Laptop computers

B. A device used to control other devices used inside a computer

C. A sophisticated numerical integrator

D. A modern device that can do millions of operations

43. The unit of measurements of information storage in a computer is known as

A. Bit B. Mother Board C. Bios D. Byte

44. What is 'Param Padma'?

A. Super Computer developed by India
B. Software to facilitate e-governance
C. Name of satellite launched by India
D. Name of a website about computers

45. Which is the satellite launched exclusively for educational programmes?

A. Ekalavya B. Edusat C. Insat 1 B D. Aryabhatta

46. Which of the following is not an example for processing?

A. Arithmetic calculations
B. Sorting a list
C. Receiving signals from key board
D. Drawing pictures

47. Distance Education System employs multi-media for curricular transactions with a view to:

A. providing upto date information to learners
B. exposing them to relevant sources of information
C. compensating the limited interpersonal interaction
D. giving a global thrust to education

48. Under which element of communication would you classify the doubts raised by students in a class?

A. The Source B. Feedback C. Medium D. Message

49. Classroom communication by a teacher will be most effective when:

A. the teacher has an impressive personality
B. the teacher is capable of making humorous situations
C. the teacher supports his systematic presentation of ideas in simple language with illustrative examples
D. the students are given full freedom to ask questions and discuss ideas among themselves.

50. The major problem causing distortion of communication in the classroom is:

A. noisy classroom environment
B. lack of attention by students
C. lack of clarity in teachers explanation
D. use of highflown language and lengthy sentences

51. The quality of classroom communication can be improved once:

A. the teacher indicates the topic for teaching atleast one day earlier

B. the students are drawn into a focused discussion on the basic constructs to be taught

C. the teacher asks probing questions to direct the students thought process

D. all this above

52. Read the two assumption (a) and (b), and statement (c) which is a conclusion drawn from the assumption (a) and (b).

(a). All employees in office 'X' are members of organization 'Y'

(b). Raju is an employee of offfice 'X'

Conclusion:

(c). Raju is a member of organization 'Y'. This argument could be described as

A. an inductive argument

B. a deductive argument

C. an inductive - deductive

D. none of the above

53. If AZB = ZAY, BYC = ?

A. YBX B. XCY C. YCX D. XCW

Study the diagram given below and answer the question.

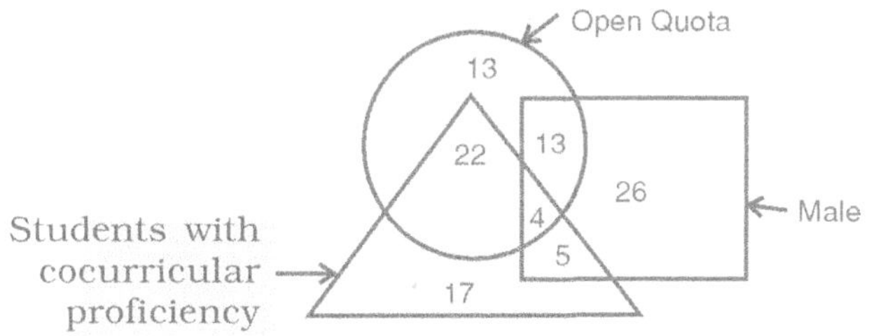

54. The number in each figure indicates the percentage of students admitted to a course from different categories. If the total number of students for the course is 250, how many were admitted with weightage given for their extra curricular performance?

A. 220 B. 200 C. 180 D. 120

55. Which of the following defines best a 'model of teaching'? A model of teaching is:

A. an instructional system with supporting aids

B. material used for giving concrete instructional experiences

C. the application of a learning theory for dividing the sequence of an instructional programme for achieving the expected educational objectives optimally

D. the ideal model to be adopted by students for optimising learning

56. Which one of the following is least important for effective communication in the classroom?

A. Clear perecption of the instructional objectives

B. Use of appropriate instructional aids

C. Integrating reinforcement strategies

D. The handsome appearance of the teacher

57. Which one of the following sampling procedures is most suitable for conducting a study in education on:

"A survey of the attitude of secondary school students of Delhi towards academic work".

A. Random sampling

B. Proportional Random sampling

C. Proportional satisfied sampling

D. Cluster sampling

58. Which one of the rights is a constitutional right but not a fundamental right as per the Indian constitution?

A. Right to freedom of religion

B. Right to property

C. Cultural and educational right

D. Right against exploitation

59. Which part of a computer is regarded as its brain?

A. The monitor B. The key board

C. The C.P.U D. The mouse

60. The Vice-Chancellor of a state university is appointed by:

A. The syndicate of the university

B. The Education Minister of the State

C. The Chairman of the UGC

D. The chancellor of the University who is also the Governor of the state.

Answer keys

1.D	2.D	3.B	4.A	5.C	6.D	7.C	8.B	9.B	10.B
11.C	12.D	13.C	14.C	15.C	16.C	17.C	18.D	19.A	20.D
21.D	22.B	23.C	24.A	25.A	26.D	27.A	28.A	29.B	30.B
31.D	32.A	33.D	34.C	35.B	36.A	37.D	38.C	39.D	40.B
41.A	42.B	43.D	44.A	45.B	46.C	47.C	48.B	49.C	50.C
51.D	52.B	53.A	54.D	55.C	56.D	57.C	58.B	59.C	60.D

MODEL QUESTION PAPER - 10

Note : This paper contains **sixty** (60) multiple choice questions, each carrying **two** (2) marks. Answer any **fifty** (50) questions. The total time for complete the paper is 75 minutes and the total marks for the paper is 100.

1. **The major focus of teaching in classrooms should be:**

   A. to make all students active participants in their learning

   B. to create situations for building new learning on what is already known

   C. to develop learning procedures which will lead to knowledge construction by the learners either by themselves or in groups

   D. a combination of all these

2. **One of the following is not a proper description of good teaching. Which is that?**

   A. Teaching is a process of carefully designed interaction between the teacher and the taught to achieve desired instructional outcomes

   B. Teaching is a deliberate process intended to help students to attain the expected goals of learning

   C. Teaching is giving all help to learners is their learning

   D. Teaching is a process of transfering knowledge from the lecturer to the learner

3. **Teaching model is a way to:**

   A. select the learning experiences in such way that the pupils react with the expected response

   B. teach in a formal as well as informal way

   C. adopt a new outlook on instruction where instructional experiences are organised, classified and interpreted to achieve better impact are the learners

   D. none of the above

4. **Division of all the teaching models under the title 'Modern Teaching Model' was carried out by:**

   A. John Dewey B. Percy Nunn C. Bruce. R. Joyce D. Montessoni

5. **Teaching is done in sequential steps. These steps are called:**

   A. Processes B. Programmes C. Phases D. paradigms

6. **The quality of a research in education is judged by the:**

   A. Experience of the researcher

   B. Impact of the research theme on professional practice

C. Methodology used for research

D. The theoretical base used for research

7. Which one of the following types of research procedures is used most by the media?

A. Natural Experimentation B. Sematic Differential

C. Content Analysis D. Internal criticism

8. Research and teaching are two different professions which:

A. cannot go together

B. can go together if the researcher is also a good teacher

C. can go together if there is a genuine researcher in the teacher

D. can go together only at the expense of quality

9. Which one of the following is the aim of educational research?

A. Control the quality of education

B. Revealing effective educational practices and principles hitherto unknown to practitioners

C. Improving Human welfare through new knowledge about teaching

D. Prediction of the level of a dependent variables upon the independent variable

10. A research paper is a piece of academic writing that requires:

A. a sound training in scientific reporting

B. ability for interpreting a finding in a very unusual but convincing manner

C. both A & B

D. none of the above

Read the following passage and answer the questions 11 to 15:

There are a wide variety of ways in which one individual stands out from others in their social behaviour. The group of social behaviours which are associated with leadership are complex and varied. So diverse are these ways that any one concept attempting to encompass them all, as "leadership" loses the specificity and precision that is necessary to scientific thinking. In general, it is an essential feature of the concept of leading that influence is exerted by one individual upon another, or more commonly that one or few individuals influence a large number. Influence, however, is itself a non-specific term. One may be influenced by another's disapproved-of behaviour to act antagonistically toward him or in a direction quite contrary to what he represents or advocates. It is usual in such circumstances to say that one is driven to act thus, rather than led. "Leading" implies a shared direction and this, in turn, often implies that all parties to the leadership relation have a common goal or at least similar or compatible goals. In the words of Hollander and Julian, is the influence of leaders that make a positive contribution towards the attainment of these goals." Thus, any act of leading implies an inter-individual relationship, and leading is one form of inter-individual influence. Definition of the simplest unit of analysis in leadership as "the act of leading" has led to the identification of four basic elements in the relationship (1) the *leader*, with the characteristics of ability and personality and his "resources relevant to goal attainment" (Hollander & Julian 1964); (2) the *followers*, who also have relevant abilities, personality, characteristic and resources; (3) the *situation* within which the relationship occurs : and (4) the *task* with which the interacting individuals are confronted. The nature of the leader-influence relationship and the characteristics of the act of leading are to be understood in terms of interaction between these four sets of variables.

11. The group of behaviour associated with the concept of leadership are:

A. vast and varied
B. specific and limited
C. not easily explained
D. far too many to be usefully discussed

12. Leading implies:

A. exerting influence upon one individual to change his views
B. exerting mental pressure upon one or few individuals by another
C. forcing others to accept another's views
D. persuading a group to accept a common direction

13. Hollander and Julian are of the opinion that:

A. a leader is the one who unnecessarily interferes with the decision making of others
B. a leader's role in the attainment of a common goal is often negligible
C. a leader's influence makes a positive impetus towards the attainment of certain common goals
D. a leader very often tends to misguide others

14. The act of leading implies that:

A. the leader isolates from his followers
B. the leader forges a close relationship with his followers
C. the leader stabilizes his relationship with followers using his leadership
D. the leader uses his ability to develop hero-worship among his followers

15. For a leader, the followers are:

A. mere puppets in his hands
B. those who contribute collectively to perform a common task
C. with their meagre abilities remain passive and follow the leader
D. using their collective strength sometimes to surpass the strength of the leader

16. Which one of the following is the most likely qualities to be a successful communicator?

A. One who sometimes demonstrates his inferiority before the receiver

B. One who knows a lot, but is unable to impress the receivers because of his reserved attitude

C. One who is able to use the language used by his listeners

D. One who has the ability to present the content in a precise manner

17. The oldest newspaper in India is:

A. Statesman B. Tribune

C. The Hindu D. The Times of India

18. Which of the following will reduce the quality of communication in a classroom?

A. A statement which gives the listeners the freedom to draw their own conclusions about its meaning

B. A precise statement using technical terms coined by experts

C. An ambiguous statement conveying differing interpretations

D. A lengthy statement

19. Which one of the following is not a proper way of communication in promoting literacy among the people of villages?

A. Large-group presentations using formal talks

B. Use TV and Film Projection for presentations followed by group discussions

C. Film or CD presentations of successful literacy programmes practised elsewhere

D. Small group discussions about the advantages of literacy programmes

20. Computer can best be used in education for:

A. evaluating student's progress

B. computer-based animation for science teaching and working of machines

C. calculations in arithmetic teaching

D. teaching of pronunciation

Directions: The four segments of population in a given region are represented by four diagrams intersecting with each other. Circle represents villagers, triangle stands for educated, square for agricultural labourers, and rectangle for hard working persons. Different regions in the diagram are numbered from 1 to 10. Study the diagram carefully and choose the correct answers for the following questions numbered 21-25:

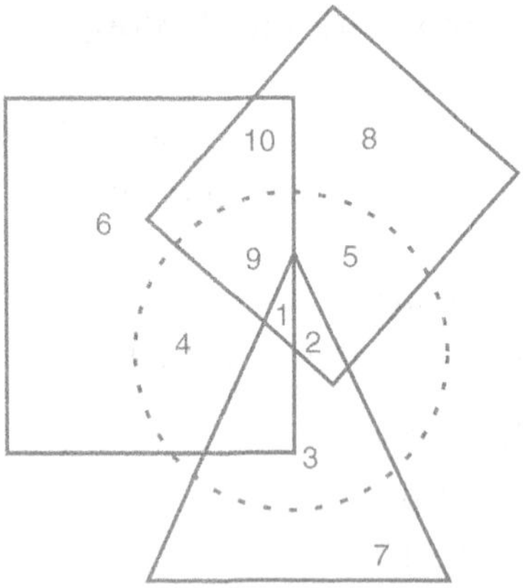

21. Among the villagers, hardworking agricultural labourers are indicated by:

A. 1 B. 5 C. 9 D. 10

Hint: Intersection of the circle, of angle and square

22. Educated, hardworking agricultural labourers in the village are indicated by:

A. 1 B. 2 C. 3 D. 4

23. Educated hardworking villagers are indicated by:

A. 1 B. 2 C. 3 D. 4

24. Which number indicates hardworking villagers ?

A. 2 B. 4 C. 6 D. 5

25. Indicate the numbered region which stands for neither educated nor hardworking agricultural labourers outside the village:

A. 5 B. 6 C. 7 D. 8

26. A teacher needs to know that Learning Disability (i) is contagious (ii) can be genetic (iii) is associated with low intelligence and/or (iv) involves developmental lag and difference.

A. (ii) and (iv) B. (i) and (ii) C. (ii) and (iii) D. (iii) and (iv)

Directions: The following question begin with a statement which is followed by two arguments. Which one of the four conclusions is strong?

27. *Statement:*

Should we impose fine on the parents who refuse to send their children to school?

Arguments:

I. Yes, this is the only way to eradicate illiteracy

II. No, parents might have their own personal problems, that's, why they are not sending their wards to schools.

A. Only argument I is strong

B. Only argument II is strong

C. Both arguments are strong

D. None of the two arguments is strong

28. Find the odd man from the following alternatives:

A. Elf

B. Sorcerer

C. Goblin

D. Fairy

29. Which out of the given options has similar relationship as Vein: Blood.

A. Wire : Electricity

B. Eye : Vision

C. Lungs : Air

D. Bone : Bone marrow

30. The Following question consists of two statements followed by two conclusions, select the valid conclusion from the four alternatives:

Statements:

I. Some helicopters are made of metal

II. All aeroplanes are metals

Conclusions:

I. All helicopters are aeroplanes

II. Some metals are aeroplanes

A. Only conclusion I follows

B. Both follows

C. Only conclusion II follows

D. None of the above

31. The average age of the four members of a family is 19 years. After 2 years their average age will increase by nearly:

A. 8%   B. 10.05%

C. 11.2%   D. 12.8%

32. Research shows that there is a direct relationship between growth and calorie intake of human beings. The graph indicates that most girls complete their physical growth:

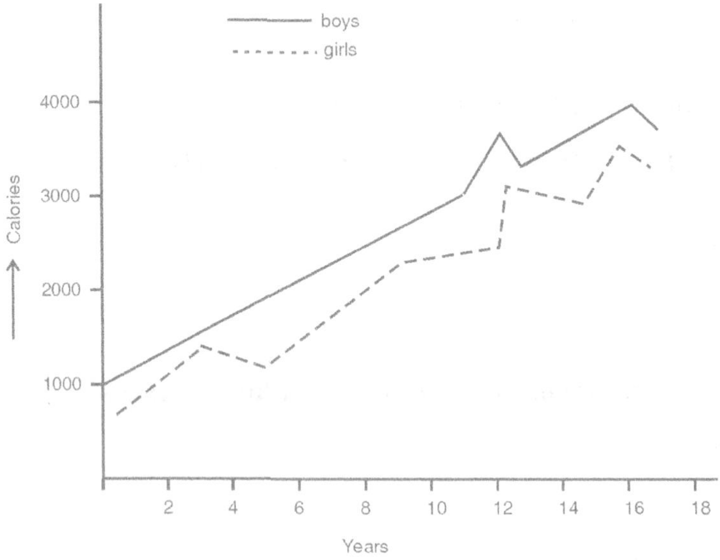

A. a few months earlier than boys
B. almost at the same time as boys
C. after they attain 18 years of age
D. a few months later than boys

Read the table and answer the questions

Use of pesticides in tonnes

Pesticides	1996	1997	1998	1999	2000
BHC	15300	18540	18500	17500	16640
DDT	2000	3970	2934	1294	2450
Malathion	430	750	640	875	943
Others	19242	19477	20173	16984	19855
Total	36972	42537	42247	36653	3988

33. The use of the three pesticides together BHC, DDT and Malathion - 'X' percent of total pesticides used in India in 1998. Then 'X' was approximately.

A. 48% B. 52.3%
C. 55.5% D. 53.5%

Study the pie-chart which represents the proportion of the expenditure on differentitem by an average family in the city. Answer the questions (34 and 35) that follow:

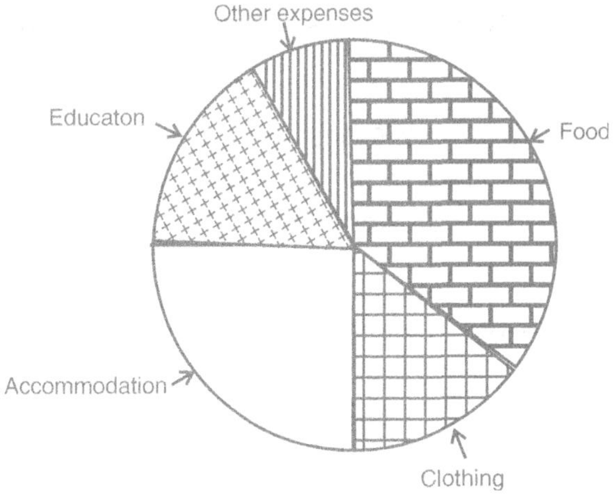

34. What percent of total expense was incurred by the family for accommodation?

A. 90% B. $33\frac{1}{3}\%$ C. 25% D. 15%

35. The expenditure incurred by the family on food is as much as on:

A. Education and accommodation

B. Education and other expenses

C. Accommodation and clothing

D. Other expenses

36. A 32-bit microprocessor can at a time handle:

A. 32 bits B. 32 bytes

C. 32 kilobytes D. 32 megabytes

37. Pick the odd one out

A. PC B. PC/XT

C. Minicomputer D. PC/AT

38. Which does not display graphics?

A. MA B. CGA

C. EGA D. VGA

39. Which one of the following statements about computer parts is true?

A. All diskettes can be made bootable

B. A bootable diskette is one which contains operating system files

C. The place where IO.SYS and MSDOS.SYS files, present on the disk, is fixed

D. All the above are true

40. The date field in the directory entry is:

A. 2 bytes long B. 8 bytes long

C. 6 bytes long D. None of the above

41. What is sericulture?

A. Study of various cultures in a community

B. Artificial rearing of fish

C. Art of silkworm breeding

D. Science of the manufacturing various kinds of serum

42. The Nagarjuna-Sagar Project is located on which one of the following rivers ?

A. Godavari B. Krishna

C. Cauvery D. Tungabhadra

43. Which one of the following states has the highest number of sandalwood in its forests?

A. M.P. B. A.P.

C. Kerala D. Karnataka

44. What is "Cirrus"?

A. A hail-bearing cloud

B. A cloud found in high altitudes

C. A rain-bearing cloud

D. A low cloud found is law altitudes

45. Which one of the following stands for a cold stream ?

A. Hakuna Hatata B. Labrador

C. Gulf Stream D. Eurasia

46. "Education is life, not a preparation for life." This statement summarizes the important principle in the educational philosophy of:

A. John Dewey B. Mahathma Gandhi

C. Rabindranatha Tagore D. Comenius

47. Which one of the following agencies does not have the authority to declare a University as a Deemed University in India

A. The University grants commission

B. The Parliament

C. Central Ministry of Human Resource Development

D. A State Legislature

48. Navodaya Vidyalayas have been primarily established to provide:

A. educational facilities for children of backward classes

B. free residential school benefits to select children

C. quality education to rural poor, with less expense

D. coaching to poor children for higher profession

49. Which of the following is not correct?

A. Eight state level tests have been accredited at par with NET

B. The student-teacher ratio in the Indian higher education is 1:21

C. There is a system of National - Eligibility Test for selection of school teachers in the states

D. NET is being conducted by the UGC

50. The Indira Gandhi National Open University came into existence in:

A. 1977 B. 1978 C. 1985 D. 1986

51. A teacher can develop a good rapport with his pupils if he:

A. accepts them for what they are

B. is willing to guide them properly

C. possesses good communication skills

D. All of the above

52. Which of the following is not important in sampling design?

A. the universe identified for study

B. the significant strata to be represented in the sample

C. the size of the sample and the method used for identifying the sample

D. All these

53. Which of the following doesn't have a state network of Doordarshan?

A. Delhi B. Bihar C. UP D. MP

54. If 9/12/2001 happens to be a Sunday, then 9/11/2005 was a

A. Wednesday B. Thursday C. Friday D. Saturday

55. Find the odd term in the series below.

12, 20, 30, 42, 55, 72

A. 78 B. 58 C. 57 D. 55

56. 'Liberty' is related to 'Slavery' in the way 'Danger' is related to:

A. Safety B. Hostility

C. Stability D. Authority

57. Circle A represents the set of orators B represents the set of actresses and C represent the set of actors in a populations. If the numbers in each set is represented as below, ie n A = 20, n B = 30 and n C = 40 then number of person of this group who have only one ability is:

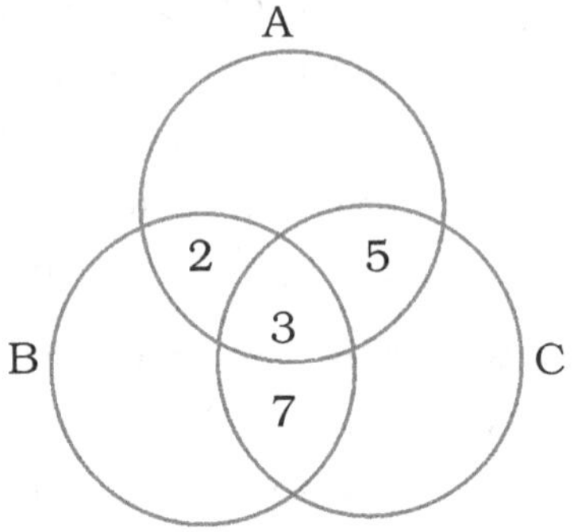

A. 62 B. 57 C. 63 D. 53

58. A huge network of computers, which links many different types of computers all over the world is known as:

A. the e-mail B. the website

C. the internet D. the intra net

59. ULSD stands for :

A. Unused lead selenium Dioxide

B. Undissolved Lead Sulphur Dioxide

C. Ultra Low Sulphur Diesel

D. None of the above

60. In India, a political party is recognized as a National or Regional Party by the:

A. Government of India

B. Election Commission of India

C. The Law Commission of India

D. Union Parliament in consultation with the State Legislatures

Answer keys

1. D	2.D	3.C	4.C	5.C	6.B	7.C	8.C	9.B	10.C
11.A	12.D	13.C	14.B	15.B	16.B	17.D	18.B	19.A	20.B
21.C	22.A	23.B	24.D	25.B	26.A	27.B	28.B	29.A	30.D
31.B	32.A	33.B	34.C	35.C	36.A	37.C	38.D	39.D	40.A
41.C	42.B	43.D	44.B	45.B	46.A	47.C	48.C	49.C	50.C
51.D	52.D	53.A	54.C	55.D	56.A	57.D	58.C	59.C	60.B

MODEL QUESTION PAPER - 11

Note : This paper contains **sixty** (60) multiple choice questions, each carrying **two** (2) marks. Answer any **fifty** (50) questions. The total time for completing this paper is 75 minutes and the total marks for this paper is 100.

Read the following passage carefully and answer questions 1 to 6

I am familiar with the superstition that self-realization is possible only in the fourth stage of life, ie Sannyasa (renunciation). But it is a matter of common knowledge that those who defer preparation for this invaluable experience until the last stage of life attain not self-realization, but old age amounting to a second and pitiable childhood, living as a burden on earth. I have a full recollection that I held these views even whilst I was teaching, though I might not then have expressed them in identical language. How then was this spiritual training to be given? I made the children memorize and recite hymns and read to them from books on moral training. But that was far from satisfying me. As I came into closer contact with them, I saw that it was not through books that one could impart training of the spirit. Just as physical training was to be imparted through physical exercises, and intellectual through intellectual exercises, even so the training of the spirit was possible only through the exercise of the spirit entirely dependent on the life and character of the teacher. The teacher had always to be mindful of his P's and Q's whether he was in the midst of his students or not.

1. Which among the following is the most suitable title for the passage?

A. Spiritual development as an intellectual training

B. Spiritual development through spiritual training

C. Superstitions about the practice of spiritualism

D. Spiritualism with teacher as model

2. The superstition among people about self-realization is that; it is to be practised:

A. without the help of a teacher

B. when one becomes a burden to others

C. during the last phase of one's life

D. using the model of life followed by old people

3. Spiritual training of the children according to the author is to be hinged mainly upon the character of:

A. parents

B. peer groups

C. social leaders

D. teachers

4. **The common knowledge quoted by the author about old age was that it is:**
   A. those who consider old age as most mature for Sanyasa
   B. those who wait for this old age to practise renunciation lead a miserable life as old men
   C. one can take a different view about renunciation as a teacher from that of a common man
   D. old men are a burden to others

5. **What does the author indicate through P's and Q's of the teacher, in this passage?**
   A. the spiritual and moral qualities of the teacher
   B. his concern as a teacher about spiritual training for youngster's
   C. the commitment of teachers to society
   D. the strengths and weaknesses of teacher is developing moral values

6. **Which of the following is not endorsed by the author?**
   A. Physical training is possible through physical exercises
   B. Intellectual development can be brought about through intellectual exercise
   C. Spiritual development is facilitated by exercising the spirit
   D. Spiritual development depends entirely on one's personal convictions

7. **Which one of the following will help to prevent distortion of communication in the classroom?**
   A. clear explanations by the teacher to help students to draw their own conclusions
   B. Extempore talks by the teacher to inspire the learners
   C. Objective-based deliberations and practice of focused learning experience by learners
   D. Teacher quoting various authors to support his arguments

8. **Classroom interaction based on the topic will be more effective if an outline of the topic of discussion is:**
   A. made available to students earlier
   B. a summary of the topic is written on the blackboard before beginning the class
   C. theme reduced to a short heading and written on the black board before commencing teaching
   D. not revealed until the students discover it during the presentation in class

9. An effective teacher will design his lesson using:

A. competition between the students

B. mutual acceptance by students

C. co-operation in developing different sub-areas of the main theme

D. teacher's presentation of the main theme

10. Choose the most essential roles of a teacher in a classroom for achieving quality student learning:

(i) develop a focussed and sharply defined theme for his presentation

(ii) motivate students by giving meaning to the theme presented

(iii) organize learning experiences which will help learners to construct knowledge of their own.

(iv) to prepare students for the final examinations

(v) locate information sources for learning the select topic

(vi) dictate notes to help learners to recall this informations presented

A. (i), (ii), (iii) and (v)

B. (i), (ii), (iv) and (vi)

C. (iii), (iv), (v) and (vi)

D. (i), (iv), (v) and (vi)

11. If students are found to be scoring poor marks in a test based on a specific topic by a teacher, it is better for this teacher to:

A. conduct the test again after giving feedback

B. teach the topic once more using teaching aids and longer explanations

C. diagnose the reasons for the scoring poor marks and apply remedial measures

D. suggest better learning strategies and give another test

12. Classroom communication will be most effective when we use one of the following combinations of processes. Identify the most effective combination from among the four choices:

A. reversing, evaluating, focussing

B. exaggerating, illustrating, evaluating

C. focussing, reversing, illustrating

D. evaluating, focussing, illustrating

13. The characteristics of some teachers are listed below. Which combination of characteristics is most appropriate for a teacher in higher education?

(i) A continuous learner of the subject keeping abreast of modern a developments in higher education

(ii) Strict and regimented with regard to student discipline and student learning

(iii) Deep insight into student needs and their problems
(iv) Dedication to the profession and to learning
(v) Political affiliation and aspiration for higher positions in education

A. (i), (iii) and (v)   B. (ii), (iv) and (v)
C. (i), (iii) and (iv)   D. (i), (ii) and (iv)

14. Which is the most important cause of absenteeism in the lecture halls in colleges?

A. students not properly motivated to learn
B. the teacher lacking in skills to present a complex subject area comprehensible to most of the students
C. the over dependence of teachers on verbal presentation
D. all the above

15. Good teaching is mostly to be attributed to the:

A. academic qualifications of the teacher
B. the dynamism and leadership of the head of the educational institution
C. teacher's professionalism and sincerity
D. support facilities available in the institution

16. Which of the following is associated with the element 'feedback' in the classroom communication?

A. regular attendance of students
B. questions raised by students during and after teacher's presentation
C. the quality and variety of the illustrations used by a teacher
D. respect and acceptance given to that teacher

Study the Pi-diagram and answer the questions 17 and 18, based on the details given there in:

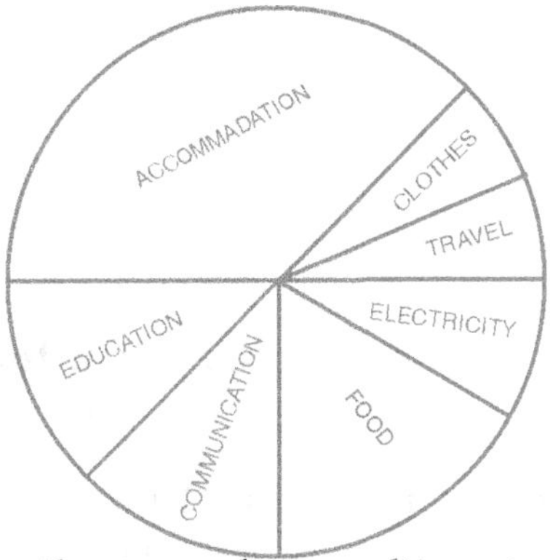

(Pi-diagram indicating the annual expenditure incurred by a family)

17. The family spends as much as on education as on:

A. communication

B. food

C. accommodation

D. travel

18. The percentage of expenditure incurred on food, electricity and travel together will be

A. more than three-fourth of the total family expenditure

B. less than one fourth of the total family expenditure

C. half of the total family expenditure

D. one-third of the total family expenditure

The graph given below shows rainfall in the cities E, F, G and H from the year 1991 to 1995. Study the graph and answer questions 19 and 20.

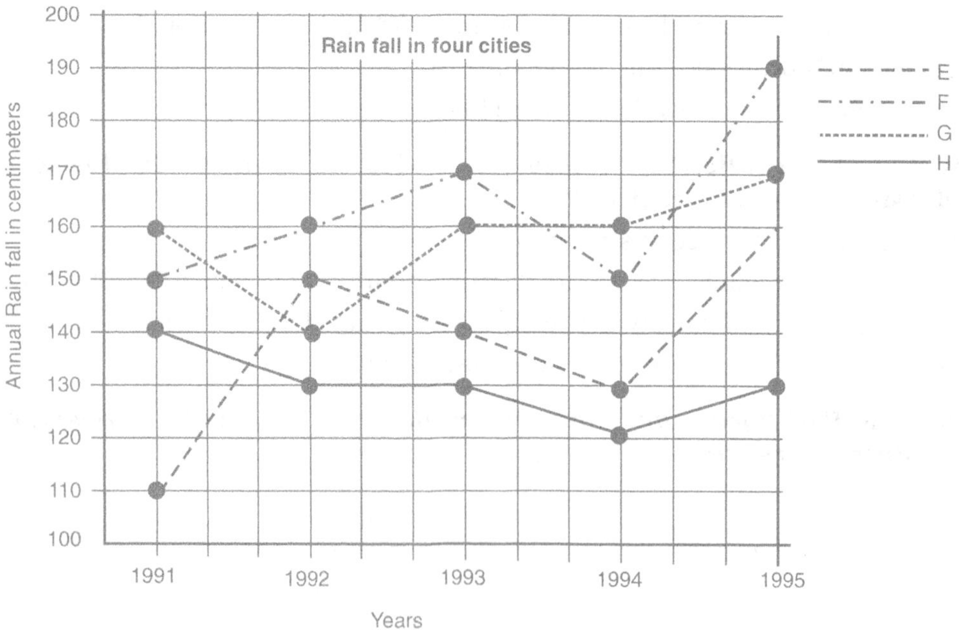

19. Which city has recorded the minimum rainfall during the five-year period?

A. G B. F C. E D. H

20. Which city had the highest rainfall in 1993?

A. G B. F C. E D. H

Study the following table showing the various causes of death in different years from 1970 to 2000.

Causes	1970	1980	1990	2000
Cancer	12.7%	16.5%	17.1%	18.00%
Cardio Vascular	36.2%	39.8%	42.3%	40.1%
Violence	8.7%	10.8%	12.1%	14.0%
Earth quakes	4.4%	4.9%	2.1%	1.1%
Accident	10.5%	8.00%	9.2%	8.2%
Floods	5.0%	5.00%	2.0%	1.0%
Others	22.5%	15.00%	15.2%	17.6%

21. Two inferences based on the data in the table are given. Which is true? Statement:

(i) violence shows a steady increase from the year 1970-2000

(ii) Floods have shown a steady decline during the period from 1970-2000

A. Both (i) and (ii) are false

B. Both (i) ans (ii) and true

C. Only (ii) is true

D. Only (i) is true

22. Who is regarded as the father of biodiversity?

A. Charles Darwin B. E.O.Wilson

C. Rachel Carson D. John Muir

23. Nature has enough to meet man's needs, but not enough to satisfy man's greed". This famous statement is by:

A. Winston Churchil B. Jawaharlal Nehru

C. Mahatma Gandhi D. Albert Einstein

24. The part of the earth where life exists is called:

A. the atmosphere B. the ecosphere

C. the environment D. the biosphere

25. What are known as 'keystone species'?

A. The extinction of the species which cause a catastrophic effect on an ecosystem.

B. The species which are on the threat of extinction

C. The species upon which many other species depend

D. The endangered species in an ecosystem

26. Bio-magnification is caused mainly by:

A. toxic substances concentrating through food chains

B. the green-house effect

C. the concentration of carbondioxide in the atmosphere

D. the pollutants contained in the atmosphere

27. Find out the next two missing items in the following series.

4,81,9,64,16,49,25........,

A. 39, 46 B. 36, 36

C. 48, 48 D. 38, 56

28. Which is the missing item?

calligrapher: photographer:: ......?....... : camera

A. paint brush B. photocopier

C. paper knife D. pen

29. Find out the item that does not belong to the group.

A. 7391 B. 3719

C. 2973 D. 9173

30. BEDA: QTSP:: ADCB: ...?

A. BDEA B. PRQS C. PQRS D. PSRQ

31. Out of 100 students in a college 25 study all the three subjects, Physics, Chemistry and Biology. 20 study Physics and Chemistry, 15 study Chemistry and Biology and 10 study Physics and Biology. Equal number of students study only one of these subjects. If so how many students study Physics?

A. 65 B. 60 C. 68 D. 70

32. Read the following statements and classify them in terms of Assumptions, Advice, Prejudice, Opinion and Fact.

(a): Consumption of tobacco is a major reason for oral Cancer

(b): No party should be in power for more than two terms

(c): Listen to criticisms patiently because it may help you to correct your mistakes.

(d): She is from an affluent family. She must be arrogant

(e): Women cannot come up, even if seats are reserved for them

	Fact	Opinion	Prejudice	Assumption	Advice
A.	(a)	(e)	(d)	(b)	(c)
B.	(a)	(b)	(e)	(d)	(c)
C.	(e)	(c)	(a)	(d)	(b)
D.	(d)	(e)	(b)	(a)	(c)

33. The world Trade Organisation believes in Intellectual Property Rights and Liberalised Trade Regime. Their belief is based on the assumption that:

A. Modern economy bestows equal benefits to all

B. Knowledge-based economy and globalization are a realities

C. All countries are well-equipped for modern trade

D. Rich countries will always help poor countries

34. The relationship between an Affiliating University I, an Affiliating College II and a University Department III is best represented by:

A. 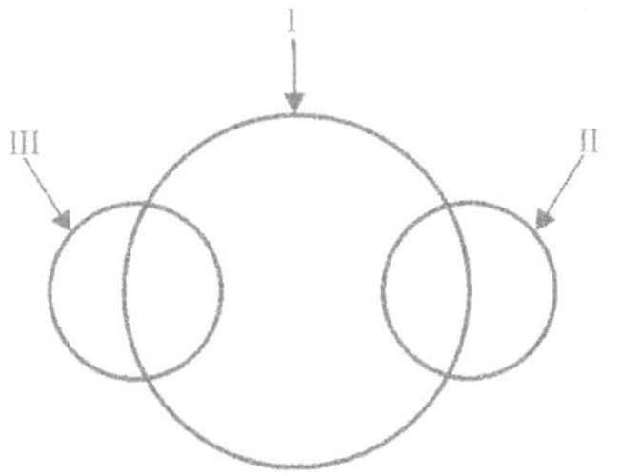

B. 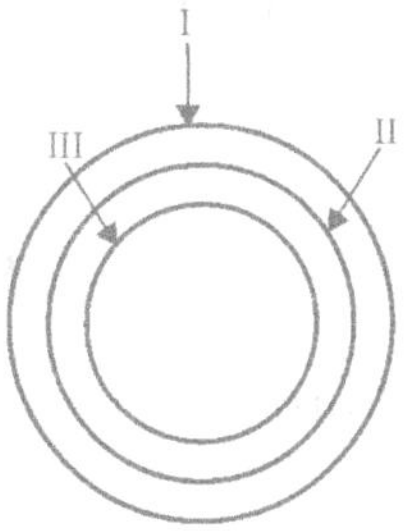

C. 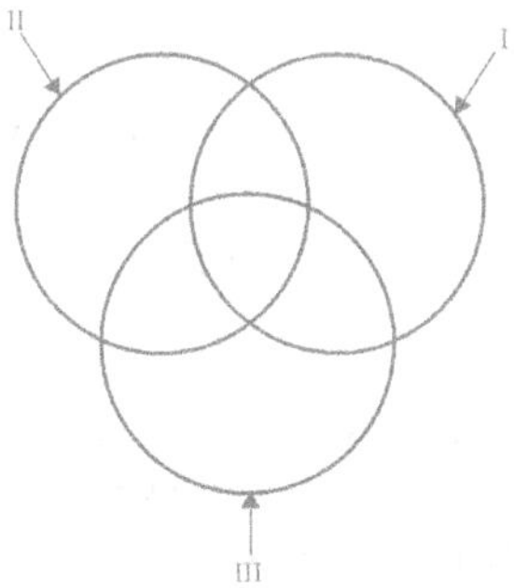

D. 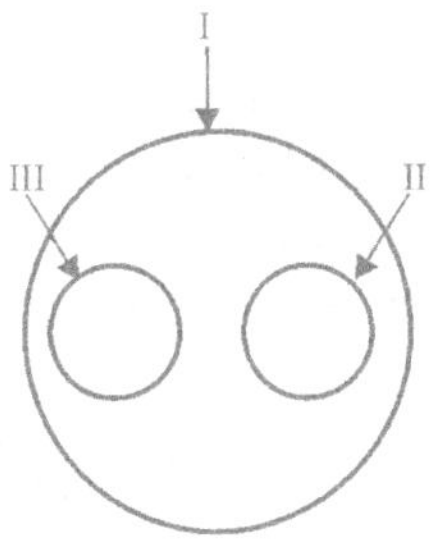

35. Given below are two statements followed by two conclusions. Which conclusion (s) can be logically derived from the statements?

Statements:

A: All furniture are wooden.

B: All wooden items are costly.

Conclusions:

(i) All furniture are costly.

(ii) All costly items are wooden.

A. Only (i)

B. Only (ii)

C. Both (i) and (ii)

D. Neither (i) nor (ii)

36. "Two of the very poor candidates were selected by a selection committee. There is lot of corruption in the selection procedure". The opinion in the above statement is:

A. valid B. invalid C. long-drawn D. doubtful

37. A research endeavour is best explained as:

A. An insightful process

B. A trial and error process

C. A process of unifying the findings of other researchers

D. A scientific paradigm for arriving at the solution to a crucial problem in an area

38. One of the given alternatives is not the purpose of research. Identify this alternative.

A. Research attempts to validate a new theory or a novel practice using the accepted method of science

B. Research is a hypothetico-deductive process of approaching a problem and verifying the hypothesis around which a study is conducted

C. Research is an attempt to add to one's academic status and to enable him to get higher placement in the area of specialization

D. Research aims at contributing to the existing fund of knowledge through discoveries using logically accepted methods.

39. Very many research projects are being undertaken in academic institutions. But discoveries are very rare. This is because:

A. Many researchers are using convergent thinking in conducting research

B. Most of the researchers do not have indepth-knowledge in the subject in which they do their research

C. Researchers capable of intelligent and patient efforts are not coming forward to do research

D. Adequate facilities are not available to most researchers in India

40. Which one of the following modalities is to be adopted by researcher?

A. Try to explore every sub-problem in connection with the topic of one's research

B. Concentrate on a group of sub-areas connected with the topic of research and go deeply into what one has selected

C. Patiently wait until solution flashes in his mind

D. Reject any finding which contradicts with his hypothesis

41. A researcher is engaged in the investigation of the causes and course of a phenomenon after its occurrence. What is the term used for this type of research?

A. Experimental Research

B. Survey Research

C. Ex-post facto Research

D. Action Research

42. What is 'Windows Vista'?

A. A Computer Virus

B. A Super Computer

C. Robot

D. An Operating System

43. Which Indian news agency was recently sold out to a private agency?

A. PTI B. UNI

C. PTI-Bhasha D. Tharang

44. The first technopark in India was established at:

A. Bangalore

B. Hyderabad

C. Thiruvananthapuram

D. Pune

45. The world-wide-web that takes you to another location or document when clicked is the:

A. URL

B. Address Bar

C. Browser

D. Hyperlink

46. 20th September 2004 is the day of:

A. Starting the programme called Ekalavya

B. The date on which lap-top computer was introduced
C. The date of launching of the 'Edusat'
D. The date in which America's Surveyor started sending satellite photographs of Mercury

47. Match the institutions in Column 'I' with their locations in Column 'II'

Column I

(i) Gandhigram Rural University
(ii) Centre of Advanced Studies in Education
(iii) National Institute of Mental Health and Neuro Sciences
(iv) English and Foreign Languages University (EFLU)
(v) Santhi Nikethan

Column II

(a) -Bangalore
(b) -New Delhi
(c) -Hyderabad
(d) -Madurai
(e) -Kolkotta
(f) -Baroda

A. (i) (d), (ii) (f), (iii) (a), (iv) (c), (v) (e)
B. (i) (d), (ii) (e), (iii) (f), (iv) (a), (v) (c)
C. (i) (e), (ii) (f), (iii) (b), (iv) (c), (v) (d)
D. (i) (f), (ii) (f), (iii) (a), (iv) (b), (v) (c)

48. A university without affiliating colleges, but has its own constituent colleges is known as:

A. A Central University
B. A Federal University
C. A Unitary University
D. A Deemed University

49. The Prime Minister of India is appointed by:

A. The President of the party which enjoys majority in the Lok Sabha
B. The Speaker, LokSabha
C. The Central Cabinet
D. The President of India

50. Which among the following is not an agency for funding of universities, colleges and other academic bodies in India?

A. UGC B. ICAR C. ICMR D. NAAC

51. Which one among the following is a Central University?

A. Mumbai University B. Delhi University

C. Madras University D. Kolkotta University

52. Question by students to clarify their doubts is treated as one of the elements of communication; which is this element?

A. message B. source

C. channel D. feedback

53. Communication boosters like film clippings, LCD projectors, etc. are used in the classroom for:

A. providing more accurate information

B. leading the students to original sources of information

C. making the presentation interesting and effective

D. all of the above.

54. Study the diagram given below and answer the question.

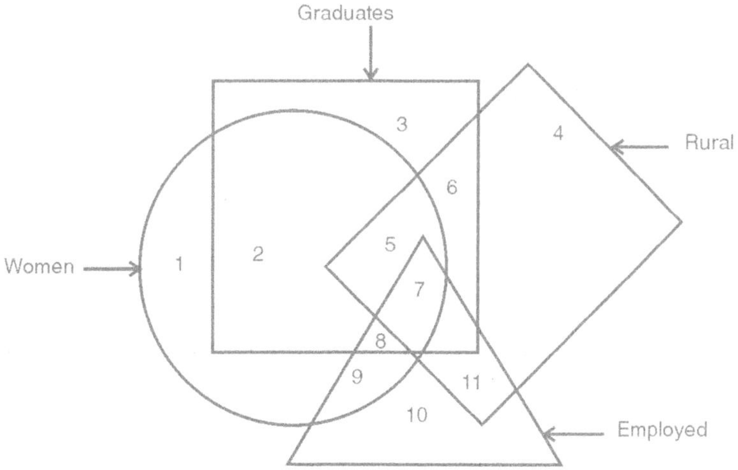

Employed women graduates from Rural area are represented by the number:

A. 8 B. 5 C. 7 D. 6

55. The side of the sun that is visible to us is called:

A. The Chromosphere

B. The Lithosphere

C. The Photosphere

D. The Troposphere

56. Where is 'Tidal Park' situated?

A. Delhi
B. Kolkotta
C. Chennai
D. Mumbai

57. Find out the missing number in the following diagram.

5	7		4	8		9	2		6	3
74			80			85			?	

A. 45
B. 53
C. 68
D. 71

58. Read the following proposition and select the most logical conclusion.

"All trains do not stop in Station X"

A. 'X' is an unimportant station

B. Some trains stop in this station

C. Only passenger trains stop here

D. Express and superfast trains will not stop here.

59. The AICTE and NCTE are:

A. Central Government Agencies

B. Bodies with the power to start new Engineering Colleges/Colleges of Education.

C. Independent statutory bodies with regulatory powers

D. Bodies functioning under the UGC.

60. The major difference between an 'administrator' and 'researcher' is that:

A. The administrator is interested in practical aspects of problems, whereas the researcher is interested in the theoretical sides

B. The administrator perceives the problem holistically whereas the researcher perceives the problem from an academic angle.

C. The administrator is concerned about the economic aspects of a decision, but the researcher is interested in the economic, academic and social outcome of a decision

D. The administrator is interested only in the outcomes of a problem, but the later is interested in the processes used for solving the problem.

Answer keys

1.B	2.C	3.D	4.B	5.A	6.C	7.C	8.A	9.C	10.A
11.C	12.D	13.C	14.D	15.C	16.B	17.A	18.D	19.C	20.A
21.B	22.B	23.C	24.D	25.A	26.A	27.B	28.D	29.C	30.D
31.A	32.B	33.B	34.D	35.A	36.C	37.D	38.C	39.A	40.B
41.C	42.D	43.B	44.C	45.D	46.C	47.A	48.B	49.D	50.D
51.B	52.D	53.D	54.C	55.C	56.C	57.A	58.B	59.C	60.B

MODEL QUESTION PAPER - 12

Note : This paper contains **sixty** (60) multiple choice questions, each carrying **two** (2) marks. Answer any **fifty** (50) questions. The total time for completely this paper is 75 minutes and the total marks for the paper is 100.

1. Fill in the following series.

9, 25, 49, 81, 121 ....

A. 169 B. 141 C. 172 D. 232

2. Find out the missing number in the following diagram.

5	25	35
6	?	48
7	49	63

A. 56 B. 42 C. 36 D. 64

3. In a row of six persons R is the third from X. V is the neighbour of both S and X. X is the fourth from Y. Z is the neighbour of Y. Who are at the extreme ends?

A. ZY B. XY C. RY D. RX

4. Seed, Tree, Forest has the same relationship as:

A. Nurse, Doctor, Pharmacy

B. Classroom, Lecturehall, Convention hall

C. Infant, Man, Crowd

D. Infant, Man, Meeting

5. Out of 50 players in a college, 6 play all the three games, cricket, hockey and football, 10 play cricket and hockey, 5 play hockey and football-8 play cricket and football- Equal number of players play only one of these games- If so how many play cricket?

A. 27 B. 31 C. 26 D. 29

6. Find out the item that doesnot belong to the group

A. Replace B. Rectify

C. Improve D. Modify

7. **'If Mahatma Gandhi was alive today, he should have led Sathyagraha against corruption' This statement is:**

A. a fact B. an opinion
C. an assumption D. a prejudice

8. **Read the statement and the two conclusions based on it. Identify the correct answer**

Statement:

Fortune favours the brave.

Conclusion:

1. People who take risks have greater chance of success
2. Cowards are never fortunate.

A. only 1 is implied
B. only 2 is implied
C. Both 1 and 2 are implied
D. Neither 1 nor 2 is implied

9. **Assuming that the proposition given below is true, indicate which of the conclusions can be validly drawn from it.**

Proposition:

Teachers seldom enjoy classroom teaching.

Conclusions:

A. Teachers frequently enjoy classroom teaching
B. Teachers invariably enjoy classroom teaching
C. Teachers do not enjoy classroom teaching
D. Many teachers do not like teaching

10. **"Non violence doesnot mean tolerating any injustice patiently, nor is it a weakness." This sentence implies that:**

A. Non violence is a fight against injustice
B. Non violence is a synonym for bravery
C. Tolerating any injustice is a weakness
D. Non-violence is a peaceful way of resisting injustice with courage

11. **If all birds can fly, and if the penguin is a bird, the penguin can fly. The conclusion drawn in this argument is:**

A. logical B. invalid
C. long drawn D. valid

12. If A is B's son, B and C are sisters. D is C's mother and E is the son of D. Which of the following is the correct inference?

A. E and A are cousins

B. E is the maternal uncle of A

C. C is A's grand mother

D. C and E are sisters

***Read the following passage and answer* questions 13-18:**

The British pattern of education in the pre-independence and later in independent India had a great influence on the generation of quality of educated manpower in India. Earlier it was meant to serve the Britishers during the colonial period and later it aided the fulfillment of scientific and technical manpower needs of various institutions abroad. That is why the Indian scientists and technologists could excel in foreign countries as there exists a slot for them in the growth of interdisciplinary areas at the prestigeous institutions abroad rather than in India. We too need our brilliant young scientists and technologists here, not one or two, but in large numbers to further the process of industrialization, as well as to enhance the prestige of India in the world market. A critical analysis suggests that soon after independence, a model was adopted which aimed at industrialization through technology import, followed by efforts aimed at import substitution and development of indigenous technology for attaining overall economic development of the country. It was believed that through industrialization there would be enough production and prosperity to gradually take care of many of our day to day problems. This has happened not as much as one would have liked; benefits following out of our developmental efforts have not reached many of our people, especially the poor and the rural ones. Science in India needs introspection. There is a need to restructure the present Indian model of development of science, technology and industry in the country. The monitoring and evaluation of Indian science has now assumed great significance in view of globalization. Industrial progress needs a proper technological base which in turn requires strong scientific temper among the people in the country. All efforts were directed in the past to develop a science base in India. It appers that there exist very weak linkages both backwards and forwards among the academic, R&D and Industrial sectors.

13. The most suitable title for the passage is:

A. Industrialization

B. Education and Development

C. Science base in Technology

D. Co-ordination between academy & Industry

14. The main approach adopted by Indian scientists in doing outstanding scientific research abroad is:

A. There were slots awaiting them in many foreign countries
B. Use the expertise they developed serving the Britishers during the colonial period
C. Excel in educated manpower within the country and outside
D. Excel in the interdisciplinary research area in prestigious foreign institutions.

15. Industrialization in India emphasises least upon:

A. Globalizaton
B. Foreign technology
C. Indigenous technology
D. Export technology

16. At present the greatest need in the development of science and technology in India is:

A. Research and development
B. Monitoring and evaluation
C. Material collection and production
D. Technical education and commercialization

17. The Indian model of development in the post-independence period is aimed at:

A. Imports of technology for industrialization
B. Import substitution and development
C. Indigenous technology development
D. Economic development

18. Scientific and technology development in India is important because:

A. younger generation need a scientific temperament to succeed
B. globalization warrants it
C. there are weak linkages of science and technology with development
D. We have to reconceive the existing model of development

19. The major difference between an affiliating university and a unitary university is that:

A. The later is more or less residential
B. There are no colleges affiliated to a unitary university
C. There are several schools for performing academic and administrative functions in an Affiliating University
D. The method of management of the two types of Universities are different

20. Which of the following universities in India is best described as a Federal University?

A. Aligarh Muslim University

B. Banares Hindu University

C. Delhi University

D. Indira Gandhi National Open University

21. The curriculam designing of an institution under an Affiliating University is done by:

A. the senate of the University

B. the syndicate of the University

C. the Academic Council and Boards of Studies of the University

D. all these bodies in combination

22. An institution is declared as a Deemed University taking into account:

A. its previous record of excellence

B. the quality of the faculty members

C. the unique curricular programmes offered by it

D. the recommendation of the elected representatives connected with the institution

23. The Central Institute of Indian Languages is situated in:

A. Delhi

B. Mysore

C. Bangalore

D. Chennai

24. The major objective of distance education is to provide:

A. opportunities for all those who aspire for higher education

B. technological support to higher education

C. accessibility to quality education is the youth

D. compensatory measures to correct the defiencies of the regular system

25. One will be able to communicate effectively if he:

A. is able to inject humour into his preventation

B. has histrionic talents to support his communication

C. can communicate by quoting several important authorities in the area concerned

D. is very clear about the objectives and the content of his communication

26. Which one of the following is most desirable for making classroom communication effective?

A. Extempore preventation by the teacher supporting illustrations

B. Expository presentation by the teacher based on a prepared design for organizing subject matter

C. Expository presentation followed by a discussion with the participation of the standards

D. Use of communication boosters like LCD projector

27. The questions asked by students after the teacher's presentation refer to which one of the following elements of communication?

A. Receiver

B. Message

C. Source

D. Feedback

28. Multimedia approach is adopted in distance education so as to:

A. compensate for the deficiency of interpersonal interaction between the teacher and the learners in the group

B. lead the students to original sources of information

C. expose the students to presentation by specialist teachers

D. to develop the impression that the quality of the course is excellent

29. Which one of the following is a good example for non-verbal communication?

A. A scribbled piece of paper is exchanged by the students while a class is going on

B. A message sent while the phone is in silent mode

C. A traffic policeman showing signals to proceed

D. A poster displayed on the college notice board

30. Verbal communication is least effective in developing:

A. Attitudes

B. Values

C. Concepts

D. Skills

Four students PQR and S appeared for four subject papers I, II, III and IV. Their percentage scores for each of the papers are given in the table. Study the table and answer questions 31 and 32.

Papers / Students	I	II	III	IV
P	60	81	45	55
Q	59	43	51	04
R	74	04	71	65
S	72	76	04	68

31. Which candidate scored aggregate between 60-65%?

A. P B. Q C. R D. S

32. In which paper did the students perform badly?

A. I B. II C. III D. IV

Study the following diagram and answer questions 33 and 34.

Distribution of Graduate Students in a college in 10 optional Subjects

1. Physics 2. Chemistry 3. Biology 4. Mathematics
5. Commerce 6. Psychology 7. English 8. History
9. Micro Biology 10. Economics

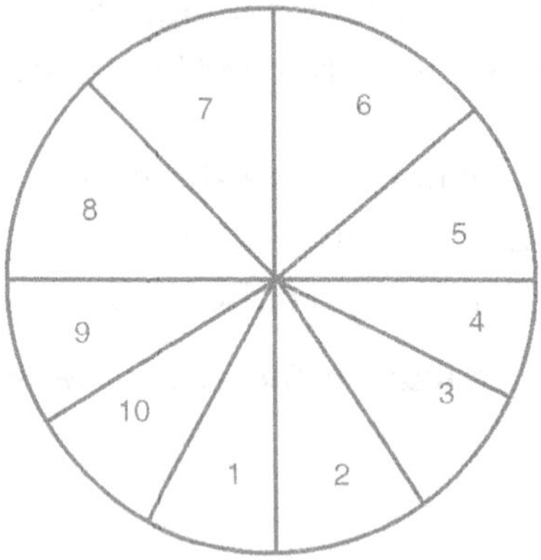

33. If the total number of graduates enrolled is 2500, How many are studying in History and English put together?

A. 360 B. 478

C. 625 D. 600

34. Which one of the following statements is correct if the total number of graduates is 1250?

A. Total number of students in Physics, History, Commerce & Psychology are 625

B. There are more students in Physics, Chemistry & Biology combined than in Maths, Commerce and Psychology combined

C. Equal number of students are enrolled in Psychology & Commerce

D. Total number of students in English, Maths & Microbiology are 400

Study the graph showing variation in temperature in a city over a week and answer questions 35 and 36.

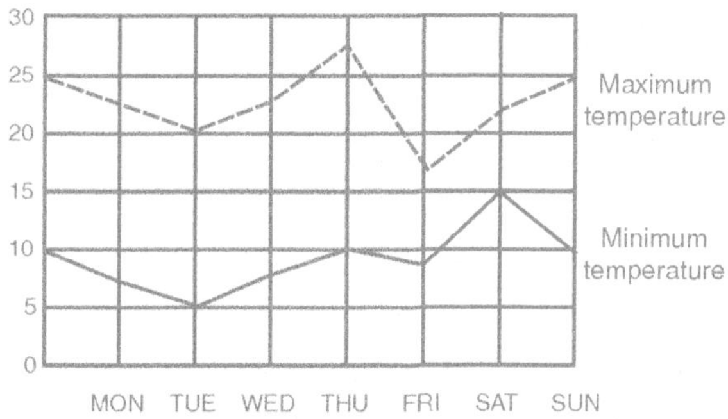

35. On which day of the week did the maximum temperature of the city come closest to the minimum temperature?

A. Saturday B. Thursday

C. Friday D. Monday

36. On which day was the highest difference between the maximum and minimum temperature reported

A. Monday B. Wednesday

C. Thursday D. Friday

37. Internet requires:

A. an international agreement to connect computers

B. a local area network

C. a commonly agreed set of rules to communicate between computers

D. a world wide web

38. Services available on the world wide web are:

(i) encryption

(ii) HTTP

(iii) HTML

(iv) Fire walls

A. (i) and (ii) B. (ii) and (iii)

C. (iii) and (iv) D. (i) and (v)

39. A search engine is a programme to search:

A. for information

B. web pages

C. web pages for specified index terms

D. web pages for information using specified search items

40. HTML is similar to:

A. word processing language

B. screen editor

C. scripting language

D. search engine

41. VIRUS in computers stands for:

A. Virtual Information Resource Under Security

B. Virtual Interactive Resource Under Siege

C. Virtual Information Resource Under Seige

D. Virtual Interactive Resource Under Security

42. Which computer generation has the property of Artificial Intelligence?

A. Sixth Generation

B. Fifth Generation

C. Fourth Generation

D. None of these

43. Which of the following combination of professional competencies are most desirable for a teacher in higher education?

(i) competency to prepare for the exam and deliver between in a disciplined classroom

(ii) Motivate the learners, convent students into cuscicutioun learners

(iii) Evaluator of student learning, arbitrator for resorting conflicts among students

(iv) Dictating notes, giving leadership in the social activities

(v) Facilitator of learning, councillor student

A. (i), (ii) and (iii)
B. (ii), (iii) and (iv)
C. (iii), (iv) and (v)
D. (ii), (iii) and (v)

44. The most formidable challenge for the generation teacher in higher education is:
A. evening students presence in the lecture hall
B. evaluating large numbers of answer scripts
C. motivating students to accept world-class higher education
D. acting as per the dictates of trade unions

45. Which one of the following statements about teachers in higher education would you endorse?
A. A teacher in higher education should be a strict disciplinarian
B. A teacher should prepare for lectures, quoting authorities in his subject
C. A teacher should be able to assert his superiority in his lecture hall
D. A teacher should be capable of understanding the needs and the mentality of his students

46. Which strategy is most appropriate for curriculum transaction in higher education?
A. Full lecture presentations, students preparing their own notes
B. Short lectures followed by note dictation on topics useful for final exams
C. Library arrangement after a short lecture
D. Expository teaching ( ) around group discussions and seminar presentation

47. Some activities related to the development phase of a lecture are given below. Find out the item that does not relate to that phase.
A. Motivating the student
B. Citing illustrations
C. Using communication boosters
D. Progressive differentiation & evaluation

48. What according to you, is the most important intention of higher education?
A. Help in acquiring higher qualifications
B. Help in getting higher employment
C. Assistance in total personality development
D. Identifying content which we help are to score top marks in common exams

49. Which of the following is not biodegradable?

A. Vegetables
B. Fruits
C. Earthworms
D. Aluminium foil bags

50. Air pollution is caused mainly by:

A. insecticides
B. sewage
C. smoke
D. loud speakers

51. Which of the following diseases is caused by water pollution?

A. Scurvey
B. Typhoid
C. Malaria
D. Anemia

52. Vanamahotsava is observed on:

A. Second October
B. First December
C. Tenth August
D. First July

53. What is not an indirect service of the world's eco systems?

A. Atmospheric gas regulation
B. Water supply
C. Nutrient cycling
D. Climatic regulations

54. Which one of the following articles does not contain mercury-based chemicals?

A. Computer discs
B. Blinking lights in sneakers
C. Fluorescent light bulbs
D. Thermometers

55. Reliability of research is concerned with the:

A. replicability of findings
B. generalizability of conclusions
C. interpretability of results
D. consistency of findings when replicated

56. A research tool is valid when it:

A. measures what it is meant to measure

B. yields the same scores on repeated administration

C. has inter researcher agreement

D. provides discriminating scores of different research variables

57. Survey study that does not require the use of a sample is called:

A. A Historical Survey
B. Causal-comparative Survey
C. Census Survey
D. None of the above

58. The best definition for a case study is:

A. a detailed study about a person

B. an indepth study of a phenomenon

C. a cross sectional study of a social system

D. a longitudinal study of a social unit

59. A research report should essentially have all the qualities except:

A. statement of hypothesis in operational terms

B. explanation of methodology, tools and techniques

C. stylistic language for reporting

D. the details of the major findings and conclusions

60. One of the following is not an objective of research; identify that:

A. to find the truth about a phenomenon scientifically and contribute to the existing fund of knowledge

B. to add to one's reputation as a scholar and increase his opportunities for placement in higher positions

C. to verify the existing theories and their relevance in changing scenario

D. to explain a newly experienced phenomenon

Answer keys

1.A	2.C	3.C	4.C	5.B	6.A	7.B	8.A	9.C	10.D
11.C	12.B	13.B	14.D	15.D	16.B	17.A	18.B	19.B	20.C
21.C	22.C	23.B	24.A	25.D	26.C	27.D	28.A	29.C	30.D
31.A	32.C	33.C	34.C	35.A	36.C	37.C	38.B	39.D	40.B
41.C	42.B	43.D	44.C	45.D	46.D	47.A	48.C	49.D	50.C
51.B	52.D	53.B	54.A	55.D	56.A	57.C	58.D	59.C	60.B

APPENDIX

APPENDIX - I

About the UGC Test

In early eighties, there was a general perception among the public and the leading educationists that well qualified persons were not being attracted towards teaching profession. Concerns were also expressed about the criteria that were employed for the selection of teachers. It was increasingly realized that quite a large number of people who had neither the competence nor the aptitude for teaching made an easy entry into the profession.

The Committee formed by the UGC in 1983 on revision of pay scales of teachers in the universities and colleges, under the Chairmanship of Prof. R C Mehrotra, recommended the following qualifications for the post of Lecturer:

i. Master's degree in the subject concerned with at least 55 % marks or its equivalent grade.

ii. Pass in the National Test conducted for the purpose by the UGC or any other agency approved by the UGC.

The Committee suggested that the qualifications should not be relaxed even for candidates possessing M.Phil/Ph.D. degree. The Committee observed that the stipulation of M.Phil/Ph.D. as an essential qualification for Lecturers had not been followed in most institutions. What is worse, these research qualifications do not contribute to the raising of standards of teaching and research. The committee was of the view that the prolification of research qualifications led to the dilution of research standards. The rush for acquiring research degrees further diluted the standard of research. In view of the diversity of standards among universities, the Mehrotra Committee recommended that passing a national qualifying examination before recruitment be made an essential pre-requisite for all teachers.

The National Commission of Teachers on Higher Education headed by Prof. Rais Ahmed had strongly recommended the need for adopting more definable methods of selection: it recommended the need for evolving a rigorous merit- based selection for the entry level of the teaching profession.

The National Policy on Education, 1986 too had underlined the need for adopting more rational methods of recruitment of teachers to ensure merit, objectivity and conformity with regional and functional requirements. The Programme of Action prepared in pursuance of the National Policy of Education, 1986, recommended that the teachers will be recruited on the basis of a common qualifying test, the details of which are to be formulated by the UGC.

With a view to working out the modalities for the conduct of such a test, the UGC constituted a Committee, which developed strategies for the conduct of a national level eligibility test for the recruitment of teachers in universities and colleges. Consequently, the Government of India, through a notification in 1988 entrusted the task of conducting the eligibility test for lectureship to the UGC. Thereby, the UGC has been conducting the National Eligibility Test for Junior Research Fellowship and eligibility for Lectureship since 1989.

The National Educational Testing Bureau of University Grants Commission (UGC) conducts National Eligibility Test (NET) for deciding the eligibility for lectureship and for the award of Junior Research Fellowship (JRF) for Indian nationals in order to ensure minimum standards for the entrants in the teaching profession and for entry level researching.

For candidates who desire to pursue research, the Junior Research Fellowship (JRF) is available for five years subject to fulfillment of certain conditions. The UGC has allocated a number of fellowships to the universities for the candidates who qualify for the JRF. The JRFs are awarded to the meritorious candidates from among the candidates qualifying for eligibility for lectureship in the NET. The JRFs are available only to the candidates who opt for it in their application forms.

1. SCOPE OF NET

a. Eligibility for Lectureship

Clearing of NET confers eligibility for lectureship upon Indian nationals, i.e. the NET qualified candidates are eligible to apply for the post of lecturer in the area,in all Indian universities/Institutes/colleges.

b. Junior Research Fellowship

The candidates who qualify the Junior Research Fellowship (JRF) Examination of the UGC are also eligible for the post of lectureship. In addition, they are also eligible to receive Fellowships (UGC) under various schemes, subject to the candidates finding their placement in the universities. The validity of the offer is for two years w.e.f. the date of issue of the JRF award letter. The validity period of the offer has been raised from one year to two years for the JRF Award Letters issued on or after 1st April, 2005. However, in case the candidates who have already joined for M.Phil. /Ph.D., the date of commencement of fellowship will be from the date of declaration of the NET examination result or date of their joining, whichever is later.

2. CONDITIONS OF ELIGIBILITY

i. Candidates who have secured at least 55% marks (without rounding) in Master's Degree or equivalent examination from universities/institutions recognised by the UGC in Humanities (including languages) and Social Sciences, Computer Science & Applications, Electronic Science etc. are eligible for this Test. The Scheduled Caste (SC)/Scheduled Tribe (ST) including candidates from Lakshadweep/ Physically Handicapped (PH)/Visually Handicapped (VH) category candidates who have secured at least 50% marks (without rounding) in Master's degree or equivalent examinations are eligible for this Test.

ii. Candidates who have appeared or will be appearing for the qualifying Master's degree (final year) examination and whose result is still awaited or candidates whose qualifying examinations have been delayed may also apply for this Test. However, such candidates will be admitted provisionally and shall be considered eligible for award of the JRF/Lectureship eligibility only after they have passed their Master's degree examination or equivalent with at least 55% marks (50% marks in case of SC/ST/PH/VH category candidates). Such candidates must complete their P.G. degree examination within two years from the date of the NET result with required percentage of marks, failing which they shall be treated as disqualified.

iii. The Ph.D. degree holders whose Master's level examination had been completed by 19th September, 1991 (irrespective of date of declaration of result) shall be eligible for a relaxation of 5% in aggregate marks (i.e., from 55% to 50%) for appearing the NET.

iv. Candidates are advised to appear in the subject of their post-graduation only. The candidates, whose subject for post-graduation is not covered in the list of subjects, may appear in a related subject.

v. Candidates seeking concession in fee are required to submit attested copy of their OBC(Non-creamy layer)/SC/ST/PH/VH certificate along with on-line printout of their Application Forms (obtained while applying on-line). Other candidates are not required to submit any certificates/documents in support of their eligibility along with the printout of their Application Form. Therefore, the candidates, in their own interest, must satisfy themselves about their eligibility for the Test. In the event of any ineligibility being detected by the Commission at any stage, their candidature will be cancelled and they shall be liable for legal action.

vi. Candidates with post-graduate diploma/certificate course(s), should in their own interest, ascertain the equivalence of their course(s) with Master's degree of recognized Indian universities from Association of Indian Universities, New Delhi.

Exception (Eligibility for Lectureship)

i. The NET shall remain the minimum eligibility condition for recruitment and appointment of Lecturers in Universities/Colleges/Institutions. However, candidates, who are or have been awarded Ph.D. Degree in compliance of the "University Grants Commission (minimum standards and procedure for award of Ph.D. Degree), Regulation 2009, shall be exempted from the requirement of the minimum eligibility condition of the NET for recruitment and appointment of Assistant Professor or equivalent positions in Universities/Colleges/Institutions." The candidates who have passed the UGC JRF examination prior to 1989 are also exempted from appearing in the NET.

ii. For SET Candidates: The candidates who have cleared the State Eligibility Test (SET) accredited by the UGC for eligibility for Lectureship held prior to 1st June 2002, are exempted from appearing the NET, being eligible to apply for Lectureship anywhere in India. For SET held from 1st June 2002 onwards, the qualified candidates are eligible to apply for the post of lecturer only in the universities/colleges belonging to the state from where they have cleared their SET.

3. AGE LIMIT & RELAXATION

i. **Junior Research Fellowship:** Not more than 28 years. A relaxation up to 5 years is provided to the candidates belonging to SC/ST/OBC/PH/VH categories and to women applicants. Relaxation will also be provided to the candidates having research experience, limited to the period spent on research in the relevant/related subject of post-graduation degree, subject to a maximum of 5 years, on production of a certificate from appropriate authority. Three years relaxation in age will be permissible to the candidates possessing L.L.M. Degree. Total age relaxation on the above ground(s) shall not exceed five years under any circumstances.

ii. **Lectureship:** There is no upper age limit for applying for lectureship eligibility.

4. SCHEME AND DATE OF THE TEST

i. The Test will consist of three papers. All the three papers will be held in two separate sessions as under:

Session	Paper	Marks	Duration
First	I	100	1¼ Hours (09.30 A.M. to 10.45 A.M.)
First	II	100	1¼ Hours (10.45 A.M. to 12.00 NOON)
Second	III	200	2½ Hours (01.30 P.M. to 04.00 P.M.)

Paper-I shall be of general nature, intended to assess the teaching and research aptitude of the candidate. It will primarily be designed to test the aptitudes in teaching and research, reasoning ability, comprehension, divergent thinking and general awareness of the candidate. Sixty (60) multiple choice questions of two marks each with four alternatives will be given, out of which the candidate would be required to answer any fifty (50). In the event of the candidate attempting more than fifty questions, the first fifty questions attempted by the candidate will be evaluated.

Paper-II shall consist of questions based on the subject selected by the candidate. This paper will consist of a Test Booklet containing 50 compulsory objective type questions of two marks each. Each question will be followed by four alternatives.

The candidate will have to mark the responses for questions of Paper-I and Paper-II on the Optical Mark Reader (OMR) Sheet provided along with the Test Booklet. The detailed instructions for filling up the OMR Sheet will be sent to the candidate along with the Admit Card.

Paper-III will consist questions from the subject selected by the candidate. The candidate will be required to attempt questions in the response sheet provided in the Test Booklet. The structure of Paper-III has been revised from June, 2010 UGC-NET.

Paper-III will be evaluated only if the candidate qualifies in Paper I and II as per the table given below:

CATEGORY	MINIMUM QUALIFYING MARKS		
	PAPER - I	PAPER - II	PAPER-I+PAPER-II
GENERAL	40	40	100 (50 %)
OBC/PH/VH	35	35	90 (45 %)
SC/ST	35	35	80 (40 %)

The minimum qualifying criteria for award of JRF are as follows:

CATEGORY	MINIMUM QUALIFYING MARKS			
	PAPER - I	PAPER - II	PAPER-I+ PAPER-II	PAPER – III
GENERAL	40	40	100 (50 %)	100 (50 %)
OBC/PH/VH	35	35	90 (45 %)	90 (45 %)
SC/ST	35	35	80 (40 %)	80 (40 %)

However, the final qualifying criteria for Junior Research Fellowship (JRF) and Eligibility for Lectureship shall be decided by the UGC before declaration of result.

ii. For Visually Handicapped (VH) candidates thirty minutes' extra time will be provided separately for paper-I and Paper-II. For paper-III, forty five minutes' extra time will be provided. They will also be provided the services of a scribe who would be a graduate in a subject other than that of the candidate. Those **Physically Handicapped (PH)** candidates who are not in a position to write in their own hand-writing can also avail these services by making prior request (at least one week before the date of UGC-NET) in writing to the Co-ordinator of the test centre. Extra time and facility of scribe will not be provided to other Physically Handicapped candidates.

iii. Syllabus of the Test: Syllabi for all NET subjects can be downloaded from the UGC Website www.ugc.ac.in and are also available in the libraries of all Indian Universities. The UGC will not send the syllabus to individual candidates.

iv. In Paper III, candidate has the option to answer either in Hindi or in English in all subjects except the languages where the candidate is required to write in the languages concerned. In case of Computer Science & Applications, Electronic Science and Environmental Sciences, the question papers have to be answered in English only.

v. In case any discrepancy found in the English and Hindi versions, the questions in English version shall be taken as final.

5. SUBJECTS

The list of NET subjects along with their respective codes is as given below:

Subject Code	Name of the Subject
01	Economics
02	Political Science
03	Philosophy
04	Psychology
05	Sociology
06	History
07	Anthropology
08	Commerce
09	Education
10	Social Work
11	Defence and Strategic Studies
12	Home Science
14	Public Administration
15	Population Studies*
16	Music
17	Management
18	Maithili
19	Bengali
20	Hindi
21	Kannada
22	Malayalam
23	Oriya
24	Punjabi
25	Sanskrit
26	Tamil
27	Telugu
28	Urdu
29	Arabic
30	English
31	Linguistics
32	Chinese
33	Dogri

34	Nepali
35	Manipuri
36	Assamese
37	Gujarati
38	Marathi
39	French
40	Spanish
41	Russian
42	Persian
43	Rajasthani
44	German
45	Japanese
46	Adult Education/ Continuing Education/ Andragogy/ Non Formal Education
47	Physical Education
49	Arab Culture and Islamic Studies
50.	Indian Culture
55	Labour Welfare/Personnel Management/Industrial Relations/ Labour and Social Welfare/Human Resource Management
58	Law
59	Library and Information Science
60	Buddhist, Jaina, Gandhian and Peace Studies
62	Comparative Study of Religions
63	Mass Communication and Journalism
65	Performing Arts – Dance/Drama/Theatre
66	Museology & Conservation
67	Archaeology
68	Criminology
70	Tribal and Regional Language/Literature
71	Folk Literature
72	Comparative Literature
73	Sanskrit Traditional Subjects (including Jyotisha/ Sidhanta Jyotisha/ Navya Vyakarna/ Vyakarna/ Mimamsa/ Navya Nyaya/ Sankhya Yoga/ Tulanatmaka Darsana/ Shukla Yajurveda/ Madhva Vedanta/ Dharma Sastra/ Sahitya/ Purana-itihasa/Agama/Advaita Vedanta)

74	Women Studies
79	Visual Arts (including Drawing & Painting/Sculpture/ Graphics/Applied Art/History of Art)
80	Geography
81	Social Medicine & Community Health
82	Forensic Science
83	Pali
84	Kashmiri
85	Konkani
87	Computer Science and Applications
88	Electronic Science
89	Environmental Sciences
90	International and Area Studies
91	Prakrit
92	Human Rights and Duties
93	Tourism Administration and Management

* The candidates with Master's Degree in Geography (with specialization in Population Studies) or Mathematics/Statistics are also eligible to appear in the subject "Population Studies" (Code 15).

6. TEST CENTRES

The Test Centres with their respective codes are given below. Printout of Online Application Form should be addressed to the Registrar of the respective University Test Centres. However, candidates desirous of appearing at the Centre Code No. 65 shall address their Application Forms to the Principal of the College. Please note that change of centre will not be allowed under any circumstances.

Centre Code	Name of the Centre
01	Aligarh Muslim University, Aligarh – 202 002.
02	University of Allahabad, Allahabad – 211 002.
03	Andhra University, Visakhapatnam – 530 003.
04	Rajiv Gandhi University, Rono Hills, Itanagar – 791 111.
05	Banaras Hindu University, Varanasi – 221 005.
06	Bangalore University, Bangalore – 560 056.
07	M.P. Bhoj Open University, Raja Bhoj Marg, Bhopal – 462016.
08	Berhampur University, Berhampur – 760 007.
09	Bharathiar University, Coimbatore – 641 046.

10	Bharathidasan University, Tiruchirapalli – 620 024.
11	University of Burdwan, Burdwan – 713 104.
12	University of Calcutta, Kolkata – 700 073.
13	University of Calicut, Kozhikode – 673 635.
14	Ch. Charan Singh University, Meerut – 250 005.
15	Chhatrapati Shahu Ji Maharaj University, Kanpur – 208 024.
16	Cochin University of Science and Technology, Kochi – 682 022.
17	Jamia Millia Islamia, Jamia Nagar, New Delhi – 110 025.
18	Devi Ahilya Vishwavidyalaya , Indore – 452 001.
19	Dr. B. S. A. Marathwada University, Aurangabad – 431 004.
20	Gauhati University, Guwahati – 781 014.
21	Goa University, Goa – 403 203.
22	Deendayal Upadhyaya Gorakhpur University, Gorakhpur–273 009.
23	Gujarat University, Ahmedabad – 380 009.
24	Gulbarga University, Gulbarga – 585 106.
25	Guru Nanak Dev University, Amritsar – 143 005.
26	Himachal Pradesh University, Shimla – 171 005.
27	University of Jammu, Jammu (Tawi) – 180 006.
28	Jai Narain Vyas University, Jodhpur – 342 001.
29	Jiwaji University, Gwalior – 474 011.
30	Karnatak University, Dharwad – 580 003.
31	University of Kashmir, Srinagar – 190 006.
32	University of Kerala, Thiruvananthapuram – 695 034.
33	Kurukshetra University, Kurukshetra – 132 119.
34	University of Lucknow, Lucknow – 226 007.
35	M.S. University of Baroda, Vadodara – 390 002.
36	University of Madras, Chennai – 600 005.
37	Madurai Kamraj University, Madurai – 625 021.
38	Mangalore University, Mangalore – 574 199.
39	Manipur University, Imphal – 795 003.
40	Mohanlal Sukhadia University, Udaipur – 313 001.
41	University of Mumbai, Mumbai – 400 032.
42	Nagarjuna University, Guntur – 522 510.
43	Nagpur University, Nagpur – 440 001.

44	North Bengal University, Darjeeling – 734 430.
45	North Eastern Hill University, Shillong – 793 022.
46	Osmania University, Hyderabad – 500 007.
47	Pt. Ravishankar Shukla University, Raipur – 492 010.
48	Panjab University, Chandigarh – 160 014.
49	Patna University, Patna – 800 005.
50	University of Pune, Pune – 411 007.
51	University of Rajasthan, Jaipur – 302 004.
52	Ranchi University, Ranchi – 834 008.
53	Rani Durgavati Vishwavidyalaya, Jabalpur – 482 001.
54	H.N. Bahuguna Garhwal University, Srinagar-246 174
55	Sambalpur University, Sambalpur – 768 019.
56	Saurashtra University, Rajkot – 360 005.
57	Sri Venkateswara University, Tirupati – 517 502.
58	Tilka Manjhi Bhagalpur University, Bhagalpur – 812 007.
59	Tripura University, Agartala – 799 004.
60	Utkal University, Bhubaneswar – 751 004.
61	Dr. Bhim Rao Ambedkar University, Agra – 282 004.
62	Maharshi Dayanand Saraswati University, Ajmer – 305 009.
63	Mizoram University, Mizoram, Post Box No.190, Aizawl –796012.
64	Nagaland University, P.B.341, Lumani, Kohima –797 001.
65	Jawaharlal Nehru Rajkeeya Mahavidyalaya, Andaman & Nicobar Islands, Port Blair – 744 104.
66	Dr. Awadesh Pratap Singh University, Rewa – 486 003.
67	Assam University, Silchar – 788 011. (Assam)
68	Dibrugarh University, Dibrugarh – 786 004.
69	Sikkim University, 6th Mile, Samdur, P.O. Tadong-737 102. (Gangtok, Sikkim)
70	Tezpur University, Tezpur – 784 028.
71	Maharaja Ganga Singh University, Bikaner, Rajasthan
72	Maharishi Dayanand University, Rohtak – 124001
73	Punjabi University, Patiala – 147002
74	University of Mysore, Crawford Hall, Mysore – 570005

7. NET EXAMINATION

a. Examination Schedule

UGC conducts NET twice a year, i.e., in the months of June and December. The notifications announcing the June and December examinations are published in the months of March and September respectively in the weekly journal of nation-wide circulation, viz, Employment News.

b. Results Declaration Schedule

The result of June, UGC Test is declared generally in the month of October. Similarly December, UGC Test result is usually declared in the month of April. The UGC Test results published in the Employment News are also available on UGC website.

c. N E T for Science Subjects

The NET in Major Science Subjects, viz., Chemical Sciences; Earth Atmospheric Ocean & Planetary Sciences; Life Sciences; Mathematical Sciences and Physical Sciences is conducted jointly with the Council of Scientific and Industrial Research (CSIR), New Delhi. The notifications concerned are issued separately by the CSIR.

8. SUBMISSION OF THE APPLICATION FORMS FOR APPEARING THE UGC TEST

The procedure for applying for UGC Test is described in detail in the notification for the relevant examination. The notification is published in the Employment News generally in the months of March and September and is also uploaded on the UGC website www.ugc.ac.in.

a. Enclosures to be sent with the application

The candidates should send the following documents with print out of their online application form (two copies), Attendance Slip (one copy) and Admission Card (one copy on separate A-4 size papers):

i. Copy of Bank Chelan (UGC copy).
ii. Attested copies of SC/ST/Visually Handicapped/Physically Handicapped/ OBC (Non creamy layer) certificates, in case applicable.
iii. Certificates duly attested by a Gazetted Officer to prove educational qualification/ research experience, in case applicable, entitling the candidate for age relaxation.
iv. Two self addressed unstamped envelopes of 10" X 4" size.

b. Examination Fee

General Candidates	₹ 450/-
Other Backward Classes	₹ 225/-
SC/ST/PH/VH candidates	₹ 110/-

c. Mode of payment

- The candidate is expected to fill the Bank Chelan form in triplicate (Bank Copy, the GC Copy & Candidate's Copy) as given in the Notification.
- All the three copies of the Chelan form have to be submitted in any branch of State Bank of India along with the bank charges (commission) of ₹ 20/-.
- The bank will retain one copy and return two copies of the Chelan to the candidate.
- The candidate has to attach the UGC copy of the Chelan with the printout of online Application Form which he/she has to submit to the Registrar of the UGC Test Centre opted by the candidate.
- Fee submitted by any other mode like money order, demand draft, IPO etc. will be rejected.
- Fee once paid will not be refunded under any circumstances.

d. Checklist for filling the online application form

The candidates are advised to ensure the following points before filling the Online Application Forms:

i. whether they fulfil the eligibility conditions for the Test as prescribed under the heading 'CONDITIONS OF ELIGIBILITY' and 'AGE LIMIT'.

ii. that they have filled their CATEGORY, viz., GEN/SC/ST/OBC (non-creamy layer), in the relevant column correctly.

iii. that they have filled their subject and test centre in the relevant columns correctly.

iv. that the VH/PH candidates have filled the relevant column in the Online Application Form. Only VH/PH candidates have to fill this column and the others have to leave it blank.

v. whether they have signed the printout of Online Application Form Admission Card and Attendance Slip.

vi. whether they have enclosed the required documents with the Application Form before submission at the Test Centre.

vii. whether they have kept a copy of the submitted documents for their own record.

Ref: www.ugc.ac.in

APPENDIX - II

NET SYLLABUS

PAPER – I

SUBJECT: GENERAL PAPER ON TEACHING AND REASEARCH APTITUDE

The main objective is to assess the teaching and research capabilities of the candidates. Therefore, the test is aimed at assessing the teaching and research aptitude as well as their awareness. They are expected to possess and exhibit cognitive abilities like comprehension, analysis, evaluation, understanding the structure of arguments as well as deductive and inductive reasoning. Candidates are also expected to have a general awareness and knowledge of sources of information. They should be aware of interaction between people, environment and natural resources and their impact on quality of life. The details are given in the following sections:

Note: i. Each section gets equal weightage: five questions and 10 marks from each section.

ii. Whenever pictorial questions are set for the sighted candidates a passage followed by equal number of questions should be set for the visually handicapped candidates.

I. Teaching Aptitude

1. Teaching: Nature, objectives, characteristics and basic requirements
2. Learner's characteristics
3. Factors affecting teaching
4. Methods of teaching
5. Teaching aids
6. Evaluation systems.

II. Research Aptitude

1. Research: Meaning, characteristics and types
2. Steps of research
3. Methods of research
4. Research Ethics
5. Paper, article, workshop, seminar, conference and symposium
6. Thesis writing: its characteristics and format.

III. Reading Comprehension

1. A passage to be set with questions to be answered.

IV. Communication

1. Communication: Nature, characteristics, types, barrier and effective classroom communication.

V. Reasoning (Including Mathematical)

1. Number series; letter series; codes
2. Relationships; classification

VI. Logical Reasoning

1. Understanding the structure of arguments
2. Evaluating and distinguishing deductive and inductive reasoning
3. Verbal analogies: Word analogy – Applied analogy
4. Verbal classification
5. Reasoning Logical Diagrams: Simple diagrammatic relationship, multi-dia grammatic relationship
6. Venn diagram; Analytical Reasoning.

VII. Data Interpretation

1. Sources, acquisition and interpretation of data
2. Quantitative and qualitative data
3. Graphical representation and mapping of data.

VIII. Information and Communication Technology (ICT)

1. ICT: meaning, advantages, disadvantages and uses
2. General abbreviations and terminology
3. Basics of internet and e-mailing.

IX. People and Environment

1. People and environment interaction
2. Sources of pollution
3. Pollutants and their impact on human life, exploitation of natural and energy resources
4. Natural hazards and mitigation.

X. Higher Education System: Governance, Polity and Administration

1. Structure of the institutions for higher learning and research in India; formal and distance education; professional/technical and general education; value education: governance, polity and administration; concept, institutions and their interactions.